Using the *Write Source* Book

Your *Write Source* book is loaded with information to help you learn about writing. One section that will be especially helpful is the "Proofreader's Guide" at the back of the book. This section covers all of the rules for language and grammar.

The book also includes four units covering the types of writing that you may have to complete on district or state writing tests. At the end of each unit, there are samples and tips for writing in science, social studies, and math.

Write Source will help you with other learning skills, too—test taking, note taking, and speaking. This makes *Write Source* a valuable writing and learning guide in all of your classes.

Your *Write Source* guide . . .

With practice, you will be able to find information in this book quickly, using the guides explained below.

The **TABLE OF CONTENTS** (starting on the next page) lists the six major sections in the book and the chapters found in each section.

The **INDEX** (starting on page **751**) lists the topics covered in the book in alphabetical order. Use the index when you are interested in a specific topic.

The **COLOR CODING** used for "Basic Grammar and Writing" (blue), "A Writer's Resource" (green), and the "Proofreader's Guide" (yellow) make these important sections easy to find.

The **SPECIAL PAGE REFERENCES** in the book tell you where to turn for additional information about a specific topic.

If, at first, you're not sure how to find something in *Write Source,* ask your teacher for help. With a little practice, you will find everything quickly and easily.

HOUGHTON MIFFLIN HARCOURT

WRITE SOURCE

Authors

Dave Kemper, Patrick Sebranek, and Verne Meyer

Illustrator

Chris Krenzke

GREAT SOURCE®

HOUGHTON MIFFLIN HARCOURT

Reviewers

Ilene R. Abrams
Cobb County School District
Marietta, GA

Dawn Calhoun Bray
Houston County School System
Warner Robins, Georgia

Doreen A. Caswell
Mary G. Montgomery
Semmes, Alabama

Tricia Dugger
St. Lucie County Schools District
Ft. Pierce, FL

Vallie J. Ericson
Sheboygan Area School District
Sheboygan, Wisconsin

Paula Denise Findley
Arkansas River Educational Cooperative
White Hall, Arkansas

Mary M. Fisher
Arlington Public Schools
Arlington, MA

Michelle Harden-Brown
Savannah-Chatham Southwest Middle
Savannah, Georgia

Kevin F. Harrington
Baldwin Middle School
Baldwin, New York

Beverly Canzater Jacobs
Solon City Schools
Solon, Ohio

Alissa Lowman
Hillside Middle School
Northville, Michigan

Elizabeth F. Manning
A.E. Phillips Laboratory School
Ruston, Louisiana

Rhea Mayerchak
Omin Middle School
Boca Raton, Florida

Steve Mellen
Prince George's County Public Schools
Temple Hills, Maryland

Diana L. Mooney
Lake Denoon Middle School
Muskego, Wisconsin

Ellen Nielsen
Clovis Unified School District
Clovis, California

Geraldine Ortego
Lafayette Parish District Office
Lafayette, Louisiana

Deborah Richmond
Ferry Pass Middle School
Pensacola, FL

Addie Rae Tobey
Shaker Heights Middle School
Shaker Heights, Ohio

Jodi Turchin
Silver Lakes Middle School Board
of Broward County
North Lauderdale, FL

Bridget Wetton
Alpine Union School District
San Diego, California

Susan Wilson
South Orange/Maplewood School District
South Orange, New Jersey

Robert Wright
Sebastian River Middle
Sebastian River, FL

Peggy Zehnder
Bellingham School District
Bellingham, Washington

Printed in the U.S.A.

ISBN 978-0-547-48504-1

9 10 1083 19 18 17 16 15

4500536365 A B C D E F G

Quick Guide

contents

The Writing Process

The Forms of Writing

DESCRIPTIVE WRITING

NARRATIVE WRITING

EXPOSITORY WRITING

PERSUASIVE WRITING

RESPONSE TO LITERATURE

CREATIVE WRITING

RESEARCH WRITING

The Tools of Learning

SPEAKING TO LEARN

WRITING TO LEARN

Basic Grammar and Writing

WORKING WITH WORDS

BUILDING EFFECTIVE SENTENCES

CONSTRUCTING STRONG PARAGRAPHS

A Writer's Resource

Strengthening Word Choice and Vocabulary

Improving Sentence Fluency

Enhancing Your Presentation

Proofreader's Guide

Test Prep!

The "Proofreader's Guide" includes test-prep pages to help you study for tests on punctuation, mechanics, usage, sentences, and the parts of speech.

Why Write?

The following story by Mr. James Pearson, a high school basketball coach, will help answer this question.

When I was in eighth grade, basketball was my life. But I couldn't try out for the team unless I improved my grades.

I started with language arts and asked Ms. Libby what I could do. She told me to spend more time on my writing, and she gave me this advice: *Write down what you are thinking. Then read your writing. Write some more and then read it again. Do some more writing, and so on. Back and forth.* I followed her advice and found out that I could write.

That advice helped me through middle school, high school, *and* college. It also helped me get the grades to play basketball. If I hadn't listened to Ms. Libby back then, I might not be a coach today.

Writing can do many things if you give it a chance. For one thing, it can help you reach your goals, just like it helped Coach Pearson reach his. Read on to find out more about the value of writing.

What's Ahead

- **Reasons to Write**
- **Creating a Writing "SourceBank"**

Reasons to Write

Writing makes you a better thinker because it helps you explore your experiences. Writing also makes you a better learner because it helps you understand the subjects you are studying. And finally, the writing you do now will make you a better writer next month, next year, and forever.

Writing for All the Right Reasons

Explore Your Personal Thoughts

Writing in a personal journal helps you learn important things about yourself and feel more confident in your ability to write. (See pages 431–434 for more information.)

Better Understand New Ideas

Writing in a classroom journal or a learning log helps you make sense of what you are learning, and it helps you remember things better. (See pages 435–440 for more information.)

Show Learning

Writing essays, developing reports, and answering essay-test questions can show teachers what you have learned. These forms of writing can also help you assess your own understanding of classroom material.

Share Your Ideas

Writing stories and poems to share brings out the best in you as a writer because you are writing for an interested audience, such as your classmates.

Think of your writing as a special opportunity to learn and to grow, and you will soon understand its value—in school and in life. So what should you do? Just start writing for all the right reasons!

Write to learn. Write for 5 minutes about the following quotation: "Writing is one of the best learning tools for all students in all subjects." In your writing, explain one or more ways that writing has helped you learn about something in school or in your personal life.

Creating a Writing "SourceBank"

To think like a writer, you should act like one. You can do this by creating your own "SourceBank" of possible writing ideas. The activities listed below will get you started. (Also see pages **544–547**.)

Look around you for ideas. Be on the lookout for writing inspiration anywhere, anytime. For example, while walking along, you and a friend might see a well-cared-for, healthy plant perched in front of a rundown building. A "flower in the rough" scene like this could give you an idea for a story, a poem, or an essay.

Carry a small pocket notebook to record ideas. (It's hard to remember everything!) You might also want to write about some of the "found" ideas in your personal journal.

Get involved in your community. Visit museums, historical sites, businesses, and churches. Volunteer your services to a local day care or the park district. Each new experience will give you fresh ideas for writing.

Explore available resources. Surf the Internet and prowl around your library for writing ideas. Make a list of Web sites, articles, and books that you would like to explore. Also become a regular reader of your local newspaper.

Create a personal almanac. Take a close look at your life up to now and list people, places, and things that have mattered the most to you. Here's what you might include:

- Personal skills and interests (singing)
- Memorable firsts (learning to ski)
- Memorable lasts (breaking my ankle)
- School memories (joining the track team)
- Unforgettable people (my great-aunt)
- Unforgettable places (McKinley Hill)
- Favorite books and movies (*The Giver*)
- Things to change (homework routine)

Develop an almanac. Copy the headings above into your writing notebook. Leave plenty of space after each. Then list personal ideas under the headings and continue to add ideas throughout the school year. Use some of these ideas as starting points for your writing.

publish EDIT write

The Writing Process

Academic Vocabulary

Work with a partner. Read the meanings and share answers to the questions.

1. An **experience** is one or more events that happen to you.
   What is an interesting experience you have had?
2. Something that is **valuable** is very important or useful.
   What writing skill do you find most valuable?
3. You can't forget something that is **unforgettable**.
   What is an unforgettable experience you've had?
4. To **concentrate** means to pay close attention.
   Why is it important to concentrate when studying?

Understanding the Writing Process

Most people simply look up at the night sky and say, "Ahh!" Serious stargazers, however, follow a process. They memorize star charts, check weather reports for best viewing times, set up their equipment, and gaze at the right corner of the sky at the right time. The process they follow allows them to see things that most people would miss.

Serious writers also follow a process. There is nothing instant about developing effective writing. It results from prewriting, writing, revising, and editing. This chapter will help you learn more about the writing process and build some valuable writing habits.

What's Ahead

Building Good Writing Habits

Professional writers aren't born with a special writing gene. They have had to do a lot of practicing to develop their skills. Follow the tips below and you will begin to improve your own writing skills.

Keep a writer's notebook or folder.

Reserve a part of a folder or notebook for your personal writing. Underline any ideas you might want to use in a writing assignment.

> Keep a diary [or writer's notebook]. It's a place to write about things that happen, and also to write about the feelings you're having. —William Zinsser

Write every day, preferably at a set time.

Get into a regular writing routine, and stick to it. You set aside time to practice other skills. Do the same with your writing.

> The idea is to get the pencil moving quickly.
>
> —Bernard Malamud

Write with feeling.

How do you truly feel about your subject? Relax and let those emotions hit the page. (You can always tone them down later if you need to.)

> Every time I sit down and write, I know it's going well when it sort of takes over and I get out of the picture.
>
> —Sandra Bolton

Write about a quotation. **Write nonstop for 5 to 8 minutes about one of the quotations on this page. Consider what it means to you.**

The Writing Process

Good writing almost always goes through a series of changes before it is ready to share. That is why writing is called a *process*. The steps in this process are described below.

The Steps in the Writing Process

Prewriting

At the start of an assignment, a writer explores possible topics before selecting one to write about. Then the writer collects details about the topic and plans how to use them.

Writing

During this step, the writer completes the first draft using the prewriting plan as a guide. This draft is a writer's *first* chance to get everything down on paper.

Revising

After reviewing the first draft, the writer changes any ideas that are not clear or complete. A wise writer will ask at least one other person to review the draft, as well.

Editing

A writer then checks his or her revised writing for correctness before preparing a neat final copy. The writer proofreads the final copy for errors before sharing or publishing it.

Publishing

This is the final step in the writing process. Publishing is to a writer what an exhibit is to an artist—an opportunity to share his or her work with others.

Analyze your process. How would you classify yourself as a writer? Are you carefree, creative, dramatic, private, public, detailed, and so on? Or are you a combination of some of these? Explain.

The Process in Action

The next two pages show you the writing process in action. Use this information as a general guide for each of your writing assignments. The graphic below reminds you that, during an assignment, you can move back and forth between the steps in the writing process.

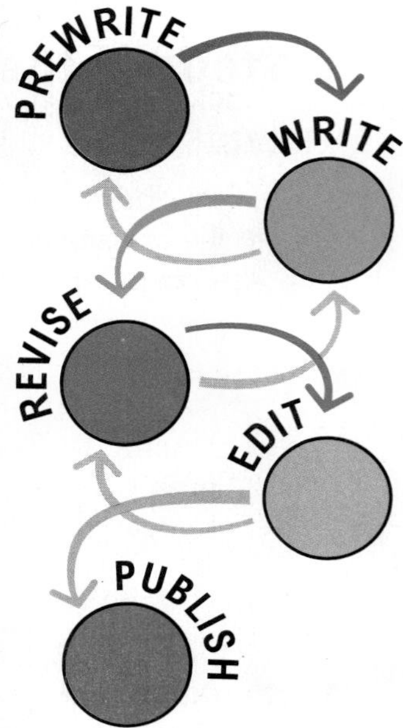

Prewriting Selecting a Topic

- Search for possible writing topics that meet the requirements of the assignment.
- Select a specific topic that really appeals to you.

Gathering and Organizing Details

- Learn as much as you can about the topic before you start your first draft.
- Consider the purpose of the assignment and what to emphasize in the writing—either an interesting part of the topic or your personal feelings about it. This will be the focus, or thesis, of your writing.
- Decide which details you want to include in your writing. Also decide on the best way to organize the details and form a plan.

Writing Developing the First Draft

- When you write your first draft, concentrate on getting your ideas on paper. Don't try to produce a perfect piece of writing.
- Use the details you collected and your prewriting plan as general guides, but feel free to add new ideas as you go along.
- Make sure your writing has a beginning, a middle, and an ending.

Write on every other line and on only one side of the paper when using pen or pencil and paper. Double-space on a computer. This will give you room for revising, the next step in the process.

Revising Improving Your Writing

- Review your first draft, but only after setting it aside for a while.
- Use these questions as a general revising guide:
  - **Do I sound truly interested in my topic?**
  - **Do I say enough about my topic?**
  - **Does the beginning draw the reader into the writing?**
  - **Are the ideas clear and in the right order?**
  - **Does the closing remind the reader about the importance of the topic?**
  - **Are the nouns and verbs specific?**
  - **Are the modifiers (adjectives and adverbs) clear and colorful?**
  - **Are the sentences varied? Do they read smoothly?**
- Try to have at least one other person review your work.
- Make as many changes as necessary to improve your first draft.

Editing Checking for Conventions

- Edit for correctness by checking for punctuation, capitalization, spelling, and grammar errors. Also ask someone else to check your writing for errors.
- Then prepare a neat final copy of your writing. (See pages **24–26** for tips and an example.) Proofread this copy for errors before sharing it.

Publishing Sharing Your Writing

- Share your finished work with your classmates, teacher, friends, and family members.
- Consider including the writing in your portfolio.
- Think about submitting your writing to your school newspaper or some other publication. (See pages **57–64** for ideas.)

Consider the process. The graphic on page 8 reminds you that you sometimes have to go back and repeat a step before you can move forward in your writing. In a brief paragraph, describe a writing assignment in which you had to move back and forth between the steps in the writing process.

Getting the Big Picture

Coaches know what it takes to build a successful basketball team: strong rebounders, tough defenders, and good shooters. Experienced writers also know what it takes to produce successful writing: strong *ideas*, clear *organization,* effective *word choice*, and so on.

Of course, these same traits are important in your own writing as well. You should deal with them as they become important at different points in the writing process. Remember that the writing process helps you to slow down and give each trait or part of writing the proper attention.

- ☐ Ideas
- ☐ Organization
- ☐ Voice
- ☐ Word Choice
- ☐ Sentence Fluency
- ☐ Conventions

Use the writing process. Imagine that you are doing a writing assignment. On your own paper, match each activity on the left to its proper place in the writing process on the right.

___ **1.** Check the first draft for voice and personality.	A. Prewriting
___ **2.** Organize your details for writing.	B. Writing
___ **3.** Display the final copy on your Web site.	C. Revising
___ **4.** Double-check the punctuation of dialogue.	D. Editing
___ **5.** Develop an ending that gets the reader thinking.	E. Publishing

Extra Credit: Suppose you had to explain the writing process to a group of younger students who were just beginning to write paragraphs and brief stories. On your own paper, write down what you would say to them.

One Writer's Process

Writers need the freedom to choose and to experiment when they write. Without this freedom, writing has little meaning or importance to them. For this reason, you must think of writing as a process. You will do your best work when you select topics that truly interest you and decide how you want to write about them.

This chapter shows the process used by student writer Linda Kerklin as she wrote about her visit to *Freedom Schooner Amistad*. As you will see, this writing had special meaning to Linda because she was writing about people who were fighting for their freedom.

What's Ahead

- **Previewing the Goals**
- **Prewriting**
- **Writing**
- **Revising**
- **Editing**
- **Publishing**
- **Assessing the Final Copy**
- **Reflecting on Your Writing**

Previewing the Goals

Before Linda Kerklin began writing, she looked at the goals for her personal narrative assignment, which are shown below. These goals helped her get started. She also previewed the rubric for narrative writing on pages 130–131.

Goals of Narrative Writing

Ideas

Use specific details and dialogue that make the reader want to know what happens next.

Organization

Make sure that the details are organized chronologically, and the beginning, middle, and ending are clear to the reader.

Voice

Make the writing sound like you, and use dialogue to show each speaker's personality.

Word Choice

Use words that express how you feel about the experience.

Sentence Fluency

Use a variety of sentence lengths and beginnings to create an effective style.

Conventions

Be sure that your punctuation, capitalization, spelling, and grammar are correct.

To understand the important goals for Linda's assignment, answer the following questions:

1. What type of topic should Linda select? Why?
2. Why is chronological organization important in a narrative?
3. What's one way Linda can add personality to her story?

Reviewing Linda's First Revision

After Linda reviewed her first draft, she made the following revisions to the ideas, organization, and voice of her essay.

A key idea is moved.

New details make the ideas clearer.

A personal feeling is added.

Last summer, the Freedom Schooner Amistad sailed to Chicago. I couldn't wait to get aboard. My excitement at seeing this beautiful ship was soon forgoten when I heard the terrible story.

I've always loved stories about the high seas. I've always wanted to climb up a ship's pole and shout, Land ho"!

"The ceiling in here would have been three ft. lower" said the Captain ^ *as we stood in the small cargo bay of the boat. He lowered his hand from just over his head to the middle of his waist. He told us that in this room, the captives sat in chains* ^ *for three days in the heat of the tropics.*

The wooden ceiling and walls seemed to close on me. The ship moved a little, even docked here. I could only imagine how much it tossed on the high seas.

^ *The heat, the room, the fact that All these people had been kidnaped from there homes in Africa and were being sold into slavery* ^ *—it all made me feel sick. I moved to steady myself, and my ankles and wrists tingled.*

One night, a captive broke free from his chains and freed the other prisoners. He opened . . .

Review Linda's revisions. Identify two of the changes that seem the most effective. Explain your choices.

Revising Using a Peer Response Sheet

One of Linda's classmates read her essay. He used a rubric like the one on pages 130–131 and spotted more places that could use improvements. Linda's classmate wrote his comments on a "Peer Response Sheet."

Peer Response Sheet

Writer: *Linda Kerklin* Responder: *William Becker*

Title: *Freedom Ho!*

What I liked about your writing:

** You got my attention right away.*

** You mix the captain's words and your own thoughts.*

** You sound really interested in the experience.*

Changes I would suggest:

** In the beginning, could you tell why you like sea stories?*

** What "terrible story" do you mean?*

** How many captives were there?*

** Where is the ship docked?*

Review the classmate's suggestions for improvements listed above. Which one do you think is the most important? Explain. Also think of one suggestion of your own. Focus on the ideas, organization, and voice in the writing.

Revising with a Peer Response

Using the comments made by her classmate, Linda revised her story again. She added some important details.

What do you love about sea stories?

What terrible story?

What kind of captives? How many were there?

Where is the ship docked?

I've always loved stories about the high seas with their sailors, cannons, and pirates. *I've always wanted to climb up a ship's pole and shout, Land ho"! Last summer, the Freedom Schooner Amistad sailed to Chicago. I couldn't wait to get aboard. My excitement at seeing this beautiful ship was soon forgoten when I heard the terrible story* of the original Amistad.

"The ceiling in here would have been three ft. lower" said the Captain as we stood in the small cargo bay of the boat. He lowered his hand from just over his head to the middle of his waist. He told us that in this room, the forty-nine african *captives sat in chains for three days in the heat of the tropics.*

The wooden ceiling and walls seemed to close on me. The ship moved a little, even docked here at navy pier. *I could only imagine how much it tossed on the high seas. The heat, the room, the fact that all these* 49 *people had been kidnaped from there homes in Africa and were being sold into slavery—it all made me feel sick. I moved to steady myself, and my ankles and . . .*

Discuss with your classmates the changes the writer makes (shown on pages 17 and 19). Which additions seem the most effective? What other types of changes does she make? How effective are the changes?

Revising Focusing on Words and Sentences

Once Linda was done revising for ideas, organization, and voice, she went back to the rubric again, checking her work for word choice and sentence fluency. Her comments tell how she planned to revise her writing for style.

Word Choice

Use words that express how you feel about the experience.

"My language is easy to understand, but some of my nouns and verbs could be stronger. I'll also check the Internet for specific sailing terms."

Sentence Fluency

Use a variety of sentence lengths and beginnings to create an effective style.

"In some places, the sentences don't flow. I'll try using transitions to connect them. Also, I'll combine the short, choppy sentences in the middle paragraphs."

Try It Team up with a partner to review Linda's revised writing on page 19 for style. Identify two nouns, verbs, or adjectives that could be more specific, vivid, or colorful. Then find one or two sentences that could be improved.

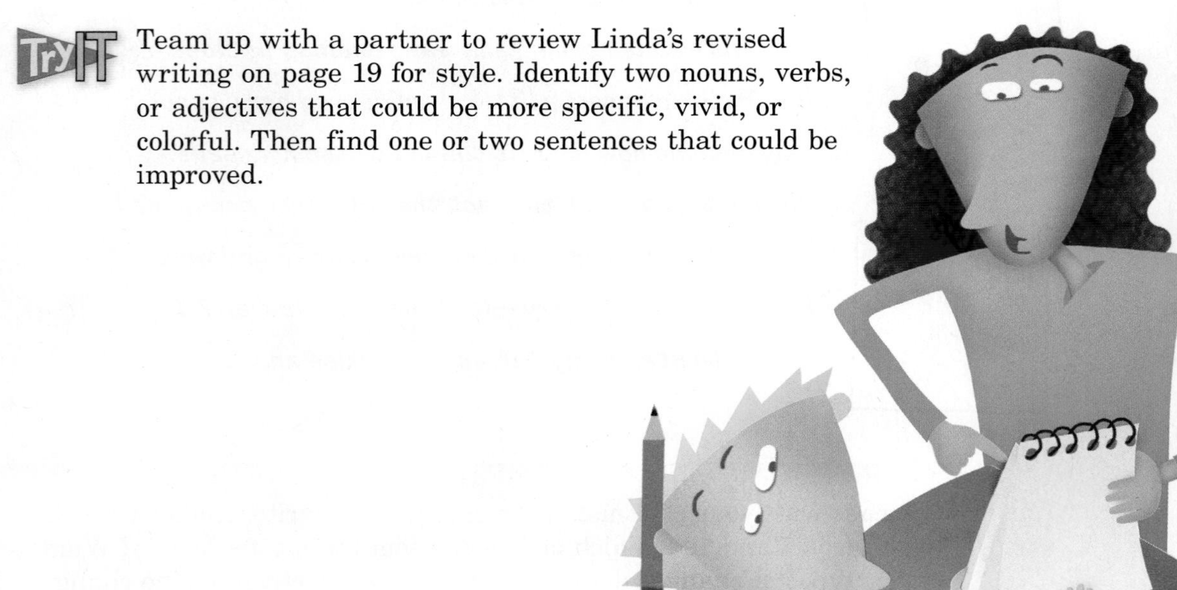

Checking Linda's Improvements in Style

Linda's next step was to concentrate on the style of her writing. She paid special attention to the clarity and flow of the words and the sentences.

Nautical terms improve the level of language.

Combined sentences and transitions improve fluency.

Stronger words are chosen.

I've always loved stories about the high seas, with their ~~sailors~~ swashbuckelers, cannons, and pirates. I've always wanted to climb up a ship's ~~pole~~ mast and shout, Land ho"! So ~~L~~last summer, when the Freedom Schooner Amistad sailed to Chicago~~.~~, I couldn't wait to get aboard. My excitement at seeing this beautiful ship, though, was soon forgoten when I heard the terrible story of the original Amistad.

"The ceiling in here would have been three ft. lower" said the Captain as we stood in the small cargo bay of the ~~boat~~ schooner. He lowered his hand from just over his head to the middle of his waist ~~. He told us~~ and added that in this tiny room, the forty-nine african captives ~~sat~~ crouched in chains for three days in the blistering heat of the tropics.

The wooden ceiling and walls seemed to close on me. The ship ~~moved~~ rolled a little, even docked here at navy pier. I could only imagine how much it must have tossed on the high seas. The heat, the ~~room~~ cramped quarters, the fact that all these 49 people had been kidnaped from . . .

Compare your ideas for changing Linda's writing (page 20) with the changes she has made. How are her changes alike or different from your recommendations?

Editing Checking for Conventions

At last it was time for Linda to edit her story for *conventions.* If she had worried about grammar, punctuation, capitalization, and spelling too soon, she may have forgotten to make the other changes that dramatically improved her work. Her comment tells how she planned to edit her writing for one of the conventions.

Conventions

Be sure that your punctuation, capitalization, spelling, and grammar are correct.

"I'll carefully check my narrative for punctuation."

For help with conventions, Linda turned to the "Proofreader's Guide" in the back of her *Write Source* book. She also used the editing checklist shown below.

Editing Checklist

PUNCTUATION

_____ **1.** Do I use end punctuation after all my sentences?
_____ **2.** Do I use commas correctly?
_____ **3.** Do I punctuate dialogue correctly?

CAPITALIZATION

_____ **4.** Do I start all my sentences with capital letters?
_____ **5.** Do I capitalize all proper nouns?

SPELLING

_____ **6.** Have I spelled all my words correctly?
_____ **7.** Have I double-checked words my spell-checker might miss?

GRAMMAR

_____ **8.** Do I use correct forms of verbs (*had gone,* not *had went*)?
_____ **9.** Do my subjects and verbs agree in number? (*Each* of them *has* a chance to win.)
_____ **10.** Do I use the right word (*to, too, two*)?

Team up with a partner. Using the checklist above, find two or three errors in Linda's revised draft on page 21.

Checking Linda's Editing for Conventions

Linda edited her narrative for spelling, punctuation, capitalization, and grammar. (See inside the back cover of this text for the common editing and proofreading marks.)

Spelling errors are corrected.

Punctuation mistakes are fixed.

Treatment of measurements and numbers is corrected.

Capitalization errors are corrected.

I've always loved stories about the high seas, with their swashbuckelers, cannons, and pirates. I've always wanted to climb up a ship's mast and shout, Land ho"! So last summer, when the Freedom Schooner Amistad sailed to Chicago, I couldn't wait to get aboard. My excitement at seeing this beautiful ship, though, was soon forgoten when I heard the terrible story of the original Amistad.

"The ceiling in here would have been three ft. lower" said the Captain as we stood in the small cargo bay of the schooner. He lowered his hand from just over his head to the middle of his waist and added that in this tiny room, the forty-nine african captives crouched in chains for three days in the blistering heat of the tropics.

The wooden ceiling and walls seemed to close on me. The ship rolled a little, even docked here at navy pier. I could only imagine how much it must have tossed on the high seas. The heat, the cramped . . .

(Editing marks: swashbuckelers → swashbucklers; " inserted before Land; !" transposed; forgoten → forgotten; ft. → feet; comma inserted after lower; Captain → captain; forty-nine → 49; african → African; in inserted after close; navy pier → Navy Pier)

Review Linda's editing for conventions in the paragraphs above. Did you find some of the same errors when you edited her earlier draft on page 21?

Publishing Sharing Your Writing

Linda used the tips below to help her write the final copy of her story. (See pages 25–26.)

Focus on Presentation

Tips for Handwritten Copies

- Use blue or black ink and write neatly.
- Write your name according to your teacher's instructions.
- Skip a line and center your title; skip another line and start your writing.
- Indent every paragraph and leave a one-inch margin on all four sides.
- Write your last name and page number on every page after page 1.

Linda Kerklin

Freedom Ho!

I've always loved stories about the high seas, with their swashbucklers, cannons, and pirates. I've always wanted to climb up a ship's mast and shout, "Land ho!" So last summer, when the Freedom Schooner Amistad sailed to Chicago, I couldn't wait to get aboard. My excitement at seeing this beautiful ship, though, was soon forgotten when I heard the terrible story of the original Amistad.

"The ceiling in here would have been three feet lower," said the captain as we stood in the small cargo bay of the schooner. He lowered his hand from just over his head to the middle of his waist and added that in this tiny room, 49 African captives crouched in chains for three days in the blistering heat of the tropics.

The wooden ceiling and walls seemed to close in on me. The ship rolled a little, even docked here at Navy Pier. I could only imagine how much it must have tossed on the high seas. The heat, the cramped quarters, the fact that all these 49 people had been kidnapped from their homes in Africa and were being sold into slavery—it all made me feel sick. I crouched to steady myself, and my ankles and wrists tingled as if I wore invisible shackles.

One moonless night, though, a captive named Sengbe Pieh broke free from his chains and freed the other prisoners. He opened the hatch and crept onto the deck, where the crew slept. Only the man at the helm was awake. Sengbe and the captives attacked. In the fight, one African was killed, as well

Kerklin 2

"One moonless night, though, a captive named Sengbe Pieh broke

Linda Kerklin

Freedom Ho!

I've always loved stories about the high seas, with their swashbucklers, cannons, and pirates. I've always wanted to climb up a ship's mast and shout, "Land ho!" So last summer, when the *Freedom Schooner Amistad* sailed to Chicago, I couldn't wait to get aboard. My excitement at seeing this beautiful ship, though, was soon forgotten when I heard the terrible story of the original *Amistad*.

"The ceiling in here would have been three feet lower," said the captain as we stood in the small cargo bay of the schooner. He lowered his hand from just over his head to the middle of his waist and added that in this tiny room, 49 African captives crouched in chains for three days in the blistering heat of the tropics.

The wooden ceiling and walls seemed to close in on me. The ship rolled a little, even docked here at Navy Pier. I could only imagine how much it must have tossed on the high seas. The heat, the cramped quarters, the fact that all these 49 people had been kidnapped from their homes in Africa and were being sold into slavery—it all made me feel sick. I crouched to steady myself, and my ankles and wrists tingled as if I wore invisible shackles.

Tips for Computer Copies

- Use an easy-to-read font and a 12-point type size.
- Double-space and leave a one-inch margin around each page.

Linda's Final Copy

Linda was proud of her finished story. Presenting it to the class allowed her friends to share the eye-opening experience of being aboard the *Freedom Schooner Amistad.*

Linda Kerklin

Freedom Ho!

I've always loved stories about the high seas, with their swashbucklers, cannons, and pirates. I've always wanted to climb up a ship's mast and shout, "Land ho!" So last summer, when the *Freedom Schooner Amistad* sailed to Chicago, I couldn't wait to get aboard. My excitement at seeing this beautiful ship, though, was soon forgotten when I heard the terrible story of the original *Amistad.*

"The ceiling in here would have been three feet lower," said the captain as we stood in the small cargo bay of the schooner. He lowered his hand from just over his head to the middle of his waist and added that in this tiny room, 49 African captives crouched in chains for three days in the blistering heat of the tropics.

The wooden ceiling and walls seemed to close in on me. The ship rolled a little, even docked here at Navy Pier. I could only imagine how much it must have tossed on the high seas. The heat, the cramped quarters, the fact that all these 49 people had been kidnapped from their homes in Africa and were being sold into slavery—it all made me feel sick. I crouched to steady myself, and my ankles and wrists tingled as if I wore invisible shackles.

One moonless night, though, a captive named Sengbe Pieh broke free from his chains and freed the other prisoners. He opened the hatch and crept onto the deck, where the crew slept. Only the man at the helm was awake. Sengbe and the captives attacked. In the fight, one African was killed, as well as two crew members. The rest of the crew were captured and tied up. The next morning, Sengbe told the crew to "sail toward the rising sun, toward Africa."

When the captain said the name "Africa," it was as if he had said the word "freedom." For a moment, I felt better. But the story wasn't over. Every night, the crew secretly turned the ship around, heading west. That way, they wasted two months at sea, and the lack of food and water killed 10 more of the captives. At last, *La Amistad* was found by an American ship, which brought it to shore at Long Island Sound.

"That's when they were set free, right?" I asked.

The captain turned toward me, and his brown eyes looked old and sad, as if he'd seen all these things himself. "That's when they were charged with mutiny and murder."

I couldn't stand up anymore and sat down on those rough boards to listen to the story. The Africans had become captives again. The question was whether they were legal slaves in Cuba or were illegal slaves taken from Africa. Numerous trials led finally to the Supreme Court, where John Quincy Adams argued their case. He helped the captives win their freedom.

When we came up out of that cramped and hot hold into the cool winds off Lake Michigan, I felt like I had been freed. I wanted to climb the mast and shout, "Freedom ho!"

Assessing the Final Copy

Linda's teacher used a rubric like the one that appears on pages 130–131 to assess Linda's final copy. A 6 is the very best score that a writer can receive for each trait. The teacher also included comments under each trait.

5 Ideas

You have selected an excellent experience to share. I want to take the same tour.

5 Organization

Your writing has a clear beginning, middle, and ending.

5 Voice

Your personal feelings come through in your writing.

4 Word Choice

A few more nautical terms would have added a special touch to your narrative.

4 Sentence Fluency

Your sentences are easy to follow. You could have varied some of your sentence beginnings.

6 Conventions

Your essay is free of careless errors.

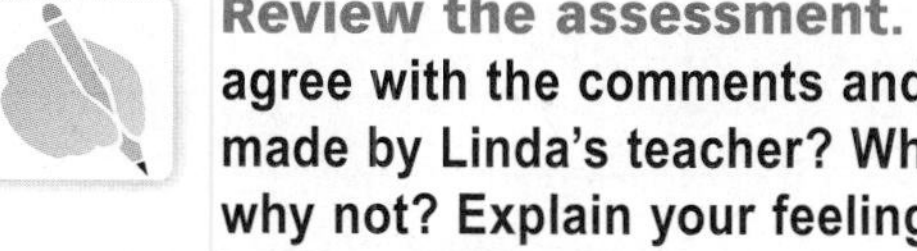

Review the assessment. Do you agree with the comments and scores made by Linda's teacher? Why or why not? Explain your feelings in a brief paragraph.

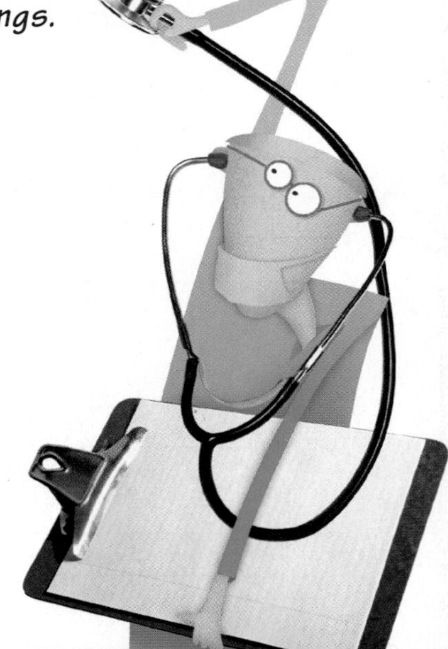

Reflecting on Your Writing

After the whole process was finished, Linda filled out a reflection sheet. This helped her think about the assignment and plan for future essays.

Linda Kerklin

My Personal Narrative

1. *The strength of my narrative is . . .*
   that I was able to connect my own experience with a tragic historical event.

2. *The part that still needs work is . . .*
   the amount of detail I included. I could have made the Africans' experiences easier for the reader to follow.

3. *The main thing I learned about writing a personal narrative is . . .*
   that it must build in suspense and drama to hold the reader's interest.

4. *In one of my next assignments, I would like to . . .*
   write a fictionalized story based on the theme of freedom.

5. *Here is one question I still have about writing a personal narrative:*
   What are some creative ways to write endings for narratives?

Peer Responding

Sharing a piece of writing with your classmates can be a nerve-racking experience. Even professional writers like Mem Fox sometimes get nervous when reading their own work aloud to others: "In those sessions in which each of us reads our writing to the class, we shake with nerves."

The truth is, though, that you—and all writers—need an audience. You need someone to let you know what makes sense and what is unclear. You get the best feedback from your peers in response sessions.

This chapter is all about sharing your writing and making the best possible use of the responses you get from your fellow writers.

What's Ahead

- **Peer-Responding Guidelines**
- **Sample Peer Response Sheet**

Peer Resp

Writer: Lana

Title: Changing Faces

What I liked about your writing:

* The general comments in th
the essay.

* Your description of each fam

* I learned a lot about Albert Ei
paragraph.

Changes I would suggest:

* Could you include more details
did you include her as one of th

* Your essay would b

Peer-Responding Guidelines

At first, you may work with only one person: a teacher or a classmate. This person does not expect your writing to be perfect. He or she knows that you are still working on your paper.

Later, you may have a chance to work with a small group. After a while, you will find that responding to someone's writing is much easier than you thought it would be.

The Author's Role

Select a piece of writing to share and make a copy of it for each group member.

Guidelines	Sample Responses
• **Introduce your piece of writing.** But don't say too much about it.	*This paper is about our dependence on the automobile. I decided on this topic after watching a TV show.*
• **Read your writing out loud.** Or ask group members to read it silently.	*Automobiles are a primary cause of pollution. They are very dangerous. They present many problems. . . .*
• **Invite your group members to comment.** Listen carefully.	*Okay, everyone, now it's your turn to talk. I'm listening.*
• **Take notes** so you will remember what was said.	*So, which statistics should I add?*
• **Answer all questions** the best you can. Be open and polite.	*Yes, the automobile is the number one cause of global warming.*
• **Ask for help from your group** with any writing problems you are having.	*In my ending, is it clear what I want the reader to do?*

The Responder's Role

Responders should show an interest in the author's writing and treat it with respect.

Guidelines	Sample Responses
Listen carefully. Take notes so that you can make helpful comments.	*Notes: What is the problem with sport utility vehicles?*
Look for what is good about the writing. Give some positive comments. Be sincere.	*Most of your statistics are convincing.*
Tell what you think could be improved. Be polite when you make suggestions.	*Could you discuss alternatives to car travel?*
Ask questions if you need more information.	*Where did you get your statistics about the number of roads in our cities?*
Make other suggestions. Help the writer improve her or his work.	*Could you include a stronger call to action?*

Helpful Comments

In all your comments, be as specific as you can be. This will help the writer make the best changes.

Instead of . . .	Try something like . . .
Your beginning doesn't work.	**Your focus statement sounds a little too wordy.**
Your writing is boring.	**Most of your sentences begin with "It is" or "It may."**
I can't understand one part.	**The part about road rage needs more explanation.**

Suppose you are the responder to one of the essays on pages 136–137, 200–201, or 262–263. Carefully read the essay. Then write responses to it using the samples at the top of this page as a guide.

Sample Peer Response Sheet

Your teacher may want you and a classmate to react to each other's writing by completing a response sheet like the one below. (Sample comments are included.)

Peer Response Sheet

Writer: *Lana* Responder: *Jesse*

Title: *Changing Faces*

What I liked about your writing:

** The general comments in the beginning drew me into the essay.*

** Your description of each famous person is very clear.*

** I learned a lot about Albert Einstein in the fifth paragraph.*

Changes I would suggest:

** Could you include more details about Helen Keller? Why did you include her as one of the changing faces?*

** Your essay would be even better if it contained a little bit more of your personality. Could you let people know that you really care about these people?*

Practice. **Exchange a recent piece of writing with a classmate.**

1. **Read the paper once to get an overall feel for it.**
2. **Then read the paper again, paying careful attention to its strengths and weaknesses.**
3. **Fill out a response sheet like the one above.**

Understanding the Traits of Writing

What are your favorite foods? Popcorn? Pancakes? Watermelon? Whatever they are, you wouldn't dump them all into a taco shell and take a bite. That wouldn't make sense.

In the same way, there's more to writing than putting a bunch of words on the page. Effective writing contains well-chosen *ideas*, clear *organization*, and an appropriate *voice*. Experienced writers also pay attention to *word choice, sentence fluency*, and *conventions*. This chapter will teach you how to use these six traits of writing. Before you know it, you'll be using words in ways that clearly express your best thoughts and feelings.

What's Ahead

- Introducing the Traits
- Understanding Ideas . . . Organization . . . Voice . . . Word Choice . . . Sentence Fluency . . . Conventions

Introducing the Traits

The traits listed below identify the main features found in the best writing. If you write with these traits in mind, you will be pleased with the results.

Ideas

Effective writing has a clear message, purpose, or focus. The writing contains plenty of specific ideas and details.

Organization

Strong writing has a clear beginning, middle, and ending. The overall writing is well organized and easy to follow.

Voice

The best writing reveals the writer's voice—or special way of saying things. The voice also fits the audience.

Word Choice

Good writing contains strong words, including specific nouns and verbs. Strong words help deliver a clear message.

Sentence Fluency

Effective writing flows smoothly from one sentence to the next. Sentences vary in length and begin in a variety of ways.

Conventions

Good writing is carefully edited to make sure it is easy to understand. The writing follows the rules for punctuation, grammar, capitalization, and spelling.

One additional trait to consider is the **presentation** of your writing. The best writing looks neat and follows guidelines for margins, indenting, spacing, and so on. The way the writing looks on the page attracts the reader and makes him or her want to read on.

Understanding Ideas

All writing starts, and ends, with ideas. Your job as a writer is to find the best ideas to use in your stories, essays, and reports. As writer Mark Van Doren says, "Bring ideas in and entertain them royally."

How can I select the best topic for writing?

Selecting a topic is different for each form of writing. Use the information below as a guide for selecting the best topics.

Descriptive Writing

Purpose: To present clear pictures of people, places, and objects
Key reminder: Select topics that you know well or that you can observe or research.
Example topics: Describing a neighbor, the bus stop, a special outfit

Narrative Writing

Purpose: To share memorable experiences
Key reminder: Select experiences that you can recall in great detail.
Example topics: Remembering meeting a relative, experiencing stage fright, getting lost

Expository Writing

Purpose: To share information, to explain
Key reminder: Select topics that you can research.
Example topics: Sharing information about tornadoes, pasta, peer pressure

Persuasive Writing

Purpose: To convince the reader to agree with your opinion
Key reminder: Select topics that you have strong feelings about and that you can research to find supporting facts and details.
Example topics: Arguing for or against study halls, final exams, curfews

Try It Write "Topics for Writing" at the top of a piece of paper. Down the left-hand margin list the following headings (leave five to seven lines after each heading): *Personal Narrative Writing, Descriptive Writing, Expository Writing,* and *Persuasive Writing.* Under each heading, list possible writing topics for each type of writing. Add to the list throughout the school year.

How should I write about a topic?

Writer William Zinsser says, "Clutter is the disease of American writing." You can avoid this disease by creating a focus for your writing. A focus statement tells what specific part of a topic you will cover. With a focus in mind, you won't clutter your writing with unnecessary details.

> The peregrine falcon, a lightning-quick bird of prey *(topic)*, is an endangered species *(a certain part)*.

What should I do first to gather details?

The first thing you should do is find out what you already know about a topic. Here are three ways to collect your thoughts about a writing topic:

Freewriting Write freely for at least 5 to 10 minutes, exploring your topic from a number of different angles. The key is to keep your fingers or your pen moving to see what thoughts come to mind.

Listing Jot down things that you already know about your topic, and any questions you have about it. Keep your list going as long as you can.

Clustering Create a cluster with your specific topic as the nucleus word. (See page 95.)

How can I gather additional details?

Collecting additional details may be a problem unless you have a variety of gathering strategies to use. Here are four of them to choose from.

Ask questions. List questions that come to mind and then find answers to them. You can also ask the 5 W's—*Who? What? When? Where?* and *Why?*—about your topic. Add *How?* for even better coverage.

"Talk" about your topic. Write a dialogue between two people who talk about your topic. (You may or may not want to be one of the speakers.) The two speakers should build on each other's comments as they go along. Keep the conversation going as long as you can.

Focus on a specific audience. Write about your topic to a specific group or audience. You could write to a classroom of preschoolers, a live television audience, the local school board, or the readers of a popular teen magazine. This focus will help you see your topic in new ways.

Read about your topic. Refer to the Internet, nonfiction books, magazines, and newspapers for information. Take notes as you read. (See pages 442–448 for help.)

How many different levels of detail should I use?

Usually, each main point in a piece of writing is developed in a separate paragraph. A well-written paragraph should contain at least three different levels of detail.

LEVEL 1: A topic sentence names the main point of a paragraph.

Water is natural and important to life.

LEVEL 2: Secondary sentences make the main point clearer.

It is in rivers, ponds, and lakes, and, of course, inside the human body. Water is the life-giving element that makes up a large percentage of each human being.

LEVEL 3: Additional sentences add specific details to complete the point.

Minerals and salts are essential in the human body, too, but an individual can get enough of these two things from eating healthy food and drinking clear water.

What special features can I use?

To add style to your writing, try including figures of speech and anecdotes.

Figures of speech are creative comparisons that help you explain something or create a special effect. Two common figures of speech are similes and metaphors.

- A **simile** compares two things using *like* or *as*.
  The fire leaped like an attacking panther onto the helpless van in the driveway.
- A **metaphor** compares two things without using *like* or *as*.
  In most high schools across the country, football is king during the fall season.

Anecdotes are brief "slices of life," or ministories, that help you make a point about your topic. They allow you to show your readers something rather than tell them matter-of-factly.

Joe and Ki, two elderly Koreans, shake hands and formally bow to each other. Samantha and Susan, two Americanized Korean teenagers, give each other a kiss on the cheek and then hug.

(These brief anecdotes, or slices of life, come from an expository essay comparing Korean and American culture.)

Try It Gather details for one of the topics that you listed (page 35). Start by freewriting about the topic; then continue by asking and answering questions about it. Finish by writing a simile, a metaphor, or an anecdote about the topic.

PROCESS

Understanding Organization

Strong writing is well organized from start to finish. Writer Stephen Tchudi (pronounced "Judy") calls organizing a paper the "framing" process: "Just as a carpenter puts up a frame of a house before tacking on the outside walls, a writer needs to build a frame for a paper."

How can transitions help me organize my writing?

Linking words and phrases (transitions) can help you organize the details in each mode of writing. (Also see pages 572–573.)

Descriptive: You can use the following transitions, which show location, to arrange details in your descriptions.

above   across   below   beneath   on top of   to the right   in back of

On top of the track our car groaned to a halt. Then the rain suddenly rushed down. . . . Below us a huge pool of water waited. . . .

Narrative: You can use the following transitions, which show time, to arrange details in your narratives.

after   before   during   first   second   today   next   then

I squeezed my grandmother's hand, holding on with all my strength. First, when we entered the classroom, I let go and walked around. Then I headed back toward my grandmother—only she wasn't there.

Expository: You can use the following transitions to organize comparisons and contrasts.

(when comparing)	like	also	both	in the same way	similarly
(when contrasting)	but	still	yet	on the other hand	unlike

Both fossil fuels and sunlight can produce energy to run cars and heat homes. . . . But solar energy has some distinct advantages. . . .

Persuasive: You can use the following transitions to organize the details in your persuasive essays.

in fact   in addition   equally important   all in all

In fact, more cars and more roads lead to more congestion in busy areas. . . . All in all, the automobile is the leading cause of air pollution. . . .

How else can I organize my writing?

Many of the essays that you will be asked to write require two different types of thinking about a topic. There's the comparison-contrast essay, the problem-solution essay, and so on. To organize these types of essays you have to consider the two parts of the topic.

Creating a Two-Part Focus Statement

To help you organize a two-part essay, you need to develop an effective focus statement, but only after you have gathered enough facts and details. If you can't think of a focus statement for your two-part essay, complete one of the patterns below. (See pages 548–549 for two-part graphic organizers.)

For problem-solution essays:

. . . could be fixed if . . .
. . . won't change until . . .

The lack of open gym time for basketball (part 1) could be fixed if **the community center extended its hours** (part 2).

For cause-effect essays:

Because of . . . we now . . .
When . . . happened, I *(we, they)* . . .

Because of **the stricter grade requirements** (part 1), we now **have fewer students going out for sports** (part 2).

For comparison-contrast essays:

_____ and _____ are both . . . but they differ in . . .
While _____ and _____ have . . . in common, they also . . .

Sharks and **dolphins** are both **fascinating sea creatures** (part 1), but they differ in **many significant ways** (part 2).

For before-after essays:

Once I *(we, they, it)* . . . , but now . . .
I *(we, they, it)* . . . until . . .

Once I **had trouble understanding American culture** (part 1), but now **it makes much better sense to me** (part 2).

Write a focus statement for each two-part essay shown above. Think of topics that you know well or have strong feelings about. Share your statements with your classmates for discussion.

Understanding **Voice**

Author Sandra Belton says, "I write for myself because that's who I have to please first." When someone writes for her- or himself, the person's writing voice shines through.

How can I sound confident in my writing?

You will sound confident in your writing if you . . .

- show genuine interest in your topic,
- know a great deal about it, and
- share your honest thoughts and feelings.

Writing Without Confidence

For my history project, I thought I might build a model castle and then write about it.

To build the castle, I will need to learn a lot about castles and figure out how to build one. Maybe I could use some plywood, clay, and stuff like that.

My project should give the class some idea about medieval castles. If you think I might be on the right track, please let me know.

Writing With Confidence

For my history project on medieval life, I plan to build a scale model (2' x 2') of an English castle and write an essay on the construction of castles for protection.

To complete this project, I will need books on medieval castles, a 3' x 3' plywood board for the base, modeling clay for the walls, toilet paper rolls for the frame of the towers, toothpicks and glue for . . .

My project will help the class understand how a castle was built and how it was used. I would appreciate any suggestions before I get started.

Should I sound enthusiastic in my writing?

Yes, your readers will appreciate it if you sound enthusiastic because it means that you truly care about your topic. However, be careful not to sound too enthusiastic. Too much excitement in your voice will sound phony.

Write a brief note to a coach, a director, an advisor, or a parent displaying a confident voice.

Understanding **Word Choice**

Using the best words is an important part of writing. The best words are the ones that sincerely reflect your feelings about your topic. As author Stephen King says, "One of the really bad things you can do is dress up your vocabulary, looking for long words."

How can I improve the verbs that I use?

Here are some strategies that you can use to improve the verbs in your writing:

- After writing a first draft, list the verbs that you have used. If many of your sentences contain linking verbs (*is, are, was, were,* and so on) or overused verbs (*look, see, talk,* and so on), replace some of them.
  A sentence containing an overused verb:
  The play director talked to the unprepared cast members.
  The revised sentence containing a more specific verb:
  The play director lectured the unprepared cast members.
- Use verbs that are active and move the writing forward. Make it clear in your sentences that your subject is actually doing something.
  A sentence that is slow moving because of the verb:
  A surplus of calories is necessary for growth in children.
  The revised sentence that is more direct and active:
  Children require plenty of calories for growth.

How does word choice affect the tone of my writing?

The tone of your writing is the feeling that your writing produces. If the purpose of your writing is to explain or persuade, use words that suggest a serious tone. On the other hand, if the purpose of your writing is to share or to entertain, use words that suggest a more personal tone.

Word choice suggesting a serious, somewhat formal tone:

The automobile has become the main means of transportation, making many aspects of daily life much easier. However, too many people have become overly reliant on the automobile.

Word choice suggesting a personal, more informal tone:

Suddenly I heard these slurping, snorting noises coming from our campsite. I crept to the door. I saw a big brown bear munching on our marshmallows.

Review one of your latest first drafts and circle any verbs that could be improved. Replace some of these verbs with more effective ones. Also check the tone of your draft. Do all of the words reflect your intended tone?

Understanding Sentence Fluency

All writers build their stories, arguments, or explanations one sentence at a time. Author Gloria Naylor clearly understands the importance of each sentence in her work: "The bottom line for me is the sentence in front of my face. If nine out of ten of them hit the mark, then I am satisfied."

How can I test my writing for fluency?

Sentences are fluent when they all work together to make your writing enjoyable to read. Use the following strategies to test your sentences.

- When you edit your writing, list the opening words in each of your sentences. Decide if you need to vary some of your sentence beginnings.
- Then identify the number of words in each sentence. Consider changing the length of some of your sentences if too many of them have the same number of words.
- Also check your writing for transitions—*first of all, in addition,* and so on. When you revise your writing, add transitions as needed to make the connections between your sentences easier to follow.
- Have someone else read your writing aloud. As this person reads, listen for any sentences that cause the reader to stumble. Then decide if you should revise those sentences to make them easier to read.

How can sentence modeling help me?

You can learn a lot about fluency by studying the sentences and passages of some of your favorite authors. When you come across sentences that you really like, practice writing sentences of your own following that pattern. This process is called **modeling**. (See pages 521–522 for more information.)

A professional sentence from *A Solitary Blue* by Cynthia Voight:

> **Jeff couldn't see the musician clearly, just a figure on a chair on the stage, holding what looked like a misshapen guitar.**

A student model:

> Larisa couldn't identify the person immediately, just a shadow in the dark alley behind the store, carrying what appeared to be a heavy box.

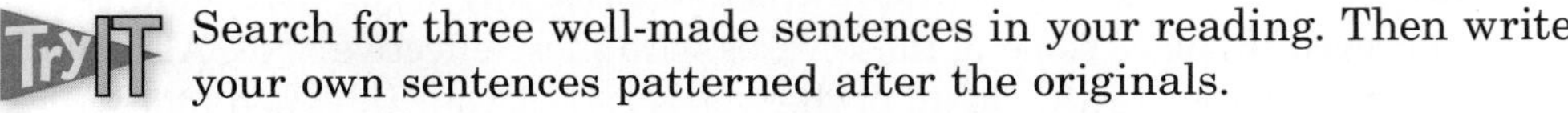

Try It Search for three well-made sentences in your reading. Then write your own sentences patterned after the originals.

What are different ways I can start my sentences?

You can vary your sentence beginnings in many different ways. Some of the key ways are listed below:

- **Start with a single-word modifier.**
  Before: **Susan Lue confidently stepped into the batter's box.**
  After: Confidently, **Susan Lue stepped into the batter's box.**
- **Start with a participial phrase.**
  (See pages 514 and 520.)
  Before: **She tripped and fell right next to us,** chasing after the pop fly.
  After: Chasing after the pop fly, **she tripped and fell right next to us.**
- **Start with an infinitive phrase.**
  (See pages 514 and 520.)
  Before: **I decided to interview my grandfather** to learn about his days as a baseball player.
  After: To learn about my grandfather's days as a baseball player, **I decided to interview him.**

Carefully review one of your recent pieces of writing. Look for parts in which the sentences all seem to start in the same way. Vary some of these sentences using the information above as a guide.

What types of sentences add style to writing?

Look for the following types of sentences whenever you read, and practice writing your own versions.

- A **loose sentence** expresses the main idea near the beginning (underlined below) and adds details as needed.

  <u>Wil nodded to himself and slipped away</u>, softly as a mouse, toward the back of the house where tourists were never taken.

  —"A Room Full of Leaves" by Joan Aiken

- A **balanced sentence** includes two or more parts that are equal or parallel in structure. (The parallel parts are underlined below.)

  He <u>goes out onto his baseball field</u>, <u>spins around second base</u>, and <u>looks back at the academy</u>.

  —*The Headmaster* by John McPhee

Understanding **Conventions**

Good writing follows the conventions, or basic rules, of the language. These rules cover punctuation, capitalization, grammar, and spelling. When you follow these rules, the reader will find your writing much easier to understand and enjoy.

How can I make sure my writing follows the rules?

A checklist like the one below can guide you as you look over your writing for errors. When you are not sure about a certain rule, refer to the "Proofreader's Guide" (pages 578–749).

Conventions

PUNCTUATION

_____ **1.** Do I use end punctuation after all my sentences?

_____ **2.** Do I use commas correctly in compound sentences?

_____ **3.** Do I use commas correctly in a series?

_____ **4.** Do I use apostrophes correctly to show possession (*that girl's purse* and *those girls' purses*)?

CAPITALIZATION

_____ **5.** Do I start every sentence with a capital letter?

_____ **6.** Do I capitalize the proper names of people and places?

SPELLING

_____ **7.** Have I checked my spelling using a spell-checker?

_____ **8.** Have I also checked the spelling by myself?

GRAMMAR

_____ **9.** Do I use correct forms of verbs (*had gone,* not *had went*)?

_____ **10.** Do my subjects and verbs agree in number (*the boy eats* and *the boys eat*)?

_____ **11.** Do I use the right word (*to, too,* or *two*)?

Have at least one other person check your writing for conventions. Professional writers have trained editors to help them with this step in the process. You should ask your classmates, teachers, and family members for help.

Using a Rubric

How can a writer be measured? A tape measure can tell the writer's hat size, but it can't even begin to measure the person's *ideas,* unique writing *voice,* and *word choice.* A rubric can measure these things.

Rubrics have other uses as well. They can help to prepare a writer at the beginning of a project. They can also guide a writer through the development of a first draft and aid in the revising and editing process. By using the rubric throughout the writing process, a writer can also make sure that his or her final work is ready for assessment. In this chapter, you will learn about all these uses of a rubric—and more!

What's Ahead

- **Understanding Rubrics**
- **Reading a Rubric**
- **Getting Started with a Rubric**
- **Revising and Editing with a Rubric**
- **Assessing with a Rubric**
- **Assessing in Action**
- **Assessing a Persuasive Essay**

Understanding Rubrics

Rubrics are rating scales. Have you ever rated books or movies on a scale from a high of 10 (perfect) down to a low of 1? With rubrics, you can rate your writing—in this case on a scale from 6 to 1.

Any piece of writing has a number of different traits or qualities—*ideas, organization, voice, word choice, sentence fluency,* and *conventions*. (For more about the traits, see pages **33–44**). In a single essay, the ideas might be amazing (6), but the word choice might be merely okay (3). See the rating guide below.

Rating Guide

This guide will help you understand the rating scale.

A **6** means that the writing is truly amazing.
It goes way beyond the requirements for a certain trait.

A **5** means that the writing is very strong.
It clearly meets the main requirements for a trait.

A **4** means that the writing is good.
It meets most of the requirements for a trait.

A **3** means that the writing is okay.
It needs work to meet the main requirements for a trait.

A **2** means that the writing is poor.
It needs a lot of work to meet the requirements for a trait.

A **1** means that the writing is incomplete.
It is not yet ready to assess for a trait.

Reading a Rubric

In this book, the rubrics are color-coded according to the traits. *Ideas* appear in a green strip, *organization* in a pink strip, and so on. Within each strip, the trait is ranked from 6 to 1.

Rubric for Persuasive Writing

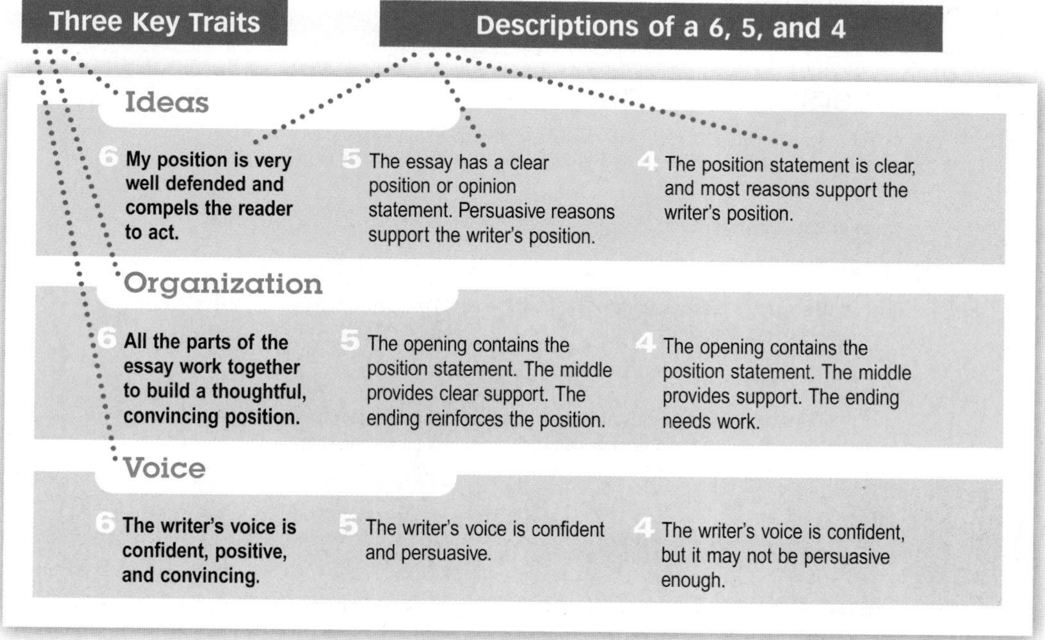

Three Key Traits	Descriptions of a 6, 5, and 4		
Ideas	**6 My position is very well defended and compels the reader to act.**	5 The essay has a clear position or opinion statement. Persuasive reasons support the writer's position.	4 The position statement is clear, and most reasons support the writer's position.
Organization	**6 All the parts of the essay work together to build a thoughtful, convincing position.**	5 The opening contains the position statement. The middle provides clear support. The ending reinforces the position.	4 The opening contains the position statement. The middle provides support. The ending needs work.
Voice	**6 The writer's voice is confident, positive, and convincing.**	5 The writer's voice is confident and persuasive.	4 The writer's voice is confident, but it may not be persuasive enough.

Guiding Your Writing

A rubric helps you . . .

- **plot your course**—knowing what is expected,
- **create a strong first draft**—focusing on *ideas, organization,* and *voice,*
- **revise and edit your work**—considering each trait, and
- **assess your final copies**—rating the traits and the whole assignment.

Think about the rubric. Read the level 5 descriptions above for *ideas, organization,* and *voice*. What makes an opinion statement clear? What makes reasons persuasive? How are the opening, middle, and ending best organized? What makes a writer's voice confident and persuasive? The following pages will use rubrics to help you answer questions like these.

Getting Started with a Rubric

Each of the writing units in this book begins by outlining your writing goals. The page below provides the goals from the persuasive rubric. By previewing the writing rubric, you will understand the main requirements for the unit.

224

Understanding Your Goal

Your goal in this chapter is to write a well-organized persuasive essay that defends a position. The traits listed in the chart below will help you plan and write your essay.

Traits of Persuasive Writing

Ideas

Use specific reasons to defend a position about an issue in your school or community.

Organization

Create a beginning that states your position, a middle that provides support and answers an objection, and an ending that restates your position.

Voice

Use a persuasive voice that balances facts and feelings.

Word Choice

Choose fair words and qualifiers to strengthen your position.

Sentence Fluency

Write clear, complete sentences with varied beginnings.

Conventions

Check your writing for errors in punctuation, capitalization, spelling, and grammar.

Literature Connections: For another example of persuasive writing, read the editorial "Should the Driving Age Be Raised to 18?" by Alex Koroknay-Palicz.

A Closer Look at Understanding Your Goal

The following steps will help you use the "Understanding Your Goal" rubric at the beginning of each writing unit.

1. **Read through the whole chart** to understand your general goals in writing.
2. **Focus on *ideas, organization,* and *voice*** in your prewriting and writing, since these traits are the foundation of excellent writing. (See the chart below.)
3. **Identify goals** for each trait (such as "specific reasons" or "defend a position").
4. **Ask questions** if you aren't sure about any part of the assignment.

A Special Note About the Traits

Different traits are important at different times during your writing. The following chart shows which traits are important at what times.

During **Prewriting** and **Writing**, focus on the *ideas, organization,* and *voice* in your writing.

During **Revising**, focus on *ideas, organization, voice, word choice,* and *sentence fluency.* (For some assignments, your teacher may ask you to concentrate most of your attention on one or two of these traits.)

During **Editing** and proofreading, focus on *conventions.*

When **Assessing** a final copy, consider all six traits. (For some assignments, your teacher may ask you to assess a piece of writing for just a few of the traits.)

Write a paragraph. Review the goal rubric on page 48. Then write a short paragraph stating your position about an issue in your school or community. Keep the traits in mind as you write.

Revising and Editing with a Rubric

6 My position is very well defended and compels the reader to act.

5 My position is supported with logical reasons, and I respond to an important objection.

4 Most of my reasons support my position. I respond to an objection.

In this book, the sections on revising and editing each start with a rubric strip that focuses on one trait and the activities presented on those pages. It provides ratings from 6 to 1. The rubric strip above focuses on the *ideas* of persuasive writing.

How can rubric strips help me rate my writing?

A rubric strip can help you look objectively at your writing. By knowing how your work measures up, you will be better able to revise or edit. Follow these steps when considering each trait.

1. Begin by checking the number 5 description (a rating of *strong*).
2. Decide if your writing rates a 5.
3. If not, check the 6 or 4 descriptions.
4. Continue until you find the rating that matches your writing.
5. Notice how levels 3, 2, and 1 suggest ways to improve your writing.

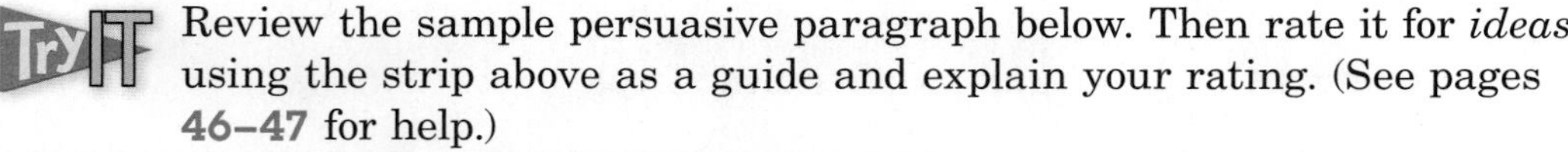

Try It Review the sample persuasive paragraph below. Then rate it for *ideas* using the strip above as a guide and explain your rating. (See pages **46–47** for help.)

Songs and jingles that get stuck in my head drive me crazy. Songs like this are called earworms because they enter a person's ear and burrow into the brain and won't go away. Pop stars and ad companies come up with the tunes. Special techniques make a song stick. There's no cure for earworms except to turn off all electronic media.

PROCESS

3 I need more supporting reasons and a more convincing response to an objection.

2 I need to rethink my position from start to finish.

1 I need to learn how to defend a position.

How can rubric strips help me revise and edit?

Once you have rated your writing for a given trait, you will see ways to improve your score. The writer of the paragraph on page 50 rated her ideas as a 3. The description of a 3 for ideas told her just what she needed to do to improve her work.

In the main writing units, each rubric strip is followed by minilessons that will help you revise or edit your writing to improve that trait.

In order to create more logical reasons and provide a convincing response to an objection, the writer made the following changes.

Ideas
Details are made more specific.

An objection is answered in a convincing way.

Songs and jingles that get stuck in my head drive me crazy. "The Sweet Escape" once haunted me for weeks. Songs like this are called earworms because they enter a person's ear and burrow into the brain and won't go away. Pop stars and ad companies come up with the tunes using simple lyrics and catchy rhythms to ~~Special techniques~~ make a song stick. Some people don't mind ~~There's no cure for~~ earworms, but others should just ~~except to~~ turn off all electronic media.

Assessing with a Rubric

When you use a rubric like the one on the facing page, follow these four steps to assess your writing.

1. **Create an assessment sheet.** Use the sample at the right to create your own sheet. Write each of the key traits from the rubric, preceded by a short line. Under each trait, leave two or three lines to allow for comments.

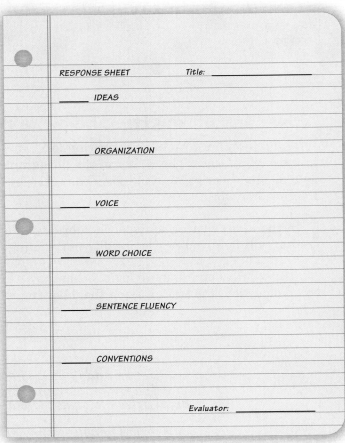

RESPONSE SHEET Title: ____________

_____ IDEAS

_____ ORGANIZATION

_____ VOICE

_____ WORD CHOICE

_____ SENTENCE FLUENCY

_____ CONVENTIONS

Evaluator: ____________

2. **Read the final copy.** First, read straight through to get an overall sense of the writing. Then read more carefully, paying attention to the traits.

3. **Assess the writing.** Use the rubric to rate each trait by checking the description for 5 and shifting up or down the scale until you discover the correct rating. Write down the number next to the right trait.

4. **Provide comments.** Under each trait, write one thing you liked and one thing that could be improved.

Assess your persuasive paragraph. Make an assessment sheet like the one above. Then evaluate your paragraph (from page 49) using the rubric on pages 256–257. For each trait, write something you did well and something you'd like to improve. (See the sample on page 55.)

PROCESS

Rubric for Persuasive Writing

Refer to the following rubric for guiding and assessing your persuasive writing. Use it to improve your writing using the six traits.

Trait	6	5	4
Ideas	**My position is very well defended and compels the reader to act.**	The essay has a clear position or opinion statement. Persuasive reasons support the writer's position.	The position statement is clear, and most reasons support the writer's position.
Organization	**All the parts of the essay work together to build a thoughtful, convincing position.**	The opening contains the position statement. The middle provides clear support. The ending reinforces the position.	The opening contains the position statement. The middle provides support. The ending needs work.
Voice	**The writer's voice is confident, positive, and convincing.**	The writer's voice is confident and persuasive.	The writer's voice is confident, but it may not be persuasive enough.
Word Choice	**The writer's choice of words makes a powerful case.**	The writer's word choice helps persuade the reader.	Some changes would make the word choice more persuasive.
Sentence Fluency	**The sentences spark the reader's interest in the essay.**	Variety is seen in both the types of sentences and their beginnings.	Varied sentence beginnings are used. Sentence variety would make the essay more interesting to read.
Conventions	**The writing is error free.**	Grammar and punctuation errors are few. The reader is not distracted by the errors.	Grammar and punctuation errors are seen in a few sentences. They distract the reader in those areas.

Each complete rubric lets you review all six traits of writing.

3	2	1
		A new position statement and reasons are needed.
		The organization is unclear and incomplete.
		The writer has not considered voice.
Many more precise and persuasive words are needed.	The words do not create a clear message. Some unfair words are used.	Word choice has not been considered.
Varied sentence beginnings are needed. Sentence variety would make the essay more interesting.	Most sentences begin the same way. Most of the sentences are simple. Compound and complex sentences are needed.	Sentence fluency has not been established. Ideas do not flow smoothly.
There are a number of errors that may confuse the reader.	Frequent errors make the essay difficult to read.	Nearly every sentence contains errors.

PERSUASIVE

The rubrics provide a scale in which 6 is the highest rating. A 1 is the lowest.

Assessing in Action

In the following persuasive essay, the writer both states his position on an issue in his school and defends his position against an important objection. Read the essay, paying attention to its strengths and weaknesses. Then read the self-assessment on the following page. **(The essay contains errors.)**

Lend a Helping Hand

For the last few years, Wentworth school board has considered creating a student mentoring program. Students who do well in their studies would receive extra credit for helping students who struggle. After years of debate, its time to make student mentoring a reality.

First of all, student mentoring would help create cooperation rather then competition. Right now, after each test, a few students come out "on top" and the others get bummed. With student mentoring, students work together rather than competing. Grades should be about learning, not "winning."

Student mentoring would also help teachers. With a student-teacher ratio of 30 to 1, teachers can't give much one-on-one attention to students. A mentoring program would put extra "teachers" in each class. So more kids could get individual attention.

Most important, student mentoring would help learning. Many struggling students would get the help of a student mentor. Mentors would learn by sharing knowledge. A win-win situation!

Admittedly, a mentoring program would take time to get organized. Teachers would have to choose and train mentors. Still, the program would save time in the long run.

Wentworth Middle School needs student mentoring. The program would create cooperation, help teachers, improve learning, and save time overall. For all these reasons, school board members should vote "yes" for mentoring.

Sample Assessment

The student who wrote "Lend a Helping Hand" created an assessment sheet to evaluate his essay. He used the persuasive rubric on pages 256–257. Under each trait, he wrote one strength and one weakness.

RESPONSE SHEET Title: Lend a Helping Hand

4 IDEAS
1. My position statement is clear, and I include persuasive details.
2. A few more details would have made my essay stronger.

4 ORGANIZATION
1. I followed the plan for my paragraphs.
2. Some of my transitions sound kind of unnatural.

4 VOICE
1. My voice is confident, positive, and persuasive.
2. In a few places, I'm not formal enough.

3 WORD CHOICE
1. Most of my words are accurate.
2. The word "bummed" really sticks out.

3 SENTENCE FLUENCY
1. I tried to vary sentences.
2. Two fragments got past me!

4 CONVENTIONS
1. I caught many of my errors.
2. I should have proofed the final copy one more time.

Evaluator: Jason Rollingcloud

Review the assessment. **On your own paper, explain why you agree with the response above (or why you don't). Consider each trait carefully.**

Assessing a Persuasive Essay

Read the essay that follows and focus on the strengths and weaknesses in it. Then follow the directions at the bottom of the page. (**The essay contains errors.**)

Our Turn to Shine

Jonesburg Jr. High doesn't have a drama program, so junior high students have to try out for senior high plays. Upper-class actors get all the good parts, and younger students end up in the chorus or as extras. It's time for Jonesburg Jr. High to start its own drama club.

First of all, a junior high drama club would give students a chance at the lead roles. Instead of always standing in the background, they could learn lines, sing solos, and be the stars. As it is, junior high students don't get to feel much pride in senior high plays.

A drama club in the junior high would also help students learn about drama. It doesn't take much acting skill to sit in the background and pretend to make conversation or to stand and hold a spear. Also, junior high students often feel like they are "trespassing" when they participate in senior high plays. Instead of learning about drama, many younger students are learning that they don't want to be involved in drama.

Some people object that a junior high drama club would compete against the senior high program. However, a junior high program would actually support drama at the upper levels. It would train students in acting, singing, and dancing and would help set up drama supporters for the years to come.

Jonesburg Jr. High needs to start its own drama club. It would teach students about drama and help the senior high program. If someone asks about junior high drama, say, "It's long overdue!"

Use a persuasive rubric. Assess the persuasive essay you have just read using the rubric on pages 256–257 as a guide. Before you get started, create an assessment sheet like the one on page 52. *Remember:* After each trait, add comments (something good, something to improve).

Publishing Your Writing

To build a kite, you begin with simple things: paper, a frame, and plenty of string. Still, when these elements are put together well, the kite will leap into the sky and soar, and everyone for miles around will be able to marvel at it.

Writing is the same way. An essay begins with paper, a framework of ideas, and a string of thought. Put the pieces together well, and you'll create something that will soar. After you finish your work, you'll naturally want everyone to see it. For that, you will need to know your publishing options.

This chapter will help you get your writing ready to publish and give you a variety of publishing ideas. (Also see "Creating a Portfolio" on pages 65–69.)

What's Ahead

- Sharing Your Writing
- Preparing to Publish
- Designing Your Writing
- Making Your Own Web Site
- Publishing Online

Sharing Your Writing

Some publishing ideas are easy to carry out, like sharing your writing with your classmates. Other publishing ideas take more time and effort, like entering a writing contest. Try a number of these publishing ideas during the school year. All of them will help you grow as a writer.

Performing

- Sharing with Classmates
- Reading to Various Audiences
- Preparing a Multimedia Presentation
- Videotaping for Special Audiences
- Performing Onstage

In School

- School Newspapers
- Classroom Collections
- School Literary Magazines
- Writing Portfolios

Self-Publishing

- Family Newsletters
- Greeting Cards
- Bound Writings
- Online Publications

Posting

- Classroom Bulletin Boards
- School or Public Libraries
- School Display Cases
- Business Windows
- Clinic Waiting Rooms
- Literary/Art Fairs

Sending It Out

- Local Newspapers
- Area Historical Society
- Young Writers' Conferences
- Magazines and Contests
- Various Web Sites

Plan your publishing. Select three or four pieces of writing that you feel are your best work. Using the lists above, decide which specific type of publishing (performing onstage, business windows, and so on) would be the best for each of your selected works. Then make specific proposals for publishing each one.

Preparing to Publish

Your writing is ready to publish when it is clear, complete, and correct. Getting your writing to this point requires careful revising and editing. Follow the tips below to help you prepare your writing for publication.

Publishing Tips

- **Ask for advice during the writing process.**
  Be sure your writing answers any questions your readers may have about your topic.
- **Check the ideas, organization, voice, word choice, and sentence fluency in your writing.**
  Every part of your writing should be clear and complete.
- **Work with your writing.**
  Continue working until you feel good about your writing from beginning to end.
- **Check your writing for conventions.**
  In addition, ask at least one classmate to check your work for correctness. Another person can catch errors that you miss.
- **Prepare a neat finished copy.**
  Use a pen (blue or black ink) and write on one side of the paper if you are writing by hand. If you are writing with a computer, use a font that is easy to read. Double-space your writing.
- **Know your options.**
  Explore different ways to publish your writing. (See page 58.) Start small; then venture into more demanding—and creative—options.
- **Follow all publication guidelines.**
  Just as your teacher wants assignments presented in a certain way, so do the newspapers, magazines, or Web sites. Check for submission guidelines.

Save all drafts for each writing project. If you are preparing a portfolio (see pages 65–69), you may be required to include early drafts as well as finished pieces.

Designing Your Writing

Whenever you write, always focus on *what you say* before worrying about *how it looks*. Only when you're satisfied with content and style should you concentrate on design. For handwritten papers, write the final copy neatly in blue or black ink on clean paper. When using a computer, follow the guidelines below.

Typography

- Use an easy-to-read font. Generally, a serif font is best for the body, and a sans serif style is used for contrast in headings.

  The letters of serif fonts have "tails"—as in this sentence.

  The letters of sans serif styles are plain—as in this sentence.

- Use a title and headings. Headings break writing into smaller parts, making the writing easier to follow.

Spacing and Margins

- Use one-inch margins on all sides of your paper.
- Indent the first line of every paragraph.
- Use one space after every period and comma.
- Avoid awkward breaks between pages. Don't leave a heading or the first line of a paragraph at the bottom of a page or a column. Never split a hyphenated word between pages or columns.

Graphic Devices

- If appropriate, use bulleted lists in your writing. Often, a series of items works best as a bulleted list (like the ones on this page).
- Consider including graphics. A table, a chart, or an illustration can help make a point clearer. But keep each graphic small enough so that it doesn't dominate the page. A larger graphic can be displayed by itself on a separate page.

Analyze effective design. Working with a partner, compare the design features of articles from two different magazines. How are the design features of the two articles the same? How are they different? Decide which one is the most effective based on its audience and purpose.

Computer Design in Action

The following two pages show a well-designed student report. The side notes explain all of the design features.

The title is 18-point type.

The main text is 12-point type and double-spaced throughout.

Headings are 14-point type.

A graphic is inserted for visual interest.

Numbered lists identify main points.

John Swift

Running Toward Health

Joggers, runners, and walkers are everywhere. People who are thinking about taking up running should consider its benefits and what it takes to get started.

Looking at Benefits

Studies have shown that exercise produces definite health benefits. In addition to the proven advantages, people often report other reasons that they like physical activity. Here are three of the most important incentives for staying in shape.

1. **Strength.** Doctors recommend walking, jogging, and running because regular physical activity strengthens muscles and increases stamina.
2. **Weight Control.** Regular exercise helps change the way the body uses calories, which helps control weight.
3. **Long-Term Benefits.** Joggers say they feel better after exercising. Medical studies show that regular exercise early in life helps keep a person fit throughout life.

The writer's name and page number appear on every page starting with page 2.

A bulleted list helps organize the essay.

Margins are at least one inch all around.

Swift 2

Getting Started

Getting started is simple. Compared to many forms of exercise, jogging is easy and inexpensive because a fancy gym or costly equipment is not needed. The following suggestions can help someone start off "on the right foot."

- **Finding the right clothes.** Wear good quality, comfortable running shoes; they are really the only special equipment required. Light, roomy jogging clothes are best. More thin layers can be added in cold weather.
- **Setting aside time.** Block out 30 to 60 minutes for exercise every day. Make jogging a regular part of your schedule.
- **Running regularly.** Gradually increase time and distance. Don't try to run 10 miles the first day.

After a few weeks of regular jogging, the initial aches and pains will disappear. Then more options open up such as jogging for longer periods of time and for longer distances. There are also long-distance races, which can be very rewarding. Joggers who keep running are becoming healthier and stronger all the time.

Design a page. Create an effective design for an essay or a report you've already written. Share your design with a classmate to get some feedback: Does your design make the writing appealing to the reader? Is it clear and easy to follow? Does your design distract the reader in any way?

Making Your Own Web Site

You can make your own Web site if your family has an Internet account. Be sure you get the permission of your parents or guardians. Then ask your provider how to get started. If you are using a school account, ask your teacher for help. Use the questions and answers below as a starting point.

How do I plan my site?

Think about the purpose of your Web site and how many pages you need. Do you want a single page, or would several linked pages work better? Check out other sites for ideas. Then make sketches to plan your pages.

How do I make the pages?

Start each page as a text file by using your computer. Many word processing programs let you save a file as a Web page. If yours doesn't, you will have to add HTML (Hypertext Markup Language) codes to format the text and make links to graphics and other pages. You can find instructions for HTML on the Net or at the library.

How do I know whether my pages work?

You should always test your pages. Using your browser, open your first page. Then follow any links to make sure they work correctly. Also make sure that all the graphics appear and that the pages look perfect.

How do I get my pages on the Net?

You must upload your finished pages to the Internet. Ask your Internet provider how to do this. After the upload, visit your site to make sure it still works. Also, check it from other computers if possible.

How do I let people know about my site?

Once your site is up, e-mail your friends and tell them to visit it!

Try It Plan your own Web site. You might consider a site about your family or one of your special interests. Answer the following questions to help you get organized: What will be the title of the site? What would be a good picture or illustration for the opening page? Where will the links on the opening page lead your visitors?

Publishing Online

The Internet offers many publishing opportunities, including online magazines and writing contests. The information below will help you submit your writing for publication on the Net. (At home, always get a parent's approval first. In school, follow all guidelines for computer use.)

How should I get started?

Check with your teacher to see if your school has its own Web site where you can post your work. Also ask your teacher about other Web sites. There are a number of online magazines that accept student writing. Visit some of these magazines to learn about the types of writing they usually publish.

How do I search for possible sites?

Use a search engine to find places to publish. Some search engines offer their own student links.

How do I submit my work?

Before you do anything, make sure that you understand the publishing guidelines for each site. Be sure to share this information with your teacher and your parents. Then follow these steps:

- **Send your writing in the correct form.**
  Some sites have online forms. Others will ask you to send your writing by mail or e-mail. Always explain why you are sending your writing.
- **Give the publisher information for contacting you.**
  However, don't give your home address or any other personal information unless your parents approve.
- **Be patient.**
  A site may contact you within a week to confirm that your work has arrived. Be patient, though; it may be several weeks before you hear whether your writing will be used or not.

Search for Web sites. Use the guidelines above to search the Internet for sites that publish student work. Create a list of sites to share with the class. When you complete writing assignments, consider submitting your work for publication using one of the Web sites from your class list.

Creating a Portfolio

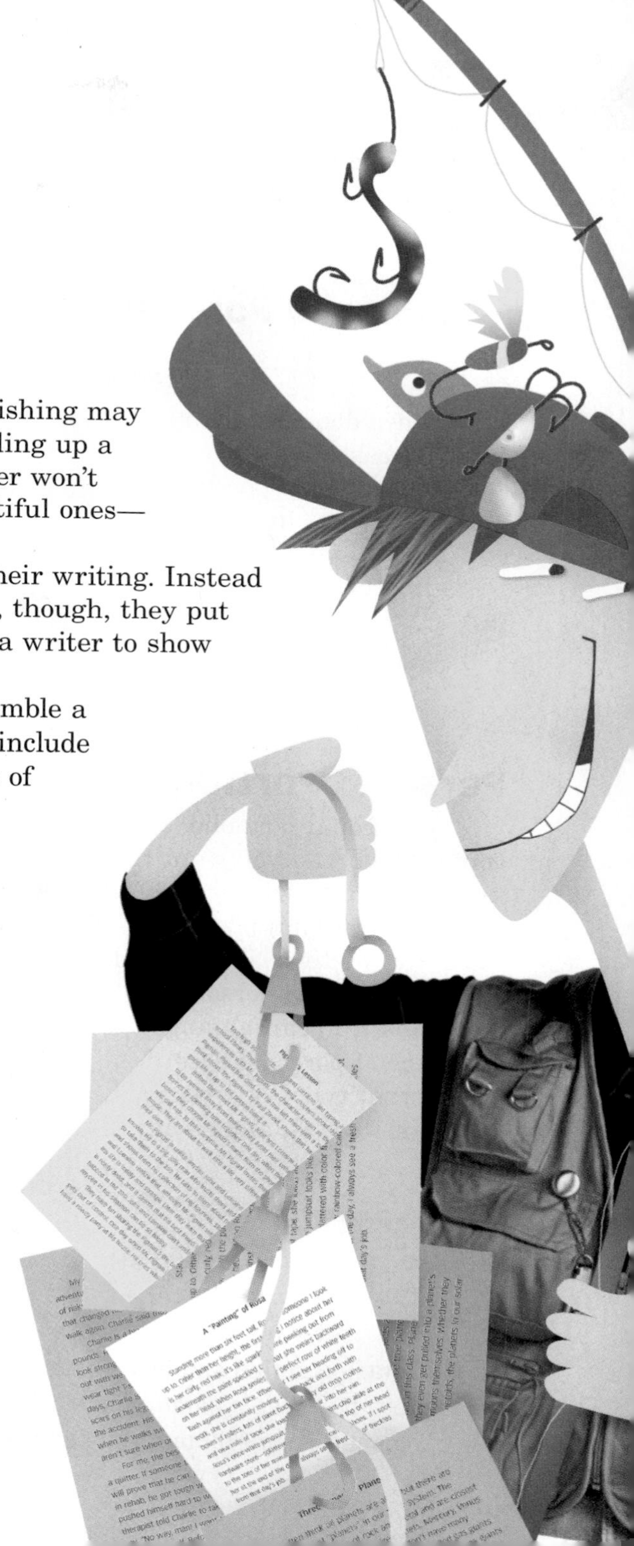

A person who has spent the day fishing may get his or her picture taken while holding up a stringer of fish. Of course, that stringer won't hold the small fish, only the big, beautiful ones—the "keepers."

Writers do the same thing with their writing. Instead of hanging their "keepers" on a string, though, they put them in a portfolio. A portfolio allows a writer to show off his or her best work.

This chapter will help you to assemble a writing portfolio. The following pages include information about the types and parts of portfolios, plus planning ideas.

What's Ahead

- **Types of Portfolios**
- **Parts of a Portfolio**
- **Planning Ideas**
- **Sample Portfolio Reflections**

Types of Portfolios

There are four basic types of portfolios you should know about: a showcase portfolio, a growth portfolio, a personal portfolio, and an electronic portfolio.

Showcase Portfolio

A showcase portfolio presents the best writing you have done in school. A showcase is the most common type of portfolio and is usually put together for evaluation at the end of a grading period.

Growth Portfolio

A growth portfolio shows your progress as a writer. It contains writing assignments that show how your writing skills are developing:

- writing beginnings and endings,
- writing with voice,
- using specific details, and
- using transitions.

Personal Portfolio

A personal portfolio contains writing you want to keep and share with others. Many professional people—including writers, artists, and musicians—keep personal portfolios. You can arrange this type of portfolio according to different types of writing, different themes, and so on.

Electronic Portfolio

An electronic portfolio is any type of portfolio (showcase, growth, or personal) available on a CD or a Web site. Besides your writing, you can include graphics, video, and sound with this type of portfolio. This makes your writing available to friends and family members no matter where they are!

Showcase your strengths. Review your writing from the most recent grading period and then select the pieces that you consider your best efforts. Write a paragraph that summarizes the strengths of your work. Also mention one skill that you still need to develop.

Parts of a Portfolio

A showcase portfolio is one of the most common types of portfolios used in schools. It may contain the parts listed below, but always check with your teacher to be sure.

- A **table of contents** lists the writing samples you have included in your portfolio.
- A **brief essay** or **letter** introduces your portfolio—telling how you put it together, how you feel about it, and what it means to you.
- A **collection of writing samples** presents your best work. Your teacher may require that you include all of your planning, drafting, and revising for one or more of your writings.
- A **cover sheet for each sample** explains why you selected it.
- **Evaluations**, **reflections**, or **checklists** identify the basic skills you have mastered, as well as those skills that you still need to work on.

Gathering Tips

- **Keep track of all your work.** Include your prewriting notes, first drafts, and revisions for each writing assignment. Then, when you put together a portfolio, you will have everything that you need.
- **Store all of your writing in a pocket folder or computer file.** This will help you keep track of your writing as you build your portfolio.
- **Set a schedule for working on your portfolio.** You can't put together a good portfolio by waiting until the last minute.
- **Take pride in your work.** Make sure that your portfolio shows you at your best.

Write your cover sheets. For each piece of writing that you include in your portfolio, write a cover sheet. Explain why the writing is a good example of your work. Tell what makes it stand out from other writing you have done. Finally, tell why you included it in your portfolio.

Planning Ideas

The following tips will help you choose your best pieces of writing to include in your portfolio.

1 Be patient.

Don't make quick decisions about which pieces of writing to include in your portfolio. Just keep gathering everything—including all of your drafts—until you are ready to review all of your writing assignments.

2 Make good decisions.

When it's time to choose writing for your portfolio, review each piece. Remember the feelings that you had during each assignment. Which piece makes you feel the best? Which one did your readers like the best? Which one taught you the most?

3 Reflect on your choices.

Read the sample reflections on page 69. Then answer these questions about your writing:

- Why did I choose this piece?
- Why did I write this piece? (What was my purpose?)
- How did I write it? (What was my process?)
- What does it show about my writing ability?
- How did my peers react to this writing?
- What would I do differently next time?
- What have I learned since writing it?

4 Set future writing goals.

After putting your portfolio together, set some goals for the future. Here are some goals that other students have set:

I will write about topics that really interest me.

I will spend more time on my beginnings and endings.

I will make sure that my sentences read smoothly.

I will support my main points with convincing details.

Set your goals. After you finish putting together a portfolio, set some goals for your future writing. Review the student goals listed above and then identify three goals that would improve your writing.

Sample Portfolio Reflections

When you take time to reflect on your writing assignments, think about the process that you used to develop each one. Also think about what you might do differently next time. The following samples will help you with your own reflections.

Student Reflections

Of all the writing in my portfolio, I am proudest of my persuasive essay about volunteering at the Humane Society. It was a challenge. To write persuasively, I had to understand my topic, my feelings about it, and my reader's feelings. Every word mattered. I worked hard on that essay, but in the end, it helped convince two of my friends to volunteer.

—Melissa Breen

My expository essay turned out really well because I was interested in my topic. It was easy to break the subject down into its parts because I understood it. I seem to have trouble whenever I have to summarize information from other sources, because it's hard to organize the information in a way that is different from the original. The strongest part of my expository essay is the way I used comparisons with everyday things to help explain difficult ideas.

—Thad Molumba

Professional Reflections

As you continue writing and rewriting, you begin to see possibilities you hadn't seen before.

—Robert Hayden

The only way, I think, to learn to write short stories is to write them, and then try to discover what you have done.

—Flannery O'Connor

SPECIFY
picture

WRITE SOURCE Online
www.hmheducation.com/writesource

Descriptive Writing

Writing Focus

- **Descriptive Paragraph**
- **Describing a Person**

Grammar Focus

- **Verbs and Adjectives**

Academic Vocabulary

Work with a partner. Read each meaning and then answer the questions.

1. Words that give you a picture in your head are **descriptive**.
   Name a descriptive word for the color of the sky.
2. Something's **appearance** is the way it looks.
   Describe the appearance of your school.
3. A **challenge** is a task that requires a lot of effort.
   When have you faced a challenge at school?
4. A **feature** is a part of something that gets attention.
   What feature stands out in your favorite game?
5. When a person is **inspired**, he or she has strong feelings to do something.
   Tell about a time that you felt inspired.

express
describe
portray

Descriptive Writing

Descriptive Paragraph

By skillfully brushing paint onto a canvas, an artist can create a vision of a distant landscape or an image of an amazing person. When you write descriptively, you can do the same thing. By carefully arranging words on a piece of paper, you can create a vision of a faraway place or a wonderful likeness of a person.

In this unit, you will write a paragraph that paints a picture of a person. Your goal is to write a description that makes the person come alive for the reader.

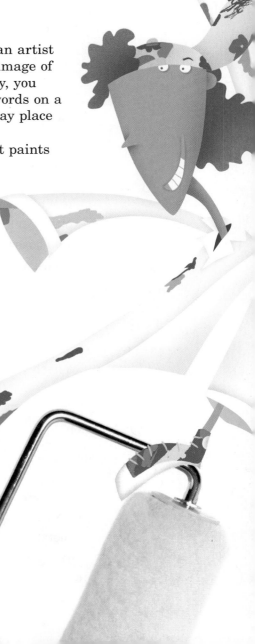

Writing Guidelines

Subject: A favorite person
Form: Descriptive paragraph
Purpose: To describe what a person looks like
Audience: Classmates

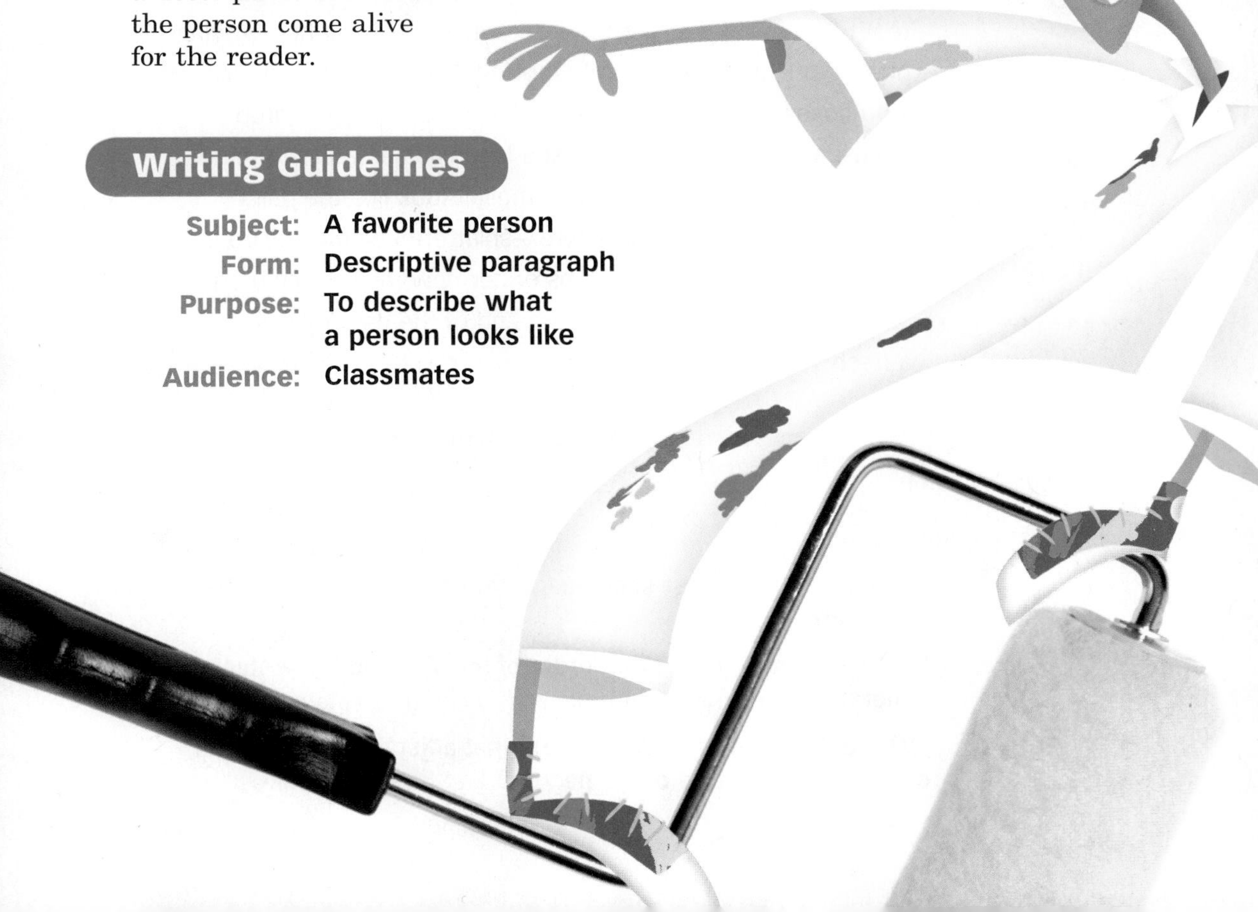

Descriptive Paragraph

A descriptive paragraph offers a detailed picture of a person, a place, a thing, or an event. It begins with a **topic sentence** that tells what the paragraph is about. The sentences in the **body** include descriptive details about the topic, and the **closing sentence** wraps up the paragraph. In the paragraph below, the writer used specific details to describe a painter.

Topic Sentence

Body

Closing Sentence

A "Painting" of Rosa

Standing more than six feet tall, Rosa is someone I look up to. Other than her height, the first thing I notice about her is her curly, red hair. It's like sparks of fire peeking out from underneath the paint-speckled cap that she wears backward on her head. When Rosa smiles, her perfect row of white teeth flashes against her tan face. Whenever I see her heading off to work, she is constantly moving. Zipping back and forth with boxes of rollers, lots of paint buckets, bulky old drop cloths, and new rolls of tape, she loads all her gear into her van. Rosa and her once-white jumpsuit look like the paint-chip aisle at the hardware store—splattered with color from the top of her head to the toes of her now rainbow-colored canvas shoes. If I spot her at the end of the day, I always see a fresh set of freckles from that day's job.

Respond to the reading. On your own paper, answer each of the following questions.

- ☐ Ideas **(1) In the first sentence, what detail gets the reader's attention?**
- ☐ Organization **(2) What order of location did the writer generally follow *(top to bottom, left to right)*? Explain.**
- ☐ Voice & Word Choice **(3) What adjectives are used to create a clear picture of the person? List three of them.**

Prewriting Selecting a Topic

First, you must choose a person to write about. Listing is a good way to get started. The writer of the paragraph on page 72 made lists of people whose physical appearances were interesting to him.

People I Know	People I See Often
* Dr. Willard, the eye doctor	* The old man who feeds the ducks
* My great-grandpa Salvatore	* The little kid who hangs out near my grandma's
* Ron, the junk guy	* Rosa the painter
* My oldest sister, the chef	

Select a topic. Make lists of interesting people you know or often see during your daily activities. Then circle one to describe in a paragraph.

Gathering Details

Your descriptive paragraph should show instead of tell. Before you write your paragraph, jot down concrete details that show what your person looks like from head to toe.

Collect your details. To get started, answer the following questions about your person.

1. Is there any feature that is immediately noticeable (height, color of hair, smile, freckles, posture, and so on)?
2. How can I describe the person's hair, face, and posture?
3. What type of clothes does this person wear?
4. Do the clothes have anything to do with a particular job?
5. Does the person move in a special way or wear unusual shoes?
6. What one word comes to mind when I see this person?

Writing Creating Your First Draft

The goal of a first draft is to get all of your ideas and details down on paper. Follow the guidelines below.

- Start with a topic sentence that catches your reader's attention. Include a noticeable feature of the person you're describing.
- Use order of location (head to toe) to organize the details in the body of your paragraph. Include the details that you gathered on page 73.
- End with a sentence that keeps the reader thinking about the person.

Write your first draft. Get all your ideas and details down on paper, thoroughly describing your topic from head to toe. When you are finished, give your paragraph a title.

Revising Improving Your Writing

Now that you have finished your first draft, you need to review it and make revisions. Add, delete, or move parts to make your paragraph clear and interesting to your reader.

Revise your paragraph. Use the following questions as a guide.

1. Does my topic sentence introduce the person and mention a noticeable feature?
2. Have I included details that create a clear picture of the person?
3. Have I organized the details from head to toe?
4. Do I sound interested in the description?
5. Do I use specific nouns, verbs, and adjectives?
6. Do I use complete sentences that read smoothly?

Editing Checking for Conventions

Carefully edit your revised paragraph for capitalization, spelling, grammar, and punctuation. Then write a neat final copy.

Edit and proofread your work. Use the checklist on page 128 to check your writing for errors. Then write a neat final copy of your paragraph.

Descriptive Writing

Describing a Person

Every person is unique. Think of people you know and admire. What do they look like? What are their personality traits? What makes them interesting or special? Answering these questions will give you a variety of details to include in a descriptive essay about a person.

In this unit, you will read an essay describing a person who loved to snowmobile. Then you will write an essay that describes a person who has influenced you in a positive way.

Writing Guidelines

Subject: A person who has positively influenced you

Form: Descriptive essay

Purpose: To describe a person

Audience: Classmates

Descriptive Essay

In this sample essay, the writer describes his cousin Charlie. As you read the description, look at the notes in the left margin. They explain the important parts of the essay.

Beginning

The beginning introduces the person.

Middle

The first middle paragraph describes the physical appearance (from head to toe).

The next middle paragraph describes the personality.

The Price of Danger

My older cousin Charlie was always up for an adventure, especially if it was dangerous. Charlie took lots of risks. Then, one day, he had a snowmobile accident that changed his life. The doctors said that he might never walk again. Charlie said they were wrong.

Charlie is a big guy who is more than six feet tall and weighs 260 pounds. His size, along with his long, black hair, makes him look strong, like a fullback or a wrestler. Because he works out with weights, his arm muscles are like iron. He likes to wear tight T-shirts to show off his biceps and abs. These days, Charlie is wearing baggy sweatpants to cover up the scars on his legs, which are banged up and twisted from the accident. His feet sometimes drag along the ground when he walks with his forearm crutches. The doctors aren't sure when or if Charlie will ever fully recover.

For me, the best thing about Charlie is that he's not a quitter. If someone tells him he can't do something, he will prove that he can. In the beginning, when Charlie was in rehab, he got tough with himself. At every session, he pushed himself hard to walk again. When the physical therapist told Charlie to take a break, my cousin would say,

"No way, man! I want to do this now." Charlie kept pushing himself. Before long he was getting around pretty well without any help. However, I know Charlie. He's not going to be satisfied until he can walk without his crutches.

Middle
The third middle paragraph shares an anecdote.

Before the accident, Charlie liked riding his snowmobile and his motorcycle and jogging with his black Lab, Tex. These days he's finding other ways to keep active. When the whole family got together at Thanksgiving, Charlie couldn't play on our pickup football team. That didn't stop him. He did a super job of coaching us from the sidelines.

Ending
The ending tells how the person influenced the writer.

My cousin Charlie has taught me two important lessons. First, I realize I should check out all the safety rules before I try something risky. Second, the best way to get through bad times is to have the right attitude. Charlie's attitude is just as strong as he is. I believe that someday Charlie will walk the way he did before, just like he says he will.

Respond to the reading. Answer the following questions about the essay.

- ☐ **Ideas** (1) What special challenge does the subject of the essay face? (2) What physical features does the writer describe to create a picture for the reader? (3) What details give the reader an insight into the subject's personality?
- ☐ **Voice & Word Choice** (4) What words or phrases show that Charlie has had a positive influence on the writer? List two.

Literature Connections: For another example of descriptive writing, read author Richard Peck's description of his grandmother in *A Year Down Yonder.*

Prewriting Selecting a Topic

Your essay should describe the person's appearance and personality. It should also tell how the person inspired you in a positive way. A chart, like the one below, can help you choose a person to write about and identify the ways in which he or she has influenced you.

Topic Chart

Person	Positive Influence
Dr. Julie, the veterinarian	– caring person – honest person – generous with her time
Mr. Hayes, the chorus director	– patient teacher – explores different types of music – teaches foreign language songs
Adamay, my neighbor	– loves adventure

Create a topic chart. In the first column, list at least three people who interest you. In the second column, tell how each person has influenced you in a positive way. Choose one of the people as the subject of your essay.

Gathering Details

Next, analyze your subject as you gather details. Think carefully about the person's appearance, personality, special skills, talents, and interests.

Collect details. Answer the following questions to help you find information to include in your essay.

1. What does the person look like? (Describe him or her from head to toe.)
2. What personality traits does the person have? (Think about feelings and emotions. Is this person quiet? Funny? Outgoing? Kind?)
3. Which of the personality traits is most clear to you? (Think of an experience or event during which this personality trait was evident.)
4. How has this person positively influenced you?

Organizing Your Details

Your essay should describe the person's physical appearance (from head to toe) and personality. You should also include a short story (anecdote) to illustrate your subject's key personality trait. A list can help you organize your details.

Organizing List

Subject	Dr. Julie, the veterinarian
Physical Appearance	short, big smile, white lab coat, blue jeans, red sneakers
Key Personality Trait	kind
Anecdote	caring for Snoops

Organize your details. Create a list like the one above. List details about the person's physical appearance and a key personality trait. Also include an anecdote to illustrate that trait.

Using Verbs and Adjectives

Interesting and specific words help create a strong voice and add personality to your writing. Keep the following tips about word choice in mind as you write:

- Use specific verbs to show action.
  attacked wandered examined
- Use adjectives to help readers "see" the scene.
  tiny woman straight, blond hair five feet tall

Make a list of specific verbs and adjectives to describe your person's actions and appearance. Use the best ones in your essay.

Writing Starting Your Essay

The beginning paragraph should catch your reader's interest and introduce your topic—a person who has positively influenced you. Here are two approaches.

Beginning Paragraph

- **Briefly explain how you know the person.** Is he or she a family member? Friend? Teacher? Include some interesting details to draw the reader into your essay.

The writer makes a personal connection.

Dr. Julie is the veterinarian for our family's pets. She gives shots to our dogs and cats every year, and she took care of our parakeet, Squeeker, when he broke his wing last fall. The most important thing she ever did for us was to save our spaniel, Snoops, when he was attacked by a coyote that wandered into our yard.

- **Begin with an important fact.** Share one important reason why you admire the person; tell something interesting that the person did, or something unusual that happened to him or her.

The writer shares an interesting detail.

If it weren't for Dr. Julie, our veterinarian, Snoops would be dead. She saved our spaniel's life after he was attacked by a coyote that had wandered into our yard last fall.

Using an Engaging Voice

Voice is the special way that a writer expresses ideas and emotions. It shows that the writer really cares about the subject and the audience. When you write, keep the following tips about voice in mind:

- Write as if you were telling a friend about this person.
- Show enthusiasm for your subject.
- Express your true feelings about the person.

Write your beginning paragraph. Choose one of the approaches above to get started. If you don't like how your first attempt turns out, try another one.

Developing the Middle Part

The middle part of your essay will include three paragraphs. The first describes the person's appearance, and the second focuses on personality. The third should include an anecdote that demonstrates a key personality trait.

Middle Paragraphs

The first paragraph describes Dr. Julie with specific physical details.

Dr. Julie is a tiny woman, about five feet tall, who always greets everyone with a big smile. Her blond hair is pulled up into a twist. Seeing her in her white lab coat, blue jeans, and red tennis shoes, a person would never guess that she would be strong enough to handle large animals. But the day Snoops was attacked, she hoisted him up onto the examining table just as if she were lifting a cat.

The second paragraph describes Dr. Julie's personality.

Dr. Julie is hardworking and caring. Whenever she examines a pet, she talks quietly the whole time to calm the animal. She also carefully explains what she's doing as her strong hands gently feel for a trouble spot. Everyone is thankful that Dr. Julie takes emergency calls both day and night.

Finally, the writer shares an anecdote about Dr. Julie.

The day that Dr. Julie examined Snoops, she was honest with her diagnosis. "He has some very bad bites, and he's lost a lot of blood," she said. "However, I'm not going to give up on him." Dr. Julie stated that Snoops needed surgery to save his life. It was hard to leave him at the clinic, but Dr. Julie was very reassuring. That's another great thing about her. She cares about animals, and she also cares about people. When the surgery was over, I could hear the happiness in her voice, and I knew that Snoops was going to be fine.

Write your middle paragraphs. Use the details you gathered (page 78) and your organizing list (page 79). Describe your person's appearance and personality. Include an anecdote to illustrate a key personality trait.

Writing Ending Your Essay

The ending clearly signals that your description is complete. In your last sentence or two, leave the reader with a final idea or image—something that will keep him or her thinking about your topic.

Ending Paragraph

The writer makes a final personal connection.

From watching Dr. Julie, I've learned that sincerely caring about people and animals is so important. Every time Snoops comes and lays his head in my lap, I think of Dr. Julie and smile.

Write your ending paragraph. Wrap things up by explaining how the person has had a positive influence on you.

Revising and Editing

A first draft can always be improved. By adding, deleting, or reorganizing some details, you can make your description better.

Revise your first draft. Revise your first draft using the questions below as a guide. Then add a title.

- ☐ **Ideas** Have I included enough specific details about the person's appearance and personality? Did I include an anecdote?
- ☐ **Organization** Do I have a clear beginning, middle, and ending? Do I describe my subject from head to toe and share an anecdote according to time order?
- ☐ **Voice** Do I sound interested in the person and in my audience?
- ☐ **Word Choice** Do I use specific verbs and adjectives?
- ☐ **Sentence Fluency** Do my sentences flow smoothly? Do I vary sentence lengths and beginnings?

Edit

Edit your description. Once you have completed your revising, use the checklist on page 128 to edit your essay for errors. Then write a clean final copy to share.

Descriptive Writing

Across the Curriculum

Since its creation in 1876, the telephone has been used to carry descriptions of people, places, and things across the land. A clear phone description lets the listener feel as if he or she is "right there" with the speaker. A clear written description can do the same thing for readers.

You will use descriptive writing in almost all of your classes. In social studies, you may be asked to write an eyewitness report about a famous historical person. In math, your teacher may require you to describe an object using geometric terms. In science class, you may need to describe a place you visited on a field trip. Your description will be successful if your readers can clearly imagine the topic in their minds.

What's Ahead

- **Social Studies:** Writing an Eyewitness Report
- **Math:** Describing an Object
- **Science:** Writing a Field-Trip Report
- **Practical Writing:** Writing a Project Proposal

Social Studies:
Writing an Eyewitness Report

An eyewitness report is a type of descriptive writing. The writer of the following report describes what it might have been like to witness Alexander Graham Bell inventing the telephone.

The **beginning** shares some important background information.

The **middle** describes the subject and what he is doing.

The **ending** leaves the reader with something to think about.

The World's First Phone Call

It is March 10, 1876. I find myself inside a small, dusty electrical shop in Boston, Massachusetts. Alexander Graham Bell and his assistant, Thomas Watson, are here working on Bell's invention, the electrical speech machine.

Bell is a young man with wavy, black hair and a wild beard. Under his shop apron, he wears a white shirt and brown pants. His right foot taps impatiently as he adjusts the machine's transmitter. A long wire connects it to the receiver, which is with Watson in another room in the shop.

Accidentally, Bell's left elbow knocks over a small container of battery acid. He watches helplessly as the acid oozes onto the wire.

As I rush into the other room, I hear Mr. Bell's voice shouting, "Mr. Watson, come here. I want you!" Watson's eyes widen with surprise as he hears Bell's voice coming through the machine's receiver.

"We've done it!" he shouts to Bell. "We've transmitted human speech through a wire!"

It looks as if this accident has made the invention work! Who knows how the electrical speech machine will be used in the future?

Writing Tips

Before you write . . .

- **Choose a famous inventor.** Select an inventor you have studied in class.
- **Do your research.** Learn about the person and his or her invention. Study pictures of the person. From your research, try to imagine the setting in which the person tested the invention and discovered that it worked.
- **Take notes.** Collect important details that will help make your description interesting and clear.

During your writing . . .

- **Write as if you are observing the inventor at the moment the invention first works.** Tell when the event takes place. Briefly describe the inventor and the setting. End with a final thought to keep the reader thinking about the topic.
- **Show, don't tell.** Use descriptive details that show the reader what is happening, as if he or she were seeing it firsthand.
- **Organize your thoughts.** Use order of location (*top to bottom, front to back, left to right, head to toe*) or time order (*first, next, then,* and so on) to organize your details.
- **Use an engaging voice.** Your voice should sound interested, knowledgeable, and excited about being an eyewitness.

After you've written a first draft . . .

- **Check for completeness.** Make sure that you have included enough information to give the reader a clear picture of the inventor and the invention.
- **Check for correctness.** Proofread your essay to make sure there are no mistakes in punctuation, capitalization, spelling, and grammar.

Choose a famous inventor. Learn about the person and the invention. Write a creative eyewitness account describing the inventor at the moment the invention works.

Math: Describing an Object with Geometric Terms

Sometimes an object can be described with geometric terms. The writer of this essay describes a quartz crystal as a hexagonal prism.

The **beginning** introduces the object.

The **middle** describes the top, bottom, and side views of the object.

The **ending** makes a final comment.

A Crystal Clear Hexagon

In the world, both natural and man-made objects have geometric shapes. Triangles, rectangles, squares, circles, cubes, cones, and pyramids can be seen in nature and in the world every day. Another common hexagon in nature is the glasslike quartz crystal.

A hexagonal prism crystal is a shape with six sides. The base of a quartz crystal is a hexagon with equal sides and equal angles. A perpendicular rectangle rises from each side from the base. The six rectangles of equal size rising from the base form a six-sided or hexagonal box. The top of the crystal is the same shape as the base.

When looking at the bottom or the top of the crystal, the viewer will see a perfect hexagon. A side view will reveal three long rectangles. From this view, the top and the bottom rectangles are each attached to the middle rectangle at an angle of 60 degrees.

Focusing on geometric shapes to describe an object can help someone else visualize it. Describing something in geometric terms may also make it easier to remember facts and information about the object.

Writing Tips

Before you write . . .

- **List some geometric terms that could be used to describe a flat or three-dimensional object.**
  Make notes or sketches on the list. Review any terms you are unsure of.
- **Choose an object that can be described with geometric terms.**
  Study the object and look at it from all different angles.
- **Make notes as you observe the object.**
  Jot down specific geometric terms you could use to enable a reader to visualize the object.

During your writing . . .

- **Write a clear beginning, middle, and ending.**
  Introduce the object and then describe it using geometric terms. End with a final comment about your topic or about using geometric terms to describe everyday objects.
- **Organize your description.**
  Describe your object using a spatial method of organization (top to bottom, left to right, and so on).
- **Use correct terms.**
  Include specific and correct geometric terms in your description. The reader should be able to picture the shape you describe.

After you've written a first draft . . .

- **Check for completeness.**
  Have you included enough details to clearly describe your object?
- **Check for correctness.**
  Proofread your writing for punctuation, capitalization, spelling, and grammar errors.

Write a short essay using geometric terms to describe an object. Share your essay with your classmates.

Science: Writing a Field-Trip Report

In science class, you may be asked to describe your observations on a recent field trip. This student writer describes a field trip to a planetarium.

The **beginning** introduces the topic.

The **middle** clearly describes the planetarium program.

The **ending** makes a final observation.

Blain Planetarium

On March 3, our class visited Blain Planetarium. As the bus rounded the curve, I saw the huge white dome. I was anxious to see what was inside.

Stepping into the main room, my eyes followed the curve of the high, dome-shaped ceiling. The guide told us that this would be our movie screen. Scanning the room, I noticed that the planetarium is actually a large circular room. All the seats follow the shape of the room and face the center. We were quickly ushered to a row of red cushioned seats that tilted way back so we could look at the dome. In the center, there is a machine called a star projector.

Then the lights dimmed, quiet music played, and a beautiful sunset in the western sky faded to a black sky filled with stars. A man's voice narrated as we observed the Milky Way, planets, meteorites, and the colorful aurora borealis. Among the stars were constellations like Ursa Major and Orion. Even Halley's comet swept across the sky.

A sunrise in the eastern sky signaled that the show was finished. I felt as if I had been in a dream. I had been zooming through space so close to the planets that I could almost touch them.

Writing Tips

Before you write . . .

Sensory Chart

Subject:				
Sights	Sounds	Smells	Tastes	Feelings

- **Choose a topic that interests you.**
  Select a recent field trip related to your class.
- **List main ideas you want to include.**
  You can't tell everything about the field trip, so choose one or two impressive things to write about.
- **Gather specific details.**
  Think about your destination. Use sensory details to describe the sights and sounds of the place.

During your writing . . .

- **Write a clear beginning, middle, and ending.**
  Introduce the topic in the beginning part. In the middle, describe the place by including specific details. Close by sharing a final thought about the experience.
- **Organize your details.**
  You may organize your details by order of location (*left to right, top to bottom, near to far*) or time order (*first, second, next, last*). Choose the pattern that works best for your description.
- **Use strong words.**
  A strong description contains specific nouns, action verbs, and well-chosen adjectives.

After you've written a first draft . . .

- **Check for completeness.**
  Make sure that you have included all the details that make it possible for the reader to see the place in his or her mind.
- **Check for correctness.**
  Proofread your report for punctuation, capitalization, spelling, and grammar errors.

Select a recent or a past field trip and describe it following the tips above.

Practical Writing:
Writing a Project Proposal

Descriptive writing comes in many different forms. For example, you may be asked to describe a project you plan to do. The following proposal, written by a student team, describes a tutoring project.

The **heading** identifies the writers and their proposed project.

Date: January 12, 2012
To: Mrs. Munn, Room 210
From: The Titan Group: Todd Davis, LaToya Wilson, Jacque Trevino, Becky Jackson
Subject: Volunteer Tutoring

The **beginning** describes the project.

Project Description: An article in our school paper stated that Lincoln Elementary School needed eighth-grade students to tutor third graders in reading. We would like to volunteer our services starting February 3.

The **middle** part gives details about the project.

What We Need: We need written permission from you, our parents, and our principal. We also need written approval from the principal and the third-grade teachers of Lincoln Elementary School.

What We Will Do: On Tuesdays and Thursdays, during our fourth-period study hall, we will walk across the playground to Lincoln School to our assigned classrooms. We will help third-grade students by listening to them read, helping them with their reading assignments, and reading to them.

Outcome: At the end of this project, we will report on the students' progress and show a videotape of our students reading during one of our last sessions. It will show how the tutoring helped.

The **ending** asks for approval of the project.

We hope you will approve our proposal. If you have any suggestions or changes, please let us know.

Writing Tips

Before you write . . .

- **Choose a project that interests you.**
  Working alone or with a team of classmates, choose a project you will enjoy doing.
- **Do your research.**
  Decide specifically what you will do and what you will need to complete your project.
- **Plan your proposal.**
  Collect details in order to describe the project to your teacher. Your goal is to present a clear description of the work you plan to do.

During your writing . . .

- **Write a clear beginning, middle, and ending.**
  In the *heading* give the date, your teacher's name and room number, the names of your team members, and the subject of your project. Next, clearly describe the project. For the other parts of your proposal, follow the model on page 90.
- **Order your ideas.**
  Make sure you've included all the information in the correct order.
- **Use precise words.**
  Make your description clear and easy to follow. Use specific nouns and verbs.

After you've written a first draft . . .

- **Check for completeness.**
  Make sure that you have included all the details that your teacher needs to understand the project.
- **Check for correctness.**
  Proofread your proposal for punctuation, capitalization, spelling, and grammar errors.

Select a project that you or your team would like to do. Write a project proposal using the tips above.

tell
relate
WRITE SOURCE Online
www.hmheducation.com/writesource

Narrative Writing

Writing Focus

- Narrative Paragraph
- Phase Autobiography
- Biographical Narrative

Grammar Focus

- Subject-Verb Agreement

Academic Vocabulary

Work with a partner. Read the meanings and share answers to the questions.

1. Something that is **extended** is longer than normal.
   What would happen if you stayed in the bathtub for an extended period of time?
2. An **interview** is a meeting in which one person asks questions of another person to get information.
   Who would you like to interview? Why?
3. Something that is **memorable** is worth remembering.
   Tell about a memorable time you spent with a friend.

narrate
remember
share

Narrative Writing

Narrative Paragraph

Has anyone ever offered you a "penny for your thoughts"? Has anyone ever pulled a quarter out of your ear?

Actually, your thoughts are worth much more than pennies and quarters. By the end of eighth grade, a typical public school system has spent more than $60,000 to educate *each student*. To you, your thoughts are even more valuable. Your mind is a treasure trove of discoveries and "aha!" moments.

One way to count up the treasures in your head is to write about them. A narrative paragraph gives you a chance to record a moment of discovery and share it with others. It's a trick as neat as pulling a quarter out of your ear!

Writing Guidelines

Subject: A moment of discovery
Form: Narrative paragraph
Purpose: To entertain
Audience: Classmates

Narrative Paragraph

A "moment of discovery" is a perfect subject for a narrative paragraph. In the student model below, Eric describes a special moment when he figured out his first magic trick. The **topic sentence** introduces the topic, the **body** explains what happened, and the **closing sentence** wraps things up with a final thought.

Topic Sentence

Body

Closing Sentence

A Handy Trick

Grandpa grinned and held out his hand in front of me. He snapped his fingers, and a quarter appeared in his palm. Rapidly, he rolled his fingers, and the quarter vanished. I'd seen this trick a hundred times, but today I was determined to figure it out. The quarter appeared again, and vanished again. I stared carefully at Grandpa's hands. He held his left hand out to his side, palm open. His right hand was in front of him and open underneath, with the back facing me. He turned his right hand over, and I glimpsed the quarter in his clenched fist. I snatched the quarter from his hand and held it just as he had shown me. Then, with a grin of my own, I snapped my fingers, and the quarter appeared. Grandpa still had many tricks up his sleeve, but that was one trick I had learned.

Respond to the reading. Answer the following questions on your own paper.

- ☐ Ideas **(1) What moment of discovery is the story about?**
- ☐ Organization **(2) Are the details of the paragraph organized by importance, time, or some other pattern of organization?**
- ☐ Voice & Word Choice **(3) What vivid verbs help re-create the moment of discovery?**

Prewriting Selecting a Topic

Whenever you learn something new, you have a moment of discovery. To find a topic for his narrative paragraph, Eric made a cluster of these moments.

Topic Cluster

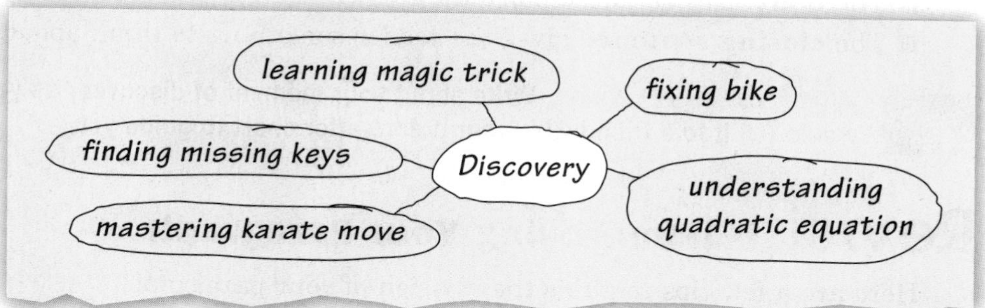

Create a cluster. On your own paper, write "Discovery" and circle it. Make a cluster of four or five of your own moments of discovery. Choose one of these moments to write a paragraph about.

Gathering Details

One way to gather details about the moment of discovery is to use a before-after chart. Eric created the following chart about his "aha!" moment.

Before-After Chart

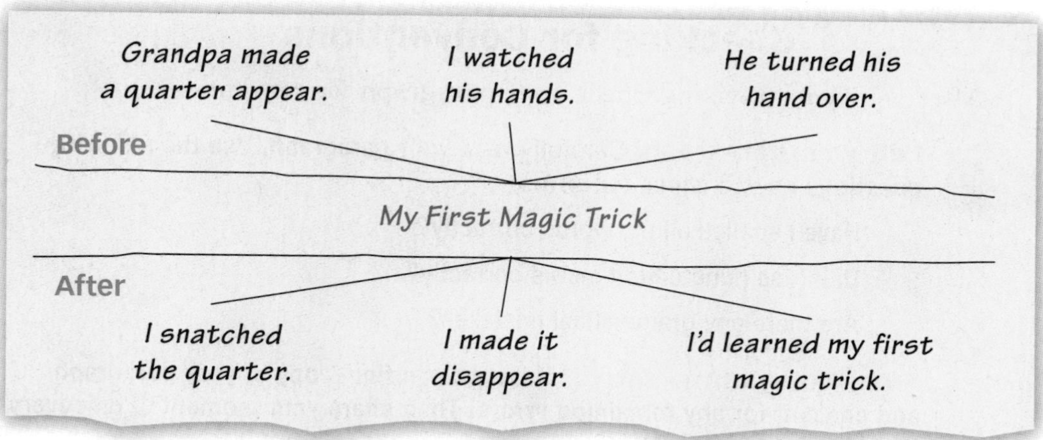

Create a before-after chart. Make a chart like the one above. Write what happened before and after your moment of discovery.

Writing Creating Your First Draft

A well-written narrative paragraph should have a topic sentence, a body, and a closing sentence.

- The **topic sentence** introduces or starts the narrative.
- The **body** uses action to move the story along.
- The **closing sentence** gives the reader something to think about.

Write your first draft. Write about your moment of discovery as you would tell it to a friend. Use your before-after chart to guide you.

Revising Improving Your Paragraph

Here are a few tips to guide the revision of your paragraph.

- **Show, don't tell.** Instead of telling the reader that "Jenna was excited," show it: "Jenna clapped her hands and screamed at the top of her lungs."
- **Build to the high point.** Lead up to the moment of discovery.
- **Rewrite sentences if needed.** Check for sentences that are awkward or unclear. Rewrite them so that they flow nicely.

Revise your paragraph. Focus on ideas, organization, voice, word choice, and sentence fluency as you revise your narrative paragraph.

Editing Checking for Conventions

After you finish revising, check your paragraph for conventions.

Edit your paragraph. Carefully read your paragraph. Use the following questions as you check for errors.

1. Have I spelled all my words correctly?
2. Did I use punctuation marks correctly?
3. Are there any grammatical mistakes?

Proofread your narrative. Make a clean final copy of your paragraph and check it for any remaining errors. Then share your moment of discovery with your classmates.

Narrative Writing

Writing a Phase Autobiography

At one time or another, most students have had to write a narrative entitled "What I Did Last Summer." Many of those essays could be summed up this way: "I mowed the lawn—over and over and over. . . ." A more thoughtful narrative, though, would focus on a few related experiences the writer had and would show how those experiences changed him or her in some way.

A phase autobiography is a narrative essay about an extended period of time in your life. An effective phase autobiography shows how the period of time changed you or taught you an important lesson. The key to this form of writing is to focus on just the main actions and events. By the end of the writing experience, you will become much wiser about life—and what it has to offer.

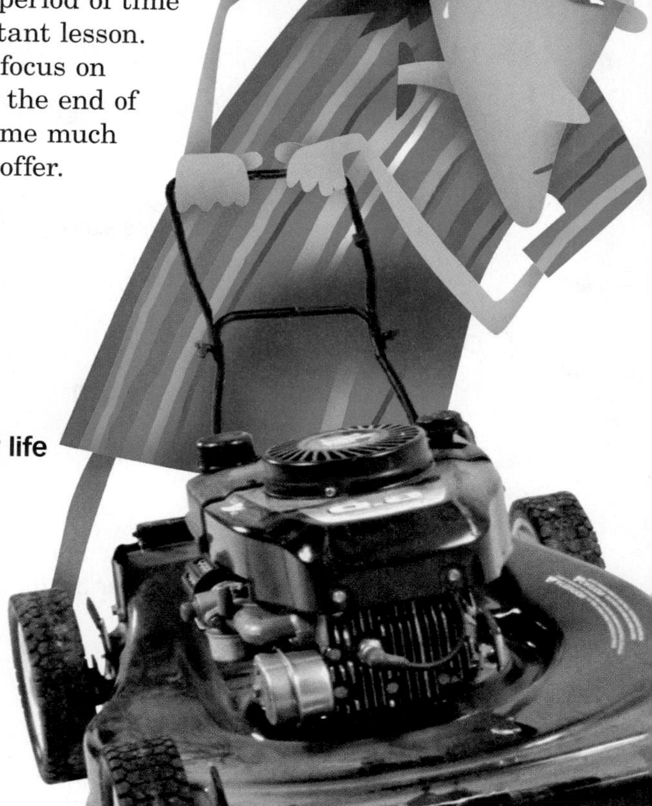

Writing Guidelines

Subject: An extended period of time in your life
Form: Phase autobiography
Purpose: To share a part of your life
Audience: Classmates

Understanding Your Goal

Your goal in this chapter is to write about a time in your life when you changed. The following traits will help you plan and write your phase autobiography. Use the rubric on pages 130–131 to guide your writing.

Traits of Narrative Writing

Ideas

Select an important time in your life. Include events and details that show how you changed.

Organization

Present the events in chronological order with a strong beginning, middle, and ending. Consider using dialogue.

Voice

Use an active voice and match the tone to your experience.

Word Choice

Choose specific words with appropriate feelings or connotations.

Sentence Fluency

Make your sentences flow smoothly by combining and expanding them.

Conventions

Be sure that your punctuation, capitalization, spelling, and grammar are correct.

Literature Connections: For another example of a personal narrative, read *My First Free Summer* by Julia Alvarez.

Phase Autobiography

In this sample narrative, the student author tells how he changed after getting to know his elderly neighbor. The key parts of the phase autobiography are described in the left margin.

Beginning
In the beginning, the writer gets the reader's attention and introduces the period of time.

Middle
The writer uses a variety of specific details to tell what happened during this period of time.

Getting to Know Joe

I live in an old two-story home in Newark. My neighbors are mostly retired people with perfect front yards. One of the retirees, Joe Perez, lives on the corner. Because of our time together last summer, he and I have built a special relationship.

At the start of the summer, Joe and I didn't hit it off too well. He was very picky about his yard. Every morning he was doing something to make the lawn look better. If we goofed around and stepped on his grass, Joe would yell at us from his front porch.

Through mid-July his yard was perfect, but then I noticed some changes. I didn't see Joe outside as much. His grass was getting brown and shaggy, and some weeds were growing in his flower beds. It wasn't like Joe to let things go. I didn't dwell on it, but when I walked by his place, I wondered why he wasn't taking care of his yard.

One day I was sitting on the curb waiting for one of my buddies to show up when Joe came out on the porch. I expected him to yell at me for sitting on his grass. Instead, he swayed back and forth. Then he fell down! I ran to my house and dialed 911. "My neighbor, Mr. Perez, just passed out! He lives on the corner of Garden and Mills," I blurted. Then I hurried back to the porch to see what I could do. Joe was awake, but he was as white as a ghost. He stared blankly at me.

Middle
The writer uses dialogue to explain what was said.

"W-What happened to me?" he mumbled.

"You passed out, Mr. Perez," I said, trying to catch my breath. "But help is on its way."

The paramedics came and took Joe to the emergency room. It turned out that Joe had been forgetting to take his blood pressure medication. He was going to be all right, and I was glad about that. He could be a grump at times, but I guess I cared about Joe more than I realized. I couldn't imagine my neighborhood without him.

Joe thanked me for helping. Then I asked him, "Is there anything I can do for you, Mr. Perez?" Little did I know that one question would change everything.

Joe found lots of things I could do. Soon I was cutting his grass, weeding his flowers, trimming his bushes, and edging the grass along his sidewalk. Before long, I was planting things like a pro and telling kids to stay off the grass. Instead of yelling at me from his porch, Joe now waved and smiled.

Ending
The ending tells how the writer changed.

A whole year has passed, and each week I help Joe. I realize that I can make a difference, so I also help some of the other older neighbors. Joe taught me that helping people is what life is all about.

Respond to the reading. Why is "Getting to Know Joe" a good piece of writing? To find out, answer these questions.

- ☐ **Ideas (1) What memorable phase of his life does the writer tell about?**
- ☐ **Organization (2) What organizational pattern does the writer use?**
- ☐ **Voice & Word Choice (3) Which words help the writer create an appropriate voice? Identify three.**

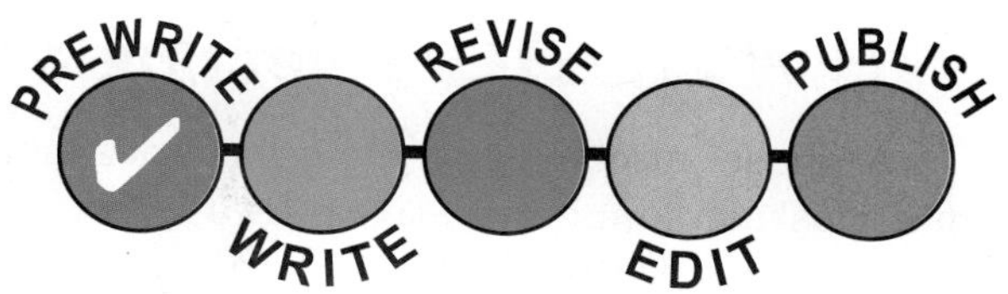

Prewriting

Before you can begin writing your phase autobiography, you need to choose an extended period of time to write about. In your prewriting, you will choose a topic, gather details, and organize your thoughts.

Keys to Effective Prewriting

1. Think about several important times in your life.
2. Choose one main time to share with your readers.
3. Identify the key events related to this time.
4. Organize your ideas chronologically.
5. Gather specific details and feelings.
6. Consider using dialogue.

Prewriting **Selecting a Topic**

A phase autobiography is a form of narrative writing, but it is different from most personal narratives. In a typical personal narrative, you share one specific event or experience. In a *phase autobiography,* you write about an extended period of time that has changed you in some important way.

One way to find a topic for your autobiography is to list the meaningful things that have happened in your life. The list below shows important times in one writer's life.

Life List

Was hospitalized with an appendicitis attack
Took a train trip with my grandmother
Went canoeing with the youth group
Participated in the school's spelling bee
Joined the Junior Drum and Bugle Corp
Volunteered at the local nursing home
Transferred to a new school
Helped my neighbor take care of her dog

Reason: I chose this topic because it changed me in so many ways.

Make a "Life List." List a number of important times in your life. Circle the time you want to use as the topic of your phase autobiography. Then write your reason for choosing this topic.

Focus on the Traits

Ideas Phase autobiographies are often written about getting to know new friends, participating in an extracurricular activity, experiencing a change in family life, and so on.

Focusing Your Topic

After you have chosen a period of time in your life that has changed you in some important way, you should write a sentence or two that will give your phase autobiography a good focus. You should mention both the phase and the way in which it changed you. The examples below will help you understand how the two parts work together.

Weak Focus

One Saturday night a year ago, I learned that my friends are not always right.
("One Saturday night" is not an extended period of time.)

The last month of track meets really taught me something.
("Really taught me something" should be more specific.)

Strong Focus

The last month of track meets taught me that champions are made from discipline, determination, and sweat.

First, carefully read the following sentences. Then identify the ones you feel would make a good focus for a phase autobiography.

1. Felicia and I had played in tennis tournaments all summer, but we learned more about friendship and dedication than about tennis.
2. I met my grandfather for the first time at my cousin's wedding.
3. I surprised my mother by making supper.
4. I lived with my grandparents for a semester while my parents were busy starting a new business.
5. When my little sister was born, my life changed completely.

Focus your topic. Using the topic you selected (page 102), write a sentence or two that will give your phase autobiography a good focus. Be sure you state both the period of time and the important way in which your life changed.

Prewriting **Freewriting**

Now that you have chosen a phase to write about, you need to search your memory for information. Freewriting is an excellent way to recall details without worrying about organization or correctness.

The example of freewriting below was done by the writer of the essay on pages 109–112. Notice that after she finished her writing, she located and underlined the key events. These key events eventually became part of the topic sentences in the middle paragraphs.

Freewriting

The drum and bugle flyer I brought home from school really got Dad talking about his days in the drum corps. His stories convinced me to sign up for summer band camp. I felt excited and nervous on that first day of camp. I heard Mr. D, the director, was very strict. He was! My first day of practice was unbelievable. All of our practices were tough. We marched like soldiers. My friend, Marcia, quit during the first week. I didn't have that choice. (Our family has this rule: Whatever you start, you finish.) I have to admit that I really liked being in the parades. Field competitions were the best. We always placed somewhere in the top three. In August we traveled to Canada for a competition. I thought the name of it—a tattoo—was weird. We came in first and won an international trophy. . . .

Freewrite. **Write nonstop for 5 to 10 minutes about your topic. Write down all your thoughts and don't stop to revise or correct your writing. Then read through your paper and underline the key events that took place.**

Gathering Details

Now that you've listed your key events, it's time to recall specific details and feelings connected with them. As the writer of the essay on pages 109–112 thought about each event, she wrote down specific details and feelings in a chart. Then she used the chart to write her middle paragraphs.

Specific Details Chart

Key Events	Details	Feelings
First day of practice	hot summer day sore feet Mr. D.—very strict	nervous frightened
Daily practices	intense practices kept bumping into people quickly improved	wanted to quit was exhausted determined to get better
Parades and competitions	teamwork performed in all kinds of weather	was overwhelmed could face difficult challenges
The tattoo	packed stadium competed with the best marching bands	felt confident was motivated

Create a chart. Make a details chart like the one above. Record key events in the first column. Jot down details and feelings you remember about each.

Focus on the Traits

Organization Narrative writing is almost always organized chronologically to help the story flow smoothly from beginning to end. For other patterns of organization, see page 551.

Prewriting

Understanding Tone and Connotation

When you write about an important phase in your life, your voice should show clearly how you feel about the events. Your attitude toward your subject is called *tone*. One way to create tone is to choose words with a strong feeling, or *connotation*.

In the examples below, note how the writer replaces neutral words with words that have a strong connotation.

Neutral: **Mr. D. was a man with short hair.**
Strong: **Mr. D. was a drill sergeant with a crew cut.**

Neutral: **Mr. D. walked before us and spoke loudly.**
Strong: **Mr. D. paced before us and barked loudly.**

Read the following sentences. For each, indicate which of the words in parentheses has the stronger connotation.

1. The tough schedule *(affected, shook)* my confidence.
2. Mr. D. told me my playing added *(spark, something)* to the trumpet section.
3. Before the competition, Mr. D. *(huddled, met)* with us like a *(leader, football coach)*.
4. As we took the field, we marched like a *(conquering army, big group)*.
5. The *(hard, grueling)* practices paid off when we *(won, dominated)* the competition.

Gather words with feeling. Review your "Specific Details Chart" (page 105). For each feeling shown in the right column, write at least one word or phrase that expresses that feeling strongly. Try to use these words as you write your first draft.

Focus on the Traits

Voice When you write a phase autobiography, you need to use a voice that sounds like you. Since you're writing about an important part of your life, it should be easy for you to use a natural-sounding voice.

Writing

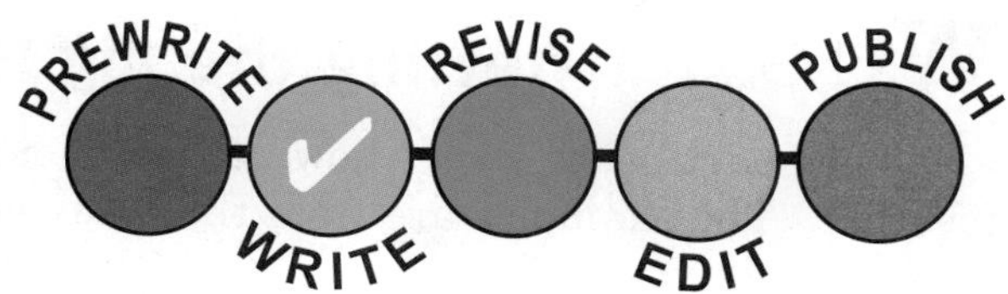

Now that you have gathered and organized your details, you can begin writing the first draft of your phase autobiography.

Keys to Effective Writing

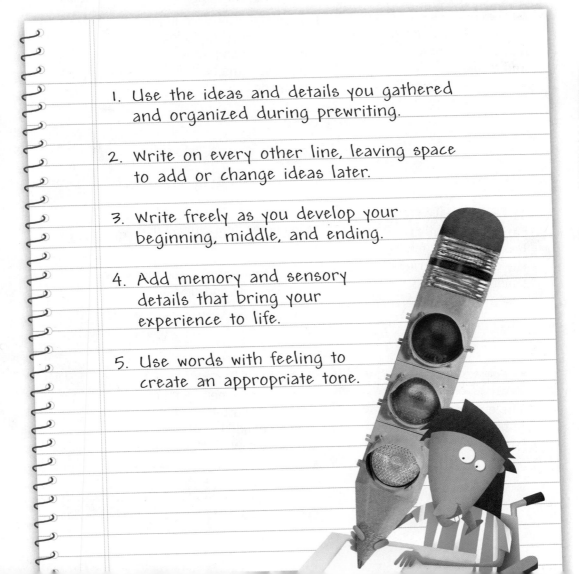

1. Use the ideas and details you gathered and organized during prewriting.
2. Write on every other line, leaving space to add or change ideas later.
3. Write freely as you develop your beginning, middle, and ending.
4. Add memory and sensory details that bring your experience to life.
5. Use words with feeling to create an appropriate tone.

Writing Getting the Big Picture

The chart below shows how the parts of a phase autobiography fit together. (The examples are from the essay on pages 109–112.) You're ready to write once you've . . .

- collected plenty of details about the experience and
- organized the details chronologically.

Beginning

The **beginning** gives background information and focuses on the phase.

Opening Sentences

I was never interested in joining any group or sport during the summer. . . . so I decided to give it a try. It was the best decision I've ever made.

Middle

The **middle** part uses a variety of details to show how the writer felt during the extended period of time.

I will never forget my first day of practice . . .

Many times during those first weeks, . . .

The best part of that summer was our tattoo in Windsor, Canada.

Ending

The **ending** explains the importance of this time in the writer's life.

Closing Sentences

After last summer, I am not the same Julie Patterson anymore. . . . I am a confident, outgoing person who enjoys working with others.

Starting Your Phase Autobiography

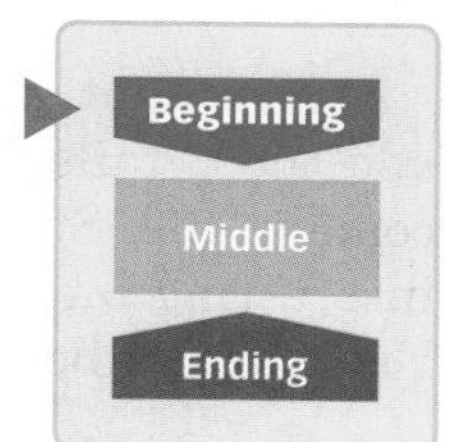

Now that you've selected a topic and gathered details, you are ready to begin writing. In the opening, you need to do three things.

- **Grab the attention of your reader.**
- **Include necessary background information.**
- **State the topic or phase that you will write about.**

Beginning Paragraph

The writer sets the scene and introduces the phase she plans to write about.

I was never interested in joining any group or sport during the summer. I figured I got plenty of that during the school year. Besides, I liked being free to hang out with my friends and do some odd jobs to earn a little spending money. But then last summer, I saw a flyer for the Warrentown Junior Drum and Bugle Corps. I knew they were a very good group and got to travel a lot, so I decided to give it a try. It was the best decision I've ever made.

Using Transitions

Transitions help you move your reader smoothly through time. You should choose transitions that sound natural in your writing. Below is a chart of transitions that you can use to show time and make your sentences read smoothly. For a chart of other transitions, see pages 572–573.

Transition Words and Phrases

about	but	now	this time	usually
as soon as	during	recently	today	when
before	later	so far	until	whenever
besides	next	then	until now	while

Write your beginning. On your own paper, write the beginning of your phase autobiography. Use transitions to connect your ideas.

NARRATIVE

Writing Developing the Middle Part

Now that you have your reader's attention, it's time to add the details that will make the middle of your writing come to life. Stay focused on the most important and interesting information about the extended period of time. Use the tips below to maintain your reader's interest.

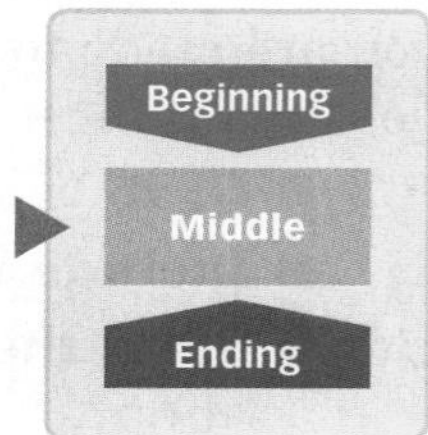

- **Use sensory details to add interest.**
- **Choose words with feeling to help create an appropriate tone.** (See page 106.)
- **Use some dialogue.**

Middle Paragraphs

The writer tells about key events related to this period of time.

I will never forget my first day of practice with the drum and bugle corps. The director, Mr. DeRusha, stepped onto the football field and ordered us all to sit along the 50-yard line. I nervously tapped the keys of my trumpet. I'd heard that Mr. D. had a reputation for being tough. He looked like one of those army drill sergeants on TV. He was tall and had a fresh crew cut, and when his voice exploded through the bullhorn, I shivered, even though it was almost 70 degrees outside.

Dialogue is used to show the personality of an important person.

"Listen up, people!" he barked. "Welcome to the Warrentown Junior Drum and Bugle Corps. Being in a drum and bugle corps means you are alert and prepared at all times. Is that understood?"

He paced back and forth in front of us. "By the end of the summer, you will learn to respect this organization, yourselves, and each other." Then his shadow stopped over me. He must have read my name tag.

I couldn't even look up when I heard him call my name and tell me to polish my horn.

"Yes, sir, " I answered, almost choking on the words.

The writer shows her feelings about the experience.

Many times during those first weeks, when the demands of practice were shaking my confidence, I thought about quitting. That's when Mr. D. came along and announced, "Miss Patterson, you add a spark to this trumpet section. Good job." Sometimes I wondered if Mr. D. could read minds. He always seemed to know just who needed to hear encouraging words.

The best part of that summer was our tattoo in Windsor, Canada. A tattoo is a type of nighttime marching competition. We were competing for an international trophy. Just before our performance, Mr. D. huddled with us like a football coach.

Strong sensory details help the reader see and feel the experience.

"You are the finest band here tonight," he said. "You know it. I know it. Now go out there and make sure everyone else knows it!"

"Yes, sir!" we shouted.

Marching in a strong, straight line, we were a band with a mission. The explosions of applause we heard during our performance propelled us to hit clearer notes and create sharper steps. We had never sounded so good. At the end, the audience went crazy and rewarded us with a standing ovation. We did it. We dominated the competition and came home with a trophy.

Write your middle paragraphs. Before you begin, review the drafting tips on page 110. Then use your "Specific Details Chart" (page 105) to write the middle part of your essay.

Writing Ending Your Phase Autobiography

The ending explains the importance of the period of time covered in the essay. Your ending should be thoughtful and should come soon after the most important part of your story. Below are several different ideas for endings.

Beginning
Middle
▶ Ending

- **Coming Full Circle**
  You can "come full circle" if you include the same key idea in both the beginning and the ending. This approach could have been used in this phase autobiography.

Key Idea in the Beginning

I snapped to attention when the band director hurried onto the marching field, barking orders.

Key Idea in the Ending

Now, three months later, I still snap to attention whenever Mr. D. barks orders, but I do it because I respect him, not because I'm afraid of him.

- **Explaining Your Change**
  The writer of the essay about the marching band chose to explain how she had changed. (See the model below.)

Ending Paragraph

The writer tells how she changed.

I still get goose bumps when I think about the band. Mr. DeRusha is a great director who taught me about discipline and respect. After last summer, I am not the same Julie Patterson anymore. I now look forward to summer and being with the band. More importantly, I am a confident, outgoing person who enjoys working with others.

Write your ending. Complete your phase autobiography by writing the final paragraph. You may want to use one of the above ways to end your essay.

Form a complete first draft. Put together a complete first draft. Then move on to the revising process.

Revising

You've worked hard while writing your first draft. During the next step in the writing process, you'll have the chance to go back and improve it. By adding, deleting, or moving parts, you will make your writing even better.

Keys to Effective Revising

1. Set your writing aside for a while so you'll have a fresh perspective as you begin to revise.
2. Read your writing out loud to see how well your beginning, middle, and ending work.
3. Mark any spots that seem confusing or incomplete.
4. Listen to your writer's voice, making sure it sounds like you.
5. Check your words and sentences.
6. Use the editing and proofreading marks inside the back cover of this book.

Revising for Ideas

6 My writing includes great details that totally engage the reader.	**5** I use a variety of details that hold my reader's interest.	**4** I use a variety of details, but they are not the most interesting ones.

When you revise for *ideas*, check for a variety of details and make sure those details add interest to your writing. Use the rubric strip above to guide you through your revisions.

Do I include the right kinds of details?

As you write about a phase in your life, you need to become aware of what you felt and thought. Three kinds of details help you recall and reflect on a past time in your life.

- **Sensory details** allow your reader to use his or her senses to see, hear, smell, taste, or touch what you experienced.
- **Memory details** bring your past experiences to life for the reader.
- **Reflective details** allow your reader to know what you wonder about, hope for, or wish.

Try It Identify each type of detail below. Tell if it is a sensory, memory, or reflective detail.

1. Jagged bluffs . . .
2. We packed the van and . . .
3. What if . . .
4. Tires squealed as . . .
5. Blackened embers . . .
6. The announcer introduced . . .
7. My favorite picture book reminds . . .
8. Maybe someday I'll . . .
9. Last Sunday, our dog . . .
10. Noxious fumes polluted . . .

Check your details. Read through your first draft. Label details with either "S" for sensory, "M" for memory, or "R" for reflective to make sure your writing has a variety of details.

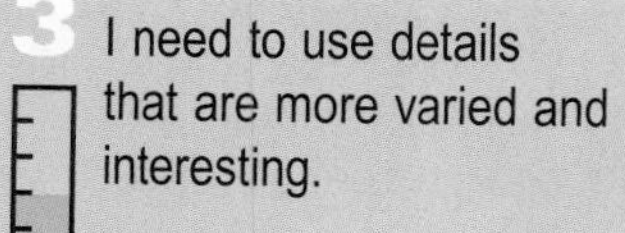

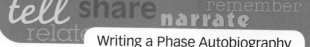

3 I need to use details that are more varied and interesting.

2 I need to use more details.

1 I need to collect details about my topic.

How do I know if my ideas interest my audience?

One way to find out if your writing interests classmates is to share your first draft with them. The following tips can help you organize a small group to discuss your work. (See also pages 420–421.)

Group Discussion Tips

1. Provide a copy of your work to two to five classmates.
2. Allow them to read your work before you meet.
3. Ask for title suggestions, which can start the conversation and show whether readers understand the main point of the narrative.
4. Ask group members what they feel or think about different points in the narrative.
5. Ask what could be improved, added, or cut.

Meet with peers. Gather a small group of classmates and share your work with them. Follow the tips above. (See also pages 29–32.) Make changes to improve your narrative.

Ideas
A variety of details adds interest.

. . . means you are alert and prepared at all times. Is that understood?"

He ~~walked out~~ paced back and forth in front of us. "By the end of the summer, you will learn to respect this organization, yourselves, and each other." Then his shadow stopped over me. He must have read my name tag.

Revising for Organization

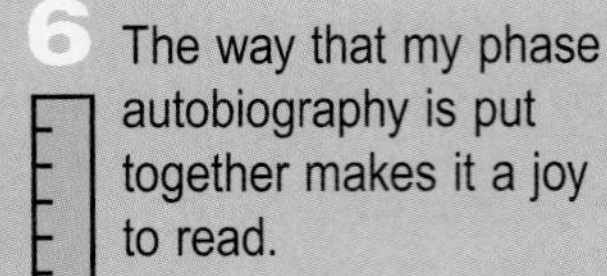

6
The way that my phase autobiography is put together makes it a joy to read.

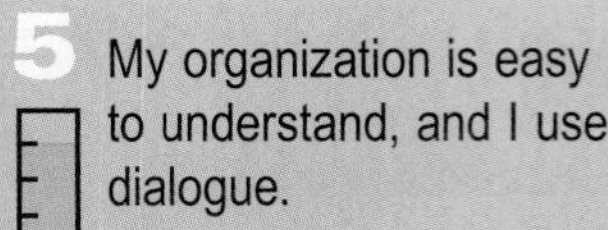

5
My organization is easy to understand, and I use dialogue.

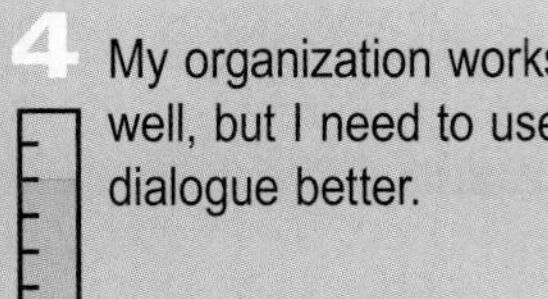

4
My organization works well, but I need to use dialogue better.

When you revise for *organization*, consider using dialogue to develop your narrative. Also check your beginning, middle, and ending. Use the rubric strip above to guide you.

How can dialogue help me develop my narrative?

Dialogue lets you show what people in your story say. There are two ways to write dialogue.

- **Direct Dialogue**
  Direct dialogue lets you show the exact words of a person. Use direct dialogue when the things a person says reveal an idea very clearly or show something about the person.

  My little brother Jake looked up at me. "When I'm 14, I'll boss you around."

  "When you're 14," I said, "I'll be 22."

  He shook his head sadly. "All right, I'll wait till I'm 23."

- **Summarized Dialogue**
  Summarized dialogue allows you to *tell* what the speaker says. Use summarized dialogue when you want to keep the action moving, rather than show the speaker's actual words.

  I corrected Jake again, telling him I would be 30 when he was 23. He was persistent, upping the age to 31, then 39, and on until I was 111 years old. I told him I probably wouldn't last that long.

Check your quotations. Find places where dialogue could help you develop your autobiography. **(See page 556 for tips on punctuating dialogue.)**

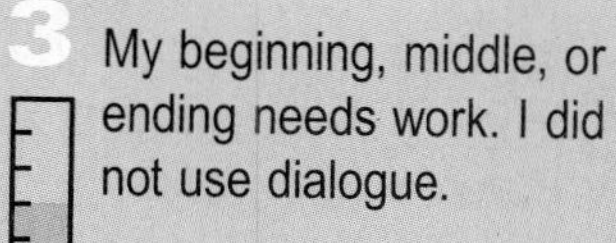

3 My beginning, middle, or ending needs work. I did not use dialogue.

2 I do not have a beginning, a middle, and an ending.

1 I need to learn how to organize my paper.

Do my beginning, middle, and ending work well?

You will know if your phase autobiography is organized well after you answer the following questions.

1. Does my beginning introduce a phase of my life and grab my reader's attention?
2. Have I presented the middle in chronological order?
3. What time transitions have I used? (See page 109.)
4. In the ending, do I tell the reader how my life changed because of this phase?

Revise

Check the parts of your phase autobiography. **Read through each part of your essay, while answering the questions above. Make needed changes.**

NARRATIVE

Organization
Direct and summarized dialogue improve the autobiography.

I couldn't even look up *when I heard him call my name and tell me to polish my horn.* ~~*"Miss Patterson. It is an important rule here at the Warrentown Junior Drum and Bugle Corps for everyone to clean his or her trumpet!"*~~

"Yes, sir," I answered, almost choking on the words. ~~*I mumbled that I understood what he said.*~~

Many times during those first weeks, when the demands of practice were shaking my confidence, I thought about quitting. . . .

Revising for Voice

6	5	4
The voice and tone in my autobiography perfectly capture this special time in my life.	My voice is active, and my tone matches my experience.	My voice is active. At times my tone doesn't match my experience.

When you revise for *voice*, check to see that you have used an active voice in most of your writing and that the tone of your voice fits the experience. Use the rubric strip above to guide you through your revision.

Have I used an active voice?

You have used an active voice if the subject in a sentence is doing the action. See the examples below. Active voice adds energy and clarity. (See 726.1.)

Passive Voice

The tornado was photographed by a student.
(The subject *tornado* is not doing the action.)

Active Voice

A student photographed the tornado.
(The subject *student* is doing the action.)

Rewrite each of the following sentences, changing the passive voice to active voice.

1. Due to severe storms the film festival at the community center was canceled by officials.
2. My sisters and I were told the news by our parents, who had planned an all-day party.
3. An alternative plan for a "Davis Family Film Festival" was made by my parents.
4. Old videos from the time we all were kids were pulled out of storage by Dad.
5. Movies such as *Aladdin* and *The Iron Giant* were enjoyed by everyone, and popcorn was eaten by us in mass quantities.

Check for active voice. Check your sentences to be sure that most of your subjects are doing the action. Rewrite sentences as needed.

3 I need to change my passive voice in some sentences. My tone doesn't match my experience.	**2** My voice is passive. My tone doesn't match my experience.	**1** I need to find out how to write with an active voice.

Does my tone match my experience?

Your tone matches your experience if it reveals your attitude about your topic. It's important that your details "show" your reader how you feel.

Read the following paragraphs. What is the tone of the writer? What details create that tone?

Having never traveled in the mountains, I tightly close my eyes while the bus chugs up the steep, narrow mountain road. Silently, I pray we don't meet another vehicle coming down the road. The passengers' "ooh's" and "aah's" accompany each bend. After what seems like eternity, the wheels stop and, instinctively, my eyes open.

"We've made it," I say to myself.

Stepping off the bus, the cool air welcomes me. Now I see why everyone is so excited. Towering, snowcapped mountains surround a Cinderella-type castle. I take a deep breath. This view was worth the ride.

Check the tone of your voice. **As you read through your writing, think of the attitude you want to reveal. Include details that reflect that attitude.**

Voice
A silly phrase is deleted because it doesn't fit the tone.

The best part of that summer was our tattoo in Windsor, Canada. A tattoo~~, not the kind that you get on your body,~~ is a type of nighttime marching competition. We were . . .

NARRATIVE

Revising for Word Choice

6 The word choice in my autobiography perfectly captures the action for the reader.	**5** I use specific nouns. My words create an appropriate tone.	**4** My writing contains specific words. I need to change some words to improve the tone.

When you revise for *word choice,* be sure you have used specific nouns, verbs, and adjectives. Also be sure you have chosen words with feeling to create an appropriate tone. Use the rubric strip above to guide your revision.

Have I used specific words?

Specific words present clear details for your reader. The chart below shows how a writer could make a general noun, verb, or adjective more specific.

Nouns		Verbs		Adjectives	
General	*Specific*	*General*	*Specific*	*General*	*Specific*
teacher	instructor coach professor	**tell**	narrate report relate	**good**	well-behaved obedient mannerly
park	square woods commons	**walk**	march stroll plod	**different**	distinct unique unusual

Do this activity with a partner:

1. Write a sentence that has several nouns, verbs, or adjectives and give it to your partner.
2. Let your partner choose one to three general nouns, verbs, or adjectives in your sentence and make them more specific.
3. See if you can make another round of changes on the same words.
4. Repeat the process, using a sentence your partner wrote.
5. Discuss how these specific words improved the sentences.

Check for specific words. Look at your nouns, verbs, and adjectives. Have you chosen specific words to make your ideas clear and to match your tone? If not, replace your general words with specific ones.

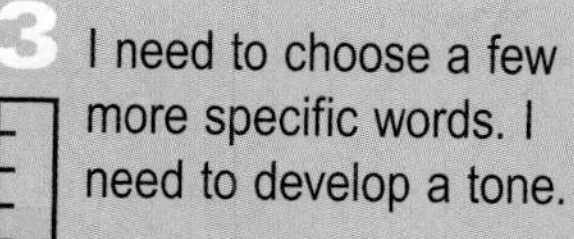

3 I need to choose a few more specific words. I need to develop a tone.

2 Most of my words are general. I need to develop a tone.

1 I need to learn more about specific words and developing a tone.

How can word choice help me develop the tone?

Words that show a specific feeling can help you control the tone of your writing. By changing some neutral words to words with stronger connotations, you can create a more effective tone.

Read the following sentences. In each, replace the neutral underlined word to create the tone indicated in parentheses.

1. I sat in my seat and waited for the test. *(nervous)*
2. After my name was called, I walked across the room. *(angry)*
3. My friend spent the whole lunch hour talking. *(bored)*
4. Down the alley came a dog. *(fearful)*
5. I walked down a(n) group of hallways. *(confused)*

Check connotations. Read through your autobiography, noting words that could be replaced to create a stronger tone. Make changes where appropriate.

Word Choice
Specific words with feeling create a stronger tone.

~~Walking~~ Marching in a strong, straight line, we were ~~a big group of people~~ a band with a mission. The ~~sound~~ explosions of applause we heard during our performance ~~made~~ propelled us to hit ~~right~~ clearer notes and ~~make better~~ create sharper steps. We had never sounded so good. At the end, the audience went crazy and rewarded us with a standing ovation. We did it.

NARRATIVE

Revising for Sentence Fluency

6 The style of my sentences perfectly captures my thoughts and feelings about this critical time in my life.	**5** I have combined and expanded sentences to make them flow smoothly.	**4** I have combined sentences to make them flow smoothly, but I need to expand some sentences with details.

When you revise for *sentence fluency,* check that you have expanded and combined short, choppy sentences. Use the rubric strip above and the suggestions below as you revise your sentences.

How can sentence expanding improve my writing?

Sentence expanding lets you add important information to basic sentences. One way is to add an *appositive*. An appositive is a word, phrase, or clause that follows a noun or pronoun and renames it.

Another way is to add a prepositional phrase. A *prepositional phrase* is a group of words that begins with a preposition, includes an object of the preposition, and functions as an adjective or adverb. See the samples below. (See also page 519.)

Basic Sentence	Expanded Sentences
Mr. Nelson took me fishing.	Mr. Nelson, **my neighbor,** took me fishing. (An appositive is added.)
We caught five bass.	**In less than an hour,** we caught five bass. (A prepositional phrase is added.)

Expand the following sentences by adding the type of phrase asked for in the parentheses.

1. Miss Phram contacts the radio station. *(appositive phrase)*
2. The program manager speaks with her. *(prepositional phrase)*
3. Tomorrow Jordan will speak to our class. *(appositive phrase)*
4. When we arrived, Maurice was waiting for us. *(appositive phrase)*
5. Maly watches the eagle soar. *(prepositional phrase)*

Check your sentences. Skim your writing for short, choppy sentences. Try expanding some of them by using appositive or prepositional phrases.

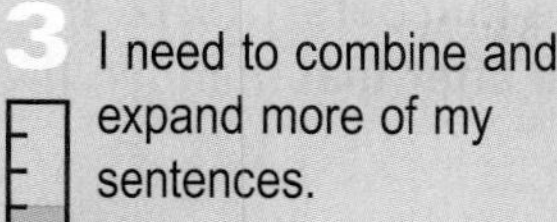

3 I need to combine and expand more of my sentences.

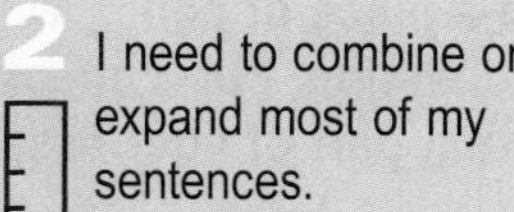

2 I need to combine or expand most of my sentences.

1 Most of my sentences need to be rewritten.

How can sentence combining improve my writing?

Sentence combining lets you eliminate short, choppy sentences and improve sentence style. The examples below show sentence combining using an infinitive phrase ("to" followed by a verb) or a participial phrase (a phrase beginning with an *ing* or *ed* word and functioning as an adjective). (See also page 520.)

Short Sentences	Combined (Infinitive Phrase)
The kids yelled, waved, and jumped. They would attract a crowd.	**The kids yelled, waved, and jumped to attract a crowd.**

Short Sentences	Combined (Participial Phrase)
The siren blared. It signaled that a tornado was approaching.	**Blaring loudly, the siren signaled that a tornado was approaching.**

Revise

Combine shorter sentences. **Skim your writing, looking for short, choppy sentences. See if you can combine any of them with either an infinitive or a participial phrase.**

Sentence Fluency

Prepositional phrases expand short, choppy sentences.

At the end, the audience went crazy and rewarded
with a standing ovation
us. We did it. We dominated the competition and
with a trophy
came home.

Revising Using a Checklist

Check your revising. On a piece of paper, write the numbers 1 to 12. If you can answer "yes" to a question, put a check mark after that number. If not, continue to work with that part of your essay.

Ideas

_____ **1.** Do I tell about one phase of my life?
_____ **2.** Do I include a variety of details?
_____ **3.** Do my ideas interest my audience?

Organization

_____ **4.** Do I use dialogue effectively?
_____ **5.** Have I checked my beginning, middle, and ending?
_____ **6.** Do I use transitions effectively?

Voice

_____ **7.** Have I used an active voice?
_____ **8.** Does my tone match my experience?

Word Choice

_____ **9.** Do I use specific words?
_____ **10.** Do I use words with feeling?

Sentence Fluency

_____ **11.** Do I expand short sentences with details?
_____ **12.** Do I combine choppy sentences?

Make a clean copy. When you've finished revising your essay, make a clean copy before you begin to edit.

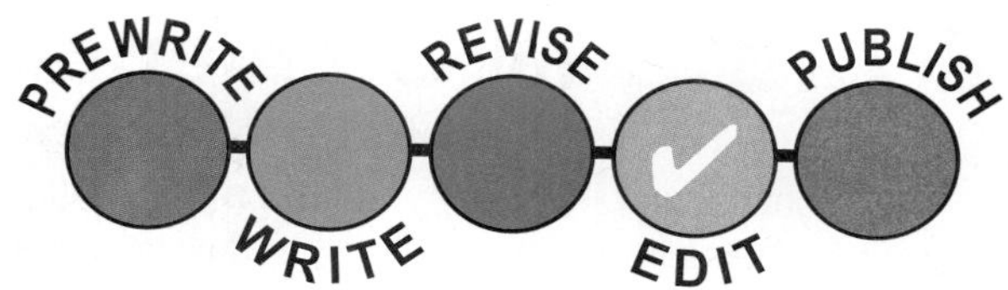

Editing

After you have finished revising your writing, it's time to edit your work for conventions: punctuation, capitalization, spelling, and grammar.

Keys to Effective Editing

1. Use a dictionary, a thesaurus, and the "Proofreader's Guide" in the back of this book.
2. Check for any words or phrases that may be confusing to the reader.
3. Check your writing for correctness of punctuation, capitalization, spelling, and grammar.
4. Edit on a printed computer copy and then enter your changes on the computer.
5. Use the editing and proofreading marks inside the back cover of this book.

Editing for Conventions

6 My grammar and punctuation are correct, and the copy is free of spelling errors.	**5** I have a few minor errors in punctuation, spelling, or grammar, but they won't confuse the reader.	**4** I have some errors in punctuation, spelling, or grammar that may distract the reader.

When you edit for *conventions*, you check spelling, grammar, capitalization, and punctuation. The rubric strip above will help you with your editing.

How can I check for subject-verb agreement?

As you check for subject-verb agreement, you need to remember that subjects and verbs must always agree in number. That means if the subject is singular, the verb must be singular; and if the subject is plural, the verb must be plural. (See pages **508–509**.)

Don't forget that most nouns ending in *s* or *es* are plural, and most verbs ending in *s* are singular.

Singular Subject-Verb Agreement

Beth volunteers at the city's food pantry.

Plural Subject-Verb Agreement

Her friends volunteer at the city's park department.

Choose a verb for each subject, making sure the two agree in number. Then write a complete sentence for each subject-verb pair. Finally, label each subject-verb pair as singular or plural.

Subjects	*Verbs*	
1. The semi driver	take	arranges
2. Voters	draws	read
3. They	collect	is
4. Maurice	receive	blinks
5. Lights	glows	fade

Check your subject-verb agreement. Make sure that your subjects agree with the verbs in each of your sentences. Make any necessary corrections.

3 I need to correct the errors because they confuse the reader.

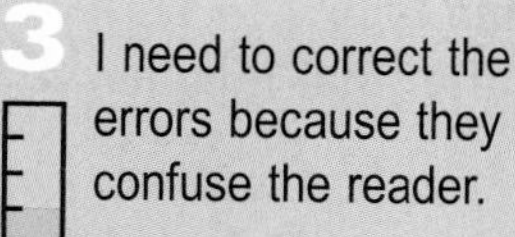

2 I need to correct many errors that make my phase autobiography hard to read.

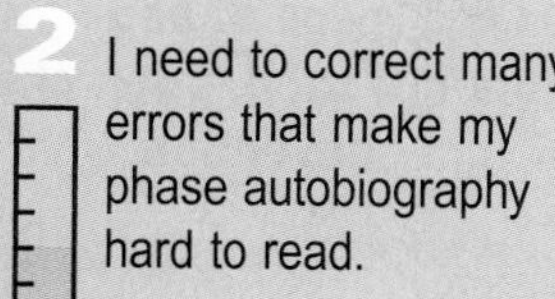

1 I need help making corrections.

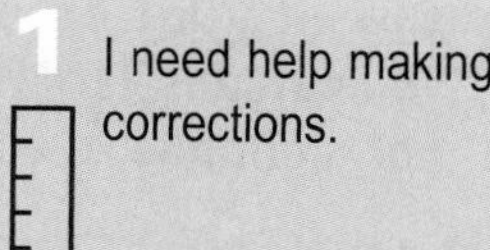

Do my verbs agree with their compound subjects?

To check your subject-verb agreement with compound subjects, you need to remember the following rules.

- If the compound subject uses *and* as a connector, use a plural verb.
  Lia and Ramon carry the school's banner in the Memorial Day parade.
- If the compound subject uses *or* or *nor* as a connector, the verb must agree with the subject closest to it.
  Either band members or Mr. Kurz needs to collect the flags.

Read each of the following sentences. Write "A" if the subject and verb agree in number. If they don't agree, rewrite the sentence.

1. Terry and Jose wants to study German.
2. Neither Colby nor Ramon sings in the chorus.
3. Every weekend, Jason and Leela volunteer at the animal shelter.
4. Their older brother and sister works at the grocery store.
5. After the race, Jodie or Chantell congratulate the winner.
6. Neither the flowers nor the cats triggers Alex's allergies.
7. The music and video games echo through the halls.
8. Every Sunday, Ling and Jules meets at the bowling alley.

Check your compound subjects. **Make sure your compound subjects agree in number with their verbs.**

Conventions
Subject-verb agreement errors are corrected.

I still ~~gets~~ get goose bumps when I ~~thinks~~ think about the band. Mr. DeRusha is a great director who . . .

NARRATIVE

Editing Using a Checklist

Check your editing. On a piece of paper, write the numbers 1 to 12. If you can answer "yes" to a question, put a check mark after that number. If not, continue to edit for that convention.

Conventions

PUNCTUATION

_____ **1.** Do I use end punctuation after all my sentences?

_____ **2.** Do I use commas after introductory word groups and transitions?

_____ **3.** Do I use commas between equal adjectives?

_____ **4.** Do I punctuate dialogue correctly?

_____ **5.** Do I use apostrophes to show possession (*a boy's bike*)?

CAPITALIZATION

_____ **6.** Do I start all my sentences with capital letters?

_____ **7.** Do I capitalize all proper nouns?

SPELLING

_____ **8.** Have I spelled all my words correctly?

_____ **9.** Have I double-checked the words my spell-checker may have missed?

GRAMMAR

_____ **10.** Do I use correct forms of verbs (*had gone,* not *had went*)?

_____ **11.** Do my subjects and verbs agree in number? (She and I *were* going, not She and I *was* going.)

_____ **12.** Do I use the right words (*to, too, two*)?

Creating a Title

- Use strong, colorful words: **Marching to Confidence**
- Give the words rhythm: **Step High, Work Hard**
- Be imaginative: **About-Face for Julie**

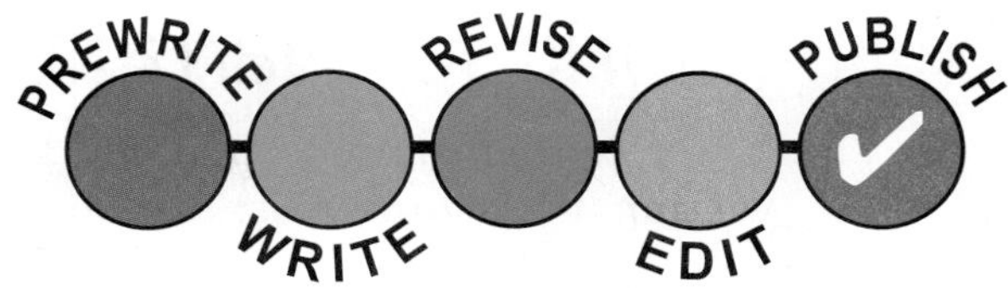

Publishing

Sharing Your Phase Autobiography

After you have worked so hard to improve your writing, make a neat, final copy to share. You may also decide to present your story in the form of a class magazine, a reading, or a recording. (See the suggestions below.)

Make a final copy. When you write your final copy, follow your teacher's instructions or use the guidelines below to format your story. (If you are using a computer, see pages 60–62.) Create a clean copy of your phase autobiography and carefully proofread it.

Focus on Presentation

- **Use blue or black ink and write neatly.**
- **Write your name in the upper left corner of page 1.**
- **Skip a line and center your title; skip another line and start your writing.**
- **Double-space your essay.**
- **Indent every paragraph and leave a one-inch margin on all four sides.**
- **Write your last name and the page number in the upper right corner of every page after the first one.**

Create a Class Magazine
Encourage your classmates to submit their writings for a class magazine. Staple them together and keep them in the class.

Share with a Group
Share your writing with a small group of peers. Allow them to ask questions or offer positive comments.

Make a Recording
Record your phase autobiography. Be sure to use an expressive voice. Give the recording and a printed copy of it to someone as a gift.

Rubric for Narrative Writing

Use this rubric for guiding and assessing your narrative writing. Refer to it whenever you want to improve your writing.

Ideas

6	5	4
The narrative captures an unforgettable time. The details make the story come alive.	The writer shares an interesting experience. Details help create the interest.	The writer tells about an interesting experience. More details are needed.

Organization

6	5	4
The way the narrative is put together makes it enjoyable to read.	The narrative is well organized, with a clear beginning, middle, and ending. Transitions are used well.	The narrative is well organized. Most of the transitions are helpful.

Voice

6	5	4
The voice in the narrative perfectly captures the special time or experience.	The writer's voice creates interest in the story.	The writer's voice could be stronger.

Word Choice

6	5	4
The writer's exceptional word choice captures the experience.	Specific nouns, verbs, and modifiers create clear pictures.	Some of the words need to be more specific to create clear pictures.

Sentence Fluency

6	5	4
The style of the sentences captures this time or experience.	The sentences are skillfully written and original.	The sentences show variety, but some should read more smoothly.

Conventions

6	5	4
The narrative is error free.	The narrative has a few minor errors in punctuation, spelling, or grammar.	The narrative has some errors that may distract the reader.

3	2	1
The writer tells about an experience or time. Many more details are needed.	The writer needs to focus more specifically on one experience or time.	The writer needs to select a topic suitable for a narrative.
The order of events needs to be corrected. More transitions need to be used.	The beginning, middle, and ending all run together. The order is unclear.	The narrative needs to be organized.
A voice can sometimes be heard. The writer needs to show more feelings.	The voice cannot be heard.	The writer has not gotten involved in the story.
Many more specific words need to be used.	The writer has given little consideration to word choice.	The writer has not yet considered word choice.
A better variety of sentences is needed. Sentences do not read smoothly.	Many short or incomplete sentences make the writing choppy.	Few sentences are written well. Help is needed.
Several errors confuse the reader.	Many errors make the narrative truly confusing and hard to read.	Help is needed to make corrections.

Evaluating a Phase Autobiography

As you read the phase autobiography below, focus on the writer's strengths and weaknesses. **(The essay contains some errors.)** Then read the student self-evaluation on page 133.

Under Two Hours!

My heart pounds with excitement, as Dad and I line up for this year's Charity Run. It's my first race. I've been working out. I feel great. I know I'm ready. Bang! We're off. As we run side by side, Dad is panting, "Coop, don't forget . . . how hard you worked . . . to get here."

Yes. Dad and I had started training several months ago. Each day in our early morning walks, we'd go faster and faster. Slowly, the walks turned into jogging. Then they finally turned into running. At first, I had a tough time keeping up with Dad. Sometimes he would slow down for me.

At that time, I have to admit, I was a couch potato. Still, I felt like I should be able to outrun my Dad. So every chance I got, I started working out on my own. After a while, I wasn't panting for breath. I was actually keeping up with Dad. I knew the 10-mile run would be a big challenge. I began to believe that I could do it.

As time went by, I began to think that Dad was actually trying to keep up with me on our morning runs. I would find myself slowing down, so that he wouldn't feel bad just as he had done for me in the beginning.

Suddenly, I hear Dad panting beside me. He tells me to go on. So I take off like a racehorse roaring ahead. My body works in rhythm—legs, arms, muscles, lungs. Just a bit farther . . . pounding toward the waiting crowd . . . I sprint across the finish line. The big race clock shows 1:57:15. I feel so proud, as I turn to cheer on my Dad who is just minutes behind me. He's grinning and panting, "We did it, Coop, under two hours." I think to myself, *Not bad, Coop. Not bad at all.*

Student Self-Assessment

The assessment below shows how the writer of "Under Two Hours!" rated his essay. He used the rubric and number scales on pages 130–131 to rank each trait. Then he made two comments for each trait. The first one showed something he liked or did well in his essay. The second comment pointed out something that he felt he could have done better.

5 Ideas

1. *My topic will interest my classmates.*
2. *I could tell more about my workouts.*

4 Organization

1. *Transitions help me tell my story smoothly.*
2. *My last sentences don't fit well in the narrative.*

4 Voice

1. *My tone perfectly fits my subject.*
2. *I could have used more dialogue.*

4 Word Choice

1. *My title makes readers want to read my narrative.*
2. *I overused some words, like "panting."*

4 Sentence Fluency

1. *I use a variety of sentences.*
2. *I could have combined some short sentences.*

4 Conventions

1. *I spell all words correctly.*
2. *Commas give me trouble.*

Use the rubric. Assess your narrative using the rubric shown on pages 130–131.

1. On your own paper, list the six traits. Leave space after each trait to write one strength and one weakness.
2. Then choose a number (from 1 to 6) that shows how well each trait was used.

Reflecting on Your Writing

You've worked hard to write a phase autobiography that your classmates will enjoy. Now take some time to think about your writing. Finish each of the sentence starters below on your own paper. Thinking about your writing will help you see how you are growing as a writer.

My Phase Autobiography

1. *The strength of my phase autobiography is . . .*
2. *The part that still needs work is . . .*
3. *The main thing I learned about writing a phase autobiography is . . .*
4. *In my next phase autobiography, I would like to . . .*
5. *Here is one question I still have about writing a phase autobiography:*

Narrative Writing

Biographical Narrative

What would it be like to live another person's life? Imagine being your brother on his first day at army boot camp or your grandmother as she decided to leave Peru and travel to the United States.

Writing a biographical narrative gives you the chance to take a walk in someone else's shoes. By learning about another person's life experiences and writing about them, you can feel as if you are experiencing the events yourself.

In this chapter, you will read a biographical narrative about a young girl's decision to leave her homeland. Then you will write your own biographical narrative.

Writing Guidelines

Subject: An experience of someone you know
Form: Biographical narrative
Purpose: To tell a story
Audience: Classmates

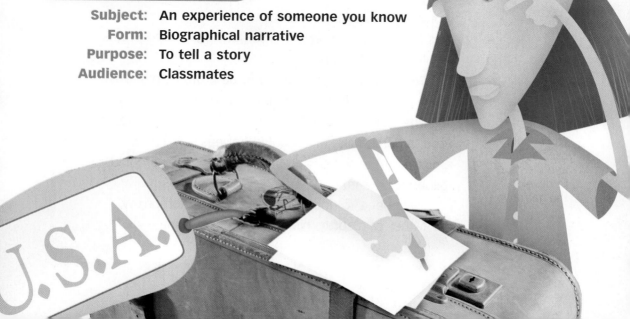

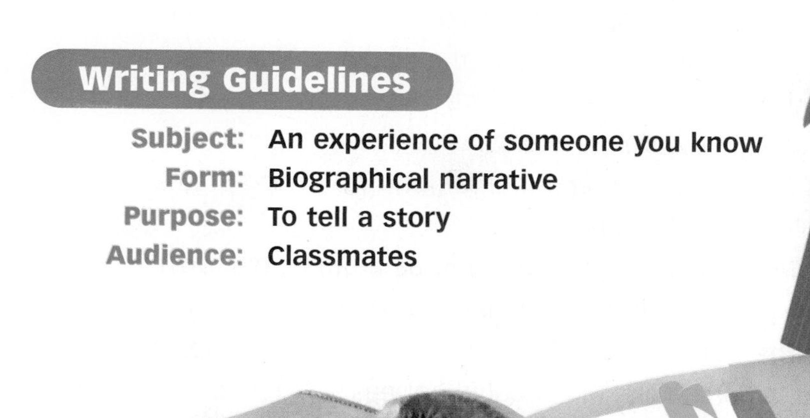

Biographical Narrative

A biographical narrative tells a true story from someone else's life. Alayna wrote about her grandmother Maria's decision to come to America as a student from Peru.

Beginning

The beginning introduces the main character and the choice she faces.

Middle

The middle uses action and dialogue to develop the narrative.

A Life-Changing Decision

"So, Maria," asked her father, paging nervously through his newspaper, "have you decided yet?"

"No, Papa," Maria answered as she stared out the living room window.

It was the spring of 1965, and Maria had a life-changing decision to make. Would she stay with her family and friends in Lima, Peru, or accept the scholarship she was being offered at a university in the United States? She knew the choice would change her life forever.

Maria gazed out at the plaza in front of her home and the beautiful cathedral in the distance. Her eyes wandered then to her father's bookstore, where she worked, just walking distance away. Maria sighed. Lima was so comfortable and familiar, but the United States would let her fulfill her dream.

Maria had always wanted to be a nurse, but when she had been a little girl, polio had withered her right leg. The disease had left her with a permanent limp. In Peru, a person like Maria could not easily become a nurse, but in the United States she knew she could follow her dream.

"We need to notify the university by tomorrow," her father said softly, his newspaper crinkling.

Middle
The tension builds to a high point.

Maria's heart started pounding, and her mind raced. The future was so uncertain, but part of her loved that fact! Did she have the courage to go to America? Could she bear to stay in Peru?

"Papa, I want to go to America!"

Maria's father jumped up and came to her, hugging her tightly. His eyes looked sad, but he smiled and said, "You will be able to do so much in the United States. They have a modern way of thinking, and if you work hard, they'll give you a chance to live your dreams."

A few months later, Maria's family and friends took her to the airport. They held hands in a circle while they sang "La Flor de la Canela," a Peruvian folk song about love and family. Maria waved one last good-bye before disappearing down the long hallway. With each step, she knew she was growing up.

Ending
The ending shows how the experience changed the person.

As the plane lifted off the ground, Maria felt in her heart that she would never come back to Peru to live. Through tear-filled eyes, she watched the cities, villages, and lush, green mountains of her home get smaller and smaller. She closed her eyes and took a deep breath. Her new life had begun.

Respond to the reading. **Answer the following questions about the biographical narrative.**

- ☐ **Ideas & Organization** **(1) What details help the reader experience the story? (2) How does the writer organize the details?**
- ☐ **Voice & Word Choice** **(3) What words or phrases show how the people in the narrative felt?**

Literature Connections: **For another example of biographical writing, read *Harriet Tubman: Conductor on the Underground Railroad* by Ann Petry.**

Prewriting Selecting a Topic

To find a topic for her biographical narrative, Alayna made a line diagram. She began by writing down people she knew well. Under each name, she wrote interesting stories they had told her.

Line Diagram

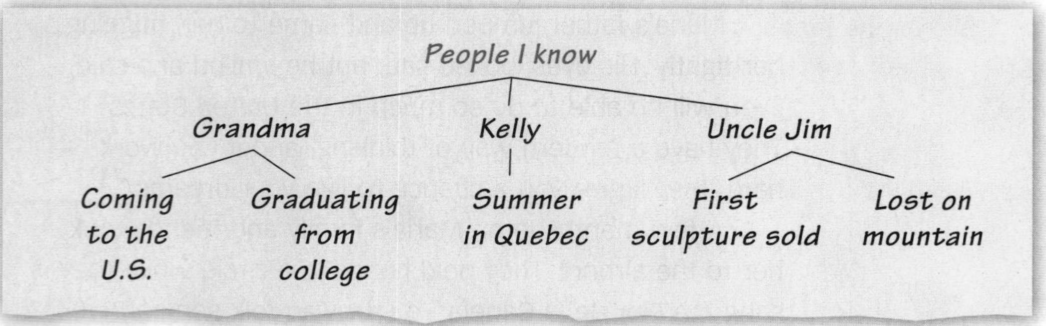

Choose your topic. Create your own line diagram. Think of people you know and interesting stories they have told you. Choose a story that you would like to learn about and share with others.

Gathering Details

Before you write, gather details about the story. Alayna used the 5 W's and H to interview her grandmother about coming to the United States.

5 W's Chart

1. *Who was involved? Maria, Papa, and her family and friends*
2. *What happened? Maria decided to leave Peru for the U.S.*
3. *When did the event happen? Spring of 1965*
4. *Where did the event happen? Lima, Peru*
5. *Why did it happen? Maria's dream to be a nurse*
6. *How did she feel about the event? Scared, sad, and excited*

Gather details. Write down questions based on the 5 W's and H. Then ask your subject to tell his or her story. Write down answers to your questions. Afterward, ask any other questions you might have.

Organizing Details

Most biographical narratives are organized chronologically. Alayna used a time line to organize the details she had gathered about her grandmother's story. Above the line, she wrote events in the story. Below it, she wrote details to include.

Time Line

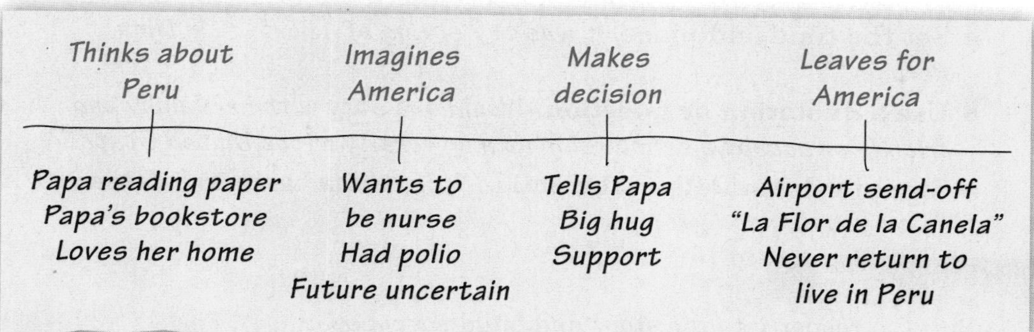

Create a time line. Use the model above to help you organize your details into a time line. Above the line, list key events. Below it, list details you would like to include in your biographical narrative.

Focus on the Traits

Organization

Narratives follow the classic shape of a plot line. The **beginning** grabs the reader's attention and sets the stage for the narrative. Then **rising action** builds suspense. The **high point** brings the person and the conflict face-to-face, and the **ending** tells how the person is changed.

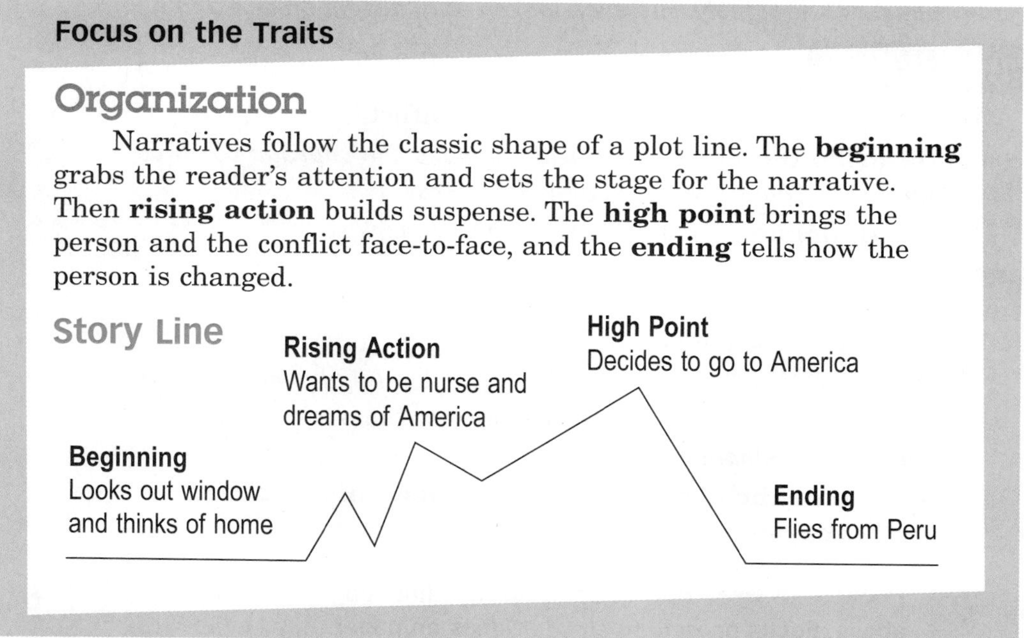

Writing Creating Your First Draft

As you write your first draft, be sure to follow your time line. Use the tips below as a guide.

Beginning

Grab the reader's attention and set the stage for your story.

- **Set the time and place.** *It was the spring of 1965 . . . in Lima, Peru.*
- **Use a quotation or question.** *Would she stay with her family and friends or accept a scholarship at a university in the United States?*
- **Start in the middle of the action.** *"So, Maria," asked her father, "have you decided yet?"*

Rising Action

Pull the reader into the story and build suspense.

- **Include thoughts and feelings.** *Lima was so comfortable and familiar, but the United States would let her fulfill her dream.*
- **Use action.** *Maria's heart started pounding, and her mind raced.*
- **Use sensory details.** *Maria's father jumped up and came to her, hugging her tightly. His eyes looked sad, but he smiled and said, . . .*

High Point

Bring the person face-to-face with the conflict.

- **Describe the high point.** *Did she have the courage to go to America? Could she bear to stay in Peru?*
- **Use dialogue.** *"Papa, I want to go to America!"*

Ending

Describe how the person changed.

- **Describe the final scene.** *Through tear-filled eyes, she watched the cities, villages, and lush, green mountains of her home get smaller and smaller.*
- **Show how the event changed the person.** *She closed her eyes and took a deep breath. Her new life had begun.*

Write the first draft. Use your time line (page 139) and follow the tips above. Focus on getting all your ideas on paper.

Revising Improving Your Writing

Once you finish your first draft, take a break. When you come back to your story, it will be easier for you to see the parts that need improvement. Check your work for the following traits of writing.

- ☐ **Ideas** Make sure you have included sensory details as well as thoughts and feelings to bring your story to life.

  Maria gazed out at the plaza in front of her home and the beautiful cathedral in the distance. Her eyes wandered then to her father's bookstore, where she worked, just walking distance away. Maria sighed.

- ☐ **Organization** Add transitions where you need to show a shift in time.

  A few months later, Maria's family and friends took her to the airport.

  As the plane lifted off the ground, Maria felt in her heart that she would never come back to Peru to live.

- ☐ **Voice** Make sure that the voice fits the person and the event.

  The future was so uncertain, but part of her loved that fact!

- ☐ **Word Choice** Use descriptive and active words.

  Maria waved one last good-bye before disappearing down the long hallway.

- ☐ **Sentence Fluency** Read your story out loud and listen to the flow of your sentences. Combine any short, choppy sentences.

Choppy

They held hands in a circle. They sang "La Flor de la Canela." It was a Peruvian folk song about love . . .

Combined

They held hands in a circle while they sang "La Flor de la Canela," a Peruvian folk song about love . . .

Revise your narrative. Use the guidelines above as you review your story and make changes.

NARRATIVE

Editing Checking for Conventions

When you're finished revising, it's time to edit your biographical narrative for conventions.

Conventions

Review your punctuation, capitalization, spelling, and grammar. The following checklist can help you.

PUNCTUATION

_____ **1.** Do I use commas correctly?

_____ **2.** Do I include punctuation at the end of every sentence?

_____ **3.** Do I put quotation marks and punctuation in the right place?

_____ **4.** Do I use apostrophes to show possession (*Maria's trip*)?

CAPITALIZATION

_____ **5.** Do I capitalize all proper nouns?

_____ **6.** Do I begin every sentence with a capital letter?

SPELLING

_____ **7.** Have I checked my spelling?

GRAMMAR

_____ **8.** Do I use correct forms of verbs (*had done,* not *had did*)?

_____ **9.** Do my subjects and verbs agree in number?
(We *were* going, not We *was* going.)

_____ **10.** Do I use the right words (*their, they're, there*)?

Edit your biographical narrative. **After you edit, let someone else look over your work for anything you missed. Then create a final copy and proofread it.**

Publishing Sharing Your Writing

A biographical narrative can bring you closer to friends and family. Share your story with the person who lived it.

Share your biographical narrative. **Read your story to the person who experienced it and give him or her a copy to keep.**

Narrative Writing
Across the Curriculum

Narratives set a course for adventure. In history class, you could write a historical narrative about being the barrel maker aboard the *Mayflower*. In math, you might write about your adventures learning new math concepts. For science class, you might even write a narrative about being a gigantic thunderhead!

This chapter contains samples of narratives like these. It also helps you create e-mails and respond to prompts on writing tests. No matter what the class or assignment, narrative writing can bring any subject to life.

What's Ahead

- **Social Studies:** Recalling a Historical Moment
- **Math:** Writing a Math Autobiography
- **Science:** Writing About a Natural Formation
- **Practical Writing:** Creating an E-Mail Message
- **Writing for Assessment**

Social Studies: Recalling a Historical Moment

American history is filled with important events. In the narrative below, a student writes about a historical moment as if he had experienced it firsthand.

The **beginning** introduces the narrator and sets the scene.

The **middle** builds to a moment of realization.

The **ending** reflects on the event.

America the Beautiful

Finally, after months crossing the Atlantic, I see land! As the *Mayflower* brings us closer to shore, I am surprised by how wild the New World looks. There are trees everywhere, a deep, dark forest. The only sounds are the creaking of the ship and the waves crashing against the rocky coast. We are all alone here. My stomach used to feel seasick, but now it feels homesick. What use is a barrel maker in a place like this?

"Landing party, to the boats!" shouts Mr. Carver, who will govern our colony.

Soon I help row a boatful of settlers ashore. The boat comes aground on a big rock, and I climb out onto it and stand on the New World.

Mr. Carver follows me. He draws a deep breath and announces, "Our new home!"

Suddenly I can almost see the new settlement. There are rows of houses, people busy with their tasks, and ships from England to trade with us. We have a lot of work ahead of us, but Mr. Carver's confidence makes me believe that we can make this new frontier feel like home.

Writing Tips

Before you write . . .

- **Select a topic.**
  Choose a historic moment to write about, such as Paul Revere's ride, the driving of the golden spike in Utah, or the day Teddy Roosevelt refused to shoot a bear. Page through your history textbook for other ideas. Select a single important moment so that you can write a well-focused narrative.
- **Research your topic.**
  Read about the event and gather details about the place and time.

During your writing . . .

- **Write as if you experienced the event.**
  Use the "I" voice. Imagine yourself to be part of this event in order to get a feel for the experience. Then record what you would see, hear, and so forth. Include thoughts and feelings.
- **Create other characters.**
  Imagine the different kinds of people you might meet. Make them historically accurate. Use dialogue to bring the characters to life.
- **Show how the event affects you.**
  Make sure that the moment isn't important only in history, but also to the main character of your narrative—you!

After you've written a first draft . . .

- **Revise your first draft.**
  Check your story's organization to be sure it is easy to follow.
- **Check for accuracy.**
  Double-check your historical facts—dates, names, and so on.
- **Edit for correctness.**
  Check for errors in punctuation, spelling, and grammar.

Select a moment from American history. Research the event and place yourself in the middle of it. Write a narrative that is both historically accurate and enjoyable to read.

Math: Writing a Math Autobiography

A math autobiography lets students reflect on their experiences with math. In the following autobiography, a student writes about how she has used math in the past and in the present, and how she expects to use it in the future.

The **beginning** reflects on the student's first experiences with math.

The **middle** gives details about the way the student currently uses math.

The **ending** suggests how she will use math in the future.

Math Matters

I remember the first day I stopped using my fingers to add and subtract. It felt so good to finally "get it." I've come a long way since then, but I still feel just as good every time I learn a new math skill.

I use math a lot in my daily life. When I was younger, I used math to do simple things like make change. Now I can solve more difficult problems. For example, my dad and I put a wood floor in our game room. We took measurements and used equations to find the square footage. That was especially tough because the game room has two small closets. Afterward, Dad and I were able to decide how much wood to buy.

I've come so far in math that now I'm a math tutor. I helped one boy, Chris, understand how to isolate variables. Suddenly, all those equations didn't scare him anymore. He finished his assignment and got an A on it.

I feel great that I can do so many things with math. It's even better now that I can help other kids. I know I'll find many new ways to use my math skills in the future for school, work, and everyday life.

Writing Tips

Before you write . . .

- **Remember thoughts and feelings about math.** Think of math experiences that made you proud, nervous, excited, or confused. Remember the first time you learned to multiply and the times you've used math in everyday life.
- **Select specific examples to mention.** Sift through your memories and choose a few examples of ways that you have used math.

During your writing . . .

- **Focus on examples.** Describe specific times that math has been helpful—or difficult—for you.
- **Show the big picture.** Demonstrate how you relate to math overall. Let your reader know whether you like math or struggle with it, and why.

After you've written a first draft . . .

- **Revise your first draft.** Add any examples that would clarify your experience and remove examples that don't.
- **Check your organization.** Make sure the details in your autobiography are organized in a logical way.
- **Edit for correctness.** Check for errors in punctuation, capitalization, spelling, and grammar.

Write your own math autobiography. Share specific examples that tell the reader about your overall experience with math.

Science:
Writing About a Natural Formation

When you use "personification" in your writing, you give human qualities or characteristics to a nonhuman thing. In science, you can use personification to imagine being a natural formation. In the narrative below, a student personified a thunderhead.

The **beginning** introduces the natural formation.

The **middle** provides details from the point of view of the formation.

The **ending** completes the narrative.

I'm All Grown Up!

People sometimes call me a cumulonimbus. That may not sound like a compliment, but for me it is. In the beginning, I was just a cumulus. That's right, I'm a cloud. I'm made of tiny water droplets that attach to dust, sea salt, and even pollution. As water droplets gather, I grow into a flat-topped thunderhead.

The first half of my name, cumulus, means "heap." That describes how I begin my life, like a heap of puffy cotton balls. I fly low and constantly change shape to look like different animals. It is a fun way to pass the time on warm, sunny days, but I have bigger things in my future.

The second half of my name, nimbus, means "precipitation." As the sun warms the air close to the ground, I grow from a cumulus cloud to a cumulonimbus—a thunderhead. The warm air rises rapidly, pushing the tiny water droplets higher and higher. They bump into each other and form raindrops. I don't even realize what is happening until I am over 40,000 feet tall!

It's exciting to be that tall, but it does make my stomach drop. My negatively charged electrons get attracted to the positively charged protons in the ground. Then the positive and negative charges crash in a shocking bolt of electricity. I immediately hear a rolling round of applause. It's great to be a cumulonimbus.

Writing Tips

Before you write . . .

- **Select a topic that interests you.**
  Check your science book for natural formations to write about. Consider formations such as waterspouts, hurricanes, glaciers, fault lines, craters, or canyons.
- **Research the topic.**
  Check your textbook, an encyclopedia, or a Web site to learn about the formation you have chosen.

During your writing . . .

- **Write from the point of view of the formation.**
  Use the "I" voice and imagine yourself as the formation. Tell about where you come from, what you do, and how you change.
- **Include thoughts and feelings.**
  Indicate what your formation does and thinks, likes and dislikes.

After you've written a first draft . . .

- **Revise your narrative.**
  Make sure your essay is organized logically. Check to see that it is informative and easy to follow.
- **Check for accuracy.**
  Double-check the facts in your story.
- **Edit for correctness.**
  Review your work, looking for errors in punctuation, spelling, capitalization, and grammar.

Select a natural formation that you'd enjoy writing a narrative about. Research your topic and write a story from the point of view of the formation. Share your narrative with your classmates.

Practical Writing:
Creating an E-Mail Message

E-mail has become an important link between teachers and students. In the following narrative e-mail, a student tells a teacher about a tour she went on for extra credit.

The **heading** includes sending information and a subject line.

The **beginning** tells the reason for the e-mail.

The **middle** describes the events of the day.

The **ending** closes in a thoughtful way.

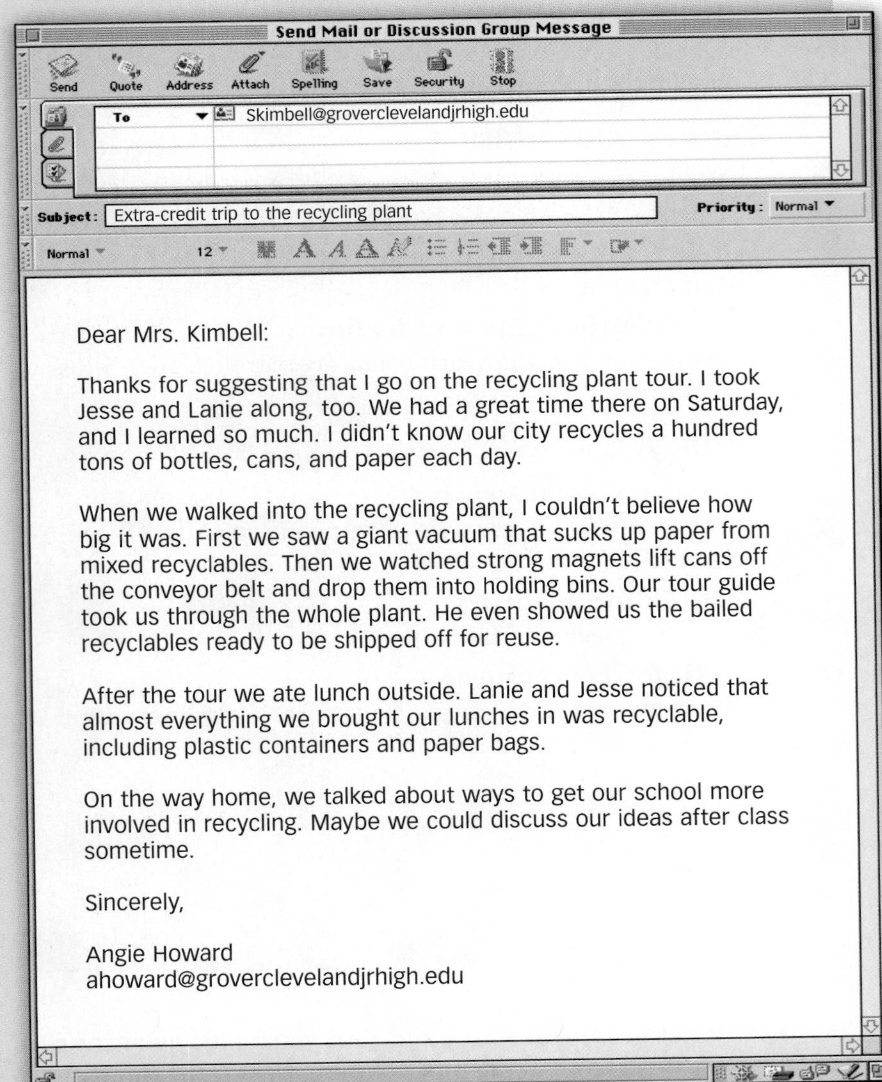

Send Mail or Discussion Group Message

Send Quote Address Attach Spelling Save Security Stop

To Skimbell@groverclevelandjrhigh.edu

Subject: Extra-credit trip to the recycling plant

Priority: Normal

Normal 12

Dear Mrs. Kimbell:

Thanks for suggesting that I go on the recycling plant tour. I took Jesse and Lanie along, too. We had a great time there on Saturday, and I learned so much. I didn't know our city recycles a hundred tons of bottles, cans, and paper each day.

When we walked into the recycling plant, I couldn't believe how big it was. First we saw a giant vacuum that sucks up paper from mixed recyclables. Then we watched strong magnets lift cans off the conveyor belt and drop them into holding bins. Our tour guide took us through the whole plant. He even showed us the bailed recyclables ready to be shipped off for reuse.

After the tour we ate lunch outside. Lanie and Jesse noticed that almost everything we brought our lunches in was recyclable, including plastic containers and paper bags.

On the way home, we talked about ways to get our school more involved in recycling. Maybe we could discuss our ideas after class sometime.

Sincerely,

Angie Howard
ahoward@groverclevelandjrhigh.edu

Writing Tips

Before you write . . .

- **List the details you want to report.**
  Write down your experience, putting events in time order.

During your writing . . .

- **Complete the e-mail heading.**
  Fill in the address line and make sure each character is correct. Then write a subject line that clearly indicates the reason for the e-mail.
- **Greet the reader and give your reason for writing.**
  Start with a polite greeting. Follow by telling why you are sending the e-mail.
- **Be conversational but proper.**
  Make sure your sentences are clear and complete. You may use an informal voice, but your grammar should be correct.
- **Describe what happened and what was said.**
  Describe your experience and include any important conversations you had.
- **End politely.**
  Close with "Sincerely," or another closing you might use in a letter. Type your name below.

After you've written a first draft . . .

- **Reread your e-mail.**
  Don't simply press "Send." Make sure your e-mail is clear and complete.
- **Check for correctness.**
  Check for errors in punctuation, capitalization, spelling, and grammar.

Think of a school-related event that you enjoyed and select a teacher or mentor who was involved with the event. Write an e-mail message to the person, sharing your experience. (You can send the e-mail or merely treat it as a class assignment.)

Narrative Writing

Writing for Assessment

Many state and school writing tests include a narrative prompt that asks you to recall a personal experience or respond to a "what if" question. Study the following sample prompt and student response.

Narrative Prompt

Life is one long string of learning experiences. From the time that you were a newborn to your eighth-grade year, you have learned many lessons. Think back to an experience that taught you an important lesson. Write a narrative essay describing the experience and what you learned.

Response to a Narrative Prompt

The **beginning** sets up the experience.

Whenever I face a challenging situation, I tell myself, "This will make a good story—if I ever get through it!" Challenges may not be fun, but they often teach important lessons. Just last summer at camp, I faced a rope course that taught me to believe in myself and other people as well.

I stood in front of a 50-foot-tall climbing tower built out of telephone poles. Handholds were bolted to the sides of the poles, and I wore a special harness with belaying ropes. Still, the climb to the top would take all the arm and leg strength I had, as well as faith in two people I hardly knew.

Each **middle** paragraph describes events that took place.

The rope attached to my harness went up over the top of the tower and back down into a locking device held by my cabin mate, Eric. Another boy named Taylor backed him up, but I wasn't sure I could trust either of them. It was too late to turn back, though. I didn't want Eric, Taylor, or other campers to see me lose my nerve.

Numbly, I stepped to the base of the tower. I grabbed a pair of handholds. The rope on my harness drew tight as Eric pulled on it. Swallowing my fear, I lifted myself up onto the pole. As I rose, Eric and Taylor drew in the slack of my belaying rope. Soon I was 10 feet off the ground, and then 20, and then 30. I paused, smiling as I caught my breath. I should have believed in myself.

Suddenly I slipped, tumbling away from the tower. My belaying line snapped tight, and I hung there, 25 feet up.

"I got you," Eric called out. "Swing back over and grab on."

I did, and realized I should have believed in Eric and Taylor, too. Panting a little, I continued to climb until I reached the platform at the top. When I got there, I cheered, and so did Eric, Taylor, and everyone down below.

The **ending** paragraph reflects on the experience.

That day, I learned that it took two things for me to climb that tower. First, I had to believe in myself. Second, I had to believe in others. That's a lesson I'll be able to use throughout my life.

Respond to the reading. Answer the following questions about the sample response.

- ☐ **Ideas** **(1) What is the focus of this narrative essay? (2) What did the writer learn from the experience?**
- ☐ **Organization** **(3) How did the writer organize the paragraphs in the essay?**
- ☐ **Voice & Word Choice** **(4) What words and phrases express how the writer's mood changed throughout the narrative?**

Writing Tips

Use the following tips as a guide when responding to a narrative writing prompt.

Before you write . . .

- **Understand the prompt.**
  Remember that a narrative prompt asks you to tell a story.
- **Plan your time wisely.**
  Take several minutes to plan your writing. Use a graphic organizer like a time line to help with planning your writing.

Time Line

Subject: ______

First: ______

______

______

______

Finally: ______

During your writing . . .

- **Decide on a focus for your narrative.**
  Use key words from the prompt as you write your focus statement.
- **Be selective.**
  Tell only the main events in your experience.
- **End in a meaningful way.**
  Reflect on the importance of the narrative.

After you've written a first draft . . .

- **Check for completeness and correctness.**
  Present events in order. Delete any unneeded details and neatly correct any errors.

Narrative Prompts

- According to an old saying, "The best way to have a friend is to be a friend." Recall a time when you did something to help one of your friends. Write a narrative essay about the experience. Focus on the way that your actions affected your friendship.
- Think about a time when you were new to a group. Perhaps it was your first day at your middle school or junior high. Perhaps it was the first practice for a school play or sports team. Write a narrative about your experience and how you learned to fit in.

Plan and write a response. Respond to one of the prompts above. Complete your writing within the period of time your teacher gives you. Afterward, list one part that you like and one part that could be better.

Narrative Writing in Review

Purpose: In narrative writing, you *tell a story* about something that has happened.

Topics: Narrate . . . an experience that taught you something,
an experience that covers a period of time,
a story about another person's life,
a time of personal change, or
a memorable event.

Prewriting

Select a topic from your own (or another's) life. List important times in your life to use as possible topics. (See page 102.)

Organize key events. Do some freewriting to arrange key events in chronological order. (See page 104.)

Remember the details by creating a chart of details and feelings. (See page 105.)

Writing

In the beginning, grab the reader's attention and use transitions to smoothly move the reader through your opening paragraph. (See page 109.)

In the middle, use dialogue, sensory details, and personal feelings. "Show, don't tell," to help the reader understand the experience. (See pages 110–111.)

In the ending, tie the beginning to the ending or explain the importance of the event or experience. (See page 112.)

Revising

Review the ideas, organization, and voice first. Then check **word choice** and **sentence fluency**. Combine and expand sentences to eliminate choppy writing. (See pages 114–124.)

Editing

Check your writing for conventions. Check your writing for subject-verb agreement, and ask a friend to check the writing, too. (See pages 126–128.)

Make a final copy and proofread it for errors before sharing it with other people. (See page 129.)

Assessing

Use the narrative rubric to assess your finished writing. (See pages 130–131.)

describe define

Expository Writing

Writing Focus

- Expository Paragraph
- Classification Essay
- Comparison-Contrast Essay

Grammar Focus

- Apostrophes to Show Possession
- Subordinating Conjunctions

Academic Vocabulary

Read the meanings and share answers to the questions.

1. An **expository** essay is one that explains something.
   What might you write an expository essay about?
2. A **category** is a group of similar things.
   Oranges, apples, and bananas can be put into what category?
3. To **compare** is to say how two or more things are alike.
   Compare your two favorite books.
4. To **contrast** is to say how two or more things are different.
   Contrast your two favorite books.

solve explain inform

Expository Writing

Expository Paragraph

Astronomers estimate that the universe contains ten thousand billion billion stars. That's a 1 with 22 zeroes after it! Even so, those innumerable stars fall into just seven main types. Seven is a much more manageable number than ten thousand billion billion!

Whenever you separate something into types or parts, you are classifying it. In this chapter, you will write a classification paragraph that will break a topic into categories. When you are finished, you can share with your reader a part of your universe.

Writing Guidelines

Subject: A topic that can be broken down into categories
Form: Expository paragraph
Purpose: To share information
Audience: Classmates

Expository Paragraph

The classification paragraph is a simple way to present the parts of a topic. It begins with a **topic sentence** that tells what the paragraph will be about. The **body** sentences that follow present the categories along with specific details about each. Finally, the **closing sentence** wraps up the paragraph. The following paragraph classifies the types of "planets" in our solar system.

Topic Sentence

Body

Closing Sentence

Three Types of Planets

People often think all planets are alike, but there are actually three types of planets in the solar system. The terrestrial planets are made of rock and metal and are closest to the sun. These include the midsize planets Mercury, Venus, Earth, and Mars. They rotate slowly and don't have many moons. Farther from the sun are the planets called gas giants, Jupiter, Saturn, Uranus, and Neptune. They are called gas giants because they are formed from gases such as hydrogen and helium. Gas giants rotate fast and have many moons. Finally, planetoids are objects made up of rock and ice and are too small to be true "planets." Planetoids sometimes even get pulled into a planet's gravitational field and become moons themselves. Whether they are terrestrials, gas giants, or planetoids, the planets in the solar system are fascinating.

Respond to the reading. On your own paper, answer each of the following questions.

- ☐ **Ideas** (1) What three categories does the writer give?
- ☐ **Organization** (2) How does the writer organize the specific categories (order of location, order of importance, time order)?
- ☐ **Voice & Word Choice** (3) What words or phrases show that the writer is knowledgeable about the topic?

Prewriting Selecting a Topic

To select a topic, make a diagram. Select two things you know about and write them at the top. Then list the different categories that can be found in each topic. The writer of the paragraph on page 158 created the following diagram and put a star next to the topic she wanted to write about.

Line Diagram

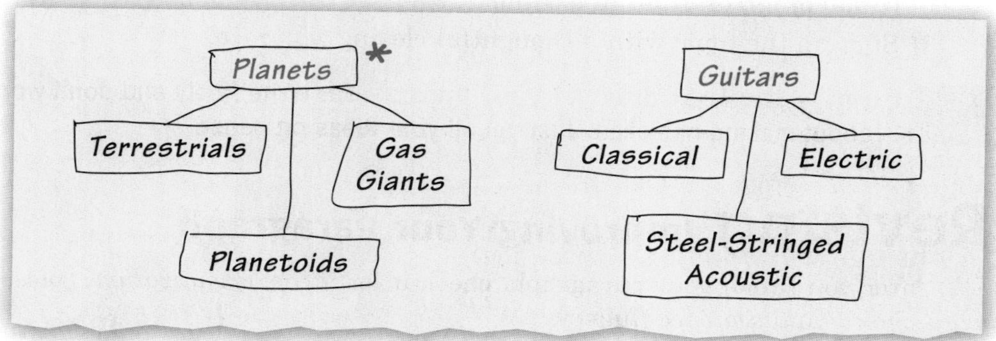

Create a diagram and select a topic. Using the diagram above as a guide, create your own, listing two or three topics that interest you along with their categories. Put a star next to the topic you would like to write about.

Writing a Topic Sentence

Many subjects are too broad for a single paragraph. You can't sum up the universe, for example, in one paragraph. However, you can explain the types of planets in our solar system. Your topic sentence should (1) name the topic, and (2) mention its categories. A simple formula follows.

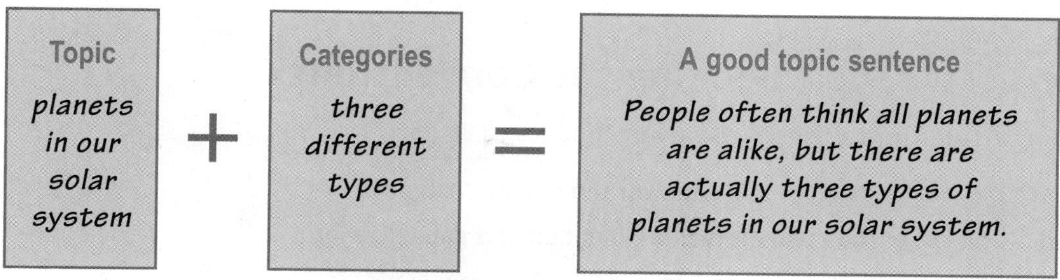

Write your topic sentence. Use the basic formula above to write a topic sentence for your paragraph. You may need to try a few different versions to make this sentence say exactly what you want it to say.

EXPOSITORY

Writing Developing Your First Draft

A classification paragraph consists of a topic sentence, a body that explains the categories—with supporting details—and a closing sentence.

- Include your topic sentence at the beginning of the paragraph.
- Write body sentences explaining your topic's categories and arrange them in the best possible order: order of importance, chronological (time) order, or order of location. (See page 551.)
- Sum up the topic with a thoughtful closing sentence.

Write the first draft of your paragraph. Write freely and don't worry about making mistakes. Just get all your ideas on paper.

Revising Improving Your Paragraph

After you finish your paragraph, check it for *ideas, organization, voice, word choice,* and *sentence fluency.*

Review your paragraph. Think about the following questions as you revise your writing.

1. Is my topic sentence clear? What details should I add or remove?
2. Are my categories and details organized in the best way?
3. Do I sound knowledgeable about my topic?
4. Are my words clear and precise?
5. Do my sentences flow smoothly? Have I included a thoughtful closing?

Editing Checking for Conventions

After you revise your paragraph, check it for *conventions.*

Edit your work. Answer the questions below.

1. Did I use correct punctuation and capitalization?
2. Have I checked my spelling and grammar?

Proofread your paragraph. After making a neat copy of your paragraph, check it one more time for errors.

Expository Writing

Classification Essay

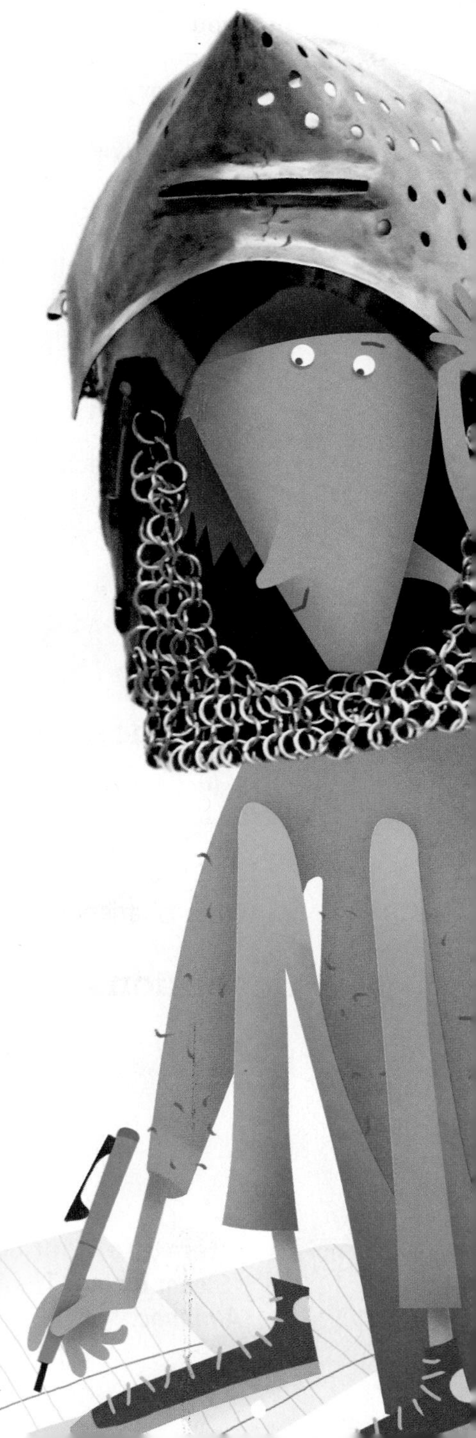

Medieval soldiers came in three varieties: foot soldiers, archers, and knights. Foot soldiers dressed in mismatched armor and carried simple weapons such as poleaxes or flails. Archers often wore no armor, but stood behind other troops to shoot their long bows. Knights wore suits of armor, fought from horseback, and used swords, lances, and shields.

When you identify the types or categories of something, you are using classification. In this chapter, you will write a classification essay. The key is to select a topic that you know well and can separate into categories.

Writing Guidelines

Subject: A topic that can be broken down into categories
Form: Classification essay
Purpose: To share information
Audience: Classmates

Understanding Your Goal

When you plan your expository essay, keep the following traits in mind. Understanding these traits will help you reach your goal of writing an excellent expository essay.

Traits of Expository Writing

Ideas

Choose a topic that can be broken down into at least three classes or categories. Then support each with a variety of interesting details.

Organization

Develop a precise pattern of organization for each category and clearly connect your details.

Voice

Use words and details that fit your purpose and connect with the reader.

Word Choice

Select precise words that clearly explain each of the categories.

Sentence Fluency

Write a variety of sentences that connect your ideas smoothly.

Conventions

Use punctuation, capitalization, spelling, and grammar correctly.

Literature Connections: For another example of expository writing, read "Steam Rising: The Revolutionary Power of Paddleboats" from *The World Almanac.*

Classification Essay

In the expository essay below, the writer identifies and explains three types of armor that have been developed over thousands of years of history. The key parts of the expository essay are listed in the left margin.

Beginning

The beginning introduces the topic and presents the focus statement (underlined).

Centuries of Protection

Officer T. J. Cosford, a guest speaker at Cooper School, showed students a bulletproof vest. This type of body armor once saved his partner's life. While armor has been used throughout the ages, the materials used to make it have changed a great deal over time. From chain mail to steel suits to Kevlar vests, armor has protected people for centuries.

Middle

The first middle paragraph describes the first category and explains its drawbacks.

Even though armor had been around for more than 2,500 years, the first important change in armor took place around 1000 C.E. That was when soldiers began wearing chain mail. Chain mail was made of thousands of little metal rings hooked together. The thin rings formed a kind of metal cloth that could be draped around a soldier's body. It was lighter than a metal plate and could cover large areas of a soldier's body. However, chain mail was not perfect. It did very little to stop the impact of a blow from a sword. The chain mail wearer still could be injured or killed.

The second category is explained.

The next type of armor, the steel suits worn by knights in the 1400s, was a step up from chain mail. A complete suit had the following parts: a breastplate, a back plate, flexible arm and leg covers, gloves, shoes, and a helmet with a hinged door that protected the face. Besides being extremely heavy, the armored suits were expensive to make. Only the rich could afford to wear them. A knight needed people to help him get dressed and mount his horse for battle. Although these steel

Middle
The third middle paragraph describes the third category and explains its advantages.

Ending
The ending considers the overall importance of the topic.

suits offered excellent protection from weapons, they made movement very awkward. If he was knocked from his horse, a soldier in a suit of armor was as good as dead.

Today, the newest armor is made of plastics and man-made fabrics. One of these is Kevlar, invented in the 1970s. Kevlar is a lightweight fiber that is stronger than steel and more flexible than chain mail. With enough layers, Kevlar can stop a speeding bullet. The protective clothing items—helmets, jackets, vests, and boots—worn by today's soldiers contain Kevlar.

People have always needed to protect themselves in battle, and through the years, they found newer and better ways to do it. Types of protection have evolved from chain mail and metal suits to man-made materials. Battle armor will continue to evolve as long as it is needed. Science fiction suggests that someday people may be protected by invisible force fields. In the meantime, people like Mr. Cosford will continue to rely on the latest forms of armor.

Respond to the reading. Answer the following questions about the essay you just read.

- ☐ **Ideas (1) What is the writer's topic? (2) What three main categories does the writer cover?**
- ☐ **Organization (3) Can you find the pattern that is used to organize each middle paragraph? Explain it. (4) How does the writer tie the ending to the beginning?**
- ☐ **Voice & Word Choice (5) How does the writer show personal interest in and knowledge of the topic? Give an example of each.**

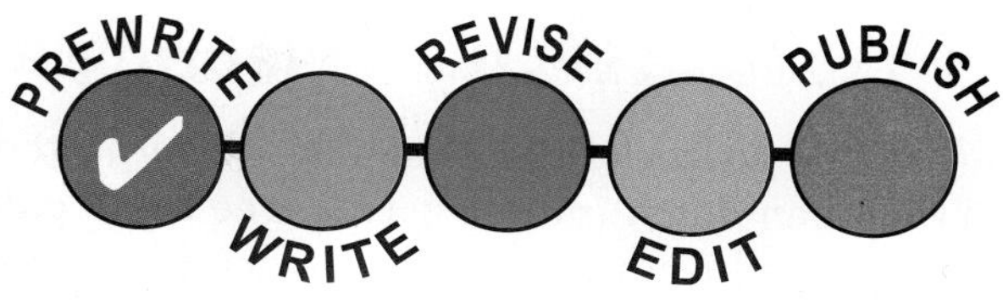

Prewriting

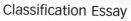

Prewriting is the first step in the writing process. It involves selecting a topic, gathering specific details, and organizing your ideas.

Keys to Effective Prewriting

1. Select a topic that you know well or one you would like to know more about.
2. Write a focus statement that clearly states the topic and mentions its main types or categories.
3. Gather details that will make your essay clear and interesting.
4. Organize your details into three or four main categories.
5. Plan your essay using an organized list or an outline.

Prewriting Selecting a Topic

The writer of the model essay on protective armor chose a topic that could be broken down into at least three main categories. Choose from the following general subjects for the brainstorming activity below.

clothing	*education*	*health*	*occupation*
exercise	*friends*	*machines*	*recreation*
food	*goals*	*art/music*	*science*

Brainstorm for topics. **To brainstorm for topics, you think freely about all the possibilities. You don't stop to think about any one idea. Just keep listing.**

1. **Select four general subjects that appeal to you from the list above.**
2. **On your own paper, draw a gathering chart like the one shown below. Write your four subjects on the top line.**
3. **List possible writing topics under each general subject.**
4. **Star the two topics that interest you the most. (You will use these topics in the next exercise.)**

Gathering Chart

RECREATION	GOALS	ART/MUSIC	SCIENCE
biking *	climbing a mountain	photography	animal defenses *
canoeing		popular music	storms
skateboarding			

Focus on the Traits

Ideas The writer of the sample essay on pages 163–164 wrote about a topic that interested both him and his classmates. The topic worked well because it could be divided into three main categories that could be supported with specific details.

Sizing Up Your Topic

Once you have selected two possible topics, you should test them to see if they can be broken down into three or four categories. Use the guidelines below to test your topics:

Too Broad . . . Topics that are too broad have too many categories to explore. For example, "animals" has so many categories that you couldn't possibly cover them all in one essay.

Too Narrow . . . If a topic can't be easily broken down into categories, it is too narrow. For example, "octopus ink" would be too narrow.

Just Right . . . "Animal defenses" could include three or four natural methods that animals use to protect themselves. It is just right.

Choose your topic. On your own paper, write the two topics you starred in the exercise on page 166. Beneath each one, list at least three main categories of the topic. When you are finished, ask yourself the following questions about each topic. Then choose the better topic.

1. **Does this topic have three or four main categories?**
2. **Could I find enough details to support each main category?**
3. **Is this topic *too broad, too narrow,* or *just right*?**

Focusing Your Topic

Once you have selected a topic, it's time to write a *focus statement* (also called a *thesis statement*). An effective focus statement identifies the topic you will write about and how it can be broken down. (Sometimes you may wish to actually name the specific categories in your focus statement.)

The following formula was used to write a focus statement for an essay about animal defenses.

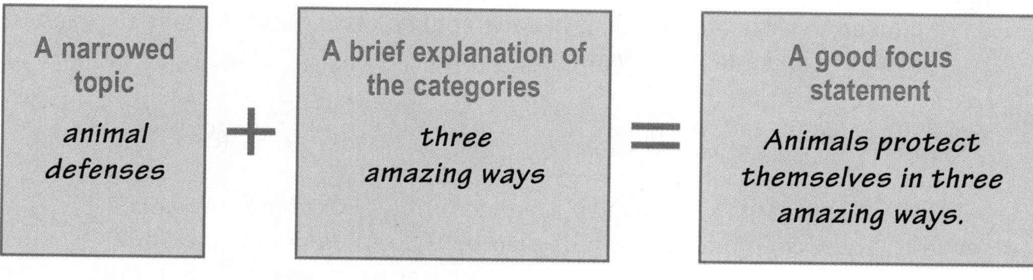

Write your focus statement. Using the formula shown above, write a focus statement for your classification essay.

Prewriting Gathering and Sorting Details

Now that you have selected your topic and written your focus statement, you can begin gathering and sorting details. Sorting helps you see how many details you have for each category. Study the sorting chart below from the student essay about how animals protect themselves.

If you think of something you would like to add to your list, but you don't know enough about it, write it down as a question and circle it. Do whatever reading or researching is necessary to answer your questions.

Sorting Chart

Changing Colors	Using Chemicals	Releasing Body Parts
- Snowshoe rabbits turn white in winter.	- Skunks spray a stinky liquid.	- Starfish drop arms.
- Cuttlefish turn colors.	- Some frogs taste bad.	Do they regrow their lost parts?
Is there a color that cuttlefish can't change to?	- Octopuses shoot dark, cloudy ink.	- Salamanders can regrow a leg or tail.

Create your sorting chart. On your own paper, draw a sorting chart like the one above. At the top, write the three or four main categories you've chosen to write about. Then, in each column, list specific details for each category and add any questions you may have.

Focus on the Traits

Organization If you are able to divide your topic into three or four main categories, you will also be able to easily divide your essay into clear paragraphs. Remember that each paragraph should address one main category of the topic.

Writing Topic Sentences

The topic sentence of each middle paragraph should clearly identify one of the categories. Each topic sentence should also include a transition that moves the reader smoothly from one category to the next. The writer of the essay on animal defenses used the topic sentences below to rate the defenses from least to most unusual. (For more information on topic sentences, see pages 552–553.)

Topic Sentences

Topic sentence 1: *One common way animals protect themselves is by changing color to blend in with their environment.*

Topic sentence 2: *A more unusual way animals avoid attack is by giving off a chemical that smells bad or clouds the surroundings.*

Topic sentence 3: *Perhaps the most amazing way animals protect themselves is by releasing a tail or another body part to get away when captured.*

Write your topic sentences. Use the above models to help you write your topic sentences.

1. Keep your focus statement in mind as you write each topic sentence.
2. Be sure each topic sentence addresses one of the main categories mentioned in the focus statement.
3. Include a transition to introduce or say something important about the category. (For more information on transitions, see pages 572–573.)

Focus on the Traits

Voice In a classification essay, you want to sound both interested and knowledgeable. Search for fascinating details and amazing facts to include in your writing.

Prewriting Organizing Your Ideas

The focus statement identifies the overall topic and main categories of the classification essay. Each category becomes a topic sentence in the actual essay.

Directions	Organized List
Write your focus statement (thesis).	*Animals protect themselves in three amazing ways.*
Write the first category.	*1. Changing color to blend in with surroundings*
List your first example.	*– Rabbit turns brown in summer, white in winter*
List your second example.	*– Cuttlefish changes to color of surroundings*
Write the second category.	*2. Using chemicals*
List your first example.	*– Skunk repels attackers with foul-smelling liquid*
List your second example.	*– Octopus squirts dark, inky fluid*
Write the third category.	*3. Releasing body parts*
List your first example.	*– Salamander and starfish drop a limb*
List your second example.	*– Gecko drops its tail to get away*

Make sure you have approximately the same number and kinds of details for each main category in your essay. When you revise, you will check for a balance of information from one paragraph to the next.

Make an organized list. To create your list, follow the "Directions" in the sample above. You will use this list as you write your essay.

Go Online!

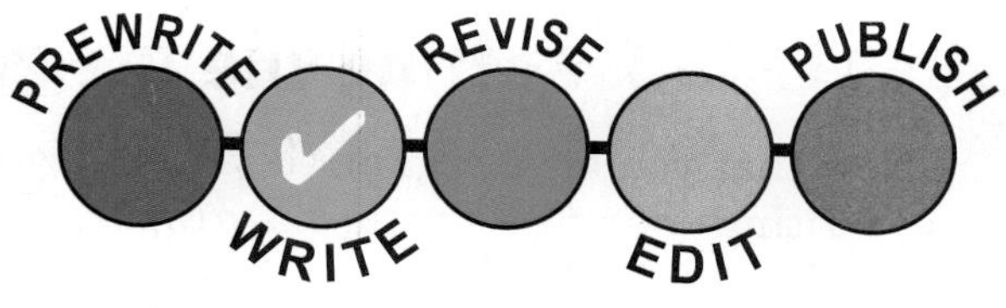

Writing

Once you've finished your prewriting, it's time to write your first draft. You're ready to write a first draft when you know enough about your topic and have written a clear focus statement.

Keys to Effective Writing

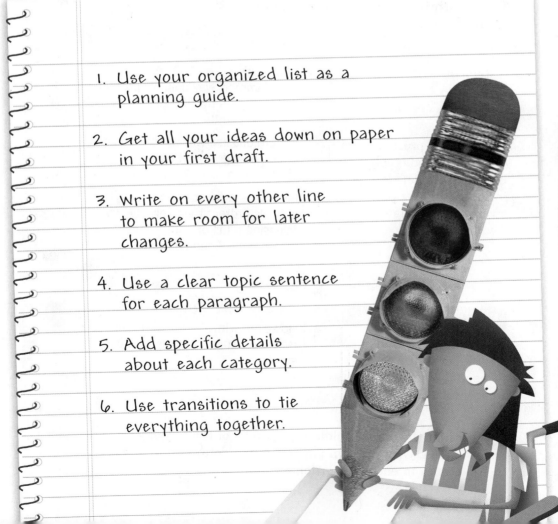

1. Use your organized list as a planning guide.
2. Get all your ideas down on paper in your first draft.
3. Write on every other line to make room for later changes.
4. Use a clear topic sentence for each paragraph.
5. Add specific details about each category.
6. Use transitions to tie everything together.

Writing Getting the Big Picture

Now that you have organized your categories into a logical order, you can begin writing your first draft. The graphic below shows how a classification essay is put together.

The opening paragraph contains a clear focus statement. The middle contains several supporting paragraphs, each one covering one main category of the topic. The closing paragraph sums up the essay. (The examples used below are from the sample essay shown on pages 173–176.)

Beginning

The **beginning** captures the reader's interest, introduces your topic, and gives your focus statement.

Focus Statement

Animals protect themselves in three amazing ways.

Middle

The **middle** presents each category of your topic. Each middle paragraph includes one category and strong supporting details.

Three Topic Sentences

One common way animals protect themselves is by changing color to blend in with their environment.

A more unusual way animals avoid attack is by giving off a chemical that smells bad or clouds the surroundings.

Perhaps the most amazing way animals protect themselves is by releasing a tail or another body part to get away when captured.

Ending

The **ending** reminds the reader of the essay's focus and suggests the importance of the topic.

Closing Sentence

However, without their amazing defenses, some animals would not survive.

Look at the three middle paragraphs of the model essay on pages 163–164. On your own paper, list the details that support the topic sentence in each paragraph.

Starting Your Essay

Begin by writing your opening paragraph as freely as you can. This paragraph should make the reader want to read your entire paper. It should also introduce the focus statement.

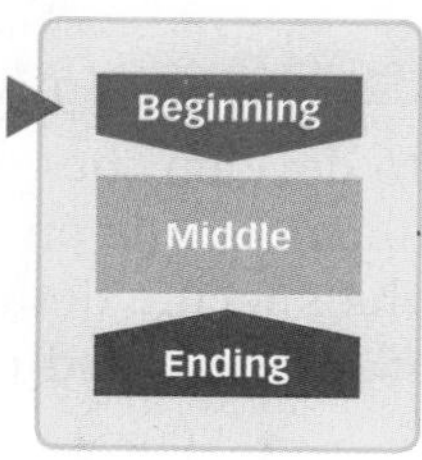

Several ways to begin a classification essay are shown below. Each of these examples is written in a different voice, but any would offer an interesting beginning. You might use one or more of these to start your essay.

- **Share interesting or surprising details about the subject.** *They sting! They stink! They taste bad! What could "they" possibly be? They are animals that protect themselves in amazing ways.*
- **Ask a question.** *What if you could suddenly change colors and blend into the background?*
- **Give interesting background information.** *For years, people have found many ways to protect themselves. Today, they wear camouflage uniforms and shoot pepper spray.*

Beginning Paragraph

In the beginning paragraph below, the writer combines interesting details with a question to introduce the focus statement.

The writer provides interesting background information and asks a question.

The writer includes a focus statement (underlined).

For years, people have found many ways to protect themselves. Today, they wear camouflage uniforms and shoot pepper spray. Where did people get the ideas for these forms of protection? They may have come from the unusual ways animals defend themselves. Animals protect themselves in three amazing ways.

EXPOSITORY

Write an opening. Write two beginning paragraphs, using one or more of the techniques given above. Ask yourself which opening will better capture the reader's attention and which one has a stronger voice.

Writing Developing the Middle Part

After writing your beginning paragraph, you are ready to develop the middle of your essay. Each middle paragraph should focus on one main category of your topic and include the specific details from your organized list (page 170). A well-organized paragraph uses a variety of details.

Beginning
Middle
Ending

1. The **topic sentence** introduces the topic of the paragraph. (See the underlined sentence in the paragraph below.)
2. The **specific details** in each paragraph support the topic sentence. Here are several different ways to add details to your writing:
   - **Include facts and examples.**
   - **Explain a term.**
   - **Make a comparison.**
   - **Write about a personal experience.**
3. The **closing sentence** ends the paragraph and provides a final thought.

Middle Paragraphs

Topic Sentence	*One common way animals protect themselves is by changing color to blend in with their environment.*
Specific Details	*A good example of this is the snowshoe rabbit. This rabbit turns from brown in summer to white in winter. Its change in color makes it hard for predators to see the rabbit in dry summer grass and winter snow. Cuttlefish also change color to blend with their surroundings. Without the ability to change color, some species of animals would probably be extinct by now.*
Closing Sentence	*Humans have borrowed this idea to make camouflage clothing.*

Topic Sentence

<u>A more unusual way animals avoid attack is by giving off a chemical that smells bad or clouds the surroundings.</u> The skunk defends itself by releasing a foul-smelling chemical from glands found beneath its tail. Because the chemical can severely sting eyes, and the smell is enough to send predators hurrying away, any animal that tangles with a skunk surely won't do it twice! An octopus squirts a dark, inky fluid in front of its attackers. The ink clouds the water and lets the octopus escape. Did these protective methods give someone the idea for pepper spray?

Specific Details

Closing Sentence

Topic Sentence

<u>Perhaps the most amazing way animals protect themselves is by releasing a tail or another body part to get away when captured.</u> When a limb is trapped, these animals simply release it and go. A salamander's tail will fall off to allow escape, and a starfish's detached arm will grow into a new starfish! The gecko, a tropical lizard, can drop its tail, which then keeps moving to distract the attacker. After the animal escapes, the lost body part will grow back. Wouldn't it be amazing if humans possessed the ability to regrow parts?

Specific Details

Closing Sentence

Write your middle paragraphs. Use your organized list (page 170) to help you write your middle paragraphs. Also consider the drafting tips listed below.

Drafting Tips

Here are some tips for writing your middle paragraphs.

- **Keep your purpose and audience in mind.**
- **Follow your plan or outline.**
- **Add new details if they fit the topic sentence.**

Writing Ending Your Essay

In your ending paragraph, you need to restate your focus and make a final statement. Below are two different ending paragraphs for the essay on animal defenses.

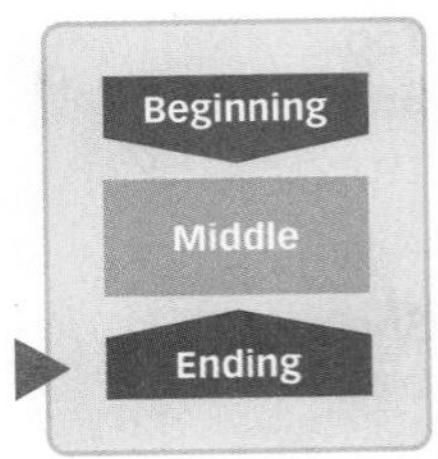

Ending Paragraphs

The writer asks the reader to think about the topic and then offers a final thought.

Imagine that an individual's skin turned color when he or she went from a red carpet to green grass. What if someone simply dropped a leg if he or she got hurt in an accident, only to have a new leg grow back? Some ways animals use to protect themselves may seem like science fiction. However, without their amazing defenses, some animals would not survive.

Your final paragraph could also

- summarize all your main points, and
- emphasize the special importance of the overall topic.

The writer suggests the importance of the essay and its information.

Nature has provided animals with many different ways to protect themselves. They blend in with their surroundings, give off bad-tasting or bad-smelling chemicals, or even drop a captured limb. Over the years, humans have observed and copied many of these defenses. Human beings may be more intelligent, but they can still learn a lot from animals.

Write your ending paragraph. Write a final paragraph for your essay using the suggestions above.

Write your complete first draft. Bring all the parts of your first draft together to form a complete essay.

Revising

A first draft never turns out quite right. One part may need more details. Another part may not be clear enough. Another part may be too dull. To fix or improve these parts, you need to carefully revise your first draft.

Keys to Effective Revising

1. Read through your entire draft to get a feeling for how well your essay works.
2. Make sure your focus statement states your topic clearly.
3. Check your paragraphs to make sure the details relate to the topic sentence and are in logical order.
4. Be sure you've used a knowledgeable, interested voice.
5. Check your writing for precise words and a variety of sentences.
6. Use the editing and proofreading marks inside the back cover of this book.

Revising for Ideas

6 My essay presents a variety of fascinating and surprising details for each category.

5 My essay presents different kinds of interesting details.

4 My essay has different kinds of details, but they are all basic details.

As you revise for *ideas*, check to see if you used different kinds of details. In a classification essay, you should also be offering information that is new and interesting to your reader. Use the above rubric strip to help you check your ideas.

How can I use different kinds of details?

You can use details to define, explain, or compare ideas in your essay.

- **Definitions** usually answer the question "What is it?"
  Octopus ink makes it hard for predators—**the animals attacking the octopus**—to see where the octopus is going.
- **Explanations** answer the question "What does it do?" or "Why or how does it do it?"
  An octopus squirts ink **to cloud the water and let the octopus escape.**
- **Comparisons** answer the question "What is it like?"
  The ink the octopus squirts is **like the dust that hides a car on a dirt road.**

Below are six sentences from a classification essay on types of clocks. For each, tell whether the detail used is an explanation, a definition, or a comparison. Use the above questions to help you.

1. Ancient people often used the sun to tell time with an obelisk, a tall, tapered structure with a pyramid-like top.
2. Like obelisks, sundials also use the sun to tell time.
3. Modern watches are more accurate than nature's clocks.
4. Quartz crystals keep accurate time by using an electric field.
5. Quartz watches use an LCD, or liquid crystal display, to show time.
6. Atomic clocks are accurate to one-millionth of a second per year.

Review your writing. Look for ideas that may need more explanation and for terms that need defining. Also consider making a comparison if it would make your ideas clearer.

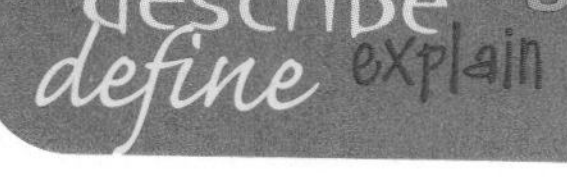

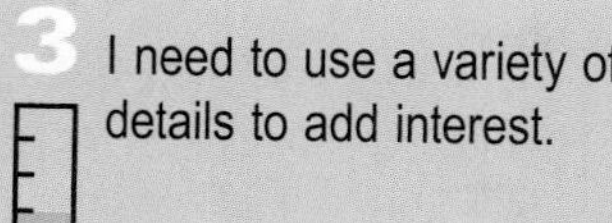
3 I need to use a variety of details to add interest.

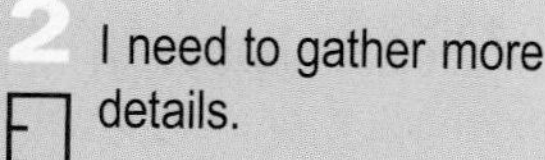
2 I need to gather more details.

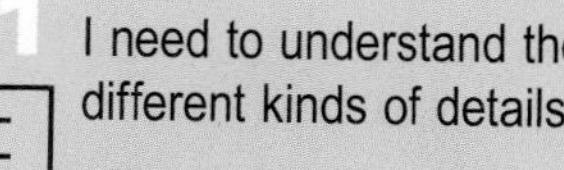
1 I need to understand the different kinds of details.

How can I go beyond basic details?

You know you have gone beyond basic details if a reader says, "Wow, I didn't know that!" For example, most people are familiar with the way a hedgehog rolls up into a ball to protect itself. But many people would not know that when it curls up, the animal also crawls into a protective bag created by its own skin! That's a detail that goes beyond "basic."

- **Basic detail**

  A frog can use its eyeballs for more than just seeing.

- **Surprising detail**

  A frog's eyeballs can drop down against the roof of its mouth to help push food down its throat.

Read the following paragraph. Then write down two details that are surprising or especially interesting. Explain why you chose them.

Whales breathe through blowholes, exhaling air at over 300 mph. These watery explosions don't happen that often because whales can hold their breath for as long as 90 minutes. Then they must actually remember to breathe. When whales sleep, they float near the surface with half of their brain awake. It's that half that reminds the whales to breathe.

Check your writing. Read through your essay to check for surprising details. If necessary, add some details that go beyond basic information.

Ideas
A surprising detail is added.

which then keeps moving to distract the attacker
The gecko, a tropical lizard, can drop its tail. After the animal escapes, the lost body part . . .

Revising for Organization

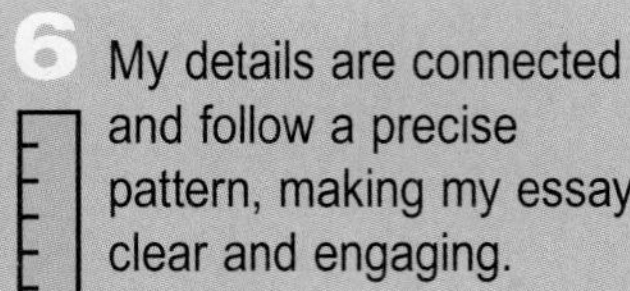

6 My details are connected and follow a precise pattern, making my essay clear and engaging.

5 My details are clearly connected with key words and transitions. I follow a precise pattern.

4 My details are connected, but the pattern isn't clear.

When you revise for *organization*, you need to check your details carefully. In a classification essay, the details should be clearly connected. They should also be arranged in the same pattern in each middle paragraph. The above rubric strip will help you check your essay for organization. (For additional information on organization, see pages 550–551.)

Are my details clearly connected?

Your details are clearly connected when they build from one idea to the next. Here is a strategy to help you tie your ideas together.

- **Repeating a key word.**
  The hermit crab's shell does not cover its soft abdomen. To protect its abdomen, the crab backs into an abandoned shell and adopts it as its own. (The key word *abdomen* connects the details.)

Read the following paragraph and then list four key words that help to connect the sentences.

Seals, sea lions, and walruses are members of the same family, but each has its unique characteristics. The walrus, for example, has unique tusks that make it easy to pick out in a crowd. The tusks are actually huge canine teeth that the walrus uses to establish dominance and secure the best basking spots. To get to these prime spots, the walrus uses its tusks to help pull itself onto rocky or icy shores. Once on shore, the walrus is able to keep other sea-going mammals away by simply displaying its super-sized teeth.

Check your details. Read through your essay to check for clearly connected details. If you need to, add key words or transitions to create a link between your ideas.

3 I connect some details, but I do not use a pattern.

2 Most of my details are not connected. I do not use a pattern.

1 I need to completely reorganize my paragraphs.

Do I follow a precise pattern in my essay?

You have followed a precise pattern if each main category is covered in the same way, with about the same number and types of details. You can establish this pattern in your organized list or outline. (See page **170**.)

Read the following paragraph. Then number your paper from 1 to 4 and arrange the four sentences below so they follow the same pattern used in the paragraph.

The folk guitar neck is designed for playing popular music. The neck is tightly glued or bolted to the body to hold up to the tension of the steel strings. The strings are close together on the slender neck, making it easier to use a pick. Because the neck joins the body at the 14th fret, the musician can reach very high notes.

1. Because nylon strings cause less pressure, the wide neck can be carved together with the body.
2. The neck joins the body at the 12th fret to keep the tones low.
3. If you enjoy playing "art" music, the classical guitar is for you.
4. The wide neck keeps the strings spaced for easy finger picking.

Check for paragraph pattern. **Review each middle paragraph of your essay to see if you have followed the same pattern for each category.**

Organization
A sentence is moved for a more precise pattern.

A good example of this is the snowshoe rabbit. Its change in color makes it hard for predators to see the rabbit in dry summer grass and winter snow. This rabbit turns from brown in summer to white in winter.

EXPOSITORY

Revising for Voice

6 My voice makes my reader feel I am speaking directly to him or her.	5 My voice is appropriate for my purpose and connects with my audience.	4 My voice is acceptable for my purpose, but it does not always connect with my audience.

When revising for *voice* in a classification essay, you must be certain that your voice fits your purpose and reaches the audience. The above rubric strip can guide you in your revising.

How can I tell if my voice fits my purpose?

You can tell if your voice fits your purpose in a classification essay if your writing presents interesting information without sounding too informal.

Try It Below are four passages from classification essays. Decide which of the passages present the facts in a clear and interesting way without sounding too personal or informal.

1. The saguaro cactus survives in the desert by storing water in its stem. The stem tissue can swell up to three times its size as it absorbs the rain.

2. Pitcher plants are really cute. Their leaves are kind of like water pitchers filled with a gross nectar that attracts insects. The bugs then slip on the slimy sides, plop into the liquid, and become plant food.

3. I was bowled over when I learned that the giant redwood tree actually needs a forest fire to reproduce! It's true—the heat of the fire forces the pine cones to open and drop their seeds. Cool!

4. Prairie grasses have adapted to the many fires common to their habitat. The growing structure of the plant is actually located under the ground. This way, when the top of the plant is burned away, new growth can spring up within a few days.

Check your voice. Answer the following questions. If your voice is not quite right for the purpose of your essay, change some words or sentences.

1. Do I state the facts in a clear and interesting way?
2. Do I avoid words that sound too informal or personal?

3
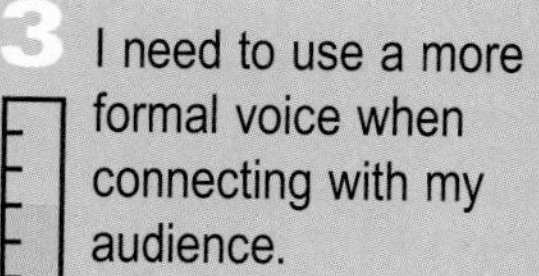
I need to use a more formal voice when connecting with my audience.

2
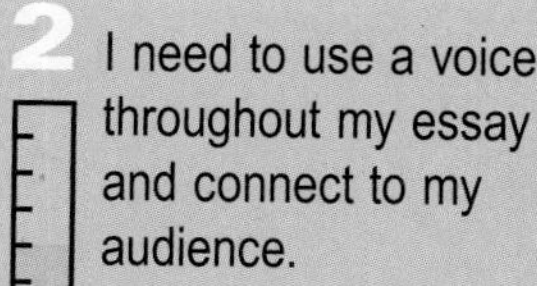
I need to use a voice throughout my essay and connect to my audience.

1
I need to learn about voice.

Does my voice connect with my audience?

Your voice will connect with your audience if your essay is informational and engaging. You can make this connection with your audience in several ways.

- **Use specific examples.** Specific examples can make your thoughts clearer and more interesting to the reader.
  Giant redwood trees can have bark two feet thick. The bark helps the trees survive droughts, insect attacks, and even forest fires.
- **Share an anecdote.** A brief anecdote or story can make your information easier to understand.
  People who are sprayed by a skunk try everything from bathing in tomato juice to covering themselves in baking soda.
- **Relate your topic to the reader.** Allow your audience to see how the topic affects their lives.
  If prairie grasses hadn't adapted to survive fires, the prairies would have eventually dried up and blown away. The loss of prairies would have changed the ecology of the entire country.

Check reader reaction. Ask a classmate to read your essay and suggest ways you could create a stronger connection. Use the strategies above as you revise.

Voice
A sentence has been added to connect the topic with the reader's life.

After the animal escapes, the lost body part will grow back. ^Wouldn't it be amazing if humans possessed the ability to regrow parts?

Imagine that an individual's skin turned color when he or she went from a red carpet to green grass. . . .

Revising for Word Choice

6 Precise words and modifiers make my essay informative and enjoyable to read.	**5** Precise words and modifiers make my essay informative.	**4** Most of my words are precise; however, I need to check for unnecessary modifiers.

Use precise words and phrases to give your writing clarity. Also avoid the trap of overusing modifiers. The above rubric can help you check for *word choice*.

How can I find precise words?

One way to find just the right word for your essay is to use a thesaurus. A thesaurus is a book that lists synonyms and antonyms. If your thesaurus is arranged alphabetically, look up your word as you would in a dictionary. If you are using a traditional thesaurus, look up your word in the index.

Part of speech
Entry word
Synonyms, explanations, and examples

run ***verb*****—when used as a verb, the word run might suggest:**
(1) *to move quickly.* sprint, scuttle, scamper, dart, dash, rush, hurry (2) *to flow.* stream, trickle, pour out, course, gush, spill, flood (3) *to proceed.* happen, go, progress, move along, pass, move forward, go by, pass by (4) *to manage.* administer, govern, lead, control, be in charge, handle, manipulate, direct, rule, organize (5) *to function.* operate, process

Not every synonym for a word has the same meaning. Note how the above thesaurus entry is numbered to show the different meanings of the word. When you use a synonym, be sure it fits your meaning.

Using the thesaurus entry above, find two synonyms to replace the word "run" in each of the following sentences. Make certain your choice fits the meaning of each sentence.

1. Once the skunk has stopped the attack, it can run to safety.
2. Li was selected to run the school garage sale.
3. Whenever it rains, the water runs over the dam.

Check your essay for precise word choice. Go through your essay and circle two or three plain words. Use a thesaurus to replace them with more interesting words. Be sure each new word has the precise meaning you need.

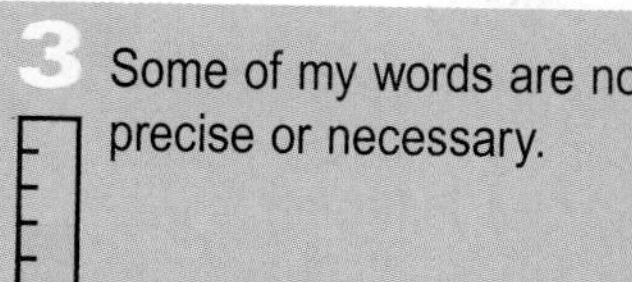

3 Some of my words are not precise or necessary.

2 My words are not precise, and I need to delete unnecessary modifiers.

1 I need help finding precise words and identifying unnecessary modifiers.

Have I used any unnecessary modifiers?

You can check your writing for wordiness by being sure to avoid the problems shown below.

- **Unnecessary Modifiers** (Delete "kind of," "sort of," and "really.")
  It's sort of important to really keep these fish well fed.
  Better: **It's important to keep these fish well fed.**
- **Strings of Adjectives** (Select the best one or two.)
  The tiny, cute red sea horse was fun to watch.
  Better: **The tiny red sea horse was fun to watch.**
- **Unnecessary Adjectives** (Don't restate the obvious.)
  The penguins waddled across the cold, frozen ice.
  Better: **The penguins waddled across the ice.**

Rewrite each sentence to eliminate wordiness.

1. The hippopotamus can kind of walk on the bottom of the river.
2. The giraffe's horns are really hard, bony, hairy knobs.
3. A giraffe has the same number of neck bones as a small, little child has.

Check for wordiness. Circle unnecessary modifiers in your essay and rewrite any sentences that seem wordy.

Word Choice
Precise words are used, and unnecessary modifiers are cut.

Today, they wear ~~kind of different-colored outfits~~ camouflage uniforms and shoot ~~sort of different stuff from cans.~~ pepper spray. Where did people get the ideas for these forms of protection?

Revising for Sentence Fluency

6 My sentences are skillfully written and easy to follow.

5 Most of my sentences flow because I have used subordinating conjunctions and avoided rambling sentences.

4 Most of my sentences are well written, but I could combine some.

When you revise for *sentence fluency*, you should consider combining short sentences by using dependent clauses. At the same time, you should watch out for long, rambling sentences that have too many conjunctions. Your goal is to write smooth sentences of varying types and lengths.

How can I combine sentences using subordinating conjunctions?

You can combine two closely related sentences into one complex sentence by using a subordinating conjunction. (See pages 517 and 744.)

Cats get frightened by loud noises. They arch their backs and hiss.

By adding the subordinating conjunction "when," you create a subordinate clause and turn the two short sentences into one complex sentence.

When cats get frightened by loud noises, they arch their backs and hiss.
(or) Cats arch their backs and hiss when they get frightened by loud noises.

When the dependent clause begins a sentence, it is followed by a comma. Usually, when the dependent clause comes at the end of a sentence, no comma is used.

Combine the following sentence pairs by using the subordinating conjunction given in parentheses.

1. Porcupine fish are usually left alone by predators. Their bodies are covered with sharp spines. *(because)*
2. Puffer fish gulp water to expand their size. Larger fish can't get puffer fish into their mouths. *(when)*
3. The red panda has an extra thumb like the giant panda. It is more closely related to the raccoon. *(although)*

Combine short sentences. Underline any closely related sentences in your essay. Try to combine some of them using subordinating conjunctions.

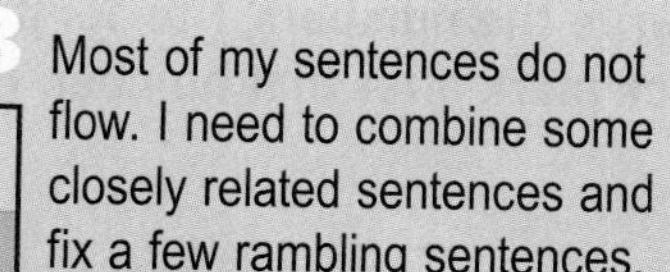

3 Most of my sentences do not flow. I need to combine some closely related sentences and fix a few rambling sentences.

2 Many of my sentences are choppy or rambling. I need to fix them.

1 I need to learn about subordinating conjunctions and rambling sentences.

How can I fix rambling sentences?

You can start fixing a rambling sentence by removing some of the *and*'s and replacing them with periods. Capitalize words as needed. (See page 505.) After you break up a rambling sentence, you may also improve the flow of the writing by using a subordinating conjunction or another sentence-combining method.

GRAMMAR Try It On your own paper, correct the rambling sentence below by cutting some of the *and*'s and adding periods. Then try to combine a couple related sentences.

Small animals need the most protection and they might use chemicals to keep themselves safe and these chemicals often cause pain to attacking animals and this pain teaches attackers to leave the small animals alone.

Revise **Check for rambling sentences.** Review your essay for sentences that go on and on. Make whatever corrections are needed.

Sentence Fluency

A rambling sentence is made into two sentences. The second sentence begins with a subordinating conjunction.

The skunk defends itself by releasing a foul-smelling chemical from glands found beneath its tail ~~and~~. Because the chemical can severely sting eyes, and the smell is enough to send predators hurrying away, ~~so~~ any animal that tangles with a skunk surely won't do it twice! An octopus squirts a dark, inky fluid in . . .

Revising Using a Checklist

Check your revising. On a piece of paper, write the numbers 1 to 15. If you can answer "yes" to a question, put a check mark after that number. If not, continue to revise that part of your essay.

Ideas

_____ **1.** Do I cover at least three specific categories of my topic?
_____ **2.** Do I have a clear focus statement?
_____ **3.** Do I include different kinds of interesting details?

Organization

_____ **4.** Does my beginning grab the reader's attention?
_____ **5.** Do the details in each paragraph support the topic sentence?
_____ **6.** Are my ideas and details clearly connected?
_____ **7.** Do I follow a precise pattern?
_____ **8.** Does the ending paragraph restate my focus and make a final statement?

Voice

_____ **9.** Does my voice fit my purpose?
_____ **10.** Have I used different ways to connect with my audience?

Word Choice

_____ **11.** Do I know how to use a thesaurus?
_____ **12.** Do I use precise words?
_____ **13.** Have I deleted unnecessary modifiers?

Sentence Fluency

_____ **14.** Have I combined closely related sentences?
_____ **15.** Is my writing free of rambling sentences?

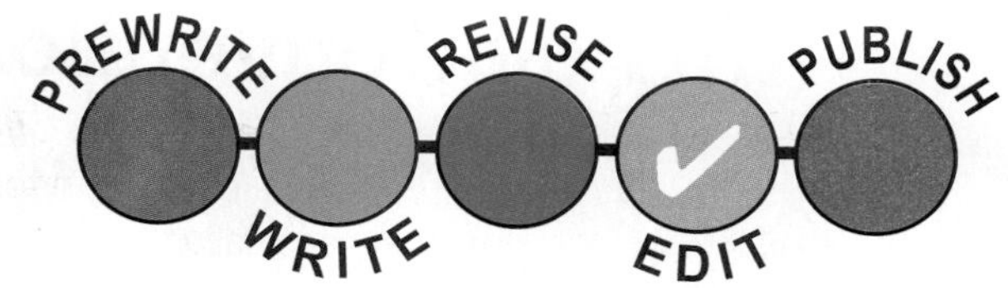

Editing

After you've finished revising your essay, it's time to edit your work for conventions: punctuation, capitalization, spelling, and grammar.

Keys to Effective Editing

1. Use a dictionary, a thesaurus, and the "Proofreader's Guide" in the back of this book.
2. Check your writing for correctness of punctuation, capitalization, spelling, and grammar.
3. If you're using a computer, edit on a printed computer copy. Then enter your changes on the computer.
4. Use the editing and proofreading marks located inside the back cover of this book.

Editing for Conventions

6 My grammar and punctuation are correct, and I have no spelling errors.	**5** I have a few minor errors in punctuation, spelling, or grammar.	**4** I need to correct errors in punctuation, spelling, or grammar.

When you edit for *conventions*, you are checking your essay for spelling, grammar, capitalization, and punctuation. Use the rubric strip above to guide you through this step in the editing process.

How can I use apostrophes to show possession?

You can show possession of singular words by adding an apostrophe and *s*. For plural words ending in *s*, just add an apostrophe. Be careful, though, because there are some exceptions to these rules. (See 604.4 and 606.1–606.4.)

- When a singular noun of two or more syllables ends with an *s* or *z* sound, add either an apostrophe or an apostrophe and *s*.
  cactus' needles *(or)* **cactus's needles**
- Plural words not ending in *s* need an apostrophe and an *s*.
  children's books **women's decisions**
- To show shared possession of more than one noun, add an apostrophe and *s* to the last noun in the series.
  Sadako, Nina, and Kim's project (The three share one project.)
- When possession is by individuals in a series of nouns, add an apostrophe and *s* to each noun.
  Sadako's, Nina's, and Kim's projects (Each has her own project.)

Write the correct possessive form of each underlined noun in the following sentences.

1. The grasses long blades offered excellent camouflage.
2. The men tan clothing hid them so they could watch the birds.
3. They heard the crow, dove, and robin calls.
4. The ibis red feathers were sighted at last.
5. Luz binoculars were passed around.

Check your work. **Look through your essay for any possessives you may have used and make sure you have punctuated them correctly.**

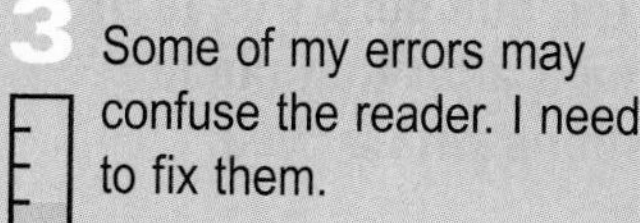

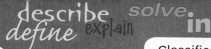

3 Some of my errors may confuse the reader. I need to fix them.

2 I need to correct many errors that make my essay confusing and hard to read.

1 I need help making corrections, especially with my commas.

How should I use commas with subordinating conjunctions?

When the dependent clause is at the beginning of the sentence, place a comma after it. Generally, do not use a comma when the dependent clause comes after the main clause. (See page **503** and **746.1**.)

> **Because the viceroy butterfly looks like the bad-tasting monarch, many predators leave it alone.**
>
> **The stonefish is often ignored by predators because it looks just like a rock on the ocean floor.**

Write the following complex sentences on your paper, placing commas where necessary.

1. Because some birds can puff up their feathers to appear larger than they are predators leave them alone.
2. The turtle's shell is a fortress when the animal is under attack.
3. Unless it moves a fawn can hide in the brush from a predator.
4. Hedgehogs can avoid being eaten when they roll into a tight ball.
5. Though the lowland gorilla seems aggressive it is passive.

Edit your essay. Check to be sure that you correctly punctuated any dependent clauses.

Conventions
Errors with apostrophes and commas are corrected.

When a limb is trapped, these animals simply release it and go. A salamander's tail will fall off to allow escape, and a starfish's detached arm will . . .

EXPOSITORY

Editing Using a Checklist

Check your editing. On a piece of paper, write the numbers 1 to 10. If you can answer "yes" to a question, put a check mark after that number. Continue editing until you can answer all the questions with a "yes."

Conventions

PUNCTUATION

_____ **1.** Do I correctly punctuate dependent clauses?

_____ **2.** Do I use apostrophes to show possession?

CAPITALIZATION

_____ **3.** Do I capitalize proper nouns and adjectives?

_____ **4.** Do I begin each sentence with a capital letter?

SPELLING

_____ **5.** Have I spelled all my words correctly?

_____ **6.** Have I used the spell-checker on my computer?

_____ **7.** Have I double-checked the words my spell-checker may have missed?

GRAMMAR

_____ **8.** Do I use correct forms of verbs *(had come,* not *had came)*?

_____ **9.** Do my subjects and verbs agree in number?

_____ **10.** Have I used the right words *(there, their, they're)*?

Creating a Title

For a classification essay, the title should do one of the following:

- Name the topic: **Ways Animals Defend Themselves**
- Catch the reader's imagination: **Animal Armor**
- Establish the tone: **Staying Alive: Animal Adaptations**

Go Online!

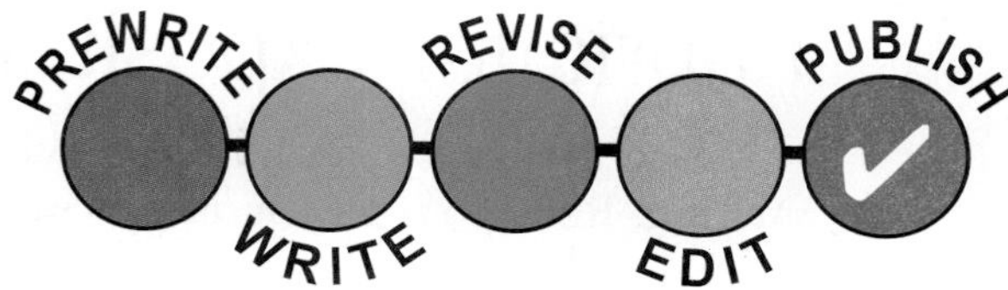

Publishing

Sharing Your Essay

After you have worked so hard writing your essay, you'll want to proofread it and make a neat copy to share. You may also decide to display your essay in the library or present it as a book or a poster. (See the suggestions below.)

Make a final copy. Follow your teacher's instructions or use the guidelines below to format your essay. (If you are using a computer, see pages 60–62.) Create a clean final copy of your essay and carefully proofread it.

Focus on Presentation

- Use blue or black ink and write neatly.
- Write your name in the upper left corner of page 1.
- Skip a line and center your title; skip another line and start your writing.
- Indent every paragraph and leave a one-inch margin on all four sides.
- Write your last name and the page number in the upper right corner of every page after the first one.

Produce a Book
Turn your essay into a picture book by adding pictures with captions. Make a cover out of cardboard and include your title and name. Punch holes along the left side and fasten the pages together with yarn or secure with brads.

Display Your Essay in School
Ask your teacher if there is a special section or showcase for student papers.

Create a Poster
Attach your essay pages to a large piece of tagboard and add illustrations and informative side notes for each section. Include Web site addresses for further information on each main idea.

Rubric for Expository Writing

Use this rubric for guiding and assessing your expository writing. Refer to it as you improve your writing using the six traits.

Ideas

6 The topic, focus, and details make the essay truly memorable.

5 The essay is informative with a clear focus and specific details.

4 The essay is informative with a clear focus. More specific details are needed.

Organization

6 The organization and transitions make the essay clear and easy to read.

5 The beginning interests the reader. The middle supports the focus. The ending works well. Transitions are used.

4 The essay is divided into a beginning, a middle, and an ending. Some transitions are used.

Voice

6 The writer's voice sounds confident, knowledgeable, and enthusiastic.

5 The writer's voice sounds knowledgeable and confident. It fits the audience.

4 The writer's voice sounds knowledgeable most of the time and fits the audience.

Word Choice

6 The word choice makes the essay very clear, informative, and enjoyable to read.

5 Specific nouns and action verbs make the essay clear and informative.

4 Some nouns and verbs could be more specific.

Sentence Fluency

6 The sentences are skillfully written, and readers will enjoy them.

5 The sentences read smoothly.

4 Most of the sentences read smoothly, but some are short and choppy.

Conventions

6 The essay is error free.

5 The essay has a few minor errors in punctuation, spelling, or grammar.

4 The essay has some errors in punctuation, spelling, or grammar.

3	2	1
The focus of the essay needs to be clearer, and more specific details are needed.	The topic needs to be narrowed or expanded. Many more specific details are needed.	A new topic needs to be selected.
The beginning or ending is weak. The middle needs a paragraph for each main point. More transitions are needed.	The beginning, middle, and ending all run together. Paragraphs and transitions are needed.	The essay should be reorganized.
The writer sometimes sounds unsure, and the voice needs to fit the audience better.	The writer sounds unsure. The voice needs to fit the audience.	The writer needs to learn about voice.
Too many general words are used. Specific nouns and verbs are needed.	General or missing words make this essay difficult to understand.	The writer needs help finding specific words.
Many short, choppy sentences need to be rewritten to make the essay read smoothly.	Many sentences are choppy or incomplete and need to be rewritten.	Most sentences need to be rewritten.
Several errors confuse the reader.	Many errors make the essay difficult to read.	Help is needed to make corrections.

Evaluating an Expository Essay

As you read through Simcha's classification essay below, focus on its strengths and weaknesses. **(The essay contains several errors.)**

Choose Your Entertainment

Once there were only three or four TV channels available. Now, with cable and satellite TV, people might have to choose from hundreds of channels and thousands of programs. It's easy to choose a show if they know what type they are looking for. Three popular types of TV shows include sitcoms, dramas, and reality shows.

If viewers want to laugh and forget their troubles, they could watch a sitcom. Sitcoms—short for situation comedies—are half-hour shows that have one group of people with a different problem each week. These problems are always solved in 30 minutes—minus commercials. They can be either adult or family shows. They have a live audience or a recorded laugh track to let the viewers know when something is funny.

If viewers like serious dramas, they can find plenty of those on TV as well these are usually an hour long. Some are on late at night, when kids shouldn't be up to see them, but some dramas are on at earlier times. Dramas also usually focus on one group, but the story can go on for the whole season. These shows do not have a laugh track.

Finally, there are the so-called "reality" shows. These shows take people and place them in funny or dangerous situations—and then videotape how they react. These shows can be funny—or embarrassing—depending on the people. Sometimes they are scary. They are usually an hour long, but "specials" can be longer and the same people are usually on the show for a while.

People can choose the kind of TV show they want to watch. Depending on their mood, they might want to laugh, have a good scare, or enjoy a classic drama. Thinking about it, though, there are times they'll be better off just reading a good book!

Student Self-Assessment

The assessment below includes comments by Simcha, who evaluated his own essay (on page 196). Notice that he includes a positive comment first. Then he points out an area of his writing that could be improved. (The writer used the rubric and number scale on pages 194–195.)

3 Ideas

1. *I know my audience will be interested in my topic.*
2. *My ending is weak, and I don't have enough details.*

5 Organization

1. *I include a clear topic sentence for each paragraph.*
2. *I should rearrange my last middle paragraph to fit the pattern.*

3 Voice

1. *The reader can tell I like TV.*
2. *What I say about reality shows is too negative.*

3 Word Choice

1. *I explain terms like "sitcom."*
2. *I could use more-effective modifiers.*

4 Sentence Fluency

1. *I vary my sentence beginnings.*
2. *I have a run-on sentence and sometimes ramble.*

4 Conventions

1. *I don't have many spelling errors.*
2. *I use too many dashes where I should use commas.*

Use the rubric. Assess your essay using the rubric on pages 194–195.

1. On your own paper, list the six traits. Leave room after each trait to write one strength and one weakness.
2. Then choose a number (from 1 to 6) that shows how well you used each trait.

Reflecting on Your Writing

Now that you've completed your classification essay, take a moment to reflect on it. Complete each starter sentence below on your own paper. These thoughts will help you prepare for your next writing assignment.

My Classification Essay

1. *The strength of my essay is . . .*
2. *The part that still needs work is . . .*
3. *The main thing I learned about writing a classification essay is . . .*
4. *The prewriting activity that worked best for this essay was . . .*
5. *In my next essay, I would like to . . .*
6. *Here is one question I still have about writing a classification essay:*

Expository Writing
Comparison-Contrast Essay

"Day One: I was about to begin my dive in the Amazon when I noticed a strange school of fish below my canoe. They look like harmless pacus, but they may be their close cousins, piranhas. I wish I could decide which they were. . . ."

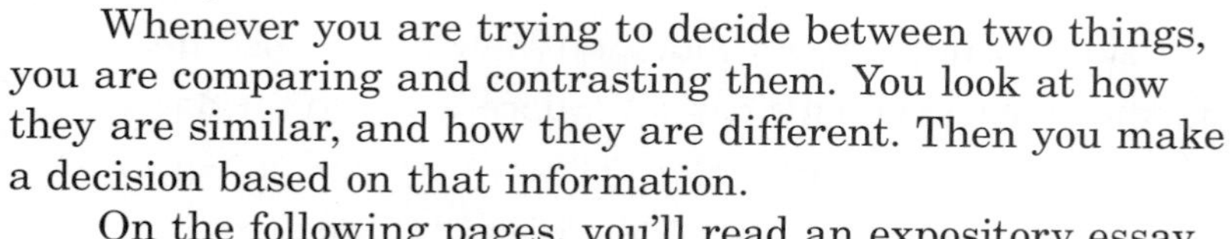

Whenever you are trying to decide between two things, you are comparing and contrasting them. You look at how they are similar, and how they are different. Then you make a decision based on that information.

On the following pages, you'll read an expository essay comparing and contrasting two American cities. The guidelines that follow will help you write your own comparison-contrast essay.

Writing Guidelines

Subject: Two similar topics that interest you
Form: Comparison-contrast essay
Purpose: To explain
Audience: Classmates

Comparison-Contrast Essay

Making comparisons can result in new insights about a topic: two American cities, two types of sports, two admirable people. For the following essay, the writer compares two cities.

Beginning

The topics are introduced, and the focus statement (**underlined**) sets up the comparison.

Cities Between the Waters

Brad Janty lives in Madison, Wisconsin, and loves it. When his cousin Jim from Seattle visits, Brad shows him the sights. They shop for music on State Street, visit the farmer's market on the capitol square, and end the day listening to jazz on the Union Terrace overlooking Lake Mendota. When Brad visits Jim in Seattle, Jim shows him the sights there. They go to the shops in Pike Place Market, explore Underground Seattle, and eat lunch in the Space Needle. Madison and Seattle may seem different, but they have much in common.

Middle

The first middle paragraph addresses the differences point by point.

Of course, there are plenty of differences between the cities. At 540,000 people, Seattle is more than twice the size of Madison, which has 205,000 people. Seattle is the largest city in its state, and though Madison is not Wisconsin's largest city, it is the state capital. The Madison area's main products are milk and cheese. Seattle, on the other hand, is known for its cutting-edge technology. Seattle is surrounded by majestic natural wonders, such as mountains, rain forests, and the ocean. Madison's surroundings are a little more humble. It has hills instead of mountains, oak groves instead of rain forests, and lakes instead of the ocean. Madison is in the Midwest and has hot summers and cold winters, while Seattle is on the West Coast and has a temperate climate.

The second middle paragraph addresses the similarities point by point.

Despite their differences, Madison and Seattle have many similarities. Both cities sit on narrow strips of land between two bodies of water. In Madison, we have Lake Mendota and Lake Monona. Seattle lies between Lake Washington and Puget Sound. Both cities are in the northern part of the country. Madison's latitude is 43 degrees, and Seattle's is 47. Each has a huge state university, the University of Wisconsin and the University of Washington, and both are UW's. Madison and Seattle even lie on the same Interstate, I-90, although they're 2,000 miles apart. Either is worth a trip, though, because both are exciting and fun places to visit.

Ending

The ending adds a final reflection about the comparison.

In some ways, none of these features define the two cities. Madison and Seattle have the same soul. Both places are full of tie-dyed clothes, well-worn jeans, and leather sandals. Both have an exciting music scene. It's the atmosphere in each city that most makes them similar. Whether Jim is visiting Brad or Brad is visiting Jim, they always feel at home.

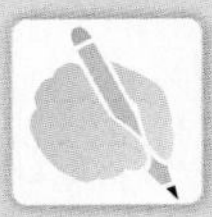

Respond to the reading. On your own paper, write answers to the following questions about the sample essay.

- ☐ **Ideas** (1) What two things does the writer compare? (2) What two similarities and two differences interest you?
- ☐ **Organization** (3) How do the two middle paragraphs support the focus statement?
- ☐ **Voice & Word Choice** (4) What words and phrases reveal how the writer feels about the two cities? (5) How does the writer show knowledge about the two cities?

Literature Connections: For another example of comparison-contrast writing, read Michael Dorris' essay titled "Americans All."

Prewriting Selecting a Topic

Your teacher may assign a general subject for your essay. For the subject "American Cities," the writer used freewriting to find two cities to write about.

Freewriting

Well, let's see. American cities. There's the big three, of course: New York, Chicago, and L.A. But I've never visited any of these cities. The only city I know something about is Madison from visiting my good friend there. Mad Town's cool. I've also heard from my friend that Seattle is cool. I think I'll compare these two cities, if I can find enough about both of them. . . .

Select your topic. **Do a freewriting to find two topics you know enough about to compare and contrast.**

Gathering Details

After you have finished your freewriting and found two topics, list details you can use in your essay. Make a gathering chart with two columns like the one below. In each column, write details for one of the topics. If you think of additional details, add them as you go.

Gathering Chart

Madison, WI	*Seattle, WA*
Lakes Mendota and Monona, Farm products, Latitude 43°, UW, 205,000 people, State capital, Snowy–31", Babcock Hill ice cream, Historical museums, Hills, Near Wisconsin Dells . . .	*Largest city in state, 540,000 people, Rainy-34", I-90, Mountains, Space Needle, Puget Sound, West Coast, Known for technology, Latitude 47°, UW, Pike Place Market . . .*

Create a gathering chart. **Fill in a gathering chart like the one above. If you can't think of many details, you may want to find another topic.**

Organizing Details

The writer used the following Venn diagram to organize ideas for his essay. In the center, he wrote the similarities between the cities. In the outer circles, he listed the contrasting ideas from his gathering chart, matching a point about one city to a corresponding point about the other city. If a fact for one city did not have a matching idea for the other, he did not use it in the essay.

Venn Diagram

Madison, WI	Both Cities	Seattle, WA
Midwest	I-90	West Coast
Hills, trees	UW	Mountains, rain forest
Population 205,000	Lots to see	Population 540,000
Milk and cheese	Latitude (43°/47°)	Computers, technology
State capital	Precipitation (31"/34")	Largest city in state
Snowy		Rainy

Create a Venn diagram. Make a Venn diagram like the one above to organize the similarities and differences of your topics.

Forming a Focus Statement

A good focus statement gives the topics to be compared and introduces a general comparison.

Sample Focus Statements

Madison and Seattle may seem different, but they have much in common.

Many people confuse viruses and bacteria, but if you examine them closely, you'll find they are totally different organisms.

Although the sequoia and giant redwood seem similar, they are in fact very different.

Write a focus statement. Using the samples given above, write a focus statement for your comparison-contrast essay.

Writing Creating Your First Draft

When you write your comparison, pay close attention to each of the main parts: beginning, middle, and ending.

- **Beginning** Grab your reader's attention by starting strong. Then provide details that lead up to your thesis, or focus statement.
- **Middle** Organize your middle paragraphs by discussing each topic point by point, as the writer did on pages 200–201.
- **Ending** Bring the writing to an effective close. One way is to sum up the comparison. Another way is to reflect or comment on it.

Write your first draft. **Refer to your Venn diagram and focus statement to help you write the first draft of your comparison-contrast essay.**

Revising Improving Your Writing

After you finish your first draft, review your work for the following traits.

- ☐ **Ideas** Does the focus statement name my two topics and state my focus? Will the details grab the reader's attention?
- ☐ **Organization** Does the essay have a clear beginning, middle, and ending? Does each paragraph focus on one part of the comparison-contrast theme?
- ☐ **Voice** Is my voice appropriate for the topic?
- ☐ **Word Choice** Do I use strong nouns, verbs, and modifiers?
- ☐ **Sentence Fluency** Do my sentences vary in length?

Revise your writing. **Ask yourself the questions listed above after each trait. Decide how you will revise for ideas, organization, voice, and so on. Make whatever changes are needed.**

Editing Checking for Conventions

When you finish revising, edit your essay for conventions.

- ☐ **Conventions** Have I checked my punctuation, capitalization, and spelling? Have I checked for grammar errors?

Edit your work. **Ask yourself the above questions. Make your corrections, write a neat final copy, and proofread it carefully.**

Expository Writing

Across the Curriculum

Explanations are handy in all sorts of places. For example, imagine that you and six hungry friends need to share one pizza. Can you explain a way to cut the pizza so everyone gets a fair share? Perhaps you could divide 360° by 7 to discover that each piece should be 51.42°. The rest is a matter of working with the protractor and the pizza cutter. On the other hand, you could simply let each person cut a piece of the pizza, and afterward, in reverse order, choose the piece he or she will eat!

This section includes many amazing explanations. You will read a news report about the death of Julius Caesar, an explanation of a mathematical operation, a summary of a science experiment, and a memo giving an update. You'll even learn how to respond to an expository writing prompt. So turn to these pages anytime you've got some explaining to do.

What's Ahead

- **Social Studies:** Writing a News Report
- **Math:** Explaining a Mathematical Operation
- **Science:** Writing an Observation Report
- **Practical Writing:** Writing a Memo
- **Writing for Assessment**

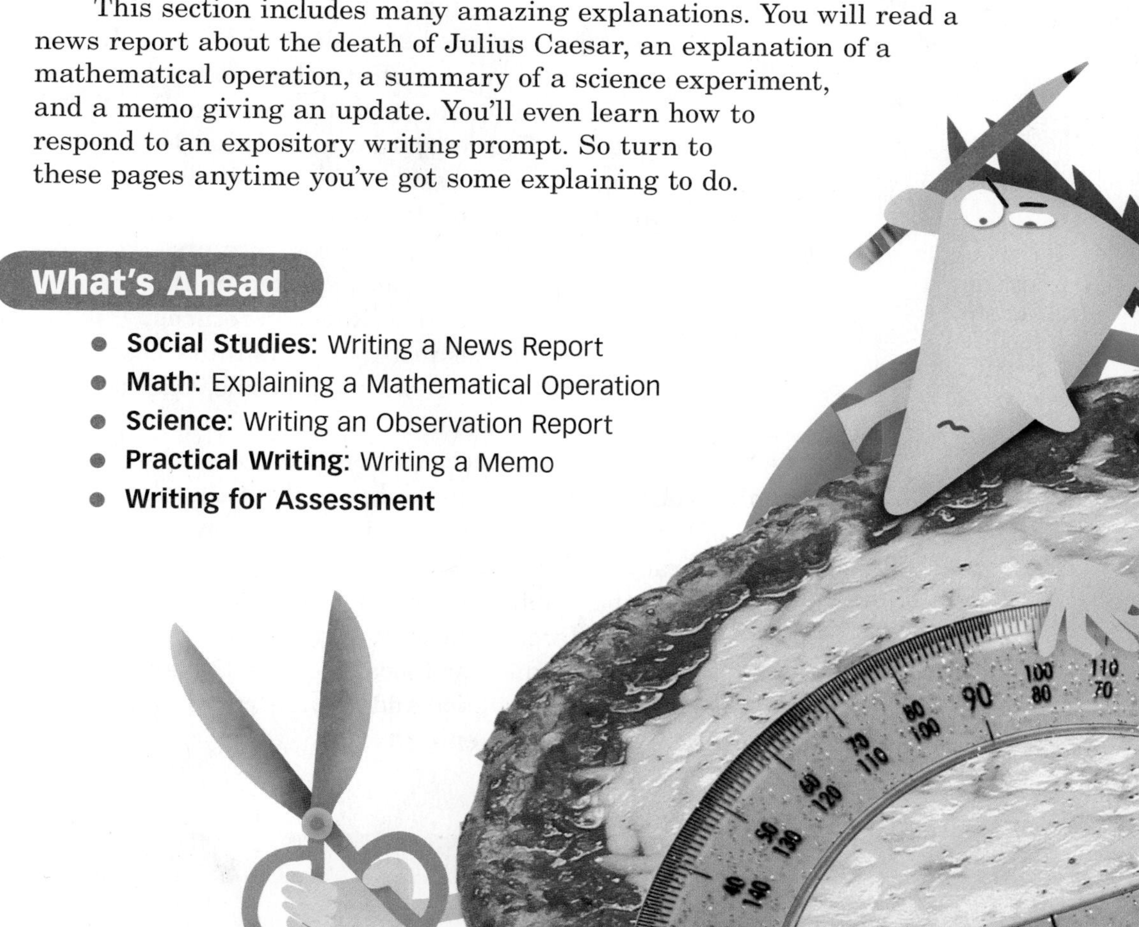

Social Studies: Writing a News Report

One way to understand a historical event is to write a news story about it. The following news story was written for a history class. Notice how the student reports the story as if it were a current event.

The **beginning** includes a strong headline that grabs the reader's attention. The most important details come first.

Caesar Slain on Senate Floor

MARCH 15, ROME: Julius Caesar is dead. Caesar had just arrived in the senate when a mob of senators with knives leapt up and attacked him. Caesar's own friend, Brutus, was allegedly among the attackers. He reportedly stabbed Caesar, too.

Caesar's autopsy recorded 23 stab wounds, though witnesses estimate the number of attackers to have been much higher. One senator, who did not want his name given, stated, "The conspiracy included at least 60 senators, but Brutus and Cassius were the ringleaders."

The **middle** includes facts reported in an interesting way.

Brutus and Cassius did little to hide their guilt. Following the attack, they and other conspirators paraded through the streets. Crowds picked up the shouts, "Tyranny ends" and "The Republic returns!"

This latest shock comes just five years into Caesar's reign. Though always popular with the people, Caesar had many enemies in the senate.

"I warned him," a soothsayer outside the senate building claimed. Asked how he knew about the plot ahead of time, the soothsayer denied any involvement in the conspiracy.

The **ending** avoids editorializing (giving an opinion).

Hope for the empire now rests with a new group: Gaius Octavius, Marcus Anthony, and Marcus Lepidus. Though hiding in undisclosed locations, the three have made pledges to raise armies and battle Brutus and Cassius across the whole empire.

Writing Tips

Before you write . . .

- **Select a topic.**
  Your teacher may assign a topic, or you may choose an event you are familiar with or are studying about.
- **Gather details.**
  Use the 5 W's and H to help you gather key information.
- **Consider the participants.**
  Consider the event and the people involved.
- **Think of your audience.**
  What information would be most important to them?

During your writing . . .

- **Organize your report.**
  Use the inverted pyramid style of organization. Place the most important information in the very first sentence. Then answer as many of the 5 W and H questions as you can. Add less important information later.

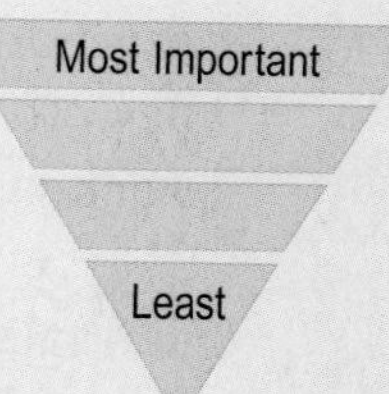

- **Focus on voice.**
  As you write, use active verbs, strong sentences, and brief paragraphs. Avoid editorializing (giving your opinion).

After you've written a first draft . . .

- **Write a strong headline.**
  Make sure your headline grabs the reader's attention and has a subject and a verb.
- **Check for completeness and correctness.**
  Read to make sure you have included the information your reader needs to understand the story. Check your use of conventions.

Choose an interesting historical event from the time period you are studying. Write it up as a news story. Get your facts right, but make it interesting, too.

Math: Explaining a Mathematical Operation

In math class, you may be asked to explain a mathematical operation. The writer of this essay was asked to show how percentages are used to calculate discounts and sales tax.

The **beginning** tells why the operation is important.

The **middle** uses specific details to explain the operation.

The **ending** makes a final observation.

Using Percentages

Discount and sale signs are posted everywhere on shops. Before shoppers get to the checkout line, they may want to know how much they're going to save on a sale item, and how much they need to pay. To do this, shoppers need to understand how to work with percentages.

Suppose someone finds a really cool pair of sandals on sale for 20% off the original price of $19. To find out the discount, a shopper should multiply $19 by 20%. The product, $3.80, is the discount. Next, he or she should subtract $3.80 from the original price of $19. The sale price is $15.20. Figuring out the cost of sale items requires two simple steps: (1) multiply the price by the percentage, and (2) subtract the product from the original price.

To figure the sales tax, a shopper should follow almost the same process. He or she should multiply the price of the item by the sales tax percentage (5%, 6%, 7% . . .), and then, instead of subtracting the product from the cost, add it. A shopper must remember that if there's a sales tax, he or she will need more money at checkout time.

Understanding how to work with percentages will help shoppers in many ways. They'll especially need to know all about them when they visit their favorite stores in the mall.

Writing Tips

Before you write . . .

- **Choose a familiar mathematical operation.**
  If your teacher has not assigned a particular mathematical operation, search for one in your notes or math textbook.
- **Study the operation.**
  Make sure you thoroughly understand the process needed to perform the operation. Think of how the operation can be applied to everyday life.
- **Plan the steps.**
  Break your operation into manageable steps and list them in the correct order. Then check the steps by working through the process.

During your writing . . .

- **Write a clear beginning, middle, and ending.**
  Begin by introducing the operation. Next, explain the process (or steps) in a clear manner. Provide an example of how the operation can be applied to everyday life. End with a thought that leaves the reader thinking about the operation.
- **Organize your explanation.**
  Decide on the order of organization that would clearly present the operation to your reader (time order, numbered steps, and so on).
- **Use specific terms.**
  Include words that are associated with the specific math operation.

After you've written a first draft . . .

- **Check for completeness.**
  Make sure that you have included all the information a reader needs to understand the process you are explaining.
- **Check for correctness.**
  Edit and proofread your work to eliminate errors in spelling, punctuation, and other conventions.

Write directions for a mathematical operation that you are learning in math class. Use specific examples and clear steps.

Science: Writing an Observation Report

Experiments are at the heart of science. A good way to review and analyze an experiment is to write an observation report. The following report is based on a student's experiment involving root growth.

The **beginning** identifies the focus of the experiment.

The **middle** identifies the process.

The **ending** explains what the writer has learned.

Do Bean Roots Always Grow Downward?

Scientific question: Do bean roots always grow downward?

Hypothesis: The roots of beans placed in different growing positions will always grow downward toward the center of the earth.

Procedure: Four lima beans were glued onto a sponge with the concave sides facing different directions: down, up, left, and right. The sponge was moistened and placed in a zippered plastic bag. Several small slits were cut in the bag and the bag was tacked to a bulletin board. The bag was watered daily through the slits.

Observations:

Day 3: Small sprouts have appeared from each bean.

Day 5: The roots from the beans facing left and right are growing horizontally, the bean facing down has roots growing downward, and the bean facing up has roots growing upward.

Day 7: The roots from the left- and right-facing beans have bent downward. The bean facing down grew its roots straight down. The roots from the bean facing up have curved to the right and now go over the bean.

Day 9: The roots from all of the beans are growing downward.

Conclusion: Lima bean roots may initially sprout upward or horizontally but will always bend to finally grow downward.

Writing Tips

Before you write . . .

- **Take notes during the experiment.**
  Take careful notes so that you will have enough information to write an effective summary.
- **Follow the correct form.**
  Use the form your teacher requests or the one used for the sample on page 210. Remember that observation reports usually follow the scientific method and include these five parts: *scientific question, hypothesis, procedure, observations,* and *conclusion.*

During your writing . . .

- **Explain the focus of the experiment.**
  Identify the scientific question and the hypothesis that you explored.
- **List the steps in the procedure.**
  Make sure each step is clear and in the correct order.
- **Include all of your observations.**
  List your personal observations chronologically.
- **Base your conclusions on what you observed.**
  Make careful observations so that your conclusions are accurate.

After you've written a first draft . . .

- **Use accurate terminology.**
  Find out the correct scientific terms for things you observe and use those terms in your report.
- **Check for completeness and correctness.**
  Go over your report to make sure that there are no mistakes. Answer any questions that the reader might have about the experiment. Then check your writing for errors.

Your teacher will tell you what experiment to perform and how to perform it. Pay close attention and take good notes.

Practical Writing: Writing a Memo

In school and in the workplace, memos allow people to communicate quickly and effectively. Memos also provide a handy written record. The following memo reports the progress on the "sets" for a school musical.

Standard memo format is used.

Date: Friday, March 6, 2009

To: Mrs. Lee, Technical Director

From: Corrine Stier, Student Director

The subject of the memo is clearly stated.

Subject: Progress on the *Brigadoon* Sets

Here is the first weekly update on the progress of the *Brigadoon* sets.

Important details are listed.

- Dave Dye has sketched a 15-foot-long set. One side will show the living room of the Campbell cottage, with a thatched roof on top and a window at the back. The other side will be cathedral ruins for the wedding scene. The whole piece will be on wheels, so we can spin it around for scene changes.
- Julie Reynolds primed the four old flats from *My Fair Lady* and drew trees on them. We'll use them on a dark stage along with two freestanding trees to make the forest for the chase scene.
- I want to repaint an old drop curtain to look like the backdrop in the movie. I've attached my drawings for your approval.

A polite but businesslike voice is used.

Thanks for your confidence in me, Mrs. Lee. I won't let you down!

Writing Tips

Before you write . . .

- **Use the correct format.**
  At the left margin, write or type these four headings: *Date, To, From*, and *Subject*. Each word should be followed by a colon and the appropriate information. Double-space between each line; triple-space before beginning the body of the memo.
- **Get right to the point.**
  Make sure the subject line states the topic of the memo. Then, in the body, begin with the most important information.

During your writing . . .

- **Keep it short.**
  Include only the essential information.
- **Organize your thoughts.**
  Provide information in a clear, well-organized way. If you need a response, state your request clearly and politely.
- **Use an appropriate voice.**
  Be polite and businesslike.

After you've written a first draft . . .

- **Check for completeness.**
  Revise your work, asking yourself these two questions:
    - *What does the reader already know?*
    - *What does the reader need to know?*

  Then fill in any missing information and delete the unnecessary details.
- **Check for correctness.**
  Remember: A memo represents you. In order to make a good impression, check your writing for errors. Once everything is clear and correct, your memo is ready to share.

Write a memo updating your teacher about your progress on a current school project or assignment.

Expository Writing

Writing for Assessment

Many state and school writing tests ask you to respond to an expository prompt. An expository prompt will ask you to explain something or share information. Study the sample prompt and the student response below.

Expository Prompt

There are many inventions that have made life easier. Think of one invention that has had a significant impact on modern life. Then write an expository essay explaining several ways this invention has changed the way people live.

Response to an Expository Prompt

The **beginning** paragraph states the focus or thesis (**underlined**).

Technology is everywhere: supercomputers, MP3 players, hybrid cars, GPS tracking systems, and even greeting cards that play "Celebration." But sometimes the best tech is the old tech. Just now, a library full of students sits at writing carrels, crouching over tests, and every one of them holds a pencil. The lowly pencil has shaped the world.

Each **middle** paragraph covers one main point.

The pencil put writing in everybody's hands. In the old days, writing was limited to professors with hand-carved goose quills and pots of India ink. Now, carpenters have pencils sticking out of their jeans. Kindergartners and congresspeople use pencils, too. The pencil has made writing democratic.

The pencil also introduced the world to a new concept: the eraser. Before that, writing was permanent. From the time of calligraphy

The writer's engaging voice will be a welcome relief to essay graders.

on a letter sealed with a wax blob all the way back to Egyptians chiseling hieroglyphics in rocks—writing had been permanent. Then, along came the eraser, and for the first time writers got to change their minds with no trouble at all. Watch out for a writer with a pencil, because that person is probably a free spirit.

Varied examples make the writing lively.

Maybe the biggest way the pencil has changed the world is that it was a computer before there were computers. Pencils can do word processing. They can perform the most complex mathematical calculations. They can create art and doctor photos—often by adding mustaches and beards. And instead of costing $500.00, the typical pencil costs $.05. That's one ten-thousandth of the price—a fact that this very pencil calculated.

The **ending** adds an amusing final thought.

While most people get excited by all the new technology around them, a few people should take the time to admire the old technology, too. Write with it, erase with it, chew on it, but don't forget the pencil.

Respond to the reading. Answer the following questions about the sample essay.

- ☐ **Ideas (1) What is the writer's topic? (2) What three main parts of the topic does the writer cover?**
- ☐ **Organization (3) Does the writer organize the essay by time, by order of importance, or by location?**
- ☐ **Voice & Word Choice (4) What words tell that the writer cares about the subject?**

Writing Tips

Before you write . . .

- **Understand the prompt.**
  Remember that an expository prompt asks you to explain.
- **Plan your time wisely.**
  Take several minutes to plan your writing. Use a graphic organizer like a cluster to help with planning your writing.

Cluster

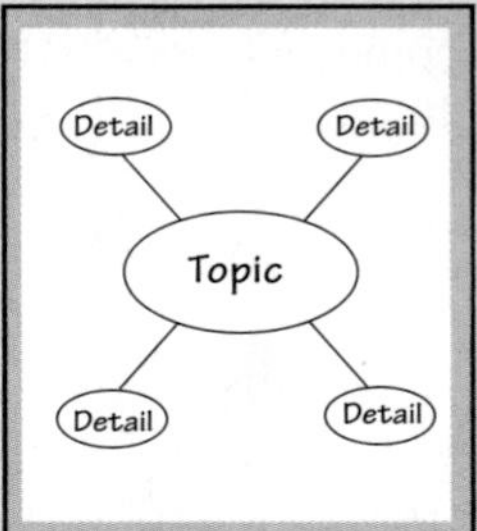

During your writing . . .

- **Decide on a focus for your essay.**
  Keep your main idea or purpose in mind as you write.
- **Be selective.**
  Use examples and explanations that directly support your focus.
- **End in a meaningful way.**
  Remind the reader about the importance of the topic.

After you've written a first draft . . .

- **Check for completeness and correctness.**
  Present your details in a logical order and correct errors in capitalization, punctuation, spelling, and grammar.

Expository Prompts

- Each of us owns something we treasure. Your object may not seem special to anyone else, but it has meaning to you. Write an essay explaining why this object is so important in your life.
- Write an essay explaining why a certain person is deserving of your admiration. You may or may not personally know this individual.

Plan and write a response. Respond to one of the prompts above. Complete your writing within the period of time your teacher gives you. Afterward, list one part of your essay that you like and one part that could have been better.

Expository Writing in Review

Purpose: In expository writing, you *explain* something to readers.

Topics: Explain . . . the kinds of something,
how things are similar or different,
how to do or make something,
the causes of something, or
the definition of something.

Prewriting

Select a topic that you know something about or one you want to learn more about. (See pages 166–167.)

Gather and sort details and organize them chronologically, point by point, or in order of importance. (See pages 168 and 170.)

Write a focus statement, telling exactly what topic you plan to write about. (See page 167.)

Writing

In the beginning, introduce your topic, say something interesting about it, and state your focus. (See page 173.)

In the middle, use clear topic sentences and specific details to support the focus. (See pages 169 and 174–175.)

In the ending, summarize your writing and make a final comment about the topic. (See page 176.)

Revising

Review the ideas, organization, and voice first. Then review for **word choice** and **sentence fluency.** Make sure that you use terms that are precise and connect with the reader. (See pages 178–188.)

Editing

Check your writing for conventions. Also have a trusted classmate edit your writing. (See pages 190–192.)

Make a final copy and proofread it for errors before sharing it. (See page 193.)

Assessing

Use the expository rubric to assess your finished writing. (See pages 194–195.)

persuade
argue

Persuasive Writing

Writing Focus

- Persuasive Paragraph
- Defending a Position
- Personal Commentary

Grammar Focus

- Avoiding Double Subjects
- Pronoun Antecedent Agreement

Academic Vocabulary

Learning these words will help you understand this unit.

1. A **controversy** is something that people disagree about.
   Name a controversy that occurred at your school.

2. When you **debate** a topic, you discuss the reasons for and against it.
   What topic might you debate with your parents?

3. To **convince** is to make someone believe something.
   How would you convince a friend to play a game?

convince
reason
support

Persuasive Writing

Persuasive Paragraph

Where do you stand on the new weekend curfew? What's your position on the cancellation of school dances? When you "take a stand" or "defend a position," you state what you think about an important issue.

What positions have you, or could you, defend? One way to defend a position is to write a persuasive paragraph in which you state your position and provide reasons to support it. In this chapter, you will read a sample persuasive paragraph defending the position that winning in sports is about more than trophies. Afterward, you'll write a "position" paragraph of your own.

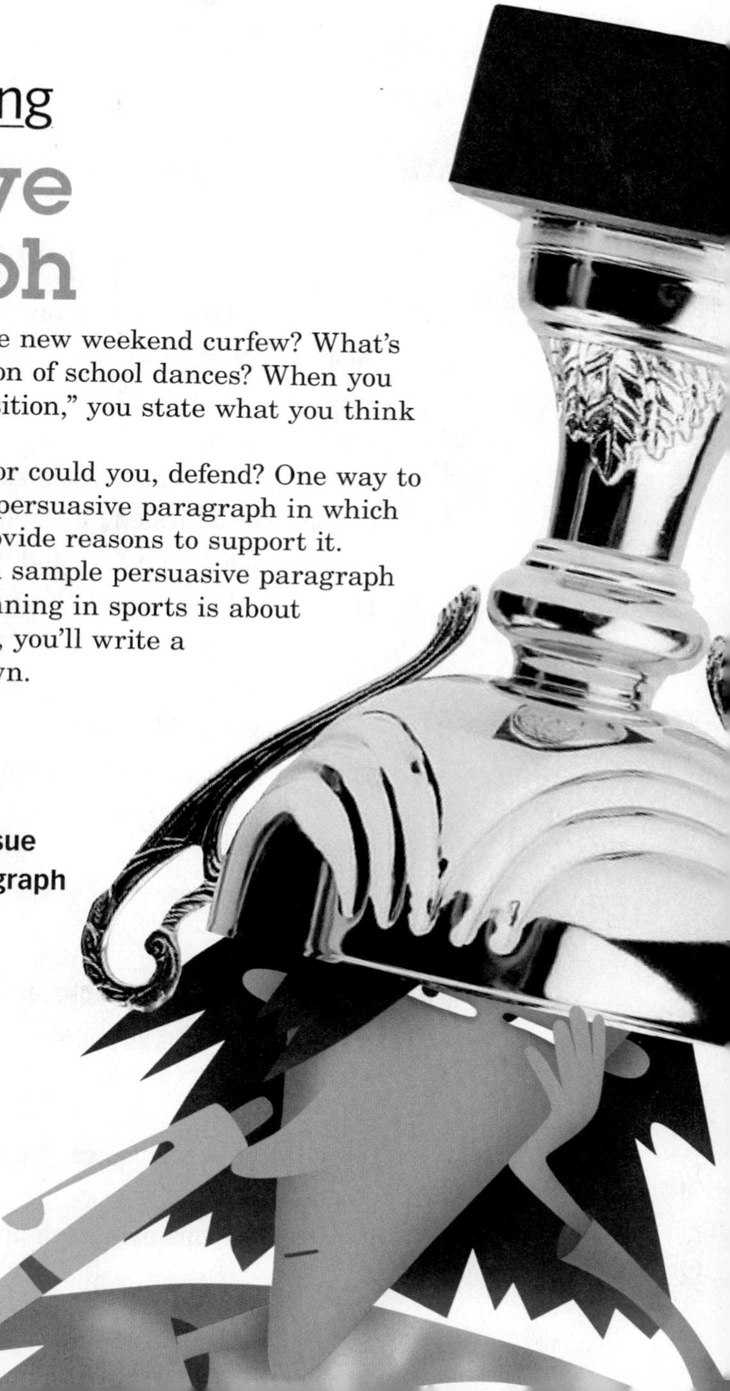

Writing Guidelines

Subject: An important issue
Form: Persuasive paragraph
Purpose: To support your position
Audience: Classmates, parents, guardians

Persuasive Paragraph

In a persuasive paragraph, you state your position in the **topic sentence**. The **body** of the paragraph supports the position, and the **closing sentence** restates it. The following paragraph was written by Ellen, a student who took the position that participating in sports makes for healthy living.

Topic Sentence

Body

Closing Sentence

Join a Winning Team

Sports tone up students' bodies and also their minds. To start with, sports are a fun way to stay healthy and physically fit. Growing kids need physical activity to build strong bones and improve hand-eye coordination. Sports also improve muscle strength, flexibility, and the cardiovascular system. In addition, sports teach students to work well with others and have a good attitude. The challenge of the game helps players learn to keep going and never give up. Because they learn determination, students who play sports often do better in school. Playing sports is good for the body and mind, so no matter who scores the most points, everybody wins!

Respond to the reading. After reading the paragraph above, write answers to the following questions.

- ☐ **Ideas** (1) What is the writer's position? (2) What reasons support the position?
- ☐ **Organization** (3) What transitions does the writer use in the body sentences of the paragraph?
- ☐ **Voice & Word Choice** (4) What specific words or phrases make this paragraph persuasive? Find two.

Prewriting Selecting a Topic

Think about a debate you recently had with another person. Ellen charted recent debates to find a position she wanted to write about.

Topics Chart

Debates

I said . . .	The other person said . . .
School lunch is too expensive.	It's cheaper than fast food.
I need more allowance.	Then do more chores.
* Sports are good for students.	Sports make students too competitive.
School starts too early.	It's better than getting out too late.

Select a position. Create a chart like the one above. List debates you have had with other people. Write down what you said and what the other person said. Then select a position you would like to write about in a paragraph.

Gathering Reasons

Next you need to gather reasons to support your position. Ellen gathered supporting reasons by turning her position into a question that started with "Why?" Then she answered the question in as many ways as she could.

Supporting Reasons

Why are sports good for students?

- ~~Lots of people enjoy them.~~
- Participating in sports improves flexibility.
- Sports activities help build strong bones and muscles.
- ~~Athletes are more popular than other kids.~~
- Sports teach kids to keep trying and never give up.
- Kids who play sports often do well in school.

List your reasons. Turn your position into a question that starts with "Why?" Then answer the question in as many ways as possible. Review your list and cross out any reasons that are not very persuasive.

Writing Creating Your First Draft

As you write the first draft of your paragraph, follow these tips.

- Write a **topic sentence** that clearly states your position. Try different versions until you feel satisfied with the sentence.
- Create **body sentences** that provide your supporting reasons. Use transitions to help connect the ideas in your sentences.
- Write a **closing sentence** that restates your position in a fresh, different way.

Write your first draft. Use the tips above and your prewriting to guide you. The purpose of your first draft is to get your ideas on paper.

Revising Improving Your Writing

Once your first draft is finished, it's time to revise it. Check your *ideas, organization, voice, word choice,* and *sentence fluency.*

Revise your paragraph. Let the questions below guide the revision of your paragraph.

1. Does the topic sentence clearly state my position?
2. Do the reasons support my position?
3. Do my reasons appear in an effective order? Do I use transitions to tie my ideas together?
4. Does my word choice make my paragraph sound persuasive?
5. Do my sentences flow smoothly?

Editing Checking for Conventions

After you revise your paragraph, check it for *conventions.*

Edit your paragraph. Ask yourself the following questions.

1. Have I used the correct spelling, punctuation, and capitalization?
2. Have I checked for errors in grammar?

Proofread your paragraph. Make a final copy of your paragraph and check it one more time before sharing it with your audience.

Persuasive Writing

Defending a Position

Hubbub, tussle, scrap, ruckus, hoo-hah, squabble, tiff—English has hundreds of words that describe differences of opinion. Anytime you get a large group of people together, whether in a school or in a community, differences of opinion are bound to come up.

Perhaps people in your school disagree about creating an open study hall. Maybe school board members are debating a change in the school mascot. It might even be that your city is squabbling over a new housing development.

One form of persuasive writing helps you deal with differences of opinion. By stating a position and defending it, you can convince others to agree with you. In this chapter, you will write a position essay about a controversy in your school or community.

Writing Guidelines

Subject: A controversy in your school or community

Form: Persuasive essay

Purpose: To defend a position

Audience: Classmates and community members

Understanding Your Goal

Your goal in this chapter is to write a well-organized persuasive essay that defends a position. The traits listed in the chart below will help you plan and write your essay.

Traits of Persuasive Writing

Ideas

Use specific reasons to defend a position about an issue in your school or community.

Organization

Create a beginning that states your position, a middle that provides support and answers an objection, and an ending that restates your position.

Voice

Use a persuasive voice that balances facts and feelings.

Word Choice

Choose fair words and qualifiers to strengthen your position.

Sentence Fluency

Write clear, complete sentences with varied beginnings.

Conventions

Check your writing for errors in punctuation, capitalization, spelling, and grammar.

Literature Connections: For another example of persuasive writing, read the editorial "Should the Driving Age Be Raised to 18?" by Alex Koroknay-Palicz.

Position Essay

In a position essay, you take one side of a controversy and state clearly where you stand on the issue. By stating and defending a position, you can convince others to agree with you. In the sample essay that follows, the student writer defends his position on allowing students more options during study hall.

Beginning
The beginning introduces the topic and states the position (**underlined**).

Middle
The middle paragraphs support the writer's position.

Open Study Halls

"Study hall is for studying!" Most students at Carr Middle School have heard Mr. Spencer say these words in study hall, especially when people are talking or making trouble. He's right. Many students really count on their time in study hall to do homework and get ready for tests. The best way to make study hall more effective is to make it more open.

First of all, an open study hall would let hardworking students go where they need to go to get more work done. A person who needs to do research could go to the library. A student who has to write a report could go to the computer lab. If a person needs to finish an art project, he or she could go to the art room. By allowing hardworking students to move around, an open study hall would actually help them accomplish more.

Secondly, an open study hall would motivate students to take study hall more seriously. When hardworking students earned the privilege of leaving the room, other students would want to earn the same privilege. The only way would be to study.

Most importantly, an open study hall would teach responsibility. Teachers are always saying that students should take responsibility for their education. After all, in high school, nobody will hold their hands. Now is when they should learn how to manage their time. An open study hall would help. Students who used it well would have more free time after school, and students who abused the privilege would wind up back at their desks. An open study hall would reward kids for being responsible.

The last middle paragraph defends the position against an important objection.

Understandably, Principal MacGregor and some teachers are worried about students just wandering the halls. But just because study hall would be open doesn't mean students could wander. They would still have to use hall passes and arrange with specific teachers to come to their rooms. Students caught wandering would be sent back to study hall, and their privilege would be taken away.

Ending

The ending restates the writer's position.

Study hall would be more effective if it were open. An open study hall would allow students to accomplish more, would motivate kids to work harder, and would teach responsibility. Though some people are worried that kids would abuse the system, hall passes could take care of those problems. Principal MacGregor should give this proposal serious attention. Open the doors of study hall!

Respond to the reading. Answer the following questions about the sample essay.

- ☐ **Ideas (1) What three reasons support the writer's position?**
- ☐ **Organization (2) Which paragraph deals with the most important reason? (3) Which paragraph answers an objection?**
- ☐ **Voice & Word Choice (4) Does the writer sound knowledgeable and persuasive? Explain.**

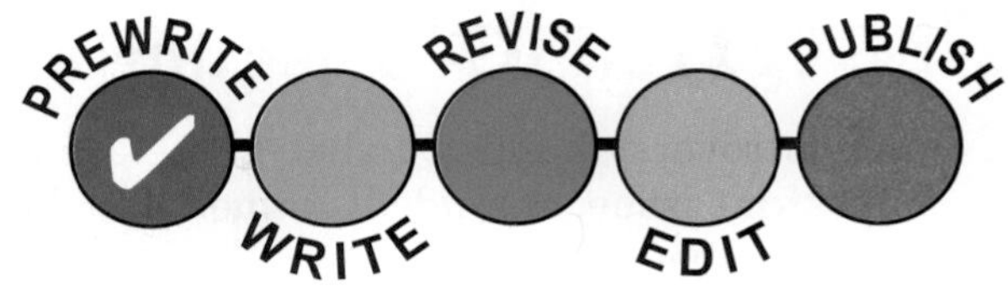

Prewriting

In prewriting, you will select a controversial issue, gather reasons and details, and organize your ideas. Solid prewriting makes persuasive writing much easier.

Keys to Effective Prewriting

1. Select a controversial issue in your school or community and decide what your position is.
2. Gather reasons and details that support your position.
3. Select an important objection that you can address.
4. Write a clear position statement to guide you.
5. Create a list or an outline as a planning guide.

Prewriting Selecting a Controversy

A controversy happens when there are differing opinions concerning an important issue. A student named Janelle used sentence starters to brainstorm about controversies in her school and community.

Sentence Starters

People at my school disagree about . . .
- *whether we should go to block scheduling.*
- *45-minute bus rides.*
- *all the fund-raisers.*
- *whether graduation should be a bigger deal.*

People in my neighborhood disagree about . . .
- *what should happen to that empty lot.*
- *all the "no skateboarding" signs.*
- *the woods for sale next to the school.* *
- *the 10:00 p.m. curfew.*
- *the Labrador that barks all night.*

List controversies. On your own paper, complete the two sentence starters above. Try to come up with at least three endings for each sentence. Choose a controversy that you feel strongly about and write a sentence that states your position.

I think Belmer Woods should be turned into a park.

Focus on the Traits

Ideas Choose an issue that you feel strongly about. You'll have an easier time finding support and defending a position that you really believe in.

Gathering Reasons to Support Your Position

Once you have stated your position, you need to gather reasons to support it. A table diagram can help. The tabletop presents your position. The table legs support that position by answering the question "Why?" The following table diagram helped Janelle gather reasons for her position.

Table Diagram

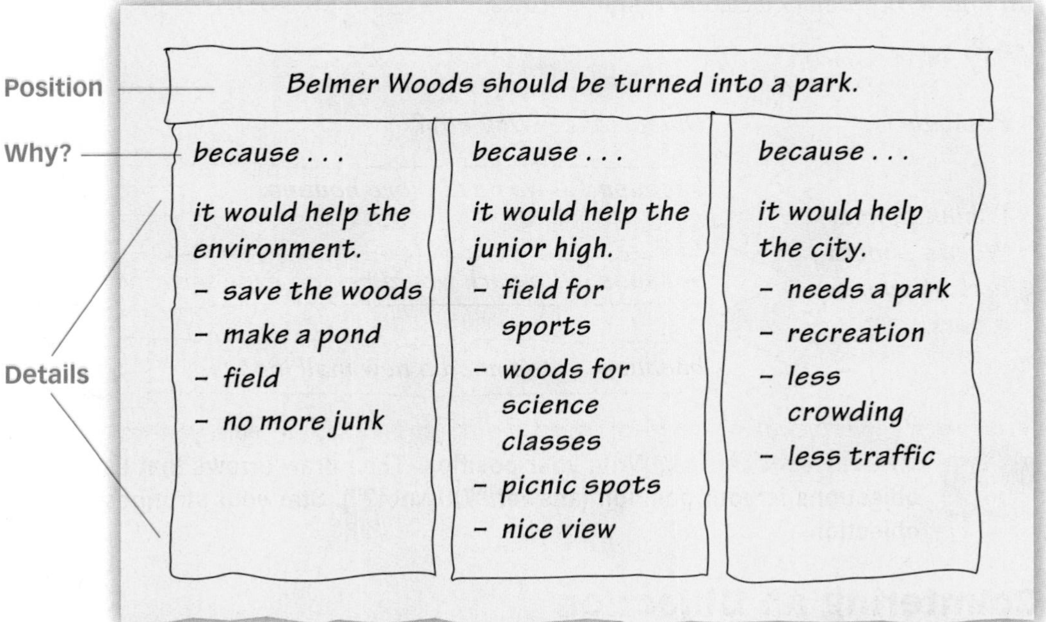

Position
Why?
Details
Belmer Woods should be turned into a park.
because . . .
it would help the environment.
– save the woods
– make a pond
– field
– no more junk
because . . .
it would help the junior high.
– field for sports
– woods for science classes
– picnic spots
– nice view
because . . .
it would help the city.
– needs a park
– recreation
– less crowding
– less traffic

Create a table diagram. **Use the sample as a guide to create your own table diagram. In the top box, write your position. In three or four boxes beneath it, write reasons that answer the question "Why?" Then add details about each reason.**

Focus on the Traits

Organization A table needs at least three legs to keep from wobbling and falling over. In the same way, your position essay needs at least three supporting reasons. In your essay, you will organize these reasons by building toward the most important one.

Prewriting Gathering Objections

Answering the question "Why?" helped you gather support for your position. Next, answering the question "Why not?" will help you gather possible objections. If you understand objections the reader might have, you can defend against them and make your position stronger. One way to think of objections is to imagine arrows the reader might shoot at your position. Janelle wrote her objections inside arrows.

Why Not Chart

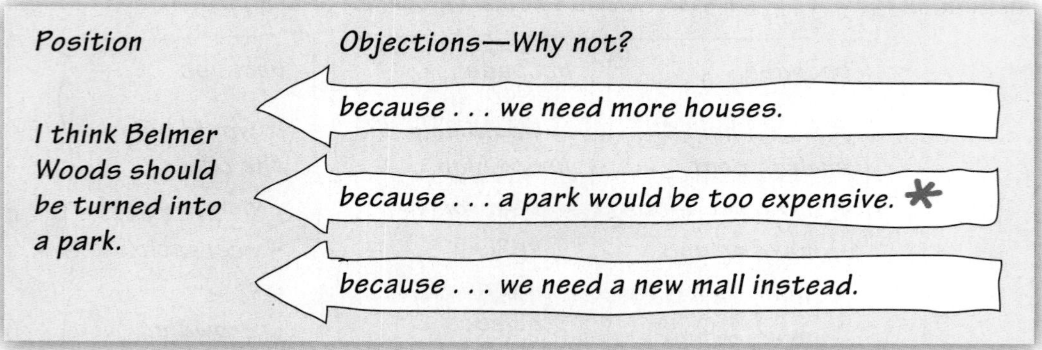

Position
Objections—Why not?
I think Belmer Woods should be turned into a park.
because . . . we need more houses.
because . . . a park would be too expensive. *
– A strip mall would require wider roads—big $$$.
– A referendum could pay for a park.
because . . . we need a new mall instead.

Gather objections. Write your position. Then draw arrows that list objections to your position (answer "Why not?"). Star your strongest objection.

Countering an Objection

When you counter or address an objection, you simply argue against it. Janelle countered the following objection with the reasons listed below it.

Counterargument Chart

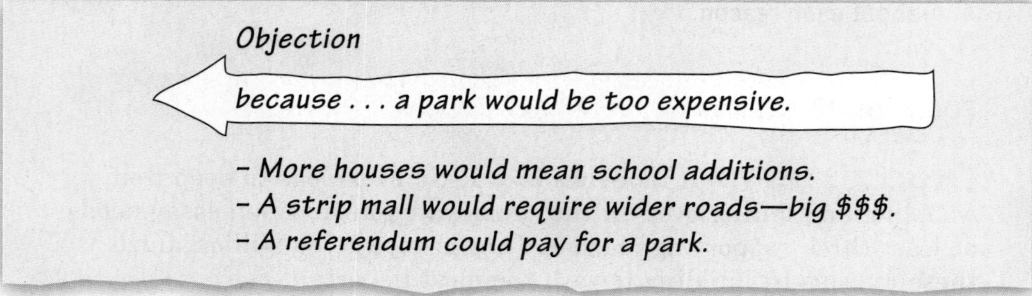

Counter an important objection. Write down the strongest objection to your argument and list the reasons you disagree.

Writing a Position Statement

Your position statement should clearly tell what you think about the controversy. Janelle wrote down her position. Then she tried two other ways to state it. She put a star next to the statement that worked best.

Position Statements

Belmer Woods should be turned into a park.

The best way to develop Belmer Woods would be to make it a park. *

Instead of more houses or stores, the land should become a park.

Write your position statement. Write three different versions. Then choose the statement you feel works best.

Writing Topic Sentences

Next, you need to write topic sentences for your middle paragraphs. Janelle used a chart. She wrote her reasons in the left column and corresponding topic sentences in the right column.

Outline Chart

Reasons	*Topic Sentences*
It would help the environment.	*First of all, a park would be the right choice for the environment.*
It would help the junior high.	*Turning Belmer Woods into a park would also help the junior high.*
It would help the city.	*The most important reason to create a new park is that the whole city would benefit.*
Objection: A park would be too expensive.	*Some people say the city doesn't have enough money to create a park.*

Write topic sentences. Make an outline chart like the one above. In the left column, list the reasons from your table diagram (page 229) and the objection you chose (page 230). In the right column, create topic sentences.

Prewriting Organizing Your Essay

The following directions can help you create an organized list for your essay. The organized list brings together all the ideas of your prewriting and prepares you to write your first draft.

Directions	Organized List
Write your position statement.	*The best way to develop Belmer Woods would be to make it a park.*
Write your first topic sentence.	*1. First of all, a park would be the right choice for the environment.*
List facts and details.	*– save part of forest – make pond and field – stop pollution and graffiti*
Write your second topic sentence.	*2. Turning Belmer Woods into a park would also help the junior high.*
List facts and details.	*– field for sports teams – forest for science classes – picnic areas for clubs*
Write your third topic sentence.	*3. The most important reason to create a new park is that the whole city would benefit.*
List facts and details.	*– no parks on west side – west side already crowded – houses/strip mall not needed*
Write your fourth topic sentence.	*4. Some people say the city doesn't have enough money to create a park.*
List facts and details.	*– new houses = school additions – new strip mall = road work – cheaper to make park*

Create an organized list. Use the "Directions" above to organize your position statement, topic sentences, and details. This list will guide you as you write your first draft.

Writing

After you create a plan for your essay, you are ready to get all of your ideas on paper.

Keys to Effective Writing

1. Use your organized list or outline as a planning guide.
2. Get all your ideas on paper in your first draft.
3. Write on every other line to make room for later changes.
4. State your position in the first paragraph.
5. Use specific details to support your position.
6. Address an important objection.

Writing Getting the Big Picture

Now that you have finished prewriting, you are ready to create a first draft of your essay. The graphic that follows shows how the parts of your essay will fit together. (The examples are from the student essay on pages 235–238.)

Beginning

The **beginning** introduces the controversial issue and states the writer's position.

Position Statement

The best way to develop Belmer Woods would be to make it a park.

Middle

The **middle** paragraphs support the writer's position.

Topic Sentences

First of all, a park would be the right choice for the environment.

Turning Belmer Woods into a park would also help the junior high.

The most important reason to create a new park is that the whole city would benefit.

The **last middle** paragraph answers an important objection.

Some people say the city doesn't have enough money to create a park.

Ending

The **ending** revisits the position.

Closing Sentence

Many people have ideas about developing Belmer Woods, but only a park would be best for the community.

Starting Your Essay

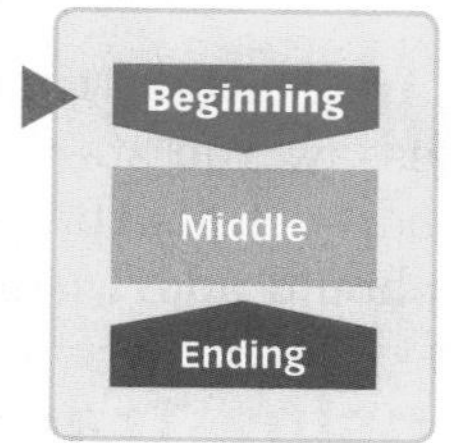

The beginning paragraph of your essay needs to get the reader's attention, introduce the topic, and state your position about it. Here are some ways you can get the reader's attention.

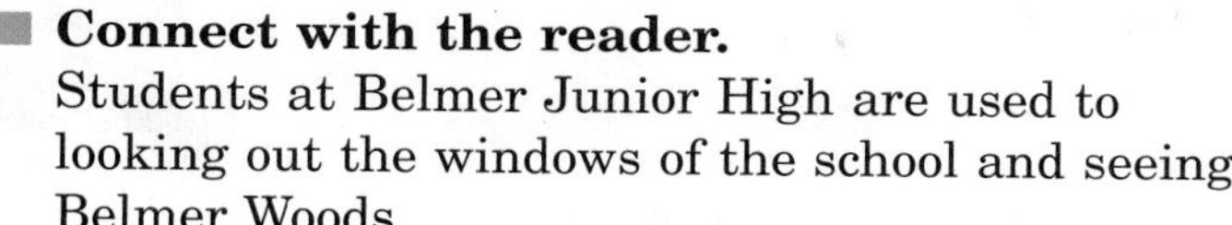

- **Connect with the reader.**
  Students at Belmer Junior High are used to looking out the windows of the school and seeing Belmer Woods.
- **Dramatize the controversy.**
  The chain saws and bulldozers are coming to Belmer Woods.
- **Ask a question.**
  Would students rather look at a park or hundreds of houses?
- **Be creative.**
  When developers look at Belmer Woods, they don't see green leaves but green stacks of cash.

Beginning Paragraph

Janelle begins her essay by making a connection with the reader. Then she introduces the topic and states her position about it.

The controversy is introduced.

Students at Belmer Junior High are used to looking out the windows of the school and seeing Belmer Woods. Now when they look out, they see a sign: "For Sale, 20 acres, Zoned Residential/ Commercial." Belmer Woods is about to change, and there are many different ideas about how it should change. <u>The best way to develop Belmer Woods would be to make it a park.</u>

The position is stated (underlined).

Write an opening. Write the beginning paragraph of your essay. Use one of the strategies above to get your reader's attention. Then introduce the topic and state your position.

PERSUASIVE

Writing Developing the Middle Part

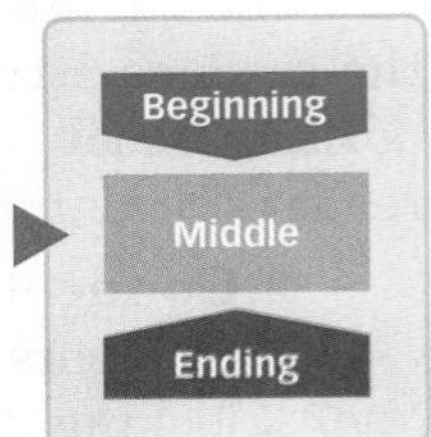

Now it's time to write the middle paragraphs of your essay. You start each paragraph with a topic sentence and add details that support it. Your last middle paragraph should address an objection.

Using Transitions

Transitions will help you show the order of importance in your paragraphs. The following sets of transitions would work well with your first three middle paragraphs.

First of all, Also, Most importantly,	To begin, Also, Finally,	To start with, In addition, Most significantly,

Middle Paragraphs

The topic sentence introduces the topic (underlined).

The body supports the topic sentence.

First of all, a park would be the right choice for the environment. Part of the forest could be saved, and earthmovers could dig out a pond. The grassy part on the north could remain as a field for soccer or baseball. Making the land into a park would also help protect the environment. Nobody would be able to dump junk or car tires there anymore or carve graffiti into the trees. A park would both preserve and protect the environment.

Turning Belmer Woods into a park would also help the junior high. Gym classes and sports teams could use the field on the north side. Science classes could study the plants, trees, and insects in the wooded spots. In addition, any clubs in the school would be able to hold events in the picnic areas. Belmer Junior High would be a better place if students had a park next door.

The middle paragraphs build to the most important reason.

<u>The most important reason to create a new park is that the whole city would benefit.</u> Currently, there are no parks on the west side of town, but there are plenty of houses. A park would give all those people somewhere to go for recreation. A new subdivision or a new strip mall would just make the west side overcrowded.

The last middle paragraph counters an objection.

<u>Some people say the city doesn't have enough money to create a park.</u> However, a subdivision or a strip mall would cost even more. If a hundred new families moved in, the city would have to add on to the schools. If a strip mall were built, the city would have to widen the roads. Those projects would cost a lot more than creating a park.

Write your middle paragraphs. Create middle paragraphs that support your position for your persuasive essay.

Drafting Tips

- **Follow the plan** in your organized list.
- **Use transitions** to show order of importance.
- **Include clear reasons** and avoid sounding emotional.
- **Respond to an objection.**

Writing Ending Your Essay

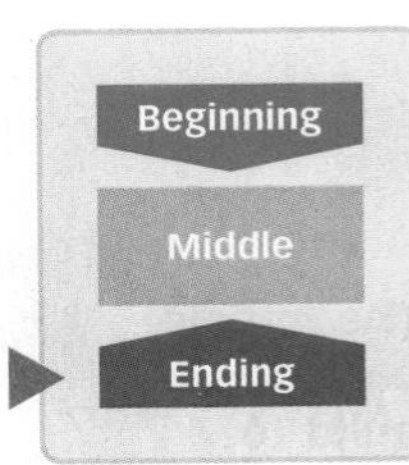

The hard work is done. You have stated your position, supported it with reasons, and responded to an objection. Now you are ready to write your ending paragraph. If you aren't sure what to write in your ending paragraph, follow these guidelines.

Sentence 1: Revisit your position.

Sentence 2: Sum up the main support for your position.

Sentence 3: Sum up the objection and your response to it.

Sentence 4: Leave the reader with a strong final thought.

Ending Paragraph

The position is restated.

The paragraph sums up support for the position.

The best way to improve Belmer Woods is to make it into Belmer Park. The park would help the environment, the junior high, and the city. In addition, the park would cost the city less than a new subdivision or strip mall. Many people have ideas about developing Belmer Woods, but only a park would be best for the community.

Write your ending. Write the final paragraph of your essay. Restate your position and sum up the reasons for it. Leave the reader with something to think about.

Form a complete first draft. Write a complete copy of your essay. Skip every other line if you write by hand, or double-space if you use a computer. This will give you room for revising.

Revising

When you revise, you add or remove details, shift parts of the essay, and work on creating a more persuasive voice. You also check your word choice and refine your sentences.

Keys to Effective Revising

1. Read your essay aloud to get a feeling for how well it works.
2. Make sure you clearly state your position.
3. Check your paragraphs to make sure they follow your writing plan.
4. Polish your voice so that it sounds convincing.
5. Check your words and sentences.
6. Use the editing and proofreading marks inside the back cover of this book.

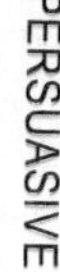

Revising for Ideas

6 My position is very well defended and compels the reader to act.	**5** My position is supported with logical reasons, and I respond to an important objection.	**4** Most of my reasons support my position. I respond to an objection.

When you revise for *ideas*, make sure you have used logical reasons and avoided "fuzzy thinking." Also look for ways to strengthen your response to any objections a reader may have. The rubric strip above can guide you.

How can I avoid "fuzzy thinking" in my essay?

You can avoid "fuzzy thinking" by making sure the reasons you use are accurate and logical. If even one of your supporting reasons is not logical, your position will be shaky, like a table with a bad leg. Here are three common types of "fuzzy thinking" errors to check for.

- **Half-truths:** Avoid telling only half of the story.
  Building a dam would help animals by giving them new habitats.
  This is a half-truth because dams also destroy habitats.
- **Exaggerations:** Avoid stretching the truth.
  Next the school board will force students to clean the highway!
  This exaggeration merely makes the writer sound unrealistic.
- **All-or-nothing statements:** Avoid oversimplifying complex issues.
  If the school bans fund-raisers, we'll never have new uniforms.
  Few people would believe that these are the only options.

Read the following sentences and identify the fuzzy thinking in each.

1. The mayor wants to put every curfew breaker into prison.
2. The school food is what is making eighth graders gain weight.
3. If the state doesn't change the tests, no one will graduate.
4. When it rains, the gymnasium is under 10 feet of water!
5. Television is the reason kids are getting bad grades.

Check for fuzzy thinking. Read the body of your essay and look for half-truths, exaggerations, and all-or-nothing statements. Revise your essay to eliminate any fuzzy thinking you may find.

3 I need more supporting reasons and a more convincing response to an objection.

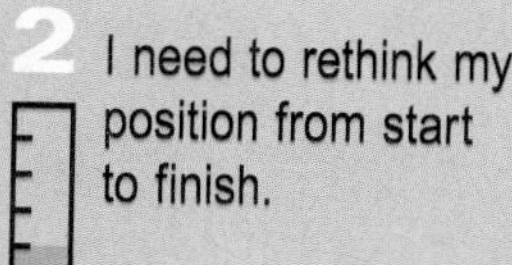
2 I need to rethink my position from start to finish.

1 I need to learn how to defend a position.

How can I check my response to an objection?

When you are defending a position, you should answer a key objection your reader may have. The best way to check your answer or response to an objection is to ask yourself the following questions:

1. Is the objection *important*?
2. What is the *main point* of the objection?
3. Do I deal with the *main point*?

Read the following objection paragraph. Use the three questions above to decide what changes could improve the paragraph.

Some teachers object to cell phones because they are too disruptive in class. That's a serious concern, but why can't teachers just start every class saying, "Please turn off all cell phones"? For that matter, students with cell phones can talk quietly enough that everyone else can still hear the lecture. Finally, students could just use cell phones for sending text messages back and forth. They are silent.

Review your objection paragraph. Ask yourself the three questions above and revise as needed to make the paragraph more effective.

Ideas
Weak reasons are replaced with more logical ones.

Some people ~~are against creating~~ [say the city doesn't have enough money to create] a park. However, a subdivision or a strip mall ~~isn't any good, either.~~ [would cost even more.] If a hundred new families moved in, the city would have ~~all kinds of problems.~~ [to add on to the schools.] If a strip mall were built, the city would have ~~even more trouble.~~ [to widen the roads.] . . .

Revising for Organization

6 All the parts of my essay work together to build a thoughtful, convincing position.

5 My overall organization is clear, and my reasons are arranged effectively.

4 Most parts of my essay are organized well except for one part.

When you revise your writing for *organization*, check the overall structure of your essay. Also be sure you have placed your reasons in the most convincing order. The rubric strip above can guide your revision.

How can I check the arrangement of my reasons?

The best way to check the arrangement of your reasons is to follow the three guidelines below.

- Save your most important reason until last.
- Use words such as "first of all," "in addition," and "most importantly" to help the reader understand the organization of your reasons.
- Use the final middle paragraph to answer an objection.

Read the following topic sentences from an essay about junior high graduation. Put them in the most effective order. Transition words and phrases will help you.

1. Junior high graduation also marks a big change for students.
2. The most important reason to treat junior high graduation more seriously is that it tells students their work is important.
3. It is true that the school board is concerned about the cost of a more elaborate graduation.
4. For one thing, parents want to make the junior high graduation a bigger event.

Check the order of your reasons. Do you build to the most important reason? Do you respond to an objection? Do you tie your paragraphs together with transitions? Revise until you can answer each of these question with a "yes."

3 I need to reorganize the middle part of my essay.

2 I need to include a beginning, a middle, and an ending in my essay.

1 I need to learn how to organize a persuasive essay.

How can I check the overall organization of my essay?

You can use the questions and the chart below to help you check the overall structure of your essay.

Beginning Paragraph
Do I get the reader's attention?
Do I state my position clearly?

Middle Paragraphs
Do I support my position with sound reasons?

Do I answer an important objection with a counterargument?

Ending Paragraph
Do I restate my position?
Do I end with a strong final thought?

Position Statement

Reason 1

Reason 2

Reason 3

Counterargument

Position Summary

Check your overall organization. Review your essay and ask yourself the questions listed above. If you can answer "yes" to every question, your overall organization is strong. If not, revise your essay until you can answer "yes" to each question.

Organization
A change helps to show the order of importance.

The most important reason is that ~~To~~ create a new park ~~would help~~ would benefit the whole city.

Currently, there are no parks on the west side . . .

Revising for Voice

6 My mature and reliable voice creates total confidence in my position.	**5** My voice is persuasive and consistent. I balance facts and feelings.	**4** My voice is consistent, but I need to balance facts and feelings.

To revise for *voice*, make sure your writing voice is persuasive, consistent, and balanced. The rubric strip above can guide you.

Do I balance facts and feelings?

You use a balanced voice if you focus on facts first and back them up with feelings. If your essay focuses on feelings first, it will sound emotional and unconvincing.

Too Emotional

The Qwik-E-Stop is a bad place. The manager seems distrustful of kids. The whole time you feel just awful. You feel as if you need to get out of there as soon as possible.

On the other hand, if your essay focuses solely on facts, it will sound too dull. Feelings give meaning to facts.

Too Dry

The Qwik-E-Stop is on Main Street. It allows only two students in at a time. The manager enforces this rule. If two kids are inside, other kids wait outside.

A persuasive voice balances facts and feelings.

A Balanced Voice

The Quik-E-Stop on Main Street allows only two students in at a time, and the manager closely watches any students who enter the store. This policy and the attitude of the manager make kids feel unwelcome.

Check your voice for balance. **Read through your essay. Do you include both facts and feelings? If your voice sounds too emotional, add facts. If it sounds too dull, add feelings. Revise until you reach a balance.**

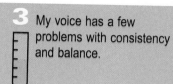

3 My voice has a few problems with consistency and balance.

2 My voice is inconsistent, and I sound too emotional and unconvincing.

1 I need to learn how to create a consistent and balanced voice.

Do I use a consistent point of view?

You can check for a consistent point of view by looking at the pronouns in your essay. A persuasive essay should use mostly third-person pronouns: *he, she, it, they.* Your teacher may also allow you to use some first-person pronouns: *I, me, we, us.* However, you should avoid second-person pronouns: *you, your.*

Read the following paragraph. Find five places where the voice shifts from third person to second person. Then suggest what changes would make the voice consistent.

Whenever students go into Quick-E-Stop, the manager watches your hands and your pockets. He asks the students if you plan to buy something. Even if the students pull out their money, the manager still scowls as if he doesn't want you there. He doesn't thank them or tell them to have a nice day, but just stares at you until you leave.

Check consistency of voice. **Read your essay, paying special attention to pronouns. Revise any spot where the voice shifts.**

Voice
An inconsistent point of view is corrected.

Students at Belmer Junior High are used to looking out the windows of the school and seeing Belmer Woods. Now when ~~you~~ they look out, ~~you~~ they see a sign: "For Sale, 20 acres, Zoned Residential/Commercial." Belmer Woods is about to . . .

Revising for Word Choice

6 My words make a powerful case for my position.

5 Carefully chosen words make my writing persuasive and effective.

4 I have avoided unfair words, but I need to add a few qualifiers.

When you check your essay for *word choice*, make sure you have chosen your words carefully and avoided unfair words. In addition, see if qualifiers (page 247) can make your writing more persuasive. The rubric strip above can guide you.

Did I use unfair words in my essay?

You used unfair words in your essay if some of them are overly negative. Unfair words make your writing seem biased and less persuasive. Notice below how unfair words can be replaced by neutral words.

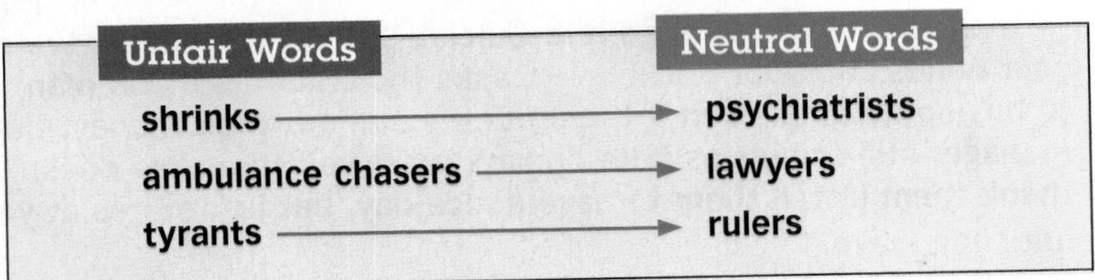

Unfair Words	Neutral Words
shrinks →	psychiatrists
ambulance chasers →	lawyers
tyrants →	rulers

Read the following sentences and find the unfair words in each. Suggest a replacement word or phrase for each unfair word.

1. The Quick-E-Stop shouldn't hire paranoid people.
2. The referendum failed because the voters are cheap.
3. Big Brother checks our lockers once a month.
4. The old gymnasium is a real pit.
5. The prison guards in study hall won't let anyone talk.
6. Old ladies volunteer over 10,000 hours annually at Fairmont Hospital.
7. Idiots cause car accidents.

Check your essay for unfair words. Read your essay and watch for overly negative words. Delete or replace them.

3 I need to change some unfair words and add qualifiers.

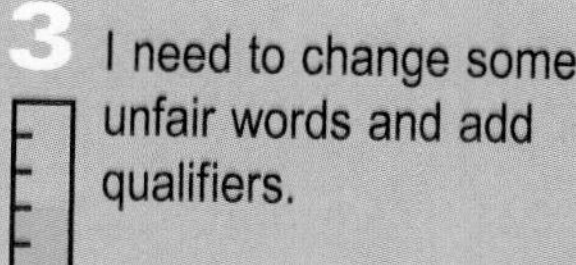

2 I need to change my unfair language to make a believable position.

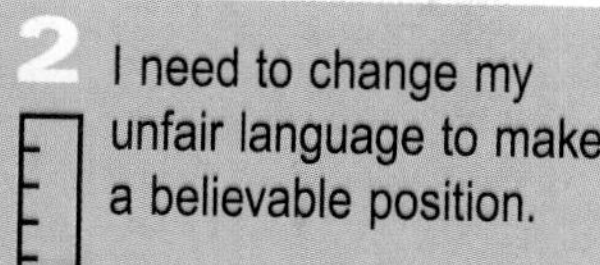

1 I need to learn what words are unfair and how to add qualifiers.

How can qualifiers make my writing more persuasive?

Qualifiers can make your writing more persuasive because they limit or "qualify" a statement. Few statements are *always* true for *everyone*. By adding a qualifier to a sentence, you can make your point or claim more believable.

Qualifiers

some	others	many	often	frequently
few	most	several	occasionally	usually

Read the following sentences. Rewrite each sentence and add a qualifier to make the claim more believable.

1. Students don't take responsibility for their own education.
2. Drivers are careless on the road behind the school.
3. Teachers don't attend the school productions.
4. Students don't care about the student council elections.
5. Parents ignore the parking rules.

Check your use of qualifiers. Review your essay, looking for sentences that need qualifiers to make your claims easier to believe.

Word Choice
A qualifier makes a claim more believable, and an unfair word is replaced.

In addition, the park would cost the city less than a new subdivision or strip mall. ~~People~~ Many people have ideas about ~~exploiting~~ developing Belmer Woods, but only a park would be best for the community.

Revising for Sentence Fluency

6 My sentences spark my reader's interest in my position.	**5** My sentences are skillfully written with varied beginnings.	**4** My sentences are complete, and most of the beginnings are varied.

To revise for *sentence fluency,* check to see that your sentences are complete and have varied beginnings. The rubric strip above will guide you.

How do I know if my sentences are complete?

Your sentences are complete if each one includes at least one subject and one predicate and expresses a complete thought. If a group of words is missing a subject, a predicate, or is not a complete thought, it is a fragment. (See pages **500–502**.)

Number your paper from 1 to 10. Read the following groups of words. If a group is a complete sentence, write an "S" after its number. If a group is a fragment, write an "F" after it. Rewrite any fragments to make them complete sentences.

1. The city should tear out the old railroad tracks and convert them into a bike path.
2. An exceptional idea.
3. Bike riders and joggers could reach the downtown with ease.
4. Would be a great way to stay in shape.
5. If the city wants to give citizens a new way to get around.
6. The trains currently go under all the major thoroughfares, so the route wouldn't stop traffic.
7. Giving people an alternative way to get to work or school.
8. Because gas prices continue to rise, bike riding and jogging are becoming more popular.
9. Although some people say that the old rail lines are too dirty for foot traffic.
10. Wish the city council would consider the proposal.

Review your sentences. Check the sentences in your essay and make sure that each contains at least one subject and one predicate. Revise any incomplete sentences.

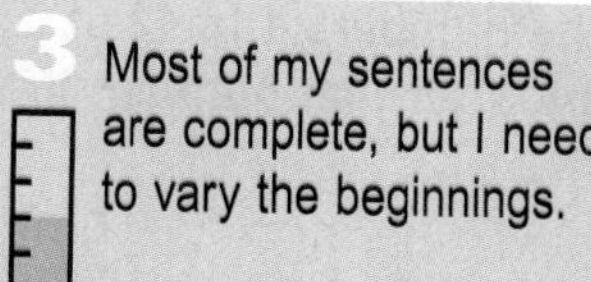

3 Most of my sentences are complete, but I need to vary the beginnings.

2 I have many incomplete sentences.

1 I need to learn what makes a sentence complete and how to vary the beginnings.

How can I vary my sentence beginnings?

If most of the sentences in a paragraph begin with a subject followed by a verb, you need to vary the beginnings. You can do so by adding a word, a phrase, or a clause. Note the difference between the following paragraphs.

Similar Beginnings

The school auditorium should be torn down and rebuilt. The roof leaks. The chairs are uncomfortable. People don't enjoy coming to our concerts. They might come if the auditorium were fixed.

Varied Beginnings

The school auditorium should be torn down and rebuilt. When it rains, the roof leaks. To make matters worse, the chairs are uncomfortable. People don't enjoy coming to our concerts. However, they might come if the auditorium were fixed.

Check your sentence beginnings. Read your essay, looking for places where your sentences all begin with a subject followed by a verb. In such places, revise by adding words, phrases, or clauses to some sentences.

Sentence Fluency
A sentence beginning is improved, and incomplete sentences are corrected.

Part of the forest could be saved, and
Earthmovers could dig out a pond. The grassy part on the north could remain. As a field for soccer or baseball. Making the land into a park would also help. To protect the environment. Nobody would be able to dump junk or car tires there anymore . . .

Revising Using a Checklist

Check your revising. On a piece of paper, write the numbers 1 to 12. If you can answer "yes" to a question, put a check mark after that number. If not, continue to work with that part of your essay.

Ideas

_____ **1.** Do I state my position clearly?
_____ **2.** Have I included reasons that support my position?
_____ **3.** Do I effectively respond to an objection?

Organization

_____ **4.** Does the overall structure of my essay work well?
_____ **5.** Are my reasons in the most persuasive order?
_____ **6.** Have I used transitions to help establish the order of importance?

Voice

_____ **7.** Are my facts and feelings balanced?
_____ **8.** Is my point of view consistent?

Word Choice

_____ **9.** Have I avoided unfair words?
_____ **10.** Have I used qualifiers to make my essay more persuasive?

Sentence Fluency

_____ **11.** Are all my sentences clear and complete?
_____ **12.** Do I vary my sentence beginnings?

Make a clean copy. When you've finished revising, make a clean copy before you edit. This makes checking for conventions easier.

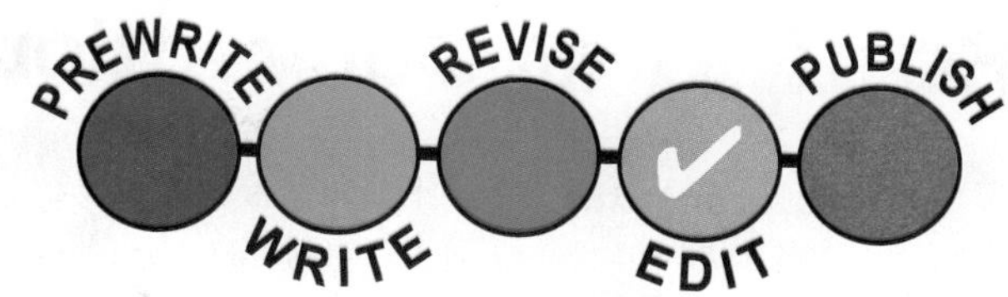

Editing

After you finish revising your essay, you are ready to edit for *conventions*: punctuation, capitalization, spelling, and grammar.

Keys to Effective Editing

1. Use a dictionary, a thesaurus, and the "Proofreader's Guide" in the back of this book.
2. Check for any words or phrases that may be confusing to the reader.
3. Check your writing for correctness of punctuation, capitalization, spelling, and grammar.
4. If you are using a computer, edit on a printed computer copy. Then enter your changes on the computer.
5. Use the editing and proofreading marks inside the back cover of this book.

Editing for Conventions

6 My essay is error free from start to finish.	**5** I have one or two errors, but they don't distract the reader.	**4** I need to correct the errors in my paper because they distract the reader.

When you edit for *conventions*, you need to pay attention to punctuation, grammar, capitalization, and spelling. These two pages will help you check your use of pronouns. The rubric strip above can guide your editing.

Do my pronouns agree with their antecedents?

Every pronoun has an antecedent. An antecedent is the noun (or pronoun) that a pronoun refers to or replaces. Pronouns and their antecedents must agree —both be singular or plural. (See pages 475–478.)

Pronoun agreement is especially tough with singular nouns that refer to people. It is incorrect to use a plural pronoun (*they, them, their*) after a singular noun (*student, teacher, parent*).

Incorrect **Every student should make sure they vote today.**
singular (student) *plural* (they)

Correct **Every student should make sure he or she votes today.**
singular (student) *singular* (he) *singular* (she)

(or) **Students should make sure they vote today.**
plural (Students) *plural* (they)

(or) **Every student should make sure to vote today.** (No pronoun)

GRAMMAR Try It Rewrite each sentence to correct pronoun-antecedent agreement.

1. No one should leave their litter in the empty lot.
2. Everyone should pick up their own trash.
3. Each student should be responsible for their own garbage.
4. A person who eats candy should put the wrapper in their pocket.
5. Every student should take pride in their school.

Check your pronouns and antecedents. Read your essay and make sure that your pronouns agree with their antecedents.

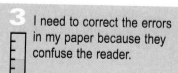

3 I need to correct the errors in my paper because they confuse the reader.

2 I need to correct the many errors because they make my essay difficult to read.

1 I need help making corrections.

How can I avoid creating a double subject?

You can avoid creating a double subject by making sure that you do not place a pronoun immediately after the subject of a sentence. (See page 510.)

Incorrect

Principal Jenson he **should support the mentoring program.**

Correct

Principal Jenson **should support the mentoring program.**

(or) He **should support the mentoring program.**

Rewrite each sentence to correct the double subject.

1. Students and teachers they need this mentoring program.
2. Ms. Dorn she will be the sponsor.
3. Students with special skills they will be the mentors.
4. Principal Jenson he should provide a work space.
5. Parents and students they should support this plan.

Check for double subjects. Read your essay and look for pronouns that immediately follow the subject. Correct any double subjects.

Conventions
A pronoun-antecedent agreement error is removed, and a double subject is corrected.

Nobody would be able to dump junk or car tires there anymore, ~~and they wouldn't be allowed to~~ or carve graffiti into the trees. A park ~~it~~ would both preserve and protect the environment.

PERSUASIVE

Editing Using a Checklist

Check your editing. On a piece of paper, write the numbers 1 to 12. If you can answer "yes" to a question, put a check mark after that number. If not, continue to edit for that convention.

Conventions

PUNCTUATION

_____ **1.** Do I use end punctuation after all my sentences?

_____ **2.** Do I use commas before coordinating conjunctions in compound sentences?

_____ **3.** Do I use a comma after a dependent clause at the beginning of a complex sentence?

_____ **4.** Do I leave out commas when a clause or phrase gives necessary information?

_____ **5.** Do I use quotation marks around direct quotations?

CAPITALIZATION

_____ **6.** Do I start all my sentences with capital letters?

_____ **7.** Do I capitalize all proper nouns and proper adjectives?

SPELLING

_____ **8.** Have I spelled all words correctly?

_____ **9.** Have I checked the words my spell-checker may have missed?

GRAMMAR

_____ **10.** Do my subjects and verbs agree in number? (She and I *are* going, not She and I *is* going.)

_____ **11.** Do my pronouns agree with their antecedents?

_____ **12.** Have I avoided double subjects?

Creating a Title

- Sum up the controversy: **Where Will the Woods Go?**
- Write a slogan: **Equal Rights for Young Shoppers!**
- Be creative: **Exploring the Halls of Education**

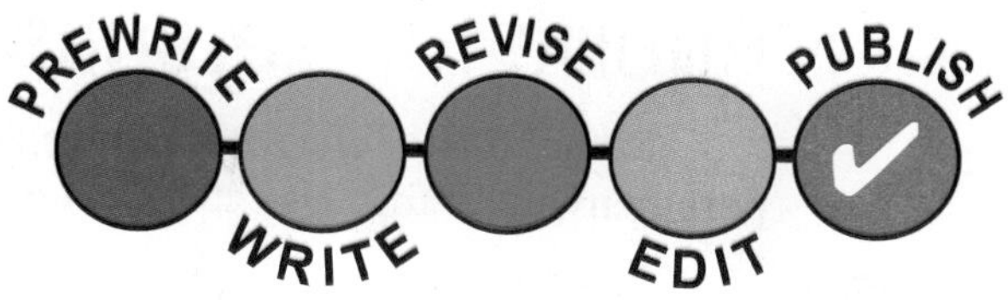

Publishing

Sharing Your Essay

After writing, revising, and editing your position essay, you'll want to make a neat final copy to share. You may also want to present your essay in a debate, publish it in a newspaper, or turn it into a speech.

Make a final copy. Follow your teacher's instructions or use the guidelines below to format your essay. (If you are using a computer, see page 60.) Create a clean final copy of your essay and carefully proofread it.

Focus on Presentation

- Use blue or black ink and write neatly.
- Write your name in the upper left corner of page 1.
- Skip a line and center your title; skip another line and start your writing.
- Indent every paragraph and leave a one-inch margin on all four sides.
- Write your last name and the page number in the upper right corner of every page after the first one.

Stage a Debate
Gather a group of classmates who have opposite opinions about the same issue. Stage a debate. Present your position, allow others to present theirs, and defend each position.

Create a Speech
Make your essay into a persuasive speech. (See pages 423–430.) Create visual aids that will help you get your point across. Then present your position to an audience that you want to persuade.

Publish in a Newspaper
Format your essay as a letter to the editor of your school or community newspaper. Check submission guidelines. Then send your work in.

Rubric for Persuasive Writing

Refer to the following rubric for guiding and assessing your persuasive writing. Use it to improve your writing using the six traits.

Ideas

6	5	4
The writer's position is very well defended and compels the reader to act.	The essay has a clear position or opinion statement. Persuasive reasons support the writer's position.	The position statement is clear, and most reasons support the writer's position.

Organization

6	5	4
All the parts of the essay work together to build a thoughtful, convincing position.	The opening contains the position statement. The middle provides clear support. The ending reinforces the position.	The opening contains the position statement. The middle provides support. The ending needs work.

Voice

6	5	4
The writer's voice is confident, positive, and convincing.	The writer's voice is confident and persuasive.	The writer's voice is confident, but it may not be persuasive enough.

Word Choice

6	5	4
The writer's choice of words makes a powerful case.	The writer's word choice helps persuade the reader.	Some changes would make the word choice more persuasive.

Sentence Fluency

6	5	4
The sentences spark the reader's interest in the essay.	Variety is seen in both the types of sentences and their beginnings.	Varied sentence beginnings are used. Sentence variety would make the essay more interesting to read.

Conventions

6	5	4
The writing is error free.	Grammar and punctuation errors are few. The reader is not distracted by the errors.	Grammar and punctuation errors are seen in a few sentences. They distract the reader in those areas.

3 The position statement may be clear. More persuasive reasons are needed.	2 The position statement is unclear. Persuasive reasons are needed.	1 A new position statement and reasons are needed.
3 The beginning has an opinion statement. The middle and ending need more work.	2 The beginning, middle, and ending run together.	1 The organization is unclear and incomplete.
3 The writer's voice needs to be more confident and persuasive.	2 The writer's voice rambles on without any confidence.	1 The writer has not considered voice.
3 Many more precise and persuasive words are needed.	2 The words do not create a clear message. Some unfair words are used.	1 Word choice has not been considered.
3 Varied sentence beginnings are needed. Sentence variety would make the essay more interesting.	2 Most sentences begin the same way. Most of the sentences are simple. Compound and complex sentences are needed.	1 Sentence fluency has not been established. Ideas do not flow smoothly.
3 There are a number of errors that may confuse the reader.	2 Frequent errors make the essay difficult to read.	1 Nearly every sentence contains errors.

Evaluating a Persuasive Essay

Read the position essay that follows and focus on its strengths and its weaknesses. Then read the student self-assessment on the next page. **(The student essay below contains some errors.)**

Service with a Smile

Delacor high schoolers don't graduate unless they have 40 hours of service learning. Now, some people are saying that middle schoolers should do service learning, too. That program works fine for high schoolers, but it wouldn't work in the middle school.

First of all, middle-school kids can't drive. It would be hard to get to the nursing home or the Humane Society. Most moms and dads already "taxi" their kids all over the place. Many of the places kids would need to get to are too far away to walk to, and too dangerous to ride a bike to. Transportation would be tough.

Middle school students are already busy. It takes time to get ready for school, time to get to school, and almost seven hours at school. Once they're home, they could have two hours of homework staring at them. Then its time for dinner, then piano practice and chores for another hour. Now, if a student gets eight hours sleep, that leaves just a couple hours to do other things. Kids certainly need a couple hours a day for themselves.

Most importantly, community service works best when it is voluntary. Already many middle school students volunteer to march in the Hope Walk for cancer research or to go door to door collecting food for the homeless. They learned the value of community service not because they were required to do it, but because they were inspired to do it.

Parents say kids aren't learning to be responsible. Actually, when those same parents were young, they didn't have to do service learning even in high school. Somehow they learned to be responsible.

Service learning works great in the high school, but it wouldn't work for middle school. Middle school students should volunteer rather than be required to serve.

Student Self-Assessment

The assessment that follows includes the student's comments about his essay on page 258. In the first comment, the student mentions something good about the essay. In the second comment, the student points out an area for possible improvement. (The writer used the rubric and number scale on pages 256–257 to complete this assessment.)

4 Ideas

1. *I have a clear position, and I support it pretty well.*
2. *Some of my ideas sound too negative.*

4 Organization

1. *I've organized my paper just the way I was supposed to.*
2. *Transitions might have helped.*

3 Voice

1. *My voice is strong.*
2. *I sound a little too emotional sometimes, and my point of view shifts.*

3 Word Choice

1. *I use pretty good words throughout.*
2. *If I used more qualifiers, my writing could sound more persuasive.*

4 Sentence Fluency

1. *All of my sentences are complete.*
2. *A little more variety could have made them better.*

4 Conventions

1. *I checked grammar, punctuation, and spelling pretty closely.*
2. *I still have problems with pronoun-antecedent agreement.*

Use the rubric. Assess your essay using the rubric on pages 256–257.

1. On your own paper, list the six traits. Leave room after each trait to write at least one strength and one weakness.
2. Then choose a number (from 1 to 6) that shows how well you think you used each trait.

Reflecting on Your Writing

Take some time to reflect on the position essay you have just completed. On your own paper, finish each starter sentence below. Your thoughts will help you prepare for your next writing assignment.

My Position Essay

1. *The strength of my essay is . . .*
2. *The part that still needs work is . . .*
3. *The prewriting activity that worked best for me was . . .*
4. *The main thing I learned about writing a position essay is . . .*
5. *In my next position essay, I would like to . . .*
6. *Here is one question I still have about writing a position essay:*

Persuasive Writing

Creating a Personal Commentary

Everyone is unique. Each person has a one-of-a-kind personality and a special way of looking at life. Even identical twins have their own viewpoints to share with the world.

In a personal commentary, a writer can express his or her personal views. News programs often provide commentaries about politics, the economy, or current events; but a commentary can deal with just about any aspect of life.

On the next few pages, you'll read a student's personal commentary about what she has learned from playing violin. Then you will learn to write a commentary of your own.

Writing Guidelines

Subject: A reflective look at life
Form: Personal commentary
Purpose: To state your personal view
Audience: Classmates

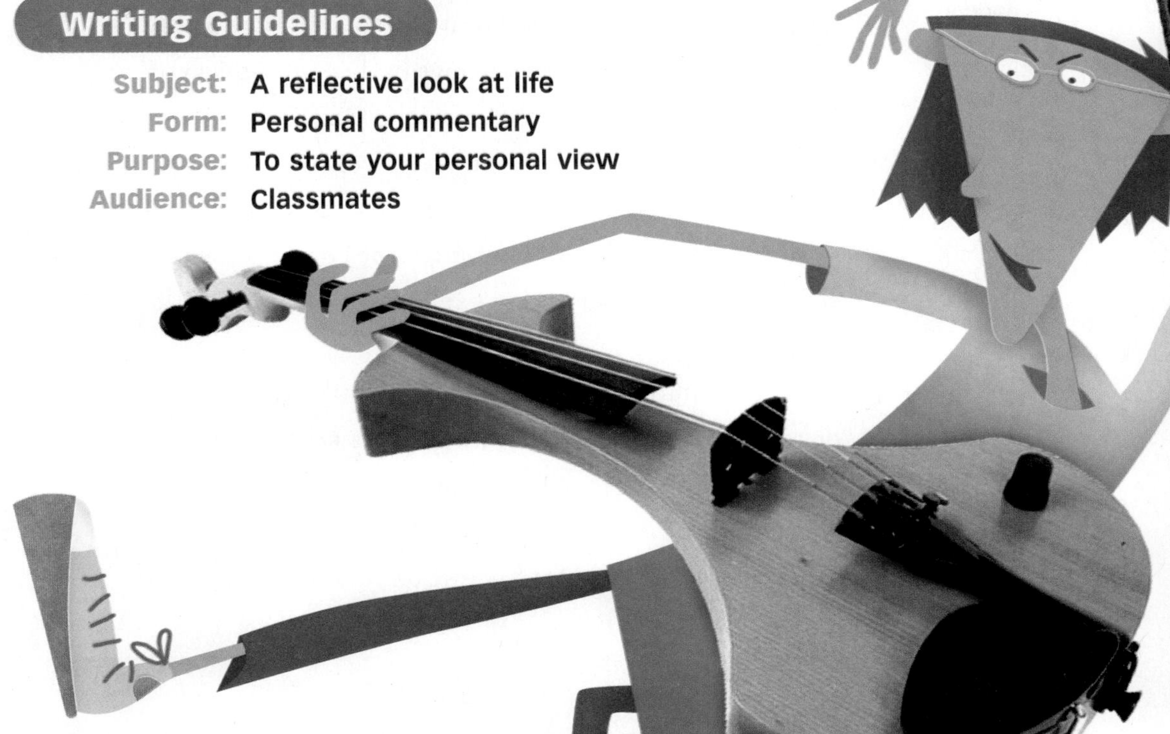

Personal Commentary

A personal commentary expresses your unique view of some aspect of life. In the commentary that follows, Aimee tells how music has taught her some important lessons about life, lessons that the whole world should learn.

Beginning
The topic is introduced, and the personal view is given (**underlined**).

Middle
The middle paragraphs support the writer's viewpoint.

Music Teaches Harmony

Some people think music is just a hobby that doesn't have any value in real life. After all, how often does a person need to know how to read notes? To me, though, music teaches some of the most important lessons of life. <u>Music teaches me how to work hard while staying in harmony with others.</u>

My experience with music began with hard work. When I was eight years old, I took my first violin lesson. It was frustrating because I didn't even get to use a real violin! Sometimes I wanted to give up, but my mom kept telling me, "Someday you'll be able to play any kind of music you want on your violin. But to reach that day, you have to keep practicing." I did keep practicing, and hard work has rewarded me. Now, whenever I have to learn something hard, I know I have to stick with it until the job is done.

Performing music brings me together with people. I'll never forget the day I joined the middle school orchestra. The sound of everyone tuning up was music to my ears! As I played the notes in front of me, I looked around at all the other people playing along. Our bows and fingers moved

Writing Tips

Before you write . . .

- **Select an issue that you care about.**
  Think about problems or issues in your school or community. Choose a topic that you feel strongly about.
- **Do your research.**
  Gather facts and details that will help you explain the topic to readers. Use the information to come up with a realistic solution.

During your writing . . .

- **State your opinion.**
  Explain the problem and why you are concerned about it.
- **Support your opinion.**
  Back up your argument with the facts from your research. Address opposing points of view. Then offer a solution.
- **Restate your opinion and call for action.**
  Ask readers to get involved.

After you've written a first draft . . .

- **Review your argument.**
  Make sure that your opinion is clear and well supported.
- **Check your facts.**
  Read your editorial carefully to make sure your facts are correct.
- **Check for conventions.**
  Correct any errors in punctuation, capitalization, spelling, and grammar.

Create your own editorial on a current issue by using the tips above. Then submit your editorial to your school paper or a local newspaper.

Math: Developing a Statistical Argument

A statistical argument uses numbers to prove the value of something. For the following assignment, a student used statistics to decide which pack of blended fruit drinks provides a better value.

The **beginning** sets up the problem.

The **middle** provides statistics and equations.

The **ending** gives the solution.

Get the Best Value

Which pack of blended fruit drinks gives a better value for the money?

* a 12-pack of 12-ounce cans that costs $3.95
* a 6-pack of 16.9-ounce bottles that costs $2.50

First, one must find out how many ounces are in each pack. To do this, a person should multiply the ounces per can or bottle by the number of cans or bottles in a pack.

Ounces per can/bottle	x	Number of cans/bottles	=	Total ounces
12	x	12 cans	=	144
16.9	x	6 bottles	=	101.4

Then a person should find the price per ounce by taking the total price for each pack and dividing it by the total number of ounces.

Total price	÷	Total ounces	=	Price per ounce
$3.95	÷	144	=	.027
$2.50	÷	101.4	=	.025

So, on an ounce-by-ounce basis, the 6-pack of larger bottles is cheaper. The 12-pack costs a little more per ounce, but if the juice is for school lunches, the smaller cans may avoid waste and allow individual servings. So value depends partly on use.

Writing Tips

Before you write . . .

- **Begin by asking a "value" question.**
  Ask a question about the value of something. For example, which package of dog food gives the best value, or which amusement park provides the best value for the entertainment dollar.
- **Plan your steps.**
  Make a list of steps and equations that you need to follow to answer the value question. Check your equations and answers for accuracy.

During your writing . . .

- **Introduce the question.**
  Begin your paper by indicating what question your argument will address.
- **Provide statistics.**
  Let readers know the facts and figures you will be using to argue your point.
- **Show the process step-by-step.**
  Write the equations you use to make your statistical argument. Lead readers through each step.
- **Interpret the statistics.**
  End by telling readers what the statistics mean.

After you've written a first draft . . .

- **Check for completeness.**
  Make sure you haven't left out important variables and steps.
- **Check for correctness.**
  Fix any errors in math, punctuation, capitalization, spelling, or grammar.

Write your own statistical argument. Choose a question of value that you can argue using statistics. Then lead your readers through the equations needed to argue your point.

Science: Creating a Persuasive Graph

A graph can quickly persuade readers about a problem. The following graph shows the increase in automobile pollution since 1998.

The **beginning** introduces the graph.

Absolutely Exhausted

Although the United States produces more carbon dioxide (the greenhouse gas CO_2) than any other country, China will soon produce more according to the Environmental Protection Agency. In the United States, total gasoline CO_2 emissions have risen by 9% since 1998.

The **middle** presents the figures visually.

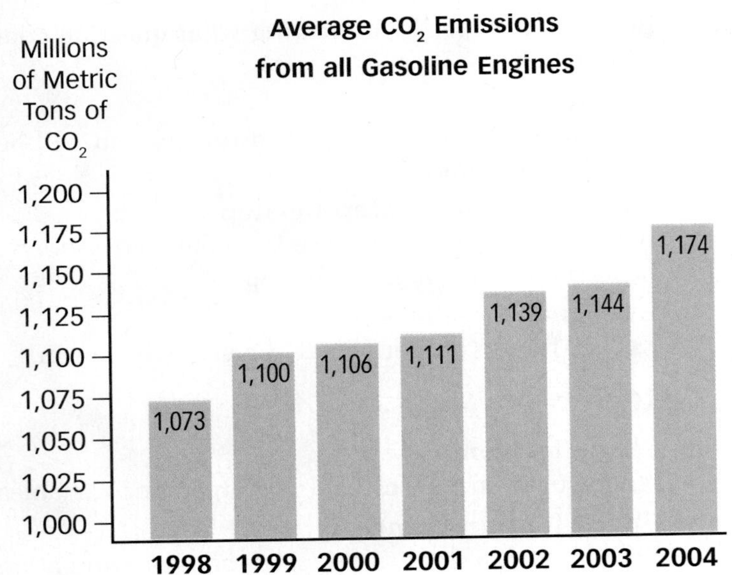

The **ending** provides the student's call to action.

This bar graph shows the increase in carbon dioxide gases per year from all gasoline engines since 1998. Carpooling, using less air conditioning, and walking are some simple ways to reduce emissions.

Writing Tips

Before you write . . .

- **Select a topic.**
  Think about a science issue that involves numbers: water quality, food production, or weather patterns, for example. Select a topic you care about and state your position about it.
- **Research your topic.**
  Find out the facts and figures behind the issue. Decide which facts would make the most persuasive graph.
- **Choose a type of graph.**
  Select a type that works best to present your argument. (See page 575 for different types of graphs.) Make sure you have all the facts you need.

During your writing . . .

- **Introduce your topic and your argument.**
  Write one or two brief paragraphs that put the facts in perspective.
- **Draw your graph.**
  Lay out your graph so that the information is clear.
- **Provide your viewpoint.**
  Sum up the figures in a persuasive way.

After you've written a first draft . . .

- **Check for completeness.**
  Make sure that you included all the necessary details and facts to support your argument. Ask another student to look at your graph to see if it is easy to understand.
- **Check for conventions.**
  Correct any errors in punctuation, capitalization, spelling, and grammar.

Pick a science issue that you care about and that includes statistics (numbers). Gather information about it and create a persuasive graph that demonstrates your position.

Practical Writing:
Drafting a Business Letter

Sometimes the best way to make a change in your school or community is to write a persuasive letter. In the following letter to his principal, Alex Hastings asks for lights on a soccer field.

The letter follows the correct format. (See pages **276–277**.)

1080 Burns Road
Orange Park, FL 32000
May 5, 2011

Principal Joseph Rodriguez
Greenberg Middle School
116 Shelton Street
Orange Park, FL 32000

Dear Mr. Rodriguez:

The **beginning** introduces the issue and asks a question.

As a soccer team member at Greenberg Middle School, I have a suggestion. We need lights for nighttime games. When school starts in the fall, it gets darker earlier and earlier. It's hard for our teams to finish games safely.

The **body** of the letter uses details to persuade the reader.

I realize that lighting is expensive. However, a lighted field could be used by the whole community, so the community could help pay for it. The soccer team could even run a citywide fund-raiser.

The **closing** includes a polite call to action.

Adding lights to our soccer field would make a huge difference for my teammates and me. Please make the request at the next school board meeting.

Sincerely,

Alex Hastings

Alex Hastings

Writing Tips

Use the following tips as a guide when you are asked to write a persuasive letter. (Also see pages 276–277.)

Before you write . . .

- **Choose a topic that you care about.**
  Make a list of problems in your school or community and think of possible solutions. Choose a problem that is important to you.
- **Gather information.**
  Learn as much as you can about the problem. Find facts to support your solution.
- **Consider your reader.**
  Determine what the person you are writing to needs to know.

During your writing . . .

- **Keep it short.**
  Make your point quickly and stay focused on the main idea. Your letter should not be longer than one page.
- **State the problem and your solution.**
  Explain why the situation exists and how it can be fixed.
- **Be polite.**
  Use a courteous voice to persuade the reader.

After you've written a first draft . . .

- **Check for completeness.**
  Make sure you did not leave out any important facts or reasons.
- **Check for correctness.**
  Read your letter several times. Double-check the address and spelling of all names. Correct any errors in punctuation, capitalization, spelling, and grammar.

Think of a problem in your school or community. Find out who can help solve it. Write a persuasive letter to that person or organization and make a strong but polite argument. (You may send the letter or simply treat it as a school assignment.)

Parts of a Business Letter

1. The **heading** includes your address and the date. Write the heading at least one inch from the top of the page at the left-hand margin.

2. The **inside address** includes the name and address of the person or organization you are writing to.
   - If the person has a title, be sure to include it. (If the title is short, write it on the same line as the name. If the title is long, write it on the next line.)
   - If you are writing to an organization or a business—but not to a specific person—begin the inside address with the name of the organization or business.

3. The **salutation** is the greeting. Always put a colon after the salutation.
   - If you know the person's name, use it in your greeting.

     Dear Mr. Christopher:
   - If you don't know the name of the person who will read your letter, use a salutation like one of these:

     Dear Store Owner:
     Dear Sir or Madam:
     Dear Madison Soccer Club:

4. The **body** is the main part of the letter. Do not indent the paragraphs in your letter; instead, skip a line after each one.

5. The **closing** comes after the body. Use **Yours truly** or **Sincerely** to close a business letter. Capitalize only the first word of the closing and put a comma after the closing.

6. The **signature** ends the letter. If you are using a computer, leave four spaces after the closing; then type your name. Write your signature in the space between the closing and the typed name.

See page 577 for more about writing letters as well as a set of guidelines for addressing envelopes properly.

Business-Letter Format

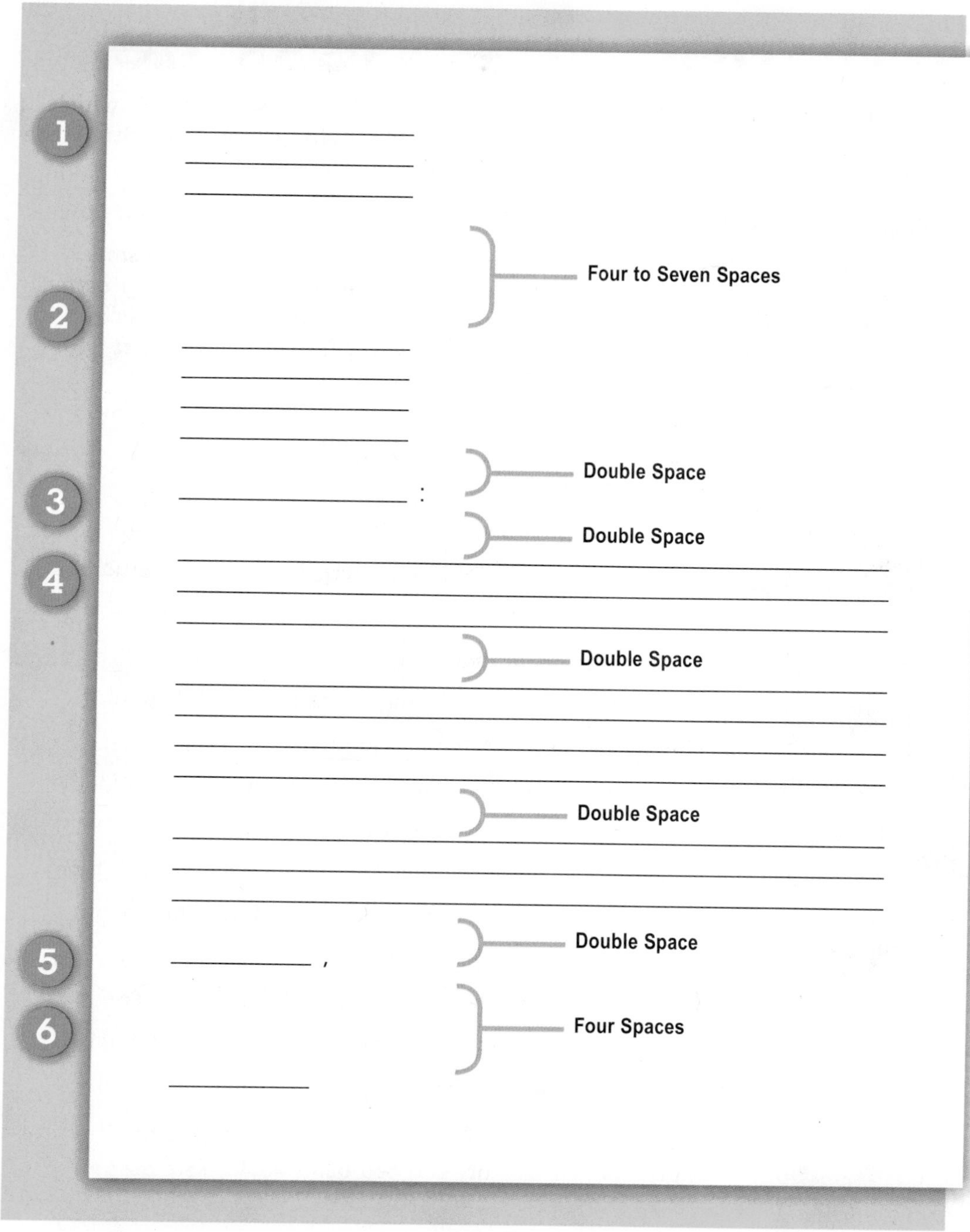

1

Four to Seven Spaces

2

Double Space

3 :

Double Space

4

Double Space

Double Space

Double Space

5 ,

6

Four Spaces

Persuasive Writing

Writing for Assessment

Many state and school writing tests contain a persuasive prompt, which asks you to state an opinion and support it with convincing reasons. Study the following sample prompt and student response.

Persuasive Prompt

A group of parents and students has asked the administration to start school one hour later. This group feels that students would perform better if school started later. Do you feel the start time should stay as it is or be changed? In an essay, state your position on this issue, support it with reasons, and defend it against an objection.

Response to a Persuasive Prompt

The **beginning** states the writer's position (**underlined**).

Some parents and students have complained that Willis Middle School starts too early. They say that students aren't awake enough at 7:30 a.m. to learn well. Because of this, they want to move the start time to 8:30 a.m. The starting time should not change because the shift would create more problems than it would solve.

Each **middle** paragraph gives reasons that support the opinion.

First of all, a later start would help only some students. Many students happen to be morning people. Moving the schedule would not help them learn better or improve their test scores. In fact, for these students, a later start might actually have the opposite effect.

For that matter, a later start would mean a later release, and that would cause problems for after-school activities. The coaches for football, basketball, and track would have an hour less for practice. The teachers who lead drama, chess club, and pep band would also lose an hour. In addition, every student would have an hour less for homework before supper.

The most important reason to keep the 7:30 a.m. start time is that a change would cause problems for the whole community. If middle school starts an hour later, high school would have to as well because of busing. High schoolers need even more time after school because of varsity sports and jobs. Some working parents also would struggle with a later start. Many parents drop off their kids by 7:30 a.m. and start work by 8:00 a.m. Their morning schedules would be much harder with an 8:30 start.

The **final middle** paragraph answers an objection.

Some people say a later start would help keep students from falling asleep during first hour. That may be true, but more students fall asleep after lunch. Shifting the school day ahead an hour would not get rid of the problem of sleepy students.

The **ending** restates the position and its supporting reasons.

A later start time at Willis Middle School would help only some students and would create problems for others. The shift would probably not end sleepiness in the classroom. For all these reasons, the Willis Middle School start time should stay right where it is.

Respond to the reading. Answer the following questions about the sample response.

- ☐ **Ideas** (1) What is the writer's position? (2) What reasons does he give?
- ☐ **Organization** (3) Where does the writer answer an objection?
- ☐ **Voice & Word Choice** (4) What words from the prompt also appear in the essay?

Writing Tips

Before you write . . .

- **Understand the prompt.**
  Remember that a persuasive prompt asks you to state and support an opinion.
- **Plan your response.**
  Spend a few minutes planning before you start to write. Use a graphic organizer (table diagram) as a guide.

Table Diagram

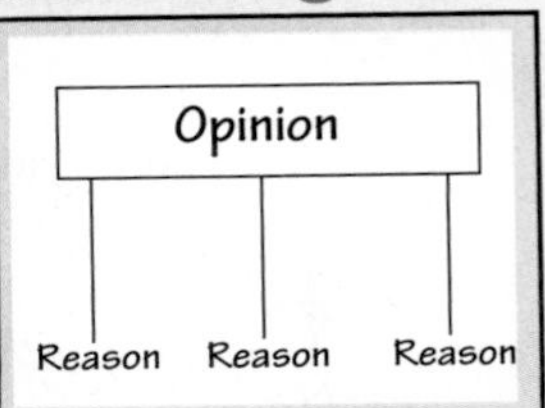

During your writing . . .

- **Share an opinion statement.**
  Think of an opinion that you can clearly support.
- **Build your argument.**
  Think of reasons that support your opinion.
- **End effectively.**
  Explain what you would like to see done.

After you've written a first draft . . .

- **Check for clear ideas.**
  Rewrite any ideas that sound confusing.
- **Check for conventions.**
  Correct errors in punctuation, capitalization, spelling, and grammar.

Persuasive Prompts

- If you could change one rule at your school, what would it be? Write a letter to your school board asking for a school rule to be changed. Make sure to give reasons why the change should happen and answer a possible objection to your idea.
- Your parent or guardian is planning a big vacation. Where would you most like to go? Write an essay proposing a trip you would like to take and indicate why it would be the best choice for your family.

Plan and write a response. Respond to one of the prompts above. Complete your writing within the period of time your teacher gives you. Afterward, list one part that you like and one part that could have been better.

Persuasive Writing in Review

Purpose: In persuasive writing, you work to *convince people* to think the way you do about something.

Topics: Persuade readers . . . to agree with your opinion or position,
to take an action,
to support a cause, or
to solve a problem.

Prewriting

Select a topic that you care about, one that you can present confidently and that is appropriate for your audience. (See page 228.)

Gather ideas about your topic. (See pages 229–230.)

Write a position statement that identifies your opinion. (See page 231.)

Organize your ideas in a list or an outline with your position statement at the top, followed by topic sentences with supporting facts or details beneath each. (See page 232.)

Writing

In the beginning, grab the reader's attention and clearly state your position. (See page 235.)

In the middle part, devote a paragraph to each reason; include supporting facts and examples. Address an objection to your position. (See pages 236–237 and 241.)

In the ending, restate your position and sum up your reasons for it. (See page 238.)

Revising

Review the ideas, organization, and voice first. Next check for **word choice** and **sentence fluency.** Avoid unfair words. Use a confident voice and a variety of sentence structures. (See pages 240–250.)

Editing

Check your writing for conventions. Ask a friend to edit the writing, too. (See pages 252–254.)

Make a final copy and proofread it for errors before sharing it with your audience. (See page 255.)

Assessing

Use the persuasive rubric as a guide to assess your finished writing. (See pages 256–257.)

experience
answer

Response to Literature

Writing Focus

- Paragraph Response
- Analyzing a Theme
- Writing a Letter to an Author

Grammar Focus

- Commas to Set Off Words and Phrases
- Punctuating Dialogue

Academic Vocabulary

Work with a partner. Read the meanings and share answers to the questions.

1. When you study something carefully, you **analyze** it.
   What might you analyze in science class?
2. To **express** an idea, you tell about it in words.
   How could you express your feelings about school?

evaluate
REACT
preview

Response to Literature

Paragraph Response

Just as the ABC's are the building blocks of words, paragraphs are the building blocks of essays. Once you can write solid paragraphs about literature, you'll be better prepared to write whole essays about the poems, stories, and novels that you read.

On the next page, you will read a sample paragraph that responds to Langston Hughes's poem, "The Kids in School with Me." It deals with learning the fundamentals of life—not just the ABC's. Then you will write a paragraph response about a short story or poem you have read recently.

Writing Guidelines

Subject: A short story or poem
Form: Paragraph
Purpose: To respond to the theme
Audience: Classmates

Paragraph Response

When you write a paragraph about a short story or poem you've read, you may be asked to focus on a theme. The **topic sentence** identifies the story, the author, and the theme. The **body sentences** explain the theme, and the **closing sentence** tells something important about it. In the following response, Mark writes about the theme of diversity in "The Kids in School with Me," a poem by Langston Hughes.

Topic Sentence

Body

Closing Sentence

"The Kids in School with Me"

In the poem "The Kids in School with Me," Langston Hughes dreams about a school where diversity would be appreciated. The poet describes kids in a classroom. The students have dark skin, freckles, black hair, or other features. Some kids are from different countries around the world, including Russia, China, Poland, Spain, and Greece. Although every student is unique in some way, they are all in the classroom together. Together they study reading and math. All of them work toward graduation, and their motto is "One for All and All for One!" This poem says that if people could only look past color and race, all students would just be kids in school.

Respond to the reading. On your own paper, answer each of the following questions.

- ☐ Ideas **(1) What theme in the poem does the writer think is most important?**
- ☐ Organization **(2) How does the topic sentence introduce the theme? (3) How does the closing sentence sum up the theme?**
- ☐ Voice & Word Choice **(4) Does the writer sound knowledgeable about the poem? Explain.**

Prewriting Selecting a Topic

Your first step in writing a response to literature is choosing a short story or poem to write about. Mark began by listing some of his favorites.

Topic List

"Raymond's Run" by Toni Cade Bambara

"The Kids in School with Me" by Langston Hughes *

"Mr. Misenheimer's Garden" by Charles Kuralt

Choose a short story or poem. Make a list of your favorite short stories or poems. Place a star (*) next to the one that interests you most.

Finding a Theme

A theme is the lesson about life in a piece of literature. The details in a story or poem are clues to the themes. Mark began his search for a theme by listing details from the poem. Then he reviewed the details and listed some possible themes.

Theme Chart

Details	*Themes*
- *America* - *students from around the world* - *different hair, eyes, smiles, skin colors* - *studying together* - *"One for All and All for One!"* - *public school* - *Polish, Greek, Russian, Chinese*	*getting along* *learning together* *appreciating diversity* *

List details and themes. Create a list of details from the short story or poem you have chosen. Beside it, list themes that relate to those details. Finally, choose one theme to write about.

Writing Creating Your First Draft

A paragraph has three main parts: a topic sentence, the body, and a closing sentence. The following tips will help you create each part.

- **Topic sentence:** Write a sentence that names the short story or poem, its author, and the theme you will focus on.
- **Body:** Write sentences that explain the theme using examples from the piece of literature.
- **Closing sentence:** End with a sentence that sums up the theme.

Write the first draft of your paragraph. Use the tips above as you write your response paragraph.

Revising Improving Your Paragraph

After you've written your first draft, you need to revise your paragraph to improve on your *ideas, organization, voice, word choice,* and *sentence fluency.*

Review your paragraph. Use the following questions as a guide to your revision.

1. Have I written about one important theme?
2. Do my sentences appear in the best order?
3. Does my interest in the story or poem show in my voice?
4. Have I used some of the same words the author used?
5. Do my sentences flow smoothly?

Editing Checking for Conventions

Next, check your paragraph for *conventions.*

Edit your work. Use the following questions to guide your editing.

1. Have I checked my punctuation, capitalization, and spelling?
2. Have I used the right words (to, two, too)?

Proofread your paragraph. After you make a neat copy of your final paragraph, check it one more time for errors.

Response to Literature

Analyzing a Theme

A great work of art is more than just paint on canvas. A masterpiece gives viewers a reason to stop and stare and get lost in the painting. It has depth and meaning.

When people talk about the depth and meaning of a piece of literature, they are referring to the literature's theme. Theme is the lesson that a book or story teaches the reader about life. In this chapter, you will write an essay that examines how the theme develops through the characters and events in a piece of literature.

Writing Guidelines

Subject: A novel or a story
Form: Essay
Purpose: To analyze a theme
Audience: Classmates

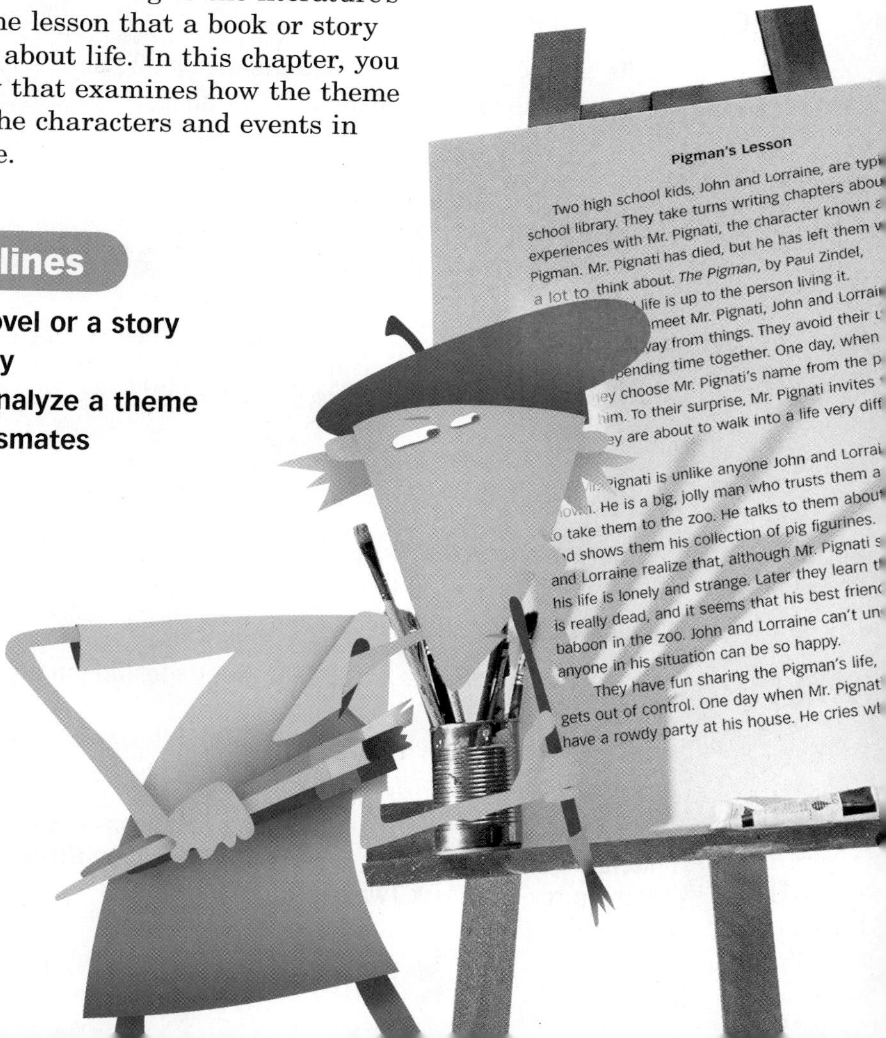

Understanding Your Goal

Your essay on a theme should explain the lesson or main idea of a story. A theme can usually be expressed as a statement about life. The chart below lists the key traits in a response to literature, with specific suggestions for this assignment.

Traits of a Response to Literature

Ideas

Write a focus statement that explains your interpretation of the theme and then select details to support that statement.

Organization

Write an opening that includes the theme, the book's title, and the author. Close with the theme's importance.

Voice

Make your writing sound natural and create a mood appropriate for the novel or story.

Word Choice

Use literary terms and words that your audience can understand and relate to.

Sentence Fluency

Write sentences that flow smoothly.

Conventions

Correct all punctuation, capitalization, spelling, and grammar errors.

Literature Connections: For an example of a student's response to literature, read "Fancy is Funnier Than Fact" by Ramon Cepero. In this piece, Ramon reviews Mark Twain's *Roughing It.*

Response Essay

The novel *The Pigman* tells about two high school students who meet an unusual man named Mr. Pignati. A student who read the book wrote this essay about the theme of the story.

Beginning
The beginning introduces the book and focuses on the theme (**underlined**).

Pigman's Lesson

Two high school kids, John and Lorraine, are typing in the school library. They take turns writing chapters about their experiences with Mr. Pignati, the character known as the Pigman. Mr. Pignati has died, but he has left them with a lot to think about. *The Pigman,* by Paul Zindel, shows that people make their own happiness.

Before they meet Mr. Pignati, John and Lorraine seem to be running away from things. They avoid their unhappy homes by spending time together. One day, when they are bored, they choose Mr. Pignati's name from the phone book and call him. To their surprise, Mr. Pignati invites them to his house. They are about to walk into a life very different from their own.

Middle
Each middle paragraph explains a different stage in the development of the theme.

Mr. Pignati is unlike anyone John and Lorraine have ever known. He is a big, jolly man who trusts them and offers to take them to the zoo. He talks to them about his wife and shows them his collection of pig figurines. Slowly, John and Lorraine realize that, although Mr. Pignati seems happy, his life is lonely and strange. Later they learn that his wife is really dead, and it seems that his best friend is Bobo, a baboon in the zoo. John and Lorraine can't understand how anyone in his situation can be so happy.

They have fun sharing the Pigman's life, but then the fun gets out of control. One day when Mr. Pignati is gone, they have a rowdy party at his house. He cries when he sees the damage and calls the police. John and Lorraine are ashamed that they have been disloyal to him, and they offer to pay for the damages. They also arrange to meet Mr. Pignati at the zoo. The two kids want to get back the happiness that they have lost.

Middle
The last middle paragraph covers the final stage in the development of the theme.

The trip to the zoo is a disaster. First of all, they discover that Bobo has died. The shock causes Mr. Pignati to collapse on the floor of the monkey house. Lorraine backs away, unable to handle what has happened. John stays with Mr. Pignati, who dies of a heart attack. John is deeply moved by Mr. Pignati's death. He is bothered by the thought that "it's possible to end your life with only a baboon to talk to."

Ending
The ending paragraph revisits the theme.

Lorraine feels extremely guilty about the way they took advantage of Mr. Pignati. John feels bad, too, but he has learned a valuable lesson. Before, he had spent too much time getting back at people. But because of Mr. Pignati's kindness, John realizes that leading a better life is completely up to him. As he states at the end of the story, "Our life would be what we made of it—nothing more, nothing less."

Respond to the reading. **Answer the following questions about the sample response to literature.**

- ☐ **Ideas** **(1) Which quotation in the essay means the same thing as the underlined theme in the first paragraph? (2) Which character seems to understand this theme?**
- ☐ **Organization** **(3) Are the steps in the theme's development in time order or order of importance?**
- ☐ **Voice & Word Choice** **(4) Does the writer sound knowledgeable about the book? Explain.**

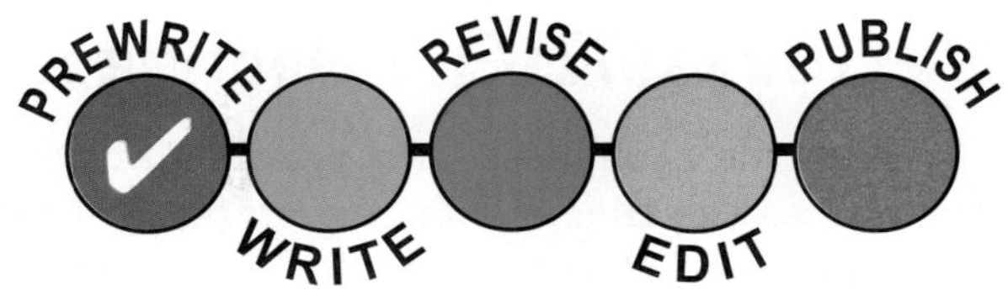

Prewriting

The first step in the writing process is prewriting. Begin by thinking about books and stories you have read recently and their themes.

Keys to Effective Prewriting

1. Select an interesting book or story that you have recently read.
2. Identify the main theme in the story.
3. Find the key stages in the development of the theme.
4. Write a clear focus statement for your essay.
5. Decide on an order of information for your middle paragraphs.
6. Write a topic sentence for each of the middle paragraphs.

PROD. NO. TAKE ROLL SCENE SOUND DATE

Prewriting Selecting a Topic

A theme is the lesson or main idea that an author expresses to the reader. Sometimes the theme is openly stated in the story, but more often it is not. Here are some places to look for clues about the theme:

- The title of the story ("Among the Brave")
- Statements about life ("Maybe we are too busy being flowers . . . instead of something worthy of respect . . . like being real people.")
- The lessons that the characters learn (John realizes that leading a better life is completely up to him.)

Think about the lessons or main ideas in the stories you have read recently. List the titles and themes of the ones that hold the most meaning for you.

Topics Chart

1. The Call of the Wild teaches you that only the strong survive.

* 2. "Raymond's Run" is about a runner who finds out what is really important in life.

3. The three children in To Kill a Mockingbird learn that prejudging people is wrong.

Reason:

* *I will write about "Raymond's Run" because we sometimes focus too much on the things in life that shouldn't really matter.*

Choose your topic. Put a star next to the story that you would like to write about. Under the list, explain the reason for your choice.

Focus on the Traits

Ideas Thinking about the characters and what they do can often help you understand the theme. Pay special attention to the main characters for clues to the author's most important ideas about life.

Gathering Details

Now that you have selected a story and a theme, you should think about how the theme develops. By reviewing the key thoughts, feelings, and actions of the main character, you can chart important stages in the development of the theme. The sample chart below is for the essay on pages 297–300.

Theme Chart

Title: *"Raymond's Run"*

Theme: *Winning isn't the most important thing in life.*

First Stage: The theme in the early part of the story

Squeaky thinks that winning the May Day race again will make her important, but she doesn't think that taking care of her brother Raymond is anything special.

Middle Stages: Important developments that follow the first stage

As the race day approaches, Squeaky concentrates so hard on training that she thinks the only way she can be successful is to win.

On the day of the race, Squeaky loses her concentration because she suddenly realizes that Raymond is kneeling down and getting ready to run, too.

Final Stage: The last stage of the theme's development

Squeaky is confused as she crosses the finish line because she realizes that something has become more important to her than winning.

Chart your theme. Write the theme at the top of a chart like the one above. Then identify three or more stages in the story that help develop or show the theme. Under each stage, list some of the main character's thoughts, feelings, and actions at that time.

Prewriting Writing a Focus Statement

Now that you have identified the main character and the stages in the development of the theme, you are ready to write your focus statement.

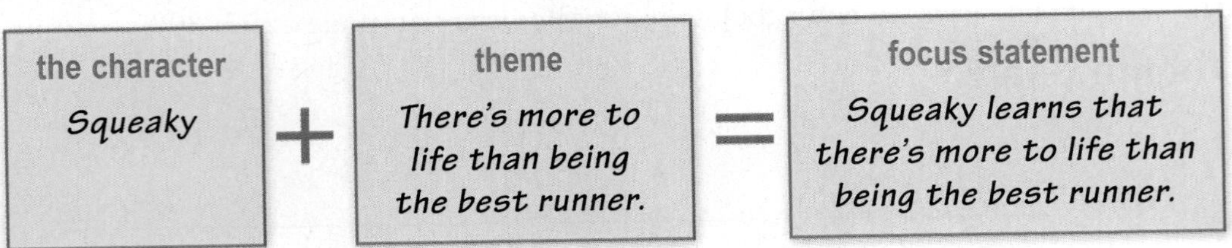
the character
Squeaky
+
theme
There's more to life than being the best runner.
=
focus statement
Squeaky learns that there's more to life than being the best runner.

Prewrite

Form a focus. Write a focus statement for your analysis of a theme using the formula above.

Organizing the Middle Paragraphs of Your Essay

After you write a focus statement, plan the middle paragraphs of your essay. Each middle paragraph should cover a different stage in the development of the theme.

Below, the writer of the sample essay on pages 297–300 planned the order of the middle paragraphs. She wrote a topic sentence for each stage.

Topic Sentences

Topic Sentence 1
Along with being a great runner, Squeaky does another thing well, too, although she doesn't take credit for it.

Topic Sentence 2
Competition is important to Squeaky, so she concentrates more and more on winning as the race day approaches.

Topic Sentence 3
The day of the race is a special day for Squeaky.

Topic Sentence 4
Squeaky can't believe what she's seeing, but she knows that something very important is about to happen.

Prewrite

Plan your middle paragraphs. Review your "Theme Chart." Add any stages you feel may be necessary. Then write a topic sentence for each of your middle paragraphs and decide the best order for the paragraphs.

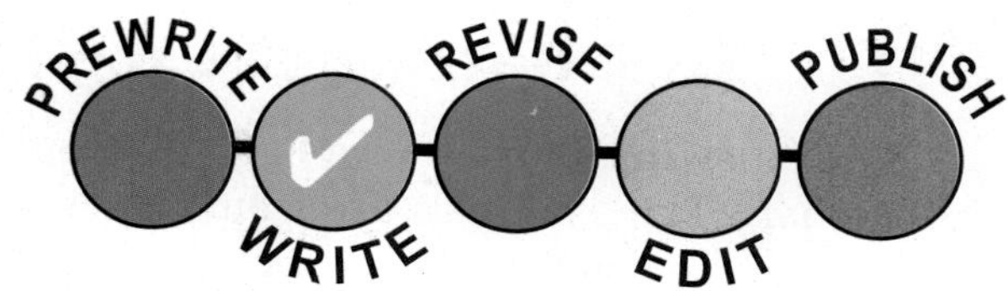

Writing

After you've done your prewriting, you can begin writing your essay. Use your focus statement, theme chart, and topic sentences as a guide.

Keys to Effective Writing

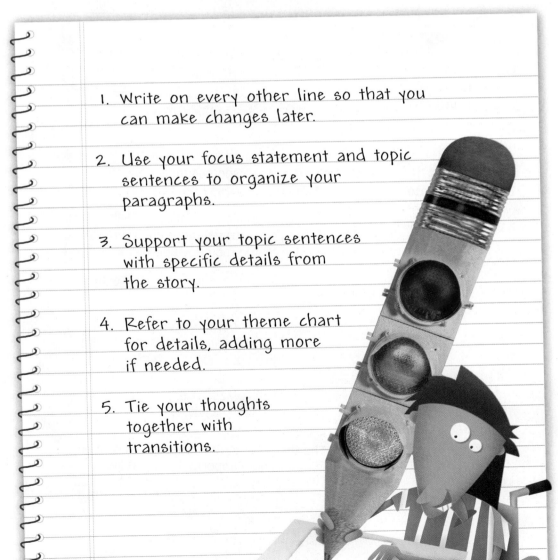

1. Write on every other line so that you can make changes later.
2. Use your focus statement and topic sentences to organize your paragraphs.
3. Support your topic sentences with specific details from the story.
4. Refer to your theme chart for details, adding more if needed.
5. Tie your thoughts together with transitions.

Writing Getting the Big Picture

The following chart shows how the three parts of a response to literature fit together. (The examples are from the essay on pages 297–300.) You're ready to write your response if you have . . .

- discovered the theme,
- written a clear focus statement that includes the theme and other information, and
- planned your paragraphs.

Beginning

The **beginning** paragraph introduces the character and states the theme.

Focus Statement

Eventually, Squeaky learns that there's more to life than being the best runner.

Middle

The four **middle** paragraphs show four stages in the development of the theme.

Four Topic Sentences

Along with being a great runner, Squeaky does another thing well, too, although she doesn't take credit for it.

Competition is important to Squeaky, so she concentrates more and more on winning as the race day approaches.

The day of the race is a special day for Squeaky.

Squeaky can't believe what she's seeing, but she knows that something very important is about to happen.

Ending

The **ending** paragraph revisits the theme and summarizes it.

Closing Sentence

The theme of the story is clear: Winning isn't the most important thing in life.

Starting Your Essay

The opening of your essay should include . . .

- background about the events and characters that help develop the theme,
- the title and author of the work, and
- your focus statement about the theme of the story.

Beginning
Middle
Ending

Beginning Paragraph

The beginning paragraph below starts with background information about the main character and ends with the focus statement about the theme.

The first part gives background.

The last sentence is the focus statement (underlined).

The main character in Toni Cade Bambara's story "Raymond's Run" is Squeaky, an aspiring runner. Squeaky is the reigning champion for her age group in the 50-yard dash at the Harlem May Day celebration. She practices running and thinks about it almost constantly as she prepares to defend her title. Eventually, Squeaky learns that there's more to life than being the best runner.

Write your beginning. Write the beginning paragraph of your essay. Include background information, the title and author, and your focus statement.

Drafting Tips

- **Talk about the story with a classmate** before you start writing.
- **Write freely,** letting your ideas flow without worrying about neatness.
- **Be sure that you have included enough details** to help your reader understand the point you're making.

Writing Developing the Middle Part

Each middle paragraph tells about one of the stages in the development of the theme. These paragraphs focus on the thoughts, feelings, and actions of important characters during each stage. Every middle paragraph should contain a topic sentence.

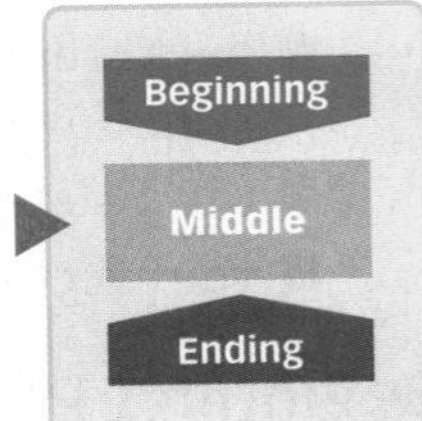

Middle Paragraphs

These paragraphs show the theme's development.

The first sentence forms a transition from the previous paragraph to this one.

Each topic sentence covers a stage of the theme (underlined).

Along with being a great runner, Squeaky does another thing well, too, although she doesn't take credit for it. Taking care of her older brother Raymond is a major responsibility in her life. Squeaky says, "He needs looking after 'cause he's not quite right." She does her duty without really thinking about it.

Competition is important to Squeaky, so she concentrates more and more on winning as the race day approaches. Her main worry is a new girl named Gretchen, who everybody says is very fast. Squeaky psychs up by picturing herself running, almost flying, to the finish line far ahead of Gretchen and the other competitors. She thinks that winning this race is the only way that she can be successful.

The day of the race is a special day for Squeaky. She has to take care of Raymond, so she sits him down on the playground swings and goes to the starting line. However, just before the race, she looks to the side, and there's Raymond on the other side of the fence, kneeling down like he's in the race, too.

Squeaky can't believe what she's seeing, but she knows that something very important is about to happen. When the gun starts the race, she sprints off, still watching Raymond. He keeps up with the leaders, and people start cheering for him. Raymond is running faster than anyone thought he could, and that makes his sister proud of him. When Squeaky crosses the finish line, she is confused and doesn't think that she has won.

The last stage in the theme's development is described in the last paragraph.

Write your middle paragraphs. **Write the middle paragraphs of your essay, using your topic sentences and theme chart as a guide. Fill in details as they are needed.**

Using Key Words for Transitions

To create a smooth flow of ideas in your middle paragraphs, tie them together with transitions. Repeating key words is a good way to connect a paragraph to the one before it. The key words below (colored) create a transition between the second and third middle paragraphs shown on page 298.

. . . She thinks that winning this race is the only way that she can be successful.

The day of the race is a special day for Squeaky. . . .

Writing Ending Your Essay

Beginning
Middle
Ending

Your essay starts with a statement about the theme. It then goes on to show how the theme develops in stages through the characters and events. Here are some suggestions to help you make your final comments about the theme.

- Show how a character has changed.
- Quote significant lines from the story.
- Predict how the theme might affect a character in the future.
- State the theme as a basic rule of life.

Quoting lines directly from the book or story can lend support to your ideas and make them stronger in the eyes of the reader.

Ending Paragraph

The ending paragraph below tells about Squeaky's realization of what is really important in life.

The last sentence restates the theme (underlined).

Finally, when things calm down, the announcer says that Squeaky came in first, and Gretchen was second. Squeaky suddenly realizes that Raymond's happiness is what is really important to her. In the past, she and Gretchen had focused on competing against each other. Now she smiles at Gretchen and thinks that maybe Gretchen would like to help her coach Raymond. Squeaky has a new reason to feel pride in her accomplishments. <u>The theme of the story is clear: Winning isn't the most important thing in life.</u>

Write your ending. Write the last paragraph of your essay. Be sure to end by revisiting the theme. (Use one of the four suggestions at the top of this page.)

Form a complete first draft. Make a complete copy of your essay. Double-space or write on every other line so that you have room for revising.

Revising

Now that you've finished your first draft, you're ready to begin revising. Focus on ideas, organization, and other traits to make changes that will improve your writing.

Keys to Effective Revising

1. To get a feel for how well your essay works, read it aloud.
2. Check your focus statement to see if it includes the topic of the essay.
3. Be sure that each detail supports its topic sentence.
4. Check your voice to see if it sounds natural.
5. Review your word choice and sentence fluency.
6. Use the editing and proofreading marks inside the back cover of this book.

Revising for Ideas

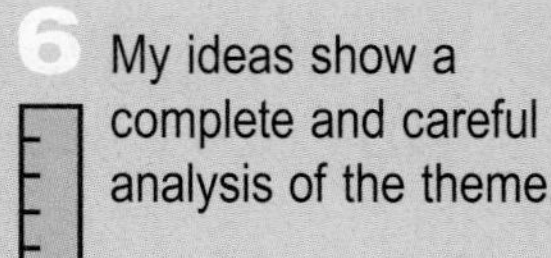
6 My ideas show a complete and careful analysis of the theme.

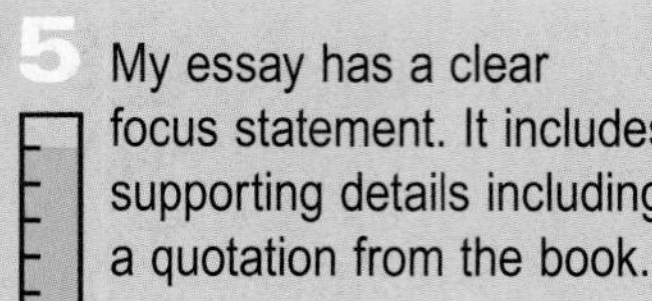
5 My essay has a clear focus statement. It includes supporting details including a quotation from the book.

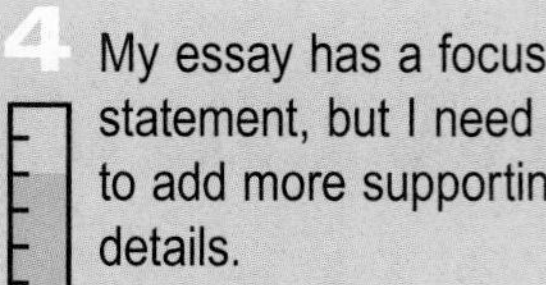
4 My essay has a focus statement, but I need to add more supporting details.

Ideas are the key elements of an essay. Use the rubric strip above and the information below as a guide to revising the ideas in your essay about a theme.

Does my focus statement introduce the story's theme?

You know your focus statement is effective when it states a specific theme and relates it to the story through the author, the title, or the characters.

Poorly Developed Focus

People don't understand each other.
(The theme is too general, and it is not related to a story.)

Well-Developed Focus

In *To Kill a Mockingbird,* the three children learn that it sometimes takes a crisis before people can see the good in others.
(The theme is specific, and it is clearly related to the story.)

The following focus statements are poorly developed. What kind of information should be added to make each one better?

1. *The Call of the Wild* is about wildness.
2. The story's main character, Vicki, realizes something about hope.
3. "The Gift of the Magi" has an interesting ending.
4. In Mark Twain's book, a boy learns that freedom carries responsibilities.
5. The story is about a boy who recovers from his injuries when he stops feeling sorry for himself.

Check your opening. Review your opening paragraph. Pay close attention to the theme in your focus statement and how it relates to the story.

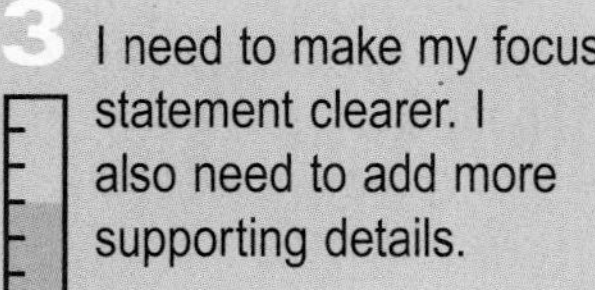

3 I need to make my focus statement clearer. I also need to add more supporting details.

2 I need a focus statement and supporting details.

1 I need to learn how to analyze a theme.

Did I use quotations to emphasize certain ideas?

Quoting directly from a book or story can be an effective way to emphasize important ideas in your essay. The quotation could . . .

- highlight an important statement by the author,
- reflect something about the character being quoted, or
- express the theme.

Read the sentences below, which come from the closing paragraph of a student essay. Why did the writer include the direct quotation? Refer to the list above to help you decide.

Atticus Finch's earliest lesson to Scout is simple: "You never really understand a person until you consider things from his point of view . . . until you climb into his skin and walk around in it." Throughout the novel, Scout is learning to understand people.

Review your first draft for ideas. Be sure that your theme is clearly stated in your opening. Also check to see whether you have used quotations effectively.

Ideas
A direct quotation is inserted.

Taking care of her older brother Raymond is a major responsibility in her life. Squeaky says, "He needs looking after 'cause he's not quite right." She does her duty without really thinking about it.

Revising for Organization

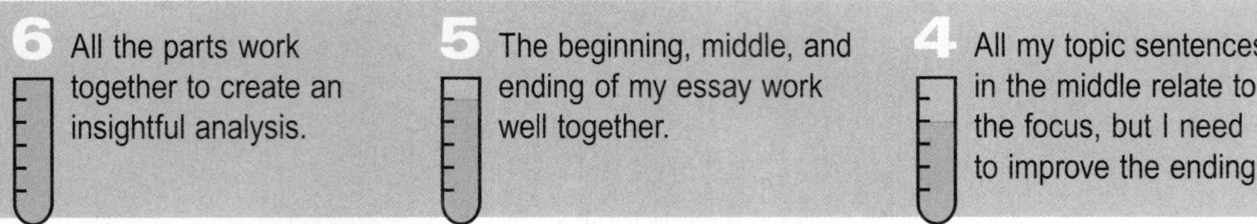

6 All the parts work together to create an insightful analysis.
5 The beginning, middle, and ending of my essay work well together.
4 All my topic sentences in the middle relate to the focus, but I need to improve the ending.

Organization is the way that you arrange your ideas within the essay. Use the rubric strip above and the following information to review and revise the organization of your essay.

Do my topic sentences relate to the focus?

The topic sentences in your middle paragraphs will relate to the focus if they sound like they flow from the focus statement in the first paragraph.

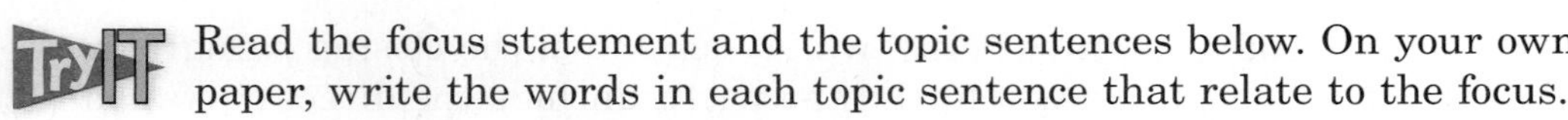

Read the focus statement and the topic sentences below. On your own paper, write the words in each topic sentence that relate to the focus.

Focus Statement

Eventually, Squeaky learns that there's more to life than being the best runner.

Topic Sentences

Along with being a great runner, Squeaky does another thing well, too, although she doesn't take credit for it.

Competition is important to Squeaky, so she concentrates more and more on winning as the race day approaches.

The day of the race is a special day for Squeaky.

Squeaky can't believe what she's seeing, but she knows that something very important is about to happen.

Check your topic sentences. Write your focus statement at the top of a sheet of paper. Then write the topic sentences from your middle paragraphs under the focus. Rewrite any topic sentences that do not relate to the focus.

3 I need to change all the topic sentences and rewrite the ending.

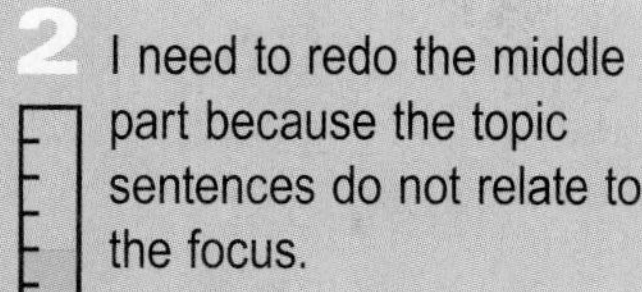

2 I need to redo the middle part because the topic sentences do not relate to the focus.

1 I need to learn how to organize a response to literature.

What's the best way to end my essay?

Your ending should revisit the theme and leave the reader with something to think about. A good way to emphasize the theme is to use one of the following suggestions.

- Show how a character has changed.
- Quote an important line from the story.
- Predict how the theme might affect a character in the future.
- State the theme as a basic rule of life: *Winning isn't the most important thing in life.*

For each of the following endings, identify the suggestion (listed above) that the writer used.

1. John now realizes that how he lives his life is completely up to him.
2. The author sees José, the "born worker," as a boy with a fine future.

Review your essay for organization. Be sure that the theme is explained clearly in the beginning and restated effectively in the ending.

Organization
A restatement of the theme is added.

Now she smiles at Gretchen and thinks that maybe Gretchen would like to help her coach Raymond. Squeaky has a new reason to feel pride in her accomplishments. ^ *The theme of the story is clear: Winning isn't the most important thing in life.*

Revising for Voice

6 My voice sounds distinctive and insightful from start to finish.	**5** My voice sounds natural. It creates the right mood for the story.	**4** My voice sounds natural, but it needs to reflect more clearly the mood of the story.

Voice is the "sound" of your writing. The rubric strip above and the information below will help you revise your essay so that it sounds natural and creates an appropriate mood.

How do I know whether my writing has a natural voice?

Your writing has a natural voice if it sounds like you and is neither too formal nor too informal. Writers sometimes create language that is too formal because they think that it sounds impressive. Others use language that is too casual or informal. Neither one will sound natural.

Too Formal

The consequence of the experience was that the adolescent female came to a new realization of what was right and what was wrong.

Too Informal

That girl sure did learn her lesson all right.

The voice in the revised sentence below sounds more natural.

Natural

Because of the experience, the girl learned a lesson about how to tell right from wrong.

The best way to hear how your essay sounds is to read it aloud. If you think it sounds unnatural, so will the reader.

Check for natural voice. Reread your essay, marking any sections that sound too formal or too informal. Rewrite those parts so that they sound more natural.

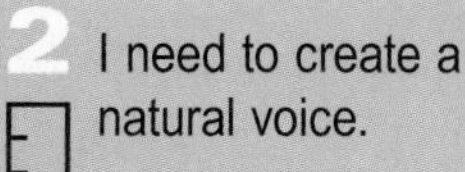

3 My voice needs to sound natural and match the mood of the story more clearly.	**2** I need to create a natural voice.	**1** I need to learn more about voice.

Does my voice create the right mood?

Mood is the feeling or reaction that your writing creates in the reader.

Read the following sentences. For each one, describe the mood (sad, suspenseful, happy, silly, fearful) that is produced by the writing.

1. At the beginning of the story, Charlise felt that something very unusual was about to happen.
2. Charlise turned from the kitchen counter, fell over the cat, dropped the pie on the floor, and sat on it as though it were a comfortable cushion.
3. Mr. Pignati felt so alone that he collapsed on the floor.

Be sure that your voice creates the right mood. Think about the mood that you wish to create in your essay. Review your writing and make necessary changes in your voice.

Voice
A sentence is deleted to keep the mood consistent. Overly formal language is rewritten.

The day of the race is a special day for Squeaky. ~~She doesn't really have a life.~~ She has to ~~give substantial assistance to~~ take care of Raymond, so she sits him down on the playground swings and goes to the starting line. However, just before the race, she looks to the side, and there's Raymond . . .

Revising for Word Choice

6 My word choice reflects my analytical thinking about literature.

5 My word choice, including literary terms, is appropriate for my reader.

4 My word choice is appropriate, but I need to add more literary terms.

When you revise your writing for *word choice*, be sure that your words effectively describe the story and that they are on the right level for your audience.

How can I improve my word choice?

When you write about literature, literary terms like *dialogue* and *mood* can help make your essay clear and effective. (See pages **351–352** for terms that you can use to write about novels and stories.)

Use each word in the following chart to complete the sentences below.

character	dialogue	mood	narrator
theme	tone	protagonist	

1. A __________ is a person or an animal in a story.
2. A story's __________ is its lesson about life.
3. __________ is the feeling that a piece of writing creates in the reader.
4. The __________ is the main character of a story.
5. The person or character who actually tells the story is the __________ .
6. __________ is the words spoken between the characters.
7. A writer's attitude toward his or her subject is the __________ .

Revise for literary terms. Check your essay for places where you might use literary terms to add clarity to your writing.

3 I need to make the word choice more appropriate for the reader.

2 I need to pay more attention to word choice.

1 I need help with word choice.

Are my words appropriate for the reader?

Your words will be appropriate if they are not too slangy or too showy.

Lorraine thought that John was acting dumb.
(This use of *dumb* is slang.)

Lorraine thought that John was acting nonsensically.
(*Nonsensically* is too showy.)

Lorraine thought that John was acting foolishly.
(*Foolishly* is an appropriate word.)

Try It Read the paragraph below and decide whether the underlined words are too slangy or too showy. Choose more appropriate words.

They have fun sharing the Pigman's life, but then everything gets nuts. One day when he is gone, they have a happening party. He cries when he sees the damage and calls the law enforcement authorities. John and Lorraine are disconsolate when they realize how much they have hurt Mr. Pignati.

Revise for word choice. Look back at the way you have used words in your essay. Replace words that are not appropriate.

Word Choice
More appropriate language is used.

Competition
~~Domination in athletics~~ is important to
concentrates more and more on
Squeaky, so she ~~freaks about~~ winning as the race day approaches. Her main worry is a new girl named Gretchen, who everybody says is very fast.

Revising for Sentence Fluency

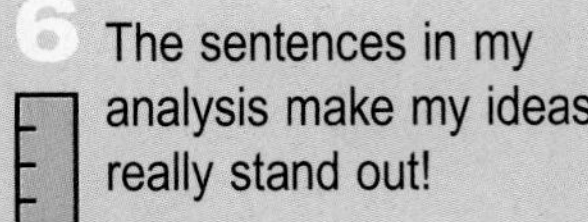
6 The sentences in my analysis make my ideas really stand out!

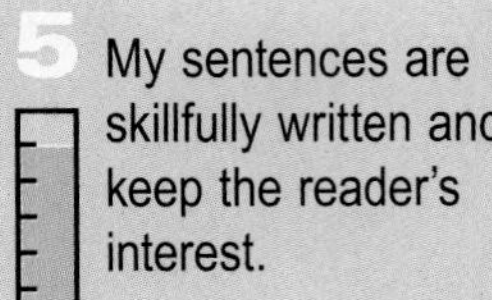
5 My sentences are skillfully written and keep the reader's interest.

4 Most of my sentences flow smoothly, but I need to cut unneeded words.

To revise for *sentence fluency*, check the clarity, flow, and smoothness of your sentences. The rubric strip above and the information below will help you.

How can I make my sentences flow more smoothly?

You can make your sentences flow more smoothly by using a relative pronoun (*who, that, which*) to join short sentences. The following example shows (1) two short sentences and (2) a combined sentence with a relative pronoun.

Two Short Sentences

José works harder than his cousin Arnie. Arnie avoids physical labor whenever possible.

Combined Sentence with a Relative Pronoun

José works harder than his cousin Arnie, who **avoids physical labor whenever possible.**

Rewrite the following sentences, using relative pronouns to combine each pair of short sentences into a longer one.

1. José is a boy with a fine future. José comes from a hardworking family.
2. José and Arnie get a job cleaning a swimming pool. The pool is owned by a friend of Arnie's father.

Use commas to set off a clause beginning with a relative pronoun if the clause is *not necessary* to the basic meaning of the sentence. (See 706.3 and 684.6).

Soccer, which is a favorite sport in many other countries**, is becoming popular in the United States.**

Commas should not set off a clause that is necessary to understand the meaning of the sentence.

Soccer that is played indoors **is a very high-scoring game.**

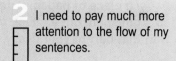

3 I need to combine short, choppy sentences and cut unneeded words.

2 I need to pay much more attention to the flow of my sentences.

1 I need to learn more about sentences.

Are some of my sentences wordy?

Your sentences may be wordy if you have used more words than you need or repeated yourself unnecessarily. (See page 506.)

When Mia opened her mouth to speak, everyone in the area around her listened.
When Mia spoke, everyone in the area listened.
(Unneeded words have been removed.)

Beyonce practices soccer on the soccer field with the other girls on her team at 3:30 p.m. in the afternoon.
Beyonce practices soccer with her team at 3:30 p.m.
(Repetitious wording has been removed.)

Rewrite the paragraph below so that it is less wordy.

Arnie goes out and gets them a job cleaning Mr. Clemens's pool at his house. While José is in the pool scrubbing the walls of the pool, Mr. Clemens accidentally falls into the pool without meaning to.

Revise for sentence fluency. **Check your essay for short sentences that can be combined. Also check for wordiness.**

Sentence Fluency
Repetitious wording and unnecessary wording are deleted.

Finally, when things calm down ~~later~~, the announcer says that Squeaky came in first, and Gretchen was second. Squeaky ~~hears the announcement and~~ suddenly realizes that Raymond's happiness is what is really important to her.

LITERATURE

Revising Using a Checklist

Check your revising. On a piece of paper, write the numbers 1 to 12. If you can answer "yes" to a question, put a check mark after that number. If not, continue to work with that part of your essay.

Ideas

_____ **1.** Have I written a focus statement that introduces my topic?
_____ **2.** Have I given the reader enough information?
_____ **3.** Did I use significant quotations?

Organization

_____ **4.** Have I included a beginning, a middle, and an ending?
_____ **5.** Do my topic sentences relate to my focus?
_____ **6.** Did I leave my reader with a clear idea of the theme's importance?

Voice

_____ **7.** Does my voice sound natural?
_____ **8.** Have I created the right mood?

Word Choice

_____ **9.** Have I used literary terms, if appropriate?
_____ **10.** Have I avoided words that are too slangy or too showy?

Sentence Fluency

_____ **11.** Have I combined short sentences?
_____ **12.** Have I eliminated unnecessary words?

Make a clean copy. When you've finished revising your essay, make a clean copy before you begin to edit.

Go Online!

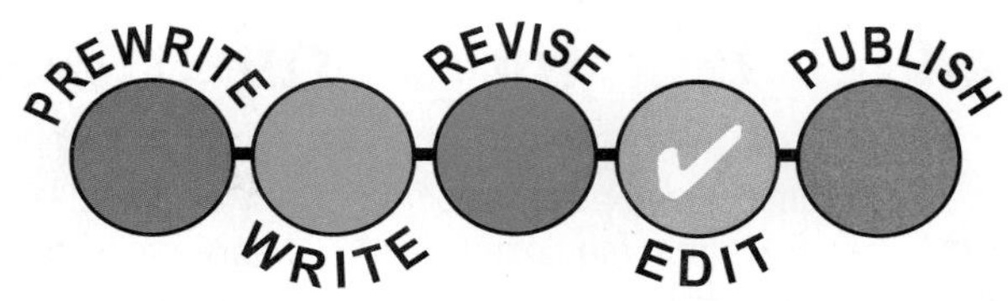

Editing

After you've finished revising your essay, it's time to edit for the following conventions: punctuation, capitalization, spelling, and grammar.

Keys to Effective Editing

1. Use a dictionary, a thesaurus, and the "Proofreader's Guide" in the back of this book.
2. Check quotations for correct punctuation.
3. Check your writing for correctness of punctuation, capitalization, spelling, and grammar.
4. If you use a computer, edit on a printed copy and enter your changes on the computer.
5. Use the editing and proofreading marks inside the back cover of this book.

Editing for Conventions

6 My grammar and punctuation are correct, and the copy is free of all errors.	**5** My essay has one or two errors that do not interfere with the reader's understanding.	**4** I need to correct the few errors in punctuation, spelling, or grammar.

Conventions are the rules you follow for punctuation, capitalization, grammar, and spelling. To edit for conventions, use the rubric strip above and the information below.

Have I used commas correctly to set off words and phrases?

A word or phrase should be set off with commas if the information *is not* needed to understand the basic meaning of the sentence. No commas are used if the information *is* needed to understand the sentence. (See 584.1.)

Jem, taking a shortcut home, was badly injured.

Hiding in his house, Boo Radley watched what went on in the neighborhood.

Jem didn't see the man who attacked him.
(*Who attacked him* is needed to understand which man the sentence is referring to.)

Read the following sentences. Decide whether the italicized words should be set off with commas.

1. Scout *who is only six when the book begins* is quick to judge.
2. She lives in a place *where people are known by what their families are like.*
3. The Cunninghams *as Scout explains to her teacher* do not like to owe people.

Edit for commas. Check your essay to make sure that you have used commas correctly to set off words and phrases.

3 I need to correct the errors because they confuse the reader.

2 I need to pay more attention to conventions so the reader can follow my writing.

1 I need to learn about conventions.

How do I punctuate direct quotations?

Use quotation marks to enclose direct quotations. An indirect or reworded quotation needs no quotation marks. Read the following paragraph and note the way the blue quotations are punctuated.

Colonel Sanders said, "Mr. Leghorn won't be with us tonight." The Colonel also told us that Leghorn had been detained in the kitchen. Everyone in the audience was upset by the news, and one of the dancers asked, "Can it be true?" Others wondered who could possibly call the square dance as well as the trusty Mr. L. Finally, a voice from the back of the room suggested that Mr. Terpsichore would make a good substitute. At that, Mr. Terpsichore stepped forward, looked at the band, and said, "Hit it, boys!"

Copy the following paragraph, inserting any punctuation needed for quotations. (See **598.1** and **600.1**.)

José's father sometimes exclaims, Life is hard! But José is not discouraged. He feels that his muscles need to work hard, and he tells his cousin Arnie that he will not rest until he finds a job. Arnie then asks, Do you want to work together?

Edit for conventions. Check your essay for punctuation, especially punctuation used in direct and indirect quotations.

Conventions
Commas are added and quotation marks are removed.

Finally, when things calm down, the announcer says that, "Squeaky came in first, and Gretchen was second." Squeaky suddenly realizes that . . .

LITERATURE

Editing Using a Checklist

Check your editing. On a piece of paper, write the numbers 1 to 12. If you can answer "yes" to a question, put a check mark after that number. If not, continue to edit for that convention.

Conventions

PUNCTUATION

_____ **1.** Does each sentence have end punctuation?
_____ **2.** Do I use commas after introductory word groups?
_____ **3.** Do I use commas to set off parenthetical expressions?
_____ **4.** Have I correctly punctuated my quotations?
_____ **5.** Do I use apostrophes to show possession *(my parents' house)*?

CAPITALIZATION

_____ **6.** Do I start all my sentences with capital letters?
_____ **7.** Have I capitalized all proper nouns?

SPELLING

_____ **8.** Have I spelled all my words correctly?
_____ **9.** Have I double-checked the words my spell-checker may have missed?

GRAMMAR

_____ **10.** Do I use correct forms of verbs *(lying in bed,* not *laying in bed)*?
_____ **11.** Do my subjects and verbs agree in number? (*Mathematics is*, not *Mathematics are,* my favorite subject.)
_____ **12.** Have I used the right words *(its, it's)*?

Creating a Title

- Use the title of the book or story: **"Raymond's Run"**
- Refer to the character: **Squeaky's Victory**
- Be creative: **Crossing the Line**

PREWRITE WRITE REVISE EDIT PUBLISH

Publishing

Sharing Your Essay

Now that you've finished writing, revising, and editing your essay, it's time to make it look good. You may also want to present your essay in some other form: illustrations, sharing with your classmates, or a submission to a literary magazine. (See the suggestions in the boxes below.)

Make a final copy. Follow your teacher's instructions or use the guidelines below to format your paper. (If you are using a computer, see pages 60–62.) Write a final copy of your essay and proofread it for errors.

Focus on Presentation

- Use blue or black ink and write neatly.
- Write your name in the upper left corner of page 1.
- Skip a line and center your title; skip another line and start your writing.
- Indent every paragraph and leave a one-inch margin on all four sides.
- Write your last name and the page number in the upper right corner of every page after the first one.

Make Illustrations
Draw one or more illustrations of key scenes in the development of the theme. Write a caption at the bottom of each illustration and post them in your classroom.

Submit Your Essay to a Literary Magazine
If your school has a literary magazine, submit your essay for publication. Write a cover letter explaining why classmates might be interested in your essay.

Share It with Your Classmates
Give a short introduction to the book or short story you wrote about and then read your essay to the class.

Rubric for a Response to Literature

Use this rubric for guiding and assessing your writing. Refer to it whenever you want to improve your writing using the six traits.

Ideas

6 **The ideas show a complete understanding of the reading.**

5 The essay has a clear focus statement and all the necessary details.

4 The essay has a clear focus statement. Unnecessary details need to be cut.

Organization

6 **All the parts work together to create an insightful essay.**

5 The organization pattern fits the topic and purpose. All parts of the essay are well developed.

4 The organization pattern fits the topic and purpose. A part of the essay needs better development.

Voice

6 **The voice expresses interest and complete understanding. It engages the reader.**

5 The voice expresses interest in and understanding of the topic.

4 The voice expresses interest but needs to show more understanding.

Word Choice

6 **The word choice reflects careful thinking about the reading.**

5 The word choice, including the use of literary terms, creates a clear message.

4 The word choice is clear, but more literary terms would improve the essay.

Sentence Fluency

6 **The sentences in the essay make the ideas really stand out.**

5 The sentences are skillfully written and keep the reader's interest.

4 No sentence problems exist. More sentence variety is needed.

Conventions

6 **Grammar and punctuation are correct, and the copy is free of all errors.**

5 The essay has one or two errors that do not interfere with the reader's understanding.

4 The essay has a few careless errors in punctuation and grammar.

3	2	1
The focus statement is too broad. Unnecessary details need to be cut.	The focus statement is unclear. More details are needed.	The essay needs a focus statement and details.
The organization fits the essay's purpose. Some parts need more development.	The organization doesn't fit the purpose.	A plan needs to be followed.
The voice needs to be more interesting and express more understanding.	The voice does not show interest in or an understanding of the topic.	The writer needs to understand how to create voice.
The word choice is too general and more literary terms are needed.	Little, if any, attention was given to word choice.	The writer needs help with word choice.
A few sentence problems need to be corrected.	The essay has many sentence problems.	The writer needs to learn how to construct sentences.
The errors in the essay confuse the reader.	The number of errors make the essay hard to read.	Help is needed to make corrections.

Evaluating an Analysis

Read through the following analysis of a theme, focusing on the essay's strengths and weaknesses. Then read the student's self-evaluation on the next page. **(There may be errors in the essay below.)**

Honest Work

In the story "Born Worker," writer Gary Soto's main character, José, is a boy who comes from a hardworking family. José himself enjoys hard work, and even though his father complains, "Life is hard," the boy loves to use his muscles doing physical labor. His cousin, Arnie, thinks that he can make money without working. Soto's theme is that those who do honest work are more responsible than those who avoid it.

José wants to work whenever he is not in school. Arnie has a plan for both of them to make money. The plan is that Arnie will find jobs, José will do the work, and they will split the money. José hates asking people for jobs, so the idea that Arnie will do that part sounds good. They agree to give the plan a try, even though José will have to do all of the work.

Arnie gets them a job cleaning Mr. Clemens's swimming pool. While José is in the pool scrubbing the walls, Mr. Clemens accidentally falls in and hits his head on the bottom. José rushes to save the bleeding man, but Arnie screams that they should take off and leave him in the pool. Arnie disappears. José calls 911 and waits with Mr. Clemens, putting ice on his injured head. When the rescue team comes, Arnie suddenly reappears as though he had been there the whole time. He acts like he is in charge of Mr. Clemens's rescue. Arnie is not only lazy, he's also dishonest and irresponsible.

With Arnie telling his lies in the background, José thinks about his father, who "would have seen that José was more than just a good worker. He would have seen a good man." Gary Soto sees José, the "born worker," as a boy with a fine future. Arnie, however, will have a future full of trouble if he doesn't change.

Student Assessment

The assessment below is the student's evaluation of her essay, including her comments. The first comment is something positive, and the second comment is something she could improve. (The writer used the rubric and number scale on pages 318–319 to complete this assessment.)

5 **Ideas**

1. *My focus states the theme.*
2. *A direct quotation from Arnie would help readers understand him.*

4 **Organization**

1. *My opening and closing express the theme in different ways.*
2. *One more middle paragraph would help show the differences between José and Arnie.*

5 **Voice**

1. *My voice creates a serious mood that fits the topic.*
2. *My voice sounds too unemotional in the focus statement.*

4 **Word Choice**

1. *My words are on the right level for my audience.*
2. *I need to choose stronger words, especially verbs and modifiers.*

5 **Sentence Fluency**

1. *My sentences are well developed, not short and choppy.*
2. *Too many of my sentences start with names.*

6 **Conventions**

1. *I think my paper is free of careless errors.*
2. *I'm not sure how to use commas around quotations.*

Use the rubric. Assess your essay using the rubric on pages 318–319.

1 On your own paper, list the six traits. Leave room after each trait to write one strength and one weakness.

2 Then choose a number (from 1 to 6) that shows how well you used each trait.

Reflecting on Your Writing

Reflect on your finished analysis of a theme by completing each starter sentence below. These comments will help you check your progress as a writer.

My Analysis

1. *The strength of my essay is . . .*
2. *The part that most needs change is . . .*
3. *The main thing I learned about writing an analysis of a theme is . . .*
4. *In my next response to literature, I would like to . . .*
5. *Here is one question I still have about writing an analysis of a theme:*
6. *Right now I would describe my writing ability as . . . (excellent, good, fair, poor)*

Response to Literature

Writing a Letter to an Author

Have you ever gotten to the last page of a novel and wished it wouldn't end? What happens next? Do the characters have any more adventures? Why didn't the author write more? The best way to get answers to these questions is to write to the author.

Writing a letter to an author is a creative way to respond to literature. You can share what you liked most about the work and ask any questions you might have. Also, when you write a letter to an author, you switch roles. You're the writer for a change!

The following pages provide a sample letter to an author. Afterward, you will find guidelines to help you create your own letter.

Writing Guidelines

Subject: A book or short story
Form: Letter
Purpose: To show understanding and ask questions
Audience: Author

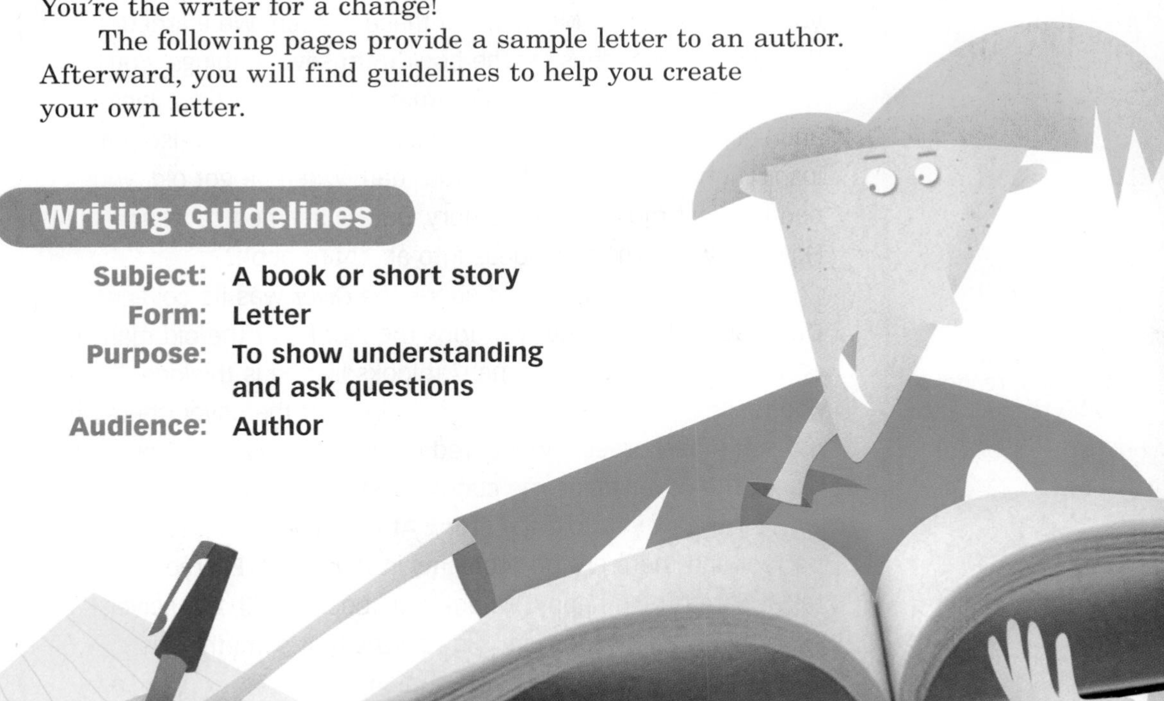

Letter to an Author

Writing a letter to an author is one way to gain a better understanding of a special book or short story that you have read. In this sample, Lupita shares her thoughts and feelings about Lois Lowry's book *The Giver.*

Beginning
The beginning introduces the reader and gives her reason for writing to the author.

Middle
The middle provides the reader's response to the book.

4214 Rose Lane
Highfield, IL 60600
October 11, 2011

Dear Ms. Lois Lowry,

I am an eighth grader in Creekside Middle School. As part of a literature class assignment, we are supposed to write to the author of a book we've read this semester. Since I really enjoyed reading *The Giver,* I decided to write you.

Before I started the book, our teacher read to us from your 1994 Newbery Medal acceptance speech. We learned that you got the ideas for the book from several things. You remembered growing up in an American part of Tokyo, Japan, and secretly riding your bike to explore the city. You also got inspiration for *The Giver* from your dad. When he got old, your dad had lost most of his memory, but he seemed content. How did you turn those ideas into an entire book?

The first thing I noticed about *The Giver* was its cover. Our teacher told us that you took the picture of the old man on the cover. Who is that man? It looks like he is thinking about something very sad. On the corner of the cover, there are some bare trees. I wondered if the man was from that place. The cover made me curious about the story.

I like how you told the story. At first, everything is perfect and there are no problems in the world. Everyone is taken care of and happy. When Jonas becomes the Receiver, everything changes for him. He realizes that something is missing from the world. Jonas searches to discover what's going on. It was really hard for me to put the book down, since I wanted to keep reading.

At first I was disappointed by the ending, but then I realized that you were leaving it up to the reader. Each person can have his or her own ending. Are you planning to write a sequel to *The Giver* someday?

Ending

The ending reflects on the importance of the book to the reader.

Our teacher told us about an interview you gave. You said, "Reading is what makes you a great writer." I think reading your work has made me a better writer. You also said that writing letters is a wonderful way to practice writing. I've started writing my grandmother a letter every week. I tell her stories about school, family, and friends. Thank you for the writing ideas and all the wonderful books you've written.

I look forward to reading more of your books.

Sincerely,

Lupita Marquez

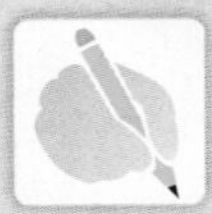

Respond to the reading. Answer the following questions about the sample letter.

- ☐ **Ideas (1) What book or short story does the writer talk about? (2) Where does the writer get her information?**
- ☐ **Organization (3) Where does the writer introduce herself and give her reason for writing?**
- ☐ **Voice & Word Choice (4) How does the writer personally connect with the author?**

Literature Connections: You may want to write your own letter to an author after reading such stories as "Hamadi" by Naomi Shihab Nye or "Rules of the Game" by Amy Tan.

Prewriting Selecting a Literary Work

To get started, select a book or story you would like to write about. Lupita began by listing novels and stories she had recently read.

Topics List

Books and Stories	*Author*
Rocket Boys	*Homer Hickman*
"Rules of the Game"	*Amy Tan*
The Giver	*Lois Lowry* *

Select a literary work. List books and short stories that you have read, along with the authors' names. Put a star (*) next to the author that you would like to write to. Have your teacher approve your choice.

Gathering Details

Sentence starters provide one way to gather information for a letter to an author. Lupita used sentence starters to think about *The Giver.*

Sentence Starters

The most interesting thing about the background of this story is . . .
that it was based on growing up in Japan.

The first thing I noticed about the story was . . .
the picture of the old man on the cover.

The thing I liked most about the story was . . .
the way it was told.

I think that the ending . . .
is open-ended; you have to decide yourself.

This story is important to me because . . .
it made me want to read more and write more.

Gather details. On your own paper, complete the sentence starters above for your book or story. Also jot down questions to ask the author.

Writing Creating Your First Draft

Now that you've selected a book and gathered details, you are ready to write the first draft of your letter. Follow the guidelines below.

- **Follow the correct format.** See the friendly letter formatting guidelines at the bottom of this page.
- **Use a polite but personable voice.** Write in a conversational voice, but avoid slang or incorrect English. Make sure your sentences are clear and complete.
- **Let your sentence starters guide your writing.** Use the sentences you completed on page 326 to help you develop each paragraph in your letter.
- **Ask questions.** Encourage the author to respond to your letter by asking questions.

Write the first draft. Follow the format and guidelines on this page as you write the first draft of your letter.

Focus on the Traits

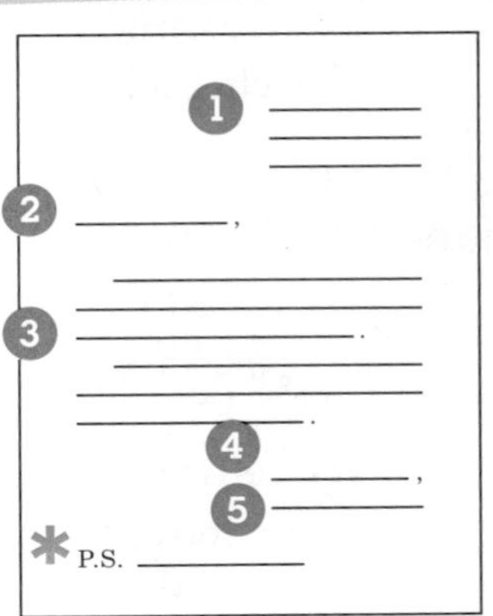

Organization A friendly letter has five basic parts. Use the following guidelines to format your letter.

1. **Heading:** The heading appears in the upper right-hand corner and includes your address and the date.
2. **Salutation:** This polite greeting begins two lines below the heading. It starts with *Dear* and ends with a comma.
3. **Body:** The body identifies the writer and the reason for writing and includes details and questions.
4. **Closing:** The closing politely says good-bye and is followed by a comma. Common closings follow:

   Sincerely, Your friend, Regards,
5. **Signature:** The signature is your signed name.

* **P.S.:** A postscript gives an optional afterthought.

Revising Improving Your Writing

After you finish your first draft, revise it for the following traits.

- ☐ **Ideas** Does my letter focus on one short story or book?
- ☐ **Organization** Do I follow the proper format? (See page 327.)
- ☐ **Voice** Do I sound as though I have read the book or short story and understand it?
- ☐ **Word Choice** Are my words clear and accurate?
- ☐ **Sentence Fluency** Are my sentences complete? Do they have different lengths and beginnings? Do they flow well?

Revise your letter. Ask yourself the questions above. Revise your letter to improve these traits of writing.

Editing Checking for Conventions

When you edit your letter to an author, focus on the *conventions* of your writing.

- ☐ **Conventions** Have I checked punctuation and capitalization? Have I checked spelling and grammar?

Edit your work. Ask yourself the questions above as you edit your letter. Make a clean final copy and proofread it.

Publishing Sharing Your Writing

Once you've finished your letter, share it. Here are some suggestions.

- Send the letter to the author if your author is still living. Check online to find the contact information for the author's publisher. Address your envelope to the author in care of (c/o) the publisher. Then attach appropriate postage and send it.
- Read the letter to your class. If any other students have read the same book or story, discuss your questions with them.
- Post the letter on a school or local library bulletin board. Ask permission first.

Share your ideas. Choose one of the publishing ideas above or come up with your own.

Response to Literature

Across the Curriculum

An old saying goes, "A picture is worth a thousand words." That's because a picture can show something that happened a thousand miles away or a hundred years ago. By responding to pictures, articles, and Web sites, you can learn about the world around you. In social studies, you can study photos from another time or place. In science, you can read articles that push the frontiers of technology. And by exploring the Web, you can see things on the other side of the world—or the universe!

After working with the different forms of response writing on the following pages, you will get a chance to practice responding to a timed test prompt.

What's Ahead

- **Social Studies:** Responding to a Historical Photo
- **Science:** Summarizing a Science Article
- **Practical Writing:** Evaluating a Web Site
- **Writing for Assessment**

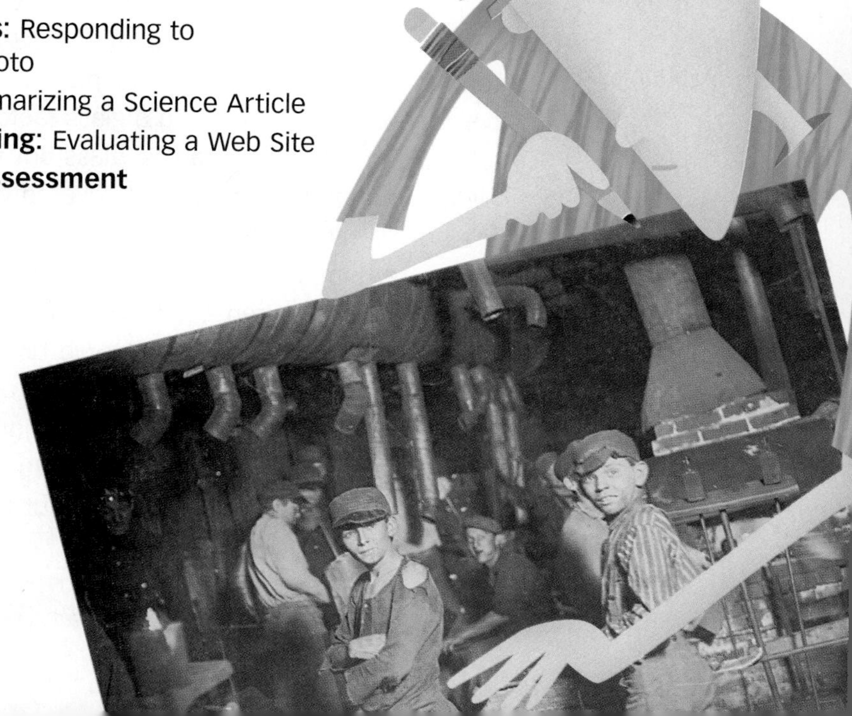

Social Studies:
Responding to a Historical Photo

Social studies explores the way people have lived in different places and at different times. A picture tells a story without any words. You can use your observational skills and information from social studies class to write a response to a historical photograph.

In her social studies textbook, Sydney saw a picture of kids working at midnight in a glass factory in the early 1900s. It showed her what life must have been like for kids who had to work to help their families make enough money.

No Time to Play

The **beginning** introduces the photo.

The **middle** describes the photo.

The **ending** reflects on the photo's value.

In the past, kids worked long hours in factories with terrible working conditions. This picture from 1908 shows child laborers at midnight in a glass factory. The dark room is crowded with pipes, tables, glass bottles, and a brick oven. Everything is smoky and covered with dirt. One of the boys wears a shirt with a big hole on the shoulder. His pants are ripped, too. A few of the boys look up toward the camera, very tired and a little surprised. Maybe they are wondering why someone would take a picture of them. Pictures like this made people want to outlaw child labor. Today, kids spend their time at school or at home with family and friends. Even though a picture may be sad to look at, it can teach valuable lessons about the country's past.

Writing Tips

Before you write . . .

- **Choose a picture.**
  Search through your history book or the Internet to find a historical picture to write about.
- **Imagine being a person in this picture.**
  Think about what it must have been like to live in another time and place.
- **Think about why this picture is important.**
  Ask yourself what this picture shows about the society of the time. Ask yourself how pictures such as this one may have brought about the changes evident in today's society.

During your writing . . .

- **Focus on the main features of the picture.**
  Start with the first thing you notice. Describe it and then shift to other details in a logical fashion.
- **Share interesting details.**
  Let the images in the photograph suggest sounds, smells, textures, and other details.

After you've written a first draft . . .

- **Revise your response.**
  Make sure you have connected the picture's historical setting to the present day. Check to see that your details appear in the best possible order.
- **Double-check important facts.**
  Make sure the names and dates in your paragraph are correct.
- **Check for correctness.**
  Check the conventions in your response. Then make a final copy of your work and proofread it for errors.

Search your textbook, the library, or the Internet for a historical photograph that interests you. Look for information that can help you understand the historical significance of the picture. Write a paragraph that responds to the photo. Use the information above as a guide.

Science: Summarizing a Science Article

Every day, magazines, newspapers, and Web sites report the fascinating discoveries of science. Summarizing an article can help you understand it. The following article, "Batteries Driving the Future," explains the technology of hybrid cars. The paragraph "Battery Included" summarizes the article.

Batteries Driving the Future

As the world's population swells, the demand for cars increases. More cars mean more pollution, but scientists and the automotive industry have found a way to reduce this problem: the hybrid car.

Hybrid cars use an electric motor and a gasoline engine. The electric motor is powered by a long-lasting battery, which is charged by a generator built into the car. This combination of devices provides an extremely efficient use of gasoline. Here's how hybrid cars work:

- When a hybrid car is starting and going slowly, the electric motor powers the car.
- At higher speeds, the gasoline engine takes over. The engine sends power to a generator, which charges the battery.
- If the car is going uphill or speeding up, the electric motor and gasoline engine work together.
- During slowing down and braking, the generator charges the battery.

Hybrid cars are becoming increasingly popular as consumers seek vehicles that lessen environmental impact. Their sleek designs make them visually appealing and aerodynamic. The fuel efficiency of hybrid cars reduces reliance on gasoline. As hybrids grow in popularity, there's no doubt that batteries will drive the future of the automotive industry.

Battery Included

Topic Sentence — *The article "Batteries Driving the Future" explains how hybrid cars use an electric motor and a gasoline engine.*

Body — *The electric motor, which works at low speeds, gets its power from a battery. The battery doesn't need to be plugged in, since it is charged by a generator in the car. Hybrid cars have a smooth shape for both style and aerodynamics, and they use less fuel, making them better for the environment.*

Closing Sentence — *The world and its people are beginning to benefit from hybrid cars.*

Writing Tips

Before you write . . .

- **Gather science magazines.**
  Check your school library for magazines such as *National Geographic* or *Current Science*. Also check the Internet for scientific articles from sources such as www.nasa.gov. Your teacher may know of other sources.
- **Read the article and take notes.**
  Read your selection once to get the overall idea of the article. Then reread the material and take notes about important information.
- **Organize your paragraph.**
  Identify the main idea of the article. Gather only the details needed to support the main idea.

During your writing . . .

- **Focus on the main idea.**
  Use your topic sentence to identify the main idea in the article. In the body, include key details to support it. End with a clear closing sentence.
- **Be brief.**
  Make sure your summary is only about a third of the length of the original article.

After you've written a first draft . . .

- **Check your facts.**
  Make sure that you have accurately recorded key facts from the article.
- **Check for conventions.**
  Correct any errors in spelling, punctuation, capitalization, and grammar.

Find an interesting science article in a magazine or on the Internet. Read the article and write a summary of it using the tips above as a guide. Make sure to double-check the facts in your response.

Practical Writing: Evaluating a Web Site

Web sites combine words and graphics to inform, persuade, or entertain. One student filled out the following form to evaluate a Web site about origami.

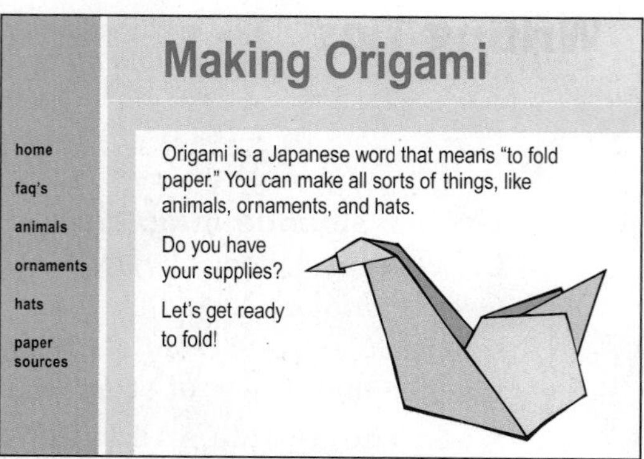

Making Origami
home
faq's
animals
ornaments
hats
paper sources
Origami is a Japanese word that means "to fold paper." You can make all sorts of things, like animals, ornaments, and hats.
Do you have your supplies?
Let's get ready to fold!

Web Site Evaluation

Complete this form by filling in the subject of the Web site, circling its purpose, and rating its parts. Then add your overall comments at the bottom.

Web-site subject: *Making Origami*

Purpose: inform persuade (entertain)

Information						
incomplete	1	2	(3)	4	5	thorough
Navigation						
confusing	1	2	(3)	4	5	simple
Layout						
distracting	1	2	3	(4)	5	helpful
Text (words)						
muddled	1	2	3	4	(5)	legible
Graphics (pictures)						
dull	1	2	3	(4)	5	engaging
Colors						
boring	1	2	3	(4)	5	appealing

The strong points: *The green and gold colors grabbed my attention. The different letter style for the title makes it stand out.*

Possible improvements: *Information about what supplies are needed and what to click next should be included.*

Writing Tips

If you are asked to evaluate a Web site, use the following tips to guide you through the process.

Before you write . . .

- **Study the form you will be using.**
  If you are given a form, review it so that you know which details to judge.
- **Review the Web site.**
  Look carefully at the site's information, navigation method, layout, and so forth. Use the form to guide you.

During your writing . . .

- **Follow all of the directions.**
  Complete the whole form.
- **Make your comments clear.**
  Give criticism that could improve the site.

After you've written a first draft . . .

- **Double-check your answers.**
  Make sure your responses are clear and complete.

Review the evaluation form on page 334. Then study the Web page below. On your own paper, write at least two "strong points" and two "possible improvements" for the Web page.

Lawrence Middle School

home calendar clubs courses schedule library sports staff contact

The field trip to Chicago is coming up. We'll visit the Museum of Natural History. They have full-size dinosaur skeletons on display. Be sure to get your permission slip in soon.

Response to Literature

Writing for Assessment

On some state and school tests, you may be asked to read a story and write a response to it. The next two pages give you an example of such a test. Read the directions, the story, and the student's comments (in blue). Then read the student's response on pages 338–339.

Response to Literature Prompt

DIRECTIONS:

- Read the following story.
- As you read, make notes. (Your notes will not be graded.)
- After reading the story, write an essay about it. You have 45 minutes to read, plan, write, and proofread your work.

When you write, focus on the author's message in the story and show your insight into the characters and ideas. Use clear organization and support your focus with examples from the text.

It Wasn't About Fish

Jake sat on his front porch and watched the road. "Any time now." Under his left elbow was a bag stuffed with a week's worth of clothes and a pair of hip waders. Under his right elbow was a five-gallon bucket loaded with a tackle box and three rods, broken down to fit in Dad's hatchback.

* "Where is he?" Jake muttered, checking his watch.

"Maybe he decided to cancel."

Jake glanced irritably over his shoulder to see his little sister grinning at him through the living room window. Her blond hair stuck out in ponytails on the sides of her face. Jake shook his head. "Yeah, right. Not two years in a row." ← Canceled before

Sarah vanished from the window and opened the front door, dragging her own pack.

"You're not going, Sarah. Mom said you couldn't."

"It's not up to Mom," she replied, sitting down beside the fishing gear. "Dad gets to decide."

Just what I need, Jake thought, *a 10-year-old sister trying to muscle in on my spring-break trip.* "You're not going. You'll get to go when you're 11. I have one more year, just me and Dad." Since the separation, Jake and Sarah had had to fight over chances like these. "Besides, you don't even like fishing."

"Maybe I do," she said. "I just need somebody to show me how."

Jake leaned back, smiling cruelly. "All right, Sis—first I'll teach you how to put worms on a hook. Then I'll teach you how to gut a fish and skin it and cut off its head."

Not nice

"Gross!" Sarah said, retreating into the house.

Laughing, Jake sighed and settled in. The fact was, he wasn't crazy about any of that stuff, either. Fishing was more about sitting in a boat with Dad and just talking, just being together on a still lake. It wasn't about fish.

"Where is he?"

He knows.

The phone rang. Jake felt his breath leave in a great gush. He knew what this call was about, even before Mom answered it. His teeth creaked against each other as he waited for the inevitable.

"Honey," Mom said, cracking the door open behind him. "Sorry. That was your dad. He's stuck at work again. He's going to have to cancel the trip. I'm sorry, Jakey."

"Don't call me Jakey," he snapped, crouching forward as if he'd just been punched in the gut. He caught his head in his hands. *Instead of fishing, I'll be stuck at home all week with Little Miss—*

The door creaked open again, and soft footsteps came on the porch behind Jake. Sarah sank down beside the fishing gear. She picked at her pack of clothes. "I wanted him to change his mind."

Jake's face flushed with anger. "You wanted him to cancel?"

Sarah stared at him, her eyes wide between her ponytails. "No, Jake. I wanted him to take me along, too."

The red in Jake's face dissolved. *Sarah wants this trip as much as I do.* Jake suddenly felt rotten. "You really want to learn to fish?"

Sarah's eyes were brimming as she nodded.

"Well, I can teach you. I know everything Dad knows."

"Honest?"

Thinks about someone else

"Sure." Jake stood up, lifting Sarah's pack and his own in one hand. His other hand hoisted the fishing gear. "Mom, fire up the minivan. I'm going to teach you two how to fish!"

Student Response

The following essay shows a student response to the story "It Wasn't About Fish." Note how the student uses details from the story to support the focus.

Beginning

The first paragraph names the story and gives a focus statement (**underlined**).

"It Wasn't About Fish" is a coming-of-age story in which a big disappointment tests the main character. Jake's father, who is separated from Jake's mother, had promised to take the boy on a fishing trip. Jake is eager to be with his dad and away from his 10-year-old sister. Then Jake's dad calls to cancel the trip for the second year in a row. <u>The way that Jake handles this disappointment shows that he is growing up.</u>

Middle

The middle paragraphs include examples and details from the story to explain characters and themes.

At first, Jake is only thinking about himself. He has packed all his things and is waiting impatiently for his dad to drive up. When Jake's sister, Sarah, says she wants to go on the trip, too, he tells her she can't. He isn't paying any attention to her feelings. Sarah doesn't give up, so Jake even scares her off by telling her, "I'll teach you how to gut a fish and skin it and cut off its head." Jake wants the fishing trip all to himself.

When Jake's dad calls to cancel the trip, Jake starts thinking in a different way. First of all, he is crushed. He feels abandoned. Afterward, when Sarah comes out, Jake gets angry. He thinks she wanted their dad to cancel. Really, she wanted to go along. Once Jake sees that Sarah feels as left out as he does, he starts to act more mature. Instead of just thinking about himself, Jake actually thinks about spending more time with his mom and his little sister.

I think the title tells a lot about the theme of this story. Jake realized that the trip "wasn't about fish," but about spending time with his dad. When the trip is canceled, Jake realizes he can go fishing anyway with the rest of his family. Instead of counting on his dad to teach him, Jake becomes the teacher.

Ending
The ending sums up the character's change and the theme.

At the beginning, Jake thinks only about himself and is pretty unhappy. By the end, he is thinking about others, and he is happy. Jake has learned that the trip is about being with family.

Respond to the reading. Answer the following questions about the student response.

- ☐ **Ideas** (1) What is the focus of the student's response? (2) What feelings does this student describe?
- ☐ **Organization** (3) How did the notes on pages 336–337 help the student organize the response?
- ☐ **Voice & Word Choice** (4) What words or phrases from the story does the writer quote? (5) Were these examples effective?

Practice Writing Prompt

Response to a literature prompt. **Carefully read the directions below. Use 10 minutes at the beginning to read the story, make notes, and plan your writing. Also leave time at the end to proofread your work.**

DIRECTIONS:

- Read the following story.
- As you read, make notes *on your own paper.*
- After reading the story, write an essay about it. You have 45 minutes to read, plan, write, and proofread your work.

When you write, focus on the author's message in the story and show your insight into the characters and ideas. Use clear organization and support your focus with examples from the text.

Mountain Encounter

Keira leaned against a large boulder and gasped for breath. She stared at the clear blue sky overhead. A small bird flew along, disappearing into the trees. Keira sighed and wished that she could fly like that bird. Instead, she was stuck here, slogging along on the trail. She looked ahead at the dirt path that switched back and forth up the steep mountainside. Her parents and little brother, Ethan, were already at the next bend.

"C'mon, Keira!" shouted Ethan. He smirked back at her as he skipped along the path.

Taking a deep breath, Keira pushed herself away from the coolness of the boulder. Her feet ached with each step. Her back was hot and sweaty under a backpack that held snacks, a bottle of water, sunscreen, and her camera. "Why did I have to come along?" Keira grumbled as she stumbled over a tree root. She just couldn't keep up with her family on these hikes. They set one pace, and Keira set another.

The voices of her family echoed from the trail ahead, and her mother's laughter floated down through the trees. Keira glared at her own feet. Puffs of dust rolled up around the boots with each arduous step. If only she could catch up . . .

Thirty agonizing minutes later, Keira slouched on a rock. "I'm taking another break!"

A faint response came from the trail ahead: "We're at the next lookout point. We'll wait for you here."

At the next lookout point . . . What beautiful things were they seeing while Keira was stuck in the dust of the trail? She slid her backpack off and grabbed her water bottle. The water was warm and tasted like plastic. Yuck. She spit it onto the ground and watched the water slowly seep into the dirt.

Maybe next year, I won't come on the family vacation. Keira reached for her backpack. Then her mouth dropped open in shock.

Just a few feet ahead on the trail stood a doe and two fawns. The deer stared at Keira with their soft brown eyes. The doe waited as her fawns skipped across the trail. They were so close, Keira wanted to reach out and touch their velvety reddish-brown coats. Instead, she held her breath and watched in quiet wonder. The fawns were so tiny and delicate. She couldn't believe how fragile they looked, and yet they playfully hopped and bounced about. All too soon, the fawns wandered off with the doe patiently following behind. As suddenly as they had appeared, the deer faded away into the woods.

Keira stared in amazement at the empty trail.

"C'mon, Keira!" Ethan called from ahead. "You're missing the view."

Nope, she thought, *I have my own view.* But out loud she replied, "I'm coming!" Keira smiled and started back up the trail, walking at her own pace.

imagine
entertain

WRITE SOURCE Online
www.hmheducation.com/writesource

Creative Writing

Writing Focus

- Writing Stories
- Writing Poems

Academic Vocabulary

Work with a partner. Read the meanings and share answers to the questions.

1. A long struggle or disagreement is a **conflict**.
   Tell about a time you experienced a conflict.
2. Something that stands in the way is an **obstacle**.
   When have you faced an obstacle at school? How did you overcome the obstacle?
3. The **plot** of a story is the events that happen.
   Describe the plot of your favorite story.
4. Something **significant** is important or has special meaning.
   Tell about a day that is significant to you.
5. A **gradual** change happens slowly or little by little.
   Why do you think it is important for some changes to be gradual and not happen all at once?

show
create
discover

Creative Writing

Writing Stories

"I'm not a kid anymore!" At some time, you may have said these words to the adults in your life. But when you cross over from adolescence to adulthood, it's a gradual process. You may not even feel it happening. Even so, at some point you suddenly realize that you have grown up.

Stories about growing up are called "coming of age" stories. The main character has a significant experience, whether big or small, that makes him or her more mature. In this chapter, you will read a "coming of age" story and then develop a story of your own to share.

Writing Guidelines

Subject: Growing up
Form: Short story
Purpose: To entertain
Audience: Classmates

Short Story

The following story is about how a young man learns to be more sensitive to others in his family.

Beginning

The beginning introduces the characters, the setting, and the conflict.

Rising Action

The rising action builds the suspense.

Shifting Gears

Ted pressed his nose against the store window that stood between him and a metallic-blue 21-speed racer. "Look at that bike, Sam! I WANT that bike!"

"Get away from there before Mr. Huan makes you clean the drool from his store window!" His friend Samantha laughed and pulled Ted away.

"Well, my birthday's tomorrow, and I've been dropping a lot of hints at home, like ads and pictures of the bike. I've just got to have it so I can go anywhere I want!"

"Your dad's out of work," Sam said quietly, "and I bet that bike's awfully expensive."

Ted didn't answer. *Yeah,* he thought, *but you only turn 13 once. Mom and Dad always promised me something special when I became a teenager.* He jumped on a hydrant and balanced a moment before jumping down again. "He'll find a job soon."

When he got home, his parents were in the kitchen talking. Ted waved to them on his way to the living room. Flopping down on the couch, he dug between the cushions for the remote. As he flipped through TV stations, he caught snatches of his parents' conversation. There were words like "overqualified" and "mortgage" and something about unemployment checks. Ted turned the volume higher.

The next morning, Ted's father woke him. "Hey, Champ, Mom had to go to work early, so I'll be making your birthday breakfast. Do you want anything special? Maybe something with wheels?" Ted was suddenly wide awake. He threw back the covers and bounded into the kitchen. There, clumsily wrapped in newspaper and tied with a crooked bow, was a bicycle-shaped package.

"Dad!" Ted tore through the newspaper, and then suddenly stopped and stared. There stood not the shiny racing bike but a secondhand 10-speed. The chrome had been shined up, and the frame was freshly painted, but it was not new—and it was not what he had hoped for. There was an awkward silence as he stared at the gift shining hopefully amidst the crumpled newspaper.

He looked away, swallowing down a lump. *Dad knows I wanted a new bike,* he thought, *not an old used one.*

High Point

The high point is when the main character has a moment of realization and moves toward adulthood.

"I know it's not exactly what you wanted, but . . . " his dad's words trailed off. Ted looked up at him and saw his own disappointment mirrored in his father's eyes. He thought of the hours his father must have spent sanding and painting, shining and oiling, to give his son something special. Suddenly, he was ashamed of himself.

"Are you kidding, Dad?" Ted hugged his father. "Hey, now I can get a paper route and help out around here." It had been a long time since they had hugged, and Ted was surprised to find he was nearly as tall as his father. "Thank you, Dad!"

The phone rang, and Ted ran to answer it.

Ending

The ending shows how the character has matured.

"Hi, Sam! Come on over and see my new bike! We can go for a ride down to the river." Ted looked over at his father, who smiled back as he picked up the crumpled paper.

Respond to the reading. Answer the following questions.

- ☐ **Ideas & Organization** (1) What does Ted want? (2) What could keep him from getting it? (3) What events make up the rising action? Name three.
- ☐ **Voice & Word Choice** (4) What words or phrases suggest the bike was disappointing? List at least two. (5) What statements suggest Ted has changed? List at least two.

Literature Connections: For another example of a short story, read Edgar Allan Poe's "The Tell-Tale Heart".

Prewriting Finding a Character

When writing a story, you should first select a main character. Next make a quick list of qualities that person might have at the beginning of your story.

The writer of "Shifting Gears" chose a teenage boy as the main character for his story and made the following quick list. He underlined the qualities he decided to use for the character.

Quick List

Character: *a boy turning 13, Ted*

Qualities: *active, heroic, selfish, unrealistic, enthusiastic, helpful, nasty, cheerful*

Make a quick list. Start with any type of person and list qualities that person might have. Underline the ones you might want to use.

Selecting a Conflict

Every story needs a conflict. A conflict is created when a character wants something and has to overcome an obstacle to get it. The writer of the story on pages 344–345 used a "What If?" chart to develop the conflict for his story.

"What If?" Chart

Character's Want	*What If? (Conflict)*
Character wants a new bicycle.	*Parents feel it's not safe.*
	* *The father is unemployed (no money).*
	The character has a physical handicap.

Create a "What If?" chart. Imagine what your character wants. Then list three or four conflicts that might keep the character from getting it. Select the conflict that you think would make the best story. (For more information on developing your story, see the plot-line graphic on page 351.)

Changing a Main Character

In a "coming of age" story, you need to focus on how your main character becomes more mature. One way to chart the change in your main character is to think about what he or she is like before and after the high point of the story.

The writer of "Shifting Gears" created a character chart to show the change in his main character. On the chart, he listed things that Ted said, thought, and did both before and after unwrapping his birthday present. The differences show that Ted is becoming more mature.

Character Chart

	What he says	What he thinks	What he does
Before	needs an expensive bike to go anywhere	doesn't want to be disappointed	avoids his parents and ignores what they are saying
After	will use the bike to get a job	realizes his father is also disappointed	hugs and thanks his father

Create a character chart. Make a chart like the one above, listing things your character could say, think, and do before and after the change.

Showing Rather Than Telling

When you focus on what a character does, you "show" instead of "tell." You can show your character's personality by describing *what* the person does and how he or she does it.

Instead of telling: **Kai felt happy.**

Show: **Kai jumped for joy.**
Kai smiled a huge grin.

Gather your details. Write down things you could have your character do to show the reader how the character feels. Write as many details as you can, even though you won't use them all. Select the details you think are clearest and most powerful.

Prewriting Using Dialogue

There are two types of dialogue. **External dialogue** is when people speak out loud. **Internal dialogue** is when the writer lets the reader know what the character is thinking.

Yeah, he thought, but you only turn 13 once.

Write internal dialogue. Imagine what your character might be thinking at some point. Be sure the internal dialogue shows the reader something important about your character.

Writing Developing Your First Draft

Once you have developed a character and a conflict, you are ready to write your first draft. The following tips will help you.

1. **Introduce your character and what he or she wants.**
   For example, the writer showed what Ted wanted through his actions.
   Ted pressed his nose against the store window that stood between him and a metallic-blue 21-speed racer.

2. **Introduce your conflict.**
   The writer used dialogue to present the obstacle.
   "Your dad's out of work," Sam said quietly, "and I bet that bike's awfully expensive."

3. **Use action verbs.**
   He jumped on a hydrant and balanced a moment before jumping down again.

4. **Build to the high point.**
   Show the character's struggle leading up to the point of decision.
   Suddenly, he was ashamed of himself.

Write your first draft. Introduce your character and conflict. Be sure the conflict is clear, and use action to build to the point when your character changes.

Revising Improving Your Writing

Once you have finished your first draft, set it aside for a while. Later, look at your story with a fresh perspective and review it for the following traits.

- ☐ **Ideas** Do I clearly present the conflict? Do I show my character through dialogue, thoughts, and action?
- ☐ **Organization** Do I build up to the moment of change? Do I end quickly after the high point?
- ☐ **Voice** Does my voice (including dialogue) sound natural and keep the reader's interest?
- ☐ **Word Choice** Do my words fit the characters? The situation?
- ☐ **Sentence Fluency** Do my sentences smoothly move the reader along?

Revise your story. Use the questions above as a guide when you revise your first draft.

Editing Checking for Conventions

After you finish revising your story, you should edit it for *conventions*.

- ☐ **Conventions** Have I begun each sentence with a capital letter? Have I ended each sentence with end punctuation and punctuated dialogue correctly? Have I checked my spelling?

Edit your story. Use the questions above to guide your editing. Then use the tips below to write a title. Create a clean final copy, proofread it, and see page 129 for publishing ideas.

Creating a Title

Your title is your first opportunity to hook the reader, so make it memorable. Here are some tips for writing a strong title.

- Use a metaphor: **Riding Through Life**
- Borrow a line from the story: **Something Special**
- Be creative: **Shifting Gears**

Story Patterns

A "coming of age" story is one of many patterns of stories you could write. Below are a few examples of common plot patterns used by writers.

The Rescue

In a *rescue* story, the main character is either in need of rescue or must rescue someone else. Adventure stories often follow this pattern.

Jori must somehow get her little brother out of a ravine.

The Union

In the *union* story, two characters must overcome one or more obstacles to be together. Many stories about friendship, family, and love use the union pattern.

Amee and Sondra are sisters adopted by different families. They must work out a way to be together.

The Underdog

In the *underdog* plot, someone overcomes adversity to achieve a goal. Main characters who are underdogs often appeal to readers.

Zhora overcomes her blindness to become a concert pianist.

The Decision

In a *decision* story, the main character is faced with a decision that will test him or her. Tension builds in the story as the decision approaches.

Anapat must choose between going on a class trip or staying with his hospitalized grandfather.

Rivalry

In a *rivalry* story, the main character must face a challenger. In this pattern, the main character is the *protagonist*, and the challenger is the *antagonist*.

Bo's team must face the team that defeated them for the state championship last year.

Choose one of the story patterns above. Think of a story that would fit that pattern. Write a single sentence that sums up the story. Be sure to include the conflict.

Elements of Fiction

The following list includes many terms used to describe the elements or parts of literature. This information will help you discuss and write about the novels, poetry, essays, and other literary works you read.

Action: Everything that happens in a story

Antagonist: The person or force that works against the hero of the story (See *protagonist*.)

Character: A person or an animal in a story

Characterization: The way in which a writer develops a character, making him or her seem believable

Here are three methods:

- Sharing the character's thoughts, actions, and dialogue
- Describing his or her appearance
- Revealing what others in the story think or say about this character

Conflict: A problem or clash between two forces in a story

There are five basic conflicts:

- **Person Against Person** A problem between characters
- **Person Against Himself or Herself** A problem within a character's own mind
- **Person Against Society** A problem between a character and society, the law, or some tradition
- **Person Against Nature** A problem with some element of nature, such as a blizzard or a hurricane
- **Person Against Destiny** A problem or struggle that appears to be beyond a character's control

Dialogue: The words spoken between two or more characters

Foil: The character who acts as a villain or challenges the main character

Mood: The feeling or emotion a piece of literature or writing creates in a reader

Moral: The lesson a story teaches

Narrator: The person or character who actually tells the story, giving background information and filling in details between portions of dialogue

Plot: The action that makes up the story, following a plan called the plot line

Plot Line: The planned action or series of events in a story (The basic parts of the plot line are the beginning, the rising action, the high point, and the ending.)

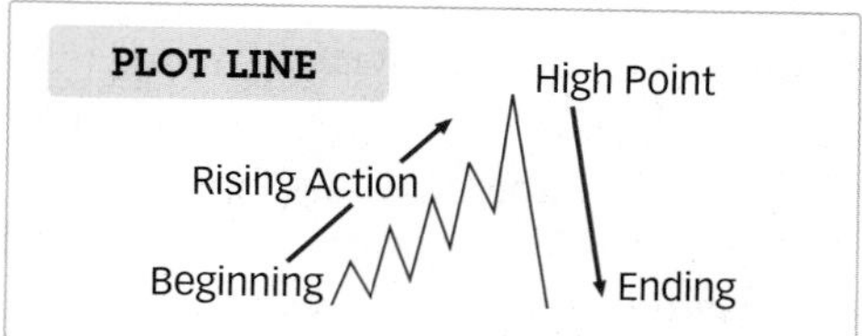

- The **beginning** introduces the characters and the setting.
- The **rising action** adds a conflict—a problem for the characters.
- The **high point** is the moment when the conflict is strongest.
- The **ending** tells how the main characters have changed.

Point of View: The angle from which a story is told (The angle depends upon the narrator, or person telling the story.)

- **First-Person Point of View** This means that one of the characters is telling the story: "We're just friends—that's all—but that means everything to us."
- **Third-Person Point of View** In third person, someone from outside the story is telling it: "They're just friends—that's all—but that means everything to them." There are three third-person points of view: *omniscient, limited omniscient,* and *camera view.* (See the illustrations on the right.)

Protagonist: The main character or hero in a story (See *antagonist.*)

Setting: The place and the time period in which a story takes place

Theme: The message about life or human nature that is "hidden" in the story that the writer tells

Tone: The writer's attitude toward his or her subject (Tone can be described by words like *angry* and *humorous.*)

Total Effect: The overall influence or impact that a story has on a reader

Third-Person Points of View

Omniscient point of view allows the narrator to tell the thoughts and feelings of all the characters.

Limited omniscient point of view allows the narrator to tell the thoughts and feelings of only one character at a time.

Camera view (objective view) allows the story's narrator to record the action from his or her own point of view without telling any of the characters' thoughts or feelings.

Select a story that you have read that fits one of the five basic conflicts on page 351. In one sentence, describe its conflict. Add a sentence that describes the protagonist.

Creative Writing

Writing Poems

The camera clicks and captures an image of one moment in time. Another way to capture a special moment is to write a poem. A well-written poem, like a thought-provoking photograph, goes beyond the surface of things and touches the heart. Poets select special words to share their deepest thoughts, feelings, and sensations.

In this chapter, you will have the best of both worlds. You'll be writing a poem based on a photograph. Your challenge, like that of the master photographer, will be to take the "picture," the photo, and then delve deeper and capture the heart of the moment.

Writing Guidelines

Subject: A picture that gives you a special feeling
Form: Free-verse poem
Purpose: To entertain
Audience: Family and classmates

Free-Verse Poem

Traditional poetry follows a specific pattern of rhythm and rhyming lines. **Free-verse poems,** on the other hand, create their own patterns and seldom use rhyming lines.

Poets who write free-verse poems carefully consider every word. The following free-verse poem expresses the poet's feelings about the photo of a soaring biplane in flight.

The Biplane

Alone
in a wide sky,
heaped clouds crowding back
against heaped hills
to make room for its dance.

Spiraling upward
for no reason, but
freedom!

Swooping downward
to chase its shadow,
waggling its wings
with a playful growl.

Its shadow passes coolly
over me,
alone and free
on this wide earth.

—Carter Williams

Respond to the reading. Reflect on the traits of the poem above.

- ☐ **Ideas & Organization** (1) Which details capture the flight of a biplane? (2) The poem is divided into four stanzas. Which special part of flight does each stanza deal with?
- ☐ **Word Choice** (3) What words work to convey a feeling of joy in this poem? List at least three.

Literature Connections: You can find another example of a free-verse poem in Langston Hughes' "I, Too."

Prewriting Selecting a Topic

To write your poem, first find a picture that gives you a special feeling. You might search family photo albums, magazines, or the Web. (Many search sites have a special option for searching pictures.) Your teacher may also offer you a choice of pictures, or you can choose one of the photos below.

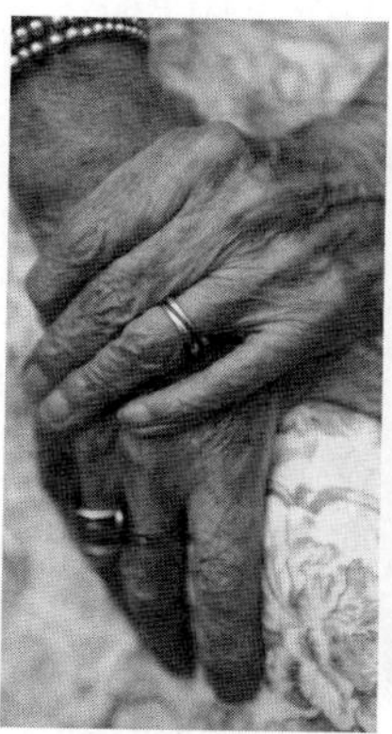

Gathering Details

Poets use sensory details to create an image in the reader's mind. As you view your photo, notice visual details. Then imagine that you are in the scene and jot down what you might hear, smell, taste, and feel. Carter created the following sensory chart, based on his biplane photo.

Sensory Chart

See	Hear	Smell	Taste	Feel
wide, brown ground wide, pale blue sky heaped shadowy mountains heaped white clouds sunlight on trees	engine buzzing, sputtering, growling hiss of wind	dry grass	dust	sun breeze flying grit heat

Create a sensory chart. Create a chart like the one above to gather sensory details about your photo. Include specific details that are in the photo as well as additional sensations that simply come to mind.

Prewriting Using Poetry Techniques

Poets play with the sounds of words. **Onomatopoeia** (*ŏn′ə-măt′ə-pē′ə*) is one example. It means using words that sound like the noises they name.

with a playful growl **wind hissing over wings**

Poets also play with the way words are placed on the page. **Line breaks**, for instance, help control the way a poem reads. In the following selection, line breaks emphasize the plane's climb and the word "freedom."

Spiraling upward
for no reason, but
freedom!

Use special techniques. On your sensory chart, underline any words that use onomatopoeia. List any other special techniques you want to use from pages 360–361.

Writing Developing Your First Draft

Now it's time to have some fun writing the first draft. Follow the tips below.

- **Study** the photo you have chosen to refresh your memory. Review your sensory chart for details.
- **Imagine** yourself in the picture. What types of things do you see and hear? Also think of experiences you have had that can help you connect with the photo.
- **Write** whatever comes to mind. There will be plenty of time for revision later.

Write your first draft. Use the tips above to guide your writing. Experiment with onomatopoeia, line breaks, and other special techniques.

Revising Improving Your Poem

"Success," you may have heard, "is 10 percent inspiration and 90 percent perspiration." Even though the first draft of your poem may be truly inspired, the work of revision can improve it. Keep these traits in mind when revising your poem.

- ☐ **Ideas** Do I use sensory details? Does my poem convey special thoughts and feelings that stem from the photo?
- ☐ **Organization** Do my line breaks and indents help express my thoughts and feelings?
- ☐ **Voice** Does my poem show personality and originality?
- ☐ **Word Choice** Are my words precise and interesting?
- ☐ **Sentence Fluency** Do my phrases and sentences have an appealing rhythm? Do I use any special poetic techniques?

Revise your poem. Using the questions above as a guide, keep revising until your poem is the best that it can be.

Editing Fine-Tuning Your Poem

Because poems are shorter than most other types of writing, every word and detail is important. Focus on the conventions of writing as you edit your poem.

- ☐ **Conventions** Is my poem free of errors that could distract the reader?

Edit your poem. Poems sometimes break the rules, but never by accident. So check your final copy one last time for errors.

Publishing Sharing Your Poem

When your poem is finished, share it with other people. Here are some good ways to do that. (See pages 57–64 for other publishing ideas.)

- **Post it.** Put it on a bulletin board, a Web site, or your refrigerator.
- **Submit it.** Send your poem to a contest or magazine.
- **Perform it.** Read your poem aloud to friends and family.

Publish your work. Poems are made to be shared, so give people a chance to read yours or hear it. Ask your teacher about other publishing ideas.

Writing a Found Poem

A found poem borrows words from day-to-day sources like street signs, package labels, recipe books, and so on. The poet then arranges those words in an interesting way. For example, the following poem uses words found at a post office and arranges them to suggest amusing meanings.

COD

BUSINESS REPLY
MAIL FIRST-CLASS
MAIL
PERMIT NO. MAIL
POST OFFICE WILL
NOT MAIL
WITH-
OUT STAMP
HELP
STAMP OUT
POSTAGE SCALE

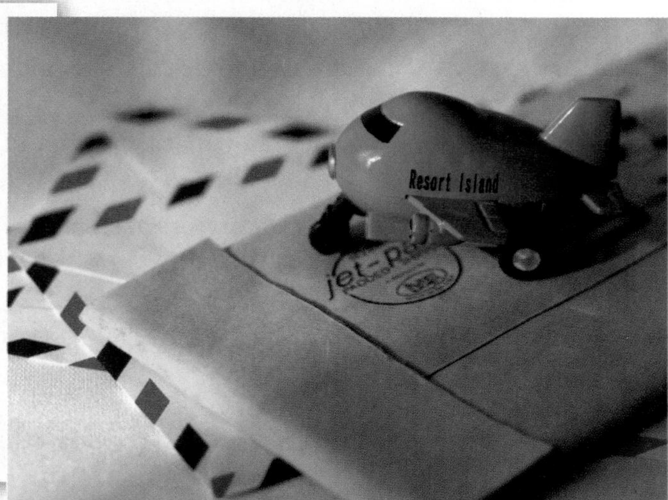

Writing Tips

- **Select a topic.** Watch for interesting words and phrases all around you—at school, at the mall, on signs, or in junk mail. What possibilities do those words and phrases suggest?
- **Gather details.** Keep a journal of things you see that could become a found poem. Collect advertisements and photographs with interesting possibilities.
- **Create a form.** Arrange your found words in unusual ways. Experiment with line breaks and indents to make your found poem one of a kind.

Create your found poem. Following the tips above, write your own found poem. Have fun making it as thought provoking as possible.

CREATIVE

Writing Other Forms of Poetry

Poetry can take many, many forms. Here are two types that could be inspired by a photograph.

Couplet

A couplet is two rhyming lines, usually of the same length and rhythm. Most couplets are in iambic pentameter format—five pairs of syllables with each pair following an unstressed-stressed pattern—like the following lines from William Shakespeare's sonnet XVIII:

So long as men can breathe, or eyes can see,
So long lives this, and this gives life to thee.

The couplet is an important building block for many rhyming forms. Taken alone, a couplet can make a concise poem itself, as in the following example.

Amber Light
Time pauses now, it seems, as this day ends
and I pause, chatting timelessly with friends.

Note that it's okay to vary from this pattern for effect. Even Shakespeare varied his rhythms sometimes!

Circle Poem

A circle poem suggests a relationship between a series of individual words or phrases. It makes these connections in a chain, eventually coming full circle to end with something close to the opening idea.

Streetlight
porch light *wet road*
clock face *night river*
floating moon

Write a poem. **Choose one of the forms on this page and write your own poem. Remember to follow the writing process on pages 355–357.**

Using Special Poetry Techniques

Poets use a variety of special techniques in their work. This page and the next define some of the most important ones.

Figures of Speech

- A **simile** (*sĭm′ə-lē*) compares two unlike things with the word *like* or *as*.

  The scrap of paper fought
  like a fish on a hook.

- A **metaphor** (*mĕt′ə-fôr*) compares two unlike things without using *like* or *as*.

  Her eyes were searchlights.

- **Personification** (*pər-sŏn′ə-fĭ-kā′shən*) is a technique that gives human traits to something that is nonhuman.

  The leaves gossiped among themselves.

- **Hyperbole** (*hī-pûr′bə-lē*) is an exaggerated statement, often humorous.

  When Guadalupe showers, the Pacific goes dry.

Sounds of Poetry

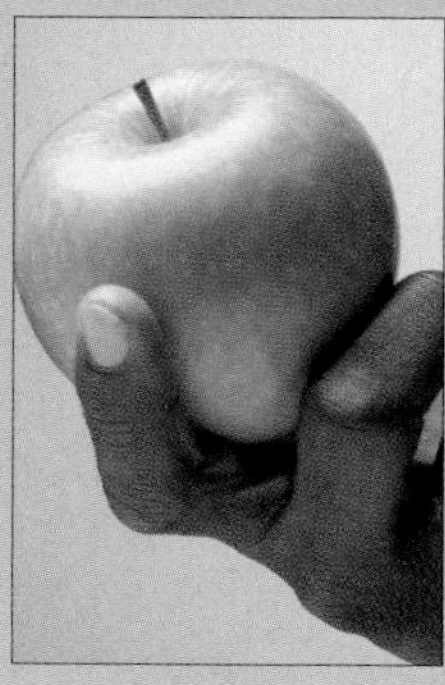

- **Alliteration** (*ə-lĭt′ə-ra′shən*) is the repetition of consonant sounds at the beginning of words.

  The kids rode a cute little carousel.

- **Assonance** (*as′ə-nəns*) is the repetition of vowel sounds anywhere in words.

  A green apple gleams at me.

- **Consonance** (*kŏn´sə-nəns*) is the repetition of consonant sounds anywhere in words.

  They plucked the anchor from the aching deep.

- **Line breaks** help to control the rhythm of a poem as it is read. Readers naturally tend to pause at the end of a line. That gives added emphasis to the last word in a line.

  In liquid heat the swimming sun
  hangs on the horizon.

- **Onomatopoeia** (*ŏn´ə-măt´ə-pē´ə*) is the use of words that sound like what they name.

  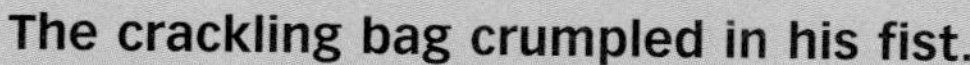

  The crackling bag crumpled in his fist.

- **Repetition** (*rĕp´ĭ-tĭsh´ən*) uses the same word or phrase more than once, for emphasis or for rhythm.

  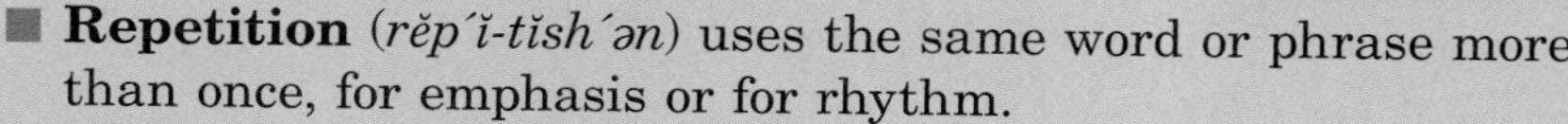

  She forced her tired feet, her tired soul, to slog along.

- **Rhyme** (*rīm*) means using words whose endings sound alike. *End rhyme* happens at the end of lines.

  Flowers grow in sidewalk cracks,
  And children grow near railroad tracks.

  Internal rhyme happens within lines.

  The smoke could choke a chimney.

- **Rhythm** (*rĭth´əm*) is the pattern of accented and unaccented syllables in a poem. The rhythm of free-verse poetry tends to flow naturally, like speaking. Traditional poetry follows a more regular pattern, as in the following example.

  In Londontown, where urchins hide,
  There lives a man of woeful mind. (a regular rhythm)

Write your own example for two or more of the techniques explained on these two pages. Then expand at least one of your examples into a complete poem.

CREATIVE

organize NOTE

WRITE SOURCE Online

www.hmheducation.com/writesource

Research Writing

Writing Focus

- **Building Research Skills**
- **Writing a Summary Paragraph**
- **Writing a Research Report**
- **Developing Multimedia Presentations**

Academic Vocabulary

Work with partner. Read the meanings and share answers to the questions.

1. A source is where you get information.
   What source would you use to find out more about outer space?
2. Media is different kinds of public communication such as television, radio, newspapers, and Web sites.
   What kinds of media have you used to find information?
3. When you do research, you use many sources to learn more about a topic.
   What is something you would like to research?

summarize RESEARCH cite

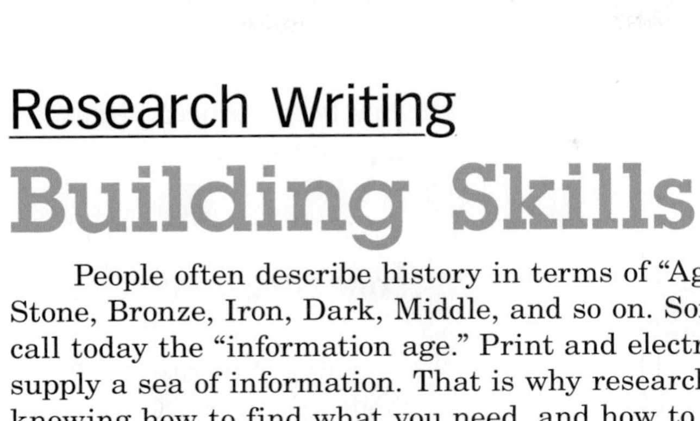

Research Writing
Building Skills

People often describe history in terms of "Ages"—Stone, Bronze, Iron, Dark, Middle, and so on. Some people call today the "information age." Print and electronic media supply a sea of information. That is why research skills—knowing how to find what you need, and how to judge what you find—are more important than ever.

In this chapter, you will learn how to use the Internet and the library to find the information you need. You'll also learn how to evaluate the sources of that information. These may be some of the most important skills you learn during your school years.

What's Ahead

Primary vs. Secondary Sources

Primary sources of information are original sources. They provide you with firsthand information.

Secondary sources contain information that has been gathered by someone else. Most nonfiction books, newspapers, magazines, and Web sites are secondary sources.

Primary Sources	Secondary Sources
1 Visiting a grocery store	**1** Visiting a Web site about salt in foods
2 Interviewing a nutritionist	**2** Reading an article about salt in foods
3 Talking to a person on a salt-free diet	**3** Watching a TV program about salt in the diet

Types of Primary Sources

- **Diaries, Journals, and Letters** You can find these sorts of primary sources in libraries and museums.
- **Presentations** Historical sites, museums, guest speakers, and live demonstrations can give you firsthand information.
- **Interviews** You can interview an expert in person, by phone, by e-mail, or through the mail.
- **Surveys and Questionnaires** To gain information from many people at once, have them answer a list of questions. Then study the results.
- **Observation and Participation** Observing a person, place, or thing is a common method of gathering firsthand information. So is participating in an event yourself.

Decide whether each of the following is a primary or a secondary source of information.

1. Listening to a scholar's presentation about an artist's life
2. Viewing an artist's work in a museum

Using the Internet

The Internet is a great place to start your research. All you need is a computer with an Internet connection to surf the World Wide Web and to send and receive e-mail. On the Web, you can find online encyclopedias, government publications, and university sites, as well as pages posted by businesses and private individuals. The tools available for searching all these sources of information are improving all the time.

If you have never used the Internet before, your teacher or librarian can show you how. Keep the following points in mind as you do your Internet research.

Points to Remember

- **Use the Web carefully.** Look for sites that have *.edu, .org,* or *.gov* in the address. These are educational, nonprofit, or government Web sites and will offer the most reliable information. If you are not sure about the reliability of a site, check with your teacher or librarian. (Also see page 374.)
- **Use a search site.** A search site such as www.google.com or www.yahoo.com is like a computer catalog for the Internet. You can enter keywords to find Web pages about your subject.
- **Look for links.** Often, a Web page includes links to other pages dealing with your topic. Take advantage of these links.
- **Be patient.** The Web is huge and searches can get complicated. New pages are added all the time, and old pages may change addresses or even disappear completely.
- **Know your school's Internet policy.** To avoid trouble, be sure to follow your school's Internet policy. Also follow whatever guidelines your parents may have set up for you.

Using the Library

While the Internet is a good place to start your research, the library may be a better place to continue your research. Library materials are often more in-depth and reliable than what you may find on the Net. In libraries, you can find books, magazines, newspapers, and videos (and maybe even a computer with Internet access). Most libraries contain the following sections.

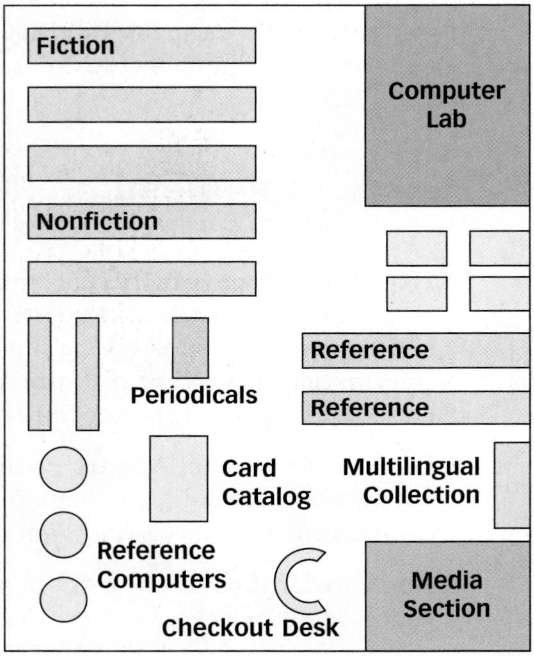

1. **Books** are usually divided into three sections.
   - The **fiction** section includes stories and novels. These books are arranged in alphabetical order by the authors' last names.
   - The **nonfiction** section contains books that are based on fact. They are usually arranged according to the Dewey decimal system. (See page 369.)
   - The **reference** section has encyclopedias, atlases, dictionaries, directories, and almanacs.

2. The **periodicals** section includes magazines and newspapers.
3. The **computer lab** has computers, often connected to the Internet. You usually sign up to use a computer.
4. The **media section** includes music CD's, DVD's, and CD-ROM's. Computer software (encyclopedias, games, and so on) may be found in this section as well.

Try It During your next visit to the library, explore a section of the library you rarely use. Take notes about the type of materials available in that section. Put your notes in your writing folder so you can use them as a reference later.

Searching a Computer Catalog

Every computer catalog is a little different. Therefore, the first time you use a particular computer catalog, it's a good idea to check the instructions for using it or to ask a librarian for help. With a computer catalog, you can find information on the same book in three ways:

1. If you know the book's **title**, enter the title.
2. If you know the book's **author**, enter the author's name. (When the library has more than one book by the same author, there will be more than one entry.)
3. Finally, if you know only the **subject** you want to learn about, enter either the subject or a keyword. (A *keyword* is a word or phrase that is related to the subject.)

If your subject is . . .	your keywords might be . . .
paper folding,	origami, paper art, paper folding, paper work.

Computer Catalog Screen

Author: Montroll, John
Title: African Animals in Origami
Published: Dover Publications, 2004
Subjects: Animals in art, decoration and ornament, origami, paper work

STATUS: Available
CALL NUMBER: 736.9822Mon
LOCATION: Adult nonfiction

Try It Create a computer catalog screen like the one above for a book you have read or one you are reading.

Searching a Card Catalog

If your library has a card catalog, it will most likely be located in a cabinet full of drawers. The drawers contain title, author, and subject cards, which are arranged in alphabetical order.

1. To find a book's **title card**, ignore a beginning *A, An,* or *The* and look under the next word of the title.
2. To find a book's **author card**, look under the author's last name. Then find the author card with the title of the book you want.
3. To find a book's **subject card**, look up an appropriate subject.

All three cards will contain important information about your book—most importantly, its call number. This number will help you find the book on the library's shelves.

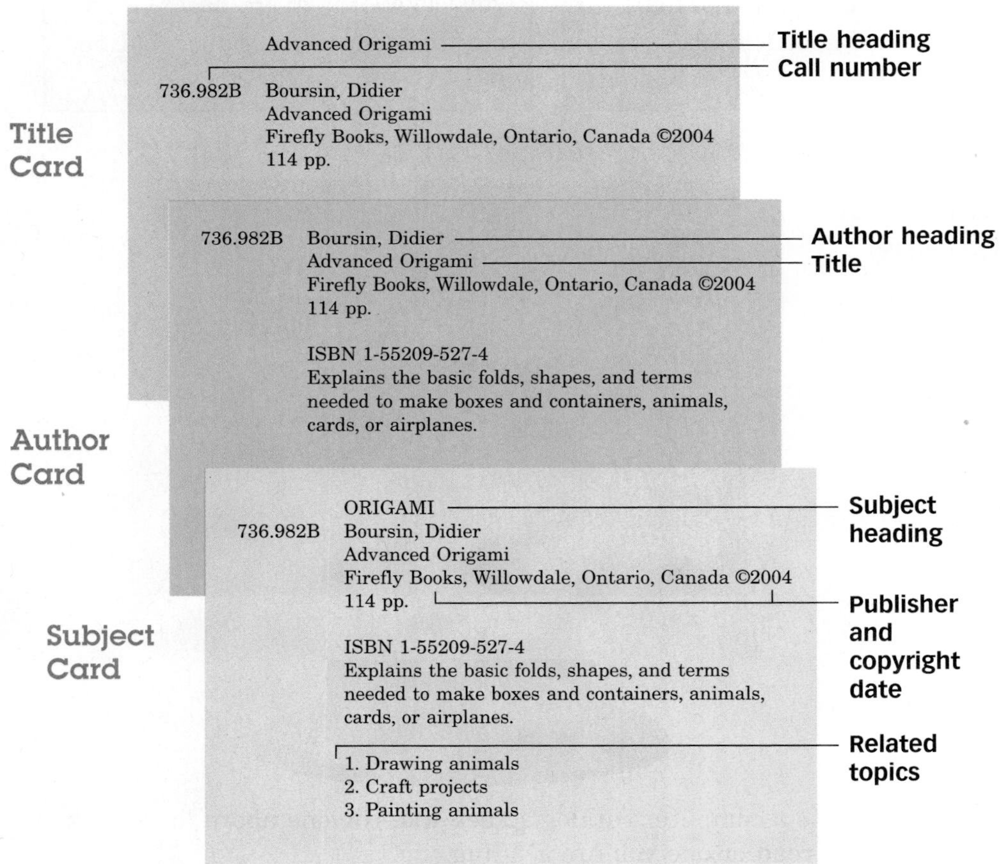

Title Card
Advanced Origami
Title heading
Call number
736.982B Boursin, Didier
Advanced Origami
Firefly Books, Willowdale, Ontario, Canada ©2004
114 pp.
Author Card
736.982B Boursin, Didier
Author heading
Advanced Origami
Title
Firefly Books, Willowdale, Ontario, Canada ©2004
114 pp.
ISBN 1-55209-527-4
Explains the basic folds, shapes, and terms needed to make boxes and containers, animals, cards, or airplanes.
Subject Card
ORIGAMI
Subject heading
736.982B Boursin, Didier
Advanced Origami
Firefly Books, Willowdale, Ontario, Canada ©2004
114 pp.
Publisher and copyright date
ISBN 1-55209-527-4
Explains the basic folds, shapes, and terms needed to make boxes and containers, animals, cards, or airplanes.
Related topics
1. Drawing animals
2. Craft projects
3. Painting animals

Finding Books

Each catalog entry for a book includes a call number that tells where to find the book on the library shelves. Most libraries organize nonfiction books by the Dewey decimal system, which has 10 subject categories.

000–099	General Works	500–599	Sciences
100–199	Philosophy	600–699	Technology
200–299	Religion	700–799	Arts and Recreation
300–399	Social Sciences	800–899	Literature
400–499	Languages	900–999	History and Geography

Using Call Numbers

A call number often has a decimal in it, followed by the first letters of an author's name. Note how the call numbers are arranged on the books below.

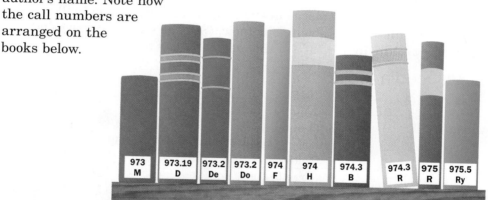

973 M | 973.19 D | 973.2 De | 973.2 Do | 974 F | 974 H | 974.3 B | 974.3 R | 975 R | 975.5 Ry

Understanding the Parts of a Book

The *title page* tells the title of the book, the author's name, and the publisher's name and city. It is usually the first page of a book. The *copyright page* comes next and includes the year the book was published. The *table of contents* lists the names and page numbers of sections and chapters in the book. Many books have at least one *appendix* near the back of the book, which holds extra information like maps, tables, and lists. The *index* is an alphabetical list of all topics and their page numbers in the book.

Get a book from your library. Write down its title and call number, its publisher's name and city, the year it was published, and the page numbers for the section names of its table of contents.

Using Reference Materials

The reference section in a library contains materials such as encyclopedias, atlases, and dictionaries.

Using Encyclopedias

An **encyclopedia** is a set of books, a CD, or a Web site with articles on almost every topic you can imagine. The topics are arranged alphabetically. The tips below can guide your use of encyclopedias.

- If the article is long, skim any subheadings to find specific information.
- Encyclopedia articles are written with the most basic information first, followed by more detailed information.
- At the end of an article, you may find a list of related topics. Use them to learn more about your topic.
- The index lists all the places in the encyclopedia where you will find more information about your topic. (See the sample below.) The index is usually in the back of the last volume of a printed set.

Encyclopedia Index

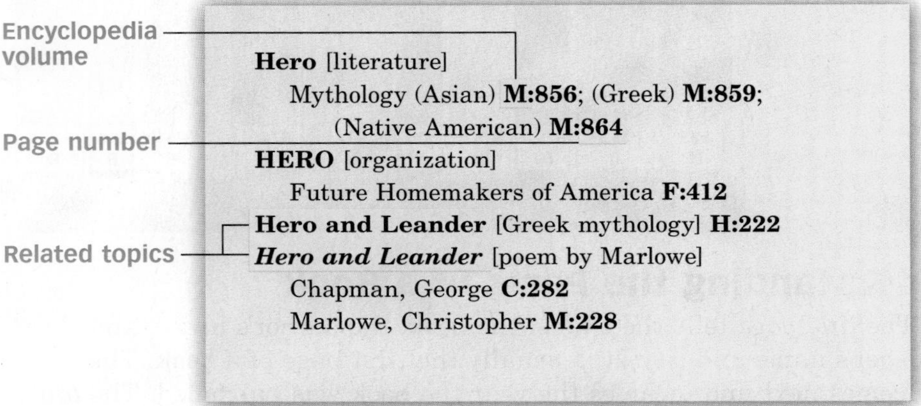

Hero [literature]
Mythology (Asian) **M:856**; (Greek) **M:859**; (Native American) **M:864**
HERO [organization]
Future Homemakers of America **F:412**
Hero and Leander [Greek mythology] **H:222**
Hero and Leander [poem by Marlowe]
Chapman, George **C:282**
Marlowe, Christopher **M:228**

Using the index entries above, list the volume and page or pages where you might find the following information.

1. A description of Leander in Greek mythology
2. Native American mythic heroes
3. A biography of the English playwright Christopher Marlowe

Finding Magazine Articles

Periodical guides are found in the reference section of the library and list magazine articles about many different topics.

- **Locate the right edition** of the *Readers' Guide to Periodical Literature* (or a similar guide). The latest edition will have the newest information, but you may need information from an older edition.
- **Look up your subject.** Subjects are listed alphabetically. If your subject is not listed, try another word related to it.
- **Write down the information** about the article. Include the name of the magazine, the issue date, the name of the article, and its page numbers.
- **Find the magazine.** Ask the librarian for help if necessary.

Readers' Guide Format

DINNER
Actually, America's still cooking, *USA Today* p6 Jn 21 2008.

DINOSAURS
Evidence of impact. J. Amadio. *Natural History* v113 no4 p15 M 2008
What wiped out the dinosaurs? E. Dobb. *Discover* v23 no6 p36–44 Jn 2006.
See also
Asteroid collisions

DIODES
Diodes and transistors demystified. Travis, Bill. *EDN* v45 no14 p28 Jl 2006.

DI SILVESTER, ROGER
Warmer climate threatens seas. Di Silvester, Roger. *National Wildlife* v42 no4 p10 Jl 2008.

Subject Entry
Title of Article
Page Number/Date
Name of Author
Cross-Reference
Name, Volume, and Number of Magazine
Author Entry

Internet-based databases are online subscription services that allow you to search for and read periodicals on the Internet.

Using the sample entries above, write answers to these questions.

1. Under what additional heading can you find more articles about dinosaurs?
2. Who wrote the article "Evidence of Impact"?
3. Which periodicals contain articles about dinosaurs?

Checking a Dictionary

A dictionary is the most reliable source for learning the meanings of words. It offers the following aids and information.

- **Guide words** are located at the top of every page. They show the first and last entry words on a page, so you can tell whether the word you're looking up is listed on that page.
- **Entry words** are the words that are defined on the dictionary page. They are listed in alphabetical order for easy searching.
- **Parts of speech** labels tell you the different ways a word can be used. For example, the word *Carboniferous* can be used as a noun or as an adjective.
- **Syllable divisions** show where you can divide a word into syllables.
- **Spelling and capitalization** (if appropriate) are given for every entry word. If an entry is capitalized, capitalize it in your writing, too.
- **Spelling of verb** forms is shown. Watch for irregular forms of verbs because the spelling can be a whole new word.
- **Illustrations** are often provided to make a definition clearer.
- **Accent marks** show which syllable or syllables should be stressed when you say a word.
- **Pronunciations** are special spellings of a word to help you say the word correctly.
- **Pronunciation keys** give symbols to help you pronounce the entry word correctly.
- **Etymology** gives the history of a word [in brackets]. Knowing a little about a word's history can make the definition easier to remember.

Open a dictionary to any page and follow the directions below.

1. Write down the guide words on that page.
2. Find a verb and write down the verb forms listed.
3. Find an entry that gives the history of the word. Write out the etymology (history).

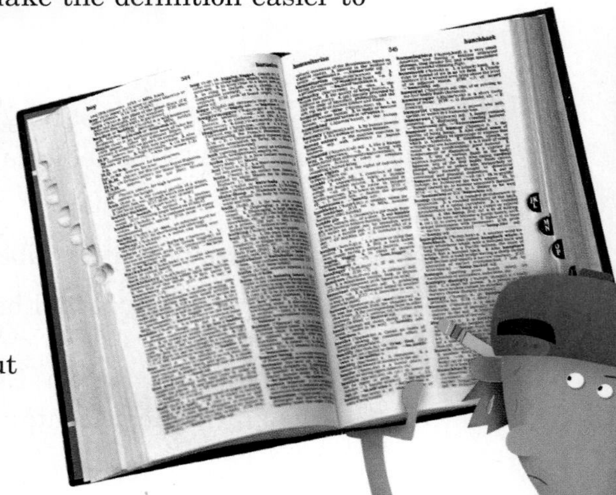

Dictionary Page

Guide words — carbon dioxide | carburetor 150

Entry word

Part of speech

Syllable division

Spelling and capitalization

Spelling of verb forms

Accent marks

Pronunciation

Pronunciation key

Etymology

carbon dioxide | carburetor 150

carbon dioxide *n.* A colorless or odorless gas that does not burn, composed of carbon and oxygen in the pro-portion CO_2 and present in the atmosphere or formed when any fuel containing carbon is burned. It is ex- haled from an animal's lungs during respiration and is used by plants in photosynthesis. Carbon dioxide is used in refrigeration, in fire extinguishers, and in carbonated drinks.

carbonic acid *n.* A weak acid having the formula H_2CO_3. It exists only in solution and decomposes readily into carbon dioxide and water.

car · bon · if · er · ous (kär´bə-**nĭf**´ər-əs) *adj.* Producing or containing carbon or coal.

Carboniferous *n.* The geologic time comprising the Mississippian (or Lower Carboniferous) and Pennsylvanian (or Upper Carboniferous) Periods of the Paleozoic Era, from about 360 to 286 million years ago. During the Carboniferous, widespread swamps formed in which plant remains accumulated and later hardened into coal. See table at **geologic time.—Carboniferous** *adj.*

car · bon · ize (kär´bə-nīz´) *tr. v.* **car · bon · ized, car · bon · iz · ing, car · bon · iz · es 1.** To change an organic compound into carbon by heating. **2.** To treat, coat, or combine with carbon.—**car´bon · i · za´tion** (kär´be-nī-zā´shən) *n.*

carbon monoxide *n.* A colorless odorless gas that is extremely poisonous and has the formula CO. Carbon monoxide is formed when carbon or a compound that contains carbon burns incompletely. It is present in the exhaust gases of automobile engines.

carbon paper *n.* A paper coated on one side with a dark coloring matter, placed between two sheets of blank paper so that the bottom sheet will receive a copy of what is typed or written on the top sheet.

carbon tet · ra · chlor · ide (tĕt´rə-**klôr**´īd´) *n.* A colorless poisonous liquid that is composed of carbon and chlorine, has the formula CCl_4, and does not burn although it vaporizes easily. It is used in fire extin-guishers and as a dry-cleaning fluid.

Car · bo · run · dum (kär´bə-**rŭn**´dəm) A trademark for an abrasive made of silicon carbide, used to cut, grind, and polish.

car · bun · cle (kär´bŭng´kəl) *n.* **1.** A painful inflammation in the tissue under the skin that is somewhat like a boil but releases pus from several openings. **2.** A deep-red garnet.

car · bu · re · tor (kär´bə-rā´tər *or* **kär**´byə-rā´tər) *n.* A device in a gasoline engine that vaporizes the gasoline with air to form an explosive mixture. [First written down in 1866 in English, from *carburet*, carbide, from Latin *carbō*, carbon.]

ă	pat	ôr	core
ā	pay	oi	boy
âr	care	ou	out
ä	father	oo	took
ĕ	pet	oor	lure
ē	be	oo	boot
ĭ	pit	ŭ	cut
ī	bite	ûr	urge
îr	pier	th	thin
ŏ	pot	*th*	this
ō	toe	zh	vision
ô	paw	ə	about

RESEARCH

Evaluating Sources

Before you use any information in your writing, you must decide if it is trustworthy. Ask yourself the following questions to help judge the value of your sources.

Is the source a primary or a secondary source?

Firsthand facts are often more trustworthy than secondhand facts. However, many secondary sources are also trustworthy. (See page 364.)

Is the source an expert?

An expert is an authority on a certain subject. You may need to ask a teacher, parent, or librarian for help when deciding how experienced a particular expert is.

Is the information accurate?

Sources that are well respected are more likely to be accurate. For example, a large city newspaper is much more reliable than a supermarket tabloid.

Is the information complete?

If a source of information provides some facts about a subject, but you still have questions, find an additional source.

Is the information current?

Be sure you have the most up-to-date information on a subject. Check for copyright dates of books and articles and for posting dates of online information.

Is the source biased?

A source is biased when it presents information that is one-sided. Some organizations, for example, have something to gain by using only some of the facts. Avoid such one-sided sources.

Research Writing

Summary Paragraph

Have you ever noticed that when you explain an idea to someone else, you actually gain a better understanding of it yourself? That is why summary writing is such a valuable skill, both for writing reports and for learning new material.

When you write a summary paragraph about an article, you identify the main idea and important supporting details so that your reader gets a clear idea of what was in the original. In this chapter, you'll read an article about salt mines in Poland, as well as a student summary of the article. Then you'll find your own article and write a clear, concise summary paragraph about it.

Writing Guidelines

Subject: A research article
Form: Summary paragraph
Purpose: To express the main idea
Audience: Classmates

Summary Paragraph

The following article, "Krakow's Salt Cellars," gives the history of two famous salt mines near Krakow, Poland. The paragraph "Polish Salt Mines" summarizes that article.

Krakow's Salt Cellars

Krakow, Poland, has two historic salt mines nearby, both of them dating back to the Middle Ages. Most famous is the 700-year-old Wieliczka mine about 20 km (12 miles) southeast of Krakow. The lesser-known Bochnia mine is 750 years old and lies about 30 km (18 miles) due east of the city.

Both mines tap into salt deposits that geologists say are left over from an inland sea that dried out 20 million years ago. Ever since the Stone Age, people have used salt from this region. At first, they boiled the brine from salt springs to get salt. In the 13th century, local farmers dug a few small shafts into the underground salt to keep themselves employed during the winter. Later, local rulers expanded the operations, using horse-powered winches to haul blocks of salt out of the mines. In the 20th century, electric power replaced the horses until the mines were finally emptied and closed in the 1990s.

Nowadays, the two mines are used mainly for guided tours. Visitors can see beautiful old chapels carved out of salt, decorated with salt statuary and chandeliers. They can view underground lakes and sports facilities where lords and ladies were once entertained. Underground museums document the history of salt mining, and cafeterias cater to the tourists. The Bochnia mine also has a sanitorium for people with respiratory ailments. The Wieliczka mine is on the United Nations' World Cultural Heritage list.

Polish Salt Mines

Topic sentence (main idea)

Body

Closing sentence

Less than 20 miles from Krakow, Poland, are two historic salt mines. The more famous is the Wieliczka mine, which dates back to the Middle Ages. The Bochnia mine is even older. Both mines were started in the 13th century and tap into deposits from a sea that dried up in prehistoric times. In the 1990s, both mines ran out of salt, but they remain open for tourists. Visitors can see chapels carved from salt, tour mining museums, and get treatment for breathing problems. The Wieliczka mine is on the United Nations' list of World Cultural Heritage sites.

Respond to the reading. Answer the following questions.

- ☐ **Ideas** (1) What details from the original are not included in the summary?
- ☐ **Organization** (2) How is the summary paragraph organized? By importance? By location? By time?
- ☐ **Word Choice** (3) Compare the first two sentences of the summary with the wording of the first paragraph of the original article. Which is simpler?

Prewriting Selecting an Article

For this assignment, you must find an article to summarize. Choose an article that . . .

- relates to a subject you are studying,
- covers an interesting topic, and
- is fairly short (three to six paragraphs).

Choose an article. Look through magazines and newspapers for an article to summarize. Choose one that has the three features listed above. Ask your teacher if the article will work for your summary paragraph.

Reading the Article

If possible, make a photocopy of your article so that you can underline important facts as you read. Otherwise, take brief notes on the article. The writer of the sample summary on page 376 underlined the key facts.

Nowadays, the two mines are used mainly for guided tours. Visitors can see beautiful old chapels carved out of salt, decorated with salt statuary and chandeliers. They can view underground lakes and sports facilities where lords and ladies were once entertained. Underground museums document the history of salt mining, and cafeterias cater to the tourists. The Bochnia mine also has a sanitorium for people with respiratory ailments. The Wieliczka mine is on the United Nations' World Cultural Heritage list.

Read your article. First read through the article. Then reread it and take notes or underline the important facts.

Finding the Main Idea

A summary focuses on the main idea of an article. Look over the material you underlined. What main idea do those facts and key details present? The writer of the sample summary wrote this main idea: "Less than 20 miles from Krakow, Poland, are two historic salt mines."

Write the main idea. Review the facts you identified in your article. What main idea do they suggest? Write the main idea as a single sentence. This sentence (or a version of it) will be the topic sentence for your paragraph.

Writing Developing the First Draft

A summary paragraph includes a topic sentence, a body, and a closing sentence. As you write each part, follow these tips.

- **Topic sentence:** Introduce the main idea of the article.
- **Body:** Include just enough important facts to support or explain the main idea. As much as possible, use your own words and phrases to share these facts.
- **Closing sentence:** Restate the main idea of the summary in a different way.

Write the first draft of your summary paragraph. Develop your topic sentence based on the main idea of the article. Add important facts that support the main idea. Then end your paragraph with a closing sentence.

Revising Reviewing Your Writing

As you revise, check your first draft for the following traits.

- ☐ **Ideas** Does my topic sentence correctly identify the main idea? Do I include only the most important facts to support it?
- ☐ **Organization** Is all of the information in a logical order?
- ☐ **Voice** Does my voice sound confident and informative?
- ☐ **Word Choice** Do I use my own words? Do I define any difficult terms?
- ☐ **Sentence Fluency** Do I use a variety of sentence types and lengths?

Revise your paragraph. First reread the article and your summary. Then use the questions above as a guide for your revising.

Editing Checking for Conventions

Focus on conventions as you edit your summary.

- ☐ **Conventions** Have I checked the facts against the article? Have I checked for errors in punctuation, spelling, and grammar?

Edit

Edit your work. Use the questions above as your editing guide. Make your corrections, write a neat final copy, and proofread it for errors.

Research Writing

Research Report

There are some amazing places in this world—many of them closer to home than you might think. For example, how many people in Detroit know that a salt mine sprawls under a quarter of their city? And how many Nevada citizens know that some trees in the White Mountains are 5,000 years old? Every region of the country has its own natural wonders and historic sites.

In this chapter, you will write a report about an important place that interests you—a building, a historic site, a monument, or a natural feature. You will explain why the place you have chosen is important, tell its history, describe its condition today, and predict something about its future. In the process, you may become something of an expert about your chosen place.

Writing Guidelines

Subject: An important place

Form: Research report

Purpose: To research and present information about an important place

Audience: Classmates

Research Report

Even though student writer Damek Soleny has lived in Detroit all of his life, he was surprised when he discovered that there is an enormous salt mine under the city. So Damek chose to write about that mine in his research report.

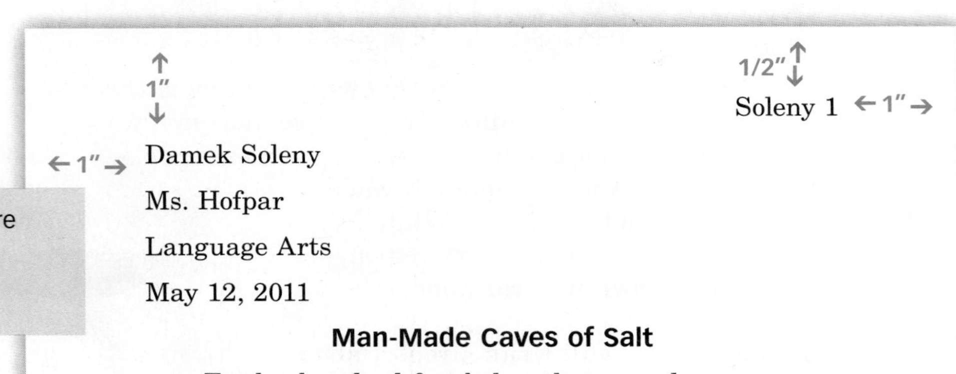

Soleny 1

Damek Soleny

Ms. Hofpar

Language Arts

May 12, 2011

The entire report is double-spaced.

Man-Made Caves of Salt

Beginning

The opening grabs the reader's attention.

Twelve hundred feet below the ground, an enormous mine has been operating almost nonstop for more than a century. A hundred miles of tunnels connect its huge chambers. It has underground roads for cars, trucks, and mining machines. This mine produces hundreds of tons of "rock" every day. However, the rock from this mine is not gold, or iron ore, or even coal; it is salt. This enormous, hundred-year-old salt mine lies beneath the city of Detroit, Michigan.

The thesis (focus) statement identifies the topic (**underlined**).

Salt is much more important than most people realize. Wars have been fought over it. In some places, people have traded salt for gold in equal measures. In ancient China, salt coins were used for money, and Roman soldiers were often paid in salt, which is where the word "salary" comes from. In the human body, salt carries electrical signals that keep a person alive. To

Middle
The first middle paragraph explains why the topic is important.

Headings help the reader to understand the paper's organization.

A map helps the reader understand the size and location of the mine.

The history of the place is explained.

Soleny 2

stay healthy, a person needs to eat about three pounds of salt a year (*Modern*). Salt is also used to preserve meat and fish, to tan leather, to soften water, and to make many different chemicals. However, most of the salt from the Detroit mine is now used to melt ice and snow on streets and highways (Zacharias).

The Salt Mine's History

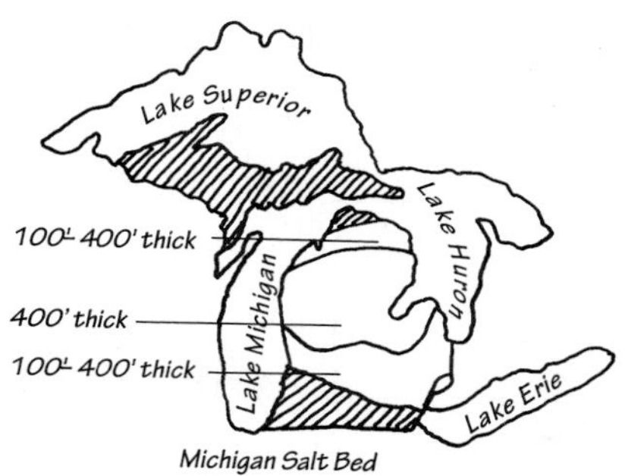

Michigan Salt Bed

Scientists say that the Detroit mine digs into a bed of salt that is several hundred million years old. From 600 million to 230 million years ago, seawater flooded the middle of North America many times. As sun and wind evaporated the water, sea salt was deposited on the submerged land. Trillions of tons of salt, collected in a layer 400 to 1,600 feet thick, reached from western Michigan all the way to New York. Eventually, it was covered by silt that became rock more than 1,000 feet thick. When people later came to the area, they found springs of salty water bubbling from the ground. Early settlers would collect that liquid and boil away the water to get the salt ("Dry").

In 1896, the Detroit salt mine was started in order to dig the salt out of the ground. It began as a shaft

RESEARCH

A source and page number are identified in parentheses.

The place is described as it exists today.

1,200 feet deep and about 6 feet wide. At first, the salt was used mainly for storing meat and fish and for making ice cream (*Detroit* 167). In 1940, though, Detroit became the first city to use rock salt on icy roads. Other cities soon followed Detroit's example, and the mine began selling most of its salt to road crews ("Dry"). In 1983, however, low sales and competition from Canadian mines caused the Detroit mine to close. Crystal Mines bought the mine, hoping to store hazardous wastes there. In 1985, while waiting for a permit, they ran public tours of the mine. In 1997, after the permit was denied, Crystal Mines sold the mine to the Detroit Salt Company, according to Kim Roberts, manager of the mine. The mine was reopened, and it again became one of the main sources of road salt in the United States.

The Salt Mine Today

Some people call the Detroit salt mine a city beneath a city. It covers 1,400 acres under Detroit and its suburbs. That's equal to 1,300 football fields. Also, it has more than 50 miles of roads where construction equipment, trucks, and cars drive. All these vehicles had to be taken apart, carried down the shaft in pieces, and reassembled in underground workshops. The seven-foot-tall tires for the dump trucks had to be compressed and bound with straps to fit down the shaft (Zacharias).

The writer's last name and page number appear on every page.

Soleny 4

The mining equipment includes many different types of big electric trucks. One type has a giant chain saw on the front, which cuts a deep groove into a salt wall at floor level. Then a drilling-machine truck bores a pattern of holes 20 feet deep into the wall to hold dynamite or other explosives. The blast from these explosives breaks hundreds of tons of rock from the wall in huge chunks. Trucks with giant shovels then scoop up tons at a time and drop them into dump trucks. The dump trucks carry the chunks back to the shaft, where a crusher breaks them into smaller pieces and sorting machines separate the pieces by size. Finally, buckets that can hold nine tons of salt run up a conveyor to the surface. There the salt is packaged and shipped ("Dry").

Each paragraph begins with a topic sentence, followed by supporting details.

The Salt Institute explains that the mine is carved out in a "room-and-pillar" method. Each room is as big and high as a school gymnasium. Between rooms, the miners leave pillars of salt about 60 feet wide to hold up the ceiling. This type of mining gets about 70 percent of the salt from the ground, leaving the other 30 percent as support pillars. Because the salt bed has never had an earthquake or other shock, it lies very flat, so the pattern of rooms and pillars stretches level from one end of the mine to the other. According to the Salt Institute, this mine "has never experienced a collapse or mine fatality" ("Dry").

A quotation is used for emphasis.

Soleny 5

Miners say that the mine is a very clean and healthy place to work. The temperature stays a cool 58 degrees year-round, and the salt keeps the humidity at an even 55 percent. There are no bugs, rats, or other animals living in the mine, because there is nothing for them to eat (Zacharias). The air itself is very clean in a salt mine, with no mold or other allergens like on the surface (*Modern*).

Ending

The final paragraph states something about the place's future and leaves the reader with something to think about.

The Salt Mine's Future

The Detroit salt mine could have a very interesting future. According to geologists, there is enough salt underneath Michigan to last for 70 million years ("Dry"). Many people worry, though, that the runoff from road salt is having a negative effect on our rivers and lakes. If people stop using salt on icy streets and highways, there may not be enough business to keep the Detroit mine open. In that case, the mine could be used to store important documents, films, and artwork, as some other salt mines do (Tanner). If nothing else, the Detroit salt mine could be turned into a public museum because it is an important part of the city's history.

A separate page alphabetically lists sources cited in the paper.

Soleny 6

Works Cited

Detroit Almanac. Detroit: Detroit Free Press, 2004. Print.

"Dry (Rock Salt) Mining." *Salt Institute*. Salt Institute, 10 May 2008. Web. 25 April 2011.

Modern Marvels: Salt Mines. A&E Television Networks, 2004. DVD.

Roberts, Kim. Message to Damek Soleny. 4 May 2011. E-mail.

Tanner, Beccy. "Salt Mine Museum Could Spark Tourist Trade." *Wichita Eagle* 8 May 2004: A9. Newspaper.

Zacharias, Patricia. "The Ghostly Salt City Beneath Detroit." *The Detroit News*. 11 May 2008. Web. 27 April 2011.

Respond to the reading. After you have finished reading the sample research report, answer the following questions about the traits of writing.

- ☐ **Ideas** (1) What is the main idea of the report? (2) List at least four details that emphasize the age and size of the mine.
- ☐ **Organization** (3) How do the headings help organize the paper?
- ☐ **Voice** (4) What words does the writer use to show his interest in this topic? Give at least two examples.

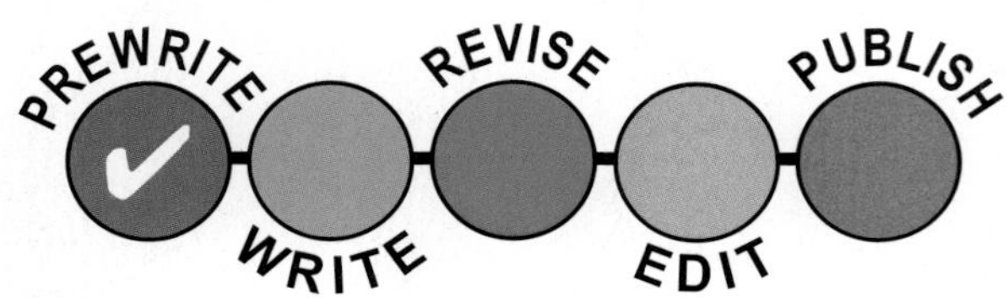

Prewriting

"Well begun is half done," Aristotle once said. When it comes to writing a research paper, a good beginning means choosing a good topic, taking careful notes during your research, writing a solid thesis statement, and preparing a good plan. Use these keys as a guide to your prewriting.

Keys to Effective Prewriting

1. For your topic, choose an important place that interests you.
2. Make a list of questions you want to have answered about that place.
3. Make sure that there are enough details about its past, present, and future.
4. Use a gathering grid and note cards to organize your research questions and the answers you find.
5. Be careful to list your sources when paraphrasing or quoting exact words.
6. Write down the publication details of all your sources for making a works-cited page.

Selecting a Topic

To find a topic for your research paper, make a list of important places that interest you. Answer the following questions to help generate ideas. (See Damek's list below as an example.)

- What interesting places have I visited?
- What interesting places have I seen on TV, in magazines, or on the Web?
- What interesting places does my social studies text mention?

TOPICS LIST

I have visited these interesting places:
- *The current Michigan State Capitol*
- *The Graystone International Jazz Museum in Detroit*
- *Yerkes Observatory in Williams Bay, Wisconsin*
- *The U.S.S. Constitution in Boston*

I have seen these places on TV, on the Web, or in a magazine:
- *The cliff dwellings at Mesa Verde, Colorado*
- * *The salt mine under Detroit*
- *The "Avenue of Giants," sequoia trees in California*
- *Fort Knox's gold vault in Kentucky*

My textbook mentions these interesting places:
- *Monticello, Thomas Jefferson's home*
- *The Alamo, a famous battle site in Texas*
- *Ellis Island, where many immigrants landed*
- *The International Space Station*

Make your list. Try to list at least three possible topics under each heading. Then choose the one that interests you the most.

Prewriting Sizing Up Your Topic

A good research report about a place should say something about the place's importance, its past, its present, and its future. Damek decided to write about the salt mine under Detroit. He searched the Internet and learned the following major facts about that mine. With this information to start with, Damek was sure he could write a good research report about the mine.

Details List

Notes About the Detroit Salt Mine

Its importance
- *The salt has been used for making chemicals, softening water, preserving food, and making ice cream.*
- *Today, it is used mainly for melting road ice.*

Its past
- *The salt bed is left from an ancient sea.*
- *The first mine shaft was dug in 1896.*
- *During the '80s its owners gave public tours.*

Its present
- *It has 100 miles of tunnels and 50 miles of roads.*
- *The rooms are each as big as a school gymnasium.*
- *Huge electric trucks do the digging and hauling.*

Its future
- *There's enough salt for 70 million years of mining.*
- *If demand for salt goes down, the mine might close.*
- *It could be used as a storage place or as a museum.*

Size up your topic. Look up your chosen topic in an encyclopedia or on the Internet. List the key details you find. Are there enough details to support a research report? If not, think of another topic.

Using a Gathering Grid

A gathering grid can help you organize the information from your research. Damek made a grid during his research about the Detroit salt mine. Down the left-hand side, he listed questions about his topic. Across the top, he listed sources he found to answer those questions. For answers too long to fit in the grid, Damek used note cards. (See pages 390–391.)

Gathering Grid

Detroit's Salt Mine	Detroit Almanac	Salt Institute	Detroit News Web site	Wichita Eagle
Importance: What is its purpose?			Rock salt for icy roads and making chemicals	
History: What is its past?	People dug a 1,200-foot shaft in 1896	See note card #1.		
Present: What does it look like?		Rooms the size of gymnasiums, pillars 60 feet wide	100 miles of tunnels, 50 miles of roads	
Future: How might it be used in the future?			It can't be use for toxic storage.	Some salt mines are used as museums.

Create a gathering grid. Make a list of questions in the left-hand column of your grid. Across the top, list the sources that you use. Fill in the squares with answers you find. Use note cards for longer, more detailed answers.

Prewriting Creating Note Cards

While a gathering grid is a great way to see all your research at one glance, sometimes an answer needs more space. You can use note cards to keep track of details from your research.

Number each new card and write a question at the top. Then answer the question with a paraphrase, a list, or a quotation. At the bottom, identify the source of the information (including a page number if appropriate). Here are three sample cards Damek made for his report on the Detroit salt mine.

Card number
Question
Answer (paraphrase)

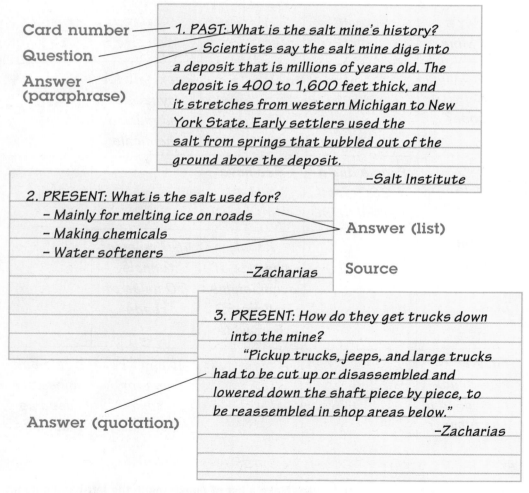

1. PAST: What is the salt mine's history?
Scientists say the salt mine digs into a deposit that is millions of years old. The deposit is 400 to 1,600 feet thick, and it stretches from western Michigan to New York State. Early settlers used the salt from springs that bubbled out of the ground above the deposit.
–Salt Institute

2. PRESENT: What is the salt used for?
– Mainly for melting ice on roads
– Making chemicals
– Water softeners
–Zacharias

Answer (list)
Source

3. PRESENT: How do they get trucks down into the mine?
"Pickup trucks, jeeps, and large trucks had to be cut up or disassembled and lowered down the shaft piece by piece, to be reassembled in shop areas below."
–Zacharias

Answer (quotation)

Prewrite

Create note cards. Make note cards like the examples above whenever your answers are too long to fit on your gathering grid.

Avoiding Plagiarism

Your research will lead you to many interesting facts and ideas to include in your paper. However, you must give credit for facts and ideas that are not common knowledge. Using other people's words and ideas without giving them credit is called plagiarism, and it is a form of stealing. Here are two good ways to avoid plagiarism.

- **Paraphrase:** Usually it's best to put the ideas from a source into your own words so that your paper sounds like you. This is called *paraphrasing*. Remember, though, to give credit to the source of the ideas. (See page 396.)
- **Quote exact words:** When a source states something so perfectly that it makes sense to use those words exactly, you may include them in quotation marks and give credit to the source. (See page 396.)

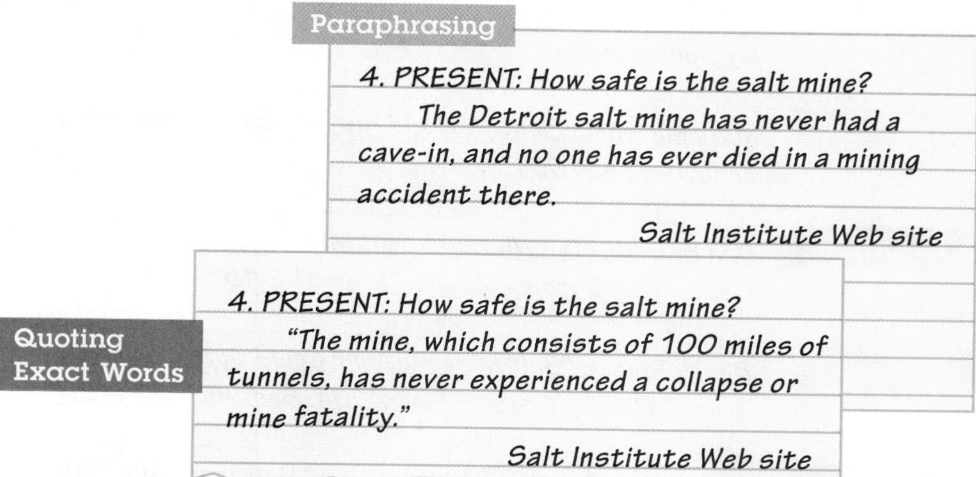

Paraphrasing
4. PRESENT: How safe is the salt mine?
The Detroit salt mine has never had a cave-in, and no one has ever died in a mining accident there.
Salt Institute Web site
Quoting Exact Words
4. PRESENT: How safe is the salt mine?
"The mine, which consists of 100 miles of tunnels, has never experienced a collapse or mine fatality."
Salt Institute Web site

Read the following excerpt from "Salt in the Michigan Basin." Then label two note cards with the question "What is salt used for?" On one card, quote a sentence from the excerpt. On the other, paraphrase the selection.

Chemically, there are several different types of salt, and they are used for many different purposes. When most people say "salt," they're talking about sodium chloride. In its purest form, sodium chloride is used for table salt. Mined rock salt usually has some impurities in it and is used for other purposes. Road crews use rock salt to melt ice and snow. Chemical companies use it to make rayon, soap, and bleach. It is also used in water softeners and as salt licks.

Prewriting Keeping Track of Your Sources

Write down the following information about the sources you find.

Encyclopedia entry: Author's name (if listed). Entry title. Encyclopedia title. Edition (if given). Publication date. Medium of publication.

Book: Author's name. Title. City of publication: Publisher's name and year of publication. Medium of publication.

Magazine: Author's name. Article title. Magazine title. Date published. Page numbers. Medium of publication.

Internet: Author's name (if listed). Page title. Site title. Date posted or copyright date. Site sponsor. Date found. Medium of publication.

Video: Title. Director's name (if given). Distributor, Release date. Medium of reception.

My Source Notes

Book *Mark Kurlansky. Salt: A World History. East Rutherford, NJ: Penguin USA, 2007. Print.*

Magazine *Don Hallett. "The Wieliczka Salt Mine." Geology Today. September/October 2006. Pages 182-185. Print.*

Newspaper *Beccy Tanner. "Salt Mine Museum Could Spark Tourist Trade." Wichita Eagle. 8 May 2004. Section A. Page 9. Print.*

Internet *No author. "Dry (Rock Salt) Mining." Salt Institute. Salt Institute. 10 May 2008. Web. 25 April 2011.*

Video *Modern Marvels: Salt Mines. A&E Television Networks. 2004. DVD.*

Interview *Roberts, Kim. E-mail interview. 4 May 2011.*

List sources. Keep a list of each of your sources with the information shown above. Whenever you find a new source, add it to the list.

Writing Your Thesis Statement

After your research is completed, you will need to write a thesis statement to guide your writing. The thesis is the main idea you want to emphasize in your report. It serves as a focus for your report to make sure all the parts work together. Use the following formula to help you write your thesis statement.

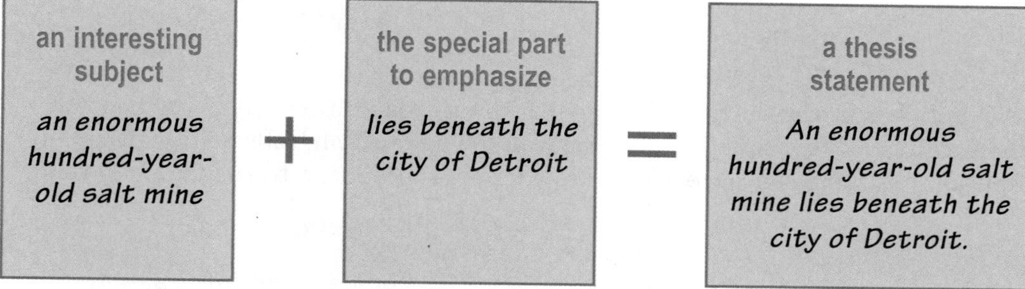
an interesting subject
an enormous hundred-year-old salt mine
+
the special part to emphasize
lies beneath the city of Detroit
=
a thesis statement
An enormous hundred-year-old salt mine lies beneath the city of Detroit.

Sample Thesis Statements

The 100-year-old Yerkes Observatory in Williams Bay, Wisconsin,
(an interesting subject)
has the largest refracting telescope in the world.
(the part to emphasize)

The "Avenue of the Giants" in northern California
(an interesting subject)
includes some giant sequoia trees that are 2,000 years old.
(the part to emphasize)

The International Space Station
(an interesting subject)
is the combined project of 16 different countries.
(the part to emphasize)

Prewrite

Form your thesis statement. Review your research notes and choose a special part to emphasize about your topic. Using the formula above, write a thesis statement for your report.

Prewriting Outlining Your Ideas

Making an outline is one way to organize your details and plan your report. You can use either a topic outline or a sentence outline to list the main ideas of your report. A topic outline lists ideas as words or phrases. A sentence outline puts ideas into full sentences. (Also see page **550**.)

Sentence Outline

Below is the first part of a sentence outline for the report on pages 380–385. Notice that the outline begins with the thesis statement for the report. Then it lists a topic sentence for each middle paragraph, followed by details to support that topic sentence. Compare this partial outline to the finished report.

Thesis Statement

THESIS STATEMENT: This enormous, hundred-year-old salt mine lies beneath the city of Detroit, Michigan.

I. Topic Sentence (for first middle paragraph)

I. *Salt is much more important than most people realize.*

A. B. C. D. Supporting Ideas

A. *Wars have been fought over salt, and it has been used for money.*
B. *It helps keep the body alive and healthy.*
C. *It is used to preserve food, to soften water, and to make chemicals.*
D. *It is used to melt the ice on roads.*

II. Topic Sentence (for second middle paragraph)

II. *Scientists say that the Detroit mine digs into a bed of salt that is several hundred million years old.*

A. . . .
B. . . .

Remember: In an outline, if you have a I, you must also have a II. If you have an A, you must also have an B.

Create your outline. Write a sentence outline for your report. Be sure that each topic sentence (I, II, III, . . .) supports the thesis statement and that each detail (A, B, C, . . .) supports its topic sentence. Use your outline as a guide when you write the first draft of your report.

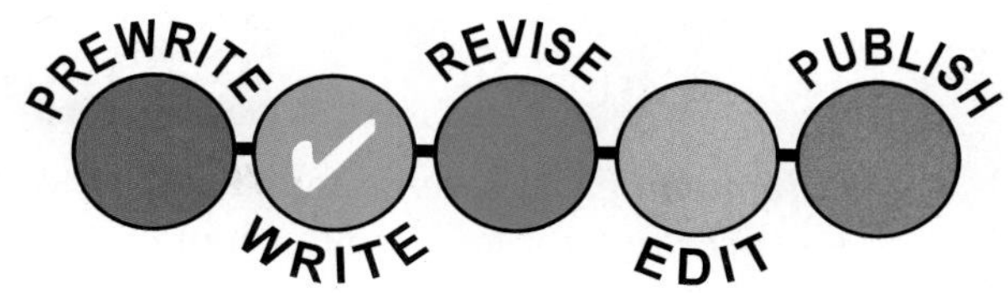

Writing

With your research finished and a plan prepared, you're ready to begin writing the first draft of your paper. You don't have to get everything perfect in this draft. Just get your ideas down on paper in a way that makes sense to you. Use the following keys to guide your writing.

Keys to Effective Writing

1. Use your first paragraph to introduce your topic, get your reader's attention, and present your thesis statement.
2. In the second paragraph, explain why the place you have chosen is important.
3. In the next few paragraphs, tell about the history of the place.
4. Next, describe the place as it exists today.
5. End your paper with a few comments about the place's future.
6. Remember to cite your sources in your paper and list those sources alphabetically on a works-cited page.

Citing Sources in Your Report

Remember: It's very important that you give credit for each of the sources you use in your report.

When You Have All the Information

- The most common type of credit (citation) lists the author's last name and the page number in parentheses.

  "Marco Polo discovered that Tibetans used salt cakes stamped with the imperial seal of the great Kublai Khan as money" (Kemper 70).

- If you already name the author in your report, just include the page number in parentheses.

  Steve Kemper explains that during the Civil War, the North sent troops to attack the South's salt producers in order to make the South weaker (71).

When Some Information Is Missing

- Some sources do not list an author. In those cases, use the title and page number. (If the title is long, use only the first word or two.)

  At first, the salt was used mainly for storing meat and fish and for making ice cream (Detroit 167).

- Some sources (especially Internet sites) do not use page numbers. In those cases, list just the author.

  The seven-foot-tall tires for the dump trucks had to be compressed and bound with straps to fit down the shaft (Zacharias).

- If a source does not list the author or page number, use the title.

  Early settlers would collect that liquid and boil away the water to get the salt ("Dry").

Rewrite the following sentence, citing Steve Kemper's article, "Salt of the Earth," from the *Smithsonian*, page 78.

Throughout history, people have soaked themselves in salt springs, believing that the salty water makes them healthier.

Writing Starting Your Research Report

The opening paragraph of your report should grab the reader's attention, introduce your topic, and present your thesis statement. To start your opening paragraph, try one of these three approaches.

Beginning
Middle
Ending

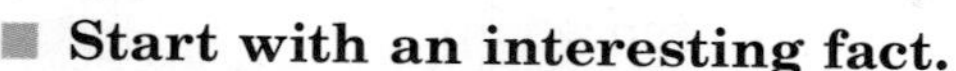

- **Start with an interesting fact.**
  Twelve hundred feet below the ground, an enormous mine has been operating almost nonstop for more than a century.

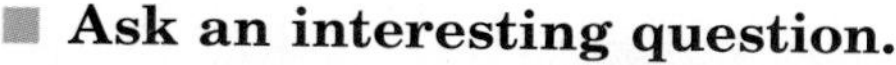

- **Ask an interesting question.**
  How many people know that there are cars and trucks driving on roads more than 1,200 feet below the city of Detroit?
- **Start with a quotation.**
  "The only dirty part of this job is getting to work," says salt miner Joel Payton.

RESEARCH

Beginning Paragraph

The beginning paragraph starts with an interesting detail and ends with the thesis (focus) statement (underlined).

Twelve hundred feet below the ground, an enormous mine has been operating almost nonstop for more than a century. A hundred miles of tunnels connect its huge chambers. It has underground roads for cars, trucks, and mining machines. This mine produces hundreds of tons of "rock" every day. However, the rock from this mine is not gold, or iron ore, or even coal; it is salt. <u>This enormous, hundred-year-old salt mine lies beneath the city of Detroit, Michigan.</u>

Write your opening paragraph. Start with something to grab the reader's attention; then introduce your topic and end with a clear thesis statement.

Writing Developing the Middle Part

The middle part of your report should begin by explaining why the place you have chosen is important. Next tell about its history, and then describe the place as it exists today.

Each middle paragraph should start with a topic sentence covering one main idea. Additional sentences in each paragraph should support that one idea. Refer to your sentence outline to guide your writing. (See page 394.)

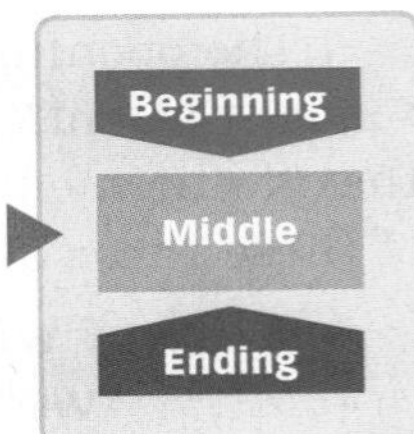

Middle Paragraphs

All the details support the topic sentence (underlined).

The first middle paragraph explains why the place is important.

The author tells about the history of the place.

Salt is much more important than most people realize. Wars have been fought over it. In some places, people have traded salt for gold in equal measures. In ancient China, salt coins were used for money, and Roman soldiers were often paid in salt, which is where the word "salary" comes from. In the human body, salt carries electrical signals that keep a person alive. To stay healthy, a person needs to eat about three pounds of salt a year (Modern). Salt is also used to preserve meat and fish, to tan leather, to soften water, and to make many different chemicals. However, most of the salt from the Detroit mine is now used to melt ice and snow on streets and highways (Zacharias).

The Salt Mine's History

Scientists say that the Detroit mine digs into a bed of salt that is several hundred million years old. From 600 million to 230 million years ago, seawater flooded the middle of North America many times. As sun and wind evaporated the water, sea salt was

Sentences are arranged so that the reader can easily follow the ideas.

Sources are included in parentheses.

Each paragraph has a topic sentence and supporting details.

deposited on the submerged land. Trillions of tons of salt, collected in a layer 400 to 1,600 feet thick, reached from western Michigan all the way to New York. Eventually, it was covered by silt that became rock more than 1,000 feet thick. When people later came to the area, they found springs of salty water bubbling from the ground. Early settlers would collect that liquid and boil away the water to get the salt ("Dry").

In 1896, the Detroit salt mine was started in order to dig the salt out of the ground. It began as a shaft 1,200 feet deep and about 6 feet wide. At first, the salt was used mainly for storing meat and fish and for making ice cream (Detroit 167). In 1940, though, Detroit became the first city to use rock salt on icy roads. Other cities soon followed Detroit's example, and the mine began selling most of its salt to road crews ("Dry"). In 1983, however, low sales and competition from Canadian mines caused the Detroit mine to close. Crystal Mines bought the mine, hoping to store hazardous wastes there. In 1985, while waiting for a permit, they ran public tours of the mine. In 1997, after the permit was denied, Crystal Mines sold the mine to the Detroit Salt Company, according to Kim Roberts, manager of the mine. The mine was reopened, and it again became one of the main sources of road salt in the United States.

The author describes the place as it is today.

The author shares interesting details with the reader.

The Salt Mine Today

Some people call the Detroit salt mine a city beneath a city. It covers 1,400 acres under Detroit and its suburbs. That's equal to 1,300 football fields. Also, it has more than 50 miles of roads where construction equipment, trucks, and cars drive. To get these vehicles down the shaft, they had to be taken apart, carried down in pieces, and reassembled in underground workshops. The seven-foot-tall tires for the dump trucks had to be compressed and bound with straps to fit down the shaft (Zacharias).

The mining equipment includes many different types of big electric trucks. One type has a giant chain saw on the front, which cuts a deep groove into a salt wall at floor level. Then a drilling-machine truck bores a pattern of holes 20 feet deep into the wall to hold dynamite or other explosives. The blast from these explosives breaks hundreds of tons of rock from the wall in huge chunks. Trucks with giant shovels then scoop up tons at a time and drop them into dump trucks. The dump trucks carry the chunks back to the shaft, where a crusher breaks them into smaller pieces and sorting machines separate the pieces by size. Finally, buckets that can hold nine tons of salt run up a conveyor to the surface. There the salt is packaged and shipped ("Dry").

A comparison of size helps the reader understand a complex idea.

The Salt Institute explains that the mine is carved out in a "room-and-pillar" method. Each room is as big and high as a school gymnasium. Between rooms, the miners leave pillars of salt about 60 feet wide to hold up the ceiling. This type of mining gets about 70 percent of the salt from the ground, leaving the other 30 percent as support pillars. Because the salt bed has never had an earthquake or other shock, it lies very flat, so the pattern of rooms and pillars stretches level from one end of the mine to the other. According to the Salt Institute, this mine "has never experienced a collapse or mine fatality" ("Dry").

Miners say that the mine is a very clean and healthy place to work. The temperature stays a cool 58 degrees year-round, and the salt keeps the humidity at an even 55 percent. There are no bugs, rats, or other animals living in the mine, because there is nothing for them to eat (Zacharias). The air itself is very clean in a salt mine, with no mold or other allergens like on the surface (Modern).

Write your middle paragraphs. Keep these tips in mind as you write.

1. Support the topic sentence for each paragraph with details.
2. Refer to your outline for help with your organization. (See page 394.)
3. Give credit to your sources in your paper. (See page 396.)

Writing Ending Your Research Report

Your ending paragraph should sum up your report and bring it to a thoughtful close. To do that, you might . . .

- **Remind the reader of the thesis of the report.**
- **Provide information about the place's future.**
- **Make a final observation for the reader.**

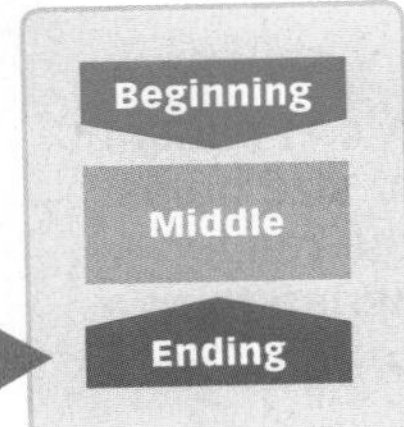

Ending Paragraph

The writer includes an interesting fact.

Some final possibilities leave the reader with something to think about.

The Salt Mine's Future

The Detroit salt mine could have a very interesting future. According to geologists, there is enough salt underneath Michigan to last for 70 million years ("Dry"). Many people worry, though, that the runoff from road salt is having a negative effect on our rivers and lakes. If people stop using salt on icy streets and highways, there may not be enough business to keep the Detroit mine open. In that case, the mine could be used to store important documents, films, and artwork, as some other salt mines do (Tanner). If nothing else, the Detroit salt mine could be turned into a public museum because it is an important part of the city's history.

Write your final paragraph. Draft your final paragraph using one or more of the three strategies listed above.

Look over your report. Read your report, checking your notes and outline to make sure you haven't forgotten anything. In the margins and between the lines, make notes about anything you should change.

Creating Your Works-Cited Page

To create your works-cited page, first format each of your sources; then list them in alphabetical order. The purpose of a works-cited page is to help other people find the sources you used.

Encyclopedias

Author (if available). Article title (in quotation marks). Title of the encyclopedia (underlined or in italics, if typed). Edition (if available). Date published. Medium of publication.

> "Sodium Chloride." Columbia Encyclopedia. 2010. Print.

Books

Author or editor (last name first). Title (underlined or in italics, if typed). City of publication: Publisher, copyright date. Medium of publication.

> Kurlansky, Mark. Salt: A World History. East Rutherford, NJ: Penguin USA, 2007. Print.

Magazines

Author (last name first). Article title (in quotation marks). Title of the magazine (underlined or in italics, if typed.) Date (day/month/year): Page numbers of the article. Medium of publication.

> Hallett, Don. "The Wieliczka Salt Mine." Geology Today Sept./Oct. 2006: 182-185. Print.

Newspapers

Author (if available, last name first). Article title (in quotation marks). Title of the newspaper (underlined or in italics, if typed) Date (day/month/year), edition (if listed): Page numbers of the article. Medium of publication.

> Tanner, Beccy. "Salt Mine Museum Could Spark Tourist Trade." Wichita Eagle 8 May 2004: A9. Print.

Internet

Author (if available). Page title (if available, in quotation marks). Site title (underlined or in italics, if typed). Name of sponsor (if available). Date posted (day/month/year, if available). Medium of publication. Date found.

> *"Dry (Rock Salt) Mining." Salt Institute. Salt Institute. 10 May 2008. Web. 25 April 2011.*

Film, Video, and So On

Title (underlined). Type of medium (filmstrip, slide program, and so on). Distributor, date released. Medium of reception.

> *Modern Marvels: Salt Mines. A&E Television Networks, 2004. DVD.*

Letter or E-Mail to the Author (Yourself)

Writer (last name first). Subject line title (if any) in quotation marks. Message to First name Last name of recipient. Date addressed (day, month, year). Medium of delivery.

> *Roberts, Kim. Message to Damek Soleny. 4 May 2011. E-mail.*

Format your sources. Check your report and your list of sources (page 392) to see which sources you actually used. Then follow these directions.

1. **Write your sources using the guidelines above and on the previous page. You can write them on a sheet of paper or on note cards.**
2. **Alphabetize your sources.**
3. **Create your works-cited page. (See the example on page 385.)**

Revising

A good research report needs more than one draft. The first time through, you work mainly with organization and ideas. In the second draft, you fill in missing information, rearrange ideas for clarity, and polish your word choice. Take the time to make your report as good as it can be.

Keys to Effective Revising

1. Read your entire draft to get an overall sense of your report.
2. Review your thesis statement to be sure that it clearly states your main point about the topic.
3. Make sure your beginning draws the reader in. Then check that your ending leaves the reader with something to think about.
4. Make sure you sound knowledgeable and interested in the topic.
5. Check for correct, specific words and complete sentences.
6. Use the editing and proofreading marks inside the back cover of this book.

Revising Improving Your Writing

A first draft is never a finished paper. There is always room for improvement. In the following sample paragraphs, Damek makes several important revisions. Each change improves the *ideas, organization, voice, word choice,* or *sentence fluency* in the writing.

Two sentences are combined for smoother reading.

An "It has" beginning is changed to improve sentence style.

A sentence is moved for better organization.

A detail is added for clarity.

Twelve hundred feet below the ground, ~~lies~~ an enormous mine ~~It~~ has been operating almost nonstop for more than a century. ~~It has~~ A hundred miles of tunnels connect~~ing~~ its huge chambers. It has underground roads for cars, trucks, and mining machines. This mine produces hundreds of tons of "rock" every day. However, the rock from this mine is not gold, or iron ore, or even coal; it is salt. This enormous, hundred-year-old salt mine lies beneath the city of Detroit, Michigan.

Salt is much more important than most people realize. In some places, people have traded salt for gold in equal measures. In ancient China, salt coins were used for money, and Roman soldiers were often paid in salt, which is where the word "salary" comes from. Wars have been fought over it. In the human body, salt carries electrical signals that keep a person alive. To stay healthy, a person needs to eat about three pounds of salt a year (Modern). Salt is also used to preserve meat and fish . . .

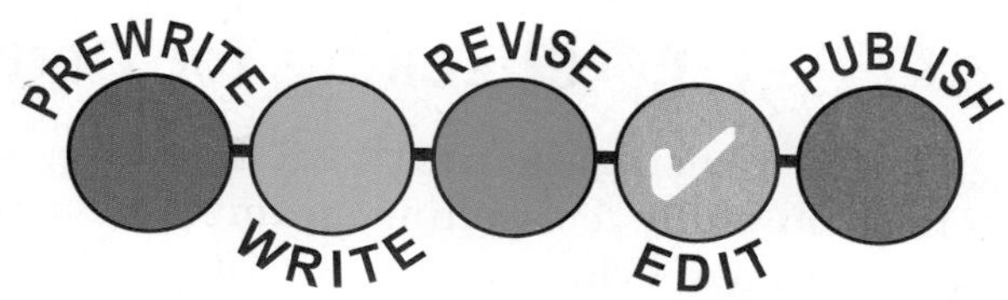

Editing

Once you have finished revising your report, edit your work for *conventions:* spelling, punctuation, capitalization, and grammar.

Keys to Effective Editing

1. Use a dictionary, a thesaurus, your computer's spell-checker, and the "Proofreader's Guide" in the back of this book.
2. Read your essay out loud and listen for words or phrases that may be incorrect.
3. Look for errors in punctuation, capitalization, spelling, and grammar.
4. Check your report for proper formatting. (See pages 380–385 and 409.)
5. If you use a computer, edit on a printed computer copy. Then enter your changes on the computer.
6. Use the editing and proofreading marks inside the back cover of this book.

Editing Checking for Conventions

After revising the first draft of his report, Damek checked the new version carefully for spelling, grammar, capitalization, and punctuation errors. He also asked a classmate to look it over. As you edit your own report, use the editing and proofreading marks inside the back cover of this book.

An error in subject-verb agreement is fixed.

A spelling error is corrected.

A missing comma is added.

A period is moved to its proper place.

Scientists says that the Detroit mine digs into a bed of salt that is several hundred million years old. From 600 million to 230 million years ago, seawater flooded the middle of North America many times. As sun and wind ~~evaperated~~ evaporated the water, sea salt was deposited on the submerged land. Trillions of tons of salt, collected in a layer 400 to 1,600 feet thick, reached from western Michigan all the way to New York. Eventually, it was covered by silt that became rock more than 1,000 feet thick. When people later came to the area, they found springs of salty water bubbling from the ground. Early settlers would collect that liquid and boil away the water to get the salt. ("Dry")

In 1896, the Detroit salt mine was started in order to dig the salt out of the ground. It began . . .

PREWRITE WRITE REVISE EDIT PUBLISH

Publishing

Sharing Your Report

After you have written and improved your report, you'll want to make a neat-looking final copy to share. You may also decide to prepare your report as an electronic presentation, an online essay, or an illustrated report.

Make a final copy. Use the following guidelines to format your report. (If you are using a computer, see page 60.) Create a clean final copy and carefully proofread it.

RESEARCH

Focus on Presentation

- Use blue or black ink and double-space the entire paper.
- Write your name, your teacher's name, the class, and the date in the upper left corner of page 1.
- Skip a line and center your title; skip another line and start your writing.
- Indent every paragraph and leave a one-inch margin on all four sides.
- For a research paper, you should write your last name and the page number in the upper right corner of every page of your report.

Creating a Title Page

If your teacher requires a title page, follow his or her requirements. Usually you center the title one-third of the way down from the top of the page. Then go two-thirds of the way down and center your name, your teacher's name, the name of the class, and the date. Put each piece of information on a separate line.

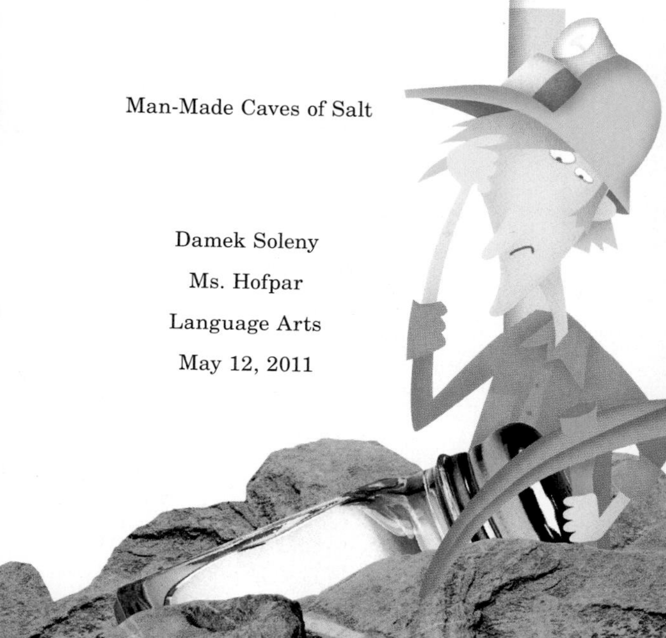
Man-Made Caves of Salt

Damek Soleny

Ms. Hofpar

Language Arts

May 12, 2011

Research Paper Checklist

Use the following checklist for your research paper. When you can answer all of the questions with a "yes," your paper is ready to hand in.

Ideas

_____ **1.** Is my research paper interesting and informative?

_____ **2.** Are my sources current and trustworthy?

Organization

_____ **3.** Does my paper have a thesis statement in the opening paragraph and a topic sentence in all other paragraphs?

_____ **4.** Does my ending paragraph cover the future of this place?

Voice

_____ **5.** Do I sound knowledgeable and interested in my topic?

Word Choice

_____ **6.** Have I explained any technical terms or unfamiliar words?

_____ **7.** Do I use quotations and paraphrasing effectively?

Sentence Fluency

_____ **8.** Do my sentences flow smoothly from one to another?

Conventions

_____ **9.** Does my first page include my name, my teacher's name, the name of the class, the date, and a title? (See page 380.)

_____ **10.** Do I correctly cite my sources? (See pages 381–384 and 396.)

_____ **11.** Is my works-cited page set up correctly? Are the sources listed in alphabetical order? (See pages 385 and 403–404.)

_____ **12.** If my teacher requires a title page, is mine done correctly? (See page 409.)

Research Writing

Multimedia Presentations

Anyone who uses a computer has seen multimedia in action on encyclopedia CD's, on Internet sites, and even in word-processing software. A multimedia presentation is a powerful means of expression that can be presented to a large group. When you can add pictures, sounds, animation, and video to a report, you bring your writing to life and keep the audience interested.

There are several kinds of software that you can use to produce multimedia presentations. With assistance from some of this software, and a little imagination, you'll be able to connect with your audience in a new, dynamic way.

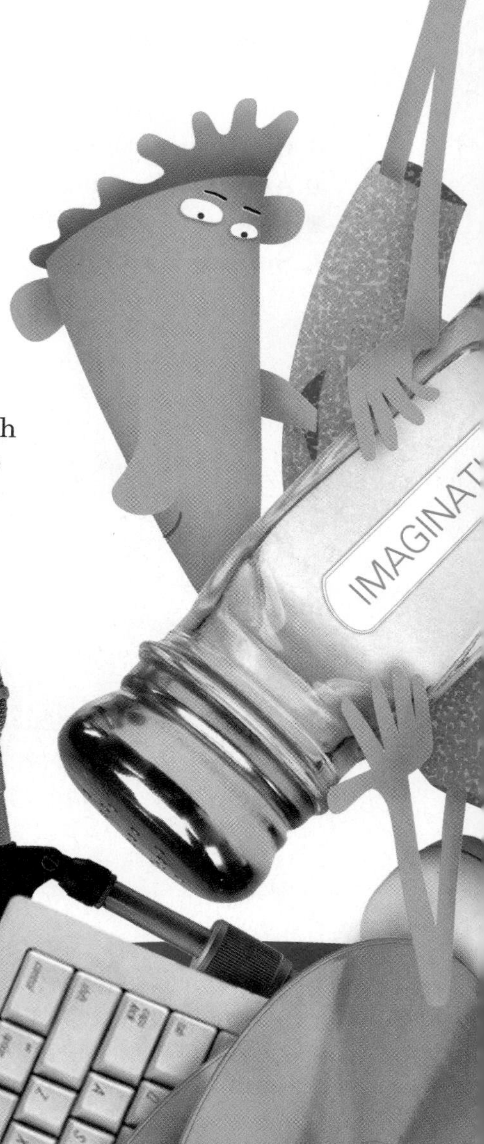

What's Ahead

- **Creating Interactive Reports**
- **Interactive Report Checklist**

Creating Interactive Reports

With the help of a computer, you can design a report that other people can interact with. Your computer-generated slides, graphics, and sound effects will make the important parts of your report clearer and more interesting.

Prewriting Selecting a Topic and Details

For your interactive report, you will want to use something you've already written, something that interests both you and your audience. After you've chosen your piece of writing, make a list of its main ideas. Then find or create one or more of the following graphics or sound effects:

- **Pictures** such as photos or clip art
- **Animations** that show a process or tell a story
- **Videos** of something you've filmed yourself
- **Sounds and music** to use as background or to make a point

Make a plan and organize your ideas by creating a list or media grid like the one below.

Media Grid

Main Ideas	Pictures or Videos	Animations or Music	Sounds
1. A hundred-year-old salt mine lies under Detroit.	photo of Detroit skyline	background music	
2. Early settlers found saltwater spring; mine opened in 1896.	picture of 1896 mine operation		mining sounds

Gather details. Select ideas from your list or from your media grid for graphics and sounds to include with each slide. Create the graphics or sounds yourself or find them on the Internet. Save the images (credit any sources) and sounds on your computer in a special folder created for this report.

Writing Preparing the Report

Before you prepare your report, you need to make a *storyboard*. A storyboard is a "map" of the slides you plan to use in your report. (See the sample storyboard on the next page.) Using your list or media grid as a guide, include each main idea in one box in the storyboard. Then add links from these boxes to additional information.

Use your computer software to design the slides. Choose a typestyle that is easy to read. Use the graphics and sounds you found earlier, and consider using bulleted lists and graphs to organize your information. Show the user how to get around in the report using easy-to-follow navigation buttons, such as arrows or the words "Next" and "Back."

Create a storyboard. Refer to your list or media grid to help you map out your report on a storyboard. Include details of what your audience will see and hear. This kind of preparation will give you an idea of how the slides should look before you actually make them on the computer.

Revising Improving Your Report

Since your audience is on their own with this type of report, it's important to double-check to make sure that it works as it should. Have several friends or family members test it for you. Ask them to tell you if it is clear, interesting, and easy to get around.

Get feedback. If your "testers" have good suggestions, revise the text and design of your report where necessary.

Editing Checking for Conventions

Check the text on each slide for spelling, punctuation, grammar, and capitalization errors. Consider asking an adult or a classmate to check your slides, too.

Make corrections. After you've made corrections, go through the report once more to make sure it works well.

Interactive Report Storyboard

Here is the map, or storyboard, for an interactive report based on the research report "Man-Made Caves of Salt." (See pages 380–385.) Since each user goes through the report on his or her own, it needs to share the essay's information as completely and clearly as possible. (The gold boxes contain additional information available by clicking a link on the original slide.)

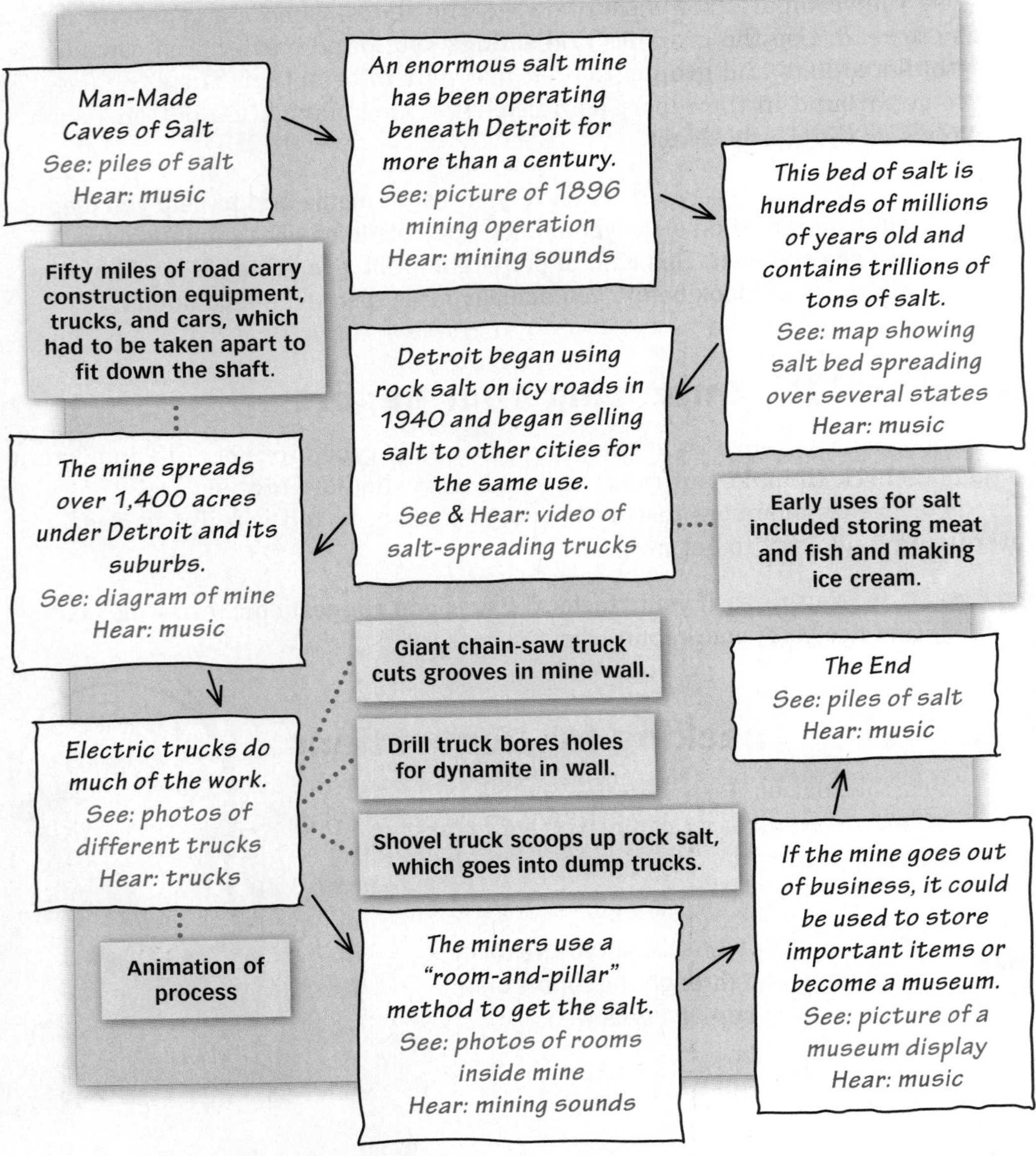
Man-Made Caves of Salt
See: piles of salt
Hear: music
An enormous salt mine has been operating beneath Detroit for more than a century.
See: picture of 1896 mining operation
Hear: mining sounds
This bed of salt is hundreds of millions of years old and contains trillions of tons of salt.
See: map showing salt bed spreading over several states
Hear: music
Fifty miles of road carry construction equipment, trucks, and cars, which had to be taken apart to fit down the shaft.
Detroit began using rock salt on icy roads in 1940 and began selling salt to other cities for the same use.
See & Hear: video of salt-spreading trucks
Early uses for salt included storing meat and fish and making ice cream.
The mine spreads over 1,400 acres under Detroit and its suburbs.
See: diagram of mine
Hear: music
Giant chain-saw truck cuts grooves in mine wall.
Drill truck bores holes for dynamite in wall.
Shovel truck scoops up rock salt, which goes into dump trucks.
Electric trucks do much of the work.
See: photos of different trucks
Hear: trucks
Animation of process
The miners use a "room-and-pillar" method to get the salt.
See: photos of rooms inside mine
Hear: mining sounds
If the mine goes out of business, it could be used to store important items or become a museum.
See: picture of a museum display
Hear: music
The End
See: piles of salt
Hear: music

Interactive Report Checklist

Use the following checklist to make sure your report is the best it can be. When you can answer all of the questions with a "yes," it's ready!

Ideas

_____ **1.** Have I chosen a strong essay or report for my interactive report?

_____ **2.** Do my graphics help communicate my ideas clearly?

_____ **3.** Does each slide fit the audience and the purpose of the report?

Organization

_____ **4.** Do I introduce my topic clearly in the beginning?

_____ **5.** Do I include the important main points in the middle part?

_____ **6.** Do I end with a summary or wrap-up thought?

Voice

_____ **7.** Do I use an interested, somewhat formal voice?

_____ **8.** Does my voice fit my audience and topic?

Word Choice

_____ **9.** Are the words on my slides easy to read?

_____ **10.** Have I chosen the best pictures and sounds for my ideas?

Sentence Fluency

_____ **11.** Does my report flow smoothly from slide to slide?

Conventions

_____ **12.** Is my report free of grammar, spelling, capitalization, and punctuation errors?

LISTEN
respect

WRITE SOURCE Online
www.hmheducation.com/writesource

The Tools of Learning

Academic Vocabulary

Work with a partner. Read the meanings and share answers to the questions.

1. Something that takes effort takes hard work.
   Tell about something you do that takes effort.
2. A lecture is a speech or talk given to an audience.
   On what subject would you like to hear a lecture by an expert?
3. To adapt means to change to fit a new situation.
   How might you adapt a report to make it a speech?

clarify speak
observe

Listening and Speaking

Is being a good listener the same thing as having good hearing? Not really. If your ears are doing one thing and your mind is doing something else, you aren't really listening. Listening, like other skills, takes practice and concentration.

Similarly, there is a big difference between speaking and merely talking. Speaking takes effort. Learning to speak effectively and listen closely will make you more successful in school and in life.

"Be a good listener. Your ears will never get you in trouble."
—Frank Tyger

What's Ahead

- **Listening in Class**
- **Participating in a Group**
- **Speaking in Class**

Listening in Class

When you really listen, you're doing more than simply hearing what is being said. Listening involves effort. The following tips will help you become a better listener.

1. **Know why you're listening.** What is the speaker trying to tell you? Is there going to be a test? Are you being given an assignment?

2. **Listen for the facts.** Listen for *who, what, when, where, why,* and *how.* The 5 W's and H will help you identify the most important information.

3. **Take notes.** When you hear important information, write it down in your notebook. Also write down questions you have and ask them later so that you can complete your notes.

4. **Put the lecture into your own words.** Paraphrase the speaker's statements as you take notes. Add your own comments and draw conclusions about the main points.

Take notes in your own words. The next time you take notes in class, practice putting the ideas in your own words. Also add your own comments as you think about the main points.

Westward Expansion
1800 to mid-1800s

Pioneer women—status different in West than in East
- *Laura Ingalls Wilder—wrote stories of westward movement (stories still popular)*
- *Annie Bidwell—social activist, Chico, CA*
- *Slave women—gained freedom in West*
- *Wyoming—gave women right to vote in 1869 (Was it the first state to do that?)*

A Closer Look at Listening and Speaking

Improving your listening and speaking skills will help you increase your confidence and effectiveness in school. Follow these basic guidelines to become a better listener and a better speaker.

Good Listeners . . .

- think about what the speaker is saying.
- pay attention to the speaker's tone of voice, gestures, and facial expressions.
- interrupt only when necessary to ask questions.

Good Speakers . . .

- speak loudly and clearly.
- maintain eye contact with their listeners.
- emphasize their main ideas by changing the tone and volume of their voice.

Focus on speaking and listening skills by doing the activity below.

1. Gather two classmates and number yourselves 1, 2, and 3.
2. Person 1 will take person 2 aside and read the paragraph below.
3. Person 2 will then take person 3 aside and repeat the paragraph from memory.
4. Person 3 will repeat the paragraph from memory to the other two classmates.
5. Compare the original paragraph to what person 3 reports.

Lieutenant Colonel Arthur Whitson was a United States Air Force pilot for 21 years. He spent some of his time flying weather planes into typhoons in the South Pacific. His crew also tracked radioactive winds, which were clues to when and where the Soviets were testing nuclear bombs. Once Whitson's plane was shot at over Vietnam. He had to dump his cargo of jet fuel, but he and his crew survived.

Participating in a Group

Working with others requires planning. Even if everyone listens politely and speaks clearly, the group needs leadership and a common goal. The guidelines below will help you organize a group discussion.

Guidelines for Group Discussion

- **Choose a chairperson.** This leader should keep the group focused and make sure everyone gets a chance to participate. Rather than choosing the same chairperson for each meeting, let each group member have a turn.
- **Select a record keeper.** The group needs someone to take notes and write down important decisions.
- **Define the topic or focus.** Be sure everyone participates when deciding on the group's goals.

Group Discussion Tips

- **Before you speak,** think about what others have said.
- **Share your thoughts** in a positive and constructive way.
- **Always be respectful,** especially when you disagree with someone.
- **Stick to the topic** or focus.

Imagine yourself in the situations below. Which of the group guidelines or discussion tips above might have prevented each situation from happening?

Situation 1 There is a disagreement about what the group decided last week.

Situation 2 You realize that you are repeating something that has already been said.

Situation 3 One group member speaks twice as often as anyone else, and another member doesn't speak at all.

Group Skills

It's fun to belong to a group that gets something done. When each member listens closely and responds clearly, the whole group can succeed. Listening and speaking in a group is actually a step-by-step process, and when everyone practices these "steps," meetings will go smoothly.

Begin by listening.

1

- Think about what the speaker is saying.
- Make eye contact with the speaker.
- Take notes on the speaker's main ideas.

Follow up by clarifying.

2

- Ask questions about things that confuse you.
- Repeat what you've heard in your own words to see if your understanding is correct.

Continue by responding.

3

- Think before you speak.
- Comment on the issue, not on the person.
- Be honest and respectful.

Try It Read and discuss with two or three of your classmates. Remember to listen, clarify, and respond.

1. **Jasmine thinks that it would be rude to criticize another person in her group.**
   Is Jasmine correct?
2. **Raul already has his mind made up about what Steve is talking about.**
   Should he sit quietly, looking out the window, until Steve finishes speaking?

Speaking in Class

Speaking in class is a skill everyone needs to master. A good classroom discussion depends on cooperation. These basic strategies will help you and your classmates become better speakers.

Before You Speak . . .

- Listen carefully and take notes.
- Think about what others are saying.
- Wait until it's your turn to speak.
- Plan how you can add something positive to the discussion.

When You Speak . . .

- Use a loud, clear tone.
- Stick to the topic.
- Avoid repeating what's already been said.
- Support your ideas with examples.
- Maintain eye contact with others in the group or class.

Play "Who Am I and Where Am I?" Warm up your speaking skills by playing the following game.

1. Form groups of five students. Have each group choose a speaker.
2. The speaker looks at the lists below and chooses one person and one place. Then the speaker begins to speak like that person in that place.
3. The first person to correctly guess the person and place becomes the next speaker.

People	Places
teacher	at the beach
athlete	in school
doctor	on a bus
police officer	in the dentist's chair
rock star	on a cattle ranch
carpenter	standing in line

Making Oral Presentations

You may not realize it, but you've been making oral presentations ever since you started school. In the early grades, your teachers coaxed you to say your name or to tell about your favorite toy. Later, you probably told your class about a book you had read or about a family vacation. Perhaps you even gave a demonstration speech or presented a report. Each year, your oral presentations become more complex, so your skill at making them should also improve.

In this chapter, you will learn how to make a persuasive speech based on an essay you have already written. You will find helpful tips for every step of the process, from planning your speech to making the presentation.

What's Ahead

- **Preparing Your Presentation**
- **Organizing a Persuasive Speech**
- **Delivering Your Speech**

Preparing Your Presentation

Adapting an essay into a persuasive speech is a different process than writing a speech from scratch. For one thing, you already have a topic and information, and you know what type of speech you will make. The following tips will help you transform your persuasive essay into a good speech.

Get Noticed	Plan Visuals	State Your Case	Cut, Cut, Cut
Use a question, fact, or anecdote to get listeners' attention. (See below.)	Note when you should use visual aids or gestures. (See page 425.)	Focus on the main persuasive points of your presentation.	Include only details that strongly support your main point.

Rewriting in Action

Below is the opening of the persuasive essay on pages 235–238. Notice that the new beginning (on gold paper) has been revised so it grabs the listeners' attention and makes an appropriate opening for an oral presentation.

Students at Belmer Junior High are used to looking out the windows of the school and seeing Belmer Woods. Now when they look out, they see a sign: "For Sale, 20 acres, Zoned Residential/ Commercial." Belmer Woods is about to change, and there are many different ideas about how it should change. The best way to develop Belmer Woods would be to make it a park.

When you look out the windows of Belmer Junior High, would you rather see the back of a strip mall or a beautiful green space? As it is now, a huge "For Sale" sign blocks the view, but the sign could be replaced by something even worse. Students should speak up now before it's too late. The best way to develop Belmer Woods is to make it a park.

Adapt your persuasive essay. **Choose a persuasive essay you've written that would make a good oral presentation. Rewrite the opening so that it gets the audience's attention. Then think of the main persuasive points that you will use in your speech.**

Using Visual Aids

Once you have written the opening of your speech and chosen your most persuasive points, you should decide where to use visual aids. Visual aids like the ones below can help you make your presentation clear and convincing.

Posters	show words, pictures, or both.
Photographs	help your audience "see" who or what you are talking about.
Charts	compare ideas or explain main points.
Transparencies	highlight key words, ideas, or graphics.
Maps	show specific places being discussed.
Objects	allow your audience to see the real thing.

Here are some tips for preparing your visual aids.

1. **Make them big.** Everyone in the room should be able to see your visual aids.
2. **Keep them simple.** Don't use sentences and paragraphs. Labels and short phrases are more effective.
3. **Design them to catch the eye.** Use color, bold lines, and basic shapes to attract attention.

List visual aids. Think about the visual aids you could use in your presentation. Then select two that would help make your points clear. Write down how you will use them.

Poster	*list reasons to create park in Belmer Woods*
Map	*show layout of possible park in Belmer Woods*

Organizing a Persuasive Speech

Now that you've written an opening and planned visual aids, you are ready to organize your speech. The purpose of a persuasive speech is to convince your audience to agree with you, so your organization should be clear and logical. Use the following tips.

Beginning	Middle	Ending
Get your listeners' attention and focus on the main persuasive point.	Put your persuasive details in the best order possible.	Close by restating your main point in a memorable way.

Using Note Cards

Writing out note cards is a simpler and more efficient way to organize your speech than writing on notepaper. Each card contains a main point that will guide you as you deliver the speech. Using cards also helps you make eye contact with your audience.

The student who adapted the essay on pages 235–238 into a speech used note cards. He included the opening, the closing, and the main ideas on cards that he used during the speech.

Note-Card Guidelines

- Write your introduction word for word on the first note card.
- Place each main idea on a separate card.
- Number each card.
- Note the main idea at the top of each card.
- Write the supporting details on the lines below the main idea.
- Mark cards that call for visual aids.
- Write your ending word for word on the last note card.

Create your note cards. Look over the note cards on the next page. Then create a note card for each important part of your persuasive speech—introduction, main points, and ending. Note where you will use visual aids.

Setting Up Your Notes

Keep separate notes for each subject. You might use a different notebook for each class or a three-ring binder with dividers. Binders allow you to remove and replace pages, which is especially helpful if you write on only one side of each sheet. The side notes below give additional tips.

page 12

Cells Nov. 9

Leave wide margins.

cell = smallest living unit of a living thing

Two kinds of living things (organisms)
1. Unicellular organism has only one cell.
2. Multicellular organism has many different types of cells.

Make sketches.

Cell parts in both animals and plants
* nucleus
* cell membrane
* ribosome
* endoplasmic reticulum
* Golgi apparatus
* vesicle
* mitochondrion

Skip a line between main ideas.

Plant cell and animal cell differences
* Plant cells have chloroplasts, a vacuole, and a cell wall.
* Animal cells have lysosomes.

Reviewing Your Notes

Take time every day to review your notes.

- **If you have any questions, write them in the margins.** Follow up by checking with your teacher or a classmate and add explanations to clarify your notes.
- **Circle words that you don't understand.** Look up the definitions and correct spellings.
- **Rewrite anything that is confusing or hard to read.** Keep your notes organized and easy to read.
- **Review your notes before the next class.** Be ready for class discussions and quizzes.

page 12

Cells — Nov. 9

cell = smallest living unit of a living thing

Two kinds of living things (organisms)
1. Unicellular organism has only one cell.
2. Multicellular organism has many different types of cells.

Cell parts in both animals and plants
* nucleus
* cell membrane
* ribosome
* endoplasmic reticulum
* Golgi apparatus
* vesicle
* mitochondrion

Here's where the DNA is.

Has another kind of DNA

Note: Some cells don't have all these parts.

Plant cell and animal cell differences
* Plant cells have chloroplasts, a vacuole, and a cell wall.
* Animal cells have lysosomes.

Review your work. **Check some class notes that you have taken recently. How well do they compare with the notes on this page? How can you improve your note taking?**

Taking Reading Notes

Taking notes as you read will help you understand and remember the information. Pause during your reading to write down important ideas and questions. Here are some tips for taking reading notes.

 Quickly skim the assignment.

Read the title, introduction, headings, and chapter summaries. Look at the charts, pictures, and illustrations. Your preview will help you when you start reading for details.

2 Read carefully and take notes.

Write down the main ideas and important details.

- **Write down each heading or subtopic.** Then write the most important information.
- **Use your own words.** You'll remember more than if you copy directly from the reading.
- **Pay attention to pictures, maps, and other graphics.** Make notes or drawings about the information.
- **Read difficult material out loud.** Hearing the information often helps you better understand and remember it.
- **Make a list of new words.** Look up the definitions in a dictionary or the glossary so that you fully understand the reading.
- **Review your notes.** After you finish reading, look over your notes and write down any questions you have.

3 Add graphic organizers whenever possible.

Graphic organizers can help you arrange your notes in a clear, logical order. You can use any of the helpful organizers on the next three pages for taking notes.

Review the tips above. Which ones do you think will be the most valuable for you the next time that you have a reading assignment?

Using a Before-After Organizer

Important events sometimes result in big changes. A **before-after organizer** can help you identify these changes by listing the way that things were before and after the event. This type of organizer can be used to help you understand what you read, especially in social studies and science.

Read the following paragraph and then note how the graphic organizer shows the main ideas.

A Chemical Reaction

A chemical reaction produces new substances by changing the way that atoms are arranged. The new substances are chemically different and may be physically different from the original. For example, if you pass an electric current through water, you can cause a chemical reaction. The water, a liquid called H_2O, becomes two gases: hydrogen (H) and oxygen (O).

Before-After Organizer

Event: When you pass an electric current through water, the chemical reaction changes the water into two gases.

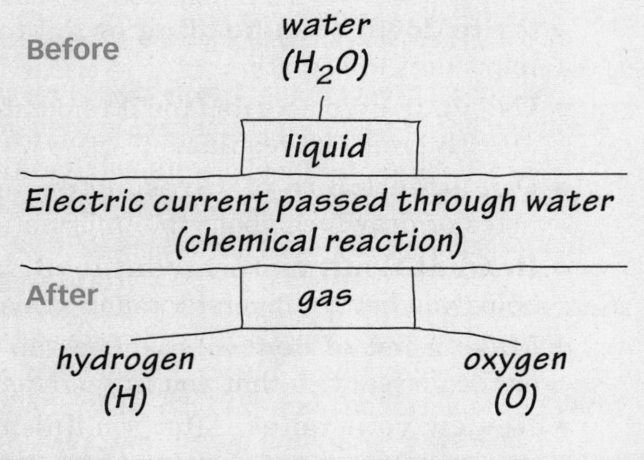

Read the following paragraph about chemical reactions. Then create a before-after organizer to diagram the information.

Chemical reactions often cause changes in temperature and appearance. For example, burning is a chemical reaction. When a piece of room-temperature white paper catches fire, its temperature jumps to over 450° F, and its color changes from white to black.

Using a Comparison-Contrast Chart

You can graph, or record, two topics' similarities and differences in a comparison-contrast chart. In this type of organizer, list the characteristics for each of the topics. After the lists are finished, underline the differences. Read the paragraphs and the corresponding comparison-contrast chart below.

Free Verse and Blank Verse

Free verse is poetry that has no regular pattern of rhyme or rhythm. Much modern poetry is free verse.

Blank verse is poetry that has a regular pattern of rhythm but does not rhyme. Blank verse became very popular during Shakespeare's time.

Comparison-Contrast Chart

Free Verse	Blank Verse
- poetry	- poetry
- no regular rhythm	- regular rhythm
- unrhymed	- unrhymed
- modern	- Shakespeare's time

Read the following paragraph comparing folktales and fables. Then create a comparison-contrast chart listing the characteristics of the two forms of writing. Underline the characteristics that are different.

People often confuse fables and folktales. A fable is a brief story that teaches a lesson. Fables sometimes feature animals. A folktale is a brief story that is passed from generation to generation. Folktales sometimes contain animals but are usually told to entertain rather than teach.

Using a Time Line

Some types of writing are organized chronologically, or according to when things happen. In histories, biographies, and narratives, for example, the order of the events is very important. When you want to take notes on this kind of writing, a time line can help you keep the flow of events organized.

Read the following short biography. Then look at the time line to see how the details are arranged.

Louisa May Alcott

By the time Louisa May Alcott died in 1888, she was famous for writing a very successful book, *Little Women*.

Louisa was born in 1832 and was raised in Massachusetts. Her first poem was published in 1851, and by 1854, she had published a book of stories and poems. *Little Women* was published in 1869. From then until her death, she wrote several other books, including several sequels to *Little Women*.

Time Line

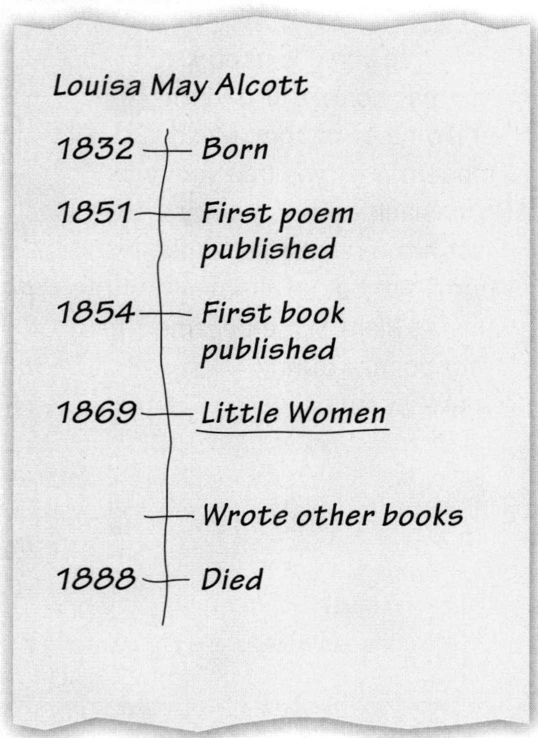

Read the following brief biography. Then create a time line that lists the important events.

In 1950, Gwendolyn Brooks became the first African American author to receive a Pulitzer Prize. She was recognized for her collection of poetry titled *Annie Allen*. Born in 1917, Gwendolyn grew up in Chicago, where her parents encouraged her to write. She was widely admired for her writing, being named poet laureate of Illinois in 1968. She died in 2000.

Completing Writing Assignments

Completing writing assignments is more than simply finishing your work before the bell goes off. Teachers give you writing assignments to make you think and "use your brains."

Did you know that your brain is more powerful than the biggest supercomputer on the planet? Computers can do certain tasks very well—recalling information, analyzing it according to a program, and applying it in a specific way. However, computers don't really understand the information, nor can they really evaluate its worth. Your brain, on the other hand, can do these things.

Next time you get a writing assignment, remember not only that you can beat the clock, but also that you can beat the computer.

What's Ahead

- **Understanding the Assignment**
- **Thinking Through Each Assignment**
- **Setting Up an Assignment Schedule**

Understanding the Assignment

Writing assignments can take many forms, including these three basic types.

Specific

If the topic is chosen for you, the assignment is specific. (Explain what causes earthquakes.)

Open-Ended

If you are allowed to select your own topic, the assignment is open-ended. (Describe a historical period in which you would like to live.)

Combination

If part of the topic is chosen for you but you are allowed to choose another part, the assignment is a combination of open-ended and specific. (Compare chimpanzees to another type of great ape.)

Decide if each of the assignments listed below is open-ended, specific, or a combination.

1. *Explain what makes planets revolve around the sun.*
2. *Compare the effects of smoking cigarettes with the effects of some other unhealthful activity.*
3. *Persuade a parent to agree with you about a family rule or something you want to do.*

Assignment Checklist

Be sure that you completely understand a writing assignment before you begin. Use the following checklist as a guide.

_____ **1. Plan your time** so that you aren't rushed at the last minute.

_____ **2. Ask what is expected** on the assignment.

_____ **3. Read the directions** carefully and ask questions if necessary.

_____ **4. Focus on key words**—*explain, contrast, describe*—so you know exactly what your writing should do.

_____ **5. Review and revise** your writing.

Thinking Through Each Assignment

Different writing assignments ask you to use different levels of thinking. These levels can range from simply recalling information to understanding, applying, analyzing, synthesizing, or evaluating it. The chart below briefly describes these thinking tasks, and the next six pages give you a closer look at each one.

Recalling means remembering information. Use this basic level of thinking when you are asked to . . .

- fill in the blanks
- define terms
- list facts or words
- label parts of something

Understanding means knowing what information means. Use understanding when you are asked to . . .

- explain something
- choose the best answer
- tell if something is true or false
- summarize something

Applying means using information. Use applying when you are asked to . . .

- follow directions
- solve a problem

Analyzing means breaking information down into different parts. Use analyzing when you are asked to . . .

- compare things
- divide things into groups
- give reasons for something
- tell why something is the way it is

Synthesizing means using information to create something new. Use synthesizing when you are asked to . . .

- create something
- add new ideas
- combine things
- predict something

Evaluating means using information to tell the value of something. Use this advanced level of thinking when you are asked to . . .

- assess something
- give your opinion of something

Recalling

When you remember information, you are *recalling* it. You can strengthen this type of thinking by listening and reading carefully, taking notes, and then reviewing the information so that you don't forget it.

You recall when you . . .

- **give details.**
- **identify or define key terms.**
- **remember main points.**

The following test questions ask the student to recall.

DIRECTIONS: Fill in the blanks below with the correct answers.

1. The American Civil War lasted __________ (number) years.
2. The United States rapidly expanded toward the __________ (direction) after the Civil War.

DIRECTIONS: Circle the correct answer in each set of parentheses.

1. The expansion into new territories was known as (Manifest Destiny, Emancipation Proclamation).
2. The "Cowboy Era" lasted from about (1865–1885, 1910–1930).

DIRECTIONS: Define each term by completing the sentence.

1. Suffragettes were ______________________________________.
2. The Underground Railroad was organized to help ____________________.

recall

Review your notes from a recent reading assignment. Set the notes aside and see how many key ideas you can recall. The next time you review your notes, underline the key ideas to help you remember them.

Understanding

When you *understand* something, you can explain what you have learned. If you can rewrite information in your own words, you are showing that you understand it.

You understand when you . . .

- **explain how something works.**
- **provide examples.**
- **summarize information in your own words.**

The following test question asks the student to show understanding, and the answer does that.

DIRECTIONS: Explain how Amendment XV to the Constitution affected voting rights in the United States.

Amendment XV of the Constitution was written to give African Americans the right to vote. It says that this right cannot be held back or changed in any way just because of a person's outer appearance. The amendment gave voting rights to people of any race or color and also applied to former slaves.

understand

Write a paragraph explaining your understanding of something you've recently learned in social studies class.

Applying

Applying information means using it. You need to understand something very well in order to apply it to a new situation or specific need.

You apply when you . . .

- think about how you can use information.
- organize the information so that it meets your specific needs.

In this assignment, the writer reviews information and chooses the most important details.

ASSIGNMENT: How did the Fair Labor Standards Act change the use of child labor in the United States? Relate these changes to the present.

Before the Fair Labor Standards Act, the United States had not put many limits on child labor. The act set minimum wages and limited the number of hours children could work. What these requirements really did was make it illegal to employ children under 16 in factories and mines. Eventually more adults realized that young people should remain in school, not get jobs. Today, most people agree that it's better to get a high school diploma than to work full-time. Some states require students to attend school until they are 18.

apply

Write a paragraph about how a law passed a long time ago still has an impact on the present day.

Analyzing

In order to *analyze* information, you need to break it down into parts so that you can see how it works.

You analyze when you . . .

- show how things are similar or different.
- identify which things are most important.
- arrange things in groups.
- give reasons.

In this assignment, the writer analyzes why some children are working more than the child-labor laws permit.

ASSIGNMENT: There are still children who work more than the labor laws allow. Give some reasons for this situation.

Children of immigrants might work rather than go to school. In farming areas, young migrant laborers move from place to place, so schools and others can't keep track of them. In big cities, young illegal immigrants often become victims of child-labor abuse because they are hidden in their neighborhoods. These children must work to help the family make enough money to support the family.

analyze

Think of something that you are good at. Write a paragraph that tells the most important skills involved in this activity.

Synthesizing

When you use information you have already learned to create something new, you are *synthesizing.*

You synthesize when you . . .

- **add new ideas to existing information.**
- **use information to create a story or other creative writing.**
- **predict what will happen based on information that you already know.**

In this assignment, the writer uses information to write an imaginary diary about being part of the Underground Railroad.

ASSIGNMENT: Imagine that you are living during the period of the Underground Railroad. Write several diary entries about your experiences.

February 8, 1864—I arrived at the Milton House Inn, where Mr. Goodrich has employed me as a maid.

February 22, 1864—Today, Mr. Goodrich spoke to me about the troubles of the runaway slaves. I told him that I support their cause. Then he told me that Milton House Inn is a station on the Underground Railroad. I said I would like to help slaves escape to freedom.

March 19, 1864—I was serving the evening meal when Mr. Goodrich suddenly said, "Mary, attend to the cabin." Going to the cellar of the inn, I crawled into the secret tunnel and up the ladder through the trapdoor into the cabin. There I met a surprised slave named Andrew Hamilton. I hid him in the basement of the inn.

Imagine living during an important time in history. Write several diary entries about your experiences.

Evaluating

When you assess the value of something, you *evaluate* it. Before you can evaluate something, you must fully understand it.

You evaluate when you . . .

- **tell your opinion.**
- **identify the good points and bad points about something.**

In this assignment, the writer evaluates a historical event.

ASSIGNMENT: What is your opinion about the westward expansion of the United States after the Civil War?

Westward expansion after the Civil War was both good and bad. On one hand, the United States is a stronger and richer nation because of the land that was settled at that time. What would this country be like without the lands west of the Mississippi? On the other hand, people should not be proud of the things that were done to Native Americans and others living in the West. It's hard to judge something that happened more than 100 years ago. To settlers, the westward expansion probably seemed like a great victory, but to Native Americans and Mexicans, it was a time of real tragedy.

Think of something that you understand very well, like a favorite sport or type of music. Write a paragraph telling both the good and bad points of the subject you have chosen.

Setting Up an Assignment Schedule

Your teacher may give you a schedule to follow for completing a writing assignment. If not, you can set up your own. Let's say that you have been asked to write a persuasive essay, and it is due in two weeks. Here's a suggested schedule.

Day	Week One	Day	Week Two
1	**Prewriting:** • Review the assignment and the assessment rubric. • Begin a topic search.	1	**Revising:** • Revise the completed draft for ideas and organization.
2	**Prewriting:** • Choose a writing topic. • Start gathering details.	2	**Revising:** • Revise the draft for voice. • Ask a peer to review it.
3	**Prewriting:** • Gather and organize details. • Find a focus for the writing.	3	**Revising:** • Check for word choice and sentence fluency.
4	**Writing:** • Begin the first draft.	4	**Editing:** • Check the writing for convention errors. • Proofread the final copy.
5	**Writing:** • Complete the first draft.	5	**Publishing:** • Share the final copy.

Change this schedule to fit your assignment. For example, if you have a week to do your work, you could focus on one step in the writing process per day.

Scheduling a Timed Writing

If you must complete a piece of writing in a single class period (for example, 45 minutes), it is very important to plan your work. Try to set aside 5 to 10 minutes at the beginning of the period to plan your writing, 25 to 30 minutes for drafting, and about 10 minutes at the end to make any necessary changes.

Taking Classroom Tests

In archery, hitting a bull's-eye doesn't just happen. It starts with the proper stance, a correctly nocked arrow, a steady draw, an eagle eye, and that all-important smooth release. In other words, a bull's-eye begins long before the arrow actually touches the target.

In the same way, an A on a test begins long before you answer the questions. By paying attention in class, taking notes, keeping up with assignments, and studying before the test, you are more likely to hit the bull's-eye. This chapter will help you learn the best way to prepare for classroom tests.

What's Ahead

- **Preparing for a Test**
- **Taking Objective Tests**
- **Taking Essay Tests**

Preparing for a Test

Preparing for a test is like building a pyramid. You begin by creating a solid foundation. You pay attention in class, take good notes, and keep up with assignments. On top of that foundation, you can build toward success. Read the chart below from the bottom up.

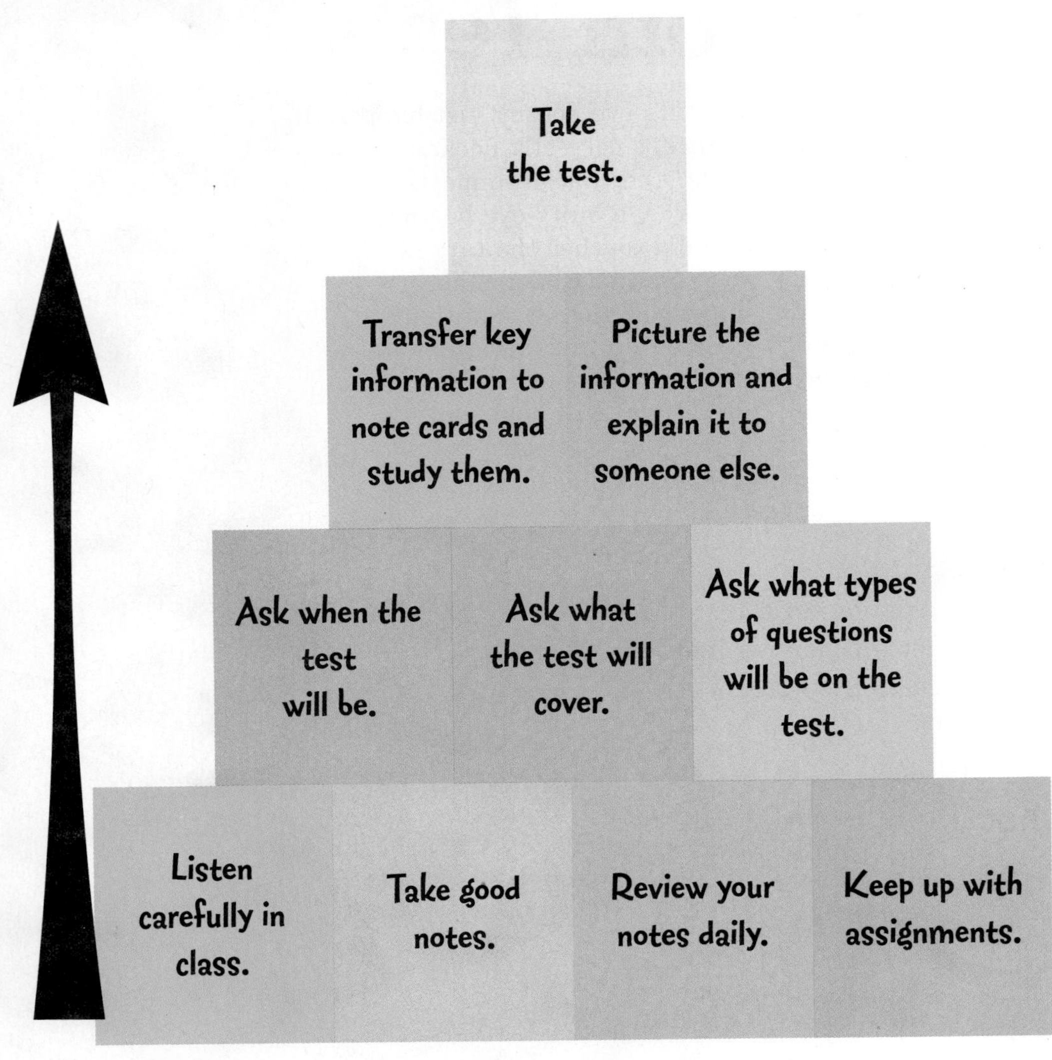
Take
the test.
Transfer key information to note cards and study them.
Picture the information and explain it to someone else.
Ask when the test will be.
Ask what the test will cover.
Ask what types of questions will be on the test.
Listen carefully in class.
Take good notes.
Review your notes daily.
Keep up with assignments.

Try It Think about a test that you took recently. Then check the illustration above. Starting from the bottom and moving up, did you follow all of the steps before taking your test?

Test-Taking Tips

Before you begin . . .

- **Listen** carefully to the instructions.
- **Ask** questions about any instructions that you don't understand.
- **Check the clock** to see how much time you have.

During the test . . .

- **Skim the whole test** so that you can plan your time.
- **Read and answer** each question carefully.
- **Skip difficult questions** and come back to them later.
- **Watch the time** so that you can answer all of the questions.

After you've finished the test . . .

- **Go back** and check your answers, if you have time.
- **Be sure** that your name is on the test.
- **Remember** the questions that were the hardest for you, in case they appear on another test.

One of the most important ways to prepare for a test is to get a good night's sleep beforehand. Also make sure to eat a good breakfast. If your body is rested and fed, your mind is free to work.

Taking Objective Tests

An objective test can contain four different types of questions: true/false, matching, multiple-choice, and fill-in-the-blanks.

True/False

On this type of question, you decide whether a statement is true or false.

- Read carefully. If *any* part of the statement is false, the answer is "false."

  False **Light-years are used to measure time.**
  (Light-years measure distance, not time.)

- Words like *always, all, every, never, none,* or *no* can be misleading. Few things are always or never true.

  False **Every solution is either acidic or basic.**
  (The word "every" makes this statement false. Some solutions are neutral.)

- Pay special attention to words meaning "not": *doesn't, don't, isn't, wasn't.* Be sure that you understand what the statement means.

  True **The different kinds of molecules in a living organism aren't all the same size.**

Matching

Matching is connecting the items from one list to the items in another.

- Read both lists and then match the items you are sure of. Next, match the more difficult items using the process of elimination. Cross out each answer after you've used it.

  B **1. Mass per unit volume** — **~~A~~. velocity**
  C **2. Upward force on an object in fluid** — **~~B~~. density**
  A **3. Direction and speed of an object** — **~~C~~. buoyancy**

- The items in a list that seem to have the closest meaning can be the hardest to match. Think about them carefully before you choose your answers.

Try It On your own paper, answer the following questions:
Which questions are harder for you, true/false or matching? Why?

Multiple-Choice

A multiple-choice question gives you several possible answers to choose from. Follow these tips:

- Be sure to follow the directions carefully. On most tests you are asked to choose the best answer, but sometimes you can choose more than one.

  1. Two of the authors of the Federalist Papers were
  A. James Madison **C. Alexander Hamilton**
  B. Franklin Roosevelt **D. Ronald Reagan**

- Pay special attention to words like *always, all, none,* and *never*.

  2. All of the following influenced the writing of the U.S. Constitution except the
  A. Magna Carta **C. English Bill of Rights**
  B. Mayflower Compact **D. Emancipation Proclamation**

- Some questions have answers like "both A and B" or "all of the above." Consider those options carefully.

  3. The women's suffrage movement was advanced by women like
  A. Elizabeth Cady Stanton **D. both A and B**
  B. Susan B. Anthony **E. all of the above**
  C. Hillary Rodham Clinton

First eliminate answers that you know are incorrect and then focus on the remaining answers.

Fill-in-the-Blanks

On a fill-in-the-blanks test, you fill in what's missing.

- Each blank usually stands for one missing answer, so three blanks mean that you should fill in three answers.

  1. The three states of matter are solid **,** liquid **, and** gas **.**

- The questions sometimes give you clues about the answers. For example, if the word before the blank is *a*, the answer you fill in should start with a consonant sound.

  2. A comet **is a small, icy object in space with a cloudy "tail."**

Taking Essay Tests

When you answer an essay-test question, you write an essay. First, you must make sure you understand the question fully. Then you need to organize your thoughts, write your essay, and check your work, all in a limited amount of time. The information on this page and on pages 465–467 will help you write effective essay-test answers.

1 Understand and Restate the Question

- Read the question very carefully.
- Identify the key word that explains what you have to do. Here are some key words and an explanation of what each asks you to do.

Compare ... tell how things are alike.
Contrast ... tell how things are different.
Define ... give a clear, specific meaning of a word or an idea.
Describe ... tell how something looks, sounds, and feels.
Diagram ... explain using lines, a web, or other graphic organizer.
Evaluate ... give your opinion about the value of something.
Explain ... tell what something means or how something works.
Identify ... answer the 5 W's about a topic.
Illustrate ... show how something works by using examples.
Prove ... present facts that show something is true.
Review ... give an overall picture of a topic.
Summarize ... tell just the key information about a topic.

- Turn the question into a statement. This often makes a good focus statement for your essay.

For each of the following essay-test questions, restate the question as a focus statement for an essay answer.

1. Identify three causes of the Civil War.
2. Describe what happens when water boils.
3. Evaluate the importance of voting in the United States.
4. How would you define the concept of democracy?

2 Plan a One-Paragraph Answer

The following guidelines will help you plan and write a one-paragraph answer for an essay-test question. Jot your planning notes on a piece of scrap paper.

- Study the essay-test question and write a focus statement.
- Use a list, an outline, or a graphic organizer to arrange the details.

Review = give an overall picture

Focus: Ireland's poor economic conditions in the 1840s forced 1.5 million of its people to come to the United States.

List
1. Economy declined for generations.
2. Government policies left farmers with little land.
3. Potato blight wiped out almost entire crop in one year.
4. Irish government encouraged people to leave country.

Social Studies Test

Review why one particular national, racial, or ethnic group immigrated to the United States during the 1800s.

Economic conditions in Ireland became so bad that 1.5 million of its people came to the United States beginning in the 1840s. For generations, the Irish people had been steadily getting poorer. Most of them were farmers, and government policies had made their farms smaller until they had only enough land to grow potatoes for their own food. Finally, the potato blight wiped out almost the entire crop in one year. The only choice the government gave the Irish was to leave Ireland or starve.

3 Plan an Essay Answer

An essay-test prompt may require you to write an answer longer than one paragraph. For example, the response to the question below should be longer than one paragraph.

- Study the essay-test question and write a focus statement.
- Quickly list the main points of your essay, leaving room under each point for details.
- Add your specific details under each main point. (See below.)

Social Studies Test Question:

Compare and contrast the reasons that two different racial, ethnic, or national groups immigrated to the United States.

Quick List

Focus Statement: Two of the largest groups to immigrate to the U.S. in the mid-1800s were the Germans and the Irish.

1. Opportunities in U.S. in 1840s
   - -plenty of land
   - -land easy to get
   - -mfg. jobs
   - -gold in CA
2. Other reasons Germans came
   - -Ger. gov. not democratic
   - -reformers came for freedom
   - -brought $ to invest
3. Contrasting reasons Irish came
   - -gov. reduced farm sizes
   - -had only potatoes for food
   - -blight wiped out crop in 1847
   - -gov. told Irish to emigrate

Think of two historical events that you could compare and contrast. Make a quick list of main points and details for your essay.

Essay Answer

The essay below uses the main points and details from the quick list on page 466.

Social Studies Test: Immigration

Compare and contrast the reasons that two different racial, ethnic, or national groups immigrated to the United States.

Two of the largest groups to immigrate to the United States in the middle 1800s were the Germans and the Irish. Both groups came for some of the same basic reasons that have drawn others, but there were also big differences between them. Those differences had a great deal to do with the conditions in their native countries.

People who came to the United States at that time were attracted by the opportunities that were available. There was a huge amount of land in America, and it was easy to get. Manufacturing jobs were increasing rapidly, and these jobs were a big attraction to those who wanted to live in the cities. Finally, there was the discovery of gold in California that lured those who wanted to get rich.

The Germans had some additional reasons to leave their native country. They had been trying to change their country's government to make it more democratic. In 1849 their efforts to write

a new constitution were ended by force. Some reformers were put in prison, and others began

...tes.
..., but
...ed
...erately
...ey
...nd
...aller,
...es
...iped
...y
...ave

compare
vary

Basic Grammar and Writing

Writing Focus

Academic Vocabulary

Work with a partner. Read the meanings and share answers to the questions.

1. When you **eliminate** something, you leave it out.
   What item would you eliminate from a picnic lunch?
2. To **transfer** an item means to move it from one place to another.
   How might you transfer your books to school?
3. When a person is **selective**, he or she chooses carefully.
   Why should a writer be selective in his or her word choice?

MODIFY CONNECT
choose

Working with Words

According to the *Oxford English Dictionary,* our language contains over a quarter of a million words—more than most other languages. No wonder a dictionary is so heavy! Lifting a dictionary can strengthen your arm, but opening one will strengthen your mind.

A sentence won't work as well without some words—*adjectives, adverbs, and conjunctions,* for instance. It won't work at all without certain other words—*nouns or pronouns,* and *verbs.* So, as you continue to read, write, and speak the English language, it will be helpful to know how, when, and where to use its parts . . . to keep it running smoothly.

What's Ahead

- Using Nouns
- Using Pronouns
- Choosing Verbs
- Describing with Adjectives
- Describing with Adverbs
- Connecting with Prepositions
- Connecting with Conjunctions

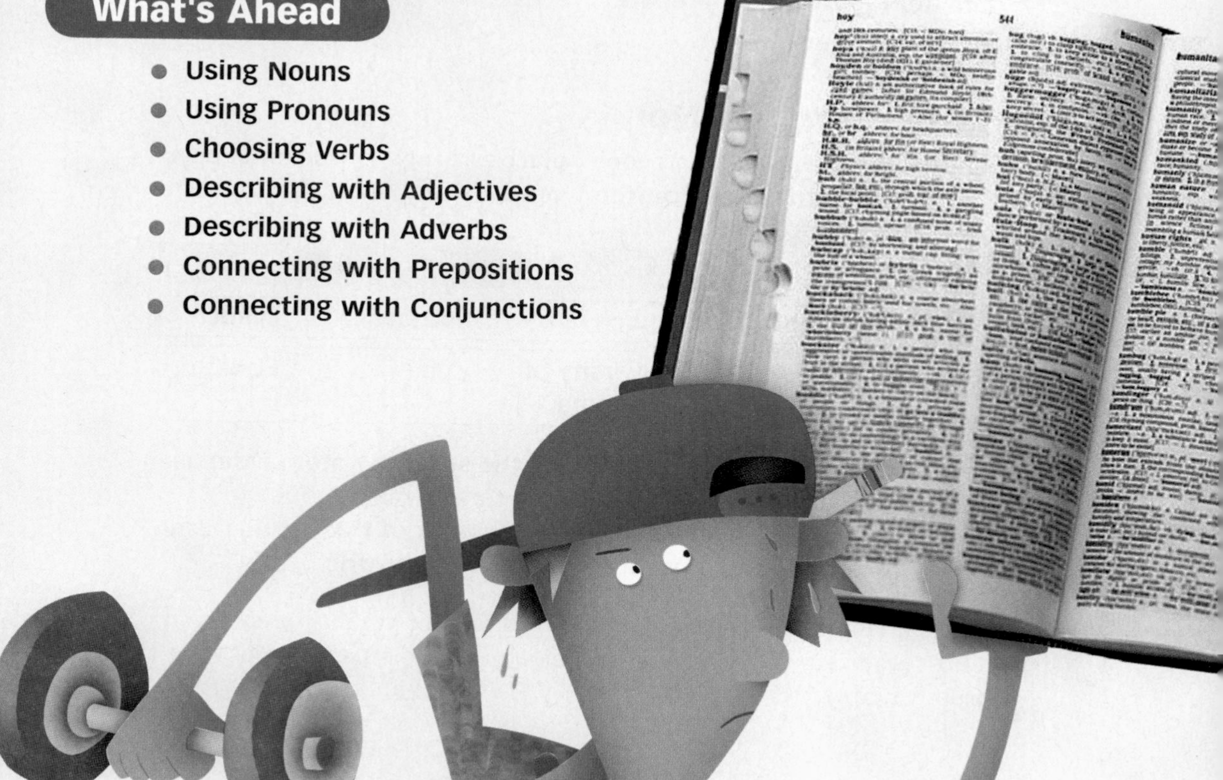

Using Nouns

A noun is a word that names a person, a place, a thing, or an idea in your writing. (See page 702.)

Person	meteorologist, Jacob Kern, students, Mayor Blain
Place	city, Chicago, sky, Tampa, middle school
Thing	Manx cat, clouds, stopwatches, thunder
Idea	day, Sunday, strength, truth, Veterans Day

Number from 1 to 8 on a piece of paper. For each of the eight underlined nouns in the paragraph below, write whether it is a person, a place, a thing, or an idea.

Weather has a very big **(1)** effect on all of the world's **(2)** citizens. In the **(3)** United States, the National Weather Service (NWS) keeps track of the **(4)** weather. Specialized **(5)** equipment at **(6)** offices across the country helps the NWS collect weather data. Its **(7)** scientists prepare forecasts and issue severe weather **(8)** warnings when necessary.

Proper and Common Nouns

Proper nouns name specific people, places, things, or ideas. Proper nouns are always capitalized. A **common noun** is any noun that is not a proper noun.

	Person	Place	Thing	Idea
Common	meteorologist	school	hurricane	event
Proper	Hank Rhodes	University of Oklahoma	Irma	El Niño

Common nouns A weather event warms the surface water of the ocean and affects weather on a faraway continent.

Proper nouns El Niño warms the surface water of the Pacific Ocean and affects weather as faraway as Africa.

Make a chart like the one above. Add four of your own common nouns and four of your own proper nouns. Be sure to capitalize the proper nouns.

Concrete, Abstract, and Collective Nouns

Concrete nouns name things that can be seen, heard, or touched.

Abstract nouns name something that you can think about but cannot see or touch.

Concrete	water	mountain	street	tree
Abstract	joy	August	dread	kindness

Identify each underlined noun in the following sentences as concrete or abstract.

Example: The fury of a tornado is hard to imagine.
abstract, concrete

1. Often a twister is preceded by a series of thunderstorms.
2. An eerie calm might settle over the area when the wind stops.
3. You won't hear a sound—no thunder, no flocks of birds, no rustling leaves.
4. Suddenly, another wave of powerful winds begins, bending the trees horizontally.
5. Tornadoes inspire fear and awe, even for a team of storm chasers.

Collective nouns name a collection of persons, animals, or things.

Persons	group	clan	tribe	squad	family
Animals	herd	flock	litter	pod	pride

In the six sentences above, identify the three collective nouns. (They are not underlined in the activity.)

General and Specific Nouns

When you use specific nouns in your writing, you give the reader a clear picture of people, places, things, and ideas. The following chart shows the difference between **general nouns** and specific nouns.

General	weatherperson	the Midwest	tool	thought
Specific	Robert Fitzroy	central Missouri	rain gauge	belief

Write specific nouns for these general nouns: *newscaster, county, storm, emotion, housing, road, animal.* Then write a brief paragraph, using as many of your specific nouns as possible.

What can I do with nouns in my writing?

Show Possession

You can make your writing more specific by naming who (or what) possesses something. See the guidelines below. (Also see 604.4 and 606.1.)

Forming the Singular Possessive

- Add an apostrophe and an *s* to a singular noun: **Emiko's raincoat.**
- For multisyllable nouns ending in an *s* or *z* sound, the possessive may be formed in two ways: **Carlos' umbrella or Carlos's umbrella.**

Forming the Plural Possessive

- Add an apostrophe for most plural nouns ending in *s*: **the boys' galoshes.**
- Add an apostrophe and an *s* for plural nouns not ending in *s*: **the women's boots.**

On a piece of paper list five singular nouns and five plural nouns. (Include at least one or two singular nouns that end in an *s* or a *z* sound.) Skip one or two lines after each noun. Then write one sentence for each noun, using the possessive form of the word.

Rename the Subject

An **appositive** renames the noun that comes before it. An appositive phrase, which is set off with commas, contains a noun.

Meteorologists predict weather changes using a barometer, a device that measures air pressure.

Cari Casey, a National Weather Service employee, gave us a tour.

List the appositive phrase in each of the following sentences.

1. Dust whirls, rotating dust clouds, surround the base of tornadoes.
2. If you live near a large lake, you may have seen a waterspout, a tornado occurring over water.
3. During the summer months, downpours, heavy and intense rains, will occur.
4. In science class we talked about humidity, the amount of moisture in the air.
5. A cap, the layer of warm air near the ground, may delay the development of a thunderstorm.

Make the Meaning of the Verb Complete

Some sentences are not complete with just a subject and a verb.

Gray clouds release. (*What* do the clouds release?)

A radio report alerted. (*Whom* did the report alert?)

When you use a transitive verb like *release or alerted* in a sentence, you need to include a **direct object** to make the meaning of the verb complete. The direct object is a noun (or pronoun) that answers the question "what" or "whom."

Gray clouds release a downpour. **A radio report alerted the family.**

To add further information, you might include a noun (or pronoun) that answers the question "to whom" or "for whom." This type of noun is called an **indirect object**. In order for a sentence to have an indirect object, it must also have a direct object. (For more about direct and indirect objects see 692.4–692.5.)

The storm gave Iesha a scare. (The storm gave a scare *to Iesha*.)

Dad built his parents a storm shelter behind their house. (Dad built a shelter *for his parents*.)

Write the direct object in each of the following sentences. If there is an indirect object as well, write it and underline it.

Example: Each year, Texas gets many tornadoes.
tornadoes

1. A recent tornado damaged many garage roofs.
2. Most thunderstorms, fortunately, do not trigger tornadoes.
3. The incredible winds show people the power of nature.
4. The twisting winds rip trees from the ground by their roots.

Add Specific Information

Another kind of object noun is the **object of a preposition**. A prepositional phrase (see 704.7) begins with a preposition and ends with an object (a noun or a pronoun). Prepositional phrases can add specific information to sentences. The object noun(s) in each prepositional phrase (underlined) below is highlighted in blue.

Tornadoes often appear <u>at the end</u> <u>of a storm</u>.

They begin high <u>off the ground</u> <u>with a specific combination of wind, temperature, and moisture</u>.

Write a brief weather-related paragraph that includes at least five prepositional phrases. Underline the object of each prepositional phrase. (For a list of prepositions, see page 742.)

Using Pronouns

A pronoun is a word used in place of a noun. The noun replaced, or referred to, by the pronoun is called the pronoun's **antecedent**. The arrows below point to each pronoun's antecedent. (Also *see* **706.1**.)

The day's temperature was so high that it broke a record.

Ms. Johnson said that she never saw people sweat so much.

The personal pronouns listed below are the most common pronouns used by writers. (For a complete list of personal pronouns, see page **710**.)

Personal Pronouns

I	**you**	**he**	**she**	**it**	**we**	**they**
me		**him**	**her**		**us**	**them**

Person and Number of a Pronoun

Pronouns show "person" and "number" in writing. The following chart shows which nominative, or subject, pronouns are used for the three different persons *(first, second, third)* and the two different numbers *(singular* or *plural)*.

		Singular	Plural
First Person	(The person speaking)	**I talk.**	**We talk.**
Second Person	(The person spoken to)	**You talk.**	**You talk.**
Third Person	(The person spoken about)	**He talks.** **She talks.**	**They talk.**

Number your paper from 1 to 4. Write original sentences that use the pronouns described below as subjects.

Example: first-person singular pronoun
(I) I don't like windy days.

1. third-person singular pronoun
2. third-person plural pronoun
3. second-person singular pronoun
4. first-person plural pronoun

Indefinite Pronouns

An indefinite pronoun refers to people or things that are not specifically named. Some indefinite pronouns are singular, while some are plural, and some can be either.

Indefinite Pronouns

Singular				Plural	Singular or Plural
another	each	more	one	both	all
anybody	everybody	nobody	some	few	any
anyone	everyone	no one	somebody	many	most
anything	everything	nothing	someone	several	none

When you use a singular indefinite pronoun as a subject, the verbs (in red below) and other pronouns that refer to the subject must also be singular. If the indefinite pronoun is plural, the verbs and other pronouns must be plural.

Singular **Everybody checks his or her rain gauge in the morning.**

Plural **Many of the gauges have more than an inch of water in them.**

To tell if the pronouns *all, any, most,* and *none* are singular or plural, you must check the noun in the prepositional phrase following the pronoun.

Singular or Plural **All of the rain is over for today, but it will return tomorrow.** (The subject *all* is singular because the noun in the prepositional phrase, *rain,* is singular.)

All of the gauges are checked daily, and then they are emptied. (The subject *all* is plural because the noun in the prepositional phrase, *gauges,* is plural.)

Number your paper from 1 to 5. Choose the correct pronoun to complete each of the following sentences. (See page 714 for more help.)

1. One of the boys left *(their, his)* umbrella at school.
2. I guess nobody thought *(they, he or she)* would need it.
3. Few of the students even wore *(their, his or her)* raincoats.
4. Most of the trail is muddy, and *(their, its)* bridges are slippery.
5. If anyone gets wet, that's *(their, his or her)* own fault.

If using *his* or *her* is clumsy, try changing the singular pronoun to a plural pronoun. For example, the first sample sentence above could be rewritten like this: **All** *of the students* check **their** *rain gauges in the morning.*

How can I use pronouns correctly?

Avoid Agreement Problems

You can make your writing clear by using pronouns properly. Remember that you must use pronouns that agree with their antecedents. (An antecedent is the noun or pronoun that a pronoun replaces or refers to.) Pronouns must agree with their antecedents in number, person, and gender. (See **712.1–712.4**.)

A cloud's electrical charges create lightning when they become separated.

Warm winds blow the positive charges high into the cloud, so its underside is full of negative charges, or electrons.

Agreement in Number

The **number** of a pronoun is either singular or plural. The pronoun must match the antecedent in number.

- A singular pronoun refers to a singular antecedent.

Since the ground does not have a lot of negative charges, it attracts the cloud's electrons.

- A plural pronoun refers to a plural antecedent.

The electrons are pulled to the ground, crashing into air molecules on their way down.

Select the correct pronouns from the following list to complete the paragraphs below. (You will use one pronoun twice.)

its	them	they	it

(1) The molecules create more charged ions as __________ are pulled down to the ground, too. **(2)** The stream of electrons moves at 240 miles per second as __________ races toward the ground.

(3) The air molecules become extremely hot when the electrons collide with __________. **(4)** As hot air expands, __________ produces the sudden earsplitting noise we know as thunder. **(5)** The lightning has completed __________ electrical connection in less than a second.

Agreement in Person

You must choose either first, second, or third person pronouns, depending on the situation. If you start a sentence in one "person," don't shift to another "person" later in the sentence.

Pronoun shift: **I have learned a lot about lightning, and with all that knowledge you can stay safe in a storm.**

Correct: **I have learned a lot about lightning, and with all that knowledge I can stay safe in a storm.**

For each sentence below, change the underlined pronoun so it doesn't cause a shift in person.

1. We are learning about weather in their science class.
2. If people knew some of the facts we're learning, you would be amazed.
3. Weather fascinates us, and they want to study it in college.
4. Once you learn about a particular kind of weather, I wish to see it up close.

Agreement in Gender

The **gender** of a pronoun *(her, his, its)* must be the same as the gender of its antecedent. Pronouns can be feminine (female), masculine (male), or neuter (neither male nor female).

Roy Sullivan, a park ranger, was struck by lightning seven times, but his injuries were never life threatening.

Grandma likes to watch lightning from her front porch.

For each of the following sentences, write the correct pronoun. Make sure it is the same gender as its antecedent.

1. The first time lightning struck Roy, __________ big toenail was knocked off.
2. One of the strikes Roy endured caused __________ to lose consciousness.
3. Roy learned that the saying "Lightning never strikes the same place twice" isn't true; __________ can, in fact, do just that.
4. Aunt Jia insists that __________ is not frightened by lightning but asks me to stay with __________ during storms anyway.

What else should I know about pronouns?

Check for Agreement with Compound Subjects and Objects

As you know, a pronoun must agree with its antecedent. When a compound subject or object is the antecedent, different rules apply depending on the conjunction that is used.

- If the compound subject or object is joined by the word *and,* use a **plural** pronoun to refer to the antecedent.

  Andre and Jerry got out their snowboards.
  (The compound subject joined by *and* requires the plural pronoun *their.*)

- If the compound subject or object is joined by the word *or* or *nor,* do one of these:
  - Use a **singular** pronoun when both subjects or objects or only the second one is singular.

    The attendant would allow neither Andre nor Jerry to ride the lift without his ticket. (The compound object joined by *nor* requires the singular pronoun *his* because *Andre* and *Jerry* are both singular.)
  - Use a **plural** pronoun when both subjects or objects or only the second one is plural.

    A blizzard or snow squalls could hamper the fun if they occur.
    (The compound subject joined by *or* requires the plural pronoun *they* because *squalls* is plural.)

For each of the following sentences, write the correct choice of pronouns (and verbs, in some cases) from those in parentheses.

Example: The cold, snow, and ice can be dangerous when *(they arrive, it arrives).*
they arrive

1. The cold causes hypothermia and frostbite, and *(this, these)* can result in physical damage to fingers and toes.
2. A collapsed roof or downed power lines *(is, are)* not only inconvenient; *(it is, they are)* also unsafe to approach.
3. Ice is treacherous for either a motorist or a pedestrian when *(they, he or she)* must travel.
4. People should wear hats when it's cold, but neither Shelby nor Selena will wear *(theirs, hers).*
5. Skis or a sled can prove *(their, its)* worth when a car can't get through the snow.

Use Intensive and Reflexive Pronouns

A pronoun with *self* attached—*myself, yourself, herself,* and so on—is either an **intensive pronoun** or a **reflexive pronoun**. The following chart shows how they differ. (Also see 708.2 and 708.3.)

Reflexive Pronoun

- *Necessary* to complete the meaning of the sentence
  Nomi fanned *(what?)* with some paper.
- Used as an object in a sentence (direct or indirect object, object of a preposition)
  Nomi fanned herself with some paper.

Intensive Pronoun

- *Not necessary* to complete the meaning of the sentence
  The temperature was not so bad.
- Used to emphasize the noun before it
  The temperature itself was not so bad.

In the sentences below, label each pronoun as either reflexive or intensive.

1. When my grandmother finds herself in the midst of a heat wave, she goes to the air-conditioned library.
2. The newspaper suggests that people wearing dark clothing while in the sun are making it very difficult for themselves.
3. Sometimes my dad pushes himself in hot weather, and that makes his body work to maintain its normal temperature.
4. I myself don't have to worry about that; I always push myself just enough.
5. Most doctors themselves know enough to avoid the extreme heat.
6. If you find yourself feeling sick because of the heat, seek shelter immediately.

Write two sentences of your own. Use a reflexive pronoun in one of the sentences and an intensive pronoun in the other one. Exchange papers with a partner. Underline the reflexive pronoun and circle the intensive pronoun in each other's sentences.

Choosing Verbs

The main verb either shows action or links the subject to another word in the sentence. A helping verb "helps" to complete the main verb.

Action Verbs

An **action verb** tells what the subject is doing. Strong action verbs can bring your writing to life.

The hurricane slammed into the coast.

High winds hurl objects through the air.

Linking Verbs

A **linking verb** connects (links) a subject to a noun or an adjective in the predicate.

Common Linking Verbs	
Forms of "be"	be, is, are, was, were, am, been, being
Other linking verbs	appear, become, feel, grow, look, remain, seem, smell, sound, taste

A hurricane is a tropical cyclone.
(The linking verb *is* connects the subject *hurricane* to the noun *cyclone*. *Cyclone* is a **predicate noun**.)

The storm grows larger, often covering a circle 500 miles wide.
(The linking verb *grows* connects the subject *storm* to the adjective *larger*. *Larger* is a **predicate adjective**.)

For each sentence in the paragraph below, write the linking verb and the predicate noun or predicate adjective that follows it. (The complex sentence has two linking verbs.)

(1) In the Pacific Ocean, the term for a "hurricane" is "typhoon." **(2)** Whatever these storms are called, they can remain a threat for up to 30 days. **(3)** They are dangerous because of their strong winds and floods. **(4)** Although some people seem fearless against the rage of such storms, many people feel powerless. **(5)** For most people it is best to evacuate the area.

Helping Verbs

The simple predicate may include a **helping verb** plus the main verb. A helping verb completes the main verb in many sentences.

A category 1 hurricane will result in minimal harm.
(The helping verb *will* helps express future tense.)

A category 3 hurricane has hit the town of Burnley.
(The helping verb *has* helps express the present perfect tense. See page 724.1.)

A category 5 hurricane does cause unbelievable damage.
(The helping verb *does* helps express ongoing action.)

Select a helping verb from the following list to complete each sentence in the paragraph below.

must	do	will	may	has	can

The United States **(1)** ________ endured two category 5 hurricanes, in 1935 and 1969. In any such storm, high winds **(2)** ________ cause the most loss of property and life. Flooding **(3)** ________ also result in losses. The government **(4)** ________ issue an order to evacuate when a hurricane strikes. Often, people **(5)** ________ leave their homes even if they **(6)** ________ not want to.

Irregular Verbs

Irregular verbs do not follow the *ed* rule. Instead of adding *ed* to show past tense, as you would with a regular verb, an irregular verb might change. (See the list of irregular verbs on page 722.) The chart below gives the three main parts for *write* and *swim*.

Present	Past	Past participle
I write. She swims.	Yesterday I wrote. Yesterday she swam.	I have written. She has swum.

On your own paper, write six sentences using the given tense of the irregular verbs listed below.

1. tear *(past)*
2. sit *(past participle)*
3. choose *(past)*
4. give *(present)*
5. get *(past participle)*
6. know *(present)*

How can I use verbs effectively?

Show When Something Happens

You can use different verb tenses to "tell time" in sentences. The three simple tenses are "present," "past," and "future." (See page 720.)

Weather controls our actions. *(present)*

We left before the thunderstorms. *(past)*

The teams will play tomorrow. *(future)*

Avoid Unnecessary Tense Shift

It may happen that you will shift from one verb tense to another in the same sentence.

Sean reported *(past)* **on hurricanes, which are** *(present)* **tropical storms that often strike** *(present)* **the Atlantic coast.**

However, in most sentences, you need to avoid a shift in verb tense because it will be confusing to the reader.

Unnecessary shift in tense:

People predicted *(past)* **the weather after they study** *(present)* **its patterns.** (The verb tense incorrectly shifts from past to present.)

Corrected sentence:

People predicted *(past)* **the weather after they studied** *(past)* **its patterns.** (Both the verbs are correctly in the past tense.)

Rewrite the following sentences to eliminate the tense shift in each one.

1. In the past, people tried to predict the weather; they use methods such as studying animal behavior and observing the heavens.
2. In the early 1600s, people invented tools that allow their users to record weather data.
3. Scientists began to understand the atmosphere, so they start making predictions.
4. Of course, it was hundreds of years later when forecasts really will become accurate.
5. Today, weather forecasters told how storms threaten this area.

Write a brief paragraph about a weather-related experience. Afterward, exchange papers with a classmate and check each other's sentences for any confusing shifts in verb tense.

Show Special Types of Action

You need perfect tense verbs to express certain types of times and actions. (See page 724 in the "Proofreader's Guide.") There are three perfect tenses.

	Singular	Plural
Present perfect tense states an action that *began in the past but continues or is completed in the present.*		
Present perfect (use *has* or *have* + past participle)	**I have studied.** **You have studied.** **He or she has studied.**	**We have studied.** **You have studied.** **They have studied.**
Past perfect tense states an action that *began in the past and was completed in the past.*		
Past perfect (use *had* + past participle)	**I had studied.** **You had studied.** **He or she had studied.**	**We had studied.** **You had studied.** **They had studied.**
Future perfect tense states an action that *will begin in the future and will be completed by a specific time in the future.*		
Future perfect (use *will have* + past participle)	**I will have studied.** **You will have studied.** **He or she will have studied.**	**We will have studied.** **You will have studied.** **They will have studied.**

Write a sentence using the stated tense of each of the following verbs. (See the list of irregular verbs on page 722.)

Example: try *(present perfect)*
Raekwon has tried to find each constellation.

1. rain *(past perfect)*
2. listen *(present perfect)*
3. grow *(future perfect)*
4. make *(past perfect)*
5. look *(present perfect)*
6. see *(future perfect)*
7. learn *(past perfect)*
8. talk *(present perfect)*
9. want *(past perfect)*
10. finish *(future perfect)*

How else can I use verbs?

Transfer Action to an Object

You will use both transitive and intransitive verbs to express specific ideas in your writing.

Transitive verbs are always action verbs. A transitive verb needs a direct object to make its meaning complete. Remember that a direct object is a noun or a pronoun that answers the question "what" or "whom." (See page 473 and 692.4.)

Mountains, cold fronts, and the jet stream cause air to rise.
(The meaning of the transitive verb *cause* would not be complete without the direct object *air*.)

The cool, expanding air holds moisture.
(The direct object *moisture* completes the meaning of the transitive verb *holds*.)

An **intransitive verb's** meaning is complete without a direct object.

The moisture condenses into droplets.
(The meaning of the intransitive verb *condenses* is complete without a direct object. *Into droplets* is a prepositional phrase.)

Ice crystals form in high altitudes.
(The meaning of the intransitive verb *form* is complete without a direct object. *In high altitudes* is a prepositional phrase.)

Depending on how a verb is used in a sentence, it may be transitive or intransitive.

All rain actually begins its life as snow.
(*Begins* is followed by a direct object, *life*. *Begins* is a transitive verb.)

All rain actually begins as snow.
(*Begins* is intransitive because there is no direct object. As *snow* is a prepositional phrase.)

Write whether the underlined verbs in the following paragraph are transitive or intransitive. For each transitive verb, write the direct object that follows it.

Ice crystals in a cloud **(1)** grow in size and weight. After a while, their weight **(2)** prevents them from staying in the cloud. As ice crystals **(3)** fall toward the earth, the warmer air below the cloud **(4)** melts the ice. As long as the surface **(5)** produces warm air, rain is the result. Otherwise, the crystals **(6)** change into snow.

Form Verbals

Verbals are words that are made from verbs but are used as other parts of speech. Verbals are used as nouns, adjectives, or adverbs, and they are often used in phrases. (See 730.2–730.4.)

Gerunds

A **gerund** is a verb form that ends in *ing* and is used as a noun.

A warning alerted us that a storm was approaching.
(The gerund warning acts as a subject noun.)

I heard the ringing of the wind chimes. (The gerund phrase *ringing of the wind chimes* acts as a direct object.)

Participles

A **participle** is a verb form that ends in *ing* or *ed* and is used as an adjective.

The pounding waves rocked the boats in the bay.
(The participle acts as an adjective describing *waves.*)

The wind whipping through town tore shingles loose.
(The participial phrase acts as an adjective describing *wind.*)

Infinitives

An **infinitive** is a verb with "to" before it. An infinitive can be used as a noun, an adjective, or an adverb.

To protect ourselves was our number one goal.
(The infinitive phrase to *protect ourselves* acts as a subject noun.)

Our plan to shut the windows was never carried out.
(*To shut the windows* acts as an adjective modifying the noun *plan.*)

We watched carefully to evaluate the danger.
(*To evaluate the danger* acts as an adverb modifying the verb *watched.*)

BASIC GRAMMAR

Write a separate sentence for each of the verbals listed below. Refer to the model sentences above as a guide.

1. breaking down the trees *(gerund phrase)*
2. to find shelter *(infinitive phrase)*
3. blowing *(participle)*
4. frightened by the wind *(participial phrase)*

Describing with Adjectives

Adjectives are words that describe or modify nouns or pronouns. Sensory adjectives help the reader see, hear, feel, smell, and taste what writers are describing. (Also see pages 732 and 734.)

Without Adjectives

Today's weather allows us to be outside. Clouds dot the sky. We can soak up the sun as we eat lunch.

With Adjectives

Today's summer-like weather allows us to be outside. Fluffy clouds dot the blue sky. We can soak up the sun as we eat our picnic lunch.

Adjectives answer four questions: *what kind? how much? how many?* or *which one?* Remember that proper adjectives can be made from proper nouns (Africa, *African;* Japan, *Japanese*) and are capitalized.

What kind?	Spanish **moss**	tall **tree**	green **apple**
How many (Much)?	six **horses**	few **computers**	some **rain**
Which one?	that **desk**	those **papers**	last **test**

For each blank in the sentences below, write an adjective of the type called for in parentheses.

1. Yesterday was a *(what kind?)* day.
2. *(What kind?)* rain fell off and on all day.
3. We had *(how many?)* separate storms go through overnight.
4. The *(which one?)* storm was the worst.
5. It left *(what kind?)* debris everywhere.
6. The window in the *(which one?)* wall was shattered.
7. Today the forecast is for a *(what kind?)* day.
8. Predictions show a *(what kind?)* chance for rain in the morning.
9. *(Which one?)* afternoon, I'll go biking.
10. A *(how much?)* exercise will energize me.

Comparative and Superlative Forms

You can use comparative adjectives to compare two things. For most one-syllable adjectives, add *er* to make the **comparative form**. To compare three or more things, add *est* to make the **superlative form**.

Positive	Comparative	Superlative
small	smaller	smallest

Comparative: **Today's rainbow is smaller than the one we saw last week.**
Superlative: **It's probably the smallest one I've ever seen.**

Add *er* and *est* to some two-syllable words and use *more* or *most* (or *less* or *least*) with others. Always use *more* or *most* with three-syllable adjectives.

Positive	Comparative	Superlative
tiny	tinier	tiniest
forceful	more forceful	most forceful

Comparative: **The wind last night was more forceful than it is tonight.**
Superlative: **The wind is most forceful during a tornado.**

NOTE Some adjectives use completely different words to express comparison. For example, *bad, worse, worst.* (See 734.6.)

Write the positive, comparative, or superlative form of the underlined adjective to fill in the blanks in each of the following sentences.

1. There were some violent storms last summer, but this past week's storms have been __________ than those. I think the __________ storm occurred last night.
2. Fargo, North Dakota, is a snowy city, and Buffalo, New York, is a __________ city, but the __________ city in the United States is Blue Canyon, California.
3. It gets __________ in Chicago, but it's __________ in Dodge City, Kansas. Mt. Washington, New Hampshire, with gusts of more than 200 miles per hour, is the windiest place in the nation.
4. Yuma, Arizona, is not a very __________ place; however, Las Vegas is even less humid than Yuma. The __________ city in the United States is Milford, Utah.

How can I strengthen my writing with adjectives?

Use Effective Adjectives

If you avoid overused adjectives (*nice, big, pretty, small, nice, good,* and so on) and use specific, colorful adjectives instead, your writing will be clear and powerful.

With Overused Adjectives

A bad storm knocked down a big tree in our yard.

With Stronger Adjectives

A fierce summer storm knocked down a century-old oak tree in our yard.

List three adjectives in the following passage that seem especially strong and two adjectives that seem overused. Then write an effective adjective next to each overused one.

I listened to the growling thunder in the distance while watching the blue-black clouds. I wondered if we would get a nice rain. The parched ground in the fields was criss-crossed with ugly cracks. The curled leaves were turned bottom side up, like hands begging for help. I hoped that the bad drought would be over.

Use Adjectives with the Right Feeling

Your choice of adjectives can really change the feeling of your writing. What an adjective suggests—its **connotation**—has a significant effect on your writing. Look at this example:

The blustery wind blew Isaac's homework against the brick wall.
What does the word *blustery* suggest to you? What if you changed it to *howling* wind or *brisk* wind? These adjectives are similar, yet each one gives the sentence a different feeling.

If you need help, check a thesaurus. This reference book offers synonyms and antonyms for words. Pick words that best fit the meaning and feeling you want to express.

Write a brief paragraph about a windy day. Concentrate on how the wind makes you feel and use adjectives with the right connotation.

Be Selective

While adjectives can make your writing engaging, don't overuse them. Compare these two sets of descriptive phrases:

Awkward, over-modified phrases	*Stronger phrases*
a sunny, inviting, warm, balmy day	**a balmy, sunny day**
the gray, threatening, windy, cloudy sky	**the gray, threatening sky**

Although the phrases in the first column have more words, they don't really say more than the second descriptions. In fact, they actually slow the reader down and disrupt the flow of ideas.

Rewrite each of the following over-modified phrases by cutting back on the number of adjectives. Keep only those adjectives that make the phrase strong. Then use each of the new phrases in an effective sentence.

1. a frigid, dark, raw, dangerous winter night
2. the intense, bright, white, shocking lightning
3. a calm, peaceful, quiet, still evening
4. the fiery, colorful, vibrant, red maple leaves
5. a plodding, struggling, weary, demoralized hiker

Be General or Specific

You can use **indefinite adjectives**, such as *few, many, more,* and *some,* to give the reader approximate (rather than *specific*) information.

Some thunderstorms produce funnel clouds.

Most storms don't cause much harm.

A **demonstrative adjective** points to a specific noun. The demonstrative adjectives are *this, that, these,* and *those.*

Those clouds over there look threatening.

This weather is not so bad.

Note that both indefinite and demonstrative adjectives must come before the nouns they modify. If they appear alone, they are pronouns.

Write about a rainy experience using two sentences with indefinite adjectives and two sentences with demonstrative adjectives. Exchange papers with a classmate and underline each other's indefinite adjectives and circle the demonstrative adjectives.

Describing with Adverbs

Adverbs describe or modify verbs, adjectives, or other adverbs. Adverbs answer *how? when?* (or *how often?*) *where?* or *how much?* in a sentence. (See pages 736 and 738.)

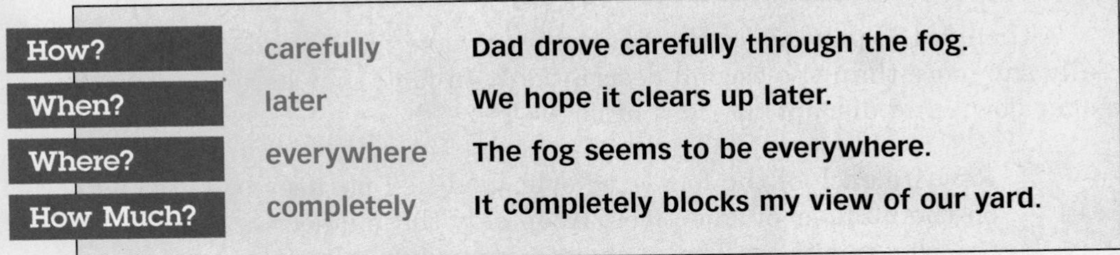

How?	carefully	**Dad drove carefully through the fog.**
When?	later	**We hope it clears up later.**
Where?	everywhere	**The fog seems to be everywhere.**
How Much?	completely	**It completely blocks my view of our yard.**

Team up with a partner, and list at least 10 adverbs from the following narrative. (There are more than 10, so keep listing if you want to.) Then write *how? when?* (or *how often?*) *where?* or *how much?* next to each adverb in your list, depending on the question it answers. If you're not sure, leave the space blank.

Grandma Abby was very disappointed when her flight was cancelled due to fog, but she probably should have expected the cancellation. Her home in the Appalachian Mountains has fog on more than 100 days annually. On those foggy days, she will go out if absolutely necessary. The morning of her flight, she optimistically journeyed to the airport, hoping that the fog would go away soon. When it didn't, she headed homeward with a heavy heart.

Obviously, Grandma could not have done anything to change the situation. Fog happens often in the Appalachians, especially in the valleys there. Nightly, the surface air cools rapidly. This colder air, full of moisture, slowly sinks into low spots. This ground fog can entirely block visibility and make driving dangerous. I'm glad Grandma stays inside when fog blankets her valley.

Special Challenge: Answer the following questions about the narrative above and about your own writing.

1. Which adverbs seem necessary to understand the story?
2. Which adverbs seem not as important?
3. Do you use adverbs very often in your writing? Explain after reviewing one of your latest pieces of writing.

Comparative and Superlative Adverbs

You can use adverbs to compare two things. The **comparative form** of an adverb compares two people, places, things, or ideas. The **superlative form** of an adverb compares three or more people, places, things, or ideas.

For most one-syllable adverbs, add *er* to make the comparative form and *est* to make the superlative form.

Positive	Comparative	Superlative
soon	sooner	soonest

While you add *er* and *est* to some two-syllable adverbs, you need to use *more* or *most* (or *less* or *least*) with others. Always use *more* or *most* with adverbs of three or more syllables.

Positive	Comparative	Superlative
early	earlier	earliest
quickly	more quickly	most quickly
importantly	more importantly	most importantly

Comparative: **It rained harder last night than it did on Sunday.**
It rains more frequently in Ohio than it does in Nevada.

Superlative: **During a storm last summer, it rained the hardest ever.**
Hawaii is the state where it rains most frequently.

Make sure that you write a complete comparison: *It rained harder last night than it did on Sunday rather than It rained harder last night than Sunday.*

Write two sentences for each adverb listed below. In the first sentence, use the comparative form of the adverb; in the second sentence, use the superlative form. Reword each sentence as needed.

Example: softly
The snow falls more softly now that it did this morning.
The snow falls most softly in the evenings.

1. early
2. loudly
3. late
4. effectively

BASIC GRAMMAR

How can I use adverbs effectively?

Describe Actions

You can make your writing more descriptive by using adverbs. Since adverbs can often appear in more than one position in a sentence, always consider the best place to include them. Remember that each different position may slightly change the meaning of the adverb.

For many years, people have tried tirelessly to control the weather.

For many years, people have tirelessly tried to control the weather.

Tirelessly, people have tried to control the weather for many years.

Rewrite the following sentences, placing the adverb (in parentheses) where you think it fits best.

1. It would be satisfying to control when and where it rains. *(certainly)*
2. Having the ability to stop severe storms would be awesome! *(absolutely)*
3. There is only one method in use that controls the weather. *(currently)*
4. "Seeding" a cloud with chemicals will produce rain. *(possibly)*
5. Whether they realize it or not, humans affect the weather. *(unfortunately)*
6. Man-made structures that trap heat and pollution can cause natural weather patterns to be unstable. *(actually)*

Special Challenge: Rewrite any four of the above sentences a second time. In each of these new sentences, place the adverb in a different position.

Add Emphasis

You can stress the importance of an idea with adverbs. Generally, use adverbs of degree—those that answer *how much?*—for this job. (See **736.4**.)

It was an unbelievably strong wind.

An extremely windy day can be scary.

Write a short paragraph about this picture that shows a windy scene. Use a few adverbs to add emphasis.

Express Frequency

With adverbs, you can describe how often something happens or how often something is done. Adverbs that tell how often include words like *sometimes, often, usually, occasionally, always,* and so on.

Storms with high winds are often frightening.

They never fail to scare me.

Write three sentences about fall weekends. Use one of the "how often" adverbs below per sentence.

regularly	never	occasionally	always	seldom	frequently

Be Precise

With adverbs, you can tell the readers exactly when or where something happens.

Adverbs answering *when?*	**first**	**then**	**yesterday**	**now**	**right away**
Adverbs answering *where?*	**here**	**there**	**nearby**	**inside**	**outside**

Shayla saw the lightning first.

Then we heard the thunder and ran inside.

Write two sentences about winter mornings using one "when" adverb per sentence. Then write two sentences about the same subject using one "where" adverb per sentence.

Connect Ideas

A **conjunctive adverb** is a special word used as a connection between two independent clauses (or complete sentences). The two sentences below show how conjunctive adverbs are used.

We wore ponchos during the storm; however, we still were drenched. (A semicolon comes before the conjunctive adverb, and a comma follows it.)

Within a few days, I came down with a cold. Nevertheless, I didn't miss a day of school. (The conjunctive adverb starts the second sentence, and a comma follows the word.)

Common conjunctive adverbs: *also, then, however, meanwhile, therefore, as a result, for example,* and *for instance*. (Also see **738.1**.)

Write sentences using three of the conjunctive adverbs listed above. Make sure that you punctuate each of your sentences correctly.

Connecting with Prepositions

A preposition is a word or words that show how one word or idea is related to another. A preposition is the first word of a prepositional phrase, a phrase that acts as an adjective or an adverb in a sentence. (See page 742 for a complete list of prepositions.)

Weather events occur even in outer space.
(The preposition in shows the relationships between the verb *occur* and the object of the preposition *outer space*. The prepositional phrase acts as an adverb telling "where.")

These cosmic storms release jets of hot gas.
(The preposition *of* shows the relationship between the noun *jets* and the object of the preposition *gas*. The prepositional phrase acts as an adjective telling "what kind.")

- **A word that is used as a preposition may also be used as an adverb.** If a word that sometimes is used as a preposition appears alone in a sentence, that word is probably an adverb.

  Ten million light-years away, space hurricanes whirl around the universe. (*Around the universe* is a prepositional phrase.)

  In the eye of these hurricanes, winds of hot gas spin around.
  (*Around* is an adverb that modifies the verb *spin*.)

- **"To" is either a preposition or part of an infinitive phrase.** If the words that follow "to" include the object of the preposition (a noun or pronoun), then "to" is a preposition. If "to" is followed by a verb or verb phrase, then "to" is part of an infinitive or infinitive phrase. (See page 485.)

  Although I might like traveling to space, I would not like getting caught in a space hurricane's million-mile-per-hour winds.
  (*To space* is a prepositional phrase.)

  Scientists use the Hubble Space Telescope to look deep into space.
  (*To look deep into space* is an infinitive phrase used as an adverb.)

Write four sentences about your favorite kind of weather. Use the word "around" as a preposition in one sentence and as an adverb in another sentence. Use the word "to" as a preposition in one sentence and as part of an infinitive in another.

How can I use prepositional phrases?

Add Information

You can use a prepositional phrase as an adjective to describe either a noun or a pronoun. Adjectives answer *what kind? how many? how much?* or *which one?*

Which one? *What kind?*

The weather report on channel 33 **predicts a cool night** with clear skies.

Write each prepositional phrase that is used as an adjective in the following paragraph. (You should find seven.)

Yesterday's forecast for a warm, sunny day was absolutely wrong. In Atlanta, we got the worst storm of the season instead. The rumbling thunder along the storm front got closer, and the lightning flashes got more intense. High winds throughout the area brought hail, and many cars across the county were damaged by it. One tree in front of our house lost a large branch. Heavy rain clogged the storm sewers. Fortunately, we still have a roof over our heads!

You can also use a prepositional phrase as an adverb to describe a verb, an adjective, or another adverb. Adverbs answer *how? when? where? how long? how often?* or *how much?*

Where? *How long?*

It hasn't rained in Middleville for three weeks.

Write a prepositional phrase that could complete each sentence below. Tell what question each one answers.

Example: The storm was heading ___________.
toward Middleville (where)

1. Clouds were heavy ___________.
2. The rain began to fall early ___________.
3. The rain did not stop ___________.
4. Some neighborhoods appeared vulnerable ___________ forcing people to flee their homes.
5. The police department acted quickly ___________ to help people find shelter.

Connecting with Conjunctions

Conjunctions connect words, groups of words, and sentences. There are three kinds of conjunctions: *coordinating, subordinating,* and *correlative*. The following sentences show some of the ways to use conjunctions. (See page **744** for a list of common conjunctions.)

Coordinating Conjunctions Connect Words and Phrases

Shawn wants to report the news and the weather on a radio station.
Does he need a science degree or a communications degree?

Connect Compound Subjects and Predicates

Hassan and Francisco want to become TV weathermen.
They continually study the weather or read about it.

Connect Sentences

Many weather reporters are meteorologists, but not all of them are.
Weather will always be a topic of interest, so reporters will never run out of work.

Subordinating Conjunctions Connect Dependent Clauses to Independent Clauses

Jalisa hopes to work at a TV station while she attends college.
Although she is a good student, she wants job experience, too.

Correlative Conjunctions Connect Phrases

Many weather forecasts today are based not only on scientific instruments and observations but also on satellite images.
People either believe the forecasts or ignore them.

Choose three of the sentences above to use as models. Write three sentences of your own imitating the three you've chosen. (Make sure to write original sentences.) Underline the conjunctions you use.

How can I use conjunctions?

Connect Phrases

You can use **coordinating** and **correlative conjunctions** to connect different types of phrases: noun phrases, verb phrases, prepositional phrases, verbal phrases, and so on. Coordinating conjunctions include words like *and, but, or, yet,* and so on. Correlative conjunctions are used in pairs: *either/ or, both/and, not only/but also,* and so on. Correlative conjunctions show a relationship between the phrases.

"Black blizzards" of the Dust Bowl (the severe drought during the 1930s) blew dry soil off the farm fields and into the air. (The coordinating conjunction *and* connects two prepositional phrases.)

A long period without rain either damages crops or prevents them from growing. (The correlative conjunctions *either* and *or* connect two verb phrases and show that they are alternatives.)

GRAMMAR Try It

Complete each sentence below using a coordinating conjunction or a set of correlative conjunctions to fill in the blanks. (See **744.2**.)

1. __________ natural elements __________ human actions were causes of the Dust Bowl.
2. Farmers learned that they must __________ change their farming practices __________ find another occupation.
3. As a result, farmers increased crop yields __________ reduced soil erosion.
4. The southern Great Plains experienced serious droughts __________ in the 1930s __________ in the 1950s.
5. High temperatures __________ low rainfall led to the five-year drought of the '50s.
6. The effects of a major drought are serious __________ for nature __________ for society.
7. Drought increases the risk of forest fires, __________ fires are necessary for certain trees to release their seeds.
8. A water shortage prevents activities as different as hog farming __________ river recreation.
9. __________ hydroelectric power __________ some manufacturing processes will work correctly during a drought.
10. To avoid the effects of drought, we can conserve water __________ find new water supplies.

Expand Sentences (with Subordinating Conjunctions)

You can use a **subordinating conjunction** to connect a dependent clause to another sentence. A dependent clause (one that *cannot* stand alone as a sentence) must be connected to an independent clause (one that *can* stand alone as a sentence). In the expanded sentences below, the dependent clause is underlined, and the subordinating conjunction is in blue.

> **Before people used satellite images to explain and predict the weather, they used folklore. As early people observed changes in the weather, they noticed how it affected insects, animals, birds, and the skies. People believed much of the weather folklore until some of it was disproved by modern science.**

- When a dependent clause begins the sentence, follow it with a comma. The comma is usually not needed when the dependent clause follows the independent clause.

Use the given subordinating conjunction (in parentheses) to combine each of the following pairs of statements into one complex sentence. Place some dependent clauses first.

Example: Some folklore turned out to be accurate. Scientists studied the weather. *(after)*
After scientists studied the weather, some folklore turned out to be accurate.

1. Other folklore was myth. It did not stop people from using the sayings anyway. *(although)*
2. Sea birds sit on the sand. There truly is a storm at hand. *(when)*
3. Wind and daylong rain is nigh. Yellow streaks the sunset sky. *(if)*
4. You see a rainbow at noon. There will be more rain soon. *(when)*
5. The dew is on the grass. Rain will never come to pass. *(as long as)*
6. We'll have a long winter over all the land. A woolly bear caterpillar has a wide brown band. *(since)*
7. A cow tries to scratch her ear. It means a shower is very near. *(whenever)*
8. I hear these different myths. I can only shake my head in wonder. *(as)*
9. I won't trust these sayings. They are proven true. *(unless)*
10. I go on a long hike. I will check the forecast for the day. *(before)*

Building Effective Sentences

Our world is a diverse place. Snow-capped mountains tower more than five miles high, and ocean trenches delve more than six miles deep. In one place, the sun pours its life-giving light on a dense tropical rain forest, while in another, it bakes sand dunes until nothing can survive. Golden fields of grain, rocky shorelines, flat-topped mesas, mazelike everglades—the beauty of the world is its diversity.

Diversity is also the beauty of writing. If every sentence is the same, a reader will soon get bored. Instead, if the sentences vary, containing pleasant surprises around some of the turns, the reader will want to keep reading. This chapter will help you create sentences that are clear, complete, and varied so that you can build beautiful landscapes of ideas.

What's Ahead

You will learn about . . .

- **writing complete sentences.**
- **fixing sentence problems.**
- **improving your sentence style.**
- **combining sentences.**
- **using different types and kinds of sentences.**
- **expanding and modeling sentences.**

Writing Complete Sentences

Every sentence has two basic parts: a complete subject (which tells who or what is doing something) and a complete predicate (which tells what the subject is doing or tells something about the subject).

Complete Subject	Complete Predicate
Who or what does something?	*What does the subject do?*
The Amazon River	**winds through the jungle.**
The Nile River	**empties into the sea.**

Divide a piece of paper into two columns. For each of the sentences below, write the complete subject in the left column and write the complete predicate in the right column.

> In the following sentences, the words that come before the verb are part of the *complete subject*. The verb and all the words that follow it are part of the *complete predicate*.

Example: Old Faithful, a geyser in Yellowstone National Park, erupts for about four minutes every hour.

Old Faithful, a geyser in Yellowstone National Park, | *erupts for about four minutes every hour.*

1. The Royal Gorge Bridge in Colorado ranks as the highest suspension bridge in the world.
2. Australia's Great Barrier Reef stretches for about 1,250 miles.
3. A moat surrounds the Imperial Palace in Tokyo, Japan.
4. Timbuktu served as the chief trading center in western Africa.
5. More than 250,000 workers built the Panama Canal for wages of about 10 cents an hour.
6. The only species of wild ape in Europe lives on Gibraltar Rock.
7. Residents of Venice, Italy, travel through canals by boat.
8. The volcano Mount Vesuvius made Pompeii, Italy, famous.
9. Antarctica is not owned by any country.
10. Jim White, a cowboy, discovered the Carlsbad Caverns in New Mexico.

Subjects and Predicates

Every sentence has a subject and a predicate. A simple subject consists of the subject without the words that modify it. A simple predicate is the verb without the words that modify it or complete the thought. In the sentences below, the **simple subjects** are orange, and the **simple predicates** are blue.

Simple Subject	Simple Predicate
Ancient Egyptians	**worshiped the Nile River.**
The distance from New York City to Los Angeles	**matches the length of the Nile.**

A simple subject may be compound, which means that it includes two or more subjects sharing the same predicate (or predicates). A simple predicate may also be compound, which means that it includes two or more verbs sharing the same subject (or subjects).

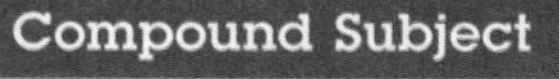

Compound Subject	Compound Predicate
Crocodiles and hippos	**live and thrive in the Nile.**

Number a piece of paper from 1 to 5, skipping a line between numbers. For each sentence below, write the simple subject on one line and the simple predicate on the next line. (Remember to look for compound subjects and predicates.)

Example: Part of the Nile River, the Blue Nile, originates in Ethiopia.
part
originates

1. Sand accumulates in the Blue Nile and turns the water brownish blue.
2. The clear White Nile gathers no sand.
3. The Blue Nile and the White Nile combine at Khartoum, Sudan.
4. The Nile River becomes dark blue at Khartoum and continues to the Mediterranean Sea.
5. The word *Nile* means "dark blue."

Write one sentence with a single simple subject and a compound simple predicate. Then write another sentence with a compound simple subject and a compound simple predicate. Ask a classmate to underline the simple subjects once and the simple predicates twice in each sentence.

How can I make sure my sentences are complete?

Check Your Subjects and Predicates

Incomplete thoughts are called fragments. Fragments may be missing a subject, a predicate, or both. Study the fragments below. Then read the complete sentences made from them. Notice that a subject, a predicate, or both have been added to make the corrections.

Fragment	Sentence
Consists of four large islands and more than 3,000 small ones.	**Japan consists of four large islands and more than 3,000 small ones.** (A subject is added.)
In Japan.	**Mount Fuji is the highest mountain in Japan.** (A subject and predicate are added.)
Shinto pilgrims this sacred mountain.	**Shinto pilgrims climb this sacred mountain.** (A predicate is added.)

Number your paper from 1 to 7. Read each group of words below. If the group of words is a complete sentence, write "C" next to the number. If it is a fragment, write "F" and tell if it needs a subject, a predicate, or both to become a complete sentence.

Example: Stands on Honshu, the largest island.
F-subject

1. Mount Fuji is named for an ancient Japanese goddess of fire.
2. Lake Biwa, Japan's largest lake, near Mount Fuji.
3. Of Japan's more than 250 volcanoes, Mount Fuji the largest.
4. In the past few hundred years, has erupted almost 20 times.
5. To hike the trail up the slopes of Mount Fuji about nine hours.
6. Open to the public only during July and August.
7. Mount Fuji remains a top tourist attraction.

Correct any fragments above by adding the missing parts to form complete sentences. Exchange papers with a classmate and check each other's work.

Check for Dependent Clauses

A dependent clause (also called a subordinate clause) contains a subject and a verb but does not express a complete thought. It cannot stand by itself as a sentence. A dependent clause needs to be connected to an independent clause to compete its meaning. A dependent clause plus an independent clause creates a complex sentence. (See 698.3.)

Dependent Clauses *(They cannot stand alone.)*	**Combined with Independent Clauses** *(Complex sentences are created.)*
Where the wilderness is mostly untouched	The Yukon Territory is located in a northerly region **where the wilderness is mostly untouched.**
Because the sun never sets during some of the summer season	**Because the sun never sets during some of the summer season,** people go to bed with the sun still shining.
That are extremely cold	Winters that **are extremely** cold can turn gasoline to slush.

A comma is needed after a dependent clause that comes at the beginning of a sentence. A comma is usually not needed if the dependent clause comes at the end. A dependent clause in the middle of a sentence may or may not need to be set off by commas. (See 584.1 and 590.1.)

Read the paragraph below. How many dependent clauses do you find? Now rewrite the paragraph, connecting each dependent clause to an independent clause that comes before or after it.

When the gold rush occurred in the 1800s. Thousands rushed to the Klondike River in the Yukon. Though many had jobs. They left home to seek their fortune. Because of the gold rush. The Royal Canadian Mounted Police went north to police the miners. The Mounties stopped travelers to be sure they had adequate supplies. Before the Mounties let them go on. Once the gold rush began. Dawson City, Yukon, grew from a tiny town to a city of 30,000. After the gold rush, only 700 residents remained in Dawson City. Suddenly the Yukon area was left with many empty log cabins. That were built earlier by the miners.

Write a brief paragraph explaining the history of a place in your city or hometown or a place you have visited or read about. Include at least two complex sentences.

Fixing Sentence Problems

Avoid Run-On Sentences

Sometimes you may accidentally write a run-on sentence by putting together two or more sentences. One type of run-on is called a *comma splice,* in which the sentences are connected with a comma only. Another type of run-on has no punctuation at all.

One way to fix run-on sentences is to add a coordinating conjunction (*and, so, or, for, but, yet, or nor*) and a comma (if not already present). Another way is to connect the two sentences with a semicolon.

Run-On Sentence	Corrected Sentences
The Rock of Gibraltar stands between Europe and Africa less than eight miles separate the continents.	**The Rock of Gibraltar stands between Europe and Africa, and less than eight miles separate the continents.**
	The Rock of Gibraltar stands between Europe and Africa; less than eight miles separate the continents.

On your own paper, correct the run-on sentences below by adding a comma and a coordinating conjunction.

Example: The Gibraltar peninsula is a thin, hilly strip of land it is connected to Spain.
The Gibraltar peninsula is a thin, hilly strip of land, and it is connected to Spain.

1. Many cargo and passenger ships visit Gibraltar's harbor the safe harbor and mild climate make it a great place to stop for repairs.
2. Storks spend winters in Africa and summers in Europe they migrate over Gibraltar.
3. This limestone mountain was legendary to Ancient Greeks they called it one of the Pillars of Hercules.
4. In ancient times, the African Moors occupied Gibraltar it has also been controlled by Spain and England.
5. People use the Rock of Gibraltar as a symbol of strength they say something strong is "as solid as the Rock of Gibraltar."

Select two of the run-on sentences above. Correct them by adding a semicolon.

Eliminate Rambling Sentences

A rambling sentence occurs when you connect too many ideas with the word *and*. Study the rambling sentence below and two ways it can be corrected.

Rambling Sentence	**Corrected Sentences** *(The and's have been eliminated.)*
Loch Ness is a large lake in northern Scotland and it is famous for its legendary monster and many tourists visit the loch and hope they see the monster. 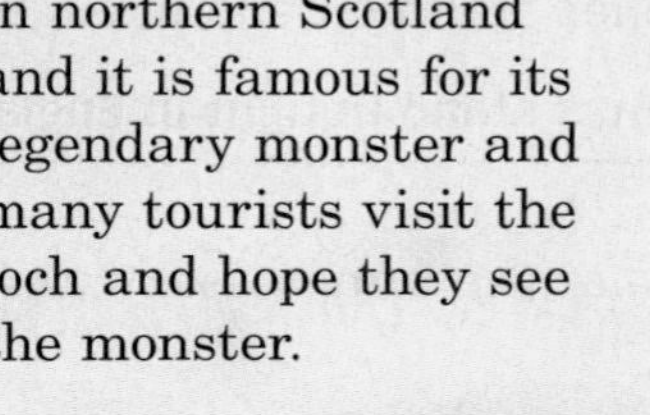 	**Loch Ness, a large lake in northern Scotland, is famous for its legendary monster. Many tourists, hoping to see the monster, visit the loch.** (An appositive phrase [see page 513] is used in the first sentence, and a participial phrase [see page 520] is used in the second sentence.) **Loch Ness is a large lake in northern Scotland that is famous for its legendary monster. Many tourists, who hope to see the monster, visit the loch.** (Two complex sentences have been created. The dependent clause in each sentence begins with a relative pronoun: *that* and *who*. See pages 515 and 517.)

It is not necessary to eliminate all of the *and's* in a rambling sentence. Some *and's* may be needed to connect compound sentences, compound subjects and predicates, and so on.

Rewrite the following rambling sentences so they contain fewer *and's*. Whenever possible, make complex sentences. (See pages 515 and 517.)

1. The water in Loch Ness stays about 42 degrees Fahrenheit (6 degrees Celsius) and it is very deep and it never freezes.
2. Scientists searched the lake with sonar equipment in the 1960s and numerous sightings of a monster were reported and this made people even more curious about the Loch Ness monster.
3. In 1972 an underwater camera took pictures in Loch Ness and scientists studied the evidence of a monster and the scientists say the creature might be a sea cow.
4. The monster legend began around the year 565 C.E. and children were not allowed to play by the lake and people began fearing attacks by the monster.

Check for Wordy Sentences

Unnecessary repetition creates wordy sentences. Removing unnecessary words improves the sentence. Study the wordy sentence below and the two ways in which it is corrected.

Wordy Sentence	Corrected Sentences *(Unnecessary words are eliminated.)*
Huge, giant stones stand on end upright in England.	**Huge stones stand on end in England.**
	Giant stones stand upright in England.

Rewrite each of the sentences below so that the unnecessary words are eliminated.

1. Approximately 4,000 years ago, 2000 B.C.E., the stones were set in place.
2. Each year thousands of visitors annually go to Stonehenge as tourists.
3. Britain has approximately about 900 stone site locations.
4. In the evening at dusk, visitors especially like to see Stonehenge while the sun is setting.
5. The rocks that make Stonehenge come from great distances far away.
6. No one is certain exactly how these gigantic stones were transported and moved.
7. Because one stone in the middle aligns in a straight line with the sun, some scientists think that people used the stones as a calendar.
8. In Great Britain, Stonehenge sits by itself on the Salisbury Plain in the southern part of England.
9. Some people think that alien beings who came from outer space created Stonehenge.
10. Careful studies show that Stonehenge was built over a long period of time taking hundreds of years.

Move Misplaced Modifiers

Misplaced modifiers occur when a descriptive phrase is improperly located in a sentence and appears to describe the wrong word or idea. To correct this error, locate descriptive phrases as close as possible to the words they modify.

Misplaced Modifier	Corrected Sentences
The largest desert in the world, Africa contains the Sahara Desert. (This sentence incorrectly makes it sound as if Africa is the desert.)	**Africa contains the Sahara Desert, the largest desert in the world.** **The Sahara Desert, the largest desert in the world, is contained in Africa.** (In both sentences the descriptive phrase is moved closer to the word it modifies.)

Rewrite each sentence below so that the descriptive modifier clearly describes the correct word or idea. (Change the sentences as needed.)

Example: Ninety percent gravel and boulders, sand actually covers a small portion of the Sahara Desert.
Sand actually covers a small portion of the Sahara Desert, which is 90 percent gravel and boulders.

1. Burrowing during the heat of the day, a visitor might see centipedes and scorpions.
2. Wearing long, protective robes and turbans, camels carry Bedouin nomads through the Sahara.
3. Supplying enough water to support a small city, people can live around a large desert oasis.
4. In sandstone shelters, the Sahara contains carvings and paintings drawn by ancient people.
5. Currently dried up, aerial photographs show that ancient rivers and lakes existed near the Sahara.

Write two sentences containing misplaced modifiers. Base your sentences on the facts below. Then exchange sentences with a classmate and correct each other's work.

Animals in the Sahara

– survive a harsh environment
– squeeze into abandoned burrows
– seek shade during the day
– are active mostly at night
– live near an oasis

What can I do to write clear sentences?

Make Subjects and Verbs Agree

Subjects and verbs in each sentence you write must agree. That means a singular subject needs a singular verb, and a plural subject needs a plural verb. (Also see 728.1.)

Single Subjects

A verb must agree with its subject in number.

- If a subject is singular, the verb must be singular, too.
  Brazil is the largest country in South America.
- If a subject is plural, the verb must be plural.
  Most beaches in Brazil have beautiful white sand.

(Don't forget that nouns ending in *s* or *es* are very often plural, and verbs ending in *s* are very often singular.)

- If an indefinite pronoun is singular, its verb must be singular, too.
  Almost everyone in Brazil lives near the Atlantic coast.
- If an indefinite pronoun is plural, its verb must be plural also.
  Many of Brazil's people speak Portuguese.

Some indefinite pronouns are tricky because they can be singular or plural when used as a subject. (See the chart on page 475.)

Number your paper from 1 to 7. For each of the following sentences, correctly write the verb to agree with the subject. If the verb or verbs are correct, write a "C" on your paper.

Example: The Amazon River flow through Brazil.
flows

1. Only some of the plants in the Amazon rain forest has been classified.
2. Amazingly, rain forest spiders grows bigger than this book.
3. Now the rain forests are endangered by civilization.
4. Something are needed to protect animals from heavy river traffic.
5. Tourists doesn't see as many animals in the rain forest.
6. Plants is also disappearing.
7. Some agencies, however, are starting to counteract the damage.

Compound Subjects Connected by "And"

A compound subject connected by the word *and* usually needs a plural verb.

Ecuador and Chile are the only South American countries that don't touch Brazil's border.

Compound Subjects Connected by "Or"

A compound subject connected by the word *or* needs a verb that agrees in number with the subject nearest to the verb.

Either concerned citizens or the World Bank manages a new rain forest conservation program.
(*World Bank,* the subject nearer the verb, is singular, so the singular verb *manages* is used.)

Unusual Word Order

When the subject is separated from the verb by words or phrases, be sure that the verb agrees with the subject.

The Amazon River basin, which extends for more than 4,000 miles, is the largest river basin in the world.
(*Basin*, not *miles*, is the subject, so the singular verb *is* is used.)

When the subject comes after the verb in a sentence, be sure that the verb agrees with the "true subject."

There is more water carried by the Amazon than by the world's 10 next largest rivers combined.
(The subject *water* and the verb *is* are both singular.)

Feeding this great river are more than 1,000 tributaries.
(The subject *tributaries* and the verb *are* are both plural.)

Number your paper from 1 to 5. Write the correct verb choice for each of these sentences.

1. The Nile and the Amazon (*is, are*) the world's longest rivers.
2. In a square mile of Amazon rain forest (*is, are*) many types of trees.
3. My aunt and uncle (*lives, live*) in Rio de Janeiro, Brazil.
4. Either Rio or the giant trees (*was, were*) highlights of my trip.
5. The screech of monkeys or the call of parrots still (*pierces, pierce*) my dreams.

Write five sentences of your own: one with a compound subject connected by "and," one with a compound subject connected by "or," and three with unusual word order. Share your work with a classmate.

What should I do to avoid nonstandard sentences?

Avoid Double Negatives

Two negative words used together in the same sentence form a double negative *(not no, barely nothing, not never).* Double negatives also happen if you use contractions ending in *n't* with a negative word *(can't hardly, didn't never).* Your writing will not be accurate if you use double negatives.

Negative Words

nothing nowhere neither never not barely hardly nobody none

Negative Contractions

don't can't won't shouldn't wouldn't couldn't didn't hadn't

Number your paper from 1 to 5. List the double negatives you find in the sentences below and then correctly rewrite each sentence. *Hint:* There is usually more than one way to correct a double negative.

Example: My sister and I never have no fun on family vacations.
never no
My sister and I never have any fun on family vacations.

1. We can't go nowhere we want to.
2. I don't hardly want to hear what the plan is this year.
3. Nobody doesn't want to go to Aunt Jessica's house again.
4. We just go there because it doesn't cost nothing.
5. Why don't we never just go to a giant water park?

Avoid Double Subjects

Avoid sentences in which a personal pronoun is used immediately after the subject—the result is usually a double subject.

Double Subject: **Mauritius it** is an island in the Indian Ocean.
Corrected Sentence: *Mauritius is an island in the Indian Ocean.*

Double Subject: **Alma she** and I want to go to Mauritius.
Corrected Sentence: *Alma and I want to go to Mauritius.*

Write four sentences. In two of them, use double negatives. In the other two, use double subjects. Exchange papers with a classmate, rewrite each other's sentences correctly, and then check each other's work.

Improving Your Sentence Style

There are a number of ways to add variety to your sentences and improve your writing style. Here are four of the most common ways.

1. **Combine short sentences.**
2. **Use different types of sentences.**
3. **Expand sentences by adding words and phrases.**
4. **Model sentences of other writers.**

When too many sentences in a paragraph are the same length or follow the same pattern, the paragraph sounds choppy. Read the following paragraph.

Little Variety

Part of Turkey is in Europe. Part of Turkey is in Asia. Turkey is a very interesting country. Ankara is the capital. The largest city is Istanbul. It exists on two continents. No other major city does this. The Bosporus Strait splits the city in two. The European part is on the western side. The Asian part is on the eastern side.

Read the following version, which has a better variety of sentences. See how using different types of sentences helps this paragraph flow more smoothly.

Good Variety

Turkey is an interesting country because part of it is in Europe and part is in Asia. Ankara is the capital city; however, the largest city is Istanbul. Istanbul is the only major city in the world that exists on two continents. The Bosporus Strait splits the city in two, with the European part on the western side and the Asian part on the eastern side.

Read the paragraph below. Then, on your own paper, rewrite the paragraph to create more sentence variety.

Turkish food is partly Asian. Turkish food is partly European. There are many kinds of dishes. Kebabs are from Turkey. Kebabs usually have meat. Some kebabs are made just with vegetables. Puddings are popular in Turkey. There are at least twelve kinds of milk pudding. There are many delicious pastries. Turkish coffee is a common drink. Turkish coffee is very strong. Tea is a common drink, too.

How can I make my sentences flow more smoothly?

Writers often combine sentences to help their writing flow more smoothly. Too many short sentences can make writing sound choppy. Combining some sentences will add variety to your writing and improve your overall writing style.

Combine with a Series

You can combine sentences using a series of words, phrases, or clauses.

Combine with a Series

Short Sentences	*Combined Using a Series of Words*
The Mississippi River was carved by melting glaciers. The Missouri and Ohio rivers were carved by melting glaciers.	**The Mississippi, Missouri, and Ohio rivers were carved by melting glaciers.**
Short Sentences	*Combined Using a Series of Words*
The Pacific Northwest has many ecosystems. It is home to over 15 million people. It is a world leader in technology industries.	**The Pacific Northwest has many ecosystems, is home to over 15 million people, and is a world leader in technology industries.**

The items in any series must be alike (or parallel). For example, if the first item is a phrase, all the items must be phrases worded in the same way. (See page **559**.) Use commas to separate items in a series.

Use a series of parallel words or phrases to combine the groups of sentences below. (Change words in the sentences as needed.)

1. The Pacific Northwest was claimed by Russia and by Spain at different times in history. It was also claimed by Britain.
2. The Rocky Mountains are in the Pacific Northwest. The Cascade Range and the Coast Ranges are also there.
3. Visitors to Olympic National Park in Washington State can take pictures of snow-topped mountains. They can also relax on ocean beaches. They can hike in rain forests.
4. Tide pools at the park are a great place to view anemones. People can also see starfish in the tide pools. They can see sand dollars in the tide pools, too.

Combine with Phrases

You can combine sentences by using appositives (see **586.1**) or prepositional phrases (see **742.1**). An appositive is a word or phrase that comes after a noun or pronoun and renames it.

Combine Using an Appositive Phrase

Short Sentences	*Combined Sentences*
Sumo wrestling began as a religious ritual. It is Japan's national sport.	**Sumo wrestling, Japan's national sport, began as a religious ritual.**

Combine Using a Prepositional Phrase

Short Sentences	*Combined Sentences*
Sumo wrestlers weigh as much as 265 kilograms. In pounds, that's about 580.	**Sumo wrestlers weigh as much as 265 kilograms, or about 580 pounds.**

Combine each of the following sets of sentences by using the method given in parentheses.

Example: The wrestling ring is a circle. The ring has a diameter of about 15 feet. *(two prepositional phrases)*
The wrestling ring is a circle with a diameter of about 15 feet.

1. The wrestling ring is raised so spectators can better see. The wrestling ring is a clay platform. *(appositive phrase)*
2. The wrestlers wear silk robes. They wear the robes before their matches. *(prepositional phrase)*
3. One way to win is to pull or push an opponent. A wrestler tries to pull or push his opponent out of the ring. *(prepositional phrase)*
4. At any one time, there are from one to four yokozuna. *Yokozuna* is the Japanese word for grand champions. *(appositive phrase)*
5. A sumo tournament consists of either seven or fifteen bouts held over two weeks. A sumo tournament is properly called a "basho." *(appositive phrase)*

Write two sentences about a sport you enjoy. Use an appositive phrase in the first sentence. Use at least one prepositional phrase in the second sentence.

Combine with Infinitive or Participial Phrases

You can combine short sentences by using infinitive phrases (see 730.4) or participial phrases (see 730.3).

Combine Using an Infinitive Phrase

Short Sentences	*Combined Sentences*
Gina interviewed her grandmother. She was interested in learning about her ancestors.	**Gina interviewed her grandmother to learn about her ancestors.**

Combine Using a Participial Phrase

Short Sentences	*Combined Sentences*
Gina's ancestors hoped for a better future. They emigrated from Italy to New York State.	**Hoping for a better future, Gina's ancestors emigrated from Italy to New York State.**

On your own paper, combine each of the following sets of short sentences using the method given in parentheses.

Example: Between 1884 and 1920, about 7 million Italians immigrated to the United States. They escaped poverty and malnutrition. *(infinitive phrase)*
Between 1884 and 1920, about 7 million Italians immigrated to the United States to escape poverty and malnutrition.

1. Gina's great-great-grandfather arrived in New York City in 1912. He was equipped with only a suitcase. *(participial phrase)*
2. Gina's great-great-grandfather settled in the Hudson Valley. He wanted a better life. *(participial phrase)*
3. Even today many immigrants come to the Hudson Valley. They can improve their lives. *(infinitive phrase)*
4. Jorge Garcia was urged to move by his uncle. Jorge Garcia came to the Hudson Valley from Mexico and now owns a restaurant. *(participial phrase)*
5. Gina is planning a trip to the Hudson Valley. She will see it for herself. *(infinitive phrase)*

Write two sentences about your ancestors. Use an infinitive phrase in the first sentence. Use a participial phrase in the second sentence.

Combine with Relative Pronouns

You can also combine sentences by using a relative pronoun to connect a dependent clause to an independent clause. Relative pronouns include words such as *who, which, that, whose, whom,* and so on.

Combine with Relative Pronouns

Two Short Sentences	*Combined Using a Relative Pronoun*
George Washington has many places named after him. George Washington was our first president.	**George Washington, who has many places named after him, was our first president.** **George Washington, who was our first president, has many places named after him.**

A dependent clause beginning with the relative pronoun *which* is always set off by commas. A dependent clause beginning with *who* or *whose* is also set off by commas if the dependent clause contains information that is not necessary to understand the independent clause.

Combine each set of sentences below by using the relative pronoun in parentheses.

Example: In the United States, "Washington" is the name of seven counties. They range from New York to Oregon. *(which)*
In the United States, "Washington" is the name of seven counties, which range from New York to Oregon.

1. Amazingly, James Madison has twenty counties named for him. James Madison was our fourth president. *(who)*
2. John Adams was the second president. His home was in Braintree, Massachusetts. *(whose)*
3. Five of the first ten presidents were all from Virginia. They were born before the U.S. became a country. *(who)*
4. Schools help us honor them. These schools are named for presidents. *(that)*
5. I attend Jefferson Middle School. It holds the best science fair in our county. *(which)*

Write freely about an adult you admire (a relative, a teacher, a coach). Explain places or organizations that could be named for this person. Afterward, underline any sentences containing relative pronouns. Also find two shorter sentences in your writing that you could combine using a relative pronoun.

BASIC WRITING

What can I do to add variety to my writing?

Varying sentence types can make your writing come alive. A good writer uses a variety of sentences to make writing clear and interesting.

Create Compound Sentences

A compound sentence is made up of two or more simple sentences (independent clauses) joined by a comma and a coordinating conjunction (*and, for, but, or, so, nor,* and *yet*) or by a semicolon. (See 590.2 and 594.1.)

Compound Sentence = Two Independent Clauses

The Bay of Bengal has an area of 1,300,000 square miles, and it is the largest bay in the world. (A comma and the conjunction and join the two independent clauses.)

Eight countries border the Bay of Bengal; its west coast is formed by India. (A semicolon joins the two independent clauses.)

On your own paper, join each of the following sets of sentences using either a comma and a coordinating conjunction or a semicolon.

Example: Ancient Greek and Roman traders sailed to the Bay of Bengal. "Modern" Europeans didn't discover the bay until the 1500s.

Ancient Greek and Roman traders sailed to the Bay of Bengal, but "modern" Europeans didn't discover the bay until the 1500s.

1. Approximately two million tons of fish are caught in the Bay of Bengal each year. The fishing industry is threatened by pollution.
2. One-fourth of the world's population lives in the countries bordering the bay. Seafood from the Bay of Bengal is very important.
3. Monsoons blow across the Bay of Bengal from the southwest in the summer. They blow from the northeast in the winter.
4. Monsoons are strong winds. They bring heavy rains.
5. Much of the country of Bangladesh is a fertile delta. Dangerous flooding there has killed many people.

Write two compound sentences about a body of water that you know about. Make sure you punctuate your sentences correctly.

Develop Complex Sentences

When you join a dependent clause to an independent clause, you form a **complex sentence**. In complex sentences, relative pronouns and subordinating conjunctions are used to connect the dependent clause to the independent clause. Subordinating conjunctions include words such as *after, although, because, before, even though, until, when,* and *while*. (See page 744 for more subordinating conjunctions.)

COMPLEX SENTENCE =

A Dependent Clause	+	An Independent Clause
Although many place names are straightforward,		some make people think twice.
An Independent Clause	**+**	**A Dependent Clause**
People can visit Santa Claus in three states (Arizona, Georgia, and Indiana)		even though it's not Christmas.

Number your paper from 1 to 5. Then write the dependent clause in each of the following complex sentences. (Also see 698.2–698.3.)

Example: You'd better be careful of what you say if you visit Secret, Nevada.
if you visit Secret, Nevada

1. Until I traveled to Rhode Island, I didn't know there was a town named Common Fence Post.
2. After you visit the town of Brothers, Oregon, you should drive on to the town of Sisters, Oregon.
3. The Romans named the Canary Islands ("Island of the Dogs" in Latin) because they found wild dogs there.
4. Because its name is only one syllable long, Maine is unique among the states.
5. Enola, Oregon, might be a solitary place since its name comes from "alone" spelled backward.

Write a short paragraph about your name. (How did you get it? How is it working for you? Or, what has happened to you because of that name?) When you finish, underline any complex sentences you use. Also try to find two shorter sentences that you could combine into a complex sentence.

Use Questions and Commands

Writers add variety to their sentences by making statements, asking questions, giving commands, or showing strong emotion. See the chart below.

Kinds of Sentences

Declarative .	Makes a statement about a person, a place, a thing, or an idea	**The diameter of Mars is slightly more than half the diameter of Earth.**	This is the most common kind of sentence.
Interrogative ?	Asks a question	**Does Mars have any interesting physical features?**	A question gets the reader's attention.
Imperative .	Gives a command or makes a strong request	**Read about it and find out.**	Commands or requests often appear in dialogue and directions.
Exclamatory !	Shows strong emotion or feeling	**What an amazing place it is!**	Use these sentences for occasional emphasis.

On a piece of paper, write the numbers 1 to 9. Classify each of the sentences below by writing "D" for declarative, "INT" for interrogative, "IMP" for imperative, or "EX" for exclamatory. Then write the correct end punctuation.

1. Did you know that Mars has two main areas
2. They are the northern lowlands and the southern highlands
3. Study the information about lava flows in the northern lowlands
4. Wow, the southern highlands are almost four miles higher than the northern lowlands
5. In the south, the Hellas Basin is more than 5.5 miles deep
6. What a crater it must be
7. When can we visit
8. For now, just read about it
9. Instead, think of the Grand Canyon, which is "only" one mile deep

Write four sentences—one of each kind—about an unusual place that you would like to visit. Be sure you punctuate your sentences correctly.

What can I do to add details to my sentences?

Expand with Prepositional Phrases

Writers add details to their sentences using prepositional phrases. These phrases function as adjectives or adverbs. *Remember:* A prepositional phrase begins with a preposition and ends with the object of a preposition. (See page 742 for a list of prepositions.)

- Prepositional phrases used as adjectives answer the questions *How many? Which one? What kind?*
- Prepositional phrases used as adverbs answer the questions *When? How? How often? How long? Where? How much?*

Prepositional Phrase	Function in Sentence
Centuries ago, settlers from Scotland and France settled Cape Breton Island.	The phrase *from Scotland and France* acts as an **adjective** to describe the noun *settlers*.
Cape Breton Island lies on Canada's eastern coast.	The phrase *on Canada's eastern coast* acts as an **adverb** to modify the verb *lies*.

Write the 10 prepositional phrases that you find in sentences 1 to 6 below.

Example: The Cabot Trail winds along Cape Breton's mountainsides.
along Cape Breton's mountainsides

1. From the road, drivers can view the ocean.
2. People often see pods of whales along the coast.
3. Moose graze near lakes and streams.
4. Visitors take tours through a museum of French history.
5. Alexander Bell, the inventor of the telephone, settled in Cape Breton.
6. Though he traveled to many places, he said, "For simple beauty, Cape Breton outrivals them all."

Use one or two prepositional phrases to add information to each of the sentences below.

1. **I can imagine going through the mountains.**
2. **I'd see whales and eagles.**
3. **The sunset would be beautiful.**

Expand with Infinitive and Participial Phrases

Writers sometimes make their sentences more interesting by adding infinitive or participial phrases. (Also see **730.3** and **730.4**.)

- An infinitive phrase consists of the word "to" plus the basic form of a verb plus any modifiers. An infinitive phrase can serve as a noun, an adjective, or an adverb.
- A participial phrase consists of a participle (a verb form usually ending in *ed* or *ing*) plus any modifiers. It serves as an adjective in a sentence.

Infinitive Phrases

To visit Death Valley is a goal of mine.
(The phrase serves as a noun—the subject of the sentence.)

Someday, I will have a chance to take this trip.
(The phrase serves as an adjective that modifies the noun *chance*.)

Many people travel to enjoy good weather.
(The phrase serves as an adverb that modifies the verb *travel*.)

Participial Phrases

Hearing about Death Valley, I thought it would be an amazing place.
(The *ing* phrase is an adjective that modifies the pronoun *I*.)

In Death Valley, recognized as one of earth's hottest places, the temperature reaches 130 degrees Fahrenheit.
(The *ed* phrase is an adjective that modifies the noun *Death Valley*.)

There is one infinitive or participial phrase in each sentence below. Copy each phrase and label it "I" for infinitive or "P" for participial.

Example: To view all of Death Valley, you should climb Telescope Peak.
to view all of Death Valley, I

1. Earth scientists, having a deep understanding of geology, can "read" Death Valley's rocks.
2. Plants and animals living in the harsh conditions are amazing.
3. Somehow, prehistoric humans were able to survive there.
4. Borax, mined in Death Valley in the late 1800s, still exists there.
5. I can't wait to visit this amazing place in person.

How can I make my sentences more interesting?

Model Sentences

You can learn a great deal about writing by studying the sentences of other writers. When you come across sentences that you like, practice writing some of your own using the same pattern. This process is called *modeling.*

Professional Models

I walked along the Grand Canyon, gazing down into its rocky gorges and dizzyingly sheer cliffs.

Goats can go where wolves cannot, following routes that spiral down canyon walls.
—*National Geographic*

Student Models

I strolled down the beach, looking out across the crashing surf and foaming breakers.

My brothers slipped through the trapdoor of the fort, swinging down ladders that hung to the ground.

Guidelines for Modeling

- Find a sentence or a short passage that you like and write it down.
- Think of a topic for your practice writing.
- Follow the pattern of the sentence or passage as you write about your own subject. (You do not have to follow the model exactly.)
- Build each sentence one part at a time and check your work when you are finished. (Take your time.)
- Review your work and change any parts that seem confusing or unclear.
- Share your new sentences with your classmates.
- Find other sentences to model and keep practicing.

On your own paper, model the following sentences. *Remember:* You do not have to follow a model sentence exactly.

1. I can tell you that when I spotted the slithery streak in the grass, my heart started to race, but my feet wouldn't move.
2. The children jumped up with surprise, broke into smiles, doubled over with laughter, and shouted for joy.
3. Although the heavy, wet snow soaked through their gloves, Tim and Matt continued building their fort.

Develop a Sentence Style

The following techniques and strategies will help you improve your writing style. (Also see page 42.)

Varying Sentence Beginnings

To add some variety to the common subject-verb pattern, try beginning a sentence with a phrase or a dependent clause.

One evening after sundown, we drove in a buggy past old Dorset's house.

—"The Ransom of Red Chief" by O. Henry

To judge by his face, Dussel is dreaming of food.

—*The Diary of a Young Girl* by Anne Frank

Moving Adjectives

Usually, you write adjectives before the nouns they modify. You can also emphasize adjectives by placing them after the nouns.

A long, low moan, indescribably sad, swept over the moor.

—*The Hound of the Baskervilles* by Sir Arthur Conan Doyle

Repeating a Word

You can repeat a word or phrase to emphasize a particular idea or feeling.

They could see her cheeks going up and down, they could see the trickle of milk leaking out of one side of her mouth, but they couldn't see what she was thinking.

—*The Fledgling* by Jane Langton

Creating a Balanced Sentence

You can write a sentence that uses parallel words, phrases, or clauses for emphasis.

Home! That was what they meant, those caressing appeals, those soft touches wafted through the air, those invisible little hands pulling and tugging, all one way!

—*The Wind in the Willows* by Kenneth Grahame

Study the sample sentences above. Then write your own sentences that follow each sample pattern. Share your sentences with your classmates.

Constructing Strong Paragraphs

What's the best way to build strong muscles? Most forms of exercise build muscle, but other factors are also important. Eating right, relaxing between workouts, and sleeping well help muscles develop.

What's the best way to build strong paragraphs? Starting with a well-written topic sentence is essential, but a paragraph doesn't stop there. The sentences in the body need to support the topic sentence and provide interesting and well-organized details. Last of all, the closing sentence should summarize or restate the topic. In the following chapter, you will exercise your brain by building strong paragraphs.

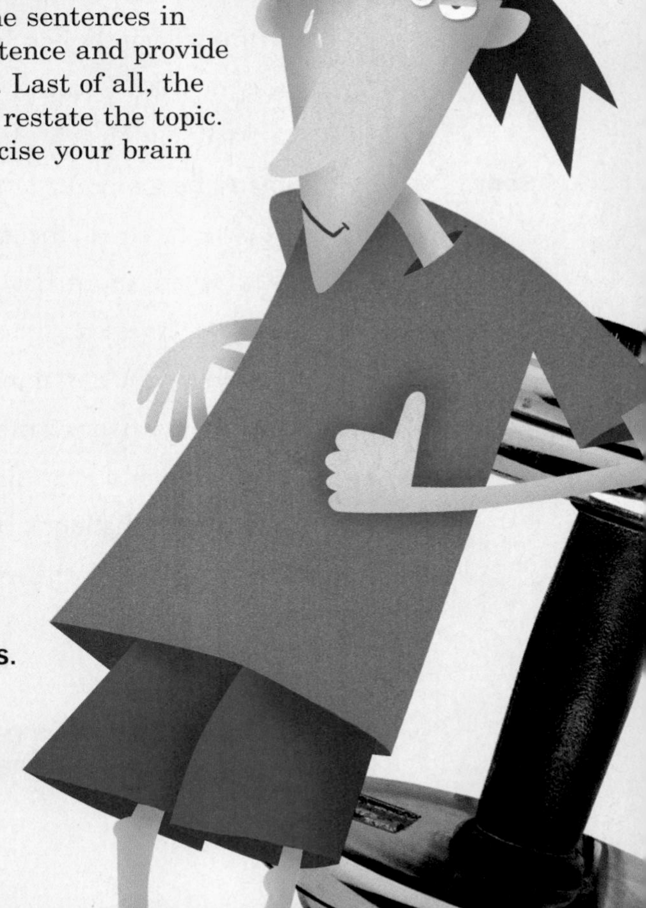

What's Ahead

You will learn about . . .

- the parts of a paragraph.
- types of paragraphs.
- writing effective paragraphs.
- adding details to paragraphs.
- gathering details.
- organizing your details.
- refining your details.
- turning paragraphs into essays.
- using a checklist.

The Parts of a Paragraph

Most paragraphs have three main parts: a topic sentence, a body, and a closing sentence. Paragraphs usually begin with a **topic sentence** that tells what the paragraph is about. The sentences in the **body** share details about the topic, and the **closing sentence** brings the paragraph to a close.

Topic Sentence

Body

Closing Sentence

Attitude Is Everything

A positive attitude can help people overcome great odds. Walt Disney didn't let a learning disability stop him from creating the best-known amusement park in the world. Helen Keller's positive attitude helped her become the first person who was hearing-, sight-, and speech-impaired to earn a bachelor of arts degree. She went on to write many books and became one of America's greatest speakers. When the famous scientist Stephen Hawking was asked about having ALS, a serious muscular disease, he said, "I try to lead as normal a life as possible and not think about my condition or regret the things it prevents me from doing." That's a positive attitude in action! Whenever people face a difficult challenge, they should remember these individuals and the power of a positive attitude.

Respond to the reading. **How many examples of positive attitude are mentioned? What do they all have in common?**

A Closer Look at the Parts

The Topic Sentence

The topic sentence tells the reader what a paragraph is going to be about. A good topic sentence (1) names the topic and (2) states a specific detail or a feeling about it. Here is a simple formula for writing a topic sentence.

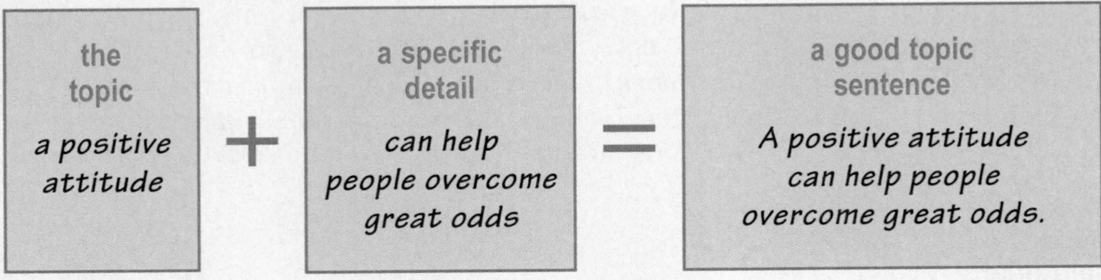
the topic
a positive attitude
+
a specific detail
can help people overcome great odds
=
a good topic sentence
A positive attitude can help people overcome great odds.

The topic sentence is usually the first sentence in a paragraph, although sometimes it comes later. It guides the direction of the sentences in the rest of the paragraph.

A positive attitude can help people overcome great odds.

The Body

The sentences in the body of the paragraph include the details needed to understand the topic.

- **Use specific details to make your paragraph interesting.** The specific details below are shown in red.

  Walt Disney didn't let a learning disability stop him from creating the best-known amusement park in the world.

- **Organize your sentences in the best possible order.** Five common ways to organize sentences are chronological (time) order, order of location, order of importance, comparison-contrast order, and logical order. (See page 551.)

The Closing Sentence

The closing sentence comes after all the details in the body. It will often restate the topic or give the reader something to think about. In an essay, it can provide a transition into a following paragraph.

Whenever people face a difficult challenge, they should remember these individuals and the power of a positive attitude.

Types of Paragraphs

There are four basic types of paragraphs: *narrative, descriptive, expository,* and *persuasive.* Each type requires a different way of thinking and planning.

Write Narrative Paragraphs

In a **narrative paragraph**, you share a personal story or an important experience with the reader. The details in a narrative paragraph should answer the 5 W's *(who? what? when? where?* and *why?)*. A narrative is often organized according to time (what happened *first, next, then, finally*).

Topic Sentence

Body

Closing Sentence

Champions

With only 15 seconds left on the clock, we needed a basket to win the Midwest Wheelchair Basketball Tournament. My teammates and I were racing toward our end of the court, and I had the ball. I scrambled between two guys and gave a strong push to the basket. Though my eyes were on all the players, my mind was on scoring. We'd worked too hard to get this far— we just had to win. When I was near the top of the key, I heard my coach yell, "Shoot it, Mo!" In one smooth motion, I squared up and let the ball fly. I remember thinking the shot was right on line, but the ball hit the back of the rim and went straight up into the air. Everyone tried to get in position under the basket. Then, just as the buzzer sounded, the ball slipped cleanly through the net. We had won the game 38–37, and the championship was ours.

Respond to the reading. How does the closing sentence connect with the topic sentence? How is suspense built into the story?

Write a narrative paragraph. Write a paragraph that tells about some memorable experience you've had. Make sure to answer the 5 W's.

Develop Descriptive Paragraphs

When you write a **descriptive paragraph**, you give a detailed picture of a person, a place, an object, or an event. Descriptive paragraphs include many sensory details (sight, sound, smell, taste, touch).

Topic Sentence

Body

Closing Sentence

My Guide Dog

I know my golden retriever Misha just about as well as I know myself. She has a firm, wide head with floppy ears that are covered with curly, silky fur. My hands slide down the top of her head and over her eyes, the eyes that see for me. Then I find her cold, damp nose and thick, smooth tongue. I can feel her warm breath on my hands. She wears a thick collar around her neck and a leather harness around her broad sides. Her silky fur ruffles in my fingers and smells like the outdoors. Her nails are stubby and hard, and her round toes are rough. Little tufts of fur, called feathers, stick out between her toes. When I hold Misha's paw, her tail thumps against the floor, almost like a greeting. Misha is an incredible dog, and I often wonder what my life would be like without her.

Respond to the reading. How many of the five senses are covered in the paragraph? Which two or three details are especially descriptive?

Write a descriptive paragraph. Write a paragraph that describes an animal. Use sensory details in your description.

Construct Expository Paragraphs

In an **expository paragraph**, you share information. You can tell how to do something, give directions, or explain a subject. Transition words like *first, next, then,* and *finally* are often used in expository writing.

What Is a TDD?

Topic Sentence

A telecommunications device for the deaf, or TDD, works like instant messaging on a computer. The TDD is made up of a keyboard, display screen, modem, and printer. First, the user types a message on the keyboard and then sends it to another TDD. When the message reaches its destination, it appears on the other user's display screen. The TDD does not ring like a regular telephone does. Instead, a flashing light tells the person at the other end that a message is waiting. Some TDD systems include a vibrating wristband to alert the person that a message has arrived. There are also message relay centers so that people using regular telephones can send messages to TDD's. Today, more than four million people in the United States have TDD's. This communication tool makes it easy for people with severe hearing disabilities to "reach out and touch somebody" with a message.

Body

Closing Sentence

Respond to the reading. What type of information about the topic is included in the paragraph? Think in terms of definitions, materials needed, and so on.

Write an expository paragraph. Write a paragraph that explains a device, small appliance, or piece of equipment that you know well. Make sure to include different types of information.

Build Persuasive Paragraphs

In a **persuasive paragraph**, you share your opinion (or strong feeling) about a topic. To be persuasive, you must include plenty of reasons, facts, and details to support your opinion. Persuasive writing is usually organized by order of importance (as in the paragraph below) or by logical order.

Topic Sentence

Body

Closing Sentence

Volunteer for Special Olympics

Students at Parkwood Middle School should volunteer to help with the Special Olympics. First of all, volunteering for this worthy event will get students involved in the community. Over time, this involvement will help them become better citizens and neighbors. Secondly, working with these special athletes will allow students to put into practice what they have learned. Parkwood coaches have taught students a lot about sports and training, so it would be satisfying to share this knowledge with other athletes. Most importantly, volunteering will help students better understand and appreciate people with different abilities and gifts. As they work with these athletes, they will surely learn a lot from them, just as they will learn from the volunteers. There are plenty of things that students can do, from working with individual athletes to helping out at the local events. How they help out doesn't matter. What is important is that students volunteer their services and make the Special Olympics a rewarding experience for everyone involved.

Respond to the reading. What is the writer's opinion in the paragraph? Name two or three reasons that support her opinion. When is the most important reason given?

Write a persuasive paragraph. Write to promote a worthwhile cause. Include at least three strong reasons that support your opinion.

Writing Effective Paragraphs

Use the following general guidelines whenever you write paragraphs.

Prewriting Selecting a Topic and Details

- Select a specific topic.
- Collect facts, examples, and details about your topic.
- Write a topic sentence that states what your paragraph is going to be about. (See page 525 for help.)
- Decide on the best way to arrange your details.

Writing Creating the First Draft

- Start your paragraph with the topic sentence.
- Write sentences in the body that support your topic. Use the details you collected as a guide.
- Connect your ideas and sentences with transitions.
- End with a sentence that restates your topic, leaves the reader with a final thought, or (in an essay) leads into the next paragraph.

Revising Improving Your Writing

- Add information if you need to say more about your topic.
- Move sentences that aren't in the correct order.
- Delete sentences that do not support the topic.
- Rewrite any sentences that are not clear.

Editing Checking for Conventions

- Check the revised version of your writing for capitalization, punctuation, grammar, and spelling errors.
- Then write a neat final copy and proofread it.

When you write a paragraph, remember that readers want . . .

- original ideas. *(They want to learn something new and interesting.)*
- personality. *(They want to hear the writer's voice.)*

How can I find interesting details?

Every paragraph needs good supporting details. Some details will come from personal experience, especially when you are writing narrative and descriptive paragraphs. Other details will come from other sources of information, especially when you are writing expository and persuasive paragraphs.

Use Personal Details

Personal details are those that you gather by using your senses, your memory, or your imagination.

- **Sensory details** are things that you see, hear, smell, taste, and touch. (These details are important in descriptive paragraphs.)

  Then I find her cold, damp nose and thick, smooth tongue. I can feel her warm breath on my hands.

- **Memory details** are things you remember from experience. (These details are important in narrative paragraphs.)

  I remember thinking the shot was right on line, but the ball hit the back of the rim and went straight up into the air.

- **Reflective details** are things you wonder about, hope for, or imagine. (These details are often used in narrative and descriptive paragraphs.)

  Misha is an incredible dog, and I often wonder what my life would be like without her.

Use Other Sources of Details

To collect details from other sources, use the following tips.

1. **Talk with someone you know.** Parents, neighbors, friends, or teachers may know a lot about your topic.
2. **Write for information.** If you think a museum, a business, or a government office has information you need, send for it.
3. **Read about your topic.** Gather details from books, magazines, and newspapers.
4. **Use the Internet.** The quickest source of information is the Internet. Remember to check Internet sources carefully for reliability. (See page 374.)

How do I know what kinds of details to gather?

The following tips will help you collect the right kinds of details for your paragraphs about people, places, objects, events, and definitions.

Writing About a Person

When writing about or describing a person, make sure you collect plenty of details that deal with his or her appearance and personality. The following guidelines will help.

Observe ■ If possible, carefully watch the person. Maybe the person laughs in a special way or wears a certain type of clothing.

Interview ■ Talk with your subject if you can. Write down words and phrases that the person uses.

Research ■ Use whatever sources are necessary—books, articles, the Internet—to find out more about this person.

Compare ■ Can your subject be compared to some other person?

Describe ■ List any physical characteristics and personality traits.

Writing About a Place

When describing or writing about a place, use details that help the reader understand why the place is important to you.

Observe ■ Study the place you plan to write about. Use photos, postcards, or videos if you can't observe the place in person.

Remember ■ Think of a story (or an anecdote) about this place.

Describe ■ Include the sights, sounds, and smells of the place.

Compare ■ Compare your place to other places.

Writing About an Object

When writing about an object, tell your reader what kind of object it is, what it looks like, how it is used, and why this object is important to you.

Observe ■ Think about these questions: How is it used? Who uses it? How does it work? What does the object look like?

Research ■ Learn about the object. Try to find out when it was first made and used. Ask other people about it.

Define ■ What class or category does this object fit into? (See "Writing a Definition" on the next page.)

Remember ■ Recall interesting stories about this object.

Writing About an Event

When writing about or describing an event, focus on the important actions or on one interesting part. Try to collect sensory details and details that answer the 5 W's. The following guidelines will help.

Observe ■ Study the event carefully. What sights, sounds, tastes, and smells come to mind? Listen to what people around you are saying.

Remember ■ When you write about something that has happened to you, recall as many details connected with the event as you can.

List ■ Answer the *who? what? when? where?* and *why?* questions for facts about the event.

Investigate ■ Read about the event and ask other people what they know about it.

Evaluate ■ Decide why the event is important to you.

Writing a Definition

When you write a definition, you need to think about three things.

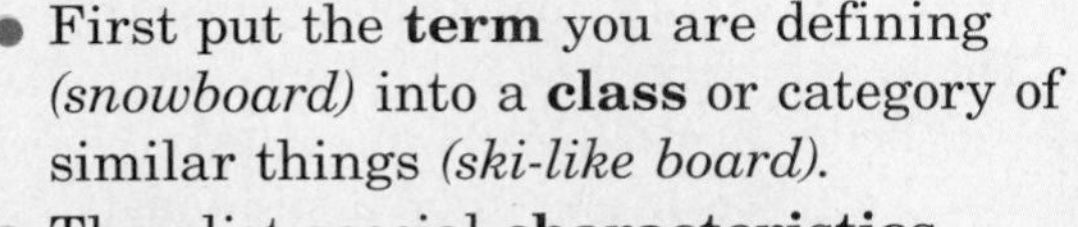

- First put the **term** you are defining *(snowboard)* into a **class** or category of similar things *(ski-like board).*
- Then list special **characteristics** that make this object different from others in that class *(ridden downhill over snow).*

Term—*A snowboard*

Class—*is a ski-like board*

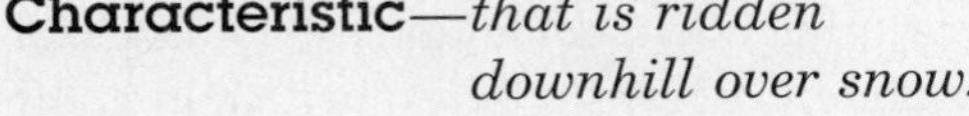

Characteristic—*that is ridden downhill over snow.*

What can I do to organize my details effectively?

After gathering your details, you need to organize them in the best possible way. You can organize a paragraph by *time, location, importance, comparison-contrast,* or *logical* order. Graphic organizers can help you keep your details in order.

Use Chronological Order

Chronological means "according to time." Transition words and phrases (*first, second, then,* and *finally*) are often used in narrative and expository paragraphs. A time line can help you organize details chronologically.

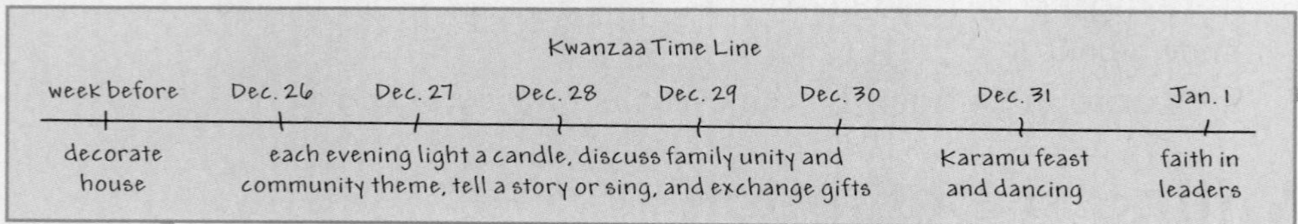

Topic Sentence

Body

Closing Sentence

Celebrating Kwanzaa

Kwanzaa is a seven-day festival that celebrates African American culture. The week before the celebration, family members decorate the home. A traditional symbol, a candleholder with seven candles, is placed on a straw mat. The candles symbolize the African Americans' struggles in the past and their hopes for the future. The celebration actually begins on the evening of December 26. Families gather, and a child lights a candle. Then the family members discuss unity of the family and the community. Next a story or song is used to illustrate the principle. Afterward, gifts may be exchanged. On each of the following four nights, this ceremony is repeated. Families discuss self-determination, community togetherness, economic cooperation, and purpose. On December 31, in addition to talking about creativity, a special feast called Karamu takes place. It features traditional food, music, and dancing. The last day of the celebration is spent discussing faith in other people, teachers, and leaders. After the seven days, the bonds of family, culture, and community have been reinforced.

Respond to the reading. **Is "Celebrating Kwanzaa" a narrative paragraph or an expository paragraph? How is time order used to organize this paragraph?**

Use Order of Location

Often, you can organize descriptive details spatially, by order of location. For example, a description may move from left to right, from top to bottom, from one direction (north) to another (south), or from the whole to its parts. Words or phrases like *next to, before, above, below, east, west, north,* and *south* may be used to show location. A drawing or map can help you organize your details.

Dancing Chinese Dragon

Topic Sentence

The grand finale of the San Francisco Chinese New Year's Parade is a giant dragon dancing down the street. As 600,000 firecrackers explode, a group of 100 people carries the 200-foot-long dragon. This special creation is made up of 29 sections of brightly colored silk and velvet. Underneath the layers of fabric, a bamboo frame supports the dragon. From head to tail, its skin is decorated with colored lights, white fur, and silver rivets. The dragon's enormous head is modeled after a camel's head. A set of curved deer horns rest on top. Between the head and the body is a serpent's slithery neck. The long, twisting body is covered in a rainbow of fish scales. The lower belly looks like the belly of a frog. A writhing, whiplike tail completes the dancing dragon. As the dragon passes, another new year begins.

Body

Closing Sentence

Respond to the reading. How are the details in this paragraph arranged—from left to right, from top to bottom, or in another order?

Use Order of Importance

Expository and persuasive paragraphs are often organized by order of importance—from *most* to *least* important, or from *least* to *most* important.

Most important		Least important
1. ______		3. ______
2. ______	**or**	2. ______
3. ______		1. ______
Least important		Most important

Topic Sentence

Ethnic Celebrations Connect People

Throughout the year, people in the United States honor and celebrate different ethnic groups. These celebrations, some lasting for an entire month, are important for many reasons. First of all, people have an opportunity to share their culture. Food is one way they can share. Pizza is Italian, egg rolls are Chinese, and so on. With these many celebrations, people have a chance to try more authentic ethnic foods such as beignets, fry bread, or pierogies. Helping ethnic groups gain a better understanding of each other is another reason for the celebrations. For example, during February, the country explores the contributions African Americans have made in science, politics, and entertainment. Most importantly, during these special times, young people get a chance to discover their own heritage. As members of different generations celebrate together, they share food, traditions, memories, and more. A bond is made that keeps each family's culture alive. As long as the celebrations continue, people will be able to appreciate the wonderful mix of cultures in this country.

Body

Closing Sentence

Respond to the reading. How are the details organized in this paragraph? On your own paper, list them in reverse order (most to least or least to most). Does one order seem to work better?

Use Comparison-Contrast Order

Expository paragraphs are often organized by comparison-contrast order, which shows how two subjects are both alike and different. A Venn diagram can be used to show differences (**A** and **B**) and similarities (**C**).

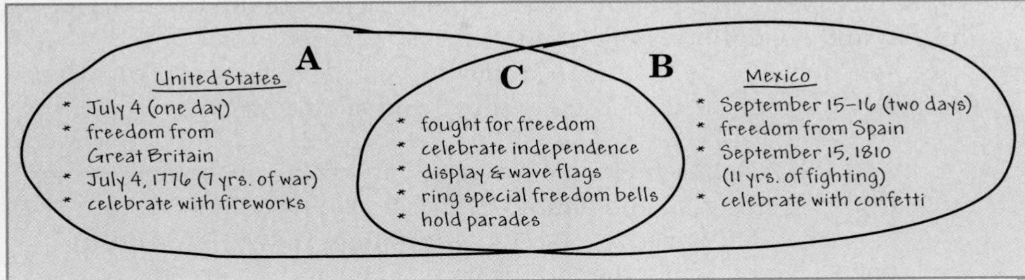

A
United States
* July 4 (one day)
* freedom from Great Britain
* July 4, 1776 (7 yrs. of war)
* celebrate with fireworks
C
* fought for freedom
* celebrate independence
* display & wave flags
* ring special freedom bells
* hold parades
B
Mexico
* September 15–16 (two days)
* freedom from Spain
* September 15, 1810 (11 yrs. of fighting)
* celebrate with confetti

Topic Sentence

Body

Closing Sentence

Two Independence Days

Both the United States and Mexico fought for their independence. July 4, 1776, marks the date when the United States declared its independence from Great Britain. It took seven years of fighting before freedom was won. Similarly, Mexico overcame Spain's control. On September 15, 1810, Father Hidalgo rang his church's bell as a signal for revolution. Mexico's battle for independence lasted 11 years. Although both countries honor freedom by celebrating their independence days, the celebrations vary slightly. Each July 4, people in the United States wave flags, hold parades, and watch fireworks. Many places have special events. For example, in Philadelphia, the Liberty Bell is rung. In Mexico, the fiesta begins on September 15, Independence Day Eve, when the Mexican president rings the same bell Father Hidalgo rang and shouts "viva Mexico, viva la independencia." Across Mexico, at the same time, people repeat the cry and throw confetti. The celebration continues through September 16 with flag-waving parades. No matter how the people celebrate, both countries enjoy the freedom that was won for them many years ago.

Respond to the reading. **Find two body sentences that include similar details. What words show the comparison?**

Write a paragraph. **Choose two festivals or holidays to compare. Use a Venn diagram to organize your details. Then write your paragraph.**

How can I be sure all my details work well?

Create Unity in Your Writing

In a well-written paragraph, each detail tells something about the topic. If a detail does not tell something about the topic, it breaks the *unity* of the paragraph and should probably be cut.

The detail shown in blue in the following passage does not fit with the rest of the paragraph. It disrupts the unity and should be cut.

> **The Pittsburgh Pirates struggled during the 1960 World Series. During series play, the Pirates had only 27 runs compared to the New York Yankees' 55 runs. In addition, the Yankees hit the ball 91 times, while the Pirates could manage only 60 hits.** The Pirates were the first modern National League champions in 1901. **However, the Pirates were victorious in the seventh game and claimed the series title for 1960 because Bill Mazeroski hit a game-winning home run in the bottom of the ninth inning.**

In the paragraph below, find three details (sentences) that *do not* support the topic sentence. Then read the paragraph aloud without those sentences. How does cutting those details affect the paragraph's unity?

> Star baseball player Roberto Clemente was born in Puerto Rico in 1934. Baseball is my favorite sport, too. At first, he played amateur baseball in Puerto Rico. Then he signed on with the Brooklyn Dodgers and played for their minor league team, the Montreal Royals. I don't know much about how he did with that team. However, he is most famous for the 18 years, 1955 through 1972, that he played with the Pittsburgh Pirates. By the way, the Pirates are doing great this year. He played in two World Series, won four batting titles and twelve Gold Glove awards, and was once voted most valuable player. Roberto was also a humanitarian. In 1972, he was on a plane carrying supplies to help people who had been in an earthquake in Nicaragua. The plane crashed, and Clemente died at the age of 38. Today he is remembered as a great athlete and the first Latino to be inducted into the National Baseball Hall of Fame.

Look at your paragraph. Study the comparison-contrast paragraph you wrote (page 537). Do all your details support your topic? Would the unity of your paragraph be improved if you cut a detail or two?

Develop Coherence from Start to Finish

An effective paragraph reads smoothly and clearly. When all the details in a paragraph are tied together well, the paragraph has *coherence* and is easy for the reader to follow. Transitions help make your writing smooth and coherent.

Number your paper from 1 to 6. Use the transitions from the following list to help tie the paragraph below together. (Use each transition only once.) Then reread the paragraph. Does it read smoothly? If not, switch some transitions.

between	after	when	until	before	finally

The Underground Railroad was made up of people who helped slaves escape from the South to the North before the Civil War. ________ (1) escaping from a slaveholder, slaves often traveled by foot, usually at night, ________ (2) they came to a "station." A station was a house or business owned by someone willing to help the slaves escape. The slaves rested and hid there ________ (3) moving on. Then the next "stationmaster" was alerted that people were coming. Once they were safe, the slaves were given food and clothing for their journey. ________ (4) it was safe, slaves moved from station to station with the help of the stationmasters. ________ (5), they crossed the border to freedom in the North. ________ (6) 1810 and 1850, approximately 100,000 slaves escaped to start new lives as free persons. Many of them used the Underground Railroad.

Read your paragraph. Read your comparison-contrast paragraph from page 537. Underline any parts that don't flow smoothly. Then use transitions to make the writing smoother. (See pages 572–573.)

How can I write essays containing strong paragraphs?

Use an Essay Plan

Writing an essay is not simply a matter of putting together a group of paragraphs. To begin with, each paragraph needs to be well written and well organized. Then follow the guidelines listed below.

1 Plan the organization.

Organize your essay in a way that fits your topic—chronological order, order of importance, order of location, and so on.

2 State the topic and focus in the first paragraph.

Begin with an interesting fact or example to catch the reader's attention. Then tell what your essay is about in a focus or thesis statement. This statement should identify the topic and a main idea or feeling about it.

3 Develop your writing idea in the middle paragraphs.

Use each paragraph in the body of your essay to explain and support one part of your focus statement. Each paragraph must have a topic sentence followed with supporting details.

4 Finish with a strong ending.

The final paragraph is usually a review of the main points in the essay. Your ending may emphasize the importance of the topic or may leave the reader with something to think about.

5 Use transition words or phrases to connect paragraphs.

For a complete list of transitions, see pages **572–573**.

A paragraph has . . .	An essay has . . .
a topic sentence.	a thesis or focus statement.
sentences that support the topic sentence.	middle paragraphs that support the focus.
a closing sentence.	an ending paragraph.

How do I know if I have a strong paragraph?

Use a Paragraph Checklist

You'll know that you have a strong paragraph if it gives the reader complete information on a specific topic. One sentence should identify the topic, and the other sentences should support it. Use the checklist below to help you plan and write effective paragraphs.

Ideas

_____ **1.** Do I focus on an interesting idea?
_____ **2.** Do I use enough specific details?

Organization

_____ **3.** Is my topic sentence clear?
_____ **4.** Have I organized the details in the best order?

Voice

_____ **5.** Do I show interest in—and knowledge of—my topic?
_____ **6.** Does my voice fit my audience? My purpose? My topic?

Word Choice

_____ **7.** Do I use specific nouns and active verbs?
_____ **8.** Do I use specific adjectives and adverbs?

Sentence Fluency

_____ **9.** Have I written clear and complete sentences?
_____ **10.** Do I use a variety of sentence beginnings and lengths?

Conventions

_____ **11.** Do I use correct punctuation and capitalization?
_____ **12.** Do I use correct spelling and grammar?

improve
support

A Writer's Resource

Academic Vocabulary

Read the meanings and share answers with a partner.

1. A **technique** is a skill or ability that helps you do something. **What is a special technique you have learned to do a specific task or job?**
2. When you **arrange** items, you put them into order. **How do you arrange the things in your room?**
3. An **effect** is something that happens because of something else. **What is the effect of being late for school?**
4. When you **quote** someone, you repeat his/her exact words. **Who might you quote in a history report?**

organize
REFERENCE
select

A Writer's Resource

Writing is a complex job. Sometimes even experienced authors have trouble knowing what to write about, where to start, or how to sound interesting. Although practice certainly helps a writer become more skillful and self-confident, everyone needs a little help once in a while.

"A Writer's Resource" contains information, tips, and guidelines to get you through your writing problems. You'll find strategies for selecting topics, ways to improve your style, and ideas on techniques to enrich your writing.

What's Ahead

You will learn how to . . .

- **find topics and get started.**
- **collect and organize details.**
- **write terrific topic sentences.**
- **use new forms and techniques.**
- **improve your voice and writing style.**
- **increase your vocabulary.**
- **improve your sentences.**
- **improve your presentation.**

How can I find the best topics to write about?

Try a Topic-Selecting Strategy

A distinguished writer once said, "There are few experiences quite so satisfactory as getting a good writing idea." This may be overstating it a little, but getting a good writing idea is certainly an important step in the writing process. Let's say, for example, you are asked to write an essay about a controversial issue in your school or community. Your first job would be to select a specific topic to write about.

General Subject Area: school or community controversy

Specific Writing Topic: new auditorium

The following strategies will help you select interesting topics that you can feel good about.

Clustering Begin a cluster (also called a web) by selecting a key word that is related to your writing assignment. Write the key word in the middle of your paper and cluster related words around it. (See page **264**.)

Journal Writing Write on a regular basis in a personal journal, recording your thoughts and experiences. Review your entries from time to time and underline ideas that you would like to write more about later, as in the model below. (See also pages **431–434**.)

Oct. 12

Today we had our last rehearsal for the fall orchestra concert. I'm first chair, so I have more responsibilities this year. I have to keep my violin really well tuned, because the whole orchestra follows me.

Mrs. Soderberg said that we did a good job and that we've come a long way since the beginning of the year. No one was practicing very much at first, but in the last two weeks, you could tell that everyone was working harder. I think they were afraid of sounding horrible in front of an audience, plus Mrs. S. really got mad one day about people not knowing their music.

The only bad thing is that after all of this work, we still have to play in the cafeteria. The sound in there is awful because of the echoes, and the cafeteria chairs make noise every time someone moves. I think we need a new auditorium in this school.

Listing Write your general subject at the top of your paper and list related ideas as they come to mind. Keep your list going as long as you can. Then look for words in your list that you feel would make good writing topics.

Freewriting Write nonstop for 5 to 10 minutes to discover possible writing ideas. Begin writing with a particular subject or idea in mind (one related to the writing assignment). Underline the ideas that might work as topics for your assignment.

Sentence Starters Complete an open-ended sentence in as many ways as you can. Try to word your sentence so that it leads you to a topic you can use for your writing assignment.

People disagree about . . .
This community should . . .
There are differences between . . .
I learned a lesson when . . .
My favorite experience was . . .
It would be interesting to meet . . .

Review the "Basics of Life" List

The words listed below name many of the categories or groups of things that people need in order to live a full life. The list provides an endless variety of possibilities for topics. Consider the first category, food. You could write about . . .

- the most unusual meal you've ever eaten,
- what's good for you and what's not, or
- the first time you tried to cook something.

food
work/occupation
clothing
faith/religion
communication
exercise
education
family
friends
purpose/goals
love
senses
machines
intelligence
history/records
agriculture
land/property
community
science
plants/vegetation
freedom/rights
energy
rules/laws
tools/utensils
heat/fuel
natural resources
personality/identity
recreation/hobbies
trade/money
literature/books
health/medicine
art/music

What can I do to get started?

Use a List of Writing Topics

The writing prompts listed below and the sample topics listed on the next page provide plenty of starting points for writing assignments.

Writing Prompts

Every day is full of experiences that make you think. You do things that you feel good about. You hear things that make you angry. You wonder how different things work. You are reminded of a past experience. These common, everyday thoughts can make excellent prompts for writing.

Describe (Descriptive)

An influential person
Your favorite celebrity
A solar eclipse
Hermit crabs
Life before television

Tell Your Story (Narrative)

Learning something about life
Overcoming a challenge
Meeting an unusual person
Visiting a special place
A sudden revelation
The perfect day
Facing a disappointment
A surprise

Classify (Expository)

Clothing styles
Scooters
Extreme sports
Types of pets
Constellations
Kinds of diets
Birds of prey

Compare-Contrast (Expository)

Soccer and football
Living in a small town/large city
Two seasons
Heroes and celebrities
Fashions now and twenty years ago
Jobs and professions

Defend (Persuasive)

Starting school later in the morning
Eating wisely and exercising
Service learning
Individuality
Sports in school
A worthwhile cause

Respond to . . . (Response to Literature)

A book that made you think
A poem that explained something
A character you identify with
The biography of someone you admire

Research (Report)

Aquifers, hot springs, glaciers
Oil wells, salt mines
Mud slides, forest fires

Sample Topics

You come across many people, places, experiences, and things every day that could be topics for writing. A number of possible topics are listed below for descriptive, narrative, expository, and persuasive writing.

Descriptive

People: best friend, favorite relative, personal idol, great leader, person you're comfortable with, someone who overcomes difficulty, teacher, coach, brother or sister

Places: hangout, garage, room, rooftop, historical place, zoo, park, hallway, barn, bayou, lake, cupboard, yard, empty lot, alley, valley, campsite, river, city street

Things: billboard, poster, video game, cell phone, bus, boat, gift, drawing, rainbow, doll, junk drawer, flood, mascot, movie

Animals: dolphin, elephant, snake, armadillo, eagle, deer, toad, spoonbill, squirrel, pigeon, pet, coyote, catfish, octopus, beaver, turtle

Narrative

moving to a new home, scoring a goal in a game, making a new friend, losing a pet, going to camp, learning a skill or sport, traveling to an interesting place

Expository

Classification: animal camouflage, natural disasters, kinds of music, types of government, religious beliefs, scientific principles, fads

Comparison-Contrast: friends, places, jobs, teachers, pets, transportation, a house cat and a lion, lakes and oceans

The causes of . . . sunburn, acne, hiccups, tornadoes, school dropouts, computer viruses, arguments

Kinds of . . . crowds, friends, commercials, dreams, neighbors, pain, clouds, joy, stereos, heroes, chores, homework, frustration

Persuasive

Community: building a skate park, beautifying the city, losing a local movie theater, opening a teen center, building sidewalks, building a superstore on the edge of town

School: assigning less homework, air-conditioning classrooms, providing more computers and printers, changing the school mascot, starting a school drama department

How can I collect details for my writing?

Try Graphic Organizers

Graphic organizers can help you gather and organize your details for writing. Clustering is one method. (See page **264**.) These two pages list other useful organizers.

Cause-Effect Organizer

Use to collect and organize details for cause-effect essays.

Subject:

Causes	Effects
•	•
•	•
•	•
•	•
•	•

Problem-Solution Web

Use to map out problem-solution essays.

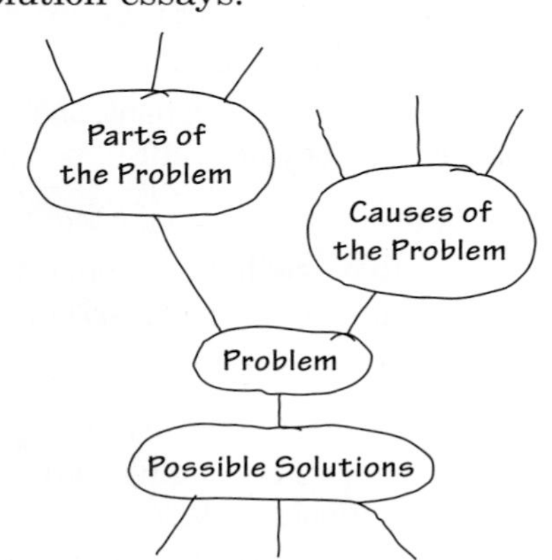

Time Line (Step-by-Step)

Use to collect details for personal narratives and how-to essays.

Subject:

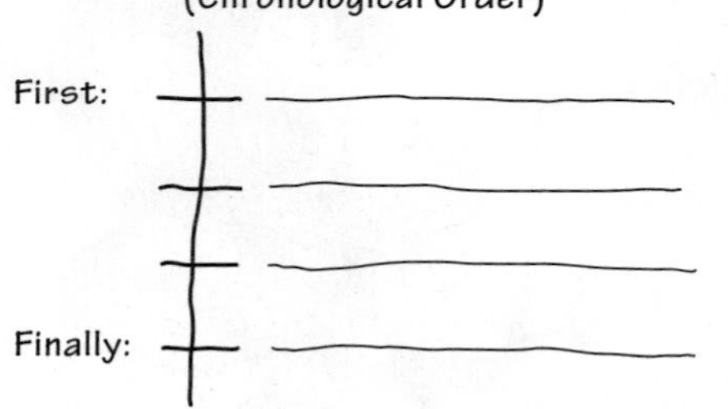

Before-After Chart

Use to collect details for narratives or expository essays.

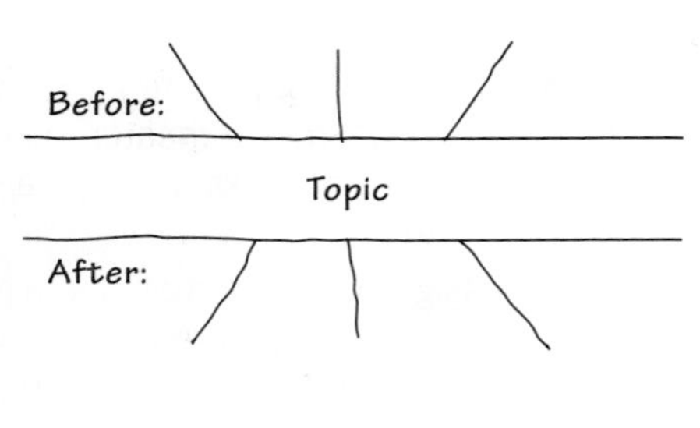

Venn Diagram

Use to collect details to compare and contrast two subjects.

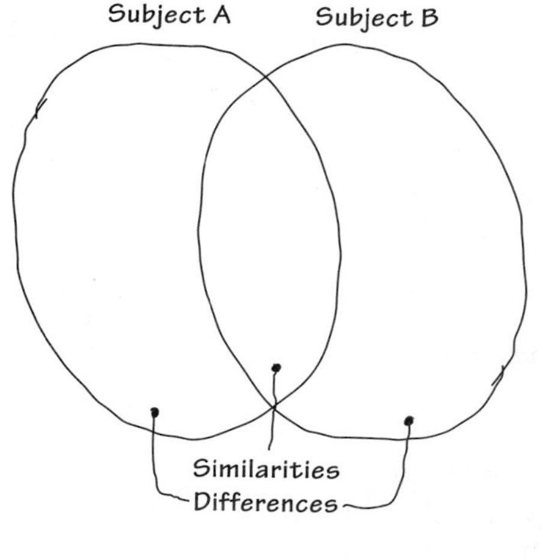

Process Chain (5-Step)

Use to collect details for science-related writing, such as how a process or cycle works.

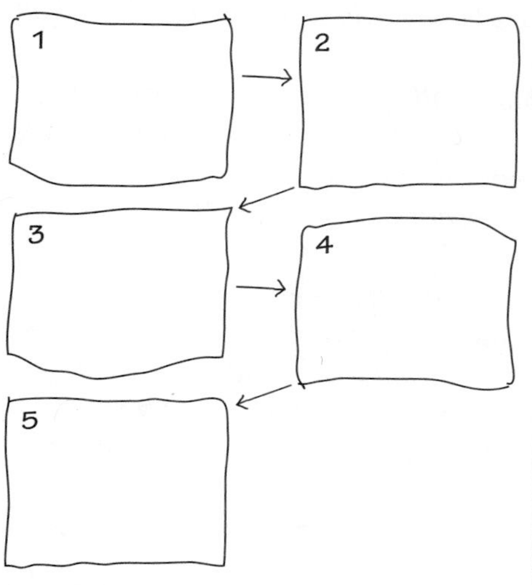

5 W's Chart

Use to collect the *Who? What? When? Where?* and *Why?* details for personal narratives and news stories.

Subject:

Who?	What?	When?	Where?	Why?

Line Diagram

Use to collect and organize details for classification or other expository essays.

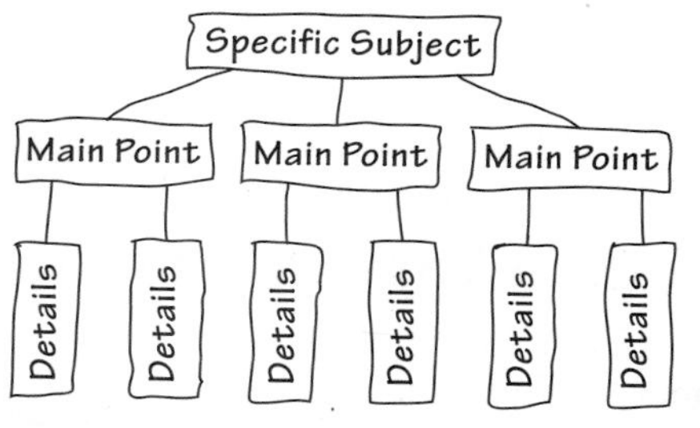

Sensory Chart

Use to collect details for descriptive essays and observation reports.

Subject:

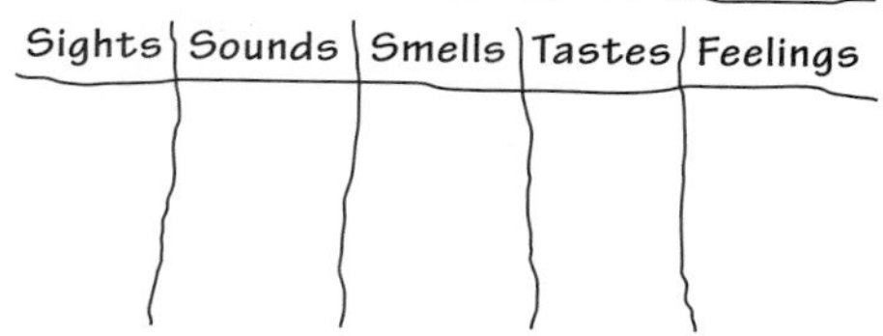

What can I do to organize my details better?

Make Lists and Outlines

List Your Details

You can use a variety of ways to organize details as you prepare to write an essay or a report. For most writing, you can make a simple list.

The importance of salt
- *wars fought over it*
- *used for money*
- *helps keep us alive*
- *preserves food*
- *softens water*
- *used to make chemicals*
- *melts ice on roads*

How Detroit salt bed formed
- *seawater flooded the area*
- *seawater evaporated, leaving salt*
- *layer 400 to 1,600 feet thick*
- *covered by layers of silt*

Outline Your Information

After gathering facts and details, select two or three main points that best support your focus. Write an outline to organize your information.

I. Salt is much more important than most people realize.
A. Wars have been fought over it.
B. In ancient China, salt coins were used for money.
C. In the human body, salt carries electrical signals that keep a person alive.
D. Salt is used to preserve meat and fish and to tan leather.
E. Salt is also used to make chemicals.
II. Scientists say that the Detroit mine digs into a bed of salt that is several hundred million years old.
A. From 600 million to 230 million years ago, seawater flooded the middle of North America many times.
B. As the sun and wind evaporated the water . . .

Use Patterns of Organization

- **Chronological (Time) Order** or **Step-by-Step** You can arrange your details in the order in which they happen *(first, then, next).* Use these patterns for narratives, history reports, and explaining a process. (See page **534**.)

  In 1896, the Detroit salt mine was started in order to dig the salt out of the ground. It began as a shaft 1,200 feet deep and about 6 feet wide. At first, the salt was used mainly for storing meat and fish and for making . . .

- **Order of Location** You can arrange details in the order in which they are located (*above, below, beside,* and so on). Use order of location for descriptions, explanations, and directions. (See page **535**.)

  Rosa and her once-white jumpsuit look like the paint-chip aisle at the hardware store—splattered with color from the top of her head to the toes of her now rainbow-colored canvas shoes.

- **Order of Importance** You can arrange details from the most important to the least—or from the least important to the most. Persuasive and expository essays are often organized this way. (See page **536**.)

  First of all, an open study hall would let hardworking students go where they need to go to get more work done. . . . Secondly, an open study hall would motivate students to take study hall more seriously. . . . Most importantly, open study hall would teach responsibility.

- **Comparison-Contrast** You can write about two or more subjects by showing how they are alike and how they are different. Compare each subject separately or compare both, point by point, as in the example below. (See page **537**.)

  The same juice comes in two different packages. Which is cheaper, a 12-pack of cans that costs $3.95 or a 6-pack of bottles that costs $2.50? The cans contain 12 ounces each, and the bottles are 16.9 ounces. Dividing the cost of each package by its total number of ounces indicates that the juice in the 12-pack is .027 cents per ounce, and the juice in the 6-pack is .025 cents per ounce. The 6-pack is a better deal.

- **Logical Order** You can organize information by beginning with a main idea followed by details, or by starting with details and leading up to the main point.

  Studies show that by eating fewer calories people can lose weight. They can also lose weight by increasing how much they exercise. However, if people eat less and exercise more, they will lose more weight and keep it off longer. Combining these methods of losing weight makes sense.

How can I write terrific topic sentences?

Try Eight Special Strategies

Writing a good topic sentence is a key to writing a great paragraph. A good topic sentence names the topic and states a specific feeling about it. Use the following strategies the next time you need to write a terrific topic sentence. (Also see page **525**.)

Use a Number

Topic sentences can use number words to tell what the paragraph will be about.

Number Words		
two	a couple	a pair
few	three	a number
several	four	many
a variety	five	a list

Several problems need to be looked at more carefully.

I have three pet peeves that drive me crazy.

Create a List

A topic sentence can list the things the paragraph will talk about.

Squeaky had to take care of her brother and train for the race at the same time.

Heat, light, and moisture can affect a plant's growth.

Start with "To" and a Verb

A topic sentence that starts with "to" and a verb helps the reader know why the information in the paragraph is important.

To identify the theme in a story, consider the thoughts and actions of the main character.

To persuade others to change their minds, you have to make a convincing argument.

Use Word Pairs

Word pairs or correlative conjunctions that come in pairs can help organize a topic sentence.

Word Pairs
if . . . then
either . . . or
not only . . . but also
both . . . and
whether . . . or
as . . . so

Whether you're the best player on the team or just average, you need to practice hard.

Both fables and folktales are entertaining, but fables are more likely to teach a lesson.

Join Two Ideas

A topic sentence can combine two equal ideas (in independent clauses) by using a comma and a coordinating conjunction: *and, but, or, for, so, nor, yet.*

Living in a small town sounds peaceful, but I think I would miss the excitement of the city.

Some fashions seem to come around every 10 or 20 years, so you can't really say that clothing stores always have new clothes, can you?

Use a "Why-What" Word

A "why-what" word is a subordinating conjunction that shows how ideas are connected.

Before you tell a story, think about the main point that you want to make.

Since we're trying to beautify the city, could we do something about the weeds along the highways?

"Why-What" Words	
So that	Once
Before	Since
Until	Whenever
Because	While
If	As long as
As	After
In order that	When

Use a "Yes, But" Word

A "yes, but" word is a subordinating conjunction that tells how two ideas are different.

Instead of discouraging strip malls, we should be sure that any new ones are well designed.

Some people think that it's all right to lie unless the lie hurts someone.

"Yes, But" Words
Although
Even though
Even if
Unless
Whether
Whereas

Quote an Expert

Sometimes the best way to start a paragraph is to quote someone who knows about your topic.

Even though I dislike football practice, I think Joe Paterno was right when he said, "The will to win is important, but the will to prepare is vital."

Helen Keller's statement "Keep your face to the sunshine and you cannot see the shadow" is a good way to define optimism.

What other forms can I use for my writing?

Try These Forms of Writing

Finding the right *form* for your writing is just as important as finding the right topic. When you are selecting a form, be sure to ask yourself who you're writing for (your audience) and why you're writing (your purpose).

Anecdote — A brief story that makes a point

Autobiography — A writer's story of his or her own life

Biography — A writer's story of some other person's life

Book review — A brief essay giving a response or an opinion about a book (See pages 287–322.)

Character sketch — Writing that describes a specific character in a story

Composition — A longer piece of writing, such as a story or an essay

Descriptive writing — Writing that uses details to help the reader clearly imagine a certain person, a place, a thing, or an idea (See pages 71–91.)

Editorial — Newspaper letter or article giving an opinion

Essay — A piece of writing in which ideas are presented, explained, argued, or described in an interesting way

Expository writing — Writing that explains by presenting the steps, the causes, or the kinds of something (See pages 157–217.)

Fable — A short story that often uses talking animals as the main characters and teaches a lesson or moral

Fantasy — A story set in an imaginary world in which the characters usually have supernatural powers or abilities

Freewriting — Writing whatever comes to mind about any topic

Historical fiction — A made-up story based on something real in history in which fact is mixed with fiction

Myth — A traditional story intended to explain a mystery of nature, religion, or culture

Narrative — Writing that relates an event, an experience, or a story (See pages 93–155.)

Novel	A book-length story with several characters and a well-developed plot
Personal narrative	Writing that shares an event or experience from the writer's personal life (See pages **93–142**.)
Persuasive writing	Writing that is meant to persuade the reader to agree with the writer about someone or something (See pages **219–281**.)
Play	A form that uses dialogue to tell a story and is meant to be performed in front of an audience
Poem	Writing that uses rhythm, rhyme, and imagery (See pages **353–361**.)
Proposal	Writing that includes specific information about an idea or a project that is being considered for approval
Research report	An essay that shares information on a topic that has been researched well and organized carefully (See pages **379–410**.)
Response to literature	Writing that is a summary or a reaction to something the writer has read (novel, short story, poem, article, and so on)
Science fiction	Writing based on real or imaginary science and often set in the future
Short story	A short piece of literature with only a few characters and one problem or conflict (See pages **343–349**.)
Summary	Writing that presents only the most important ideas from a longer piece of writing (See pages **375–378**.)
Tall tale	A humorous, exaggerated story (often based on the life of a real person) about a character or animal who does impossible things
Tragedy	Literature in which the hero is destroyed because of some serious flaw or defect in his or her character

How can I create a voice in my writing?

You can create a strong writing voice by using dialogue and by "showing instead of telling."

Use Dialogue

Each person you write about has a unique way of saying things, and well-written dialogue lets the reader *hear* the speaker's personality and thoughts. For example, notice how the message below can be spoken in several different ways.

Message: The family trip to the Grand Canyon was fun.

Speaker 1: **"The whole thing was boring until we got to ride the donkeys."**

Speaker 2: **"The view was certainly beautiful and peaceful, but those people were standing too close to the edge."**

Speaker 3: **"Wasn't the Grand Canyon great? Now, if we skip lunch, we can make it to Zion Canyon this afternoon."**

Each of the speakers above delivers the same message in a unique way. The dialogue tells as much about the speaker as it does about the topic.

One way to improve your dialogue is to think about the speaker and his or her personality. Look at the three personality webs below and try to decide which one is *Speaker 1, Speaker 2,* or *Speaker 3* from above. How does the dialogue show their personalities?

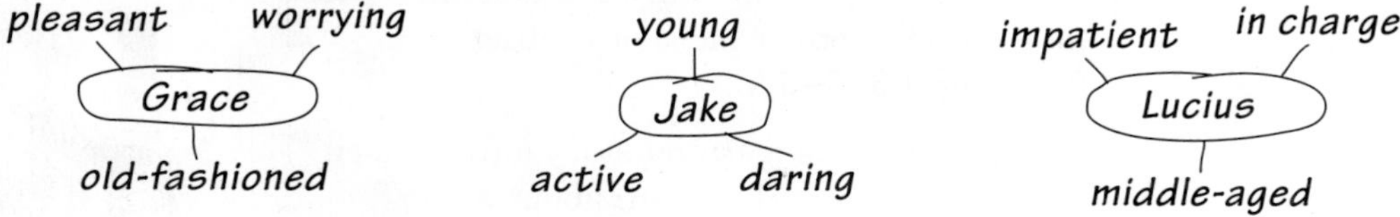

Tips for Punctuating Dialogue

- Indent every time a different person speaks.
- Put the exact words of a speaker in quotation marks.
- Set off the quoted words from the rest of the sentence by using a comma.
- At the end of quoted words, put a period or comma inside the quotation marks.

For more information and examples on how to punctuate dialogue, see **588.1**, **598.1**, and **600.1** in the "Proofreader's Guide."

Show, Don't Tell

When you tell someone that a movie is "good" or that the weather was "awful," what have you really told that person? Not much. If you really want to get your idea across, you have to *show* the details so that your reader experiences what you're describing. Notice the difference in the accounts below.

Telling: **It was really hot riding across the desert on the back of Dad's motorcycle, so we went to a movie in Phoenix.**

Showing: Before Dad and I started on our trip through the Southwest, I thought that riding on a motorcycle would cool us off. I was wrong. It was so hot and dry in the desert that we baked. The sun beat down from above, the heat radiated up from the pavement, and the engine temperature surrounded us like an oven on wheels. Our lips were burning, and our eyes got dry. One day we just stopped at a Phoenix movie theater and "chilled" all afternoon.

The sentence above *tells* the reader that the motorcycle ride was "really hot." The paragraph *shows* why the writer and his father needed to "chill."

Key Strategies for Showing

Next time you realize your writing is telling rather than showing, try one of these strategies.

- **Add sensory details.** Include sights, sounds, smells, tastes, and touch sensations. That way the reader can "experience" the event.

  Telling: **My little brother had trouble with his ice-cream cone.**

  Showing: The blast of hot air went to work on my little brother's chocolate-swirl ice-cream cone. Little streams began to drip off the rim. Jimmy licked at the sweet, sticky liquid, but he couldn't keep up, and the chocolate goo ran down his arm. As he tried to lick his arm, the ice cream tumbled out of the cone onto the sidewalk.

- **Explain body language.** Write about facial expressions and the way people stand, gesture, and move.

  Telling: **Aunt Elsa was glad to see me.**

  Showing: When I walked into the room, Aunt Elsa grinned, jumped out of her chair, and ran over to hug me.

- **Use dialogue.** Let the people in your writing speak for themselves.

  Telling: **Latrell was happy about his test.**

  Showing: Latrell gave me a high five, shouting, "Getting an A on my science test is the greatest thing I've done all year!"

What can I do to improve my writing style?

Learn Some Writing Techniques

Writers put special effects into their stories and essays in different ways. Look over the following writing techniques and then experiment with some of them in your own writing.

Analogy A comparison of similar objects to help clarify one of the objects

Personal journals are like photograph albums. They both share personal details and tell a story.

Anecdote A brief story used to illustrate or make a point

Abe Lincoln walked two miles to return several pennies he had overcharged a customer. (This anecdote shows Lincoln's honesty.)

Exaggeration An overstatement or a stretching of the truth used to make a point or paint a clearer picture (*See overstatement.*)

After getting home from summer camp, I slept for a month.

Foreshadowing Hints or clues that a writer uses to suggest what will happen next in a story

Halfway home, Sarah wondered whether she had locked her locker.

Irony A technique that uses a word or phrase to mean the opposite of its normal meaning

Marshall just loves cleaning his room.

Local color The use of details that are common in a certain place or local area (A story taking place on a seacoast would contain details about the water and the life and people near it.)

Everybody wore flannel shirts to the Friday fish fry.

Metaphor A figure of speech that compares two things without using the word *like* or *as* (See page 360.)

In our community, high school football is king.

Overstatement An exaggeration or a stretching of the truth (See *exaggeration*.)

When he saw my grades, my dad hit the roof.

Parallelism Repeating similar words, phrases, or sentences to give writing rhythm (See pages 512 and 522.)

We will swim in the ocean, lie on the beach, and sleep under the stars.

Personification A figure of speech in which a nonhuman thing (an idea, object, or animal) is given human characteristics (See page 360.)

Rosie's old car coughs and wheezes on cold days.

Pun A phrase that uses words in a way that gives them a humorous effect

The lumberjack logged on to the site to order new boots.

Sarcasm The use of praise to make fun of or "put down" someone or something (The expression is not sincere and is actually intended to mean the opposite thing.)

Micah's a real gourmet; he loves peanut butter and jelly sandwiches. (A *gourmet* is a "lover of fine foods.")

Sensory details Specific details that help the reader see, feel, smell, taste, and/or hear what is being described (See page 355.)

As Lamont took his driver's test, his heart thumped, his hands went cold, and his face began to sweat.

Simile A figure of speech that compares two things using the word *like* or *as* (See page 360.)

Faye's little brother darts around like a water bug.
Yesterday the lake was as smooth as glass.

Slang Informal words or phrases used by particular groups of people when they talk to each other

chill out   hang loose   totally awesome

Symbol An object that is used to stand for an idea

The American flag is a symbol of the United States. The stars stand for the 50 states, and the stripes stand for the 13 original U.S. colonies.

Understatement Very calm language (the opposite of exaggeration) used to bring special attention to an object or an idea

These hot red peppers may make your mouth tingle a bit.

How can I expand my writing vocabulary?

Study Writing Terms

This glossary includes terms used to describe the parts of the writing process. It also includes terms that explain special ways of stating an idea.

Antonym A word that means the opposite of another word: *happy* and *sad; large* and *small* (See page 563.)

Audience The people who read or hear what has been written

Body The main or middle part in a piece of writing that comes between the *beginning* and the *ending* and includes the main points

Brainstorming Collecting ideas by thinking freely about all the possibilities

Closing The ending or final part in a piece of writing (In a paragraph, the closing is the last sentence. In an essay or a report, the closing is the final paragraph.)

Coherence Tying ideas together in your writing (See page 539.)

Connotation The "feeling" a word suggests (See page 106 and 488.)

Denotation The dictionary meaning of a word

Dialogue Written conversation between two or more people

Figurative language Special comparisons, often called figures of speech, that make your writing more creative (See page 360.)

Focus statement The statement that tells what specific part of a topic is written about in an essay (See *thesis statement* and page 393.)

Form A type of writing or the way a piece of writing is put together (See pages 554–555.)

Grammar The structure of language; the rules and guidelines that you follow in order to speak and write acceptably

Jargon The special language of a certain group, occupation, or field

Computer jargon: byte digital upload

Journal A notebook for writing down thoughts, experiences, ideas, and information (See pages 431–434.)

Limiting the subject	Taking a general subject and narrowing it down to a specific topic General subject → Specific topic **sports → golf → golf skills → putting**
Modifiers	Words, phrases, or clauses that describe another word Our black **cat** slowly **stretched and** then **leaped** onto the wicker chair. (Without the blue modifiers, all we know is that a "cat stretched and leaped.")
Point of view	The angle from which a story is told (See page 352.)
Purpose	The specific reason that a person has for writing **to describe to narrate to persuade to explain**
Style	How an author writes (choice of words and sentences)
Supporting details	Facts or ideas used to tell a story, explain a topic, describe something, or prove a point
Synonym	A word that means the same thing as another word (*dog* and *canine*) (See page 563.)
Theme	The main point, message, or lesson in a piece of writing
Thesis statement	A statement that gives the main idea of an essay (See *focus statement.*)
Tone	A writer's attitude toward his or her subject **serious humorous sarcastic**
Topic	The specific subject of a piece of writing
Topic sentence	The sentence that contains the main idea of a paragraph (See page 525.) **Blue jeans are a popular piece of American clothing.**
Transition	A word or phrase that connects or ties two ideas together smoothly (See pages 572–573.) **also however lastly later next**
Usage	The way in which people use language (*Standard usage* generally follows the rules of good grammar. Most of the writing you do in school will require standard usage.)
Voice	A writer's unique, personal tone or feeling that comes across in a piece of writing (See pages 40 and 119.)

How can I mark changes in my writing?

Use the symbols and letters below to show where and how your writing needs to be changed. Your teachers may also use these symbols to mark errors in your writing.

Symbols	Meaning	Example	Corrected Example
≡	**Capitalize a letter.**	Lorraine Hansberry wrote *A Raisin in the sun.*	Lorraine Hansberry wrote *A Raisin in the Sun.*
/	**Make a capital letter lowercase.**	Her play tells the story of the Younger Family.	Her play tells the story of the Younger family.
⊙	**Insert (add) a period.**	This play focuses on racial attitudes It also . . .	This play focuses on racial attitudes. It also . . .
◯ or *sp.*	**Correct spelling.**	Lena Younger, the family leader, is very religous.	Lena Younger, the family leader, is very religious.
℘	**Delete (take out) or replace.**	Lena she makes a down payment on a nice house.	Lena makes a down payment on a nice house.
∧	**Insert here.**	The family wants to escape ghetto life.	The family wants to escape ghetto life.
∧ ∧ ∧	**Insert a comma, a colon, or a semicolon.**	Her son, Walter Lee, Jr. wants to buy a business.	Her son, Walter Lee, Jr., wants to buy a business.
∨ ∨ ∨	**Insert an apostrophe or quotation marks.**	Walter Lees wife hopes for a larger apartment.	Walter Lee's wife hopes for a larger apartment.
? ! ∧ ∧	**Insert a question mark or an exclamation point.**	What would Beneatha do with the money	What would Beneatha do with the money?
¶	**Start a new paragraph.**	¶The direction of the play clearly changes when . . .	The direction of the play clearly changes when . . .
∼	**Switch words or letters.**	Walter gets the possible worst news.	Walter gets the worst possible news.

What can I do to increase my vocabulary skills?

Use Context

When you come across a word you don't know, you can often figure out its meaning from the other words in the sentence. The other words form a familiar context, or setting, for the unfamiliar word. Looking closely at the surrounding words will give you clues to the meaning of the new word.

When you come to a word you don't know . . .

- Look for a synonym for the unknown word.

  Sara had an ominous feeling when she woke up, but the feeling was less threatening when she saw she was in her own room.
  (*Threatening* means the same as *ominous*.)

- Look for an antonym for the unknown word.

  Pumpkins are usually abundant in the autumn, but last year's drought made them scarce.
  (*Scarce* means the opposite of *abundant*.)

- Look for a comparison or contrast.

  Riding a mountain bike in a remote area is my idea of a great day, but some people like to ride motorcycles on busy six-lane highways.
  (A *remote* area is out of the way, in contrast to a *busy* area. The word *but* also emphasizes a contrast.)

- Look for a definition or description.

  Manatees, large aquatic mammals (sometimes called sea cows), can be found in the warm coastal waters of Florida.
  (An *aquatic* mammal is one that lives in the water.)

- Look for words that appear in a series.

  The campers spotted blue jays, chickadees, and indigo buntings on Saturday morning.
  (An *indigo bunting*, like a *blue jay* or *chickadee*, is a bird.)

- Look for a cause-and-effect relationship.

  The amount of traffic at 6th and Main doubled last year, so crossing lights were placed at that corner to avert an accident.
  (*Avert* means "to prevent.")

How can I build my vocabulary across the curriculum?

On the next several pages, you will find many of the most common prefixes, suffixes, and roots in the English language. Learning these word parts can help you increase your writing vocabulary.

Learn About Prefixes

A **prefix** is a word part that is added before a word to change the meaning of the word. For example, when the prefix *un* is added to the word fair *(unfair)*, it changes the word's meaning from "fair" to "not fair."

ambi *[both]*
ambidextrous (skilled with both hands)

anti *[against]*
antifreeze (a liquid that works against freezing)
antiwar (against wars and fighting)

astro *[star]*
astronaut (person who travels among the stars)
astronomy (study of the stars)

auto *[self]*
autobiography (writing that is about yourself)

bi *[two]*
bilingual (using or speaking two languages)
biped (having two feet)

circum *[in a circle, around]*
circumference (the line or distance around a circle)
circumnavigate (to sail around)

co *[together, with]*
cooperate (to work together)
coordinate (to put things together)

ex *[out]*
exhale (to breathe out)
exit (the act of going out)

fore *[before, in front of]*
foremost (in the first place, before everyone or everything else)
foretell (to tell or show beforehand)

hemi *[half]*
hemisphere (half of a sphere or globe)

hyper *[over]*
hyperactive (overactive)

im *[not, opposite of]*
impatient (not patient)
impossible (not possible)

in *[not, opposite of]*
inactive (not active)
incomplete (not complete)

inter *[between, among]*
international (between or among nations)
interplanetary (between the planets)

macro *[large]*
macrocosm (the entire universe)

mal *[bad, poor]*
malnutrition (poor nutrition)

micro *[small]*
microscope (an instrument used to see very small things)

mono *[one]*
monolingual (using or speaking only one language)

non *[not, opposite of]*
nonfat (without the normal fat content)
nonfiction (based on facts; not made-up)

over *[too much, extra]*
overeat (to eat too much)
overtime (extra time; time beyond regular hours)

poly *[many]*
polygon (a figure or shape with three or more sides)
polysyllable (a word with more than three syllables)

post *[after]*
postscript (a note added at the end of a letter, after the signature)
postwar (after a war)

pre *[before]*
pregame (activities that occur before a game)
preheat (to heat before using)

re *[again, back]*
repay (to pay back)
rewrite (to write again or revise)

semi *[half, partly]*
semicircle (half a circle)
semiconscious (half conscious; not fully conscious)

sub *[under, below]*
submarine (a boat that can operate underwater)
submerge (to put underwater)

trans *[across, over; change]*
transcontinental (across a continent)
transform (to change from one form to another)

tri *[three]*
triangle (a figure that has three sides and three angles)
tricycle (a three-wheeled vehicle)

un *[not]*
uncomfortable (not comfortable)
unhappy (not happy; sad)

under *[below, beneath]*
underage (below or less than the usual or required age)
undersea (beneath the surface of the sea)

uni *[one]*
unicycle (a one-wheeled vehicle)
unisex (a single style that is worn by both males and females)

Numerical Prefixes

deci *[tenth of a part]*
decimal system (a number system based on units of 10)

centi *[hundredth of a part]*
centimeter (a unit of length equal to 1/100 meter)

milli *[thousandth of a part]*
millimeter (a unit of length equal to 1/1000 meter)

micro *[millionth of a part]*
micrometer (one-millionth of a meter)

deca, dec *[ten]*
decade (a period of 10 years)
decathlon (a contest with 10 events)

hecto, hect *[one hundred]*
hectare (a metric unit of land equal to 100 ares)

kilo *[one thousand]*
kilogram (a unit of mass equal to 1,000 grams)

mega *[one million]*
megabit (one million bits)

Study Suffixes

A **suffix** is a word part that is added after a word. Sometimes a suffix will tell you what part of speech a word is. For example, many adverbs end in the suffix *ly*.

able *[able, can do]*
agreeable (able or willing to agree)
doable (can be done)

al *[of, like]*
magical (like magic)
optical (of the eye)

ed *[past tense]*
called (past tense of call)
learned (past tense of learn)

ess *[female]*
lioness (a female lion)

ful *[full of]*
helpful (giving help; full of help)

ic *[like, having to do with]*
symbolic (having to do with symbols)

ily *[in some manner]*
happily (in a happy manner)

ish *[somewhat like or near]*
childish (somewhat like a child)

ism *[characteristic of]*
heroism (characteristic of a hero)

less *[without]*
careless (without care)

ly *[in some manner]*
calmly (in a calm manner)

ology *[study, science]*
biology (the study of living things)

s *[more than one]*
books (more than one book)

ward *[in the direction of]*
westward (in the direction of west)

y *[containing, full of]*
salty (containing salt)

Comparing Suffixes

er *[comparing two things]*
faster, later, neater, stronger

est *[comparing more than two]*
fastest, latest, neatest, strongest

Noun-Forming Suffixes

er *[one who]*
painter (one who paints)

ing *[the result of]*
painting (the result of a painter's work)

ion *[act of, state of]*
perfection (the state of being perfect)

ist *[one who]*
violinist (one who plays the violin)

ment *[act of, result of]*
amendment (the result of amending, or changing)
improvement (the result of improving)

ness *[state of]*
goodness (the state of being good)

or *[one who]*
actor (one who acts)

Understand Roots

A **root** is a word or word base from which other words are made by adding a prefix or a suffix. Knowing the common roots can help you figure out the meaning of difficult words.

aster *[star]*
- **asterisk** (starlike symbol [*])
- **asteroid** (resembling a star)

aud *[hear, listen]*
- **audible** (can be heard)
- **auditorium** (a place to listen to speeches and performances)

bibl *[book]*
- **Bible** (sacred book of Christianity)
- **bibliography** (list of books)

bio *[life]*
- **biography** (book about a person's life)
- **biology** (the study of life)

chrome *[color]*
- **monochrome** (having one color)
- **polychrome** (having many colors)

chron *[time]*
- **chronological** (in time order)
- **synchronize** (to make happen at the same time)

cide *[the killing of; killer]*
- **homicide** (the killing of one person by another person)
- **pesticide** (pest [bug] killer)

cise *[cut]*
- **incision** (a thin, clean cut)
- **incisors** (the teeth that cut or tear food)
- **precise** (cut exactly right)

cord, cor *[heart]*
- **cordial** (heartfelt)
- **coronary** (relating to the heart)

corp *[body]*
- **corporation** (a legal body; business)
- **corpse** (a dead human body)

cycl, cyclo *[wheel, circular]*
- **bicycle** (a vehicle with two wheels)
- **cyclone** (a very strong circular wind)

dem *[people]*
- **democracy** (ruled by the people)
- **epidemic** (affecting many people at the same time)

dent, dont *[tooth]*
- **dentures** (false teeth)
- **orthodontist** (dentist who straightens teeth)

derm *[skin]*
- **dermatology** (the study of skin)
- **epidermis** (outer layer of skin)

fac, fact *[do, make]*
- **factory** (a place where people make things)
- **manufacture** (to make by hand or machine)

fin *[end]*
- **final** (the last of something)
- **infinite** (having no end)

flex *[bend]*
- **flexible** (able to bend)
- **reflex** (bending or springing back)

flu *[flowing]*
- **fluent** (flowing smoothly or easily)
- **fluid** (waterlike, flowing substance)

forc, fort *[strong]*
- **forceful** (full of strength or power)
- **fortify** (to make strong)

fract, frag *[break]*
- **fracture** (to break)
- **fragment** (a piece broken from the whole)

Learn More Roots

gen *[birth, produce]*
congenital (existing at birth)
genetics (the study of inborn traits)

geo *[of the earth]*
geography (the study of places on the earth)
geology (the study of the earth's physical features)

graph *[write]*
autograph (writing one's name)
graphology (the study of handwriting)

homo *[same]*
homogeneous (of the same birth or kind)
homogenize (to blend into a uniform mixture)

hydr *[water]*
dehydrate (to take the water out of)
hydrophobia (the fear of water)

ject *[throw]*
eject (to throw out)
project (to throw forward)

log, logo *[word, thought, speech]*
dialogue (speech between two people)
logic (thinking or reasoning)

luc, lum *[light]*
illuminate (to light up)
translucent (letting light come through)

magn *[great]*
magnificent (great)
magnify (to make bigger or greater)

man *[hand]*
manicure (to fix the hands)
manual (done by hand)

mania *[insanity]*
kleptomania (abnormal desire to steal)
maniac (an insane person)

mar *[sea, pool]*
marine (of or found in the sea)
mariner (sailor)

mega *[large]*
megalith (large stone)
megaphone (large horn used to make voices louder)

meter *[measure]*
kilometer (a thousand meters)
voltmeter (device to measure volts)

mit, miss *[send]*
emit (to send out; give off)
transmission (sending over)

multi *[many, much]*
multicultural (of or including many cultures)
multiped (an animal with many feet)

numer *[number]*
innumerable (too many to count)
numerous (large in number)

omni *[all, completely]*
omnipresent (present everywhere at the same time)
omnivorous (eating all kinds of food)

onym *[name]*
anonymous (without a name)
pseudonym (false name)

ped *[foot]*
pedal (lever worked by the foot)
pedestrian (one who travels by foot)

phil *[love]*
Philadelphia (city of brotherly love)
philosophy (the love of wisdom)

phobia *[fear]*
acrophobia (a fear of high places)
agoraphobia (a fear of public, open places)

phon *[sound]*
phonics (related to sounds)
symphony (sounds made together)

photo *[light]*
photo-essay (a story told mainly with photographs)
photograph (picture made using light rays)

pop *[people]*
population (number of people in an area)
populous (full of people)

port *[carry]*
export (to carry out)
portable (able to be carried)

psych *[mind, soul]*
psychiatry (the study of the mind)
psychology (science of mind and behavior)

sci *[know]*
conscious (being aware)
omniscient (knowing everything)

scope *[instrument for viewing]*
kaleidoscope (instrument for viewing patterns and shapes)
periscope (instrument used to see above the water)

scrib, script *[write]*
manuscript (something written by hand)
scribble (to write quickly)

spec *[look]*
inspect (to look at carefully)
specimen (an example to look at)

spir *[breath]*
expire (to breathe out; die)
inspire (to breathe into; give life to)

tele *[over a long distance; far]*
telephone (machine used to speak to people over a distance)
telescope (machine used to see things that are very far away)

tempo *[time]*
contemporary (from the current time period)
temporary (lasting for a short time)

tend, tens *[stretch, strain]*
extend (to stretch and make longer)
tension (stretching something tight)

terra *[earth]*
terrain (the earth or ground)
terrestrial (relating to the earth)

therm *[heat]*
thermal (related to heat)
thermostat (a device for controlling heat)

tom *[cut]*
anatomy (the science of cutting apart plants and animals for study)
atom (a particle that cannot be cut or divided)

tract *[draw, pull]*
traction (the act of pulling)
tractor (a machine for pulling)

typ *[print]*
prototype (the first printing or model)
typo (a printing error)

vac *[empty]*
vacant (empty)
vacuum (an empty space)

vid, vis *[see]*
supervise (to oversee or watch over)
videotape (record on tape for viewing)

vor *[eat]*
carnivorous (flesh-eating)
herbivorous (plant-eating)

zoo *[animal or animals]*
zoo (a place where animals are kept)
zoology (the study of animal life)

What can I do to write more effective sentences?

Study Sentence Patterns

Sentences in the English language follow the basic patterns below. Use a variety of patterns to add interest to your writing. (Also see page 571.)

1 Subject + Action Verb

S AV
The storm ended. (Some action verbs, like *ended,* are intransitive, which means that they *do not need* a direct object to express a complete thought. See 728.3.)

2 Subject + Action Verb + Direct Object

S AV DO
One mistake cost the game. (Some action verbs, like *cost,* are transitive. This means that they *need* a direct object to express a complete thought. See 728.2.)

3 Subject + Action Verb + Indirect Object + Direct Object

S AV IO DO
Jim's friends gave him a surprise party.

4 Subject + Action Verb + Direct Object + Object Complement

S AV DO OC
The director named Joyce the stage manager.

5 Subject + Linking Verb + Predicate Noun

S LV PN
Roger is an amateur ventriloquist.

6 Subject + Linking Verb + Predicate Adjective

S LV PA
Broccoli is very tasty.

In the patterns above, the subject comes before the verb. In the patterns below, the subject comes after the verb (called a *delayed subject*).

7 LV S PN
Is anyone absent? (A question)

8 LV S
There were two storms last night.
(A sentence beginning with *there* or *here*)

Practice Sentence Diagramming

Diagramming sentences can help you understand how the different parts of a sentence fit together. Here are the most common diagrams.

1 S AV
The storm ended.

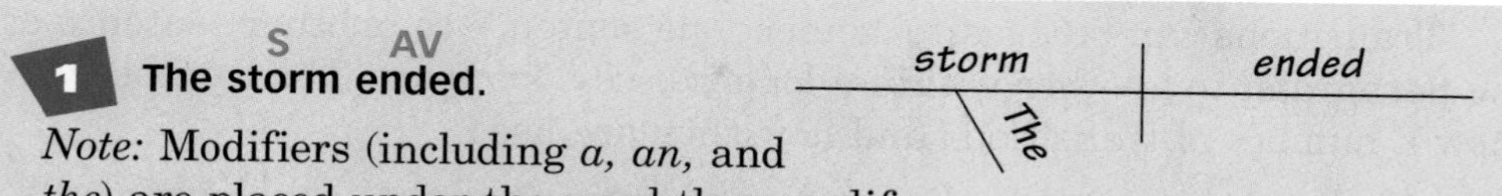

Note: Modifiers (including *a, an,* and *the*) are placed under the word they modify.

2 S AV DO
One mistake cost the game.

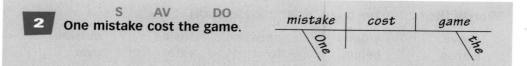

mistake | cost | game
One
the

3 S AV IO DO
Jim's friends gave him a surprise party.

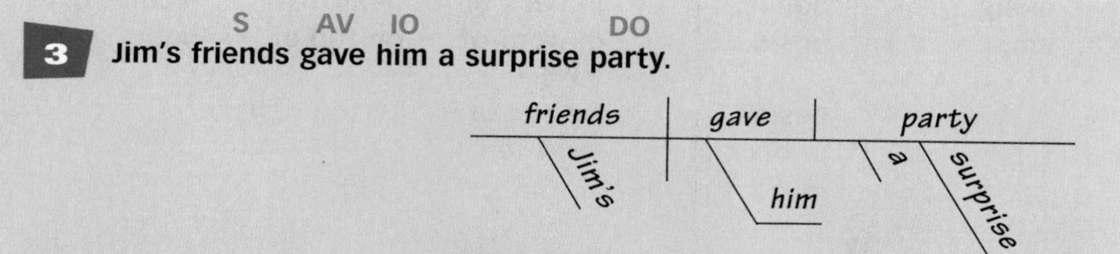

4 S AV DO OC
The director named Joyce the stage manager.

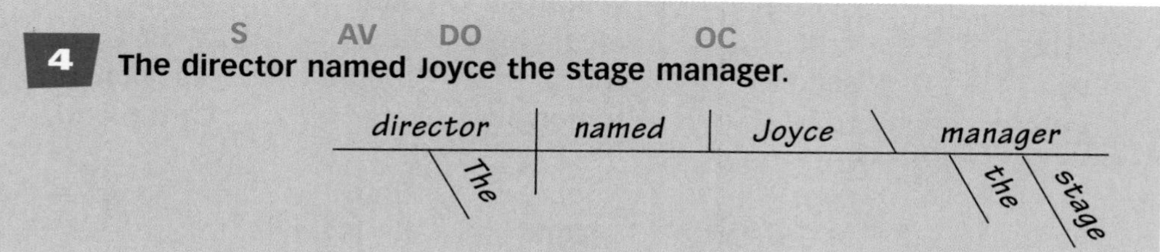

5 S LV PN
Roger is an amateur ventriloquist.

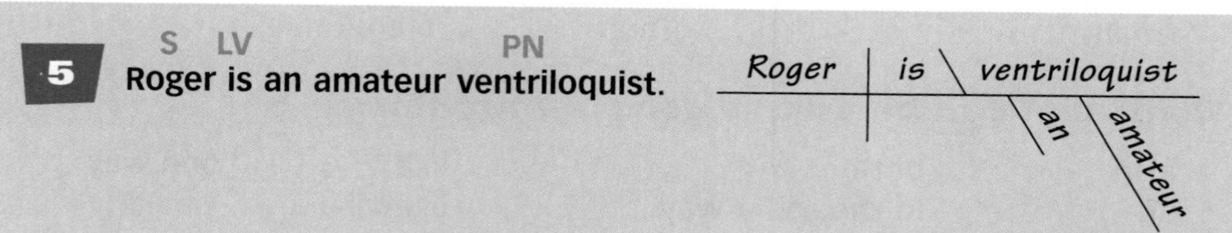

6 S LV PA
Broccoli is very tasty.

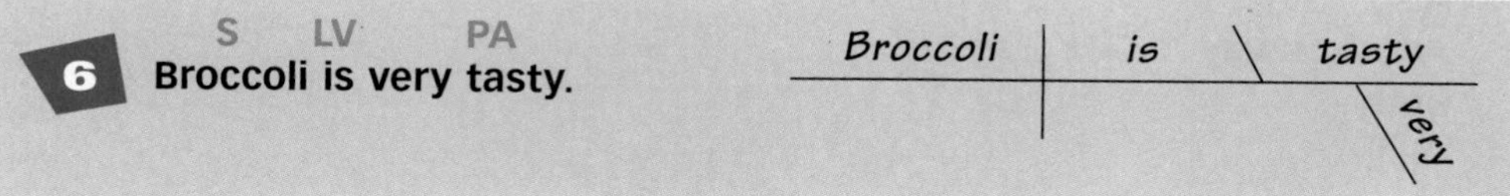

How can I connect my sentences and paragraphs?

Use Transitions

Transitions can be used to connect one sentence to another sentence or one paragraph to another within a longer essay or report. The lists below show a number of transitions and how they are used.

Note: Each **colored list** below is a group of transitions that could work well together in a piece of writing.

Words that can be used to show location

above	around	between	inside	outside
across	behind	by	into	over
against	below	down	near	throughout
along	beneath	in back of	next to	to the right
among	beside	in front of	on top of	under

Above	Beside	On top of	To the right
Below	In back of	Next to	
Beneath	In front of	To the left	

Words that can be used to show time

about	during	yesterday	until	finally
after	first	meanwhile	next	then
at	second	today	soon	as soon as
before	to begin	tomorrow	later	in the end

After	First	Now	Third
Before	In the end	Second	To begin
During	Later	Soon	To conclude
Finally	Next	Then	To continue

Words that can be used to compare two things

also	both	like	one way
as	in the same way	likewise	similarly

Also	In the same way
Another way	One way
Both	Similarly

Words that can be used to contrast things (show differences)

although	even though	on the other hand	still
but	however	otherwise	yet

Although	Nevertheless
Even though	Still
On the other hand	Yet

Words that can be used to emphasize a point

again	for this reason	to emphasize	truly
especially	in fact	to repeat	

Especially	In fact	To repeat
For this reason	To emphasize	Truly

Words that can be used to conclude or summarize

all in all	because	in conclusion	therefore
as a result	finally	lastly	to sum it up

All in all	Because	In conclusion	To sum it up
All in all	Finally	Therefore	

Words that can be used to add information

additionally	and	finally	moreover
again	another	for example	other
along with	as well	for instance	next
also	besides	in addition	

Additionally	Another	Finally	Moreover
Also	As well	For example	Next
Along with	Besides	For instance	

Words that can be used to clarify

for example	for instance	in other words	that is

Equally important	For instance
For example	In other words

What can I do to make my final copy look better?

Add Graphics to Your Writing

You can add information and interest to essays and reports by using diagrams, tables, and graphs.

Diagrams are drawings that show the parts of something.

Picture diagrams show how something is put together. A diagram may leave out some parts to show only the parts you need to learn.

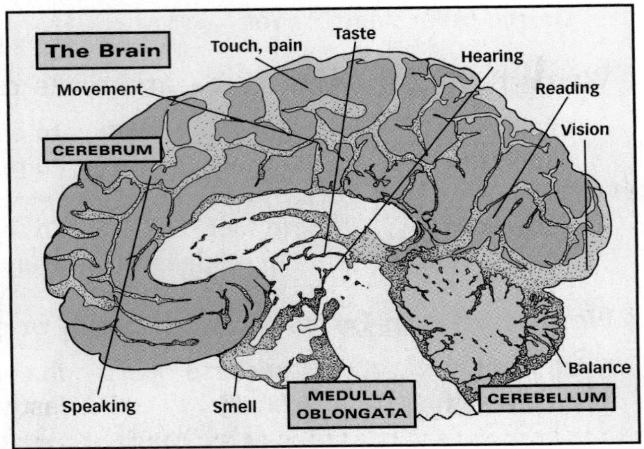

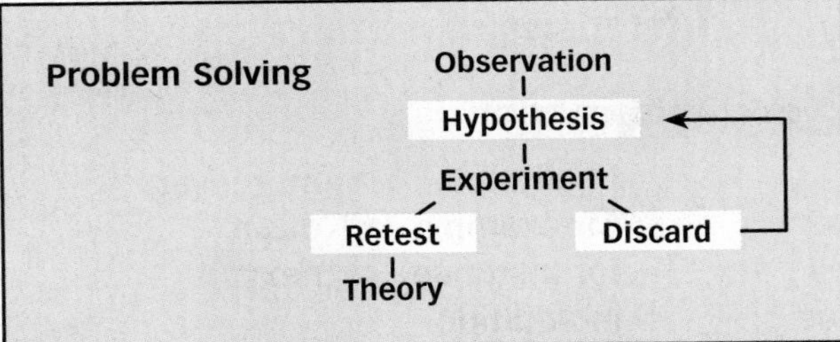

Line diagrams show something you can't really see. Instead of objects, line diagrams show ideas and relationships. The problem-solving diagram helps you understand how to solve a scientific problem.

Tables are another form of diagram. Tables have two parts: rows and columns. Rows go across and show one kind of information or data. Columns go up and down and show a different kind of data.

To read a distance or mileage table, find the place you're starting from and the place you're going to. Then find the place where the row and the column meet—that will show the distance and the driving time from one place to the other.

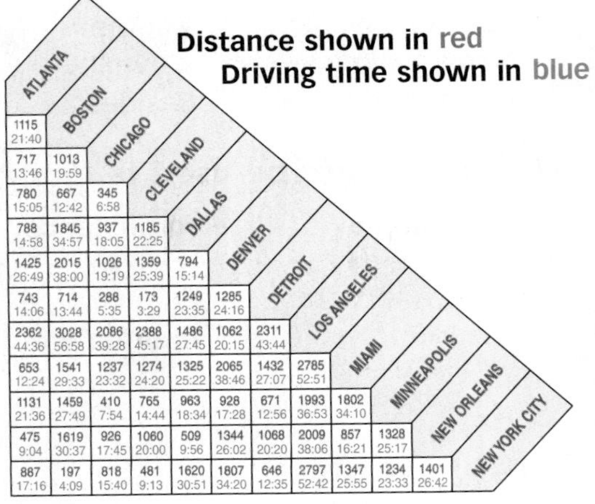

Distance shown in red
Driving time shown in blue

	ATLANTA	BOSTON	CHICAGO	CLEVELAND	DALLAS	DENVER	DETROIT	LOS ANGELES	MIAMI	MINNEAPOLIS	NEW ORLEANS
BOSTON	1115 21:40										
CHICAGO	717 13:46	1013 19:59									
CLEVELAND	780 15:05	667 12:42	345 6:58								
DALLAS	788 14:58	1845 34:57	937 18:05	1185 22:25							
DENVER	1425 26:49	2015 38:00	1026 19:19	1359 25:39	794 15:14						
DETROIT	743 14:06	714 13:44	288 5:35	173 3:29	1249 23:35	1285 24:16					
LOS ANGELES	2362 44:36	3028 56:58	2086 39:28	2388 45:17	1486 27:45	1062 20:15	2311 43:44				
MIAMI	653 12:24	1541 29:33	1237 23:32	1274 24:20	1325 25:22	2065 38:46	1432 27:07	2785 52:51			
MINNEAPOLIS	1131 21:36	1459 27:49	410 7:54	765 14:44	963 18:34	928 17:28	671 12:56	1993 36:53	1802 34:10		
NEW ORLEANS	475 9:04	1619 30:37	926 17:45	1060 20:00	509 9:56	1344 26:02	1068 20:20	2009 38:06	857 16:21	1328 25:17	
NEW YORK CITY	887 17:16	197 4:09	818 15:40	481 9:13	1620 30:51	1807 34:20	646 12:35	2797 52:42	1347 25:55	1234 23:33	1401 26:42

Graphs are pictures of information. **Bar graphs** show how things compare to one another. The bars on a bar graph may be vertical or horizontal. (*Vertical* means "up and down." *Horizontal* means "from side to side.") Sometimes the bars on graphs are called *columns*. The part that shows numbers is called the *scale*.

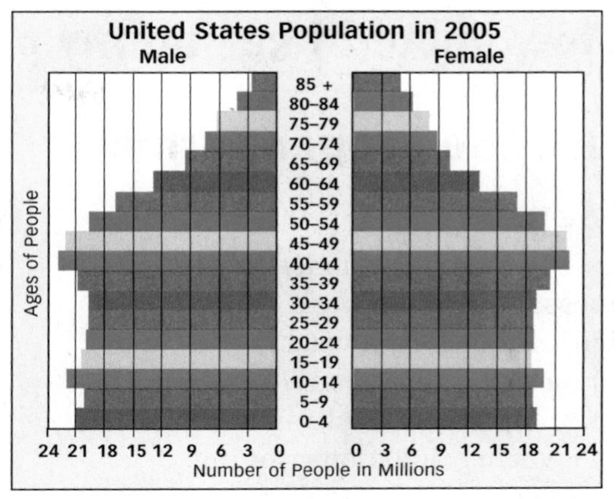

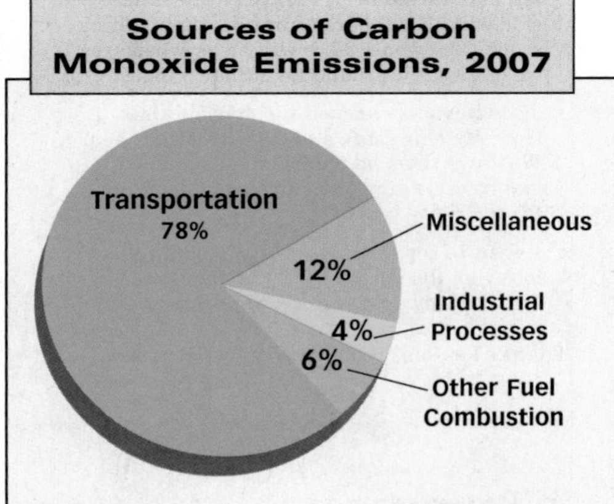

Pie graphs show how all the parts of something add up to make the whole. A pie graph often shows percentages. (A percentage is the part of a whole stated in hundredths: 35% = 35/100.) It's called a pie graph because it is usually in the shape of a pie or circle.

The pie graph to the left shows the sources of carbon monoxide emissions in 2007 and what percentage of total emissions each source produced.

Line graphs show how something changes as time goes by. A line graph always begins with an L-shaped grid. One axis of the grid shows passing time; the other axis shows quantities.

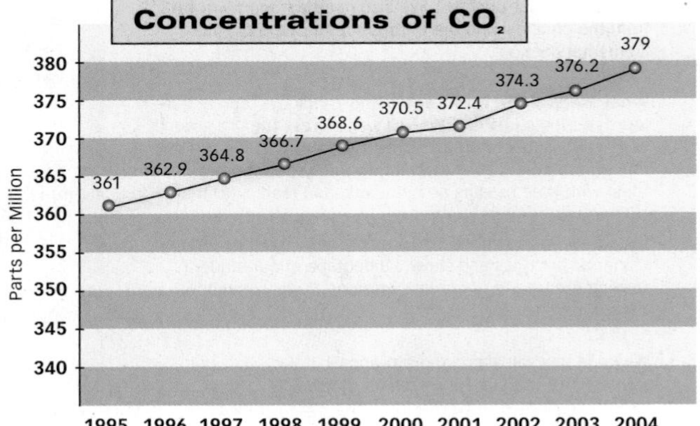

How should I set up my practical writing?

Use the Proper Format

Memos

A memo is a brief written message that you can share with a teacher, a coach, or a principal. Memos create a flow of information—asking and answering questions, giving instructions, describing work to be done, or reminding people about meetings.

Date: Friday, March 6, 2009

To: Mrs. Lee, Technical Director

From: Corrine Stier, Student Director

Subject: Progress on the *Brigadoon* Sets

Here is my first weekly update on the progress of the *Brigadoon* sets.

- Dave Dye has sketched a 15-foot-long set. One side will show the living room of the Campbell cottage, with a thatched roof on top and a window at the back. The other side will be cathedral ruins for the wedding scene. The whole piece will be on wheels, so we can spin it around for scene changes.
- Julie Reynolds primed the four old flats from *My Fair Lady* and drew trees on them. We'll use them on a dark stage along with two freestanding trees to make the forest for the chase scene.
- I want to repaint an old drop curtain to look like the backdrop in the movie. I've attached my drawings for your approval.

Thanks for your confidence in me, Mrs. Lee.

Date: January 12, 2012
To: Mrs. Munn, Room 210
From: The Titan Group: Todd Davis, LaToya Wilson, Jacque Trevino, Becky Jackson
Subject: Volunteer Tutoring

Project Description: An article in our school paper stated that Lincoln Elementary School needed eighth-grade students to tutor third graders in reading. We would like to volunteer our services starting February 3.

What We Need: We need written permission from you, our parents, and our principal. We also need written approval from the principal and the third-grade teachers of Lincoln Elementary School.

What We Will Do: On Tuesdays and Thursdays, during our fourth period study hall, we will walk across the playground to Lincoln School to our assigned classrooms. We will help third-grade students by listening to them read, helping them with their reading assignments, and reading to them.

Outcome: At the end of this project, we will report on the students' progress and show a videotape of our students reading during one of our last sessions. It will show how the tutoring helped.

We hope you will approve our proposal. If you have any suggestions or changes, please let us know.

Proposals

A proposal is a detailed plan for doing a project, solving a problem, or meeting a need.

Follow Guidelines

Letters

A letter is a written message sent through the mail. Letters follow a set format, including important contact information, a salutation (greeting), a body, and a closing signature. (See pages **274–277** for more information.)

1080 Burns Road
Orange Park, FL 32000
May 5, 2011

Principal Joseph Rodriguez
Greenberg Middle School
116 Shelton Street
Orange Park, FL 32000

Dear Mr. Rodriguez:

As a soccer team member at Greenberg Middle School, I have a suggestion. We need lights for nighttime games. When school starts in the fall, it gets darker earlier and earlier. It's hard for our teams to finish games safely.

I realize that lighting is expensive. However, a lighted field could be used by the whole community, so the community could help pay for it. The soccer team could even run a citywide fund-raiser.

Adding lights to our soccer field would make a huge difference for my teammates and me. Please make the request at the next school board meeting.

Sincerely,

Alex Hastings
Alex Hastings

Envelope Addresses

Place the return address in the upper left corner, the destination address in the center, and the correct postage in the upper right corner.

ALEX HASTINGS
1080 BURNS RD
ORANGE PARK FL 32000

PRINCIPAL JOSEPH RODRIGUEZ
GREENBERG MIDDLE SCHOOL
116 SHELTON ST
ORANGE PARK FL 32000

U.S. Postal Service Guidelines

1. Capitalize everything and leave out ALL punctuation.
2. Use the list of common address abbreviations at **634.1**. Use numerals rather than words for numbered streets and avenues (9TH AVE NE, 3RD ST SW).
3. If you know the ZIP + 4 code, use it.

capitalize SPELL
punctuate

Proofreader's Guide

Academic Vocabulary

Work with a partner. Read the meanings and share answers to the questions.

1. To feel **doubt** is to have a feeling of not believing.
   What types of details would make you feel doubt that a story was true?
2. When something is **irregular**, it does not follow the accepted rules or general pattern or order.
   What is an English word that has an irregular spelling, one that does not follow the regular rules?
3. A **combination** is something that is created by putting things together.
   Tell how a salad is an example of a combination.

Marking Punctuation

Periods

Use a **period** to end a sentence. Also use a period after initials, after abbreviations, and as a decimal point.

579.1
At the End of Sentences

Use a period to end a sentence that makes a statement or a request. Also use a period for a mild command, one that does not need an exclamation point. (See page 518.)

The Southern Ocean surrounds Antarctica. (statement)

Please point out the world's largest ocean on a map. (request)

Do not use a laser pointer. (mild command)

NOTE It is not necessary to place a period after a statement that has parentheses around it if it is part of another sentence.

The Southern Ocean is the fourth-largest ocean (it is larger than the Atlantic).

579.2
After Initials

Place a period after an initial.

J. K. Rowling (author)

Colin L. Powell (politician)

579.3
After Abbreviations

Place a period after each part of an abbreviation. Do not use periods with acronyms or initialisms. (See page 636.)

Abbreviations: **Mr. Mrs. Ms. Dr. B.C.E. C.E.**

Acronyms: **AIDS NASA**

Initialisms: **NBC FBI**

NOTE When an abbreviation is the last word in a sentence, use only one period at the end of the sentence.

My grandfather's full name is William Ryan James Koenig, Jr.

579.4
As Decimal Points

Use a period to separate dollars and cents and as a decimal point.

The price of a loaf of bread was $1.54 in 1992.

That price was only 35 cents, or 77.3 percent less, in 1972.

Question Marks

A **question mark** is used after an interrogative sentence and also to show doubt about the correctness of a fact or figure. (See page 518.)

580.1
At the End of Direct Questions

Use a question mark at the end of a direct question (an interrogative sentence).

Is a vegan a person who eats only vegetables?

580.2
At the End of Indirect Questions

No question mark is used after an indirect question. (An indirect question tells about a question you or someone else asked.)

Because I do not eat meat, I'm often asked if I am a vegetarian.

I asked the doctor if going meatless is harmful to my health.

580.3
To Show Doubt

Place a question mark within parentheses to show that you are unsure that a fact or figure is correct.

By the year 2020 (?) the number of vegetarians in the United States may approach 15 percent of the population.

Exclamation Points

An **exclamation point** may be placed after a word, a phrase, or a sentence to show emotion. (The exclamation point should not be overused.)

580.4
To Express Strong Feelings

Use an exclamation point to show excitement or strong feeling.

Yeah! Wow! Oh my!

Surprise! You've won the million-dollar sweepstakes!

Caution: Never use more than one exclamation point in writing assignments.

Incorrect: **Don't ever do that to me again!!!**

Correct: **Don't ever do that to me again!**

Grammar Practice

End Punctuation

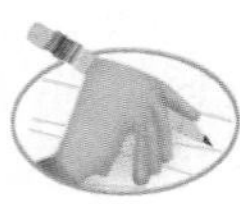

On your own paper, write whether each of the following sentences needs a period, a question mark, or an exclamation point at the end.

Example: I want to get a pet
period

1. Did you ever think about getting a ferret
2. They are from the same animal family that minks, skunks, and otters are from
3. Ferrets are active creatures and need a lot of exercise
4. The word *ferret* comes from a Latin word meaning *little thief,* so the animals also require patience
5. Oh no, a ferret might take your keys or your pens and hide them
6. Make sure you lock away anything valuable
7. A ferret's cage should be large enough to hold some toys, a water dish, and a food bowl
8. What should you feed a ferret if you can't find ferret food
9. Many ferret owners feed their animals cat food
10. Just like a cat, a ferret can be trained to use a litter box
11. Wow, a baby ferret is even called a kit
12. You might ask if ferrets need their own toys
13. They do, but they'll be happy as can be with an old sock
14. In general, ferrets will live 8 to 10 years
15. Enjoy your new pet

Next Step: Write three sentences about a pet or other animal. Use different end punctuation for each one.

Commas

Use a **comma** to indicate a pause or a change in thought. This helps to keep words and ideas from running together so that the writing is easier to read. For a writer, no other form of punctuation is more important to understand than the comma.

582.1 Between Items in a Series

Use commas between words, phrases, or clauses in a series. (A series contains at least three items.) (See page 512.)

Chinese, English, and Hindi are the three most widely used languages in the world. (words)

Being comfortable with technology, working well with others, and knowing another language are important skills for today's workers. (phrases)

My dad works in a factory, my mom works in an office, and I work in school. (clauses)

582.2 To Keep Numbers Clear

Use commas to separate the digits in a number in order to distinguish hundreds, thousands, millions, and so on.

More than 104,000 people live in Kingston, the capital of Jamaica.

The population of the entire country of Liechtenstein is only 29,000.

NOTE Commas are not used in years.

The world population was 6.1 billion by 2003.

582.3 In Dates and Addresses

Use commas to distinguish items in an address and items in a date.

On August 28, 1963, Martin Luther King, Jr., gave his famous "I Have a Dream" speech.

The address of the King Center is 449 Auburn Avenue NE, Atlanta, Georgia 30312.

NOTE No comma is placed between the state and ZIP code. Also, when only the month and year are given, no comma is needed.

In January 2029 we will celebrate the 100th anniversary of Reverend King's birth.

Grammar Practice

Commas 1

- Between Items in a Series
- To Keep Numbers Clear
- In Dates and Addresses

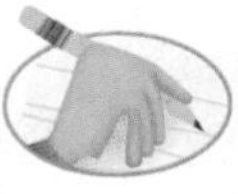

For each sentence below, write the words or numbers that need commas. Then insert the commas correctly.

Example: I started first grade on August 29 2005.
August 29, 2005

1. There are more than 1200 students at my brother's high school.
2. He has been going there since August 18 2009.
3. The school's address is 1010 Water Street Arlo Texas 80989.
4. Nikki Rasheed and Collin are hall monitors.
5. They started their "jobs" in March 2010, which was more than 1000 days ago.
6. Javier woke up late missed the bus and forgot his homework.
7. He thought of about 50000 excuses he could give the teacher.
8. The teacher gave him until October 9 2010 to turn it in.
9. Javier walked to Frank's house at 2105 Juniper Road Catalpa Texas 80990.
10. Javier did his homework Frank read a magazine and Frank's little brother bothered them.

Next Step: Write full sentences that answer each of the following questions. Be sure to use commas correctly.

- When were you born?
- What is your home address?
- What are your three favorite foods?
- What is the sum of 500 + 525?

Commas . . .

584.1
To Set Off Nonrestrictive Phrases and Clauses

Use commas to set off nonrestrictive phrases and clauses—those not necessary to the basic meaning of the sentence.

People get drinking water from surface water or groundwater, which makes up only 1 percent of the earth's water supply.
(The clause *which makes up only 1 percent of the earth's water supply* is additional information; it is nonrestrictive—not required. If the clause were left out, the meaning of the sentence would remain clear.)

Restrictive phrases or clauses—those that are needed in the sentence—restrict or limit the meaning of the sentence; they are not set off with commas.

Groundwater that is free from harmful pollutants is rare.
(The clause *that is free from harmful pollutants* is restrictive; it is needed to complete the meaning of the basic sentence and is not set off with commas.)

584.2
To Set Off Titles or Initials

Use commas to set off a title, a name, or initials that follow a person's last name. (Use only one period if an initial comes at the end of a sentence.)

Melanie Prokat, M.D., is our family's doctor. However, she is listed in the phone book only as Prokat, M.

NOTE Although commas are not necessary to set off "Jr." and "Sr." after a name, they may be used as long as a comma is used both before and after the abbreviation.

584.3
To Set Off Interruptions

Use commas to set off a word, phrase, or clause that interrupts the main thought of a sentence. These interruptions usually can be identified through the following tests:

1. You can leave them out of a sentence without changing its meaning.
2. You can place them other places in the sentence without changing its meaning.

Our school, as we all know, is becoming overcrowded again. (clause)

The gym, not the cafeteria, was expanded a while ago. (phrase)

My history class, for example, has 42 students in it. (phrase)

There are, indeed, about 1,000 people in my school. (word)

The building, however, has room for only 850 students. (word)

Grammar Practice

Commas 2

- To Set Off Nonrestrictive Phrases and Clauses
- To Set Off Titles or Initials
- To Set Off Interruptions

For each sentence below, write the parts that should be set off with commas. If commas are not necessary, write "none."

Example: When was music which plays a big role in every culture invented?
which plays a big role in every culture

1. Some scientists think it was the sounds of nature that originally inspired people to create music.
2. The songs of birds for example probably inspired many composers.
3. People were in fact making music as long as 50,000 years ago.
4. Prehistoric bone flutes which were played by cave dwellers are evidence of music's long history.
5. Egyptian paintings that show people playing instruments are also evidence of music's ancient beginnings.
6. By the Middle Ages which covered the thousand-year period from 450 to 1450 many different musical instruments were being used.
7. During the Renaissance, the recorder and reed instruments in general were very popular.
8. The years from 1825 to 1900 known as the Romantic period introduced many talented composers to the world.
9. Johann Strauss Jr. was one of these famous musicians.

Next Step: What instrument do you play (or wish you could play)? Write one sentence about it. Include a nonrestrictive phrase or clause, setting it off with commas.

Commas . . .

586.1
To Set Off Appositives

Commas set off an appositive from the rest of the sentence. An appositive is a word or phrase that identifies or renames a noun or pronoun. (See page 513.)

> **The capital of Cyprus, Nicosia, has a population of almost 643,000.** (*Nicosia* renames *capital of Cyprus*, so the word is set off with commas.)

> **Cyprus, an island in the Mediterranean Sea, is about half the size of Connecticut.** (*An island in the Mediterranean Sea* identifies *Cyprus,* so the phrase is set off with commas.)

Do not use commas with appositives that are necessary to the basic meaning of the sentence.

> **The Mediterranean island Cyprus is about half the size of Connecticut.** (*Cyprus* is not set off because it is needed to make the sentence clear.)

586.2
To Separate Equal Adjectives

Use commas to separate two or more adjectives that equally modify the same noun.

> **Comfortable, efficient cars are becoming more important to drivers.** (*Comfortable* and *efficient* are separated by a comma because they modify *cars* equally.)

> **Some automobiles run on clean, renewable sources of energy.** (*Clean* and *renewable* are separated by a comma because they modify *sources* equally.)

> **Conventional gasoline engines emit a lot of pollution.** (*Conventional* and *gasoline* do not modify *engines* equally; therefore, no comma separates the two.)

Use these tests to help you decide if adjectives modify equally:

1. Switch the order of the adjectives; if the sentence is clear, the adjectives modify equally.

   Yes: Efficient, comfortable cars are becoming more important to drivers.

   No: Gasoline conventional engines emit a lot of pollution.

2. Put the word *and* between the adjectives; if the sentence reads well, use a comma when *and* is taken out.

   Yes: Comfortable and efficient cars are becoming more important to drivers.

   No: Conventional and gasoline engines emit a lot of pollution.

Grammar Practice

Commas 3

To Set Off Appositives

For each numbered sentence below, write the appositive phrase and the noun it renames. Set off the appositive with commas.

Example: Kit houses "build-it-yourself" homes were popular in the early 1900s.
Kit houses, "build-it-yourself" homes,

(1) Sears the nationwide department store chain sold kit houses between 1908 and 1940. **(2)** One of the most popular models was the Osborn a small bungalow. **(3)** All the materials 30,000 or more pieces were neatly packed into two boxcars for rail delivery. **(4)** The home designers architects hired by the store could make changes to the floor plan the buyers wanted. **(5)** In a few months, the owners of this new house once just a big pile of materials could move in.

To Separate Equal Adjectives

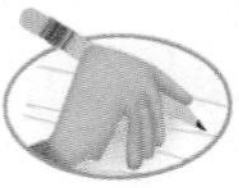

For each numbered sentence below, write the adjectives that need commas between them. Add the commas.

Example: The catalog offered 90 fashionable unique home designs.
fashionable, unique

(1) It's amazing to think that these big roomy houses—many still standing today—came from a department store catalog! **(2)** A complete ready-to-assemble kit included everything that was needed. **(3)** When people ordered their houses from the catalog, they would also order attractive modern light fixtures and sturdy plumbing fixtures. **(4)** All the pieces were delivered by rail, along with a thick detailed instruction book. **(5)** Then the buyers, along with anyone who could be persuaded to help, began the long challenging construction process.

Commas . . .

588.1
To Set Off Dialogue

Use commas to set off the exact words of a speaker from the rest of the sentence. (Also see page **556**.)

The firefighter said, "When we cannot successfully put out a fire, we try to keep it from spreading."

"When we cannot successfully put out a fire, we try to keep it from spreading," the firefighter said.

NOTE Do not use a comma or quotation marks for indirect quotations. The words *if* and *that* often signal dialogue that is being reported rather than quoted.

The firefighter said that when they cannot successfully put out a fire, they try to keep it from spreading. (These are not the speaker's exact words.)

588.2
In Direct Address

Use commas to separate a noun of direct address from the rest of the sentence. (A noun of direct address is a noun that names a person spoken to in the sentence.)

Hanae, did you know that an interior decorator can change wallpaper and fabrics on a computer screen?

Sure, Jack, and an architect can use a computer to see how light will fall in different parts of a building.

588.3
To Set Off Interjections

Use commas to separate an interjection or a weak exclamation from the rest of the sentence.

No kidding, you mean that one teacher has to manage a class of 42 pupils? (weak exclamation)

Uh-huh, and that teacher has other classes that size. (interjection)

588.4
To Set Off Explanatory Phrases

Use commas to separate an explanatory phrase from the rest of the sentence.

English, the language computers speak worldwide, is also the most widely used language in science and medicine.

More than 750 million people, about an eighth of the world's population, speak English as a foreign language.

Grammar Practice

Commas 4

- To Set Off Dialogue
- In Direct Address
- To Set Off Interjections

For each numbered sentence below, write the word or words that should be followed by commas. Add the commas.

Example: "Class we'll discuss oceans today" said the teacher.
Class, today,

1. The teacher asked "Who can define *ocean*?"
2. "It's a sea covering a large expanse Ms. Jackson" said Ralph.
3. She said "Wow that's right Ralph. Who knows which ocean is the largest?"
4. Renatta asked "Is it the Pacific?"
5. "Yes Renatta" replied Ms. Jackson.

- To Set Off Explanatory Phrases

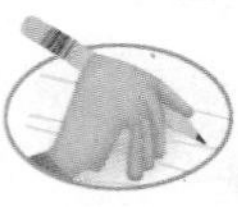

For each numbered sentence below, write the explanatory phrase that should be set off with commas.

Example: The Pacific Ocean the world's largest ocean contains nearly 50 percent of earth's water.
the world's largest ocean

1. The majority of the world's water supply 98 percent of it comes from the oceans.
2. Oceans provide fish a major source of food for many people.
3. Many huge ships cruise liners and cargo freighters provide people with opportunities for both work and play.
4. Also, shells and coral commonly used in building materials come from the oceans.
5. Ocean water which contains a lot of salt is not safe to drink.

Commas . . .

590.1
To Separate Introductory Clauses and Phrases

Use a comma to separate an adverb clause or a long phrase from the independent clause that follows it.

> **If every automobile in the country were a light shade of red, we'd live in a pink-car nation.** (adverb clause)
>
> **According to some experts, solar-powered cars will soon be common.** (long modifying phrase)

590.2
In Compound Sentences

Use a comma between two independent clauses that are joined by a coordinating conjunction (such as *and, but, or, nor, for, so,* and *yet*), forming a compound sentence. An independent clause expresses a complete thought and can stand alone as a sentence. (Also see page 516.)

> **Many students enjoy working on computers, so teachers are finding new ways to use them in the classroom.**
>
> **Computers can be valuable in education, but many schools cannot afford enough of them.**

Avoid Comma Splices: A comma splice results when two independent clauses are "spliced" together with only a comma—and no conjunction. (See page 504.)

SCHOOL DAZE
Ann, we've completed two-thirds of the quarter, and you haven't turned in one assignment. What do you have to say for yourself?

Ah . . . is there anything I can do for extra credit?

Grammar Practice

Commas 5

- To Separate Introductory Clauses and Phrases
- In Compound Sentences

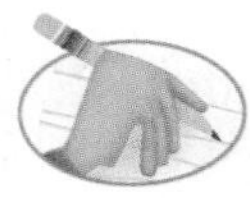

Number your paper from 1 to 13. For each line, write the words that should be followed by a comma, and put the commas after them. (Not every line needs a comma.) You should add nine commas.

Example: I didn't do my homework but I have an excuse.
homework,

This might come as a surprise to you but doing homework can be very dangerous. As I began to work on a math worksheet last night three dangerous felons grabbed me from behind and stuffed me into the trunk of a rusty, old car. After driving for quite a while the car came to a sudden stop and my kidnappers left the car. I knew I had to do something quickly or it would be too late. I didn't want to yell and alert the kidnappers so I wrote a note on the back of my worksheet and stuck it through one of the rust holes in the car. Fortunately, a passerby saw the note and notified the police. Soon after the police came and captured the kidnappers. Since the police kept my worksheet as evidence I couldn't complete my homework. For some reason my math teacher didn't buy my excuse for not having my homework done.

Next Step: Take a normal, everyday experience, such as doing homework, walking to school, taking a test, or playing a game, and turn it into a "tall tale" like the one above. Use commas with introductory word groups and in compound sentences.

Test Prep!

For each underlined part of the paragraphs below, choose the letter (on the next page) of the best way to punctuate it.

The bumps on your tongue are not your taste buds but (1) they do contain taste buds. The bumps are called papillae (2) An average person has about 10000 (3) taste buds and (4) each bud contains between 50 and 100 taste cells. Taste buds are mostly located on your tongue but (5) can also be found on the roof of your mouth your throat and part (6) of the esophagus.

What happens when you put food in your mouth (7) It gets mixed with your saliva so that the taste buds can detect the flavor. At the same time, the odor of the food in your mouth travels up into your nose so (8) specialized cells in your nose olfactory receptors (9) also play an important role in tasting. Your taste buds and olfactory receptors work together to sense true flavor.

Taste buds enable a person to experience tastes that are sweet salty sour bitter and umami (10). Umami a newly recognized taste (11) is experienced in protein-rich foods like aged cheese. Every taste cell can respond to all five sensations but (12) responds mostly to only one of them. Did you know that people are actually born liking sweet flavors and disliking bitterness (13) These traits evolved to help people desire sugars the chemicals we need for energy and growth (14) and reject bitter tastes as a protection against eating poisons.

1. Ⓐ buds, but
Ⓑ buds. but
Ⓒ buds; but
Ⓓ correct as is

2. Ⓐ papillae?
Ⓑ papillae.
Ⓒ papillae,
Ⓓ correct as is

3. Ⓐ 100,00
Ⓑ 1,0000
Ⓒ 10,000
Ⓓ correct as is

4. Ⓐ buds, and
Ⓑ buds and,
Ⓒ buds. and
Ⓓ correct as is

5. Ⓐ tongue, but
Ⓑ tongue. but
Ⓒ tongue but,
Ⓓ correct as is

6. Ⓐ your mouth, your throat and part
Ⓑ your mouth, your throat, and part
Ⓒ your mouth your throat, and part
Ⓓ correct as is

7. Ⓐ mouth?
Ⓑ mouth.
Ⓒ mouth,
Ⓓ correct as is

8. Ⓐ nose. so
Ⓑ nose, so
Ⓒ nose so,
Ⓓ correct as is

9. Ⓐ nose olfactory receptors,
Ⓑ nose, olfactory receptors,
Ⓒ nose, olfactory receptors
Ⓓ correct as is

10. Ⓐ sweet, salty, sour, bitter, and umami
Ⓑ sweet, salty, sour, bitter and umami
Ⓒ sweet salty, sour, bitter and umami
Ⓓ correct as is

11. Ⓐ Umami, a newly recognized taste
Ⓑ Umami a newly, recognized taste
Ⓒ Umami, a newly recognized taste,
Ⓓ correct as is

12. Ⓐ sensations, but
Ⓑ sensations but,
Ⓒ sensations. but
Ⓓ correct as is

13. Ⓐ bitterness.
Ⓑ bitterness,
Ⓒ bitterness?
Ⓓ correct as is

14. Ⓐ sugars, the chemicals we need for energy and growth,
Ⓑ sugars, the chemicals, we need for energy and growth,
Ⓒ sugars, the chemicals we need for energy and growth
Ⓓ correct as is

Semicolons

Use a **semicolon** to suggest a stronger pause than a comma indicates. A semicolon may also serve in place of a period.

594.1
To Join Two Independent Clauses

In a compound sentence, use a semicolon to join two independent clauses that are not connected with a coordinating conjunction. (See **744.1**.)

The United States has more computers than any other country; its residents own more than 164 million of them.

594.2
With Conjunctive Adverbs

A semicolon is also used to join two independent clauses when the clauses are connected by a conjunctive adverb (such as *as a result, for example, however, therefore,* and *instead*). (See **738.1**.)

Japan is next on that list; however, the Japanese have only 50 million computers.

You might think that the billion people of China own a lot of computers; instead, the smaller country of Germany has twice as many computers as China.

594.3
To Separate Groups That Contain Commas

Use a semicolon between groups of words in a series when one or more of the groups already contain commas.

Many of our community's residents separate their garbage into bins for newspapers, cardboard, and junk mail; glass, metal, and plastic; and nonrecyclable trash.

SCHOOL DAZE
It's true that I have only a few minutes to finish this; **however,** I am not worried.

Well, that makes one of us.

Grammar Practice

Semicolons

Write the numbers of the lines that need a semicolon in the following paragraphs. Then write the two words, separated by the semicolon.

Example: The Nintendo Playing Card Company was begun in 1889 in Japan today it's a familiar video game company.
Japan; today

In the 1960s, a Japanese company called Service Games started up the company's name was later shortened to Sega. At first, Sega created pinball games. Interactive video games were introduced in 1968 however, the first *popular* interactive game, Pong, was not developed until 1972. These early arcade video games were big machines that included speakers, video screens, and coin slots knobs, flippers, and joysticks and computer processors and software.

Things changed in 1976 when people could play video games at home on their televisions. Less than 10 years later, home computers were becoming more common as a result, Tetris became one of the first popular computer games. The first handheld video game, Nintendo's Game Boy, was introduced in 1989 it had a black-and-white screen! By 2001, online games allowed thousands of gamers to play at once.

What does the future hold for video games? One possibility is games that can "think" for themselves another is games that are controlled by eye movements. Whatever the case, these games are almost guaranteed a big audience!

Next Step: Write a compound sentence about any kind of game you've played. Punctuate it with a semicolon. Then write another compound sentence using a conjunctive adverb; again, use a semicolon to join the independent clauses.

Colons

A **colon** may be used to introduce a list or an important point. Colons are also used in business letters and between the numbers in time.

596.1 To Introduce Lists

Use a colon to introduce a list. The colon usually comes after words describing the subject of the list (as in the first example below) or after summary words, such as *the following* or *these things*. Do not use a colon after a verb or preposition.

Certain items are still difficult to recycle: foam cups, car tires, and toxic chemicals.

To conserve water, you should do the following three things: fix drippy faucets, install a low-flow showerhead, and turn the water off while brushing your teeth.

Incorrect: **To conserve water, you should: install a low-flow showerhead, turn the water off while brushing your teeth, and fix drippy faucets.**

596.2 To Introduce Sentences

A colon may be used to introduce a sentence, a question, or a quotation.

This is why air pollution is bad: We are sacrificing our health and the health of all other life on the planet.

Answer this question for me: Why aren't more people concerned about global warming?

Joaquin shared this with us: "Iceland is the world's leader in the use of renewable energy."

596.3 After Salutations

A colon may be used after the salutation of a business letter.

Dear Ms. Manners: Dear Dr. Warmle: Dear Professor Potter:
Dear Captain Elliot: Dear Senator:

596.4 For Emphasis

Use a colon to emphasize a word or phrase.

The newest alternative energy is also the most common element on earth: hydrogen.

Here's one thing that can help save energy: a programmable thermostat.

596.5 Between Numbers in Time

Use a colon between the parts of a number that indicates time.

My thermostat automatically sets my heat to 60 degrees between 11:00 p.m. and 6:00 a.m.

Grammar Practice

Colons

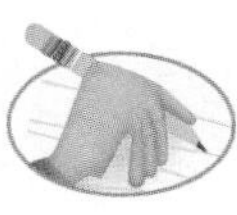

Which words or numbers in the letter below should be followed by or contain a colon? Write each one and place the colon correctly.

Example: Kangaroos are known for these features their pouches, their long legs, and their long tails.
features:

Dear Mr. Sei

Last night around 815 p.m., I saw one of the largest kangaroos I have ever seen. It entered our camping area, seemingly unafraid, and ate the plants near our tent. As I silently watched, I studied its features the long claw, the big ears, the strong forelimbs, and the soft muzzle. Although there was very little light, I could tell by the size that it could only be the giant of kangaroos the red.

I remembered a friend asking me this How much ground can a red cover in a single jump? I have seen these kangaroos easily cover 20 feet while they cruised along. I don't know if that is any kind of record, but it sure is a long hop. A park ranger says that the female red, which is gray blue in color, can hit 30 miles per hour.

After eating as much as it wanted, the big red finally disappeared into the darkness about 945 p.m. Sadly, I've heard this comment Kangaroos are giant jumping rats and cause nothing but trouble. Some kangaroos may be pests, but the one I saw makes me think only one thing They are a marvelous part of Australia.

With regards,

Franklin

Next Step: Write a brief reply to Franklin. Use colons as necessary.

Quotation Marks

Quotation marks are used in a number of ways:

- to set off the exact words of a speaker,
- to punctuate material quoted from another source,
- to punctuate words used in a special way, and
- to punctuate certain titles.

598.1 To Set Off a Speaker's Exact Words

Place quotation marks before and after a speaker's words in dialogue. Only the exact words of the speaker are placed within quotation marks.

Marla said, "I've decided to become a firefighter."

"A firefighter," said Juan, "can help people in many ways."

598.2 For Quotations Within Quotations

Use single quotation marks to punctuate a quotation within a quotation.

Sung Kim asked, "Did Marla just say, 'I've decided to become a firefighter'?"

When titles occur within a quotation, use single quotation marks to punctuate those that require quotation marks.

Juan said, "Springsteen's song 'The Rising' really inspired her."

598.3 To Set Off Quoted Material

When quoting material from another source, place quotation marks before and after the source's exact words.

In her book *Living the Life You Deserve,* Tess Spyeder explains, "Choose a job you'll enjoy doing day after day over one that will fatten your bank account."

598.4 To Set Off Long Quoted Material

If more than one paragraph is quoted from a single source, quotation marks are placed before each paragraph and at the end of the last paragraph.

Quotations that are more than four lines are usually set off from the rest of the paper by indenting each line 10 spaces from the left. Quotations that are set off in this way require no quotation marks either before or after the quoted material.

Grammar Practice

Dashes

Rewrite the sentences below, adding dashes where appropriate.

Example: We'll be outside all afternoon don't forget the sunscreen.

We'll be outside all afternoon—don't forget the sunscreen.

1. Han said, "They were going I mean they *are* going to the mall."
2. *Taraxacum officinale* that is, the common dandelion is the curse of many lawns.
3. I don't let's just wait calm down.
4. "Good morning! Here are your oops eggs," Mom said as she dropped my scrambled eggs on my lap.
5. This is Reggie's bike the bike that was stolen!

Parentheses

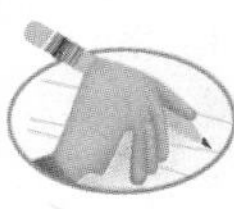

Write the parts of the sentences below that should be enclosed in parentheses. Add the parentheses.

Example: Simone's sisters Rachel, Gabby, and Naomi joined us.

(Rachel, Gabby, and Naomi)

1. Peter asked the clerk the one wearing glasses for some change.
2. Of the flower bulbs I planted, most of them 80 percent bloomed.
3. Fumiki looking quite pale excused herself from the table.
4. Vinnie my friend's first cousin has a job at the amusement park this summer.
5. Kat always peppers her e-mails with emoticons smiley faces.

Ellipses

Use an **ellipsis** (three periods) to show a pause in dialogue or to show that words or sentences have been left out. Leave one space before, after, and between each period.

614.1 To Show Pauses

Use an ellipsis to show a pause in dialogue.

> **"My report," said Reggie, "is on . . . ah . . . cars of the future. One place that I . . . uh . . . checked on the Internet said that cars would someday run on sunshine."**

614.2 To Show Omitted Words

Use an ellipsis to show that one or more words have been left out of a quotation. Read this statement about hibernation.

> **Some animals, such as the chipmunk and the woodchuck, hibernate in winter. During this time, the animal's heart beats very slowly—only a few times per minute. Its body cools down so much that it nearly freezes, and this is called going into torpor.**

Here's how you would type part of the above quotation, leaving some of the words out. If the words left out are at the end of a sentence, use a period followed by three dots.

> **Some animals . . . hibernate in winter. During this time, the animal's heart beats very slowly . . . and this is called going into torpor.**

SCHOOL DAZE

Max, where is your project? Today is the last day to turn it in!

Well . . . ah . . . can I fax it to you before midnight?

Grammar Practice

Ellipses

To Show Pauses

Rewrite the following sentences, adding ellipses where they are needed.

Example: Oh no I forgot the tickets.
Oh no . . . I forgot the tickets.

1. Did you see the disgusting uh I mean the special food we are having for lunch?
2. It's well how can I describe it?
3. Hmm does it have something healthful in it?
4. Ah you hit the nail on the head.
5. We're having let's see "Martina's Tofu Surprise."

To Show Omitted Words

Rewrite the following paragraph as a quotation for a research paper. Insert ellipses where you decide to leave out less-important information.

Sandstone is a very simple kind of sedimentary rock. It is not much more than sand pressed tightly together and mixed with clay, which acts as a kind of cement. Sandstone is porous, which means that water can pass through it; each year's freeze and thaw breaks down the rock a little more. It erodes rapidly, so wind and water can carve sandstone into unusual shapes.

Test Prep!

Number your paper from 1 to 12. For each underlined part of the paragraphs below, write the letter (from the next page) of the best way to punctuate it.

Soon you'll be thinking about an upcoming event: your (1) move from middle school to high school. Its likely that you'll (2) be going to a bigger school with many more students than attend your current school. Don't worry about getting lost; Go (3) to the freshman orientation to get valuable information—including a map—that will make your move to ninth grade easier.

You might be concerned about harder work in high school: however, (4) most students find they can keep up with it. On the other hand, you can look forward to having more choices in these areas; courses, (5) friends, and cafeteria food.

In Norton Wright (6) book *Eighth to Ninth,* (7) Wright suggests, 'It's (8) a good idea to visit the high school in the spring before you attend." He goes on to say, "If you can 'shadow' (9) another student, that's even better"! (10) An article titled "Casting Long Shadows" (11) in the newspaper "*High School Happenings*" (12) agreed with his advice.

1. (A) event: Your
(B) event; your
(C) event your
(D) correct as is

2. (A) It's likely that you'll
(B) Its' likely that you'll
(C) It's likely that you'l
(D) correct as is

3. (A) lost Go
(B) lost; go
(C) lost go
(D) correct as is

4. (A) school, however;
(B) school: However,
(C) school; however,
(D) correct as is

5. (A) areas: courses,
(B) areas courses
(C) areas: Courses
(D) correct as is

6. (A) Norton Wrights
(B) Norton Wright's
(C) Norton Wrights'
(D) correct as is

7. (A) "Eighth to Ninth"
(B) *"Eighth to Ninth"*
(C) Eighth to Ninth
(D) correct as is

8. (A) 'Its
(B) "Its
(C) "It's
(D) correct as is

9. (A) "shadow"
(B) 'shadow"
(C) "shadow'
(D) correct as is

10. (A) better!
(B) better!"
(C) better"
(D) correct as is

11. (A) Casting Long Shadows
(B) *Casting Long Shadows*
(C) *"Casting Long Shadows"*
(D) correct as is

12. (A) "High School Happenings"
(B) *High School Happenings*
(C) High School Happenings
(D) correct as is

Editing for Mechanics

Capitalization

618.1
Proper Nouns and Adjectives

Capitalize all proper nouns and all proper adjectives. A proper noun is the name of a particular person, place, thing, or idea. A proper adjective is an adjective formed from a proper noun.

Common Noun: **country, president, continent**
Proper Noun: **Canada, Andrew Jackson, Asia**
Proper Adjective: **Canadian, Jacksonian, Asian**

618.2
Names of People

Capitalize the names of people and also the initials or abbreviations that stand for those names.

Samuel L. Jackson **Aung San Suu Kyi**
Mary Sanchez-Gomez

618.3
Titles Used with Names

Capitalize titles used with names of persons; also capitalize abbreviations standing for those titles.

President Mohammed Hosni Mubarak **Dr. Linda Trout**
Governor Michael Easley **Rev. Jim Zavaski**
Senator John McCain

618.4
Words Used as Names

Capitalize words such as *mother, father, aunt,* and *uncle* when these words are used as names.

Uncle Marius **started to sit on the couch.** (*Uncle* is a name; the speaker calls this person "Uncle Marius.")

Then Uncle **stopped in midair.** (*Uncle* is used as a name.)

"So, Mom**, what are you doing here?" I asked.** (*Mom* is used as a name.)

Words such as *aunt, uncle, mom, dad, grandma,* and *grandpa* are usually not capitalized if they come after a possessive pronoun (*my, his, our*).

My aunt **had just called him.** (The word *aunt* describes this person but is not used as a name.)

Then my dad **and** mom **walked into the room.** (The words *dad* and *mom* are not used as names in this sentence.)

Grammar Practice

Capitalization 1

- Names of People
- Titles Used with Names
- Words Used as Names

Some words in the following sentences are capitalized and should not be; others need to be capitalized. Write each of the words correctly.

Example: Before he was a Governor and a President, mr. Ronald Reagan was an actor.
governor, president, Mr.

1. The first African American Congresswoman was representative Shirley Chisholm.
2. A Famous Poet, dr. Maya Angelou, read a poem at president Clinton's inauguration.
3. Abigail Adams was the Mother of President John quincy Adams.
4. Mr. Adams called his mom's brother simply "uncle."
5. President john f. Kennedy's Brother is senator Ted Kennedy.
6. The first woman appointed to the United States Supreme Court was justice Sandra day O'Connor.
7. President George w. Bush's Father is a former president: george h. w. Bush.
8. In 1997, secretary of state madeleine K. Albright became the highest-ranking woman in the history of the U.S. government.
9. Greenville, South Carolina, is the birthplace of rev. jessie Jackson, who ran for President at one time.

Next Step: Write a sentence about a famous person you are studying in school. Use a title (Dr., Ms., Senator) for this person in your sentence. Check your capitalization.

Capitalization . . .

620.1
School Subjects

Capitalize the name of a specific educational course, but not the name of a general subject. (Exception—the names of all languages are proper nouns and are always capitalized: *French, English, Hindi, German, Latin.*)

Roberto is studying accounting at the technical college.
(Because *accounting* is a general subject, it is not capitalized.)

He likes the professor who teaches Accounting Principles.
(The specific course name is capitalized.)

620.2
Official Names

Capitalize the names of businesses and the official names of their products. (These are called trade names.) Do not, however, capitalize a general word like "toothpaste" when it follows the trade name.

Old Navy **Best Buy** **Microsoft** **Kodak**
Sony Playstation **Tombstone pizza** **Mudd jeans**

620.3
Races, Languages, Nationalities, Religions

Capitalize the names of languages, races, nationalities, and religions, as well as the proper adjectives formed from them.

Arab **Spanish** **Judaism** **Catholicism**
African art **Irish linen** **Swedish meatballs**

620.4
Days, Months, Holidays

Capitalize the names of days of the week, months of the year, and special holidays.

Thursday **Friday** **Saturday**
July **August** **September**
Arbor Day **Independence Day**

Do not capitalize the names of seasons.

winter, spring, summer, fall (autumn)

620.5
Historical Events

Capitalize the names of historical events, documents, and periods of time.

World War II **the Bill of Rights** **the Magna Carta**
the Middle Ages **the Paleozoic Era**

Grammar Practice

Capitalization 2

- School Subjects
- Races, Languages, Nationalities, Religions
- Historical Events

Correctly write any incorrectly capitalized words in the following paragraphs. (Write the line number followed by the word or words.)

Example: *1* My dad speaks english, french, and spanish.
1 English, French, Spanish

Last year I took a french language class. The class was actually called french language and history, so we learned some of that country's history, too. For instance, the french wars of religion were fought by people of different christian faiths. While France was ruled by catholic kings, an army attacked a protestant church service. After many years of fighting between catholics and protestants, the french people were allowed to choose their own faith. Today, people of all faiths—christianity, judaism, hinduism, islam, and others—have freedom to worship in France.

We also talked about Bastille Day, the french holiday that's like Independence Day in the United States. In France, it celebrates the beginning of the french revolution. The Bastille was the name of a french prison for people who did not agree with the king and queen's decisions. On July 14, 1789, a crowd of frenchmen stormed the Bastille and released the prisoners. That revolution brought great changes and new freedoms to France, just as the revolutionary war gained freedom for early american colonists.

Next Step: Write two or three sentences about an American historical event you have recently studied or know something about.

Capitalization . . .

622.1
Geographic Names

Capitalize the following geographic names.

Planets and heavenly bodies . . . . **Venus, Jupiter, Milky Way**

Lowercase the word "earth" except when used as the proper name of our planet, especially when mentioned with other planet names.

What on earth are you doing here?

Sam has traveled across the face of the earth several times.

Jupiter's diameter is 11 times larger than Earth's.

The four inner planets are Mercury, Venus, Earth, and Mars.

Continents . . . . **Europe, Asia, South America, Australia, Africa**

Countries . . . **Morocco, Haiti, Greece, Chile, United Arab Emirates**

States . . . . . **New Mexico, Alabama, West Virginia, Delaware, Iowa**

Provinces . . . . **Alberta, British Columbia, Quebec, Ontario**

Counties . . . . **Sioux County, Kandiyohi County, Wade County**

Cities . . . . **Montreal, Baton Rouge, Albuquerque, Portland**

Bodies of water . . . . **Delaware Bay, Chickamunga Lake, Indian Ocean, Gulf of Mexico, Skunk Creek**

Landforms . . . . **Appalachian Mountains, Bitterroot Range**

Public areas . . . . **Tiananmen Square, Sequoia National Forest, Mount Rushmore, Open Space Park, Vietnam Memorial**

Roads and highways . . . . **New Jersey Turnpike, Interstate 80, Central Avenue, Chisholm Trail, Mutt's Road**

Buildings . . . **Pentagon, Paske High School, Empire State Building**

Monuments . . . . **Eiffel Tower, Statue of Liberty**

622.2
Particular Sections of the Country

Capitalize words that indicate particular sections of the country. Also capitalize proper adjectives formed from names of specific sections of a country.

Having grown up on the hectic East Coast, I find life in the South to be refreshing.

Here in Georgia, Southern hospitality is a way of life.

Words that simply indicate a direction are not capitalized; nor are adjectives that are formed from words that simply indicate direction.

The town where I live, located east of Memphis, is typical of others found in western Tennessee.

Grammar Practice

Capitalization 3

- Geographic Names
- Particular Sections of the Country

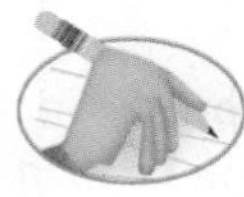

For each sentence below, write the word or words that should be capitalized but aren't. If a sentence has correct capitalization, write "correct."

Example: Kennebunk, ocean city, and St. Augustine are cities on the east coast.
Ocean City, East Coast

1. You can see giant pandas in china at the beijing zoological gardens.
2. Honolulu, Hawaii, is on the southeast coast of the island of Oahu.
3. The San Andreas Fault runs northwest to southeast along california's coastline.
4. The queen lives in buckingham palace in london, england.
5. Mt. rushmore and the crazy horse monument are in the black hills of south dakota.
6. The mississippi river runs from minnesota to the gulf of mexico.
7. Mount kilimanjaro, near the border of kenya, is the highest point in africa.
8. There are many historic trails and landmarks in the western united states.
9. The will rogers highway is one of the names for route 66, which runs from chicago to los angeles.
10. Indiana, wisconsin, iowa, and ohio are states in the midwest.

Next Step: Write complete sentences to answer the following questions. Be sure to use correct capitalization.

- What large body of water is closest to your home?
- What city in the state of New York has the greatest population?

Capitalization . . .

624.1
First Words

Capitalize the first word of every sentence and the first word in a direct quotation.

In many families, pets are treated like people, according to an article in the *Kansas City Star.* (sentence)

Marty Becker, coauthor of *Chicken Soup for the Pet Lover's Soul,* reports, "Seven out of ten people let their pets sleep on the bed." (direct quotation)

"I get my 15 minutes of fame," he says, "every time I come home." (Notice that *every* is not capitalized because it does not begin a new sentence.)

"It's like being treated like a rock star," says Becker. "Now I have to tell you that feels pretty good."

Do not capitalize the first word in an indirect quotation.

Becker says that in the last 10 years, pets have moved out of kennels and basements and into living rooms and bedrooms. (indirect quotation)

624.2
Titles

Capitalize the first word of a title, the last word, and every word in between except articles *(a, an, the),* short prepositions, and coordinating conjunctions. Follow this rule for titles of books, newspapers, magazines, poems, plays, songs, articles, movies, works of art, pictures, stories, and essays.

Locked in Time (book)

Boston Globe (newspaper)

Dog Fancy (magazine)

"Roses Are Red" (poem)

The Phantom of the Opera (play)

Daddy Day Care (movie)

"Intuition" (song)

Mona Lisa (work of art)

Grammar Practice

Capitalization 4

- First Words
- Titles

For each of the following sentences, correctly write any word that is incorrectly capitalized.

Example: Laura Ingalls Wilder once said that She had no idea she was writing history.
she

1. A collection of her letters can be found in the book *West From Home*.
2. Laura's book *Little house in The Big Woods* is about her life in Wisconsin.
3. Pa played and sang songs like "My old kentucky home."
4. the television series *Little House On the Prairie* was based on Laura's books.
5. Laura wrote articles for the *Missouri ruralist* and other magazines.
6. Laura's sister Carrie worked for a while at the *De Smet news*.
7. "I love the *Little House* books," said Heather, "Because of their descriptions about life during the 1800s."
8. Heather told us That she has all of Laura Ingalls Wilder's books.
9. "My favorite is *Little Town on the prairie*," she said. "It's the one where Laura meets Almanzo Wilder."

Next Step: Write a short paragraph about a favorite author and include the titles of some of his or her works. Exchange papers with a classmate. Are first words and titles capitalized correctly?

Capitalization . . .

626.1 Abbreviations

Capitalize abbreviations of titles and organizations.

Dr. (Doctor) **M.D.** (Doctor of Medicine)
Mr. (Mister) **UPS** (United Parcel Service)
SADD (Students Against Destructive Decisions)

626.2 Organizations

Capitalize the name of an organization, an association, or a team.

New York State Historical Society **the Red Cross**
General Motors Corporation **the Miami Dolphins**
Republicans **the Democratic Party**

626.3 Letters

Capitalize the letters used to indicate form or shape.

T-shirt **U-turn** **A-frame** **T-ball**

Capitalize	Do Not Capitalize
American	un-American
January, February	winter, spring
Missouri and Ohio rivers	the rivers Missouri and Ohio
The South is humid in summer.	Turn south at the stop sign.
Duluth Middle School	a Duluth middle school
Governor Bob Taft	Bob Taft, our governor
President Luiz Lula Da Silva	Luiz Lula Da Silva, Brazil's president
Nissan Altima	a Nissan automobile
The planet Earth is egg shaped.	The earth on Grandpa's farm is rich.
I'm taking World Cultures.	I'm taking social studies.

Grammar Practice

Capitalization 5

- Abbreviations
- Organizations

Capitalize the words in the following paragraphs that need to be capitalized. (Write the line number followed by the word or words.)

Example: The ad council donates services to organizations like the girl scouts of America.

1 Ad Council
2 Girl Scouts

The ad council is a group of volunteers in the advertising industry. They make and promote public service announcements (psa's) for many organizations. For instance, they created McGruff the Crime Dog for the National crime prevention Council. They also created Smokey Bear for the usfs (United States forest service) and Vince and Larry, the Crash Test Dummies, for the government's dot (department of transportation).

When members of the ad council see a problem that concerns people, they try to draw attention to it. Some of their recent campaigns include increasing environmental awareness (sponsored by earth share) and getting parents involved in school (sponsored by the National pta). The ad council's programs encourage people to give these subjects the notice they deserve. The hope is that positive social change will result as people take action.

Next Step: Write a brief paragraph about an issue that concerns you. Include the name of an organization that you would create to deal with the problem.

Test Prep!

For each sentence below, write the letter of the line that contains a mistake. If there is no mistake, choose "D."

1. Ⓐ "Do you want to go
Ⓑ with me and my Dad?"
Ⓒ Ryan asked.
Ⓓ correct as is

2. Ⓐ S. e. hinton
Ⓑ is the author of a book
Ⓒ called *Rumble Fish*.
Ⓓ correct as is

3. Ⓐ Tony Blair, former prime
Ⓑ Minister of Great Britain,
Ⓒ was born in Scotland.
Ⓓ correct as is

4. Ⓐ my best friend, Cory,
Ⓑ likes the new teacher
Ⓒ who teaches biology.
Ⓓ correct as is

5. Ⓐ Our english teacher
Ⓑ speaks Spanish,
Ⓒ French, and German.
Ⓓ correct as is

6. Ⓐ The Fourth of July
Ⓑ is a nickname
Ⓒ for independence day.
Ⓓ correct as is

7. Ⓐ Canada, the United
Ⓑ States, and Mexico are
Ⓒ countries in north America.
Ⓓ correct as is

8. Ⓐ At Wilson's Observatory,
Ⓑ we saw Mars, Jupiter,
Ⓒ and the Milky Way.
Ⓓ correct as is

9. Ⓐ The east coast runs along
Ⓑ the Atlantic Ocean and has
Ⓒ many interesting beaches.
Ⓓ correct as is

10. Ⓐ The story was printed
Ⓑ in the *Seattle times*
Ⓒ last winter.
Ⓓ correct as is

11. Ⓐ "When you're a singer,"
Ⓑ she told the reporter,
Ⓒ "Every song is an adventure."
Ⓓ correct as is

12. Ⓐ Maria says that
Ⓑ there are only seven
Ⓒ questions on the test.
Ⓓ correct as is

13. Ⓐ Franky plans to
Ⓑ build a large
Ⓒ a-frame storage shed.
Ⓓ correct as is

14. Ⓐ Kayle's family wants
Ⓑ to drive North to Canada
Ⓒ later this summer.
Ⓓ correct as is

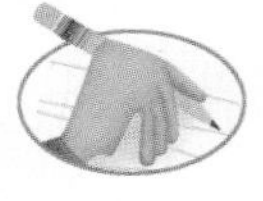

For each underlined part of the following paragraph, choose the letter (below) that shows the correct capitalization. If the underlined part is correct, choose "D."

Our Social Studies class **(15)** is learning about the cdc (Centers for disease control) **(16)**. The CDC is located in atlanta, Georgia **(17)**, and its director is dr. Julie L. Gerberding **(18)**. This agency works to improve the health of the people of the United States **(19)**. The CDC is a part of the Department of Health and human services **(20)**.

15
- (A) Social studies class
- (B) social Studies Class
- (C) social studies class
- (D) correct as is

16
- (A) CDC (Centers for Disease Control)
- (B) CDC (centers for disease control)
- (C) cdc (Centers for Disease Control)
- (D) correct as is

17
- (A) Atlanta, georgia
- (B) Atlanta, Georgia
- (C) atlanta, georgia
- (D) correct as is

18
- (A) dr. julie l. Gerberding
- (B) Dr. Julie L. gerberding
- (C) Dr. Julie L. Gerberding
- (D) correct as is

19
- (A) The people of the United States
- (B) the People of the United States
- (C) the people of the united states
- (D) correct as is

20
- (A) Department of Health and Human Services
- (B) department of Health and Human Services
- (C) Department of health and human services
- (D) correct as is

Plurals

630.1 Most Nouns

The **plurals** of most nouns are formed by adding *s* to the singular.

cheerleader — **cheerleaders** wheel — **wheels**

bubble — **bubbles**

630.2 Nouns Ending in *ch, sh, s, x,* and *z*

The plural form of nouns ending in *ch, sh, s, x,* and *z* is made by adding *es* to the singular.

lunch — **lunches** dish — **dishes** mess — **messes**

buzz — **buzzes** fox — **foxes**

630.3 Nouns Ending in *o*

The plurals of nouns ending in *o* with a vowel just before the *o* are formed by adding *s.*

radio — **radios** studio — **studios** rodeo — **rodeos**

The plurals of most nouns ending in *o* with a consonant just before the *o* are formed by adding *es.*

echo — **echoes** hero — **heroes** tomato — **tomatoes**

Exceptions: Musical terms and words of Spanish origin always form plurals by adding *s.*

alto — **altos** banjo — **banjos** taco — **tacos**

solo — **solos** piano — **pianos** burro — **burros**

630.4 Nouns Ending in *ful*

The plurals of nouns that end with *ful* are formed by adding an *s* at the end of the word.

three platefuls **six tankfuls** **four cupfuls** **five pailfuls**

630.5 Nouns Ending in *f* or *fe*

The plurals of nouns that end in *f* or *fe* are formed in one of two ways: If the final *f* sound is still heard in the plural form of the word, simply add *s;* if the final sound is a *v* sound, change the *f* to *ve* and add *s.*

roof — roofs **chief — chiefs** **belief — beliefs**
(plural ends with *f* sound)

wife — wives **loaf — loaves** **leaf — leaves**
(plural ends with *v* sound)

Grammar Practice

Plurals 1

- Nouns Ending in *ch, sh, s, x,* and *z*
- Nouns Ending in *o*
- Nouns Ending in *ful*
- Nouns Ending in *f* or *fe*

For each sentence below, write the correct plural for the underlined word. If the plural is correct, write "C."

Example: Today's four o'clock meeting is for coachs only.
coaches

1. The cooks used a whole bag of potatoes to make this soup.
2. During the night, thiefs took three signs from the parking lot.
3. Randy ate three bowlsful of his favorite cereal.
4. Sometimes countries use special taxs to control the number of imported goods.
5. These extra charges are called tariffes.
6. The winning lumberjack used six different axs during the competition.
7. The eighth-grade choir wants five more girls to be sopranoes.
8. Some people say that cats have nine lifes.
9. Allan figured he needed four bucketfuls of red paint to complete the job.
10. Angelica likes to eat mangos.
11. The newspaper reported that there were more than 50 canoes in the race.
12. In the movie *Aladdin*, does the genie grant three or four wishs?

Next Step: Write three sentences that include the plurals of these words: *studio, spoonful,* and *wax.*

Plurals . . .

632.1
Nouns Ending in *y*

The plurals of common nouns that end in *y* with a consonant letter just before the *y* are formed by changing the *y* to *i* and adding *es*.

fly — **flies** baby — **babies** cavity — **cavities**

The plurals of common nouns that end in *y* with a vowel before the *y* are formed by adding only *s*.

key — **keys** holiday — **holidays** attorney — **attorneys**

The plurals of proper nouns ending in *y* are formed by adding *s*.

There are three Circuit Citys **in our metro area.**

632.2
Compound Nouns

The plurals of some compound nouns are formed by adding *s* or *es* to the main word in the compound.

brothers-in-law **maids of honor** **secretaries of state**

632.3
Plurals That Do Not Change

The plurals of some words are the same in singular and plural form.

deer **sheep** **trout** **aircraft**

632.4
Irregular Spelling

Some words (including many foreign words) form a plural by taking on an irregular spelling; others are now acceptable with the commonly used *s* or *es* ending.

child — **children** woman — **women** man — **men**
goose — **geese** mouse — **mice** ox — **oxen**
tooth — **teeth** octopus — **octopi** or **octopuses**
index — **indices** or **indexes**

632.5
Adding an *'s*

The plurals of letters, figures, symbols, and words discussed as words are formed by adding an apostrophe and an *s*.

Dr. Walters has two Ph.D.'s.

My dad's license plate has three 2's **between two** *B*'s.

You've got too many *but*'s **and** *so*'s **in that sentence.**

For information on forming plural possessives, see **606.1**.

Grammar Practice

Plurals 2

- Nouns Ending in *y*
- Compound Nouns
- Plurals That Do Not Change
- Irregular Spelling

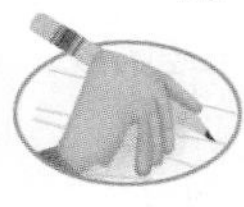

For each of the following sentences, write the plural form of the word or words in parentheses.

Example: My favorite author writes *(story)* about *(child)* in other *(country).*

stories, children, countries

1. The *(boy)* rode *(donkey)* into the Valley of the Kings.
2. There are *(county)* in Nebraska named after *(antelope)* and *(buffalo).*
3. There were six *(Bobby)* at the Malloy family reunion.
4. *(Passer-by)* saw the injured animal and called the Humane Society.
5. We saw at least two dozen *(species)* of birds on our nature walk.
6. *(Mushroom)* are edible, fleshy *(fungus).*
7. Marcus and Tyisha packed the old *(textbook)* into *(box).*
8. The zoo bought two ring-tailed lemurs and three howler *(monkey).*
9. Medical school is where *(man)* and *(woman)* study to become *(doctor).*
10. There were three *(runner-up)* in the Battle of the Bands.
11. Many Asian American *(family)* live in my neighborhood.

Next Step: Write sentences using plurals of the following words: *cavity, goose, octopus,* and *holiday.*

Abbreviations

634.1 Abbreviations

An **abbreviation** is the shortened form of a word or phrase. The following abbreviations are always acceptable in any kind of writing:

Mr. **Mrs.** **Ms.** **Dr.** **a.m., p.m.** (A.M., P.M.)

B.C.E. (before the Common Era) **C.E.** (Common Era)

B.A. **M.A.** **Ph.D.** **M.D.** **Sr.** **Jr.**

Caution: Do not abbreviate the names of states, countries, months, days, or units of measure in formal writing. Also, do not use signs or symbols (%, &) in place of words.

Common Abbreviations

AC alternating current
a.m. ante meridiem
ASAP as soon as possible
COD cash on delivery
DA district attorney
DC direct current
etc. and so forth
F Fahrenheit
FM frequency modulation
GNP gross national product
i.e. that is (Latin *id est*)
kg kilogram
km kilometer
kw kilowatt
l liter
lb. pound
m meter
M.D. doctor of medicine
mfg. manufacturing
mpg miles per gallon
mph miles per hour
oz. ounce
pd. paid
pg. (or p.) page
p.m. post meridiem
ppd. postpaid, prepaid
qt. quart
R.S.V.P. please reply
tbs., tbsp. tablespoon
tsp. teaspoon
vol. volume
vs. versus
yd. yard

Address Abbreviations

	Standard	Postal		Standard	Postal		Standard	Postal
Avenue	Ave.	AVE	Lake	L.	LK	Route	Rt.	RTE
Boulevard	Blvd.	BLVD	Lane	Ln.	LN	South	S.	S
Court	Ct.	CT	North	N.	N	Square	Sq.	SQ
Drive	Dr.	DR	Park	Pk.	PK	Station	Sta.	STA
East	E.	E	Parkway	Pky.	PKY	Street	St.	ST
Expressway	Expy.	EXPY	Place	Pl.	PL	Terrace	Ter.	TER
Heights	Hts.	HTS	Plaza	Plaza	PLZ	Turnpike	Tpke.	TPKE
Highway	Hwy.	HWY	Road	Rd.	RD	West	W.	W

Grammar Practice

Abbreviations 1

For each of the following sentences, write the correct abbreviation for the underlined word or words.

Example: Coach Chen told us to get off the field as soon as possible.
ASAP

1. On my cousin's wedding invitation, it said "please reply by May 10."
2. The district attorney for our county is Mister John B. Stepanek, Senior.
3. I wonder how long I could play my stereo on one kilowatt of electricity.
4. Grandpa always says that an ounce of prevention is worth a pound of cure.
5. At 238 miles per hour, an "Indy" car covers 350 feet of track per second.
6. Most banana plants stop growing when the temperature drops below 53 degrees Fahrenheit.
7. Noah Blain, doctor of medicine, operated on my sister's shoulder.
8. The television set we take camping uses direct current.
9. I listen mostly to frequency modulation radio stations.
10. Mom's new car averages 36 miles per gallon.
11. The cake recipe calls for one teaspoon of vanilla.
12. I was named after my uncle, Juan L. Martinez, Junior.
13. The Greek philosopher Aristotle was born in 384 before the Common Era.

Next Step: Rewrite these addresses using standard abbreviations.

123 Greenwillow Parkway
10 North Lincoln Boulevard
1659 Standish Court
13 South Linden Station
258 Willmore Terrace

Abbreviations . . .

636.1 Acronyms

An **acronym** is an abbreviation that can be pronounced as a word. It does not require periods.

WHO — World Health Organization

ROM — read-only memory

FAQ — frequently asked question

636.2 Initialisms

An **initialism** is similar to an acronym except that it cannot be pronounced as a word; the initials are pronounced individually.

PBS — Public Broadcasting System

BLM — Bureau of Land Management

WNBA — Women's National Basketball Association

Common Acronyms and Initialisms

AIDS	acquired immunodeficiency syndrome
CETA	Comprehensive Employment and Training Act
CIA	Central Intelligence Agency
FAA	Federal Aviation Administration
FBI	Federal Bureau of Investigation
FCC	Federal Communications Commission
FDA	Food and Drug Administration
FDIC	Federal Deposit Insurance Corporation
FHA	Federal Housing Administration
FmHA	Farmers Home Authority
FTC	Federal Trade Commission
IRS	Internal Revenue Service
MADD	Mothers Against Drunk Driving
NAFTA	North American Free Trade Agreement
NASA	National Aeronautics and Space Administration
NATO	North Atlantic Treaty Organization
OEO	Office of Economic Opportunity
OEP	Office of Emergency Preparedness
ORV	off-road vehicle
OSHA	Occupational Safety and Health Administration
PAC	political action committee
PIN	personal identification number
PSA	public service announcement
ROTC	Reserve Officers' Training Corps
SADD	Students Against Destructive Decisions
SSA	Social Security Administration
SUV	sport utility vehicle
SWAT	special weapons and tactics
TDD	telecommunications device for the deaf
TMJ	temporomandibular joint
TVA	Tennessee Valley Authority
VA	Veterans Affairs
VISTA	Volunteers in Service to America
WAC	Women's Army Corps
WAVES	Women Accepted for Volunteer Emergency Service

Grammar Practice

Abbreviations 2

- Acronyms
- Initialisms

Write the correct abbreviation for each phrase below. Tell whether it is an acronym or an initialism.

Example: Federal Emergency Management Agency
FEMA–acronym

1. American Kennel Club
2. telecommunications device for the deaf
3. National Basketball Association
4. personal identification number
5. Federal Bureau of Investigation
6. National Aeronautics and Space Administration
7. attention deficit disorder
8. North Atlantic Treaty Organization
9. special weapons and tactics
10. Internal Revenue Service
11. Federal Aviation Administration
12. Food and Drug Administration
13. parental guidance
14. also known as

Next Step: Make up a slogan for your school that can be abbreviated as an acronym.

Numbers

638.1
Numbers Under 10

Numbers from one to nine are usually written as words; all numbers 10 and over are usually written as numerals.

two seven nine 10 25 106

638.2
Numerals Only

Use numerals to express any of the following forms:

money	**$2.39**
decimals	**26.2**
percentages	**8 percent**
chapters	**chapter 7**
pages	**pages 287–289**
time (with "a.m." or "p.m.")	**4:30 p.m.**
telephone numbers	**1-800-555-1212**
dates	**44 B.C.E.; July 6, 1942**
identification numbers	**Highway 36**
addresses	**2125 Cairn Road**
ZIP codes	**60004**
statistics	**a vote of 23 to 4**

When abbreviations and symbols are used (for instance, in science or math), always use numerals with them.

12° C 7% 33 kg 9 cm 55 mph

638.3
Very Large Numbers

You may use a combination of numerals and words for very large numbers.

Of the 17 million residents of the three Midwestern states, only 1.3 million are blonds.

You may spell out a large number that can be written as two words. If more than two words are needed, use the numeral.

More than nine thousand people attended the concert.

About 3,011 people missed the opening act.

Grammar Practice

Numbers 1

- Numbers Under 10
- Numerals Only
- Very Large Numbers

For each of the following sentences, write the underlined number the correct way. If it is already in the correct form, write "correct."

Example: In the nineteen sixties, Americans drove large, heavy cars.
1960s

1. Many cars of that decade got only nine miles per gallon.
2. A car built in two thousand four is quite a bit more efficient than those built 40 years ago.
3. It is safest to drive under fifty-five miles per hour.
4. In 1965, there were more than 90,300,000 cars registered in the United States.
5. Today, there are about 240 million cars in use on our nation's roads.
6. In 2006, there were about 201,000,000 drivers in the United States, each averaging 14,000 miles per year.
7. Many roads in major cities get traffic jams between seven a.m. and nine a.m.
8. People would save fuel and face less traffic if more cars carried at least 2 people.
9. The business located at two forty-nine South Cheps Road requires all its employees to carpool or use public transportation.

Next Step: Complete the following sentence with your own numbers: Today, ___*(date)*___, at ___*(time)*___ it was ___*(temperature)*___ degrees.

Numbers . . .

640.1 Comparing Numbers

If you are comparing two or more numbers in a sentence, write all of them the same way: as numerals or as words.

Students from 9 to 14 years old are invited.

Students from nine to fourteen years old are invited.

640.2 Numbers in Compound Modifiers

A compound modifier may include a numeral.

The floorboards come in 10-foot lengths.

When a number comes before a compound modifier that includes a numeral, use words instead of numerals.

We need eleven 10-foot lengths to finish the floor.

Ms. Brown must grade twenty 12-page reports.

640.3 Sentence Beginnings

Use words, not numerals, to begin a sentence.

Nine students had turned in their homework. Fourteen students said they were unable to finish the assignment.

640.4 Time and Money

When time or money is expressed with an abbreviation, use numerals. When either is expressed with words, spell out the number.

6:00 a.m. or **six o'clock**

$25 or **twenty-five dollars**

SCHOOL DAZE
Jerry, haven't you finished your paper yet?

No, it's not due until three o'clock, and Mrs. Wright told me to add a few new twists and wrinkles.

Grammar Practice

Numbers 2

- Sentence Beginnings
- Time and Money

If a number in the following sentences is not in the right form, write it correctly.

Example: 14 teams compete in the girls' softball league.
Fourteen

1. The softball games at Carrey Middle School start at four p.m.
2. 40 girls from my school signed up to play softball this season.
3. It costs the school about $5 hundred a month to support all of its teams.
4. The teams practice after school on Tuesdays and Thursdays until five-thirty p.m.
5. Each player must pay 25 dollars for equipment and supplies.

- Comparing Numbers
- Numbers in Compound Modifiers

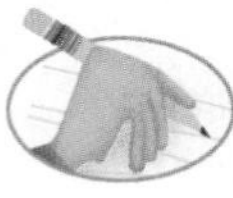

Rewrite the underlined parts of the following sentences so that they are correct.

Example: Girls from <u>nine to 14 years old</u> compete in the league.
9 to 14 years old (or) nine to fourteen years old

1. Players may participate in <u>ten to 16 games</u> each month.
2. We have <u>seven home games and 10 away games</u> this season.
3. Carlos Moy is an umpire for <u>3 90-minute games</u> each week.
4. Each team has at least <u>3 twelve-inch softballs</u>.
5. Our school has <u>4 nine-player teams</u>.

Improving Spelling

642.1
i* before *e

Write *i* before *e* except after *c,* or when sounded like *a* as in *neighbor* and *weigh.*

Some Exceptions to the Rule: *counterfeit, either, financier, foreign, height, heir, leisure, neither, science, seize, sheik, species, their, weird*

642.2
Silent *e*

If a word ends with a silent *e,* drop the *e* before adding a suffix that begins with a vowel. There are exceptions, for example, *knowledgeable* and *changeable.*

state — stating — statement **use — using — useful**
like — liking — likeness **nine — ninety — nineteen**

NOTE You do not drop the *e* when the suffix begins with a consonant. Exceptions include *truly, argument,* and *ninth.*

642.3
Words Ending in *y*

When *y* is the last letter in a word and the *y* comes just after a consonant, change the *y* to *i* before adding any suffix except those beginning with *i.*

fry — fries — frying **happy — happiness**
hurry — hurried — hurrying **beauty — beautiful**
lady — ladies

When forming the plural of a word that ends with a *y* that comes just after a vowel, add *s.*

toy — toys **play — plays** **monkey — monkeys**

642.4
Consonant Endings

When a one-syllable word ends in a consonant *(bat)* preceded by one vowel *(bat),* double the final consonant before adding a suffix that begins with a vowel *(batting).*

sum — summary **god — goddess**

When a multisyllable word ends in a consonant preceded by one vowel *(control),* the accent is on the last syllable *(contról),* and the suffix begins with a vowel *(ing)*—the same rule holds true: double the final consonant *(controlling).*

prefer — preferred **begin — beginning**

Grammar Practice

Spelling 1

- *i* before *e*
- Silent *e*
- Words Ending in *y*
- Consonant Endings

For each sentence below, write the correct spelling of any misspelled word. If no word is misspelled, write "correct."

Example: Dragon boat races are an interesting and exciteing part of Chinese history.
exciting

1. The colorful boats look like feirce dragons with scary heads, scaly bodyes, and long tails.
2. Actually, they're quite beautiful.
3. Centurys ago, some Chinese people believed that dragon boat raceing would bring them bountyful crops.
4. They rowed on the river in thier boats, beatting drums to scare fish and water dragons away.
5. They also wraped rice in leaves and threw them into the river.
6. Today, people race the dragon boats cheifly for amusment during Chinese festivals.
7. The festivals and races are enjoied by people in cities around the world.
8. Observers can expereince the thrill of all the druming and yelling.
9. Identifiing which boat will win isn't easy.
10. I am beting that the rowers are no longer nerveous about water dragons comeing to get them.

Next Step: Review the list of spelling words on pages 645–651. Choose three words that give you trouble. Write a sentence for each that will help you remember its correct spelling.

Grammar Practice

Spelling 2

- *i* before *e*
- Silent *e*
- Words Ending in *y*
- Consonant Endings

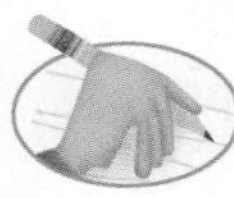

For each sentence below, write the correct spelling of any word that is misspelled. If no word is misspelled, write "correct."

Example: Angelica spent time at the art museum admireing the Renaissance paintings.
admiring

1. Ryan prefered to read about the anceint kingdoms of Egypt.
2. Borna thought that the science assignment was sensless.
3. Viu likes decorating her room with fresh flowers.
4. Our science teacher's cheif complaint is the condition of the school's microscopes.
5. He has identifyed the brand he would like to purchase.
6. Five students measured the boundarys of the school property.
7. On a hot day, Hamal faned himself with a peice of paper.
8. Everyone is talking about the wierd weather we're haveing.
9. Every morning, Principal Phipps reads the day's announcments.
10. The aviation industry plans to improve the guidance systems for its aircraft.
11. Although Shania likes shoping, she knows she is not very good at bargainning.
12. Sam twisted his right ankle, so he was hoping around on his left foot.
13. Rozene could not beleive how much snow was falling.
14. For your own safty, do not eat any food that appears to be roting.

Yellow Pages Guide to Improved Spelling

Be patient. Becoming a good speller takes time.

Check your spelling by using a dictionary or list of commonly misspelled words (like the list that follows). And, remember, don't rely too much on computer spell-checkers.

Learn the correct pronunciation of each word you are trying to spell. Knowing the correct pronunciation of a word will help you remember how it's spelled.

Look up the meaning of each word as you are checking the dictionary for pronunciation. (Knowing how to spell a word is of little use if you don't know what it means.)

Practice spelling the word before you close the dictionary. Look away from the page and try to see the word in your mind's eye. Write the word on a piece of paper. Check the spelling in the dictionary and repeat the process until you are able to spell the word correctly.

Keep a list of the words that you misspell.

Write often. As noted educator Frank Smith said, "There is little point in learning to spell if you have little intention of writing."

A

abbreviate
aboard
about
above
absence
absent
absolute (ly)
abundance
accelerate
accident
accidental (ly)
accompany
accomplice
accomplish
according
account
accurate
accustom (ed)
ache
achieve (ment)
acre
across
actual
adapt
addition (al)
address
adequate
adjust (ment)
admire
adventure
advertise (ment)
advertising
afraid
after
afternoon
afterward
again
against
agreeable
agree (ment)
ah
aid
airy
aisle
alarm
alcohol
alike
alive
alley
allowance
all right
almost
already
although
altogether
aluminum
always
amateur
ambulance
amendment
among
amount
analyze
ancient
angel
anger
angle
angry
animal

anniversary
announce
annoyance
annual
anonymous
another
answer
Antarctic
anticipate
anxiety
anxious
anybody
anyhow
anyone
anything
anyway
anywhere
apartment
apiece
apologize
apparent (ly)
appeal
appearance
appetite
appliance
application
appointment
appreciate
approach
appropriate
approval
approximate
architect
Arctic
aren't
argument
arithmetic
around
arouse
arrange (ment)
arrival
article
artificial

asleep
assassin
assign (ment)
assistance
associate
association
assume
athlete
athletic
attach
attack (ed)
attempt
attendance
attention
attitude
attorney
attractive
audience
August
author
authority
automobile
autumn
available
avenue
average
awful (ly)
awkward

B

baggage
baking
balance
balloon
ballot
banana
bandage
bankrupt
barber
bargain
barrel

basement
basis
basket
battery
beautiful
beauty
because
become
becoming
before
began
beggar
beginning
behave
behavior
being
belief
believe
belong
beneath
benefit (ed)
between
bicycle
biscuit
blackboard
blanket
blizzard
bother
bottle
bottom
bough
bought
bounce
boundary
breakfast
breast
breath (n.)
breathe (v.)
breeze
bridge
brief
bright
brilliant

brother
brought
bruise
bubble
bucket
buckle
budget
building
bulletin
buoyant
bureau
burglar
bury
business
busy
button

cabbage
cafeteria
calendar
campaign
canal
cancel (ed)
candidate
candle
canister
cannon
cannot
canoe
can't
canyon
capacity
captain
carburetor
cardboard
career
careful
careless
carpenter
carriage

carrot
cashier
casserole
casualty
catalog
catastrophe
catcher
caterpillar
catsup
ceiling
celebration
cemetery
census
century
certain (ly)
certificate
challenge
champion
changeable
character (istic)
chief
children
chimney
chocolate
choice
chorus
circumstance
citizen
civilization
classmates
classroom
climate
climb
closet
clothing
coach
cocoa
cocoon
coffee
collar
college
colonel
color

colossal
column
comedy
coming
commercial
commission
commit
commitment
committed
committee
communicate
community
company
comparison
competition
competitive (ly)
complain
complete (ly)
complexion
compromise
conceive
concerning
concert
concession
concrete
condemn
condition
conductor
conference
confidence
congratulate
connect
conscience
conscious
conservative
constitution
continue
continuous
control
controversy
convenience
convince
coolly

cooperate
corporation
correspond
cough
couldn't
counter
counterfeit
country
county
courage
courageous
court
courteous
courtesy
cousin
coverage
cozy
cracker
cranky
crawl
creditor
cried
criticize
cruel
crumb
crumble
cupboard
curiosity
curious
current
custom
customer
cylinder

daily
dairy
damage
danger (ous)
daughter
dealt

deceive
decided
decision
declaration
decorate
defense
definite (ly)
definition
delicious
dependent
depot
describe
description
desert
deserve
design
desirable
despair
dessert
deteriorate
determine
develop (ment)
device (n.)
devise (v.)
diamond
diaphragm
diary
dictionary
difference
different
difficulty
dining
diploma
director
disagreeable
disappear
disappoint
disapprove
disastrous
discipline
discover
discuss
discussion

disease
dissatisfied
distinguish
distribute
divide
divine
divisible
division
doctor
doesn't
dollar
dormitory
doubt
dough
dual
duplicate

eager (ly)
economy
edge
edition
efficiency
eight
eighth
either
elaborate
electricity
elephant
eligible
ellipse
embarrass
emergency
emphasize
employee
employment
enclose
encourage
engineer
enormous
enough
entertain
enthusiastic
entirely
entrance
envelop (v.)
envelope (n.)
environment
equipment
equipped
equivalent
escape
especially
essential
establish
every
evidence
exaggerate
exceed
excellent
except
exceptional (ly)
excite
exercise
exhaust (ed)
exhibition
existence
expect
expensive
experience
explain
explanation
expression
extension
extinct
extraordinary
extreme (ly)

facilities
familiar
family
famous
fascinate
fashion
fatigue (d)
faucet
favorite
feature
February
federal
fertile
field
fierce
fiery
fifty
finally
financial (ly)
foliage
forcible
foreign
forfeit
formal (ly)
former (ly)
forth
fortunate
forty
forward
fountain
fourth
fragile
freight
friend (ly)
frighten
fulfill
fundamental
further
furthermore

gadget
gauge
generally
generous
genius
gentle
genuine
geography
ghetto
ghost
gnaw
government
governor
graduation
grammar
grateful
grease
grief
grocery
grudge
gruesome
guarantee
guard
guardian
guess
guidance
guide
guilty
gymnasium

hammer
handkerchief
handle (d)
handsome
haphazard
happen
happiness

harass
hastily
having
hazardous
headache
height
hemorrhage
hesitate
history
hoarse
holiday
honor
hoping
hopping
horrible
hospital
humorous
hurriedly
hydraulic
hygiene
hymn

icicle
identical
illegible
illiterate
illustrate
imaginary
imaginative
imagine
imitation
immediate (ly)
immense
immigrant
immortal
impatient
importance
impossible
improvement
inconvenience
incredible
indefinitely
independence
independent
individual
industrial
inferior
infinite
inflammable
influential
initial
initiation
innocence
innocent
installation
instance
instead
insurance
intelligence
intention
interested
interesting
interfere
interpret
interrupt
interview
investigate
invitation
irrigate
island
issue

jealous (y)
jewelry
journal
journey
judgment
juicy

kitchen
knew
knife
knives
knock
knowledge
knuckles

label
laboratory
ladies
language
laugh
laundry
lawyer
league
lecture
legal
legible
legislature
leisure
length
liable
library
license
lieutenant
lightning
likable
likely
liquid
listen
literature
living
loaves
loneliness
loose
lose
loser
losing
lovable
lovely

machinery
magazine
magnificent
maintain
majority
making
manual
manufacture
marriage
material
mathematics
maximum
mayor
meant
measure
medicine
medium
message
mileage
miniature
minimum
minute
mirror
miscellaneous
mischievous
miserable
missile
misspell
moisture
molecule
monotonous
monument
mortgage
mountain
muscle

musician
mysterious

naive
natural (ly)
necessary
negotiate
neighbor (hood)
neither
nickel
niece
nineteen
nineteenth
ninety
ninth
noisy
noticeable
nuclear
nuisance

obedience
obey
obstacle
occasion
occasional (ly)
occur
occurred
offense
official
often
omission
omitted
operate
opinion
opponent
opportunity
opposite
ordinarily
original
outrageous

package
paid
pamphlet
paradise
paragraph
parallel
paralyze
parentheses
partial
participant
participate
particular (ly)
pasture
patience
peculiar
people
perhaps
permanent
perpendicular
persistent
personal (ly)
personnel
perspiration
persuade
phase
physician
piece
pitcher
planned
plateau
playwright
pleasant
pleasure
pneumonia
politician
possess
possible
practical (ly)
prairie
precede
precious
precise (ly)
precision
preferable
preferred
prejudice
preparation
presence
previous
primitive
principal
principle
prisoner
privilege
probably
procedure
proceed
professor
prominent
pronounce
pronunciation
protein
psychology
pumpkin
pure

quarter
questionnaire
quiet
quite
quotient

R

raise
realize
really
receipt
receive
received
recipe
recognize
recommend
reign
relieve
religious
remember
repetition
representative
reservoir
resistance
respectfully
responsibility
restaurant
review
rhyme
rhythm
ridiculous
route

safety
salad
salary
sandwich
satisfactory
Saturday
scene
scenery
schedule
science
scissors

scream
screen
season
secretary
seize
sensible
sentence
separate
several
sheriff
shining
similar
since
sincere (ly)
skiing
sleigh
soldier
souvenir
spaghetti
specific
sphere
sprinkle
squeeze
squirrel
statue
stature
statute
stomach
stopped
straight
strength
stretched
studying
subtle
succeed
success
sufficient
summarize
supplement
suppose
surely
surprise
syllable
sympathy
symptom

tariff
technique
temperature
temporary
terrible
territory
thankful
theater
their
there
therefore
thief
thorough (ly)
though
throughout
tired
tobacco
together
tomorrow
tongue
touch
tournament
toward
tragedy
treasurer
tried
tries
trouble
truly
Tuesday
typical

unconscious
unfortunate (ly)
unique
university
unnecessary
until
usable
useful
using
usual (ly)
utensil

vacation
vacuum
valuable
variety
various
vegetable
vehicle
very
vicinity
view
villain
violence
visible
visitor
voice
volume
voluntary
volunteer

wander
wasn't
weather
Wednesday
weigh
weird
welcome
welfare
whale
where
whether
which
whole
wholly
whose
width
women
worthwhile
wouldn't
wreckage
writing
written

yellow
yesterday
yield

Using the Right Word

652.1
a, an

A is used before words that begin with a consonant sound; *an* is used before words that begin with any vowel sound except long "u."

a heap, a cat, an idol, an elephant, an honor, a historian, an umbrella, a unicorn

652.2
accept, except

The verb *accept* means "to receive"; the preposition *except* means "other than."

Melissa graciously accepted defeat. (verb)

All the boys except Zach were here. (preposition)

652.3
affect, effect

Affect is almost always a verb; it means "to influence." *Effect* can be a verb, but it is most often used as a noun that means "the result."

How does population growth affect us?

What are the effects of population growth?

652.4
allowed, aloud

The verb *allowed* means "permitted" or "let happen"; *aloud* is an adverb that means "in a normal voice."

We aren't allowed to read aloud in the library.

652.5
allusion, illusion

An *allusion* is a brief reference to or mention of a famous person, place, thing, or idea. An *illusion* is a false impression or idea.

The Great Dontini, a magician, made an allusion to Houdini as he created the illusion of sawing his assistant in half.

652.6
a lot

A lot is not one word, but two; it is a general descriptive phrase meaning "plenty." (It should be avoided in formal writing.)

652.7
all right

All right is not one word, but two; it is a phrase meaning "satisfactory" or "okay." (Please note, the following *are* spelled correctly: *always, altogether, already, almost.*)

Grammar Practice

Using the Right Word 1

■ accept, except; affect, effect; allusion, illusion; all right

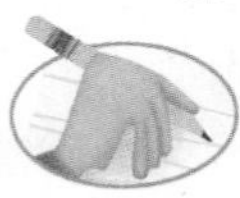

For each of the following sentences, write the correct choice from each set of words in parentheses.

Example: Dennis thought he saw pools of water in the parking lot on that hot, hot day, but it was just an *(allusion, illusion).*
illusion

1. I guess the sun can *(affect, effect)* us in many ways!
2. We will give away all the kittens *(accept, except)* the two that we're keeping.
3. Will it be *(all right, alright)* with your mom if you take one of the kittens?
4. Ms. Whitsom thinks constant cloudy weather has a bad *(affect, effect)* on a person's outlook.
5. In order for a magician to be successful, the audience must believe in the *(allusions, illusions)* he or she creates.
6. Your outfit looks *(all right, alright)* to me.
7. All the mail was addressed to Dad *(accept, except)* for one handwritten letter, which was addressed to me.
8. "Please *(accept, except)* my apology," the letter began.
9. Some students did not understand Roy's *(allusion, illusion)* to *Star Trek* in his speech during science class.

Next Step: Write three sentences that show you know the meaning of these words: *allusion, effect,* and *except*.

654.1
already, all ready

Already is an adverb that tells when. *All ready* is a phrase meaning "completely ready."

We have already eaten breakfast; now we are all ready for school.

654.2
altogether, all together

Altogether is always an adverb meaning "completely." *All together* is used to describe people or things that are gathered in one place at one time.

Ms. Monces held her baton in the air and said, "Okay, class, all together now: sing!"

Unfortunately, there was altogether too much street noise for us to hear her.

654.3
among, between

Among is used when speaking of more than two persons or things. *Between* is used when speaking of only two.

The three friends talked among themselves as they tried to choose between trumpet or trombone lessons.

654.4
amount, number

Amount is used to describe things that you cannot count. *Number* is used when you can actually count the persons or things.

The amount of interest in playing the tuba is shown by the number of kids learning to play the instrument.

654.5
annual, biannual, semiannual, biennial, perennial

An *annual* event happens once every year. A *biannual* (or *semiannual*) event happens twice a year. A *biennial* event happens once every two years. A *perennial* event happens year after year.

The annual PTA rummage sale is so successful that it will now be a semiannual event.

The neighbor has some wonderful perennial flowers.

654.6
ant, aunt

An *ant* is an insect. An *aunt* is a female relative (the sister of a person's mother or father).

My aunt is an entomologist, a scientist who studies ants and other insects.

654.7
ascent, assent

Ascent is the act of rising or climbing; *assent* is agreement.

After the group's ascent of five flights of stairs to the meeting room, plans for elevator repairs met with quick assent.

Grammar Practice

Using the Right Word 2

■ **altogether, all together; among, between; amount, number; annual, biannual, semiannual, biennial, perennial; ascent, assent**

For each of the following sentences, write the correct choice from each set of words in parentheses.

Example: The *(ascent, assent)* of Mount Everest is hard and dangerous.
ascent

1. The *(amount, number)* of climbers who successfully climb Mount Everest varies from year to year.
2. For the people of Tibet and Nepal, the arrival of climbing teams every May has become *(an annual, a biennial, a perennial)* event.
3. Some climbing routes on the mountain are more dangerous than others because of the *(amount, number)* of snow on the ridges.
4. The *(amount, number)* of days with good weather is very low.
5. Some critics believe that there are *(altogether, all together)* too many inexperienced climbers on Mount Everest.
6. Mountaineers must scramble *(among, between)* numerous ice-covered rocks.
7. Prior to a climb, each hiker must *(ascent, assent)* to doing his or her part for the team.
8. *(Altogether, All together),* team members decide on tasks for the day.
9. As two climbers make their way up the mountain, the distance *(among, between)* them is usually not very great.
10. One man who climbs once in May and once in October says his *(biannual, biennial)* climbs keep him in shape.
11. After reaching the top of Mount Everest each year during a five-year period, a seasoned mountaineer said that these *(annual, semiannual)* climbs had worn him out.

656.1
bare, bear

The adjective *bare* means "naked." A *bear* is a large, heavy animal with shaggy hair.

Despite his bare feet, the man chased the polar bear across the snow.

The verb *bear* means "to put up with" or "to carry."

Shondra could not bear another of her older sister's lectures.

656.2
base, bass

Base is the foundation or the lower part of something. *Bass* (pronounced like "base") is a deep sound or tone.

The stereo speakers are on a base so solid that even the loudest bass tones don't rattle it.

Bass (rhymes with "mass") is a fish.

Jim hooked a record-setting bass, but it got away . . . so he says.

656.3
beat, beet

The verb *beat* means "to strike, to defeat," and the noun *beat* is a musical term for rhythm or tempo. A *beet* is a carrot-like vegetable (often red).

The beat of the drum in the marching band encouraged the fans to cheer on the team. After they beat West High's team four games to one, many team members were as red as a beet.

656.4
berth, birth

Berth is a space or compartment. *Birth* is the process of being born.

We pulled aside the curtain in our train berth to view the birth of a new day outside our window.

656.5
beside, besides

Beside means "by the side of." *Besides* means "in addition to."

Besides a flashlight, Kedar likes to keep his pet boa beside his bed at night.

656.6
billed, build

Billed means either "to be given a bill" or "to have a beak." The verb *build* means "to construct."

We asked the carpenter to build us a birdhouse. She billed us for time and materials.

656.7
blew, blue

Blew is the past tense of "blow." *Blue* is a color and is also used to mean "feeling low in spirits."

As the wind blew out the candles in the dark blue room, I felt more blue than ever.

Grammar Practice

Using the Right Word 3

■ **bare, bear; base, bass; berth, birth; beside, besides**

For each of the following sentences, write a word from the list above to fill in the blank.

Example: At the ________ of the Statue of Liberty is a plaque that says her lamp is a sign of welcome to those seeking freedom.
base

1. ________ the European countries, immigrants to the United States come from Africa, Asia, and South America.
2. Pictures of immigrants in the early 1900s show children with ________ hands in cold weather.
3. The desire for freedom and opportunity was at the ________ of many immigrants' decisions to endure the journey.
4. They brought with them only the ________ minimum of belongings.
5. Many immigrants would spend most of the long voyage in a crowded ________ below the waterline of the ship.
6. From there, the passengers could hear and sometimes feel the deep ________ sound of the ship's engines.
7. The ship's crew members were occasionally called on to assist in the ________ of a baby.
8. After a two-week voyage, many passengers couldn't ________ another day at sea.
9. Tugboats ________ the ocean liners guided them into the harbor as the weary travelers celebrated.

Next Step: Find the other definitions for *bear* and *bass* explained on the facing page. Write two sentences that show your understanding of those definitions.

658.1
board, bored

A *board* is a piece of wood. *Board* also means "a group or council that helps run an organization."

The school board approved the purchase of 50 pine boards for the woodworking classes.

Bored means "to become weary or tired of something." It can also mean "made a hole by drilling."

Dulé bored a hole in the ice and dropped in a fishing line. Waiting and waiting for a bite bored him.

658.2
borrow, lend

Borrow means "to *receive* for temporary use." *Lend* means "to *give* for temporary use."

I asked Mom, "May I borrow $15 for a CD?"

She said, "I can lend you $15 until next Friday."

658.3
brake, break

A *brake* is a device used to stop a vehicle. The verb *break* means "to split, crack, or destroy"; as a noun, *break* means "gap or interruption."

After the brake on my bike failed, I took a break to fix it so I wouldn't break a bone.

658.4
bring, take

Use *bring* when the action is moving toward the speaker; use *take* when the action is moving away from the speaker.

Grandpa asked me to take the garbage out and bring him today's paper.

658.5
by, buy, bye

By is a preposition meaning "near" or "not later than." *Buy* is a verb meaning "to purchase."

By tomorrow I hope to buy tickets for the final match of the tournament.

Bye is the position of being automatically advanced to the next tournament round without playing.

Our soccer team received a bye because of our winning record.

658.6
can, may

Can means "able to," while *may* means "permitted to."

"Can I go to the library?"
(This actually means "Are my mind and body strong enough to get me there?")

"May I go?"
(This means "Do I have your permission to go?")

Grammar Practice

Using the Right Word 4

- **borrow, lend; brake, break; bring, take; by, buy, bye; can, may**

For each of the following sentences, write the correct choice from each set of words in parentheses.

Example: When I was sick at home, I asked Salvatore to *(bring, take)* me my homework.
bring

1. Suddenly the car's *(brake, break)* pedal wasn't working.
2. By pulling up on the parking *(brake, break)* lever, Sanji was able to make the car stop.
3. Our team will sit out the first round if we are given a *(by, buy, bye)* in the tournament schedule.
4. Vanessa has some black pants that she'll *(borrow, lend)* me for the choir concert.
5. I still need to *(by, buy, bye)* a white shirt, though.
6. We need to ask if we *(can, may)* hold a party for Alex.
7. We don't mind if we have to *(bring, take)* our own food.
8. I can't find the pen that is usually kept right here *(by, buy, bye)* the phone.
9. All you need is a library card to *(borrow, lend)* books, CD's, or magazines from any library in the system.
10. You never have to *(by, buy, bye)* any of that again!
11. A city's crime record is one record that its citizens really don't want to *(brake, break)*.
12. "Here, let me *(bring, take)* that for you," Maura offered as I carried my heavy suitcase.
13. "No, thanks. I *(can, may)* carry it," I said.

Next Step: Write two sentences that show your understanding of the words *borrow* and *lend.*

660.1
canvas, canvass

Canvas is a heavy cloth; *canvass* means "ask people for votes or opinions."

Our old canvas tent leaks.

Someone with a clipboard is canvassing the neighborhood.

660.2
capital, capitol

Capital can be either a noun, referring to a city or to money, or an adjective, meaning "major or important." *Capitol* is used only when talking about a building.

The capitol building is in the capital city for a capital (major) **reason: The city government contributed the capital** (money) **for the building project.**

660.3
cell, sell

Cell means "a small room" or "a small unit of life basic to all plants and animals." *Sell* is a verb meaning "to give up for a price."

Today we looked at a human skin cell under a microscope.

Let's sell those old bicycles at the rummage sale.

660.4
cent, sent, scent

Cent (1/100 of a dollar) is a coin; *sent* is the past tense of the verb "send"; *scent* is an odor or a smell.

After our car hit a skunk, we sent our friends a postcard that said, "One cent doesn't go far, but skunk scent seems to last forever."

660.5
chord, cord

Chord may mean "an emotion or a feeling," but it is more often used to mean "the sound of three or more musical tones played at the same time." A *cord* is a string or rope.

The band struck a chord at the exact moment the mayor pulled the cord on the drape covering the new statue.

660.6
chose, choose

Chose (chōz) is the past tense of the verb *choose* (cho͞oz).

This afternoon Mom chose tacos and hot sauce; this evening she will choose an antacid.

660.7
coarse, course

Coarse means "rough or crude." *Course* means "a path" or "a class or series of studies."

In our cooking course, we learned to use coarse salt and freshly ground pepper in salads.

Grammar Practice

Using the Right Word 5

■ **canvas, canvass; capital, capitol; chord, cord; coarse, course**

Write a word from the above list to properly complete each of the following sentences.

Example: Phil used ________ sandpaper to remove the paint from the old dresser.
coarse

1. When Tasha was learning how to play the guitar, she played the same ________ over and over again.
2. The class trip included a tour of the ________ building in Washington, D.C.
3. Elaine's family fits into one huge ________ tent when they go camping.
4. They tie the bulky, heavy tent to the car roof with lots of nylon ________.
5. Last year the high school offered its first ________ in German.
6. Jackson is the state ________ of Mississippi.
7. Whenever our dog would get lost, we would ________ the neighborhood looking for him.
8. On my way to school yesterday, I took a ________ through the woods that I hadn't taken before.

Next Step: Write two sentences that show your understanding of *capital* and *capitol.*

662.1
complement, compliment

Complement means "to complete or go with." *Compliment* is an expression of admiration or praise.

Aunt Athena said, "Your cheese sauce really complements this cauliflower!"

"Thank you for the compliment," I replied.

662.2
continual, continuous

Continual refers to something that happens again and again; *continuous* refers to something that doesn't stop happening.

Sunlight hits Peoria, Iowa, on a continual basis; but sunlight hits the earth continuously.

662.3
counsel, council

When used as a noun, *counsel* means "advice"; when used as a verb, *counsel* means "to advise." *Council* refers to a group that advises.

The student council asked for counsel from its trusted adviser.

662.4
creak, creek

A *creak* is a squeaking sound; a *creek* is a stream.

I heard a creak from the old dock under my feet as I fished in the creek.

662.5
cymbal, symbol

A *cymbal* is a metal instrument shaped like a plate. A *symbol* is something (usually visible) that stands for or represents another thing or idea (usually invisible).

The damaged cymbal lying on the stage was a symbol of the band's final concert.

662.6
dear, deer

Dear means "loved or valued"; *deer* are animals.

My dear, old great-grandmother leaves corn and salt licks in her yard to attract deer.

662.7
desert, dessert

A *desert* is a barren wilderness. *Dessert* is a food served at the end of a meal.

In the desert, cold water is more inviting than even the richest dessert.

The verb *desert* means "to abandon"; the noun *desert* (pronounced like the verb) means "deserving reward or punishment."

A spy who deserts his country will receive his just deserts if he is caught.

Grammar Practice

Using the Right Word 6

- **complement, compliment; continual, continuous; counsel, council; dear, deer; desert, dessert**

For each numbered sentence below, write the correct choice from the set of words in parentheses.

Example: Some *(dear, deer)* appeared on the edge of the field.
deer

(1) After a light dinner, Kiana brought some *(desert, dessert)* to the table. **(2)** She said, "I also have the perfect *(complement, compliment)* for these brownies—hazelnut ice cream."

As she and Juwan ate, he kept making "mmm" sounds. **(3)** "I'll take that as a *(complement, compliment)*," Kiana said.

(4) Then she said, "Juwan, I've noticed there's a *(continual, continuous)* buzz coming from the refrigerator recently. It just won't stop. Do you think I should have it checked?"

(5) Juwan said, "Do you want my *(counsel, council)*, or do you want me to actually check it?"

(6) "Well, yes, please see if you can fix it yourself, *(dear, deer)*. And while you're at it, take a look at the humidifier, too. **(7)** It feels like a *(desert, dessert)* in here," Kiana said.

(8) "Kiana," Juwan said, "your *(continual, continuous)* requests for me to check things are a signal. Your apartment is falling apart!"

"I know. **(9)** I'm going to bring it up at the next renters' *(counsel, council)* meeting," she said. "In the meantime, thanks for being so handy!"

Next Step: Write a few lines of dialogue between two friends. Include at least two of the words from the list at the top of the page.

664.1
die, dye

Die (dying) means "to stop living." *Dye* (dyeing) is used to change the color of something.

The young girl hoped that her sick goldfish wouldn't die.
My sister dyes her hair with coloring that washes out.

664.2
faint, feign, feint

Faint means "feeble, without strength" or "to fall unconscious." *Feign* is a verb that means "to pretend or make up." *Feint* is a noun that means "a move or an activity that is pretended in order to divert attention."

The actors feigned a sword duel. One man staggered and fell in a feint. The audience gave faint applause.

664.3
farther, further

Farther is used when you are writing about a physical distance. *Further* means "additional."

Alaska reaches farther north than Iceland. For further information, check your local library.

664.4
fewer, less

Fewer refers to the number of separate units; *less* refers to bulk quantity.

I may have less money than you have, but I have fewer worries.

664.5
fir, fur

Fir refers to a type of evergreen tree; *fur* is animal hair.

The Douglas fir tree is named after a Scottish botanist.

An arctic fox has white fur in the winter.

664.6
flair, flare

Flair means "a natural talent" or "style"; *flare* means "to light up quickly" or "burst out" (or an object that does so).

Jenrette has a flair for remaining calm when other people's tempers flare.

664.7
for, four

The preposition *for* means "because of" or "directed to"; *four* is the number 4.

Mary had grilled steaks and chicken for the party, but the dog had stolen one of the four steaks.

Grammar Practice

Using the Right Word 7

- faint, feign, feint; farther, further; fewer, less; flair, flare; for, four

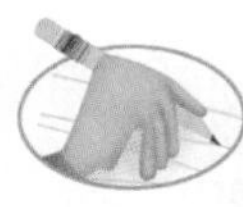

For each sentence below, write the word "correct" if the underlined word is used correctly. If it is incorrect, write the right word.

Example: During a marathon, which is just over 26 miles long, some runners feint along the way.
faint

1. Some of the runners have less stamina than others.
2. Those who can endure run further than many who begin the race.
3. Less runners finish the race than start it.
4. Near the end, a few minutes may feel like fore hours.
5. Only a surge of energy that flares up at this point will get the runner to the finish line.
6. Occasionally, a competitor will feign a move to one side before giving a burst of speed.
7. Most marathoners practice four at least a year prior to the race.
8. A few people run a marathon every year, but many are not interested in farther marathons once they've run one.
9. One runner, who has a definite flare for humor, wears a funny hat as he runs.
10. He also seems to stumble a lot, perhaps as some sort of faint.

Next Step: Write two sentences about some kind of race to show your understanding of the words *farther* and *further.*

666.1
good, well

Good is an adjective; *well* is nearly always an adverb.

The strange flying machines flew well. (The adverb *well* modifies *flew.*)

They looked good as they flew overhead. (The adjective *good* modifies *they*.)

When used in writing about health, *well* is an adjective.

The pilots did not feel well, however, after the long, hard race.

666.2
hare, hair

A *hare* is an animal similar to a rabbit; *hair* refers to the growth covering the head and body of mammals and human beings.

When a hare darted out in front of our car, the hair on my head stood up.

666.3
heal, heel

Heal means "to mend or restore to health." *Heel* is the back part of a human foot.

I got a blister on my heel from wearing my new shoes. It won't heal unless I wear my old ones.

666.4
hear, here

You *hear* sounds with your ears. *Here* is the opposite of *there* and means "nearby."

666.5
heard, herd

Heard is the past tense of the verb "to hear"; *herd* is a group of animals.

The herd of grazing sheep raised their heads when they heard the collie barking in the distance.

666.6
heir, air

An *heir* is a person who inherits something; *air* is what we breathe.

Will the next generation be heir to terminally polluted air?

666.7
hole, whole

A *hole* is a cavity or hollow place. *Whole* means "entire or complete."

The hole in the ozone layer is a serious problem requiring the attention of the whole world.

666.8
immigrate, emigrate

Immigrate means "to come into a new country or area." *Emigrate* means "to go out of one country to live in another."

Martin Ulferts immigrated to this country in 1882. He was only three years old when he emigrated from Germany.

Grammar Practice

Using the Right Word 8

- **good, well; heal, heel; hear, here; hole, whole; immigrate, emigrate**

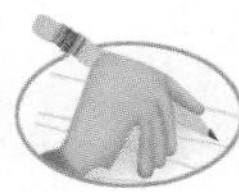

Each sentence below has a choice of words in parentheses. Write the word that makes the sentence correct.

Example: Did you *(hear, here)* the latest news?
hear

1. After her heart surgery, Granny Kasten is feeling surprisingly *(good, well).*
2. The doctor said it may take a few months for her to *(heal, heel)* completely.
3. When she *(immigrated, emigrated)* to this country, she was only 12 years old.
4. My sister Alison spends her *(hole, whole)* morning fixing her hair.
5. When Sybil broke her *(heal, heel),* she had to stay off her foot for two months.
6. My dad's parents *(immigrated, emigrated)* from Laos.
7. We often *(hear, here)* them talk about their lives there.
8. My grandparents adjusted *(good, well)* to living in this country.
9. I can't play in this weekend's concert because there is a *(hole, whole)* in my drum.
10. Deshawn is *(good, well)* at coming up with creative ideas for art projects.
11. Will this school still be *(hear, here)* in 50 years?

Next Step: Write three sentences that show you know the meaning of these words: *good, well,* and *heal.*

668.1
imply, infer

Imply means "to suggest indirectly"; *infer* means "to draw a conclusion from facts."

"Since you have to work, may I infer that you won't come to my party?" Guy asked.

"No, I only meant to imply that I would be late," Rochelle responded.

668.2
it's, its

It's is the contraction of "it is." *Its* is the possessive form of "it."

It's a fact that a minnow's teeth are in its throat.

668.3
knew, new

Knew is the past tense of the verb "know." *New* means "recent or modern."

If I knew how to fix it, I would not need a new one!

668.4
know, no

Know means "to recognize or understand." *No* means "the opposite of yes."

Phil, do you know Cheri?

No, I've never met her.

668.5
later, latter

Later means "after a period of time." *Latter* refers to the second of two things mentioned.

The band arrived later and set up the speakers and the lights. The latter made the stage look like a carnival ride.

668.6
lay, lie

Lay means "to place." (*Lay* is a transitive verb; that means it needs a word to complete the meaning.) *Lie* means "to recline." (*Lie* is an intransitive verb.)

Lay your sleeping bag on the floor before you lie down on it. (*Lay* needs the word *bag* to complete its meaning.)

668.7
lead, led

Lead (lēd) is a present tense verb meaning "to guide." The past tense of the verb is *led* (lĕd). The noun *lead* (lĕd) is the metal.

Guides planned to lead the settlers to safe quarters. Instead, they led them into a winter storm.

Peeling paint in old houses may contain lead.

668.8
learn, teach

Learn means "to get information"; *teach* means "to give information."

I want to learn how to sew. Will you teach me?

Grammar Practice

Using the Right Word 9

- **imply, infer; later, latter; lay, lie; learn, teach**

For each numbered word below, write the word "correct" if it is used correctly. If it is incorrect, write the right word.

Example: Are you inferring that I'm not smart enough?
implying

Mr. Levine was attempting to **(1)** learn us a difficult scientific concept. After answering some questions, he said, "From the looks on some of your faces, I **(2)** imply that you still don't get it."

"Mr. Levine," Davion said, "isn't there another way that we can **(3)** learn this?"

Albert added, "Why do we need to know this, anyway?"

Without being too obvious, Mr. Levine **(4)** implied that we would all fail the exam if we didn't understand it. "Furthermore," he said, "if you don't have some basic curiosity, you might as well just **(5)** lay down and sleep away your life."

(6) Latter in the week, Mr. Levine came up with a different way to **(7)** teach us about the characteristics of atoms. He asked Chaya to **(8)** lie her fleece jacket on some carpet. (He had brought a piece of the **(9)** later from home.) Then he shut off the light and told Chaya to drag her jacket back and forth on the carpet. There were sparks! Mr. Levine explained to us that static forms when one material pulls electrons away from the other. And, just like that, we had **(10)** learned something!

Next Step: Here is an easy way to remember the difference between *imply* and *infer*: "When **you** (with a *y*) imply, **I** infer." Try to think of something that will help you remember the difference between *lay* and *lie.*

670.1 leave, let

Leave means "fail to take along." *Let* means "allow."

Rozi wanted to leave her boots at home, but Jorge wouldn't let her.

670.2 like, as

Like is a preposition meaning "similar to"; *as* is a conjunction meaning "to the same degree" or "while." *Like* usually introduces a phrase; *as* usually introduces a clause.

The glider floated like a bird. The glider floated as the pilot had hoped it would.

As we circled the airfield, we saw maintenance carts moving like ants below us.

670.3 loose, lose, loss

Loose (lüs) means "free or untied"; *lose* (lo͞oz) means "to misplace or fail to win"; *loss* (lôs) means "something lost."

These jeans are too loose in the waist since my recent weight loss. I still want to lose a few more pounds.

670.4 made, maid

Made is the past tense of "make," which means to "create," "prepare," or "put in order." A *maid* is a female servant; *maid* is also used to describe an unmarried girl or young woman.

The hotel maid asked if our beds needed to be made.

Grandma made a chocolate cake for dessert.

A maid strolled in the garden before the concert.

670.5 mail, male

Mail refers to letters or packages handled by the postal service. *Male* refers to the masculine sex.

My little brother likes getting junk mail.

The male sea horse, not the female, takes care of the fertilized eggs.

670.6 main, mane

Main refers to the most important part. *Mane* is the long hair growing from the top or sides of the neck of certain animals, such as the horse, lion, and so on.

The main thing we noticed about the magician's tamed lion was its luxurious mane.

670.7 meat, meet

Meat is food or flesh; *meet* means "to come upon or encounter."

I'd like you to meet the butcher who sells the leanest meat in town.

Grammar Practice

Using the Right Word 10

- **like, as; loose, lose, loss; mail, male; main, mane**

For each of the following sentences, write the correct choice from the set of words in parentheses.

Example: The road crew set up detour signs and began repairing the village's *(main, mane)* street.
main

1. Bianca wears her hair in *(loose, lose, loss)* curls around her face.
2. For thousands of years, people have dreamed of flying *(like, as)* a bird.
3. In the 1980s, rock stars sported big, wild *(mains, manes)* of hair.
4. Most people know to avoid a bull moose, which is a *(mail, male)* moose, but a mother moose with a calf is equally dangerous.
5. Is California or Florida the *(main, mane)* producer of oranges in the United States?
6. The basketball players from Orson Middle School celebrated their victory *(like, as)* their fans screamed with joy.
7. The opposing team took their *(loose, lose, loss)* well, even though it was their last game.
8. Worrying causes many people to *(loose, lose, loss)* sleep.
9. In the hottest parts of Africa, some lions have almost no *(main, mane)*.
10. More and more people around the world now send and receive *(mail, male)* electronically.
11. I wish I had a friend *(like, as)* you.

Next Step: Write three sentences that show your understanding of the words *loss, loose,* and *lose.*

672.1 **medal, metal, meddle, mettle**

A *medal* is an award. *Metal* is an element like iron or gold. *Meddle* means "to interfere." *Mettle,* a noun, refers to quality of character.

Grandpa's friend received a medal for showing his mettle in battle. Grandma, who loves to meddle in others' business, asked if the award was a precious metal.

672.2 **miner, minor**

A *miner* digs in the ground for valuable ore. A *minor* is a person who is not legally an adult. *Minor* means "of no great importance" when used as an adjective.

The use of minors as miners is no minor problem.

672.3 **moral, morale**

Moral relates to what is right or wrong or to the lesson to be drawn from a story. *Morale* refers to a person's attitude or mental condition.

The moral of this story is "Everybody loves a winner."

After the unexpected win at football, morale was high throughout the town.

672.4 **morning, mourning**

Morning refers to the first part of the day (before noon); *mourning* means "showing sorrow."

Abby was mourning her test grades all morning.

672.5 **oar, or, ore**

An *oar* is a paddle used in rowing or steering a boat. *Or* is a conjunction indicating choice. *Ore* refers to a mineral made up of several different kinds of material, as in iron ore.

Either use one oar to push us away from the dock, or start the boat's motor.

Silver-copper ore is smelted and refined to extract each metal.

672.6 **pain, pane**

Pain is the feeling of being hurt. A *pane* is a section or part of something.

Dad looked like he was in pain when he found out we broke a pane of glass in the neighbor's front door.

672.7 **pair, pare, pear**

A *pair* is a couple (two); *pare* is a verb meaning "to peel"; *pear* is the fruit.

A pair of doves nested in the pear tree.

Please pare the apples for the pie.

Grammar Practice

Using the Right Word 11

meddle, mettle; moral, morale; morning, mourning; pain, pane

For each of the following sentences, write a word from the list above to fill in the blank.

Example: People's ________ often sags when winter drags on.
morale

1. Some people, ________ the long, warm summer days that have passed, can't see the beauty of autumn.
2. When Kaleb picked up the pile of heavy, wet clothes, he felt a sharp ________ in his back.
3. Once last winter, the extreme cold formed delicate frost flowers on the window ________.
4. Grandma thinks that the ________ values of young people have sunk to a new low.
5. "I appreciate your interest," said Alejandra, "but I really don't need you to ________ in this situation."
6. Thad is ________ the loss of his beloved dog.
7. Sometimes only time will ease the ________ of such a loss.
8. A firefighter's ________ is tested every time an emergency requires swift action.
9. I find that ________ is the best time for me to work out.
10. Is it a person's ________ obligation to help someone in need?
11. The team's high ________, despite a string of defeats, was inspiring.

Next Step: Write some sentences using one word from each of the four word groups at the top of the page.

674.1
past, passed

Passed is always a verb; it is the past tense of *pass*. *Past* can be used as a noun, as an adjective, or as a preposition.

A motorcycle passed my dad's 'Vette. (verb)

The old man won't forget the past. (noun)

I'm sorry, but I'd rather not talk about my past life. (adjective)

Old Blue walked right past the cat and never saw it. (preposition)

674.2
peace, piece

Peace means "harmony, or freedom from war." A *piece* is a part or fragment of something.

In order to keep peace among the triplets, each one had to have an identical piece of cake.

674.3
peak, peek, pique

A *peak* is a "high point" or a "pointed end." *Peek* means "brief look." *Pique*, as a verb, means "to excite by challenging"; as a noun, it means "a feeling of resentment."

Just a peek at Pike's Peak in the Rocky Mountains can pique a mountain climber's curiosity.

In a pique, she marched away from her giggling sisters.

674.4
personal, personnel

Personal means "private." *Personnel* are people working at a job.

Some thoughts are too personal to share.

The personnel manager will be hiring more workers.

674.5
plain, plane

A *plain* is an area of land that is flat or level; it also means "clearly seen or clearly understood" and "ordinary."

It's plain to see why the early settlers had trouble crossing the Great Plains.

Plane means "a flat, level surface" (as in geometry); it is also a tool used to smooth the surface of wood.

When I saw that the door wasn't a perfect plane, I used a plane to make it smooth.

674.6
pore, pour, poor

A *pore* is an opening in the skin. *Pour* means "to cause a flow or stream." *Poor* means "needy."

People perspire through the pores in their skin. Pour yourself a glass of water. Your poor body needs it!

Grammar Practice

Using the Right Word 12

- past, passed; peace, piece; peak, peek, pique; pore, pour, poor

For each sentence below, write the word "correct" if the underlined word is used correctly. If it is incorrect, write the right word.

Example: I looked up from my book and realized that my bus was now more than a mile past my stop.
correct

1. I peaked at my watch and wondered if I could possibly get to my dentist appointment in time.
2. I took out what I thought was my bus schedule and discovered that it was only a small peace of blank paper.
3. I got off the bus and saw just the pique of the building where I needed to be in 15 minutes.
4. I walked as fast as I could, and soon I was sweating from every pour on my body.
5. That would pique anyone's thirst, so I got a bottle of water from my backpack.
6. When I'd had enough, I decided to poor the rest of it on a small tree before throwing the empty bottle in a city waste can.
7. I was so focused on satisfying my thirst that I almost past the dentist's office.
8. I gratefully sat at piece in the waiting room.
9. My pore feet needed the rest.
10. I was glad that this experience was now in my passed.

Next Step: Write a paragraph about a time when you were late. Use as many of the words in the list at the top of the page as you can.

676.1
principal, principle

As an adjective, *principal* means "primary." As a noun, it can mean "a school administrator" or "a sum of money." *Principle* means "idea or doctrine."

> **My mom's principal goal is to save money so she can pay off the principal balance on her loan from the bank.**
>
> **Hey, Charlie, I hear the principal gave you a detention.**
>
> **The principle of freedom is based on the principle of self-discipline.**

676.2
quiet, quit, quite

Quiet is the opposite of "noisy." *Quit* means "to stop." *Quite* means "completely or entirely."

> **I quit mowing even though I wasn't quite finished.**
>
> **The neighborhood was quiet again.**

676.3
raise, rays, raze

Raise is a verb meaning "to lift or elevate." *Rays* are thin lines or beams. *Raze* is a verb that means "to tear down completely."

> **When I raise this shade, bright rays of sunlight stream into the room.**
>
> **Construction workers will raze the old theater to make room for a parking lot.**

676.4
real, very, really

Do not use the adjective *real* in place of the adverbs *very* or *really.*

> **The plants scattered throughout the restaurant are not real.**
>
> **Pimples are very embarrassing.**
>
> **Her nose is really small.**

676.5
red, read

Red is a color; *read,* pronounced the same way, is the past tense of the verb meaning "to understand the meaning of written words and symbols."

> **"I've read five books in two days," said the little boy.**
>
> **The librarian gave him a red ribbon.**

Grammar Practice

Using the Right Word 13

- **principal, principle; quiet, quit, quite; raise, rays, raze; real, very, really**

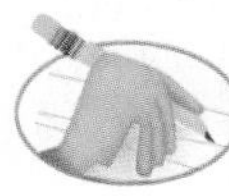

For each sentence below, write the word "correct" if the underlined word is used correctly. If it is incorrect, write the right word.

Example: The National Aeronautics and Space Administration (NASA) plans to raise some buildings to make way for new construction.
raze

1. A principle concern of NASA is the amount of debris left in space from previous space flights.
2. Although scientists keep track of the space debris, they are not quit sure they know where it all is.
3. Sound waves cannot travel in airless space, so space is a quite place.
4. At times, the raze of the sun are reflected by the shiny orbiting objects.
5. NASA worries about space debris, which is real small.
6. Even a tiny fleck of paint in space can be a real threat because it could be speeding along at almost 18,000 miles per hour.
7. Unfortunately, these very small objects cannot be tracked.
8. They rays the danger for flight crews.
9. In spite of the danger, the principle of exploration drives astronauts to travel into space again and again.
10. For a variety of reasons, some people think that the United States should quit sending rockets into space.

Next Step: Write two sentences on your thoughts about the space program. Use the words *real* and *really* correctly.

678.1
right, write, rite

Right means "correct or proper"; *right* is the opposite of "left"; it also refers to anything that a person has a legal claim to, as in "copyright." *Write* means "to record in print." *Rite* is a ritual or ceremonial act.

We have to write an essay about how our rights are protected by the Constitution.

Turn right at the next corner.

A rite of passage is a ceremony that celebrates becoming an adult.

678.2
scene, seen

Scene refers to the setting or location where something happens; it also means "sight or spectacle." *Seen* is a form of the verb "see."

The scene of the crime was roped off. We hadn't seen anyone go in or out of the building.

678.3
seam, seem

A *seam* is a line formed by connecting two pieces of material. *Seem* means "appear to exist."

Every Thanksgiving, it seems, I stuff myself so much that my shirt seams threaten to burst.

678.4
sew, so, sow

Sew is a verb meaning "to stitch"; *so* is a conjunction meaning "in order that." The verb *sow* means "to plant."

In Colonial times, the wife would sew the family clothes, and the husband would sow the family garden so the children could eat.

678.5
sight, cite, site

Sight means "the act of seeing" or "something that is seen." *Cite* means "to quote or refer to." A *site* is a location or position (including a Web site on the Internet).

The Alamo at night was a sight worth the trip. I was also able to cite my visit to this historical site in my history paper.

678.6
sit, set

Sit means "to put the body in a seated position." *Set* means "to place." (*Set* is a transitive verb; that means it needs a direct object to complete its meaning.)

How can you just sit there and watch as I set up all these chairs?

Grammar Practice

Using the Right Word 14

■ scene, seen; seam, seem; sew, so, sow; sit, set

For each of the following sentences, write a word from the list above to fill in the blank.

Example: Because even a little moisture can damage wood, please do not ________ that wet towel on the table.
set

1. "Did you notice that the ________ of this jacket is coming apart?" Mia asked.
2. "Yes," I replied, "I'm going to try to ________ it up myself."
3. Theo finally had to ________ down after standing for three hours during the football game.
4. When he ________ his soda on the bench, someone knocked it over.
5. Janelle and Rhonda stopped Craig to ask him if he had ________ their lost dog.
6. Landon wants to design his diorama to look like a ________ from the Battle of New Orleans.
7. Looking around, Jay said, "I ________ to have lost my hat."
8. Sharon promised to help her mother ________ some flower seeds in their little garden.
9. I'm trying to get extra pet-sitting jobs ________ that I will have enough money to get two kittens.
10. We ________ in assigned seats in this class.
11. My aunt does not like to be ________ without her makeup.
12. Although lemmings might ________ to jump off a ledge into the sea, they actually are looking for food and accidentally fall.
13. Khadijah is tired of her long hair, ________ she's going to get it cut short this weekend.

680.1
sole, soul

Sole means "single, only one"; *sole* also refers to the bottom surface of a foot or shoe. *Soul* refers to the spiritual part of a person.

Maggie got a job for the sole purpose of saving for a car.

The soles of these shoes are very thick.

"Who told you dogs don't have souls?" asked the kind veterinarian.

680.2
some, sum

Some means "an unknown number or part." *Sum* means "the whole amount."

The sum in the cash register was stolen by some thieves.

680.3
sore, soar

Sore means "painful"; to *soar* means "to rise or fly high into the air."

Craning to watch the eagle soar overhead, we soon had sore necks.

680.4
stationary, stationery

Stationary means "not movable"; *stationery* is the paper and envelopes used to write letters.

Grandpa designed and printed his own stationery.

All of the built-in furniture is stationary, of course.

680.5
steal, steel

Steal means "to take something without permission"; *steel* is a metal.

Early iron makers had to steal recipes for producing steel.

680.6
than, then

Than is used in a comparison; *then* tells when.

Since tomorrow's weather is supposed to be nicer than today's, we'll go to the zoo then.

680.7
their, there, they're

Their is a possessive pronoun, one that shows ownership. *There* is an adverb that tells where. *They're* is the contraction for "they are."

They're upset because their dog got into the garbage over there.

680.8
threw, through

Threw is the past tense of "throw." *Through* means "passing from one side to the other" or "by means of."

Through sheer talent and long practice, Nolan Ryan threw baseballs through the strike zone at more than 100 miles per hour.

Grammar Practice

Using the Right Word 15

- **sole, soul; sore, soar; stationary, stationery; than, then; threw, through**

If a word from the list above is used incorrectly in one of the following numbered sentences, write the correct word; otherwise, write "OK."

Example: When I finished reading Vilma's letter, I through it away.
threw

(1) I had noticed that Vilma's stationary had drawings of kites along the side of the page. That got me wondering: Why do people fly kites? **(2)** I guess the sole motive for most people is to have fun. **(3)** They would rather embrace the wind then try to fight it.

(4) Often I fly a kite, standing stationary against the raging gusts. **(5)** I watch my flying piece of art struggle in the wind, and then I gradually let out more string. **(6)** For me, the sole of kite flying is imagining myself as the kite. **(7)** Attached to the ground by only a thin string, I sore on the breeze. **(8)** I dart in and out through the clouds before diving toward earth again. **(9)** Eventually, my soar fingers mean the kite flying must end for the day. **(10)** It is time to slowly reel in the string than and put the kite away . . . until the next time a dream and the wind call me once again.

Next Step: Write two sentences about an activity you enjoy. Use the words *than* and *then* correctly.

682.1
to, too, two

To is the preposition that can mean "in the direction of." (*To* also is used to form an infinitive. See 730.4.) *Too* is an adverb meaning "very or excessive." *Too* is often used to mean "also." *Two* is the number 2.

Only two of Columbus's first three ships returned to Spain from the New World.

Columbus was too restless to stay in Spain for long.

682.2
vain, vane, vein

Vain means "worthless." It may also mean "thinking too highly of one's self; stuck-up." *Vane* is a flat piece of material set up to show which way the wind blows. *Vein* refers to a blood vessel or a mineral deposit.

The weather vane indicates the direction of wind.

A blood vein determines the direction of flowing blood.

The vain mind moves in no particular direction and thinks only about itself.

682.3
vary, very

Vary is a verb that means "to change." *Very* can be an adjective meaning "in the fullest sense" or "complete"; it can also be an adverb meaning "extremely."

Garon's version of the event would vary from day to day. His very interesting story was the very opposite of the truth.

682.4
waist, waste

Waist is the part of the body just above the hips. The verb *waste* means "to wear away" or "to use carelessly"; the noun *waste* refers to material that is unused or useless.

Don't waste your money on fast-food meals. What a waste to throw away all this food because you're concerned about the size of your waist!

682.5
wait, weight

Wait means "to stay somewhere expecting something." *Weight* is the measure of heaviness.

When I have to wait for the bus, the weight of my backpack seems to keep increasing.

682.6
ware, wear, where

Ware means "a product to be sold"; *wear* means "to have on or to carry on one's body"; *where* asks the question "in what place or in what situation?"

Where can you buy the best cookware to take on a campout—and the best rain gear to wear if it rains?

Grammar Practice

Using the Right Word 16

■ **to, too, two; vain, vane, vein; vary, very; ware, wear, where**

For each of the following sentences, write the correct choice from the set of words in parentheses.

Example: Angelica braids her hair *(to, too, two)* keep it out of her face.

to

1. The school's weather *(vain, vane, vein)* shows that the wind is from the north today.
2. A cold breeze makes me want to *(ware, wear, where)* a sweater.
3. Although the school ordered a reference guide for every class, only *(to, too, two)* arrived.
4. After searching for 15 minutes, Tony finally asked the librarian *(ware, wear, where)* the biographies were located.
5. As long as he had to talk to her, he asked her to point out the bathrooms, *(to, too, two).*
6. In a *(vain, vane, vein)* attempt to open the window, Ms. Jenkins discovered that it had been painted shut.
7. When Char glanced at the clock and realized only 20 minutes had gone by, she knew it was going to be a *(vary, very)* long day.
8. Grandpa says that sometimes a nurse cannot find a good *(vain, vane, vein)* from which to draw his blood.
9. Darren and I went *(to, too, two)* the mall yesterday.
10. Fatima is an artist who works with metal; she sells her *(wares, wears, wheres)* at festivals and county fairs.
11. Although we were told that the lunch menu would *(vary, very)* from week to week, it always seems the same to me.
12. Many fast foods have *(to, too, two)* much salt.

Next Step: Write one sentence that uses *to, too,* and *two*. For an extra challenge, write one with *vary* and *very.*

684.1
way, weigh

Way means "path or route" or "a series of actions." *Weigh* means "to measure weight."

What is the correct way to weigh liquid medicines?

684.2
weather, whether

Weather refers to the condition of the atmosphere. *Whether* refers to a possibility.

The weather will determine whether I go fishing.

684.3
week, weak

A *week* is a period of seven days; *weak* means "not strong."

Last week when I had the flu, I felt light-headed and weak.

684.4
wet, whet

Wet means "soaked with liquid." *Whet* is a verb that means "to sharpen."

Of course, going swimming means I'll get wet, but all that exercise really whets my appetite.

684.5
which, witch

Which is a pronoun used to ask "what one or ones?" out of a group. A *witch* is a woman believed to have supernatural powers.

Which of the women in Salem in the 1600s were accused of being witches?

684.6
who, which, that

When introducing a clause, *who* is used to refer to people; *which* refers to animals and nonliving beings but never to people (it introduces a nonrestrictive, or unnecessary, clause); *that* usually refers to animals or things but can refer to people (it introduces a restrictive, or necessary, clause).

The idea that pizza is junk food is crazy.

Pizza, which is quite nutritious, can be included in a healthful diet.

My mom, who is a dietician, said so.

684.7
who, whom

Who is used as the subject in a sentence; *whom* is used as the object of a preposition or as a direct object.

Who asked you to play tennis?

You beat whom at tennis? You played tennis with whom?

NOTE To test for *who/whom,* arrange the parts of the clause in a subject–verb–direct-object order. *Who* works as the subject, *whom* as the object. (See page 570.)

Grammar Practice

Using the Right Word 17

- **way, weigh; wet, whet; which, witch; who, which, that; who, whom**

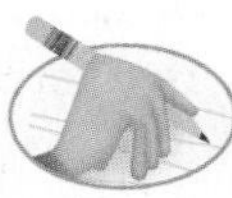

If a word from the list above is used incorrectly in one of the following sentences, write the correct word; otherwise, write "OK."

Example: Ms. Fridley, whom is our homeroom teacher, is helping us plan our year-end picnic.
who

1. The planning has really wet our desire for the end of the school year to come quickly!
2. The picnic which we planned for last year was rained out.
3. Most of us know the way to the park.
4. Lauren, that is new to the area, might not know how to get there.
5. We will use a picnic shelter that offers electricity and water.
6. Arlan suggested bringing ice for the soda, but it may way too much.
7. If Luis brings a wagon, which he did last year, we could use that for the ice.
8. Ms. Fridley still needs to decide who she will ask to organize the games.
9. I hope we play the game with water balloons that gets everyone wet!
10. A which wouldn't play that game because, according to legend, she will melt if water touches her.
11. The girl whom wore her swimsuit last year was the smart one.

Next Step: Read 584.1 and 706.3 to learn more about using *which* and *that* correctly. Then write two sentences that show your understanding of the words.

686.1
who's, whose

Who's is the contraction for "who is." *Whose* is a possessive pronoun, one that shows ownership.

> **Who's the most popular writer today?**
>
> **Whose bike is this?**

686.2
wood, would

Wood is the material that comes from trees; *would* is a form of the verb "will."

> **Sequoia trees live practically forever, but would you believe that the wood from these giants is practically useless?**

686.3
your, you're

Your is a possessive pronoun, one that shows ownership. *You're* is the contraction for "you are."

> **You're the most important person in your parents' lives.**

SCHOOL DAZE
David, you know you're supposed to be doing your homework.
I am, Mom. I'm doing firsthand research on energy conservation.
LA TACO

Grammar Practice

Using the Right Word 18

■ **who's, whose; wood, would; your, you're**

For each of the following sentences, write a word from the list above to fill in the blank.

Example: Please bring ________ journals to class tomorrow.
your

1. Five students said that they ________ be willing to help serve at the Wing Road Soup Kitchen.
2. Can anyone tell me ________ watch this is?
3. ________ planning to go on the Washington, D.C., trip?
4. The manager said, "After you put away the weights and sweep the workout room, ________ free to go."
5. This old desk is made completely of ________.
6. Make sure you have ________ lunch, and then get on the bus.

Using the Right Word Review

For each of the following sentences, write the correct choice from each set of words in parentheses.

1. My uncle living in Cuba wants to *(immigrate, emigrate)* to the United States.
2. The *(stationary, stationery)* bike is *(to, too, two)* heavy for you to move by yourself.
3. Have you *(scene, seen)* the city bus that's painted to look *(as, like)* a shark?
4. Scuba divers need a *(continual, continuous)* supply of air.
5. The magician asked Frank to *(borrow, lend)* her a coin for an *(allusion, illusion)* she would perform.
6. Larry wasn't *(quiet, quit, quite)* ready to leave the lake and the *(base, bass) (who, which, that)* got away.

Test Prep!

For each underlined part of the paragraphs below, choose the letter (on the next page) that shows the correct usage.

Last year, the company which (1) put together the Fourth of July fireworks display was Fire in the Sky. Its owned bye (2) Carlos's Uncle Diaz, whom (3) enjoys creating the biannual July 4 scene (4) in the sky. During several visits to the factory, Carlos piqued at four (5) new projects on the tables. He was as a (6) reporter, constantly asking questions. His uncle would laugh and say, "Your questions are like a (7) string of firecrackers."

On Independence Day, Uncle Diaz let Carlos walk through the mane (8) area of the display setup. Uncle Diaz pointed out an extra-special rocket, that (9) was much louder and had greater special affects then (10) any of the other fireworks. The big rocket's slow assent would sit (11) the stage for a dramatic explosion at the end of the show. A bit later, Uncle Diaz surprised Carlos with the news that he would learn (12) him how to fire the last rocket—the big rocket. Wow! What a moral (13) booster. When it was launched, the great rocket exploded with a tremendous boom, filling the sky with really long flairs (14) of light. It seemed like the birth (15) of a star. The crowd loved it! Carlos felt good about the complement (16) his uncle had given him. He wants to help his uncle again this summer.

1
- Ⓐ who
- Ⓑ whom
- Ⓒ that
- Ⓓ correct as is

2
- Ⓐ Its' owned by
- Ⓑ It's owned by
- Ⓒ It's owned bye
- Ⓓ correct as is

3
- Ⓐ who
- Ⓑ which
- Ⓒ that
- Ⓓ correct as is

4
- Ⓐ biannual July 4 seen
- Ⓑ annual July 4 scene
- Ⓒ annual July 4 seen
- Ⓓ correct as is

5
- Ⓐ peaked at for
- Ⓑ peeked at four
- Ⓒ peaked at four
- Ⓓ correct as is

6
- Ⓐ as an
- Ⓑ like a
- Ⓒ like an
- Ⓓ correct as is

7
- Ⓐ as an
- Ⓑ as a
- Ⓒ like an
- Ⓓ correct as is

8
- Ⓐ through the main
- Ⓑ threw the main
- Ⓒ threw the mane
- Ⓓ correct as is

9
- Ⓐ who
- Ⓑ whom
- Ⓒ which
- Ⓓ correct as is

10
- Ⓐ affects than
- Ⓑ effects then
- Ⓒ effects than
- Ⓓ correct as is

11
- Ⓐ assent would set
- Ⓑ ascent would sit
- Ⓒ ascent would set
- Ⓓ correct as is

12
- Ⓐ wood learn
- Ⓑ would teach
- Ⓒ wood teach
- Ⓓ correct as is

13
- Ⓐ a morale
- Ⓑ an moral
- Ⓒ an morale
- Ⓓ correct as is

14
- Ⓐ real long flares
- Ⓑ real long flairs
- Ⓒ really long flares
- Ⓓ correct as is

15
- Ⓐ seamed like the birth
- Ⓑ seamed like the berth
- Ⓒ seemed like the berth
- Ⓓ correct as is

16
- Ⓐ good about the compliment
- Ⓑ well about the compliment
- Ⓒ well about the complement
- Ⓓ correct as is

Understanding Sentences

Sentences

A **sentence** is a group of words that expresses a complete thought. A sentence must have both a subject and a predicate. A sentence begins with a capital letter; it ends with a period, a question mark, or an exclamation point.

I like my teacher this year.

Will we go on a field trip?

We get to go to the water park!

Parts of a Sentence

690.1 Subjects

A subject is the part of a sentence that does something or is talked about.

The kids on my block play basketball at the local park.

We meet after school almost every day.

690.2 Simple Subjects

The simple subject is the subject without the words that describe or modify it. (Also see page 501.)

My friend Chester plays basketball on the school team.

690.3 Complete Subjects

The complete subject is the simple subject and all the words that modify it. (Also see page 500.)

My friend Chester plays basketball on the school team.

690.4 Compound Subjects

A compound subject has two or more simple subjects. (See page 501.)

Chester, Malik, and Meshelle play on our pickup team.

Lou and I are the best shooters.

Grammar Practice

Parts of a Sentence 1

Simple, Complete, and Compound Subjects

For each of the numbered sentences that follow, write the complete subject. Underline the simple subject. (Watch for compound subjects.)

Example: Cesar Chavez was a Spanish-speaking migrant worker.
Cesar Chavez

(1) Cesar Chavez was born in Arizona in 1927. **(2)** He became an activist for farmworkers. **(3)** Many of these workers were Spanish-speaking migrants. **(4)** Chavez earned respect for using nonviolent ways to improve the working conditions on farms.

(5) In the early 1960s, Chavez organized grape pickers in California. **(6)** The workers held marches and strikes. **(7)** They picketed unfair employers. **(8)** As a result, many major growers offered farmworkers better wages, health insurance, and safer working conditions.

(9) Later in the '60s, Chavez continued his effort, and he drew attention to the situation. **(10)** People who shopped at grocery stores were asked to avoid buying grapes. **(11)** More Americans became aware of the troubles of the farmworkers. **(12)** The United Farm Workers Union gained the respect of farm employers.

(13) Chavez died in 1993. **(14)** Since then, seven states and several Southwestern cities have declared a holiday in honor of the labor leader. **(15)** Phoenix, Tempe, Los Angeles, Denver, and Santa Fe celebrate Chavez's accomplishments on his birthday, March 31. **(16)** He is remembered for making a peaceful stand for farmworkers.

Next Step: Did you remember that a compound sentence has two subjects? Review the sentences above for any of these you may have missed.

Parts of a Sentence . . .

692.1
Predicates

The predicate, which contains the verb, is the part of the sentence that shows action or says something about the subject.

Hunting has reduced the tiger population in India.

692.2
Simple Predicates

The simple predicate is the predicate (verb) without the words that describe or modify it. (See page 501.)

In the past, poachers killed too many African elephants.
Poaching is illegal.

692.3
Complete Predicates

The complete predicate is the simple predicate with all the words that modify or describe it. (See page 500.)

In the past, poachers killed too many African elephants.
Poaching is illegal.

692.4
Direct Objects

The complete predicate often includes a direct object. The direct object is the noun or pronoun that receives the action of the simple predicate—directly. The direct object answers the question *what* or *whom*. (See page 570.)

Many smaller animals need friends who will speak up for them.

The direct object may be compound.

We all need animals, plants, wetlands, deserts, and forests.

692.5
Indirect Objects

If a sentence has a direct object, it may also have an indirect object. An indirect object is the noun or pronoun that receives the action of the simple predicate—indirectly. An indirect object names the person *to whom* or *for whom* something is done. (See page 570.)

I showed the class my multimedia report on endangered species.
(*Class* is the indirect object because it says *to whom* the report was shown.)

Remember, in order for a sentence to have an indirect object, it must first have a direct object.

692.6
Compound Predicates

A compound predicate is composed of two or more simple predicates. (See page 501.)

In 1990 the countries of the world met and banned the sale of ivory.

Grammar Practice

Parts of a Sentence 2

Simple, Complete, and Compound Predicates

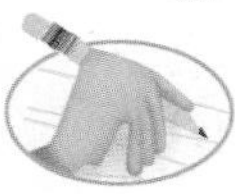

For each sentence below, write the complete predicate (or predicates for a compound sentence). Circle the simple or compound predicate.

Example: Ancient people were the first to work with copper.
(were) the first to work with copper

1. It was easy to find, and it was a fairly simple process to melt the copper.
2. Bronze is probably the first invented metal.
3. Metal workers, or smelters, melted copper and threw tin into it.
4. Smelters gradually added other substances to copper and created even stronger metals.

Direct and Indirect Objects

Write the direct object or objects that are part of the predicate in each sentence below. If the sentence has an indirect object, write it after the direct object and underline it.

Example: Metal workers produced bronze pins, jewelry, and oil lamps.
pins, jewelry, lamps

1. Sculptors could cast lifelike statues in bronze.
2. Kings sometimes gave great warriors bronze swords.
3. Wealthy people bought their families bronze trinkets.
4. Archaeologists have found many bronze artifacts.
5. Museum displays show visitors bronze objects that are thousands of years old.
6. Even today, one can see the fine designs carved into them.
7. Artists still like bronze and work with it often.

Parts of a Sentence . . .

694.1 Understood Subjects and Predicates

Either the subject or the predicate (or both) may not be stated in a sentence, but both must be clearly understood.

[You] **Get involved!** (*You* is the understood subject.)

Who needs your help? Animals [do]. (*Do* is the understood predicate.)

What do many animals face? [They face] **Extinction.** (*They* is the understood subject, and *face* is the understood predicate.)

694.2 Delayed Subjects

In sentences that begin with *there* followed by a form of the "be" verb, the subject usually follows the verb. (See page 570.)

There are laws **that protect endangered species.** (The subject is *laws; are* is the verb.)

The subject is also delayed in questions.

How can we **preserve the natural habitat?** (*We* is the subject.)

SCHOOL DAZE
John, I've got all the projects. Now which one is yours?
I'm not sure. See if there's one with a missing piece.

694.3 Modifiers

A modifier is a word (adjective, adverb) or a group of words (phrase, clause) that changes or adds to the meaning of another word. (See pages 486–493.)

Many North American **zoos and aquariums** voluntarily **participate** in breeding programs that help prevent extinction.

The modifiers in this sentence include the following: *many, North American* (adjectives), *voluntarily* (adverb), *in breeding programs* (phrase), *that help prevent extinction* (clause).

Grammar Practice

Parts of a Sentence 3

- Understood Subjects and Predicates
- Delayed Subjects

Write the simple subject in the numbered sentences below. If the simple subject is understood, write "you."

Example: There are ticks that carry disease.
ticks

(1) Imagine a tick embedded in your arm. **(2)** How do you remove it? **(3)** First of all, do not try to pull it off by force. **(4)** A portion of its head could break off and remain inside the flesh. **(5)** There is a better way to remove it. **(6)** To begin, cover the tick with rubbing alcohol, heavy salad oil, or petroleum jelly, and wait for it to relax its grip. **(7)** Then carefully remove the tick with tweezers. **(8)** What is the final step? To wash the affected area thoroughly with soap and water.

In the last sentence above, neither the subject nor the predicate is stated, but they are understood. Rewrite the sentence, stating both the subject and the predicate.

- Modifiers

List the adjectives and adverbs in each of the sentences below.

Example: Fortunately, fleas are usually not dangerous.
fortunately, usually, not, dangerous

1. An intense itch is often the only result of a flea bite.
2. Fleas really like to hide in pet fur.
3. All fleas are wingless.
4. They do not fly, but they can jump incredibly far!

Test Prep!

For each underlined part in the sentences below, choose the letter or letters from the following list that best describes it.

Ⓐ simple subject
Ⓑ complete subject
Ⓒ compound subject
Ⓓ simple predicate
Ⓔ complete predicate
Ⓕ compound predicate

1. Many diseased birds have been tagged with identification bands.
2. We decorated the gym for the dance and set the refreshment tables.
3. After school, Owen registered for the Tuesday softball league.
4. Lists and charts are two helpful brainstorming tools.
5. In the late 1800s, many pioneers traveled on the Oregon Trail.
6. Ralph Waldo Emerson was a famous American writer.
7. My oldest brother, Michael, likes to rebuild old cars.
8. One of the kittens has a kink in her tail.
9. Rachelle noisily sips and slurps her soup.
10. We are reading a pretty good book in English class.
11. Wild animals and birds in my neighborhood stay away from my dog.
12. I saw Maria talking to Jennifer after algebra class.
13. Benjamin Franklin and Alexander Hamilton are two of America's founding fathers.
14. I visited the Smithsonian and saw the White House in Washington, D.C.

Select the letter that best indicates what the direct and indirect objects are in each sentence below.

15 In the future, people will invent methods of transportation that are faster and more economical.
- (A) *direct object:* methods
- (B) *direct object:* transportation; *indirect object:* methods
- (C) *direct object:* transportation
- (D) *direct object:* faster

16 Derrick aimed his arrow at the bull's-eye on the target.
- (A) *direct object:* bull's-eye
- (B) *direct object:* arrow; *indirect object:* bull's-eye
- (C) *direct object:* arrow
- (D) *direct object:* target

17 I showed my sister the essay that I wrote for social studies class.
- (A) *direct object:* sister
- (B) *direct object:* essay; *indirect object:* sister
- (C) *direct object:* sister; *indirect object:* essay
- (D) *direct object:* class

18 Jacob gave Indira his telephone number last week.
- (A) *direct object:* Indira
- (B) *direct object:* Indira; *indirect object:* number
- (C) *direct object:* number; *indirect object:* Indira
- (D) *direct object:* week

19 Mr. Juarez coaches the girls' volleyball team.
- (A) *direct object:* girls'
- (B) *direct object:* volleyball; *indirect object:* team
- (C) *direct object:* volleyball
- (D) *direct object:* team

20 With this equation, you can calculate the percentage of a number.
- (A) *direct object:* percentage
- (B) *direct object:* percentage; *indirect object:* number
- (C) *direct object:* number
- (D) *direct object:* equation

Parts of a Sentence . . .

698.1 Clauses

A clause is a group of related words that has both a subject and a verb. (Also see pages 515–517.)

a whole chain of plants and animals is affected
(*Chain* is the subject, and *is affected* is the verb.)

when one species dies out completely
(*Species* is the subject; *dies out* is the verb.)

698.2 Independent Clauses

An independent clause presents a complete thought and can stand alone as a sentence.

This ancient oak tree may be cut down.

This act could affect more than 200 different species of animals!

Why would anyone want that to happen?

698.3 Dependent Clauses

A dependent clause does not present a complete thought and cannot stand as a sentence. A dependent clause *depends* on being connected to an independent clause to make sense. Dependent clauses begin with either a subordinating conjunction *(after, although, because, before, if)* or a relative pronoun *(who, whose, which, that)*. (See pages 710 and 744 for complete lists.)

If this ancient oak tree is cut down, **it could affect more than 200 different species of animals!**

The tree, which experts think could be 400 years old, **provides a home to many different kinds of birds and insects.**

SCHOOL DAZE
Boy, are you in for a real blockbuster next hour!

Yeah . . . Mr. Runge is showing a movie called ***A Day in the Life of a Dependent Clause.***

Grammar Practice

Parts of a Sentence 4

Clauses

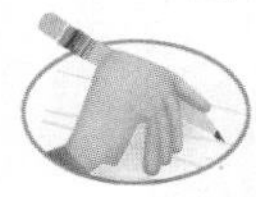

For the even-numbered sentences, write the dependent clause. (If there is no dependent clause, write "none.") Write the independent clause for the odd-numbered sentences.

Odd-numbered example: Although digital cameras take excellent pictures, they still do not see as well as the human eye.
although digital cameras take excellent pictures

1. The eye sends nerve signals through the optic nerve to the brain, which interprets the signals as sight.
2. The cornea, pupil, lens, and retina are the key parts of the eye.
3. The cornea is a clear membrane that covers the front of the eye.
4. The retina, which focuses light, is located in the back of the eye and is filled with rods and cones.
5. Cones, which are not functional in every person, make it possible to see in color.
6. Because rods sense light in black, white, and gray, they allow people to see in low light.
7. A person can also see in low light because the pupil enlarges.
8. When the light is bright, the pupil contracts.
9. Muscles stretch or compress the lens in each eye so that a person can see near or far.
10. The lenses of a person who has cataracts are not clear.
11. If someone's eye shape isn't quite right, he or she will have trouble seeing clearly.
12. Although surgery can solve many vision problems, glasses or contact lenses are still the simplest remedy.

Next Step: Write two complex sentences about your eyes. Remember that a complex sentence has both an independent and a dependent clause.

Parts of a Sentence . . .

700.1 Phrases

A phrase is a group of related words that lacks either a subject or a predicate (or both). (See pages 519–520.)

guards the house (The predicate lacks a subject.)

the ancient oak tree (The subject lacks a predicate.)

with crooked old limbs (The phrase lacks both a subject and a predicate.)

The ancient oak tree with crooked old limbs guards the house. (Together, the three phrases form a complete thought.)

700.2 Types of Phrases

Phrases usually take their names from the main words that introduce them (prepositional phrase, verb phrase, and so on). They are also named for the function they serve in a sentence (adverb phrase, adjective phrase).

The ancient oak tree (noun phrase)

with crooked old limbs (prepositional phrase)

has stood its guard, (verb phrase)

very stubbornly, (adverb phrase)

protecting the little house. (verbal phrase)

For more information on verbal phrases, see page 730.

Grammar Practice

Parts of a Sentence 5

Types of Phrases

Make three columns labeled "noun phrases," "verb phrases," and "prepositional phrases." Write each of the following phrases in the correct column.

Example:

Noun Phrases	Verb Phrases	Prepositional Phrases
a big drooling dog	quickly turned its head	toward the front door

1. my best friend's bike
2. in Washington, D.C.
3. the brown gym bag
4. ate a big dinner
5. was the captain
6. many weary people
7. at the graduation dance
8. could not swim
9. his dog's sharp teeth
10. on the piano
11. over the fence
12. traveled a long way
13. dropped a contact lens
14. an aquarium shark
15. took a walk
16. under a grocery cart
17. the modern telephone
18. through some mulberry bushes

Next Step: Choose two of the phrases above and write a sentence for each.

Using the Parts of Speech

Nouns

A **noun** is a word that names a person, a place, a thing, or an idea.

Person: **John Ulferts** (uncle) Thing: **"Yankee Doodle"** (song)
Place: **Mississippi** (state) Idea: **Labor Day** (holiday)

Kinds of Nouns

702.1 **Common Nouns**

A common noun is any noun that does not name a specific person, place, thing, or idea. These nouns are not capitalized.

woman **museum** **book** **weekend**

702.2 **Proper Nouns**

A proper noun is the name of a specific person, place, thing, or idea. Proper nouns are capitalized.

Hillary Clinton **Central Park** ***Maniac McGee*** **Sunday**

702.3 **Concrete Nouns**

A concrete noun names a thing that is physical (can be touched or seen). Concrete nouns can be either proper or common.

space station **pencil** **Statue of Liberty**

702.4 **Abstract Nouns**

An abstract noun names something you can think about but cannot see or touch. Abstract nouns can be either common or proper.

Judaism **poverty** **satisfaction** **illness**

702.5 **Collective Nouns**

A collective noun names a group or collection of persons, animals, places, or things.

Persons: **tribe, congregation, family, class, team**
Animals: **flock, herd, gaggle, clutch, litter**
Things: **batch, cluster, bunch**

702.6 **Compound Nouns**

A compound noun is made up of two or more words.

football (written as one word)
high school (written as two words)
brother-in-law (written as a hyphenated word)

Grammar Practice

Nouns 1

Concrete and Abstract Nouns

For each of the following sentences, write whether the underlined noun is "concrete" or "abstract."

Example: Pilots enjoy the challenge of flying a sailplane.
abstract

1. It's as close to soaring like a bird as a person is likely to get.
2. Fliers talk about the sense of peace they have when gliding.
3. To keep the flight going, a pilot might have to put the sailplane into a dive.
4. The dive gives the craft speed, which means more air time.
5. After the flight, the pilot returns the glider to its storage trailer so that it is ready for another day.

Compound and Collective Nouns

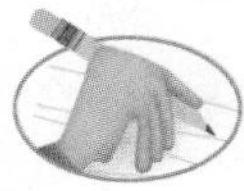

For each sentence below, write any compound or collective nouns you find. Circle the collective nouns.

Example: West of the Great Plains, groups of glider pilots take advantage of winds blowing against or over mountains.
Great Plains, groups

1. A glider's light weight and long wings, along with a small cluster of instruments, allow a pilot to take advantage of updrafts in the air.
2. With the right conditions, gliders (or sailplanes) can travel over great distances by moving along a mountain range.
3. A pilot will travel southeast along with a flock of geese over several miles.
4. Pilots can join gliding clubs that support this unique sport.
5. I think this "unique sport" would give me a stomachache.

Nouns . . .

Number of Nouns

The number of a noun is either singular or plural.

704.1 Singular Nouns

A singular noun names one person, place, thing, or idea.

boy group audience stage concert hope

704.2 Plural Nouns

A plural noun names more than one person, place, thing, or idea.

boys groups audiences stages concerts hopes

Gender of Nouns

704.3 Noun Gender

Nouns are grouped according to gender: *feminine, masculine, neuter,* and *indefinite.*

Feminine (female): **mother, sister, women, cow, hen**

Masculine (male): **father, brother, men, bull, rooster**

Neuter (neither male nor female): **tree, cobweb, closet**

Indefinite (male or female): **president, duckling, doctor**

Uses of Nouns

704.4 Subject Nouns

A noun that is the subject of a sentence does something or is talked about in the sentence.

The roots of rap can be traced back to West Africa and Jamaica.

704.5 Predicate Nouns

A predicate noun follows a form of the *be* verb *(am, is, are, was, were, being, been)* and renames the subject.

In the 1970s, rap was a street art.

704.6 Possessive Nouns

A possessive noun shows possession or ownership.

Early rap had a drummer's beat but no music.

The rapper's words are set to music.

704.7 Object Nouns

A noun is an object noun when it is used as the direct object, the indirect object, or the object of the preposition.

Some rappers tell people their story about life in the city. (indirect object: *people;* direct object: *story*)

Rap is now a common music choice in this country. (object of the preposition: *country*)

Nouns 2

Uses of Nouns

Write whether the underlined noun in each of the following sentences is a "subject," "predicate," "possessive," or "object" noun.

Example: Last year, Danika's dad found a good used all-terrain wheelchair for her.
possessive

1. It's a big improvement over her old one.
2. This wheelchair's frame and tires are very sturdy.
3. Danika recently competed in a wheelchair race.
4. A local business owner arranged the loan of a racing wheelchair for Danika.
5. The business owner is also a wheelchair user.
6. Racing wheelchairs are not the same as ordinary wheelchairs.
7. Regular wheelchairs have two large and two small wheels.
8. The made-for-racing chair features two large angled wheels but only one small wheel in the front.
9. The large side wheels tilt so the rider can more easily push the wheels.
10. The city's parks department has approved plans to make all the parks accessible to wheelchairs.
11. The parks' redesign is a definite move in the right direction.

Next Step: Write two sentences about someone in a wheelchair. Use a predicate noun and an object noun somewhere in your sentences. Underline and label each one appropriately.

Pronouns

A **pronoun** is a word used in place of a noun. Some examples are *I, you, he, she, it, we, they, his, hers, her, its, me, myself, us, yours,* and so on.

Without pronouns: **Kevin said Kevin would be going to Kevin's grandmother's house this weekend.**

With pronouns: **Kevin said he would be going to his grandmother's house this weekend.**

706.1 Antecedents

An antecedent is the noun that the pronoun refers to or replaces. All pronouns (except interrogative and indefinite pronouns) have antecedents. (See page 474.)

Jamal and Rick tried out for the team, and they both made it.
(*They* refers to *Jamal* and *Rick; it* refers to *team.*)

NOTE Pronouns must agree with their antecedents in number, person, and gender.

Types of Pronouns

There are several types of pronouns. The most common type is the personal pronoun. (See the chart on page 710.)

706.2 Personal Pronouns

A personal pronoun takes the place of a specific person (or thing) in a sentence. Some common personal pronouns are *I, you, he, she, it, we,* and *they.*

Suriana would not like to live in Buffalo, New York, because she does not like snow.

706.3 Relative Pronouns

A relative pronoun is both a pronoun and a connecting word. It connects a dependent clause to an independent clause in a complex sentence. Relative pronouns include *who, whose, which,* and *that.* (See 684.6.)

Buffalo, which often gets more than eight feet of snow in a year, is on the northeast shore of Lake Erie.

The United States city that gets the most snow is Valdez, Alaska.

706.4 Interrogative Pronouns

An interrogative pronoun helps ask a question.

Who wants to go to Alaska?

Which of the cities would you visit?

Whom would you like to travel with?

What did you say?

Grammar Practice

Pronouns 1

- Antecedents
- Personal Pronouns
- Relative Pronouns

For each blank in the sentences below, write the missing pronoun. (The type of pronoun is in parentheses.) Also write its antecedent.

Example: Field trips are enjoyable because ___*(personal)*___ allow students to learn outside of the classroom.
they (trips)

1. The student ___*(relative)*___ suggests the best field trip may propose ___*(personal)*___ to the principal.
2. The Adler Planetarium, ___*(relative)*___ is in Chicago, is a favorite field trip destination.
3. Mrs. Bogart said ___*(personal)*___ would like to go to a film festival in Boston.
4. Ben said that ___*(personal)*___ thought the class should visit a veterinary hospital.
5. Mr. Andrews suggested, " ___*(personal)*___ would like to take the class to Washington, D.C., for several days."
6. The state capitol, ___*(relative)*___ is a popular place to visit, is where we plan to go next Tuesday.
7. The students ___*(relative)*___ names are on Mr. Daly's list should attend the field trip meeting.
8. The field trip ___*(relative)*___ Susan liked best was sailing on a tall ship.
9. Mrs. Bogart and Mr. Andrews announced, "___*(personal)*___ will discuss all your suggestions."

Next Step: Write two sentences about a field trip you have taken. Use pronouns in each sentence and underline them. Exchange papers with a classmate and circle the antecedents in each other's sentences.

Pronouns . . .

Types of Pronouns

708.1 Demonstrative Pronouns

A demonstrative pronoun points out or identifies a noun without naming the noun. When used together in a sentence, *this* and *that* distinguish one item from another, and *these* and *those* distinguish one group from another. (See page 710.)

This is a great idea; that was a nightmare.

These are my favorite foods, and those are definitely not.

NOTE When these words are used before a noun, they are *not* pronouns; rather, they are demonstrative adjectives.

Coming to this picnic was fun—and those ants think so, too.

708.2 Intensive Pronouns

An intensive pronoun emphasizes, or *intensifies,* the noun or pronoun it refers to. Common intensive pronouns include *itself, myself, himself, herself,* and *yourself.*

Though the chameleon's quick-change act protects it from predators, the lizard itself can catch insects 10 inches away with its long, sticky tongue.

When a chameleon changes its skin color—seemingly matching the background—the background colors themselves do not affect the chameleon's color changes.

NOTE These sentences would be complete without the intensive pronoun. The pronoun simply emphasizes a particular noun.

708.3 Reflexive Pronouns

A reflexive pronoun refers back to the subject of a sentence, and it is always an object (never a subject) in a sentence. Reflexive pronouns are the same as the intensive pronouns—*itself, myself, himself, herself, yourself,* and so on.

A chameleon protects itself from danger by changing colors. (direct object)

A chameleon can give itself tasty meals of unsuspecting insects. (indirect object)

I wish I could claim some of its amazing powers for myself. (object of the preposition)

NOTE Unlike sentences with intensive pronouns, these sentences would *not* be complete without the reflexive pronouns.

Grammar Practice

Pronouns 2

Demonstrative Pronouns

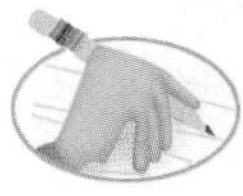

For the sentences below that have a demonstrative pronoun, write "DP." Rewrite the other sentences so that they also have demonstrative pronouns.

Example: This CD is awesome.
This is an awesome CD.

1. That was the best concert I've been to.
2. Those tickets were very expensive.
3. That drummer is the one you told me about!
4. These are my favorite cuts from the album.
5. Do you know anything about this?

Intensive Pronouns
Reflexive Pronouns

Write whether the pronouns that end in "self" or "selves" in the following sentences are intensive or reflexive.

Example: On July 4, 1845, Henry David Thoreau went by himself to live in the woods and write.
reflexive

1. Thoreau became an admired author, but he himself earned little from his writing.
2. When he went to Walden Pond, he hoped to better himself by living off the earth with just the bare essentials.
3. He himself planned and built a small cottage where he wrote in his journal and drafted his first book.
4. The cottage itself is no longer there, but the area is now a public park.
5. Someday, you may want to go somewhere by yourself to experience living quietly with just the bare essentials.

Pronouns . . .

Types of Pronouns

710.1 Indefinite Pronouns

An indefinite pronoun is a pronoun that does not have a specific antecedent (the noun or pronoun it replaces). (See page 475.)

Everything **about the chameleon is fascinating.**

Someone **donated a chameleon to our class.**

Anyone **who brings in a live insect can feed our chameleon.**

Types of Pronouns

Personal Pronouns

I, me, mine, my, we, us, our, ours, you, your, yours, they, them, their, theirs, he, him, his, she, her, hers, it, its

Relative Pronouns

who, whose, whom, which, what, that, whoever, whomever, whichever, whatever

Interrogative Pronouns

who, whose, whom, which, what

Demonstrative Pronouns

this, that, these, those

Intensive and Reflexive Pronouns

myself, himself, herself, itself, yourself, yourselves, themselves, ourselves

Indefinite Pronouns

all	both	everything	nobody	several
another	each	few	none	some
any	each one	many	no one	somebody
anybody	either	most	nothing	someone
anyone	everybody	much	one	something
anything	everyone	neither	other	such

Grammar Practice

Pronouns 3

Indefinite Pronouns

Write the indefinite pronoun in each of the following sentences.

Example: Many recognize Sondre Norheim as the father of modern skiing.
Many

1. Norheim created a new kind of ski for himself and others.
2. Each had a heel binding and curved sides.
3. Sondre had a remarkable style of skiing that everyone admired.
4. No one can deny that he promoted the joy of skiing.
5. Most credit Norheim with making skiing a popular sport.

Pronoun Review

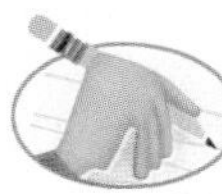

Identify the underlined pronouns in the sentences below as "personal," "relative," or "indefinite."

1. Ralph Samuelson, <u>who</u> was from Minnesota, invented water-skiing in 1922.
2. <u>Most</u> didn't believe the eighteen-year-old when he talked about skiing on water.
3. Ralph and his brother Ben set out to prove that <u>they</u> could do it.
4. They tried skis made from pieces of a barrel, <u>which</u> did not work well.
5. <u>Neither</u> thought twice about using a window-sash cord as a ski rope.
6. Ralph made <u>his</u> own skis from leather strips and lumber that he purchased.
7. <u>Everything</u> worked fine!
8. In 1925, during an exhibition <u>that</u> was held on Lake Pepin, Ralph made his first successful water-ski jump.

Pronouns . . .

Number of a Pronoun

712.1 Singular and Plural Pronouns

Pronouns can be either singular or plural in number.

Singular: **I, you, he, she, it** Plural: **we, you, they**

NOTE The pronouns *you, your,* and *yours* may be singular or plural.

Person of a Pronoun

The person of a pronoun tells whether the pronoun is speaking, being spoken to, or being spoken about. (See page **474**.)

712.2 First Person Pronouns

A first-person pronoun is used in place of the name of the speaker or speakers.

I am speaking. We are speaking.

712.3 Second Person Pronouns

A second-person pronoun is used to name the person or thing spoken to.

Eliza, will you please take out the garbage?

You better stop grumbling!

712.4 Third Person Pronouns

A third-person pronoun is used to name the person or thing spoken about.

Bill should listen if he wants to learn the words to this song.

Charisse said that she already knows them.

They will perform the song in the talent show.

Uses of Pronouns

A pronoun can be used as a subject, as an object, or to show possession. (See the chart on page **714**.)

712.5 Subject Pronouns

A subject pronoun is used as the subject of a sentence *(I, you, he, she, it, we, they).*

I like to surf the Net.

A subject pronoun is also used after a form of the *be* verb *(am, is, are, was, were, being, been)* if it repeats the subject. (See "Predicate Nouns," **704.5**.)

"This is she," Mom replied into the telephone.

"Yes, it was I," admitted the child who had eaten the cookies.

Grammar Practice

Pronouns 4

- Number of a Pronoun
- Person of a Pronoun

Write the personal pronouns in each of the following sentences and identify each as "singular" or "plural." Also tell whether it is "first," "second," or "third" person.

Example: We studied the Industrial Revolution in our history class.

We—plural, first person *our—plural, first person*

1. My history teacher asked me, "Would you do a report on the Industrial Revolution and child-labor issues?
2. It was a time when machines replaced skilled labor.
3. Many people lost their jobs during that period in history.
4. Samuel Slater and his textile mill began the Industrial Revolution.
5. Inventors Watt, Kay, and Hargreaves are known for their contributions to the textile industry.
6. My American ancestors were probably affected by the Industrial Revolution.
7. In 1886, workers formed a labor union that they called the American Federation of Labor.
8. Samuel Gompers was its first president.
9. Early unions protected workers' rights and made sure that they were paid a fair wage.
10. Of course, the teacher gave us a test on this era.
11. My friend Chris said, "I know I passed!"

Next Step: Write a short paragraph about a subject you're studying in school. Make sure your pronouns agree with their antecedents in person and number.

Pronouns . . .

Uses of Pronouns

714.1
Object Pronouns

An object pronoun *(me, you, him, her, it, us, them)* can be used as the object of a verb or preposition. (See **692.4**, **692.5**, and **742.1**.)

I'll call her as soon as I can. (direct object)

Hand me the phone book, please. (indirect object)

She thinks these flowers are from you. (object of the preposition)

714.2
Possessive Pronouns

A possessive pronoun shows possession or ownership. These possessive pronouns function as adjectives before nouns: *my, our, his, her, their, its,* and *your*.

School workers are painting our classroom this summer. Its walls will look much better.

These possessive pronouns can be used after verbs: *mine, ours, hers, his, theirs,* and *yours*.

I'm pretty sure this backpack is mine and that one is his.

NOTE An apostrophe is not needed with a possessive pronoun to show possession.

Uses of Personal Pronouns

	Singular Pronouns			Plural Pronouns		
	Subject Pronouns	Possessive Pronouns	Object Pronouns	Subject Pronouns	Possessive Pronouns	Object Pronouns
First Person	I	my, mine	me	we	our, ours	us
Second Person	you	your, yours	you	you	your, yours	you
Third Person	he	his	him	they	their, theirs	them
	she	her, hers	her			
	it	its	it			

Grammar Practice

Pronouns 5

Uses of Pronouns

For each sentence below, identify each personal pronoun as a "subject pronoun" (712.5), an "object pronoun," or a "possessive pronoun."

Example: She thinks that the invitation to the dance is from you.
She—subject pronoun, you—object pronoun

1. They asked me not to bring my brother to basketball practice.
2. When we think of our fourth-grade teacher, Mr. Wong, we remember his funny skits in the variety show.
3. Angela admits that algebra is not easy for her; it is difficult for me, too.
4. Before the game, she was afraid that her team might lose.
5. Max said, "Sunan and Elena went to the band concert without us, even after we asked them to wait."
6. The dirt bike hit some debris that caused it to crash.
7. It suffered quite a bit of damage.
8. Her sister sings in a band that plays at their school's dances.
9. Hank was late for practice today; he has been late for everything lately.
10. The coach is going to have a talk with him.
11. I thought the ball was mine, but then Jack jumped up and caught it.
12. You should check with the teacher before posting your ad on the bulletin board.

Next Step: Write a sentence with a subject pronoun and an object or a possessive pronoun. Trade sentences with a classmate. Underline the subject pronoun and circle the object or possessive pronoun.

Test Prep!

For each underlined word in the sentences below, write the letter from the following list that best describes it.

Ⓐ subject noun	Ⓓ subject pronoun
Ⓑ predicate noun	Ⓔ object pronoun
Ⓒ object noun	Ⓕ possessive noun/pronoun

Early in the twentieth century, Lloyd Loar (1) invented an electric guitar (2). The new invention, however, was not very popular in its (3) early years. Many musicians didn't like the distorted sound (4) that the guitars made.

In the 1940s, Les Paul was a well-known musician (5) and guitarist. He (6) made some changes to the instrument's (7) design. Paul created an electric guitar with a solid body rather than a hollow one (8). The new design (9) helped reduce feedback and made a better sound (10). About the same time (11), Leo Fender was developing electric guitars as a hobby. His (12) legendary Stratocaster was introduced in 1954. Together, these men are the "fathers" (13) of the electric guitar.

Jazz and country music increased the electric guitar's (14) popularity in the 1950s. By the 1960s, rock musicians had discovered it (15), and the instrument had gone mainstream. Despite an uncertain start, it (16) now has many fans (17). In fact, retailers (18) in the United States now sell more electric guitars than acoustic ones.

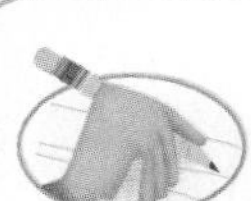

For each underlined pronoun in the sentences below, write the letter that best describes its type.

19. Darius wanted Nita and Tyree to go to the game with <u>him</u>.
Ⓐ personal Ⓑ reflexive Ⓒ indefinite Ⓓ relative

20. It is the first game of the season and the only <u>one</u> at North Park.
Ⓐ reflexive Ⓑ personal Ⓒ indefinite Ⓓ relative

21. <u>That</u> is my seat there in the third row.
Ⓐ relative Ⓑ demonstrative Ⓒ personal Ⓓ indefinite

22. <u>Who</u> left this sandwich in the refrigerator?
Ⓐ personal Ⓑ interrogative Ⓒ relative Ⓓ intensive

23. Clay said that he already gave the concert tickets to <u>you</u>.
Ⓐ interrogative Ⓑ personal Ⓒ indefinite Ⓓ relative

24. Fortunately, the man <u>whose</u> sleeve caught fire didn't get burned.
Ⓐ relative Ⓑ demonstrative Ⓒ personal Ⓓ reflexive

25. Does <u>anyone</u> know how this happened?
Ⓐ demonstrative Ⓑ indefinite Ⓒ intensive Ⓓ personal

26. Jenica <u>herself</u> doesn't understand what happened.
Ⓐ demonstrative Ⓑ reflexive Ⓒ intensive Ⓓ personal

27. They asked <u>me</u> to volunteer at my little brother's day-care center.
Ⓐ relative Ⓑ demonstrative Ⓒ personal Ⓓ interrogative

28. "Make sure you share <u>those</u> with your friends," Dad said.
Ⓐ demonstrative Ⓑ reflexive Ⓒ intensive Ⓓ personal

29. Graciela began drinking the milk <u>that</u> had turned sour.
Ⓐ personal Ⓑ interrogative Ⓒ relative Ⓓ demonstrative

30. I think I'll get <u>myself</u> a new pair of jeans.
Ⓐ personal Ⓑ reflexive Ⓒ intensive Ⓓ relative

Verbs

A **verb** is a word that shows action or links a subject to another word in a sentence.

Tornadoes cause tremendous damage. (action verb)

The weather is often calm before a storm. (linking verb)

Types of Verbs

718.1 Action Verbs

An action verb tells what the subject is doing. (See page 480.)

Natural disasters hit the globe nearly every day.

718.2 Linking Verbs

A linking verb connects—or links—a subject to a noun or an adjective in the predicate. The most common linking verbs are forms of the verb *be (is, are, was, were, being, been, am).* Verbs such as *smell, look, taste, feel, remain, turn, appear, become, sound, seem, grow,* and *stay* can also be linking verbs. (See page 480.)

The San Andreas Fault is an earthquake zone in California. (The linking verb *is* connects the subject to the predicate noun *zone.*)

Earthquakes there are fairly common. (The linking verb *are* connects the subject to the predicate adjective *common.*)

718.3 Helping Verbs

A helping verb (also called an auxiliary verb) helps the main verb express tense and voice. The most common helping verbs are *shall, will, should, would, could, must, might, can, may, have, had, has, do, did,* and the forms of the verb *be—is, are, was, were, am, being, been.* (See page 481.)

It has been estimated that 500,000 earthquakes occur around the world every year. (These helping verbs indicate that the tense is present perfect and the voice is passive.)

Fortunately, only about 100 of those will cause damage. (*Will* helps express the future tense of the verb.)

Grammar Practice

Verbs 1

Action, Linking, and Helping Verbs

For each numbered sentence in the following paragraphs, write the verb or verbs. (Remember that clauses also have verbs.) Identify each as an "action verb," a "linking verb," or a "helping verb."

Example: Pizza, which is one of the most popular foods in the world today, was also eaten by ancient people.
is-linking verb, was-helping verb, eaten-action verb

(1) Pizza is one type of food with a long history. **(2)** Its origins reach back to ancient Middle Eastern times. **(3)** People of that era ate flat bread that had been cooked in mud ovens. **(4)** Soon the Mediterraneans were eating the same flat bread with olive oil and native spices on it.

(5) Much later, in 1889, Queen Margherita was touring her Italian kingdom. **(6)** She noticed peasants who were enjoying the flat bread with spices on top. **(7)** An Italian baker, Raffaele Esposito, created a special pizza for the queen. **(8)** He topped it with tomatoes, mozzarella cheese, and fresh basil. **(9)** The pizza became the queen's favorite treat. **(10)** Today, it is known as pizza Margherita.

(11) Pizza was not a standard American food until after World War II. **(12)** American soldiers tried it for the first time while they were staying in areas of Italy. **(13)** It tasted wonderful! **(14)** When the soldiers returned home, they were hungry for this Italian treat. **(15)** Before long, everyone in America knew about pizza.

Next Step: Write a paragraph about one of your favorite foods. Use action, linking, and helping verbs. Exchange papers with a classmate. List and identify all of the verbs.

Verbs . . .

Tenses of Verbs

A verb has three principal parts: *present, past,* and *past participle.* (The part used with the helping verbs *has, have,* or *had* is called the past participle.)

All six of the tenses are formed from these principal parts. The past and past participle of regular verbs are formed by adding *ed* to the present tense. The past and past participle of irregular verbs are formed with different spellings. (See the chart on page **722**.)

720.1 Present Tense Verbs

The present tense of a verb expresses action (or a state of being) that is happening now or that happens continually or regularly. (See page **482**.)

The universe is gigantic. It takes my breath away.

720.2 Past Tense Verbs

The past tense of a verb expresses action (or a state of being) that was completed in the past. (See page **482**.)

To most people many years ago, the universe was the earth, the sun, and some stars. The universe reached only as far as the eye could see.

720.3 Future Tense Verbs

The future tense of a verb expresses action that *will* take place. (See page **482**.)

Maybe I will visit another galaxy in my lifetime.

Somebody will find a way to do it.

SCHOOL DAZE

I **know** the answer!

Okay, but I **said** you **will have** to sing the answer . . . go ahead!

Grammar Practice

Verbs 2

Present Tense, Past Tense, and Future Tense Verbs

For each of the sentences below, identify the underlined verbs as "present tense," "past tense," or "future tense."

Example: The United States Naval Academy founded its drum and bugle corps in 1914.
past tense

1. Today it boasts being the oldest drum and bugle corps in America.
2. The corps, consisting of 16 men, first performed at a baseball game.
3. It was active for eight years until it disbanded in 1922.
4. The academy's superintendent, Henry B. Wilson, said, "It is a luxury, not a necessity."
5. Some of the students thought, "The corps will return someday."
6. In 1926, the corps came back bigger and better.
7. Seeing them take the field again in full dress uniforms was an awesome sight.
8. Today the U.S. Naval Academy Drum and Bugle Corps has about 100 members.
9. The corps still plays "Anchors Away," just as it did almost a century ago.
10. You will hear its members shout, "Go, Navy!"
11. The corps provides enjoyable entertainment for people of all ages.

Next Step: Write a sentence in the present tense about some music you enjoy. Exchange papers with a classmate and write each other's sentence in the past and future tenses.

Common Irregular Verbs and Their Principal Parts

The principal parts of the common irregular verbs are listed below. The part used with the helping verbs *has, have,* or *had* is called the **past participle**. (Also see page 481.)

Present Tense:	**I write.**	**She hides.**
Past Tense:	**Earlier I wrote.**	**Earlier she hid.**
Past Participle:	**I have written.**	**She has hidden.**

Present Tense	Past Tense	Past Participle	Present Tense	Past Tense	Past Participle
am, is, are	was, were	been	lead	led	led
begin	began	begun	lie (recline)	lay	lain
bid (offer)	bid	bid	lie (deceive)	lied	lied
bid (order)	bade	bidden	make	made	made
bite	bit	bitten	ride	rode	ridden
blow	blew	blown	ring	rang	rung
break	broke	broken	rise	rose	risen
bring	brought	brought	run	ran	run
burst	burst	burst	see	saw	seen
buy	bought	bought	set	set	set
catch	caught	caught	shake	shook	shaken
come	came	come	shine (polish)	shined	shined
dive	dived, dove	dived	shine (light)	shone	shone
do	did	done	shrink	shrank	shrunk
draw	drew	drawn	sing	sang, sung	sung
drink	drank	drunk	sink	sank, sunk	sunk
drive	drove	driven	sit	sat	sat
eat	ate	eaten	sleep	slept	slept
fall	fell	fallen	speak	spoke	spoken
fight	fought	fought	spring	sprang, sprung	sprung
flee	fled	fled	steal	stole	stolen
fly	flew	flown	strive	strove	striven
forsake	forsook	forsaken	swear	swore	sworn
freeze	froze	frozen	swim	swam	swum
get	got	gotten, got	swing	swung	swung
give	gave	given	take	took	taken
go	went	gone	tear	tore	torn
grow	grew	grown	throw	threw	thrown
hang (execute)	hanged	hanged	wake	woke, waked	woken, waked
hang (dangle)	hung	hung	wear	wore	worn
hide	hid	hidden, hid	weave	wove	woven
know	knew	known	wring	wrung	wrung
lay (place)	laid	laid	write	wrote	written

Grammar Practice

Verbs 3

Irregular Verbs

For the sentences below, fill in each blank with the correct past tense or past participle form of the verb or verbs in parentheses.

Example: Mr. Malone had _____ me permission to leave early. *(give)*
given

1. Ron _____ at the ball and hit it. *(swing)*
2. It _____ in the air for a few seconds before a fielder _____ it. *(hang, catch)*
3. The alarm _____ me, but I _____ back down and _____ for another hour. *(wake, lie, sleep)*
4. When the tornado _____ through town and _____ out windows, we _____ for cover. *(tear, blow, run)*
5. I have never _____ as many e-mails as I _____ last weekend. *(write, do)*
6. My hands had almost _____ after I had _____ out in the cold temperatures for so long. *(freeze, am)*
7. Although I had _____ to the principal, we _____ detentions anyway. *(speak, get)*
8. If we had _____ that Vandana was in the track meet, we would have _____ to watch her race. *(know, come)*
9. The marching band _____ a huge crowd. *(draw)*
10. I just _____ that new action-adventure film at the cinema. *(see)*
11. I have _____ all of the movies in that series. *(see)*
12. At last night's party, I had _____ so much that the snap on my jeans _____. *(eat, break)*
13. My sister has _____ my sweater more often than I have! *(wear)*

Next Step: Write three sentences using the present tense, past tense, and past participle of the word *fly*.

Verbs . . .

Tenses of Verbs

724.1
Present Perfect Tense Verbs

The present perfect tense verb expresses action that began in the past but continues or is completed in the present. The present perfect tense is formed by adding *has* or *have* to the past participle. (Also see page 483.)

I have wondered **for some time how the stars got their names.**

A visible star has emitted **light for thousands of years.**

724.2
Past Perfect Tense Verbs

The past perfect tense verb expresses action that began in the past and was completed in the past. This tense is formed by adding *had* to the past participle. (Also see page 483.)

I had hoped **to see a shooting star on our camping trip.**

724.3
Future Perfect Tense Verbs

A future perfect tense verb expresses action that will begin in the future and will be completed by a specific time in the future. The future perfect tense is formed by adding *will have* to the past participle. (Also see page 483.)

By the middle of this century, we probably will have discovered **many more stars, planets, and galaxies.**

724.4
Present Continuous Tense Verbs

A present continuous tense verb expresses action that is not completed at the time of stating it. The present continuous tense is formed by adding *am, is,* or *are* to the *ing* form of the main verb.

Scientists are learning **a great deal from their study of the sky.**

724.5
Past Continuous Tense Verbs

A past continuous tense verb expresses action that was happening at a certain time in the past. This tense is formed by adding *was* or *were* to the *ing* form of the main verb.

Astronomers were beginning **their quest for knowledge hundreds of years ago.**

724.6
Future Continuous Tense Verbs

A future continuous tense verb expresses action that will take place at a certain time in the future. This tense is formed by adding *will be* to the *ing* form of the main verb.

Someday astronauts will be going **to Mars.**

This tense can also be formed by adding a phrase noting the future *(are going to)* plus *be* to the *ing* form of the main verb.

They are going to be performing **many experiments.**

Grammar Practice

Verbs 4

- Perfect Tense Verbs
- Continuous Tense Verbs

For each of the sentences below, write the correct form of the verb given in parentheses.

Example: Geologists _______ some strange rocks.
(discover, present perfect)
have discovered

1. During years of careful study, scientists _______ some of the ordinary-looking rocks to ultraviolet light. *(expose, past continuous)*
2. The rocks _______ with brilliant colors! *(glow, past continuous)*
3. Oddly, the rocks _______ to glow, even without the light on them. *(continue, past perfect)*
4. Now researchers _______ different levels of ultraviolet light on the rocks. *(test, present continuous)*
5. Scientists _______ these minerals unusual names, such as willemite, selenite, fluorite, aragonite, and Texas calcite. *(give, present perfect)*
6. As interest in these glow-in-the-dark minerals grows, more people _______ for them. *(look, future continuous)*
7. Geologists hope that rock hunters _______ more of these interesting objects by 2025. *(find, future perfect)*
8. In the meantime, people _______ museum displays of the minerals. *(visit, present continuous)*
9. The displays _______ museum visitors for years to come. *(amaze, future continuous)*

Next Step: Write two sentences about an interesting mineral or metal. Use continuous tense verbs.

Verbs . . .

Forms of Verbs

726.1
Active or Passive Voice

The voice of a verb tells you whether the subject is doing the action or is receiving the action. A verb is in the active voice (in any tense) if the subject is doing the action in a sentence. (See page 118.)

> **I dream of going to galaxies light-years from Earth.**
>
> **I will travel in an ultrafast spaceship.**

A verb is in the passive voice if the subject is not doing the action. The action is done *by* someone or something else. The passive voice is always indicated with a helping verb plus a past participle or a past tense verb.

> **My daydreams often are shattered by reality.** (The subject *daydreams* is not doing the action.)
>
> **Of course, reality can be seen differently by different people.** (The subject *reality* is not doing the action.)

Tense	Active Voice		Passive Voice	
	Singular	**Plural**	**Singular**	**Plural**
Present Tense	I find you find he/she/it finds	we find you find they find	I am found you are found he/she/it is found	we are found you are found they are found
Past Tense	I found you found he/she/it found	we found you found they found	I was found you were found he/she/it was found	we were found you were found they were found
Future Tense	I will find you will find he/she/it will find	we will find you will find they will find	I will be found you will be found he/she/it will be found	we will be found you will be found they will be found
Present Perfect	I have found you have found he/she/it has found	we have found you have found they have found	I have been found you have been found he/she/it has been found	we have been found you have been found they have been found
Past Perfect	I had found you had found he/she/it had found	we had found you had found they had found	I had been found you had been found he/she/it had been found	we had been found you had been found they had been found
Future Perfect	I will have found you will have found he/she/it will have found	we will have found you will have found they will have found	I will have been found you will have been found he/she/it will have been found	we will have been found you will have been found they will have been found

Grammar Practice

Verbs 5

Active or Passive Voice

For each sentence below, write the verb and tell whether it is in the active or passive voice.

Example: Elvis Presley has been called the King of Rock and Roll.
has been called (passive)

1. He is recognized by many people as an American music legend.
2. He soared to popularity with teenagers in the late 1950s.
3. By the end of his career, Elvis had recorded 81 albums and 51 singles.
4. In addition to his recording career, Elvis starred in movies.
5. Most of his best-known songs can be heard in his movies.
6. Elvis Presley died in 1977 at the age of 42.
7. His talent will be remembered for a very long time.

Rewrite each of the following sentences in the active voice. Add or delete words as necessary.

Example: Elvis Presley's movies have been enjoyed by several generations.
Several generations have enjoyed Elvis Presley's movies.

1. His films have been seen by millions of people.
2. In *Jailhouse Rock,* the part of Vince Everett was played by Elvis.
3. Elvis's films have been appreciated by audiences around the world.
4. Elvis was made famous by his singing and acting talents.

Next Step: Write a sentence in the passive voice about a famous performer. Exchange papers with a classmate and rewrite each other's sentence in the active voice.

Verbs . . .

Forms of Verbs

728.1 Singular and Plural Verbs

A singular subject needs a singular verb. A plural subject needs a plural verb. For action verbs, only the third-person singular verb form is different: *I wonder, we wonder, you wonder, she wonders, they wonder.* Some linking verbs, however, have several different forms.

First Person	Singular:	**I am (or was) a good student.**
	Plural:	**We are (or were) good students.**
Second Person	Singular:	**You are (or were) a cheerleader.**
	Plural:	**You are (or were) cheerleaders.**
Third Person	Singular:	**He is (or was) on the wrestling team.**
	Plural:	**They are (or were) also on the team.**

728.2 Transitive Verbs

A transitive verb is a verb that transfers its action to a direct object. The object makes the meaning of the verb complete. A transitive verb is always an action verb (never a linking verb). (See pages 484 and 570.)

> **An earthquake shook San Francisco in 1906.** (*Shook* transfers its action to the direct object *San Francisco*. Without *San Francisco* the meaning of the verb *shook* is incomplete.)
>
> **The city's people spent many years rebuilding.** (Without the direct object *years,* the verb's meaning is incomplete.)

A transitive verb transfers the action directly to a direct object and indirectly to an indirect object.

> **Fires destroyed the city.** (direct object: *city*)
>
> **Our teacher gave us the details.** (indirect object: *us;* direct object: *details*)

See 692.4 and 692.5 for more on direct and indirect objects.

728.3 Intransitive Verbs

An intransitive verb does not need an object to complete its meaning. (See pages 484 and 570.)

> **Abigail was shopping.** (The verb's meaning is complete.)
>
> **Her stomach felt queasy.** (*Queasy* is a predicate adjective describing *stomach;* there is no direct object.)
>
> **She lay down on the bench.** (Again, there is no direct object. *Down* is an adverb modifying *lay.*)

Grammar Practice

Verbs 6

Transitive and Intransitive Verbs

For each sentence below, write whether the underlined verb is "transitive" or "intransitive."

Example: My best friend's mother writes poetry and short stories.
transitive

1. The wolf snarled fearsomely.
2. The coach gave the player a penalty for poor sportsmanship.
3. The leaves on this bush are purple.
4. Near the end of the race, Taylor ran faster than ever before.
5. Jorge has been transferred to Jackson Park Middle School.
6. Casey told the truth when he said that he didn't do it.
7. I read a letter to the editor about rising energy costs.
8. Ted worked quietly.
9. The sound of the fire alarm blasted through the halls.
10. Eva plays the drums in a band that she and her friends put together.
11. Before eating his breakfast, Najee took a vitamin.
12. Have you ever seen a telephone with a dial?
13. The sky seems a little green this afternoon.
14. The maintenance staff cleans the pool once a week.
15. The housekeeping staff cleans regularly.

Next Step: Write two sentences with transitive verbs and two with intransitive verbs. Exchange papers with a classmate and identify each other's verbs correctly.

Verbs . . .

Forms of Verbs

730.1
Transitive or Intransitive Verbs

Some verbs can be either transitive or intransitive.

Transitive: **She reads my note.** **Albert ate an apple.**

Intransitive: **She reads aloud.** **Albert ate already.**

Verbals

A **verbal** is a word that is made from a verb but acts as another part of speech. Gerunds, participles, and infinitives are verbals.

730.2
Gerunds

A gerund is a verb form that ends in *ing* and is used as a *noun.* A gerund often begins a gerund phrase.

Worrying is useless. (The gerund is the subject noun.)

You should stop worrying about so many things. (The gerund phrase is the direct object.)

730.3
Participles

A participle is a verb form ending in *ing* or *ed.* A participle is used as an *adjective* and often begins a participial phrase.

The idea of the earth shaking and splitting both fascinates and frightens me. (The participles modify *earth.*)

Rattling in the cabinets, the dishes were about to crash to the floor. (The participial phrase modifies *dishes.*)

Why doesn't this tired earth just stand still? (The participle modifies *earth.*)

730.4
Infinitives

An infinitive is a verb form introduced by *to.* It may be used as a *noun,* an *adjective,* or an *adverb.* It often begins an infinitive phrase.

My need to whisper is due to this secret. (The infinitive is an adjective modifying *need.*)

I am afraid to swim. (The infinitive is an adverb modifying the predicate adjective *afraid.*)

To overcome this fear is my goal. (The infinitive phrase is used as a noun and is the subject of this sentence.)

Grammar Practice

Verbs 7

Verbals

For each sentence below, identify the underlined verb form as a "gerund," a "participle," or an "infinitive."

Example: In the late 1800s, Ohio artist Richard Felton Outcault began to create comics for newspapers.
infinitive

(1) Richard Outcault's comic strips became popular in America when the New York Journal decided to print his comic strip, the "Yellow Kid." **(2)** The "Yellow Kid" got his name because his distinguishing nightshirt was always printed in the color yellow. **(3)** Printing in color was new to newspapers in those days. **(4)** Soon there were more of Outcault's cartoons appearing in newspapers. **(5)** Comic strips read by people of all ages became an important part of the Sunday paper. **(6)** Reading them was fun! **(7)** Outcault went on to create several more popular strips, including one called "Buster Brown." **(8)** Then, after a while, he grew weary of creating comics, and the tired artist moved on to other things. **(9)** Advertising became his new profession. **(10)** Richard Outcault's ability to develop characters for the Sunday funnies earned him the title the Father of the Comic Strip.

For each sentence below, write the infinitive phrase and label how it is used—as a "noun," an "adjective," or an "adverb."

Example: To enjoy the funnies is a Sunday ritual.
To enjoy the funnies (noun)

1. It's a good way to begin a Sunday morning!
2. I want to read the comics before anything else.
3. I'm happy to read them to my little sister.

Adjectives

An **adjective** is a word used to describe a noun or a pronoun. Adjectives tell *what kind, how many,* or *which one.* They usually come before the word they describe. (See pages **486–489**.)

ancient dinosaurs **800 species** **that triceratops**

Adjectives are the same whether the word they describe is singular or plural.

small brain—or—small brains **large tooth—or—large teeth**

732.1
Articles

The articles *a, an,* and *the* are adjectives.

A brontosaurus was an animal about 70 feet long.

The huge dinosaur lived on land and ate plants.

732.2
Proper Adjectives

A proper adjective is formed from a proper noun, and it is always capitalized. (See **618.1**.)

A Chicago museum is home to the skeleton of one of these beasts. (*Chicago* functions as a proper adjective describing the noun *museum.*)

732.3
Common Adjectives

A common adjective is any adjective that is not proper. It is not capitalized (unless it is the first word in a sentence).

Ancient mammoths were huge, woolly creatures.

They lived in the ice fields of Siberia.

Special Kinds of Adjectives

732.4
Demonstrative Adjectives

A demonstrative adjective points out a particular noun. *This* and *these* point out something nearby; *that* and *those* point out something at a distance.

This mammoth is huge, but that mammoth is even bigger.

NOTE When a noun does not follow *this, these, that,* or *those,* these words are pronouns, not adjectives. (See **708.1**.)

732.5
Compound Adjectives

A compound adjective is made up of two or more words. (Sometimes it is hyphenated.)

Dinosaurs were egg-laying animals.

The North American Allosaurus had sharp teeth and powerful jaws.

Grammar Practice

Adjectives 1

- Demonstrative Adjectives
- Compound Adjectives
- Indefinite and Predicate Adjectives (See page 734.)

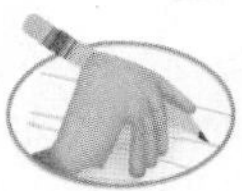

For each numbered sentence in the paragraphs below, identify the underlined word or words as one of the kinds of adjectives listed above.

Example: Most people know about the Great Chicago Fire.
indefinite

(1) On the night of October 8, 1871, an eerie, reddish orange glow filled the Chicago sky. **(2)** Some people believe that the Great Chicago Fire began in the O'Learys' barn when a cow kicked over a lantern. **(3)** (That theory was never proven, however, and the exact cause of the fire is still unknown.) **(4)** Many residents panicked and tried to flee the burning city. **(5)** Kind-hearted people did whatever they could to help, but most of Chicago was destroyed, and 300 people died.

(6) As bad as it was, another fire on the same day caused even more damage. **(7)** The Great Peshtigo Fire was huge; it covered more than a million acres in northeast Wisconsin and Michigan's upper peninsula. **(8)** Hundreds of miles of forest, dry from drought, were tinder for this firestorm. **(9)** Hurricane-force winds created by the fire pushed the blaze from town to town, and 1,500 people lost their lives. **(10)** To this day, the Great Peshtigo Fire ranks as the worst natural disaster to ever hit the United States.

Next Step: Write two or three sentences about fire safety. Use a predicate adjective, an indefinite adjective, and a demonstrative adjective in your sentences.

Adjectives . . .

Special Kinds of Adjectives

734.1 **Indefinite Adjectives**

An indefinite adjective gives approximate or indefinite information (*any, few, many, most,* and so on). It does not tell exactly how many or how much.

> **Some mammoths were heavier than today's elephants.**

734.2 **Predicate Adjectives**

A predicate adjective follows a linking verb and describes the subject.

> **Mammoths were once abundant, but now they are extinct.**

Forms of Adjectives

734.3 **Positive Adjectives**

The positive form describes a noun or pronoun without comparing it to anyone or anything else.

> **The Eurostar is a fast train that runs between London, Paris, and Brussels.**
>
> **It is an impressive train.**

734.4 **Comparative Adjectives**

The comparative form of an adjective *(er)* compares two persons, places, things, or ideas. (See page 487.)

> **The Eurostar is faster than the Orient Express.**

Some adjectives that have more than one syllable show comparisons by their *er* suffix, but many of them use the modifiers *more* or *less.*

> **It is a speedier commuter train than the Tobu Railway trains in Japan.**
>
> **This train is more impressive than my commuter train.**

734.5 **Superlative Adjectives**

The superlative form *(est* or *most* or *least)* compares three or more persons, places, things, or ideas. (See page 487.)

> **In fact, the Eurostar is the fastest train in Europe.**
>
> **It is the most impressive commuter train in the world.**

734.6 **Irregular Forms**

Some adjectives use completely different words to express comparison.

good, better, best	**bad, worse, worst**
many, more, most	**little, less, least**

Grammar Practice

Adjectives 2

Forms of Adjectives

Based on the clues in each sentence below, write the correct form (positive, comparative, or superlative) of the adjective shown in parentheses to complete each sentence.

Example: Giraffes are ______ than any other animal. *(tall)*
taller

1. The ______ snake in the world is the reticulated python. *(long)*
2. A rabbit has ______ ears than a hare does. *(short)*
3. A cheetah is a ______ runner. *(fast)*
4. Even though the whale shark feeds mostly on plankton and small fish, it is the ______ fish in the sea. *(big)*
5. The common snail is probably the ______ animal on earth. *(slow)*
6. Is the warthog really the ______ animal? *(attractive)*
7. Many people believe the polar bear is ______ than the grizzly bear. *(powerful)*
8. The Indian elephant has a ______ forehead. *(square)*
9. Even the ______ human sprinter can't outrun an elephant. *(good)*
10. Some zebras have ______ stripes than other zebras. *(many)*
11. Compared to other animals in the United States, the wolverine seems to be the one with the ______ temper. *(bad)*
12. An arctic fox in the snow is ______ than a red fox in the forest. *(visible)*
13. Long ago, the Pacific salmon was the ______ source of food in the diet of the Yakima tribe. *(important)*

Next Step: Write three sentences about different animals. Use adjectives that are positive, comparative, and superlative in your sentences.

Adverbs

An **adverb** is a word used to modify a verb, an adjective, or another adverb. It tells *how, when, where, how often,* or *how much.* Adverbs can come before or after the words they modify. (See pages 490–493.)

Dad snores loudly. (*Loudly* modifies the verb *snores.*)

His snores are really explosive. (*Really* modifies the adjective *explosive.*)

Dad snores very loudly. (*Very* modifies the adverb *loudly.*)

Types of Adverbs

There are four basic types of adverbs: *time, place, manner,* and *degree.*

736.1 Adverbs of Time

Adverbs of time tell *when, how often,* and *how long.*

tomorrow often never always

Jen rarely has time to go swimming.

736.2 Adverbs of Place

Adverbs of place tell *where, to where,* or *from where.*

there backward outside

We'll set up our tent here.

736.3 Adverbs of Manner

Adverbs of manner often end in *ly* and tell *how* something is done.

unkindly gently well

Ahmed boldly entered the dark cave.

Some words used as adverbs can be written with or without the *ly* ending. When in doubt, use the *ly* form.

slow, slowly deep, deeply

NOTE Not all words ending in *ly* are adverbs. *Lovely,* for example, is an adjective.

736.4 Adverbs of Degree

Adverbs of degree tell *how much* or *how little.*

scarcely entirely generally very really

Jess is usually the leader in these situations.

Grammar Practice

Adverbs 1

Types of Adverbs

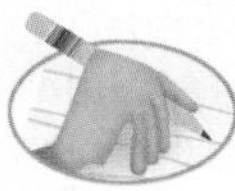

Write the adverb or adverbs that modify the underlined words in the sentences below. The number of adverbs is in parentheses. Label each as one of "time," "place," "manner," or "degree."

Example: America's national parks are always a great place to camp. *(1)*
always–time

1. Some parks, like Yosemite and Yellowstone, are often very busy. *(2)*
2. You might have to wait patiently to get a campsite. *(1)*
3. People must enjoy sleeping outside! *(1)*
4. Campers in national parks regularly go bicycling, canoeing, and hiking. *(1)*
5. Younger kids really enjoy meeting the park rangers. *(1)*
6. Frequently, national park campgrounds offer evening campfire activities. *(1)*
7. If someone brings a guitar there, people might start dancing around. *(2)*
8. Sometimes, national parks have programs to teach campers about nature and wildlife. *(1)*
9. Campers need to react quietly and cautiously when wild animals are nearby. *(3)*
10. Wherever you camp, it is important to do it safely. *(1)*
11. You should follow the park's camping rules exactly and faithfully. *(2)*
12. Never hike by yourself. *(1)*
13. Be extremely careful that your campfire does not accidentally start a forest fire. *(3)*
14. Always remember to carefully inspect your campsite before you leave. *(2)*

Adverbs . . .

Special Kinds of Adverbs

738.1 Conjunctive Adverbs

A conjunctive adverb can be used as a conjunction and shows a connection or a transition between two independent clauses. Most often, a conjunctive adverb follows a semicolon in a compound sentence; however, it can also appear at the beginning or end of a sentence. (Note that the previous sentence has an example of a conjunctive adverb.)

also	besides	however	instead
meanwhile	nevertheless	therefore	

Forms of Adverbs

Many adverbs—especially adverbs of manner—have three forms: *positive, comparative,* and *superlative.*

738.2 Positive Adverbs

The positive form describes but does not make a comparison.

Juan woke up late.

He quickly ate some breakfast.

738.3 Comparative Adverbs

The comparative form of an adverb *(er)* compares two things.

Juan woke up later than he usually did. (See page 491.)

Some adverbs that have more than one syllable show comparisons by their *er* suffix, but many of them use the modifiers *more* or *less.*

He ate his breakfast more quickly than usual.

738.4 Superlative Adverbs

The superlative form *(est* or *most* or *least)* compares three or more things. (See page 491.)

Of the past three days, Juan woke up latest on Saturday.

Of the past three days, he ate his breakfast least quickly on Saturday.

738.5 Irregular Forms

Some adverbs use completely different words to express comparison.

Positive	Comparative	Superlative
well	better	best
badly	worse	worst

Grammar Practice

Adverbs 2

Comparative Forms

For each of the sentences below, write the adverb and identify it as "positive," "comparative," or "superlative."

Example: This year, the school bus arrives earlier than it did last year.
earlier (comparative)

1. Makenna carelessly dripped paint on the floor.
2. Paul bakes walnut brownies better than I do.
3. Of everyone in our school's chorus, Marissa sings the best.
4. The play's director said, "For this role, Carmen, you have to act more mysteriously than that."
5. My old computer runs more slowly than this new one.
6. Ms. Green, who was formerly a marine, is a new teacher at our school.
7. Of any of the recent storms in the area, the wind blew the most forcefully during last night's storm.
8. My brother rides his dirt bike faster than I do.
9. Julian divided the popcorn equally among the four of us.
10. Of the Rosses' three regular babysitters, Bianca seems to be the least readily available.
11. Instant messaging was largely unknown until a few years after its introduction.
12. Shanice dresses the most plainly of anyone in her family.
13. Dimitri treats his dog roughly.
14. Paola gives classroom presentations more confidently than the other students give them.

Next Step: Write one sentence with a comparative adverb and one with a superlative adverb.

Test Prep!

For each of the following sentences, write the letter that shows the correct form of the verb in parentheses.

1. I *(see)* William when he left with his mom just before class.
   (A) seed (B) saw (C) seen (D) see
2. Latisha has *(run)* in the Labor Day marathon before.
   (A) runnen (B) ran (C) run (D) runned
3. Last summer we *(freeze)* a lot of the beans from our garden.
   (A) freezed (B) froze (C) freezen (D) frozen
4. The jockey *(lead)* the horse to the winner's circle.
   (A) lead (B) leaded (C) led (D) leaden
5. I had *(buy)* this DVD for Cruz's birthday.
   (A) bought (B) boughten (C) buy (D) buyed
6. These plants *(grow)* better inside than they did outside.
   (A) growed (B) grown (C) grew (D) grows
7. My aunt and uncle have *(drive)* their motorcycles across the country.
   (A) driven (B) drive (C) drove (D) drived
8. Since I use e-mail now, I haven't *(write)* a letter on paper in a while.
   (A) wrote (B) writed (C) writ (D) written

Label the verb in each of the following sentences. Write "I" for intransitive or "T" for transitive.

9. The students named the new mascot.
10. Syed slipped on the ice in the parking lot.
11. The class laughed at Mr. Jenkin's dumb joke.
12. Thad broke the record for the 50-yard dash.
13. Olivia read my essay.
14. Isamar read aloud.

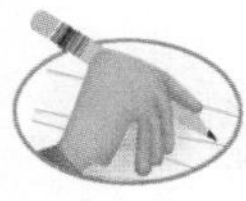

For each of the following sentences, write the letter that best describes the underlined word.

Ⓐ comparative adverb
Ⓑ comparative adjective
Ⓒ superlative adverb
Ⓓ superlative adjective

15. Could you talk more quietly, please?
16. Rocco's has the least expensive pizza in town.
17. You will have to wake up earlier when school starts in the fall.
18. This algebra test is the hardest one we've had all semester.
19. Kirstin sang better than she did yesterday.
20. This week is warmer than last week was.
21. Of everyone on the team, Claire played most energetically.
22. The classroom is more comfortable when the air conditioning is on.
23. Kevin is funnier than most of the other kids.
24. Everyone in the club worked hard, but Luis worked hardest of all.
25. Lisa's purse is the heaviest one here.

Prepositions

Prepositions are words that show position, direction, or how two words or ideas are related to each other. Specifically, a preposition shows the relationship between its object and some other word in the sentence.

Raul hid under the stairs. *(Under* shows the relationship between *hid* and *stairs.)*

742.1 Prepositional Phrases

A preposition never appears alone; it is always part of a prepositional phrase. A prepositional phrase includes the preposition, the object of the preposition, and the modifiers of the object. (See pages 494–495.)

Raul's friends looked in the clothes hamper. (preposition: *in;* object: *hamper;* modifiers: *the, clothes*)

A prepositional phrase functions as an adjective or as an adverb.

They checked the closet with all the winter coats. (*With all the winter coats* functions as an adjective modifying *closet.*)

They wandered around the house looking for him. (*Around the house* functions as an adverb modifying *wandered.*)

NOTE If a word found in the list of prepositions has no object, it is not a preposition. It is probably an adverb.

Raul had never won at hide 'n' seek before. (*Before* is an adverb that modifies *had won.*)

Prepositions

aboard	apart from	beyond	from among	near	over	toward
about	around	but	from between	near to	over to	under
above	aside from	by	from under	of	owing to	underneath
according to	at	by means of	in	off	past	until
across	away from	concerning	in addition to	on	prior to	unto
across from	back of	considering	in front of	on account of	regarding	up
after	because of	despite	in place of	on behalf of	round	up to
against	before	down	in regard to	on top of	save	upon
along	behind	down from	in spite of	onto	since	with
along with	below	during	inside	opposite	through	within
alongside	beneath	except	inside of	out	throughout	without
alongside of	beside	except for	instead of	out of	till	
amid	besides	excepting	into	outside	to	
among	between	for	like	outside of	together with	

Grammar Practice

Prepositions

Write the prepositional phrases you find in each numbered sentence below. Underline the prepositions and circle the objects of the prepositions.

Example: The Plains Indians were once the finest horse riders in the world.
in the world

(1) Plains Indians learned horse-riding skills at a very early age. **(2)** Tribesmen on horses could follow the buffalo herds, so mastering those skills meant food for the tribe. **(3)** Riding among the buffalo and using a bow involved great skill and daring. **(4)** Some of the Indian braves would ride with one foot on the top of the horse's hips while shooting arrows underneath the horse's neck at an enemy. **(5)** In the 1800s, nations like the Crow and the Lakota enjoyed a golden age because of their superb riding abilities.

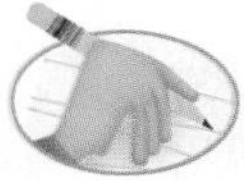

Write a prepositional phrase to complete each of the following sentences.

Example: I like tropical fish . . . *(what kind?)*
from the Caribbean Sea.

1. I was born . . . *(when?)*
2. The CD . . . *(which one?)* . . . is my favorite one right now.
3. My uncle grew up . . . *(where?)*
4. My notebook is the one . . . *(which one?)*
5. I keep my pens and pencils . . . *(where?)*
6. Please get me some candy . . . *(what kind?)*

Conjunctions

A **conjunction** connects individual words or groups of words. There are three kinds of conjunctions: *coordinating, correlative,* and *subordinating.* (See pages **496–498**.)

744.1 Coordinating Conjunctions

A coordinating conjunction connects a word to a word, a phrase to a phrase, or a clause to a clause. The words, phrases, or clauses joined by a coordinating conjunction must be equal, or of the same type.

Polluted rivers and streams can be cleaned up. (Two nouns are connected by *and.*)

Ride a bike or plant a tree to reduce pollution. (Two verb phrases are connected by *or.*)

Maybe you can't invent a pollution-free engine, but you can cut down on the amount of energy you use. (Two equal independent clauses are connected by *but.*)

NOTE When a coordinating conjunction is used to make a compound sentence, a comma always comes before it.

744.2 Correlative Conjunctions

Correlative conjunctions are conjunctions used in pairs.

We must reduce not only pollution but also excess energy use.

Either you're part of the problem, or you're part of the solution.

Conjunctions

Coordinating Conjunctions

and, but, or, nor, for, so, yet

Correlative Conjunctions

either, or — neither, nor — not only, but also — both, and — whether, or — as, so

Subordinating Conjunctions

after, although, as, as if, as long as, as though, because, before, if, in order that, provided that, since, so, so that, that, though, till, unless, until, when, where, whereas, while

Grammar Practice

Conjunctions 1

Coordinating Conjunctions

Use a coordinating conjunction to combine each pair of sentences below.

Example: Anyone may join the Polar Bear Club. He or she must be willing to swim in freezing water.

Anyone may join the Polar Bear Club, but he or she must be willing to swim in freezing water.

1. The members braved the subzero temperatures. They plunged into the icy water.
2. Club members could go into the water wearing swimsuits. They could go into the water wearing warmer clothing.
3. Participants get very cold. It is important to have a place to warm up when they get out of the water.
4. Polar Bear Club members like to have fun. They also like to help raise money for special causes.

Correlative Conjunctions

Use a different set of correlative conjunctions to combine each sentence pair below. Underline the conjunctions.

Example: Josh must decide if he wants to go to the game. Josh must decide if he wants to go to the movies.

Josh must decide whether he wants to go to the game or the movies.

1. Rain will not stop the football game. Snow will not stop the football game.
2. Volleyball is a team sport. Soccer is a team sport.
3. Sally has twin sisters. Sally also has twin cousins.
4. Maybe Ron's mom will pick us up after school. Maybe Ron's dad will pick us up after school.

Conjunctions . . .

746.1 Subordinating Conjunctions

A subordinating conjunction is a word or group of words that connects two clauses that are not equally important. A subordinating conjunction begins a dependent clause and connects it to an independent clause to make a complex sentence. (See page 517 and the chart on page 744.)

Fuel-cell engines are unusual because **they don't have moving parts.**

Since **fuel-cell cars run on hydrogen, the only waste products are water and heat.**

As you can see in the sentences above, a comma sets off the dependent clause only when it begins the sentence. A comma is usually not used when the dependent clause follows the independent clause.

NOTE Relative pronouns and conjunctive adverbs can also connect clauses. (See 706.3 and 738.1.)

Interjections

An **interjection** is a word or phrase used to express strong emotion or surprise. Punctuation (a comma or an exclamation point) is used to separate an interjection from the rest of the sentence.

Wow, **would you look at that!** Oh no! **He's falling!**

SCHOOL DAZE
Forget it! We aren't using activity money for that.
Yikes, I've told everyone that we could buy a plasma-screen TV for our classroom!

Grammar Practice

Conjunctions 2

Subordinating Conjunctions

Choose a subordinating conjunction (from the chart on page 744) to connect each pair of clauses below, forming complex sentences. Place the conjunction first in some of the sentences.

Example: Cicadas are easy to recognize. They make unique sounds.

Cicadas are easy to recognize because they make unique sounds.

1. It's not uncommon to hear dozens of them ticking, buzzing, and whining. It's hot outside.
2. They are capable of producing sounds in excess of 120 decibels. The noise might hurt your ears.
3. The king hornet preys on cicadas. Birds are even worse.
4. Unsuspecting cicadas are sitting high in the treetops. Hungry birds are watching.
5. It sounds disgusting. Some people eat cicadas.
6. You might hear the 17-year cicadas. You are in the United States east of the Great Plains.
7. These cicadas are called 17-year cicadas. They emerge in great numbers once every 17 years.
8. You know what a cicada looks like. You might mistake it for a locust or a giant fly.
9. A cicada's body temperature drops below 72 degrees Fahrenheit. It won't fly.
10. You might not like the racket that cicadas make. You have to admit that they are interesting insects.

Next Step: Would an interjection be appropriate in any of the sentences you just wrote? Add an interjection to at least four of them. Separate it from the rest of the sentence with either a comma or an exclamation point.

Quick Guide: Parts of Speech

In the English language, there are eight parts of speech. Understanding them will help you improve your writing skills. Every word you write is a part of speech—a noun, a verb, an adjective, and so on. The chart below lists the eight parts of speech.

Noun

A word that names a person, a place, a thing, or an idea

Alex Moya Belize ladder courage

Pronoun

A word used in place of a noun

I he it they you anybody some

Verb

A word that shows action or links a subject to another word in the sentence

sing shake catch is are

Adjective

A word that describes a noun or a pronoun

stormy red rough seven grand

Adverb

A word that describes a verb, an adjective, or another adverb

quickly today now bravely softer

Preposition

A word that shows position or direction and introduces a prepositional phrase

around up under over between to

Conjunction

A word that connects other words or groups of words

and but or so because when

Interjection

A word (set off by commas or an exclamation point) that shows strong emotion

Stop! Hey, how are you?

Grammar Practice

Parts of Speech Review

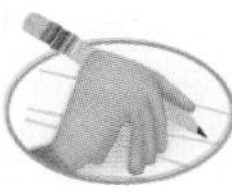

For each underlined word in the following paragraphs, write whether it is a "noun," a "pronoun," a "verb," an "adjective," an "adverb," a "preposition," a "conjunction," or an "interjection."

(1) There's a big change taking place in the Black Hills of South Dakota. **(2)** Not far from Mount Rushmore, a huge likeness of the Native American leader Crazy Horse is being carved into the side of a mountain. **(3)** Crazy Horse was a famous warrior of the Lakota tribe. **(4)** He was a committed leader who fought to preserve the traditions and values of his people. **(5)** Now, people are creating this memorial to his life. **(6)** Anyone who's in the area can see it in person.

(7) The sculptor Korczak Ziolkowski began work on the memorial in 1948. **(8)** In the beginning, he worked alone. **(9)** He worked diligently, and soon the image of Crazy Horse began taking shape.
(10) Surprisingly, he then decided to carve the entire 600-foot mountain instead of following his original plan to carve only the top 100 feet.
(11) Wow, Korczak worked on his amazing sculpture for 32 years!
(12) When he died unexpectedly in 1982 at the age of 74, he was buried in a tomb about 500 yards from the base of the mountain.

(13) Ziolkowski's project continues under the supervision of his wife.
(14) The face portion of this gigantic sculpture was dedicated in 1998.
(15) The crew will work faithfully until the project is finished.
(16) Oh, it will be years before the memorial is finished, but it will be well worth the wait.

Next Step: Write one word for each of the eight parts of speech and exchange lists with a partner. Write a sentence or two using all of each other's words.

Credits

Text:

P. 373, Copyright © 2010 by Houghton Mifflin Harcourt Publishing Company, Adapted and reproduced by permission from *The American Heritage Student Dictionary*.

Photos:

P. cover (camera), 57, 431 (b) Harcourt School Publishers; cover (desert, headlights), vi, xii, xv, xvi, 1, 3, 10, 16, 27 (t,b), 39, 45, 65, 68, 135, 143, 267 (flashlight), 323, 355 (c,r), 359, 360 (t), 363, 367, 374, 379 (rocks), 409 (rocks), 411 (plug, keyboard, mouse), 417, 431 (a), 505, 523, 533, 547 (t,b), 555 (t,b) ©Photodisc/Getty Images; cover (flame) ©Alexey Stiop/Alamy; cover (sunset), 198, 361, 555 (c) ©Corbis; cover (tires) ©picturesbyrob/Alamy; cover (video camera), x, 5, 9, 33, 43, 63, 101, 107, 113, 125, 165, 171, 177, 189, 199, 205 (pizza), 223, 227, 233, 239, 251, 255, 267 (ball), 283, 291, 295, 301, 313, 343, 347, 353 (camera), 375, 379 (salt), 386, 395, 405, 407, 409 (salt), 411 (VHS, microphone, CD, salt), 413 (remote, headset), 421, 423, 429, 483, 485, 531, 750 ©Comstock/Getty Images; endsheet, 83, 262, 265, 372, 469 ©Ablestock.com/Jupiter; ix, 329, 330 Courtesy of The Library of Congress; v, 93, 353 (clock), 413 (cardboard) Harcourt; 11 ©David Buffington/Photodisc/Getty Images; 60 ©Hemera Technologies/ Jupiter; 75 ©Corbis/Jupiter; 97, 129 ©Ingram Publishing/Jupiter; 157 ©Purestock/Jupiter; 161, 193 ©Ingram Publishing/SuperStock; 205 (protractor), 521 ©Artville/Getty Images; 219, 299 ©Ingram Publishing/Getty Images; 228 ©Randy Faris/Corbis; 238 ©Radius Images/Corbis; 269, 358 ©Jupiter; 287, 317 ©Comstock/Jupiter; 354 ©National Geographic Image Collection/Alamy; 355 (l) ©Ivan Hunter/Getty Images; 356 ©David Muscroft/Alamy; 360 (b) ©Slanted Roof Studio/ Alamy; 441, 449, 461 ©Getty Images; 492 ©NOAA; 499 ©Stockbyte/Getty Images; 535 ©Best View Stock/Alamy; Back Cover ©Digital Vision/ Getty Images.

Index

The **index** will help you find specific information in the handbook. Entries in italics are from the "Using the Right Word" section. The colored boxes will contain information you will use often.

D

F

G

H

Q

R

S

Y